本书系教育部人文社会科学研究规划基金项目"京师同文馆输入的西方法学及其术语研究——以《万国公法》为中心"（批准号：11YJA820070）结项成果

京师同文馆输入的
西方法学研究

万齐洲 ■ 著

A Study of
Western Law Introduced
by Jingshi tongwenguan

中国社会科学出版社

图书在版编目（CIP）数据

京师同文馆输入的西方法学研究 / 万齐洲著 . —北京：中国社会科学出版社，2022.12
　ISBN 978 - 7 - 5227 - 1367 - 0

　Ⅰ.①京…　Ⅱ.①万…　Ⅲ.①西方国家—法学—研究—中国—清代　Ⅳ.①D90

中国国家版本馆 CIP 数据核字（2023）第 023407 号

出 版 人	赵剑英
责任编辑	宋燕鹏　史丽清
责任校对	李　硕
责任印制	李寡寡

出　　版	中国社会科学出版社
社　　址	北京鼓楼西大街甲 158 号
邮　　编	100720
网　　址	http://www.csspw.cn
发 行 部	010 - 84083685
门 市 部	010 - 84029450
经　　销	新华书店及其他书店
印　　刷	北京明恒达印务有限公司
装　　订	廊坊市广阳区广增装订厂
版　　次	2022 年 12 月第 1 版
印　　次	2022 年 12 月第 1 次印刷
开　　本	710×1000　1/16
印　　张	33.5
插　　页	2
字　　数	500 千字
定　　价	168.00 元

凡购买中国社会科学出版社图书，如有质量问题请与本社营销中心联系调换
电话：010 - 84083683
版权所有　侵权必究

目 录

第一章 京师同文馆及其译业 ……………………………（1）
  第一节 京师同文馆的设立 ……………………………（1）
    一 《天津条约》与京师同文馆的建立 …………………（1）
    二 京师同文馆的功能 …………………………………（5）
  第二节 京师同文馆的教学与翻译工作 ………………（8）
  第三节 京师同文馆译事主要人物 ……………………（12）
    一 奕䜣、文祥 …………………………………………（12）
    二 毕利干 ………………………………………………（14）
    三 丁韪良 ………………………………………………（15）

第二章 《万国公法》的翻译与出版 ……………………（25）
  第一节 1862年以前中国与西方法学的接触 ……………（25）
  第二节 《万国公法》的翻译与出版 …………………（28）
    一 亨利·惠顿所著 Elements of International Law 及其在西方法学中的地位 ……………………………………（28）
    二 "局势对这种书的需求早已引起我的注意。"——丁韪良翻译《万国公法》的原因 ……………………………（53）
    三 "除了希伯来人之外,世界上没有一个民族曾经从古人那儿继承过这么珍贵的遗产"——丁韪良对中国文化的理解与《万国公法》的翻译 …………………………（60）
    四 《万国公法》的翻译底本问题 ……………………（64）
  第三节 《万国公法》的版本及内容 …………………（83）

第三章　京师同文馆翻译的其他国际法著作 ……………………（117）
第一节　《星轺指掌》 ……………………………………（117）
第二节　《公法便览》 ……………………………………（128）
第三节　《公法会通》 ……………………………………（143）
第四节　《中国古世公法论略》 …………………………（155）
第五节　《陆地战例新选》 ………………………………（186）

第四章　《法国律例》的翻译与出版 ……………………………（198）
第一节　《法国律例》 ……………………………………（198）
第二节　《法国律例·民律》 ……………………………（201）
第三节　《法国律例·刑律》 ……………………………（256）
第四节　《法国律例·民律指掌》 ………………………（277）
第五节　《法国律例·刑名定范》 ………………………（299）
第六节　《法国律例·贸易定律》 ………………………（318）
第七节　《法国律例·园林则律》 ………………………（330）

附录一 ……………………………………………………………（337）

附录二 ……………………………………………………………（339）

附录三 ……………………………………………………………（352）

附录四 ……………………………………………………………（360）

附录五 ……………………………………………………………（501）

附录六 ……………………………………………………………（507）

附录七 ……………………………………………………………（510）

附录八 ……………………………………………………………（519）

附录九 ……………………………………………………………（526）

参考文献 …………………………………………………………（528）

后　记 ……………………………………………………………（531）

第一章　京师同文馆及其译业[①]

第一节　京师同文馆的设立

一　《天津条约》与京师同文馆的建立

1856年，一艘名为"亚罗号"的中国走私船只被清朝水师缉拿，但因为悬挂英国国旗，英国驻广州领事巴夏礼借端生事，说该船是英国船，要求中国方面放还人犯并道歉。两广总督叶名琛屈服于英国的压力，同意交还人犯，但巴夏礼拒绝接受。10月23日，英国军舰悍然开进内河，挑起战争，第二次鸦片战争由此引发。战败的清政府被迫与英国签订了《天津条约》，其中一条规定："大清皇上特简内阁大学士尚书中一员，与大英钦差大臣文移、会晤各等事务，商办仪式皆照平仪相待。"[②]

随着双方交往的增加，清政府与西方列强建立官方外交关系不可避免，于是，奕䜣等人奏请设立总理各国事务衙门：

> 京师请设立总理各国事务衙门，以专责成也。查各国事件，向由外省督抚奏报，汇总于军机处。近年各路军报络绎，外国事务头绪纷繁，驻京之后，若不悉心经理，专一其事，必至办理迟缓，未能悉协机宜。请设总理各国事务衙门，以王大臣领之，军机大臣承书谕旨，非兼领其事恐有歧误，请一并兼管。并请另给

[①] 参见拙文《京师同文馆及其译业》，《红河学院学报》2011年第1期。
[②] 王铁崖：《中外旧约章汇编》，三联书店1982年版，第96页。

公所，以便办公，兼备与各国接见。①

1861年1月20日，经咸丰皇帝批准，总理各国事务衙门在北京正式成立，其组织依照军机处而设，由奕䜣、桂良、文祥为总理衙门大臣。起初主管外交及通商、关税等事务，后来扩大到建筑铁路、开矿、制造枪炮军火等事务，总揽了外交及与外交有关的财政、军事、教育、矿物、交通等各个方面的大权。通商、关税等事务，后来扩大到建筑铁路、开矿、制造枪炮军火等事务，总揽了外交及与外交有关的财政、军事、教育、矿物、交通等各个方面的大权。

清政府在与西方列强的交往中，长期为语言不通而困扰，"朝廷的官员，都不懂得外国语言文字，办理外交，诸多不便之处。"② 林则徐初到广州禁烟时，可供林则徐使用的翻译人员只有袁德辉、亚孟③、亚林④、梁进德⑤。这种人在当时被称为"通事"。从袁德辉翻译的滑达尔《国际法》来看，其水平（尤其是专业知识的翻译）有限。直到第二次鸦片战争时期，由于"直省并无谙习夷字人员"，⑥清政府与列强交涉都是依靠被关押在天津的犯人黄惠廉，"至夷字文书，已交熟悉夷文、去年留交天津县收管之广东人黄惠廉译出。"⑦ 与之相反，西方列强却拥有自己的翻译人才。有的是在华生活多年的传教士，如卫三畏、丁韪良；有的是高薪聘请的华人，如张彤云、梁植："现有英国翻译张彤云、梁植等——本系内地人民，现在英国，办理

---

① 李书源整理：《筹办夷务始末》卷72，中华书局2008年版。
② 张静庐：《中国近代出版史料》（二编），群联出版社1954年版，第48页。
③ 亚孟是林则徐赴广州时即随带的通事，曾在四译馆工作。他的父亲是中国人，母亲是孟加拉人。亚孟曾师从印度塞兰普尔英浸会牧师马什曼，在塞兰普尔的教会学校里念过十多年书。返华之前，亚孟在塞兰普尔帮助马什曼牧师传教。
④ 亚林即林阿适（Liaon Ashee），英文名为William Botelho。他早年留学美国，1822—1825年间在美国康涅狄格康沃尔的基督教公理会差会所办的教会学校里念书。1824年亚林曾转学宾夕法尼亚的另一所学校。1825年回国抵广州，1839年为林则徐所聘。
⑤ 梁进德即亚秩。其父将其托付给裨治文培养，意欲让他学好英文帮助自己翻译《圣经》。裨治文教亚秩学英文与希伯来文。1834年，亚秩与其父来到新加坡，他的教育由公理会负责指导，学费由马礼逊教育社负担。1837年，亚秩又回到广州去随裨治文学英文。1839年3月24日，林则徐将他聘为译员。
⑥ 李书源整理：《筹办夷务始末》卷45，中华书局2008年版。
⑦ 李书源整理：《筹办夷务始末》卷38，中华书局2008年版。

一切文案，颇深信任——嗣后，凡遇筹议事件，无不赖其调停，虽所费不赀，而颇得指臂之力。"① 他们的英语水平明显高于清朝的雇员，而清政府雇请的这些"通事"往往又是一些素质低下、品行不端的人，于中方外交十分不利。李鸿章对此论道：

> 互市二十年来，彼酋之习我语言文字者不少，其尤者能读我经史，于朝章宪典、吏治民情，言之历历；而我官员绅士绝少通习外国语言文字之人。各国在沪均设立翻译官一、二员，遇中外大臣会商之事，皆凭外国翻译官传述，亦难保无偏袒捏架情弊。中国能通洋语者，仅恃通事，凡关军营交涉事务，无非雇觅通事往来传话，而其人遂为洋务之大害。查上海通事一途获利最厚，于士农工商之外别成一业。其人不过两种：一：广东、宁波商伙子弟，佻达游闲，别无转移执事之路者，辄以学习通事为逋逃。英、法等国设立义学，招本地贫苦童稚，与以衣食而教肄之。此两种人者，类皆资性蠢愚，心术卑鄙，货利声色之外不知其他。②

1858年的《中英天津条约》规定：

> 嗣后英国文书俱用英字书写，暂时仍以汉文配送，俟中国选派学生学习英文、英语熟悉，即不用配送汉文。自今以后，遇有文词辩论之处，总以英文作为正义。此次定约，汉、英文字详细校对无讹，亦照此例。③

同年《中法天津条约》也规定：

> 凡大法国大宪、领事等官有公文照会中国大宪及地方官员，均用大法国字样，惟为办事妥速之便，亦有翻译中国文字一件附

---

① 《中国近代史资料丛刊》（《第二次鸦片战争》），上海人民出版社1978年版，第515页。
② 杨逸：《海上墨林 广方言馆全案 粉墨丛谈》，上海古籍出版社1985年版，第107页。
③ 王铁崖：《中外旧约章汇编》，三联书店1982年版，第102页。

之，其附件务尽力以相符，侯大清国京师有通事谙晓且能译大法国言语，即时大法国官员照会大清国公文应用大法国字样，大清国官员照会大法国官员公文应用大清国字样。自今以后，所有议定各款，或有两国文词辩论之处，总以法文做为正义。兹所定者，均与现立章程为然。其两国官员照会，各以本国文字为正，不得将翻译言语以为正也。①

根据国际法的规则，条约应使用双方公认的语言，19世纪一般都使用拉丁语以及签约国的语言。《天津条约》关于双方争议以英、法文字为准的规定，一方面说明西方列强对国际法规则的不尊重，一方面也表明英、法两国对清政府的不信任。虽然英、法两国政府将《天津条约》送达清政府时，附送了汉字文本，但敦促清政府及早培养自己的翻译人才。所有这些都表明，培养高水平的翻译人才已经成为当务之急。奕䜣等人在奏请设立总理各国事务衙门的奏疏中，提出组建培养语言人才的专门机构：

> 认识外国文字通解外国言语之人，请敕广东、上海各派二人来京委差，以备询问也。查与外国交涉事件，必先识其性情，今语言不通，文字难辩，一切隔膜，安望其能妥协？从前俄罗斯馆文字，曾例定设立文馆学习，具有深意。今日久视为具文，未能通晓，似宜量为鼓舞，以资观感。闻广东、上海商人，有专习英、法、美三国语言文字之人，请敕各该省督抚，挑选诚实可靠者，每省各派二人，共派四人，携带各国书籍来京。并于八旗中挑选天资聪慧，年在十三、四以下者各四、五人，俾资学习。其派来之人，仿照俄罗斯教习之例，厚其薪水，两年后，分别勤惰，其有成效者，给以奖叙。俟八旗学习之人，于文字言语悉能通晓，即行停止。俄罗斯语言文字，仍请敕令该馆，妥议章程，认真督课。所有学习各国文字之人，如能纯熟，即奏请给以优

---

① 王铁崖：《中外旧约章汇编》，三联书店1982年版，第105页。

奖，庶不致日久废弛。①

为了尽快促成此事，时隔仅有20多天，奕䜣又和桂良、文祥联奏了《总理衙门未尽事宜拟章程十条》，再次谈到了这一问题：

> 认识外国文字通晓语言之人并学生等，应酌定薪水奖励也，查臣等前定章程内，有请广东、上海挑选专习英、法、美三国语言之人，来京委差。并挑选八旗子弟学习，厚其薪水，给以奖叙。除俄罗斯馆章程，应由该馆遵旨酌议外，其英、法、美教习学习薪水奖励，应仿照俄罗斯馆议定之例办理。惟该学生原应归入俄罗斯馆，而该馆地方狭窄，难以兼容，若另设馆舍，恐其别滋事端。现查铁钱局除改作衙署外，尚有炉房，稍加修葺，堪作馆舍，免至在外滋事，臣等亦可就近稽查考核。②

二 京师同文馆的功能

几经周折，京师同文馆③于1862年夏正式建立。出于与英、法交

---

① 李书源整理：《筹办夷务始末》卷71，中华书局2008年版。
② 李书源整理：《筹办夷务始末》卷71，中华书局2008年版。
③ 同文馆设立于宋朝，最初是接待高句丽等外国使节的招待所。由于高句丽、越南等国也使用汉字，他们与宋朝同属汉字文化圈，所以以此命名。明朝将同文馆改为学习外国语言的场所，称为四夷馆（后称为四译馆）。馆中设立了管理官职——正四品的"少卿"，四译馆下设蒙古、女真、西番、西天、回回、百夷、高昌、缅甸等八馆，分别教授各种外国语言。后来四译馆规模不断扩大，增设了八百馆、暹罗馆等分支。尼布楚谈判后，清政府感到需要培养自己的翻译人才，于1708年设立了俄罗斯文馆这一机构。清人何秋涛在《朔方备乘》中介绍："内阁俄罗斯学亦谓之俄罗斯馆。会典内阁云俄罗斯馆专司翻译俄罗斯文字。选八旗官学生二十四人入馆，肄业五年后考试一次。一等授八品官，二等授九品官，三等不授官，皆留学。八品官再考列一等授七品官，九品官再考列一等授八品官。其不及原考等第者各照现考等第分别降级留学。七品官又考列一等，以主事即补。额设助教二人，于教习内奏补教习，即于考得职品各员内派委。以蒙古侍读学士或侍读一人充提调官，专司稽查课程。再由理藩院派委郎中或员外郎一人兼辖此官制也。"——转引自陈向阳：《晚清京师同文馆组织研究》广东高等教育出版社2004年版，第80页；

19世纪以后，由于学生的仕途升迁不如从前，学生的学习兴趣大减，俄罗斯文馆已是名存实亡，"顷于本年五月，该衙门传集该馆助教、副教习、学生等到署，内额设学生二十四名，除悬缺未补八名及临时不到三名外，实到学生十三名，面加考试，该学生等并不熟习俄文，其助教二员、副教习三员内，亦只国世春一人尚稍通文义。臣等公同商酌，拟将该员咨送总理衙门，仍留原奉，在新设之学堂行走，其余助教一员、副教习三员，及已、未到学生共十六人，既学无成效，自未便虚縻廪气，相应请旨裁撤；其学生所领马甲钱粮及该馆一切领项，自应一并裁去，以节縻费。"——《筹办夷务始末》卷8，中华书局1979年版。（转下页）

往的需要，起初只在俄文馆之外，设立英文馆和法文馆，英、法、俄每个语种各设一个班。由于招收的学生年龄相差悬殊、程度不一，为了便于教学，将汉语程度较高的学生编为一个班，放在前馆。主要学习外语，汉语程度较低的学生放在后馆，除学习外语之外，还要补习汉文，"本衙门设立同文馆，原为学习洋文，然必通晓汉文方能于洋文得力，故后馆学生每日洋文功课完毕时，即兼习汉文，每月底由各馆汉教习将学生功课送由提调核后，开列清单呈堂阅看，以昭核实。"①

京师同文馆旧址

（接上页）
丁韪良在《同文馆记》中描述："以成立年岁而论，俄文班本是各班之母，在一世纪以前，理藩院便设立了一个俄罗斯馆，表示中国已经知道它的北邻的地位之重要了。那个学校正式并入了同文馆；但是里面一无教员，二无学生，真不知道凭着什么来归并。他的资产只是一些章程先例而已。"毕乃德［美］在《同文馆考》中也说：俄罗斯文馆"当初成立的时候，它对于训练学生读解俄文的工作，也许果有成效，但是到了十九世纪初年，成绩便显然不很好了。此馆一直存留下来，到一八六二年，拨归新创的总理衙门管辖，方告消灭；不过馆中的师生，都是一种领干薪的性质，因为此馆在移转管辖以前，馆中师生曾一度考试，结果教习中懂得俄文的只有一个，学生则一个都没有。"1862 年，俄罗斯文馆正式归并到京师同文馆。

① 参见陈向阳《晚清京师同文馆组织研究》，广东高等教育出版社 2004 年版，第 189 页。

由于每年新入学的学生都进入后馆，后馆学生的人数逐渐增多，而且年龄、水平参差不齐，后馆学生又被分为若干个班（年级），曾在同文馆学习的齐如山回忆道："例如我，入馆一年多，升到第二班，但除第二班功课外，连第一班（彼时称头班，不说几年级，因为在一班之中，也有二三年的，也有学过四五年的，无法论几年）的功课，我都预备了，所以二年之后，我便升入了头班。按现在的情形说，在第二班把头一班的功课也预备了，这几乎可以说是不可能的，但彼时并不难。"①

后馆的学习内容比较简单，其中的优秀者，也可以进入前馆学习，"查同文馆学生，凡学有进益，补食六两膏火者，均拨入前馆肄业，仍按日兼办后馆洋文、汉文各功课，历经办理有案，现据教习毕利干单开，后馆学生恩禧、德海、金汤、双华等四名请拨前馆。"② 同样，前馆学生中汉语水平不能适应教学者，也要回到后馆补习。

在京师同文馆担任教师的既有中国人，又有外国人。起初，清政府想从国内广东、上海等沿海地区聘请外国语言教师：

> 认识外国文字通解外国言语之人，请敕广东、上海各派二人来京委差，以备询问也。查与外国交涉事件，必先识其性情，今语言不通，文字难辨，一切隔膜，安望其能妥协？从前俄罗斯馆文字，曾例定设立文馆学习，具有深意。今日久视为具文，未能通晓，似宜量为鼓舞，以资观感。闻广东、上海商人，有专习英、法、美三国语言文字之人，请敕各该省督抚，挑选诚实可靠者，每省各派二人，共派四人，携带各国书籍来京。③

但结果并不理想，广东的官员称无人可派，上海举荐的教习外语水平较低，且要价过高，最后不得不从外国人中挑选。英国人包尔腾是京师同文馆所聘任的第一位英文教习，1863年，又聘请了法国人

---

① 齐如山：《齐如山回忆录》，北京宝文堂书店1989年版，第40页。
② 参见陈向阳：《晚清京师同文馆组织研究》，广东高等教育出版社2004年版，第188页。
③ 李书源整理：《筹办夷务始末》卷7，中华书局2008年版。

司默灵、俄国人柏林分别担任新设立的法文馆和俄文馆的法文教习和俄文教习。1866年以后，除外语教习外，又陆续聘请了一批自然科学和社会科学科目的教习，如研究物理的欧礼斐硕士（C. H. Oliver, M. A.）、研究天文学的方根拔与骆三畏硕士、专攻解剖学和生理学的德贞博士、研究化学的毕利干与施德明博士。外国教习中，任职时间最长、地位最高者是丁韪良。

第二节　京师同文馆的教学与翻译工作

随着洋务运动的深入，打着"自强"、"求富"旗号的洋务派，以"师夷长技以制夷"、"中学为体，西学为用"为指导思想，先后创办了安庆军械所、江南机器制造局、福州船政局，社会对各类技术人才的需求开始增加。1866年6月25日，闽浙总督左宗棠奏请在福建马尾设立船政学堂（求是堂艺局），1867年1月6日正式开学。1866年12月11日，奕䜣等人提出在京师同文馆内添设天文馆："臣等公同商酌，现拟添设一馆，招取满汉举人及恩、拔、岁、副、优贡，汉文业已通顺，年在二十以外者，取具同乡京官印结或本旗图片，赴臣衙门考试，并准令前项正途出身五品以下满汉京外各官，少年聪慧，愿入馆学习者，呈明分别出具本旗图片及同乡官印结，一体与考，由臣等录取后，即延聘西人在馆教习，务期天文、算学，均能洞彻根源，厥道成于上，技艺成于下，数年之后，必有成效。"①

奕䜣等人不仅认识到技艺的重要，也了解到作为"术"之根源的"学"的意义：

> 因思洋人制造机器、火器等件，以及行船、行军，无一不自天文、算学中来。现在上海、浙江等处，讲求轮船各项，若不从根本上用功夫，即学习皮毛，仍无裨于实用。——盖以西人制器

---

① 李书源整理：《筹办夷务始末》卷46，中华书局2008年版。

之法，无不由度数而生，今中国议欲讲求制造轮船、机器诸法，苟不借西士为先导，俾讲明机巧之原，制作之本，窃恐师心自用，徒费钱粮，仍无裨于实际。①

但奕䜣等人的建议遭到了清政府内顽固派的反对：

朝廷命官必用科甲正途者，为其读孔、孟之书，学尧、舜之道，明体达用，规模宏远也，何必令其习为机巧，专明制造轮船、洋枪之理乎？若以自强而论，则朝廷之强莫如整纲纪、明政刑，严赏罚，求贤养民，练兵筹饷诸大端。臣民之强则惟气节一端耳。②

许多讥讽的言论也不胫而走：

有对联云："诡计本多端，使小朝廷设同文馆；军机无远略，诱佳子弟拜异类为师。"——或粘纸于前门以俚语笑骂，"胡闹胡闹，教人都从了天主教"云云。或作对句"未同而言，斯文将尽"，又曰"孔门弟子，鬼谷先生"。③

这些议论遭到了清朝最高当局的反驳，天文算学馆最终仍然得以成立。此后，化学以及法学、经济学等课程也进入了京师同文馆的课堂，京师同文馆已不再是单一的语言学习机构，它已经逐渐变成了一所综合性的类似现在大学的教育机构。许多自然科学知识，乃至于社会科学知识都成了它的教学内容。

1869年，得到赫德全力支持的丁韪良出任总教习一职。他对学习内容进行了大刀阔斧的改革，从一份1876年的课程表中看，学生除学习语言、数学、天文等课程外，还要学习各国历史、法律、经济等

---

① 李书源整理：《筹办夷务始末》卷46，中华书局2008年版。
② 李书源整理：《筹办夷务始末》卷47，中华书局2008年版。
③ 陈义杰点校：《翁同龢日记》，中华书局1979年版，第519、521页。

课程。"八年课程表：首年，认字写字、浅解辞句、讲解浅书；二年，讲解浅书、练习文法、翻译条子；三年，讲各国地图、读各国史略、翻译选编；四年，数理启蒙、代数学、翻译公文；五年，讲求格物、几何原本、平三角弧三角、练习译书；六年，讲求机器、微分积分、航海测算、练习译书；七年，讲求化学、天文测算、万国公法、练习译书；八年，天文测算、地理金石、富国策、练习译书。"① 这份课表表明，在学生八年的学习生涯中，语言、自然科学、社会科学的课程都占有一定的比例。其中，法学被安排在第七年学习，内容以国际法知识为主，由丁韪良亲自主讲。为了胜任教学工作，丁韪良于1868年返回美国耶鲁大学，师从耶鲁大学校长研习国际法。从目前所见资料来看，当时学习国际法课程的学生人数很少，"据毕乃德统计：1879年有9名学生参加了国际公法的大考；1888年为8人；1893年为12人。另外，1878年共有98人应试大考，榜单上所记参加公法学考试的学生分别为：沈铎、那三、黎子祥、徐广坤、王镇贤、文续、熙璋、斌衡、懿善。"② 当时学生接触的国际法知识已经涵盖外交与领事关系、战争法等内容，这一点从历年的考试题目中可见端倪。

1878年同文馆年考，国际公法试题为：

> 遣使之权，自主之国皆有之，何以辩之？
> 此国遣使彼国，有拒而不接者，其故何也？
> 使臣有四等，试言其序。
> 遇更易国主，驻京使臣位次何以定之，其定法不一，而各有成案，试言之。
> 头等公使得邀破格优待之礼，试言其概。

---

① 参见陈向阳：《晚清京师同文馆组织研究》，广东高等教育出版社2004年版，第111页。
② 田涛：《国际法输入与晚清中国》，济南出版社2001年版，第92页。这九名学生的情况是：沈铎，广东同文馆选送京师同文馆，曾任工部笔帖式、驻日使馆翻译；那三，广东同文馆选送，曾任京师同文馆副教习、天津电报学堂教习、新加坡总领事；黎子祥，上海广方言馆选送，后为四品衔候选知州，1906—1909年曾任驻朝鲜元山副领事；徐广坤，上海广方言馆选送，曾任驻神户领事；王镇贤，广东同文馆选送，曾任工部笔帖式、郎中；文续，曾任京师同文馆副教习、户部主事、驻德使馆随员；熙璋，曾任京师同文馆天文副教习、刑部笔帖式；斌衡，曾任京师同文馆英文副教习；懿善，曾任户部主事、驻汉城领事随员、驻元山副领事。

公使权利之尤要者，试言之。
公使职守，其尤重者在何事？
各国议立条约，所论何事居多？
公使偶不安分，有遣之出疆者，系因何事？
公使停职其故有七，试述之。①

1886 年同文馆年考，国际公法试题为：

海上盘查他国船只，限制有四，试论之。
盘查之权每有条约范围之，试述其一二。
邦国凭其自护之权，不理局外旗号，而追捕船只者，其例案如何？
英、美两国设法禁绝贩卖黑奴之事，其大端者若何？
美国与英国第二次启衅，其故有二，试言之。②

1892 年同文馆大考，国际公法试题为：

邦国之得土地者，其原不以一法，试述之。
昔者公使每争位次，其案之尤著者，试言之。
自主之国均等而仍有分别者，其义例若何？
邦国交出逃犯与否，其义例若何？
按公法之通例，其免于地方管辖者有三，试言之。
东方各国外人罪案每归领事官审问，其例由何而始？
邦国治内政，其公文有牵涉他国因而诘问者，其例案若何？
人民毁谤他国之君上，有司因而治罪，其例案若何？③

课堂之外，在丁韪良、毕利干等人的主持之下，大量西方法学著

---

① 朱有：《中国近代学制史料》，华东师范大学出版社 1983 年版，第 90 页。
② 朱有：《中国近代学制史料》，华东师范大学出版社 1983 年版第 93、94 页。
③ 孙子和：《清代同文馆之研究》，台北嘉新水泥公司文化基金会 1977 年版，第 563 页。

作被译介到中国。具体书目为：《万国公法》、《法国律例》（包含《民律》、《刑律》、《民律指掌》、《刑名定范》、《贸易定律》、《园林则例》）、《星轺指掌》、《公法便览》、《中国古世公法论略》、《公法千章》（又名《公法新编》）、《陆地战例新选》、《公法会通》、《中国古世公法论略》、《新加坡刑律》、《各国通商条约》等。

京师同文馆输入的西方法学，尤其是国际法，对于晚清外交产生了一定的影响。通过《万国公法》、《法国律例》等译作，近代知识分子进一步了解世界①。

第三节　京师同文馆译事主要人物

一　奕訢、文祥

奕訢（1832年—1898年）是清末洋务派的首领，大力支持曾国藩等人开办近代军事工业，咸丰初年被封为恭亲王。1860年，英法联军攻陷北京，被任命为全权大臣，负责谈判事宜，与英、法、俄分别签订《北京条约》。1861年主持总理各国事务衙门。咸丰帝死后，奕訢与慈禧太后发动政变，任议政王，掌握实权。奕訢在奏请设立总理各国事务衙门的同时，又奏请开办京师同文馆，并亲自操办师资选拔。奕訢起初试图从国内选拔，但不尽如人意，于是聘请外国人包尔腾为首任英文教习。在天文算学馆事件中，奕訢顶住来自顽固派的压力，不仅增设了天文算学一科，还乘势开设了化学、医学、物理等科目，将同文馆改造成为综合性的学校。对于京师同文馆的教学、考试，奕訢都十分关心。为了提高学生的实际能力，奕訢还于1866年奏请京师同文馆的学生出国考察：

> 查自各国换约以来，洋人往来中国，于各省一切情形日臻熟悉；而外国情形，中国未能周知，于办理交涉事件，终虞隔膜。

---

① 参见拙著《京师同文馆输入的国际法术语研究》，中国社会科学出版社2021年版。

臣等久拟奏请派员前往各国探其利弊，以期稍识端倪，借资筹计。惟思由中国特派使臣前赴各国，诸费周章，而礼节一层，尤难置议，是以迟迟未敢渎请。兹因总税务司赫德来臣衙门，谈及伊现欲乞假回国，如由臣衙门派同文馆学生一二名随伊前往美国一览该国风土人情，似亦甚便等语。臣等伏思同文馆学生内有前经臣等考取奏请授为八九品官及留学者，于外国语言文字均能粗识大概，若令前往该国游历一番，亦可增广见闻，有裨学业。①

此外，奕䜣还为出国考察的同文馆学生申请加官晋爵："惟该官生远涉重洋，所有副护军参领衔前襄陵县知县斌椿，可否赏给三品衔，作为臣衙门副总办官，及伊子笔帖式广英，并考取八九品官之同文馆学生凤仪、德明二名，均赏给六品顶戴，其未经授官之彦惠一名，赏给七品顶戴，以壮观瞻。"② 由此可见奕䜣对同文馆学生的厚爱。可以说，同文馆的许多重大事件都与奕䜣紧密相关，难以分割。丁韪良对他有如下的形容与评价：

> 恭亲王身形瘦削，肤色黝黑，因近视而眯缝着眼，用过去时态讲，他当时并不漂亮，尽管他现在仍然活着。然而他行为举止既和蔼又优雅，说话迅速而有力，给人以有自主力量的印象，实际上他没有。恭亲王以总理各国事务衙门主管大臣广为人知，实则掌管政务的各个分支；但他总是听从下属的意见，他的讲话不过是总结了下属的考量。作为一个皇帝的儿子和另一个皇帝的兄弟，恭亲王是中国当今统治者构成材料的良好例证。③

文祥（1818 年—1876 年）于 1859 年在军机大臣上行走，1860年随恭亲王留京议和，1861 年充总理各国事务大臣。他奉行奕䜣的主张，竭力推行洋务新政。在京师同文馆的问题上，他与奕䜣保持一

---

① 李书源整理：《筹办夷务始末》卷39，中华书局2008年版。
② 李书源整理：《筹办夷务始末》卷39，中华书局2008年版。
③ ［美］丁韪良：《花甲记忆》，沈弘等译，广西师范大学出版社2002年版，第234页。

致,是京师同文馆许多重要事件的参与者与推动者。丁韪良评价文祥:

> 他在国内政治和对外政治中的地位如此显赫,仿照普鲁塔克的先例,我应该把他列为与李鸿章平行的人物。——普鲁斯有一次向我说到文祥,称他从未遇到过更强有力的智能的人。——确切地说,中国像美国一样,并无总理一职,但文祥近十年担任军机大臣,称得上是实际上的清国总理,他影响之大,同时代的中国政治家中无人可比。①

二 毕利干

毕利干(Anatole Billequin 1837年—1894年)曾在法国著名化学家 Jean B. J. D. Boussingault (1802—1887)的实验室工作过,来华前担任另一法国化学家 Anselme Payen (1795—1871)的助手。1867年京师同文馆聘请毕利干来馆执教,担任化学教习,但迟至1871年,毕利干才正式履任。此后的20年间,他一直在京师同文馆从事化学教学工作,1891年返回巴黎,1894年在巴黎去世,时年57岁。为了方便教学,毕利干于1873年与联振子合作翻译了 Faustino Malaguti 的 Lecons elementaires de chimie,即《化学指南》,这是一本化学入门书籍,一共15卷。1882年又与京师同文馆副教习承霖、王钟祥合作翻译了 Karl R. Fresenius 的 Chemical Analysis,即《化学阐源》。除此之外,毕利干还利用闲暇时光,翻译了《法汉合璧词典》和《法国律例》。《法汉合璧词典》又名《中法文翻译名义》,法文原名为 Dictionnaire Francais-Chinose,书前有徐用仪和李鸿章的序文,于1891年同时在北京和巴黎出版。毕利干的为人及工作深受众人的好评,赫德称其为"年轻有为的法国科学家"。②王文韶在《法国律例·序》中

---

① [美]丁韪良:《花甲记忆》,沈弘等译,广西师范大学出版社2002年版,第243页。
② 【英】魏尔特:《赫德与中国海关》,陈敖才、陈琢成译,厦门大学出版社1993年版,第441页。

说："同文馆化学毕教习，系法国好学深思之士。"① 即便是遭受毕利干非议的丁韪良也认为，毕利干"在把近代化学引入作为炼金术老家的中国这件事上，他立下的功劳无疑是最大的。"② 毕利干是当之无愧的"中国化学之父"。③ 由于毕利干勤奋工作的态度以及教学、译书取得的成绩，清政府于 1885 年赏给他四品顶戴。

三 丁韪良

丁韪良（W. A. P. Martin，1827—1916）出生于美国印第安纳州里沃尼亚，祖籍爱尔兰，祖父雅各布·马丁（Jacob Martin）与祖母凯瑟琳·马丁迁居美国宾夕法利亚州。父亲威廉·马丁（William Martin）与母亲苏珊·迪皮尤（Susan Depew）育有三个儿子、五个女儿，丁韪良是最小的儿子。受父亲的影响，丁韪良与长姐马丝·维纳布尔（Marth Venable）及二哥孟丁元（Samuel Newell Martin）先后走上了传教的道路。丁韪良自幼跟随父亲学习基督教以及拉丁语、希腊语知识，1843 年进入印第安纳州立大学学习。1846 年，年仅 19 岁的丁韪良从印第安纳州立大学毕业，随即进入新阿巴尔神学院攻读神学。学习期间，丁韪良接触到苏格兰哲学"常识学派"以及威廉·佩里（William Paley）《自然神学》的思想。苏格兰"常识学派"是 18 世纪后半期到 19 世纪初英国的主要哲学流派之一，坚持外部世界和心灵的真实存在，认为这是人心的构造所产生的共同信念，是人类的常识。主要的代表人物是苏格兰哲学家 T. 里德（1710—1796）和 D. 斯图尔特（1753—1828）。自然神学指的是不依赖于信仰或特殊启示，而仅仅凭借理性与经验来构建关于上帝的教义。它以理性和日常经验为依据，试图证明上帝存在。与之相对应的是启示神学（Revealed Theology），即依靠启示与宗教经验的神学，以及先验神学（Transcedental Theology）——一种架构在先验逻辑之上的神学。丁韪

---

① ［法］毕利干编著：《法国律例·序》，日本司法省 1894 年版。
② ［美］丁韪良：《花甲记忆》，沈弘等译，广西师范大学出版社 2002 年版，第 205 页。
③ ［美］马士：《中华帝国对外关系史》第二卷，张汇文译，上海书店出版社 2000 年版，第 513 页。

良的著作《天道溯源》以及《性学举隅》均以此为理论基础。1849年，丁韪良以"物理科学之于传教士的用处（The Use of Physical Science for a Missionary）"为题发表演讲。同年 11 月，获得长老会牧师资格的丁韪良前往中国传教，他立志要"为基督教取得普遍胜利开辟一条光明大道。"①

丁韪良（W. A. P. Martin, 1827—1916）

1850 年，丁韪良到达香港，随后辗转来到美国长老会在中国传教的重要基地——宁波。他学土语，阅读中文经典，1854 年，用中文撰写了《天道溯源》一书。传教期间，丁韪良发现鬼神崇拜盛行于中国民间：

> 某个星期天的凌晨，一大帮吵吵嚷嚷的人来到了我们的门口，要求进入教堂。——走在人群前面的是一位痛哭流涕的母亲，当我问她有何贵干时，她回答说，她的小儿子"前一天把魂丢在了教堂里，所以她想进到里面来，把魂找回去"。那小孩曾经在教堂里玩过，但一回到家就开始发高烧（也许是因为受到太

---

① 陈学恂：《中国近代教育史教学参考资料》，人民教育出版社 1987 年版，第 35 页。

阳的曝晒），后来又陷入了谵妄状态。说胡话即被当地人视为丢魂，而丢魂的原因被归咎于仰望教堂的穹窿，或是因为孩子从他爬上去的某个高处摔了下来。那可怜的女人坚信，丢失的魂灵就像一只受惊的鸟儿，仍在教堂内盘旋。她拿着一捆小孩的衣服走进教堂后以后，人们就开始做祷告，祈求那"迷失的灵魂"落在那堆衣服上，并回到它原来的栖息之处。做完这些祷告，人们便起身告辞，确信他们已经捉住了那迷失的灵魂。①

为了改变人们的信仰，丁韪良在宁波南门外开设了一所日校。学校既讲授基督教教义，也传授算学、地理等近代科学知识。尽管做了许多工作，但是收效甚微。

1853年1月，洪秀全领导的太平天国起义军攻占武昌，随后顺江东下，直逼南京。洪秀全声称自己是上帝的次子、耶稣的弟弟，通过拜上帝会这一特殊的基督教组织，吸引了大量的信徒。在华传教士们"讨论起它对于传播基督教信仰可能会产生的意义"②。丁韪良认为这是在中国传播基督教的天赐良机，决意亲赴南京一探究竟。他不顾美国公使不得与叛军联系的禁令，在一个风雨交加的夜晚冒险踏上了行程：

> 在花了两天时间逆流而上之后，我们来到了镇江的附近，那儿有大运河的中转站。我们在那儿看到了停泊着的水师战舰和岸上的清军炮台。我命令我的船夫不要理会岸上哨兵的召唤，而是一直往江对岸划去，相信长江的宽度会使岸上的冷枪打不中我们。但岸上的人并没有放枪，而是派了一条船追上来。因为那条船上有很多条桨，所以很快就追上了我们。——假如他们不嫌麻烦地搜查一下的话，他们也许会在我身上找到一个危险的文件——这就是我主动提出为叛军首领服务的一封信。他们刚一转身，我就马上把信给撕了，我不想在经过下一个大营时再冒被人发现的危险。继续往上走了几英里之后，我试图劝说渔民们将我

---

① ［美］丁韪良：《花甲记忆》，沈弘等译，广西师范大学出版社2002年版，第38页。
② ［美］丁韪良：《花甲记忆》，沈弘等译，广西师范大学出版社2002年版，第86页。

带到叛军的前哨处；但我不管出什么价，他们都一口拒绝去冒这个险，因为无论从哪一方面来说都会有危险。我的船夫也因为同样的理由拒绝了我的这个请求。在芦苇丛里躲藏了一整天之后，我不情愿地让船夫在夜幕的掩护下顺流而下，以避免炮台上再次派人追上来。——在前面还有一个更大的危险在等着我们，岸上有人摇火把吸引我们的注意力，有一个声音在警告我们不要往前走，因为"不远处有海盗"。"很可能海盗就在岸上。"我对船夫说，同时船下了锚，跟两边都保持一段安全的距离。我们一直等到天亮，才继续往前赶我们的行程，一路到上海再也没有遇上进一步的干扰。①

对于西方列强帮助清政府镇压太平天国起义的行为，丁韪良颇有微词：

> 难道新教徒不比异教徒更容易皈依吗？一个自称是"耶稣·基督之弟"的统治者难道不比一个自封"天子"的人更容易臣服于罗马教廷吗？——在了解了后继事件以后，再来反思此事，我们仍然要问，当时我们对中国是否换一种政策更好？如果西方列强在中英第一次战争刚爆发时就承认太平军首领的话，它是否可能会缩短那持续了十五年之久的恐怖时期？后者最终造成了捻匪和回民的叛乱，并导致了一千五百万人的死亡。难道新政权不比旧政权更能接受新思想吗？——起义的太平军不止一次地到达了胜利的边缘，但具有偏见的近视外交家们却固执地反对他们，于是一个千载难逢的机会就从他们的手指缝中溜走了。②

宁波传教期间，丁韪良最显著的成绩在于促成《天津条约》中列入基督教传播条款。第二次鸦片战争爆发后，丁韪良感到扩大基督教在中国影响的时机到了。在美国领事裨辣理卫廉（Chales William

---

① ［美］丁韪良：《花甲记忆》，沈弘等译，广西师范大学出版社2002年版，第87页。
② ［美］丁韪良：《花甲记忆》，沈弘等译，广西师范大学出版社2002年版，第94页。

Bradley)① 以及卫三畏（Samuel Wells Williams）② 的推荐下，丁韪良成为美国对清朝谈判使团的成员，担任中文秘书一职。他怀着"加入此行可以看到许多大事，也许还可以为传教事业开辟新的领域。"③ 的目的，在谈判过程中，为基督教在中国合法传播而绞尽脑汁。1857年12月，英、法联军攻占广州。清政府被迫与英、美联军进行谈判。双方谈判期间，卫三畏送给清朝谈判代表雕版刻印的精美中国地图时，"同样给了他和随行官员一些基督教小册子和历书，后者的封面包括十诫的内容。"④ 清朝谈判代表没有接受这些书籍，同时表明了对基督教拒绝的态度：

> 在全部三十份条款中，有关宗教宽容的部分最难达成一致。起先大家认为通过就算了，但中方害怕我们以宗教之名将一些乌七八糟的东西输入内陆，因而对文件进行了严格的审查。他们也害怕这成为政治干涉的托词。他们是理智的，知道基督教这样与异教国家制度相对立的组织是不会和国家现状相调和的。——代表们今天承认皇帝曾试图阻止基督教在华传播，他之所以没有采取措施的原因是考虑到四大列强有意要传播基督教。⑤

但是，随着军事上的失败，清朝政府最后被迫签署了《天津条约》，其中第29条规定：

---

① 裨辣理卫廉，美国外交官，1849年2月7日任美国驻厦门领事。1854年1月24日改调宁波，于同月31日任美国驻宁波领事，似未就任便于3月14日改调新加坡。1856年3月7日再度调任驻宁波领事，直至1857年7月1日。

② 卫三畏，1812年9月22日出生于纽约伊萨卡。1832年7月他被美部会（美国对外传教机构）正式任命为广州传教站的印刷工。卫三畏于1833年6月起程前往中国，并于10月抵达广州，从此开始了他在中国长达四十年的工作生涯。在最初的二十年中，他的主要工作是编辑和印刷《中国丛报》。1853年和1854年他两次随美国舰队远征日本，担任翻译工作。1856年他脱离美部会，开始在美国驻华使团任职，1858年随美国公使列卫廉赴天津订立《中美天津条约》。1862年卫三畏携家眷到北京居住。从1856到1876年，二十年间他曾七次代理驻华公使职务。1877年他辞职回美国，被耶鲁大学聘为该校第一位中国语言与文学教授，被称为美国"汉学之父"。卫三畏于1884年2月16日死于康涅狄格州纽黑文。

③ 丁韪良：《花甲记忆》，沈弘等译，广西师范大学出版社2002年版，第98页。

④ ［美］丁韪良：《花甲记忆》，沈弘等译，广西师范大学出版社2002年版，第108页。

⑤ ［美］丁韪良：《花甲记忆》，沈弘等译，广西师范大学出版社2002年版，第120页。

新教及罗马天主教所遵行之基督教教旨教导人们相互帮助、相与为善。此后传习此类教规之人不应再度因其信仰而遭非难及迫害。无论合众国还是中国之教徒，只要根据教条和平传习基督教教规，便不应受到干涉或骚扰。①

从此，基督教在中国的传播就具备了合法性。

1862年8月，丁韪良来到上海，接替已故上海长老会负责人克陛存的工作。1863年夏，丁韪良离开上海，来到向往已久的北京。与清朝政府接触的过程中，丁韪良意识到走上层路线更有利于基督教的传播。而明清时期来华传教的利玛窦、南怀仁、汤若望、张诚等人通过学术传教的做法，也给丁韪良颇多启示②。为了方便与政府官员的往来，丁韪良不避忌讳，在临近总理衙门的地方购买了一处凶宅。在北京期间，他与奕䜣、文祥、李鸿章、曾纪泽等人都有密切往来。

文祥对他在北京的传教活动非常关心：

> 北京影响力最大的人，通常被称为"军机大臣"的文祥得知百姓经常聚集在礼拜堂的事后，非常关心，唯恐会发生骚乱。他和我进行了一次特别的会谈，要我告诉其他传教士让他们谨慎行事，避免引起反感，尽量在不引人注目的地方活动。这样，人们可以对看到外国人、听到他们祈祷的事逐渐习惯，就不会有什么风险了。③

---

① 王铁崖：《中外旧约章汇编》，生活·读书·新知三联书店1982年版，第97页。

② 早期来华的罗耀拉、沙勿略等人奉行"适应政策"，即顺应传教地的风俗习惯，逐渐地吸纳教徒。随后的利玛窦以学术为媒介，通过走上层路线，在中国站稳了脚跟。初到中国时，利玛窦并不急于传教，而是向人们展示钟表、油画册、三棱镜等物品，借以吸引人们的注意。事实证明这种做法收到了较好的效果。后人将利玛窦的适应策略归纳为"采纳中国的生活方式；结交精英人士并建立关系网；承担确定的社会角色；以基督教的名义提议把学习中国文化的精华作为一种必需；在基督教教义中区分出可改变的和不可改变的；运用西方文化，如科学、艺术、哲学等；采用中国社会的交流渠道和方法；建立本土化教会的基础。"八个步骤。利玛窦奉行的顺应中国文化传统的政策，收到了良好的效果，被康熙皇帝称为"利玛窦规矩"。

③ ［美］丁韪良：《花甲记忆》，沈弘等译，广西师范大学出版社2002年版，第162页。

丁韪良曾受邀参加李鸿章的七十大寿,他描述李鸿章:

> 李是所有总督中最有权势的。李身材高大,有六英尺二英寸,五官长相颇似波斯人,而非中国人,这一切衬托着他智慧和性格上的过人之处。他七十三岁时仍然思维敏捷,腿脚灵便。①

丁韪良认为李鸿章善于用人,促成了许多重要事情:"在李鸿章的支持下,清军建立了水师,装备了两处海军要塞,创办了船政和武备学堂,并开办了煤矿,组织了商船船队,在商贸领域与外国人竞争,并装备了十万新军;最后,计划与西伯利亚相接的铁路修筑到了长城终点。"② 对于李鸿章代表清政府签订《马关条约》,丁韪良提出了不同的看法:"总的说来,李的日本之行,让我对这位中国最伟大的政治家的性格更加敬仰。"③

在所有交往人员中,曾纪泽与丁韪良的关系较为密切。曾纪泽经常向丁韪良讨教英语、欧洲历史、地理、政治等方面的知识,在送给丁韪良的一把团扇上,曾纪泽用中英文题字,称赞丁韪良:

> 学究三才圣者徒,
> 识赅万有为通儒。
> 闻君兼择中西术,
> 双取骊龙颔下珠。
> To combine the reasons of Heaven, Earth, and Man,
> Only the Sage's disciple, who is, can.
> Universe to be included in knowledge,
> All men are, should,
> But only the wise man who is, could. ④

---

① [美] 丁韪良:《花甲记忆》,沈弘等译,广西师范大学出版社2002年版,第236页。
② [美] 丁韪良:《花甲记忆》,沈弘等译,广西师范大学出版社2002年版,第237页。
③ [美] 丁韪良:《花甲记忆》,沈弘等译,广西师范大学出版社2002年版,第240页。
④ [美] 丁韪良:《花甲记忆》,沈弘等译,广西师范大学出版社2002年版,第246页。

丁韪良称赞曾纪泽："性格刚毅，智力超常。——作为政治家，无论在海外代表他的国家，还是在国内参政议事，都表现出中国人最好的素质——谨慎、忍耐与坚强。"①

由于文化的差异，丁韪良通过走上层路线扩大基督教影响的企图并未取得多大成效。

北京传教期间，丁韪良还获得了赫德的支持，赫德答应从政府的资金中每年拨出1500两白银资助丁韪良创办教会学校，以培养更多的传教士。由于难以招到学生，最后也以失败告终。

尽管如此，丁韪良仍然没有放弃努力，1865年3月，在驻华外交官蒲安臣（Anson Burlingarne）和威妥玛（Thomas F. Wade）的推荐下，丁韪良就任清政府新办的语言学校——京师同文馆第三任英文教习。仅仅工作了几个月，丁韪良觉得这一工作与他所要从事的基督教传播的意图相去甚远，面对年薪白银5000两的优厚报酬，丁韪良仍然提出了辞职请求，据丁韪良所著《花甲记忆》：

就职以后，我留心规定自己在新的工作上每天只花两个小时。过了几个月之后，我觉得学院的工作没有扩展的前景，于是便请求辞职。总理衙门的两位大臣——户部尚书董恂和曾任总督的刑部尚书谭延骧，派人将我请去，竭力劝我收回辞呈。

"你为什么要辞职呢？是否嫌薪水太低？"，

"不，"我答道。"跟我付出的时间相比，薪水并不低。"

"是否有人冒犯了你？"

"根本不是，学生及所有其他人都很宽容友好，彬彬有礼。"

"那是为了什么呢？你为何请求辞职？"

"坦率地说，"我回答，"照管十个只学英语的男孩子，对我来说是太没出息了。我觉得自己是在虚度光阴。"

"假如这是你要辞职的原因，"他们说，"那你就想错了。你不会永远只教十名学生。还有你得想一下这些学生的最终前程。

---

① ［美］丁韪良：《花甲记忆》，沈弘等译，广西师范大学出版社2002年版，第257页。

我们的年龄越来越大,他们当中的有些人说不定会被委派取代我们的职位。皇帝也会感到想学外语,谁知道你的学生会不会被召去教皇帝英语呢?①

由于美国长老会对丁韪良的传教工作不甚满意,决定不再给他提供经济支持。缺少了经济保障的丁韪良被迫继续留在京师同文馆。但他依然怀抱传播基督教的雄心:"我之所以继续留在同文馆,也是因为决心要开拓比在北京街边教堂传道影响要更为广泛的领域。"②

1869年,丁韪良出任京师同文馆的总教习一职,他对京师同文馆进行了大刀阔斧的改革,不仅增设了许多新课程,而且组织人员翻译了大量的法学、经济学、地理学、数学等书籍,为清政府培养了大批人才。在同文馆工作期间,丁韪良于1872年创办了《中西闻见录》,该刊物每月发行1000份,将西方的科学技术知识适时地介绍到中国,大大开阔了人们的眼界。

1894年,丁韪良因健康原因辞职回国。1898年,清政府筹建京师大学堂,孙家鼐保举丁韪良为总教习:"阅日本使臣问答,谓聘用上等西教习,须每月六百金然后肯来,丁韪良所言亦同,今丁韪良自以在中国日久,亟望中国振兴,情愿照从前同文馆每月五百金之数,充大学堂西总教习。"③ 1900年,义和团运动爆发,京师大学堂停办,丁韪良被解聘。1902年9月,张之洞邀请丁韪良任"济美学堂总教习兼仕学院讲友":

照得湖北省城议设济美学堂,分普通中学、普通高等小学两班,专教官员子弟,免占各学堂学额。又于教吏馆内增设仕学院一所,凡府、厅、州、县佐杂各班候补人员有志讲求实学者,均可入院肄习公法、法律、财政、兵略、理化各学科。当经本部堂电咨出使美国伍大臣,代聘美国儒、前充中国京师同文馆、大学

---

① [美]丁韪良:《花甲记忆》,沈弘等译,广西师范大学出版社2002年版,第201页。
② [美]丁韪良:《花甲记忆》,沈弘等译,广西师范大学出版社2002年版,第202页。
③ 中国史学会编:《戊戌变法》,第二册,神州国光社1953年版,第437页。

堂总教习丁韪良来鄂,充当济美学堂总教习兼仕学院公法讲友。议明济美学堂总教习每月薪水银五百两,仕学院讲友每月薪水银二百两,由美来鄂川资英金一百镑等,——现查该总教习业已到鄂,本部堂实深欣悦,应即专札派以重任,为此札仰该总教习即便遵照,充当湖北济美学堂总教习兼仕学院公法学讲友,一切听受本堂节制。一面济美学堂择期开办,务期常川到堂,妥订教育课程,督学各分教习将普通学生分别等差,认真训迪。尤要在将各学生行检尽心约束,随时考察,范以准绳,务期各学生遵守礼法,奋勉向学,成效卓然可观。一面分定钟点时刻,前往仕学院将公法学与各官员切实讲解讨论,俾各知交涉事宜。该教习品端学粹,资望老成,必能启发济美学堂各学生暨仕学院各员,蔚为有用之材,本部堂有厚望焉。①

1905年7月,丁韪良离开武汉。1916年12月17日,丁韪良在北京去世,与妻子同葬于北京西直门外。丁韪良在中国工作、生活了半个多世纪,他的传教事业并未取得多少成就,但对于中国近代教育体制的建立以及中西文化的交流,丁韪良的贡献是有目共睹的。

---

① 苑书义等编:《张之洞全集》,河北人民出版社1998年版,第4232页。

第二章 《万国公法》的翻译与出版

第一节 1862年以前中国与西方法学的接触①

中西法律文化交流的历史源远流长,早在公元13世纪,意大利商人马可·波罗(Marco Polo,1254—1324年)在其游记中谈到了元朝的政制、法律情况。1554年,葡萄牙耶稣会士贝尔西奥(P. e Belchior,1519—1571年)根据别人的讲述,写了一篇涉及中国司法的文章——《中华王国的风俗和法律》。此后,西班牙人胡安·冈萨雷斯·德·门多萨(Juan Gonzales de Mendoza,1545—不详)所著《中华大帝国史》以及意大利人利玛窦所著《利玛窦中国札记》中,都以相当的篇幅介绍了中国的法律。但让西方人较为全面了解中国法律的,则是英国人托马斯·斯当东(Sir George Thomas Staunton,1781—1859年)。他将《大清律例》完整地翻译出来,并于1810年在英国伦敦出版。

中国对近代西方法学的了解源于16世纪中期传教士的著作。西班牙传教士庞迪我(Diego de Pantoja,1571—1618年)在其著作《七克》中,曾简略地描述西方的司法制度:"大西之俗,罪人有未服者,得上于他司更讞,——大西国之俗,生平尝一醉者,讼狱之人,终不引为证佐,以为不足信。"②而意大利传教士艾儒略(Giulios Aleni,

---

① 参见拙文《浅议19世纪中叶以前西方法学在中国的传播》,《惠州学院学报》2014年第2期。
② 参见王健《沟通两个世界的法律意义》,中国政法大学出版社2001年版,第22页。

1582—1649年)的介绍要详细一些:

> 官府听断不以己意裁决,所凭法律条例,皆从前格物穷理之王所立,至详至当。官府必设三堂:词讼大者先诉第三堂,不服,告之第二堂,又不服,告之第一堂,终不服,则上之国堂。经此堂判后,人无不听于理矣。讼狱皆据实,诬告则告者与证见即以所告之罪坐之。若告者与诉者指言证见是仇,或生平无行,或尝经酒醉,即不听为证者。凡官府判事,除实犯真赃外,亦不事先加刑,必俟事明罪定,招认允服,然后刑之。官亦始终不加骂詈,即词色略有偏向,讼者亦得执言不服,改就他官听断焉。吏胥廪虽亦出于词讼,但因事大小以为多寡,立有定例。刊布署前,不能多取。故官府无恃势剥夺,吏胥无舞文诈害。此欧逻巴刑政之大略也。①

从这段话,我们了解到西方审判制度的若干特色:(1) 四审终审制;最高一级称为"国堂",也就是现在的最高法院。(2) 回避制度;如果证人、审判法官与当事人有利害关系,必须回避。神志不清者不得作为证人。(3) 不得刑讯逼供。(4) 诉讼费用公开。对于当时的中国而言,这些内容都是十分新鲜的。让中国人耳目一新的还有西方的陪审员制度,当时称为"有名声的百姓"或"批判士":

> 在其国内有人犯罪,必须处治他,但不得乱拿,有证据就可以拿解到官府前问罪。要审之时,则必先招几个有名声的百姓来衙门听候,官府选出六个,又犯罪者选出六个,此十二人必坐下,听作证者之言,又听犯罪者之言,彼此比较、查察、深问、商议其事,既合意,则十二人之首,可说其被告之人有罪否,若真有罪,则审司可宣刑罚。若该人无罪,则审司可放释他也。②

---

① 爱汉者:《东西洋考每月统记传》,中华书局1997年版,第365页。
② 麦都思:《地理便童略传》转引自王健《沟通两个世界的法律意义》,中国政法大学出版社2001年版,第76页。

第二章 《万国公法》的翻译与出版

作为一名陪审员，必须是有名声的人。为体现公正，由官府与犯罪嫌疑人各选六人来审判，他们做出的判决为终审判决。关于西方这种奇特的制度，1833 年 8 月 1 日在广州创刊的中国境内出版的第一份近代中文报刊《东西洋考每月统记传》描述：

> 按察使按例缘由汇款通详察核，细加诘训，搜根寻衅，推穷义类。究其精微，就将情节明说一遍，招众者细聆其言焉。然自不定罪，却招笃实之士数位，称谓批判士发誓云：谓真而不出假言焉。此等人侍台前，闻了案情，避厢会议其罪犯有无罪否。议定了就出来，明说其判决之案焉。据所定拟者，亦罚罪人，终不宽贷。设使批判士斟酌票拟不同，再回厢商量、察夺。未定又容之出也。——批判士不俸禄，并无供职，亦不趋炎附势、指望做官，是以不畏人，而宜恭敬上帝。暗室无漏，周览天下矣。如此民畏法，而悦然服矣。①

"批判士"在参与审判之前，要指天发誓。平时不任职，也不领取薪水。这些形式的和实质的规定，最大限度地保证了审判的公正。《东西洋考每月统记传》还录有一位游历海外的侄子与其居住国内的叔父之间的通信。这些信在介绍英国著名慈善家及监狱改革家霍华德（1726 年—1790 年）的著作《英格兰和威尔士的监狱状况》时，披露了 18 世纪俄罗斯监狱的黑暗。同时，透漏了英国监狱改革的措施，1835 年，英国颁布了 17 条监狱管理条例："（1）全国之监牢，皆要同一样治理。（2）所定之章程，必先交与内阁大臣阅览盖印，方能照行。（3）设一位官员，或一月或半月到监中查探各狱卒及各犯人之行为如何。（4）监内之犯人，除了做工及听人劝教之时，其余不许聚在一处，仍各归本房内。（5）不许犯人讲话，免滋生事端及犯狱之例。（7）不许狱卒勒索出犯人做工之银。（8）犯人所得之工，不得自私，交监内管库之人，为犯人费用。（9）犯人日用之食物若干，必先对国

---

① 爱汉者：《东西洋考每月统记传》，中华书局 1997 年版，第 407 页。

内大臣说知代他允肯，给了印信，然后日日照给。（10）不许将银与犯人作柴米。（11）不许在监内食烟。（12）若有新犯人，则在始初六个月，若无上宪之命，则不许他与亲戚朋友等说话或书信往来。（13）除了睡房之外，不许犯人另有别房闲坐。惟有子之妇人，有两间可也。（14）不许狱卒人等借物件与犯人。（15）如监内有五十个犯人，则必设一位先生，教他改恶迁善。（16）又要请一位先生，教之读书写字，使日日记自己的行为，俟释放之后，能为有用之人，和睦乡里。（17）若犯大罪之人，则放他在一间黑暗的房内居住。以前所议之条款，今已遵行之。惟英吉利王仍然差人前往各监牢探视。试看还有何恶事，俾再妥为更改。"①

此外，中国与国际法的早期接触可追溯至1662年郑成功围攻热兰遮城堡时，与荷兰殖民者之间的谈判与签订的条约。②

第二节 《万国公法》的翻译与出版③

一 亨利·惠顿所著 *Elements of International Law* 及其在西方法学中的地位

惠顿（Henry Wheaton 1795—1848）是美国著名的海商法学家、外交家，1802年毕业于罗得岛学院（即如今的布朗大学），1806年至1812年间在普罗维登斯开业当律师。1812年移居纽约，担任《全国法律顾问》的编辑。两年后，被任命为美国陆军的法律顾问。1815年出版了《海上捕获法和捕获物问题汇编》一书。1815年至1819年间担任海商法院法官，1816年被任命主持美国联邦最高法院判决的汇编，以注解渊博而闻名。1827年，他被派往丹麦任代办至1835年。1835年至1846年间他先后担任驻普鲁士的代办和公使。

---

① 爱汉者：《东西洋考每月统记传》，中华书局1997年版，第421页。
② 参见拙著《京师同文馆输入的国际法术语研究》，中国社会科学出版社2021年版；拙文《台湾与国际法在中国的第一次适用》，《惠州学院学报》2014年第5期。
③ 参见拙文《丁韪良与〈万国公法〉中译本》，2011年2月5日《光明日报》理论·史学版；《〈万国公法〉翻译底本新探》，《惠州学院学报》2020年第1期。

第二章 《万国公法》的翻译与出版

惠顿 Henry Wheaton 1795—1848；美国海商法学家、外交家

惠顿于 1836 年在英国伦敦出版了 2 卷本的国际法著作 *Elements of International Law：With A Sketch of the History of the Science*，同时，在美国费城也出版了 1 卷本的版本，两者的内容基本相同。

1836 年伦敦版出自 London：B. Fellowes, Ludgate Street. 出版公司，该版的书名为 *Elements of International Law：with A Sketch of the History of the Science.* 该书在封面上介绍了惠顿的诸多头衔：Resident minister from the united states in America to the court of Berlin；Member of the American Philosophical Society of Philadelphia：of the Royal Asiatic Society of London；and of the Scandinavian Literary of Copenhagen. 书的首页为一段 Advertisement（见附录一）。

1836 年版 *Elements of International Law* 有三个部分：

第一部分分为两章，第一章 Sources and Subjects of International Law 共有 14 节；第二章 Sovereign States 共有 20 节。

第二部分 Absolute International Rights of States 分为四章，第一章 Right of self—preservation 共有 10 节；第二章 Right of Independence 共有 23 节；第三章 Right of Equality 共有 7 节；第四章 Right of Property

共有 19 节。

第三部分 International Rights of States in Their Pacific Relations 分为两章，第一章 Rights of Legation 共有 24 节；第二章 Rights of Negotiation and Treaties 共有 17 节。

紧随目录之后附有一篇 Sketch of the History of International Law（见附录二）。

此后各种版本纷纷问世，惠顿也多次予以修订，其中，1848 年在 Leipsig and Paris 出版的法语版是他生前最后一次修订的版本，而最后修订的英语版出版时间为 1846 年。

1845 年的版本中，惠顿写了一篇 History of the Law of Nations，用以取代 1836 年版中的 Sketch of the History of International Law。

1846 年，经过修订后，Elements of International Law 在费城再版。该版是第三版，也是惠顿去世前修订的最后一个版本。惠顿的 Elements of International Law 以其立论公允、例证新颖而深受学术界与外交界的好评。惠顿去世后，不断有学者对他的这本著作予以修订和增补。该版刊有惠顿于 1845 年写的一篇序言（见附录三）。

1848 年，法国巴黎的 Leipzig 出版社出版了 2 卷本的法文版。该版是 Elements of International Law 的第 4 版也是经惠顿本人修订的最后一个版本。1848 年版中有一篇写于 1847 年 4 月 15 日的序言。

1852 年德国莱比锡出版社以法文再次出版。

1854 年，在墨西哥出版了西班牙文版。

1855 年，由劳伦斯（William Beach Lawrence）编辑的一个版本在波士顿出版，1857 年，该版本被重印一次。它是 Elements of International Law 的第六版，并且是"第一个注释版"，以 1846 年作者最后修订的一个版本为依据："Sixth Edition With the Last Corrections of the Author, Additional Notes, and Introductory Remarks, Containing a Notice of Mr. Wheaton's Diplomatic Career, and of the Antecedents of His life"，出版商为：Boston: Little, Brown and Company，由 H. O. Houghton and Company 负责印刷。该书还特意注明了版权取得的途径：Entered according to Act of Congress, in the year 1855, by Catharine Wheaton, in the Clerk's Office of the District Court of the District of Massachusetts.

1855 年版 *Elements of International Law* 有四个部分：

第一部分 Definition, Sources, and Subjects of International Law 分为两章，第一章 Definition and Sources of International Law 共有 12 节；第二章 Nations and Sovereign States 共有 25 节。

第二部分 Absolute International Rights of States 分为四章，第一章 Right of self—preservation and Independence 共有 16 节；第二章 Rights of Civil and Criminal Legislation 共有 21 节；第三章 Right of Equality 共有 7 节；第四章 Right of Property 共有 19 节。

第三部分 International Rights of States in Their Pacific Relations 分为两章，第一章 Rights of Legation 共有 24 节；第二章 Rights of Negotiation and Treaties 共有 19 节。

第四部分 International Rights of States in Their Hostile Relations 分为四章，第一章 Commencement of War and its Immediate Effects 共有 23 节；第二章 Rights of War as between Enemies 共有 28 节。第三章 Rights of War as to Neutrals 共有 32 节；第四章 Treaty of Peace 共有 8 节。

最后是附录，共有 3 节

目录之后是编者写的一篇"Introductory remarks"（见附录四）。

1858 年，以 1848 年版为基础重印的法语版出版。

1860 年，译自 1848 年法语版的意大利语版由 Arlia 翻译在那不勒斯出版。

1863 年，出现了 *Elements of International Law* 注释版的第二版，1864 年再版。

1864 年，出现了 2 卷本的法语重印版。

1864 年，在清朝官员的帮助下，4 卷本的《万国公法》问世。

1865 年，《万国公法》在日本出版。

1866 年，由达纳（R. H. Dana）编辑的版本在波士顿出版。达纳为该版 *Elements of International Law* 撰写了一篇序言（见附录五）

1874 年，法语版 *Elements of International Law* 出版。

1878 年、1880 年、1889 年、1904 年，*Elements of International*

Law 由 A. C. Boyd 编辑出版。

1916 年，Coleman Phillipson 编辑的 *Elements of International Law* 出版。

1929 年，A. Berriedale Keith 编辑的 *Elements of International Law* 出版。

1936 年，惠顿的 *Elements of International Law* 作为"国际法经典丛书"的第 19 种出版，该丛书由时任美国国际法学会主席 James Brown Scott 主编。1936 年版封面上注明为 1866 年的再版：the Literal Reproduction of the Edition of 1866 By Richard Henry Dana, Jr., 编辑及注释者为哈佛大学国际法教授 Geoge Grafton Wilson，出版商为：Oxford：at the Clarendon Press；London：Humphrey Milford.

1936 年版 *Elements of International Law* 有四个部分：

第一部分 Definition, Sources, and Subjects of International Law 分为两章，第一章 Definition and Sources of International Law 共有 17 节；第二章 Nations and Sovereign States 共有 55 节。

第二部分 Absolute International Rights of States 分为四章，第一章 Right of self—preservation and Independence 共有 19 节；第二章 Rights of Civil and Criminal Legislation 共有 72 节；第三章 Right of Equality 共有 9 节；第四章 Right of Property 共有 35 节。

第三部分 International Rights of States in Their Pacific Relations 分为两章，第一章 Rights of Legation 共有 30 节；第二章 Rights of Negotiation and Treaties 共有 23 节。

第四部分 International Rights of States in Their Hostile Relations 分为四章，第一章 Commencement of War and its Immediate Effects 共有 28 节；第二章 Rights of War as between Enemies 共有 49 节。第三章 Rights of War as to Neutrals 共有 68 节；第四章 Treaty of Peace 共有 14 节。

正文之前收录了几种不同版本的序言以及评价 Henry Wheaton 及其 *Elements of International Law* 的文章，此外，还有一篇 Note[①]：（见附

---

① Henry Wheaton, *Elements of International Law*, Oxford：At The Clarendon Press, London：Humphrey Milford, 1936.

录六、附录七、附录八、附录九)

该版与1836年的第一版相比较,内容扩充了很多(见下表)。

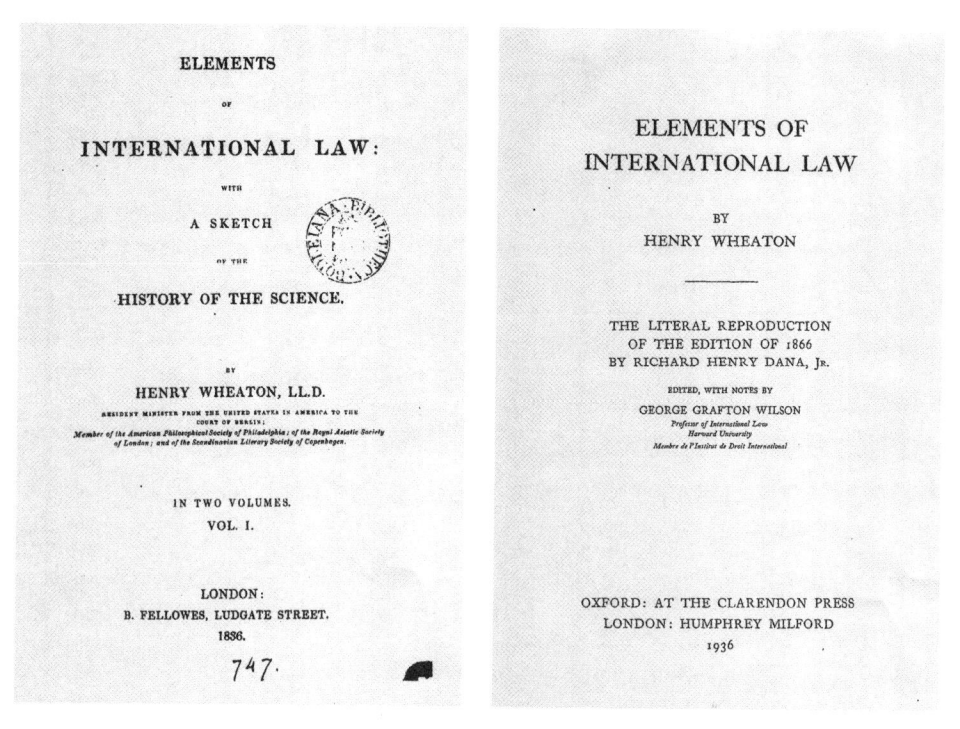

Elements of International Law 1836年伦敦版封一与1936年牛津版封一

Elements of International Law 1836年伦敦版与1936年牛津版之目录对比表[①]:

1836年伦敦版	1936年牛津版
Part First.	Part First: Definition, Sources, and Subjects of International Law
Chapter I: Sources and Subjects of International Law	Chapter I: Definition and Sources of International Law
1. Natural law defined	1. Origin of International Law

---

① Henry Wheaton, *Elements of International Law*, London: B. Fellowes, Ludgate Street. 1836. Henry Wheaton, *Elements of International Law*, Oxford: At The Clarendon Press. London: Humphrey Milford 1936.

续表

1836 年伦敦版	1936 年牛津版
2. Natural law identical with the law of God or divine law	2. Natural law defined
3. Natural law applied to the intercourse of states	3. Natural law identical with the law of God or divine law
4. Law of nations distinguished from natural law	4. Natural law applied to the intercourse of states
5. Law of natural and law of nations asserted to be identical by Hobbes and Puffendorf	5. Law of Nations distinguished from Natural Law by Grotius
6. How far the law of nations is a positive law derived from the positive consent of nations	6. Law of natural and law of nations asserted to be identical by Hobbes and Puffendorf
7. Law of nations derived from reason and usage	7. Law of nations derived from reason and usage
8. The law of nation is not merely the law of nature applied to sovereign staes	8. System of Wolf
9. There is no universal law of nations	9. Difference of Opinion between Grotius and Wolf on the Origin of the VoluntaryLaw of Nations
10. International law between Christian and Mohammedan nations	10. Systems of Vattel and Wolf
11. Definition of international law	11. System of Heffter
12. In what sens the rules of conduct between staes are called *laws*	12. *Jus and Lex*
13. Divisions of international law	13. Opinion of Savigny
14. Sources of international law.	14. Definition of international law
Chpter Ⅱ: Sovereign States	15. . Sources of international law.
1. Sovereign states defined	Chpter Ⅱ: Nations and Sovereign State
2. Limited sovereignty	1. Subjects of International Law
3. Tributary and vassal states	2. Definition of a State
4. Single or united states	3. Sovereign Princes the Subjects of International Law
5. Personal union under the same sovereign	4. Individual or Corporations the Subjects of International Law

续表

1836年伦敦版	1936年牛津版
6. *Real* union under the same sovereign	5. Terms Sovereign and States used synonymously
7. Incorporate union	6. Sovereign defined
8. Union between Russia and Poland	7. Internal Sovereignty
9. Federal union	8. External Sovereignty
10. Confederated states, each retaining its own sovereignty	9. Sovereignty, how acquired
11. Supreme federal government or composite state	10. Identity of a state
12. Germanic confederation	11. Identity of a state, how affected by Internal Revolution
13. United Staes of America	12. Conduct of Foreign States towards another Nation involved in Civil War
14. Swiss confederation	13. Parties to Civil War entitled to Rights of War against each other
15. Sovereignty when acquired	14. Identity of a State, how affected by External Violence
16. Identity of a state	15. By the Joint Effect of Internal and External Violence confirmed by Treaty
17. Identity of a state how affected by external violence	16. Province or Colony asserting its Independence, how considered by other Foreign States
18. By the joint effect of internal and external violence confirmed by treaty	17. Recognition of its Independence by other Foreign States
19. Province or colony asserting its independence, how considered by other foreign states	18. International Effects of a Change in the Person of the Soveregn, or in the Internal Constitution of the State
	19. Treaties
20. International effects of a change in the person of the soveregn or in the internal constitution of the state	20. Public Debts
Part Second Absolute International Rights of States	21. Public Domain and Private Rights of Property
Chapter Ⅰ: Right of self—preservation	22. Wrongs and Injuries
1. Absolute international rights	23. Sovereign States defined
2. Conditional international rights	24. Equity of Sovereign States
3. Right of self—preservation	25. Semi-sovereign States

续表

1836 年伦敦版	1936 年牛津版
4. Right of intervention	26. City of Cracow
5. Wars of the French Revolution	27. United States of the Ionian Islands
6. Congress of Troppau and of Laybach	28. Dependent States
7. Congress of Verona	29. Tributary and Vassal States
8. War between Spain and her American colonies	30. Relations between Ottoman Porte and Barbary States
9. British interference in the affairs of Portugal in 1828	31. Relation of Indian nations to United States
10. Interfefrence of the Christian powers of Europe in favour of the Greeks	32. Single or united States
Chapter II: Right of Independence	33. Personal Union under the same Sovereign
1. Independence of the stae in respect to its internal government	34. Real Union under the same Sovereign
2. Mediation of other foreign states for the settlement of its internal dissentions	35. Incorporate Union
3. Independence of every stae in respect to the choice of its rulers	36. Union between Russia and Poland
4. Exceptions growing out of compact or other just right of intervention	37. Charter accorded to King of Poland, 1815
5. Exclusive power of civil and criminal legislation	38. Manifesto of Emperor Nicholas, 1832
6. Droit d'Aubaine	39. Federal Union
7. Personal status	40. Confederated Staes, each retaining its own Soveregnty
8. Lex loci contractus	41. Supreme Federal Government, or Compositive State
9. Lex fori	42. Germanic Confederation
10. Foreign sovereign, his ambassador, army, or fleet, within the territory of another state	43. Germanic Confederation: internal sovereignty
11. Jurisdiction of the state over its public and private vessls on the high seas	44. Germanic Confederation: external sovereignty
12. Consular jurisdiction	45. Germanic Confederation: a system of confederated States
13. Independence of the state as to its judicial power	46. Act of the Diet of 1832

续表

1836 年伦敦版	1936 年牛津版
14. Extent of the judicial power over criminal offences	46. Act of the Diet of 1834
15. Extra-territorial operation of a criminal sentence	47. United States ofAmerica
16. Piracy under the law of nations	48. Legislative power of the Union
17. Slave trade, whether prohibited by the law of nations	49. Executive power
18. Extent of the judicial power as to property within the territory	50. Treaty-making power
19. Distinction between the rule of decision and the rule of procedure as affecting cases *in rem*	51. American Union, a supreme federal government
20. Conclusiveness of foreihn sentences *in rem*	52. Swiss Confederation
21. Extent of the judicial power over foreigners residing within the territory	53. Constitution of Swiss Confederation compared with those of other States
22. Distinction between the rule of decision and rule of proceeding in cases of contract	54. Attempts to change federal pact of 1815.
23. Conclusiveness of foreign sentences in personal action	Part Second: Absolute International Rights of Staes
Chapter III Right of Eqality	Chapter I: Right of self—preservation and Independence
1. Natural equality of states modified by compact and usage	1. Rights of Sovereign States with respect to one another
2. Royal honours	2. Right of self—preservation
3. precedence among princes and states enjoying royal honours	3. Modifications of Right of Self-defence
4. Usage of the *alteral*	4. Right of Intervention or Interference
5. Language used in diplomatic intercourse	5. Wars of the Reformation
6. Titles of sovereign princes and states	6. Wars of the French Revolution
7. Maritime ceremonials	7. Congress of Aix-la-Chapelle, of Troppau, and od Laybach
Chapter IV. Right of Property	8. Congress of Verona
1. National proprietary rights	9. War between Spain and her American colonies
2. Property of the state	10. British Interference in the Affairs of Portugal
3. Eminent domain	11. Interfefrence of the Christian powers of Europe in favour of the Greeks

续表

1836 年伦敦版	1936 年牛津版
4. Prescription	12. Intreference of Autria, &c., in the Internal Affairs of the Ottoman Empire in 1840
5. Conquest and discovery confirmed by compact and the lapse of time	13. Interference of The Great Power in Belgic Revolution of 1830
6. Maritime territorial jurisdiction	14. Independence of the State in respect to its Internal Government
7. Extent of the term *coasts or shore*	15. Mediation of a Foreign State for the Settlement of the Internal Dissensions of a State
8. Claim to contiguous portions of the sea for special purposes	16. Treaties of Mediation and Guarranty
9. Claims to portions of the sea upon the ground of prescription	17. Independence of every State in respect to the Choice of its Rulers
10. Controversy respecting the dominion of the seas	18. Exceptions growing out of Compact, or other Just Right of Intervention
11. Rivers forming part of the territory of the state	19. Quadruple Alliance of 1834
12. Right of innocent passage on rivers flowing through different states	Chapter II: Right of Civil and Criminal Legislation
13. Incidental right to use the banks of the rivers	1. Exclusive Power of Civil Legislation
14. These rights *imperfect* in their nature	2. Private International Law
15. Modification of these rights by compact	3. Conflict of Laws
16. Treaties of Vienna respecting the great European rivers	4. Application of Foreign Laws
17. Navigation of the Rhine	5. Huberus, as to the application of Foreign Laws
18. Navigation of the Mississippi	6. *Lex loci rei site*
19. Navigation of the St. Lawrence	7. *Droit d'aubaine*
Part Third: International Rights of States in Their Pacific Relations	8. Personal *status*
Chapter I: Rights of Legation	9. Naturalization
1. Usage of permanent diplomatics missions	10. Right of State over Property within its Territory
2. Right to send and obligation to receive public ministers	11. Law governing Personal Property
3. Rights of legation, to what states belonging	12. Bankruptcy

续表

1836 年伦敦版	1936 年牛津版
4. How affected by civil war or contest for the sovereignty	13. *Lex loci contractus*; application of
5. Conditional reception of foreign ministers	14. *Lex loci contractus*; defined
6. Classification of public ministers	15. *Lex loci contractus*; exceptions to
7. Letters of credence	16. Foreign Marriages
8. Full power	17. Foreign Marriages：French law
9. Instructions	18. *Lex fori*
10. Passport	19. A Foreign Sovereihn, or his Ambassador, Army, or Fleet withinthe Territory of another States
11. Public minister passing through the territory of another state than that to which he is accredited	20. Case of*The Exchange*
12. Duties of a public minister on arriving at his post	21. Exemption of the Person of a Foreign Sovereign from the Local Jurisdiction
13. Audience of the sovereign or chief magistrate	22. Exemption of Foreign Ministers
14. Diplomatic etqutte	23. Exemption of Foreign Troops passing through the Territory
15. Privileges of a public minister	24. Exemption of Foreign Ships of War
16. Exceptions to the general rule of exeption from the local jurisdiction	25. Distinction between Public and Private Vessels
17. Personal exemption extending to his family, secretaries, servants, &c.	26. Exemption of Private Vessels from Local Jurisdiction, in French Law
18. Exemption of the minister's hours and property	27. Case of*the Newton*
19. Duties and taxes	28. Qualified Exemption of Public or Private Vessels
20. Messengers and couries	29. Prize Goods on Public Vessels
21. Freedom of religious worship	30. Jurisdiction of a State over its Public and Private Vessels on the HighSeas
22. Consuls not entitled to the peculiar privileges of public ministers	31. Impressment of Seamen
23. Terminination of public mission	32. Consular Jurisdiction
24. Letter of recall	33. Independence of the State as to its Judical Power

续表

1836 年伦敦版	1936 年牛津版
Chapter II: Rights of Negotiation and Treaties	34. Extent of theJudical Power over Criminal Offence
1. Faculty of contracting by treaty, how limited or modified	35. Laws of Trade and Navigation
2. Cartels, truces, and capitulations	36. Extradition of Criminals
3. Sponsions	37. Extradition in the Constitution of the United States
4. Full power andratification	38. Extradition under the Ashburton Treaty
5. The treaty-making power dependent on the municipal costitution	39. Extradition under French Treaty of 1843
6. Auxiliary legislative measures, how far necessary to the validity of a treaty	40. Additional Article in French Treaty
7. Transitory conventions perpetual in their nature	41. Rule govering Extradition Treaties
8. Treaties, the operation of which cease in certain cases	42. Rxtraterritorial operation of Criminal Convictions
9. Treaties revived and confirmed on the renewal of peace	43. Piracy under the Law of Nations
10. Guarantees	44. Privateers
10. Distinction between *asurety and a guarantee*	45. Distinction between Piracy by the Law of Nations and under Municipal Statutes
11. Treaties of alliance	46. The Slave Trade, whether prohibited by the Law of Nations
12. Distinction between gegeral alliance and treaties of limited succour and subsidy	47. Visit and Search as a means of suppressing Slave Trade
13. *Casus foederis* of a defensive alliance	48. Decisionsof Courts of Justice in England
14. Hostages for the execution of treaties	49. *The Amedie*
15. Interpretation of treaties	50. *The Fortuna*
16. Mediation	51. *The Dians*
17. Diplomatic history	52. *The Louis*
Part Fourth: International Rights of States in Their Houtile Relations	53. *Madrazov. Willes*
Chapter I: Comeencement of War, and its Immediate Effects	54. *The Antelope*

续表

1836 年伦敦版	1936 年牛津版
1. Redress by forcible means between nations	55. Extent of Judicial Power as to Property within the Territory
2. Reprisals	56. Distinction between the Rules of Decision and of Procedure as affecting Cases in *rem*
3. Effect of reprisals	57. Transfer of Property under Foreign Bankrupt Proceedings
4. Embargo previous to declaration of hostilities	58. Extent of Judicial Power over Resident Foreigners
5. Right of making war, in whom vested	59. French Law
6. Public or solemn war	60. Proceedings against ABSENT pARTIES
7. Perfect or imperfect war	61. Distinction between the Rules of Decision and Proceeding in Cases of Contract
8. Declaration of war, how far necessary	62. Bankruptcy
9. Enemy's property found in the territory on the commencement of war, how far liable to confiscation	63. Obligation of Contract
10. Rule of reciprocity	64. Conclusiveness of Foreign Judgments in Personal Actions
11. Droits of admiralty	65. Law of England
12. Debts due to the enemy	66. Law of United States
13. Trading with the enemy, unlawful on the part of subjects of the belligerent state	67. Law of France
14. Trade with the common enemy, unlawful on the part of allied subjects	68. Foreign Divorces
15. Contracts with the enenmy prohibited	Chapter III: Rights of Equality
16. Persons domiciled in the enenmy,s country liable to reprisals	1. Natural Eqality of States Modified by Compact or Usage
17. Species of residence constituting domicil	2. Royal Honors
18. Merchants residing in the east	3. Precedence among Princes and States enjoying Royal Honors
19. House of trade in the enemy's country	4. The Great Republics
20. Converse of the rule	5. Monarchs not Crowned, and Semi-sovereigns
21. National character of ships	6. Usage of the Alternat

续表

1836 年伦敦版	1936 年牛津版
22. Siling under the enemy's license	7. Language used in Diplomatic Intercourse
Chapter II: Rights of War as Between Enemies	8. Titles of Sovereign Princes and States
1. Rights of war against an enemy	9. Maritime Ceremonials
2. Limits to the rights of war against the persons of an enemy	Chapter IV: Rights of Property
3. Exchange of prisoners of war	1. National Proprietary Rights
4. Persons exempt from acts of hostility	2. Public and Private Property
5. Enemy's property, how far subject to capture and confiscation	3. Eminent Domain
6. Ravaging the enemy's territory, when lawful	4. Prescription
7. Distinction between private property taken at sea, or on land	5. Conquest and Discovery confirmed by Compact and the Lapse of Time
8. What persons are suthorized to engage in hostilities against the enemy	6. The Papal Bull of 1493
9. Non-commissioned captors	7. Dospute concerning Nootka Sound
10. Privateers	8. Disputes concerning North-west Coast of America
11. Title to property captured in war	9. Convention of 1824, United States and Russia
12. Validity of maritime captures determined in the courts of the captor's country	10. Convention of 1825, Great Britain and Russia
13. Jurisdiction of the courts of the captor, howfar exclusive	11. Expiration of the Convention of 1824
14. Condemnation by consular tribunal sitting in the neutral country	12. Claim of United States and England to the Oregon Territory
15. Responsibility of the captor's government for the acts of its commissioned cruizers and courts	13. Treaties of 1818 and 1827 as to the Oregon Territory
16. Title to real property, how transferred in war, *jus postliminii*	14. Treaty of Washington, 1846, defining Boundary between British and American possessions in the North West
17. Good faith towards enemies	15. Maritime Territorial Jurisdiction
18. Truce or armistice	16. Extent of the Term 'coast' or 'Shore'
19. Power to conclude an armistice	17. The King's Chambers
20. Period of its operation	18. Right of Fishery

续表

1836年伦敦版	1936年牛津版
21. Rules forinterpreting conventious of truce	19. Claims to Portions of the Sea on the Ground of Prescription
22. Recommencement of hostilities on the expiration of truce	20. The Black Sea, the Bosphorus and the Dardanelles
23. Capitulations for the surrender of troopsand fortresses	21. Danish Sovereignty over the Sound and Belts
24. Passports, safe-conducts, and licenses	22. The Baltic Sea, whether *mare clausum*
25. Licenses to trade with the enemy	23. Controversy respecting the Dominion of the Seas
26. Authority to grantlicenses	24. Ports, Mouths of Rivers, &c.
27. Ransom of captured property	25. The Marine League
Chapter III: Rights of War as to Neutrals	26. Straits and Sounds
1. Rights and duties of neutrality	27. The Dardanelles
2. Neutrality modified by a limited alliance with one of the belligerent parties	28. Rivers forming part of the Territory of the State
3. Qualified neutrality, arising out of antecedent treaty stipulations, admitting the armed vessels and prizes of one belligerent into the neutral ports, whilst those of the other are excluded	29. Right of Innocent Passage of Rivers flowing through DifferentStates
4. Hostilities within the territory of the neutral state	30. Incidental Right to use River-banks
5. Passage through the neutral territory	31. Treaties of Vienna respecting the Great European Rivers
6. Captures within the maritime territerial jurisdiction, or by vessels atationed within it or hovering on the coasts.	32. Navigation of the Rhine
7. Vessels chased into the neutral territory and there capyured	33. Treaty of Mayence, 1831, as to the Navigation of the Rhine
8. Claim on the ground of violation of neutral territory, must be sanctioned by the neutral state	34. Navigation of the Mississippi
9. Restitution by the neutral state of property captured within its jurisdiction, or otherwise in violation of its neutrality	35. Navigation of the St. Lawrence
10. Limitations of the neutral jurisdiction to restore in cases of illegal capture	Part Third: International Rights of States in Their Pacific Relations

续表

1836 年伦敦版	1936 年牛津版
11. Right of asylum in neutral ports dependent on the consent of the neutral state	Chapter I: *Rights of Legation*
12. Neutral impartiality, in what it consists	1. Usage of Permanent Diplomatic Missions
13. Arming and equpping vessels, and enlisting men within the neutral territory, by either belligerent, unlawful	2. Right to send, and Obligation to receive, Public Ministers
14. Prohibition enforced by municipal statutes	3. Rights of Legation, to what States belonging
15. Immunity of the neutral territory, how far it extends toneutral vessels on the high seas	4. How affected by Civil War or Contest for the Sovereignty
16. Usage of nations subjecting enemy's goods in neutral vessels to capture	5. Conditional Reception of Foreign Ministers
17. Neutral vessels laden with enemy goodssubject to confiscation by the ordinances of some states	6. Classification of Public Ministers
18. Goods of a friend on board the ships of an enemy	7. Ambassadors
19. The teo maxims, of *free ships free goods*, and *enemy ships enemy goods*, not necessarily connected	8. Ministers of the Second Class
20. Conventional law as to *free ships free goods*	9. Diplomatic Precedence
21. Contraband of war	10. Ministers of the Third Class
22. Transportation of military persons and despatches in the enemy' service	11. Consuls and Commercial Agents
23. Penalty for the carrying of contraband	12. Letters of Credence
24. Rule of the war of 1756	13. Full-power
25. Breach of blockade	14. Instructions
26. Right of visitation and search	15. Passport
27. Forcible resistance by an enemy master	16. Duties of a Public Minister on arriving at his Post
28. Right of a neutral to carry his goods in an *armed* enemy vessel	17. Audience of the Sovereign or Chief Magistrate
Chapter IV: Treaty of Peace	18. Diplomatic Etiquette
1. Power of making peace dependent on the municipal constitution	19. Privileges of a Public Minister
2. Power of making treaties of peace limited in its extent	20. Exceptions to the General Rule of Exemption from the Local Jurisdiction

续表

1836 年伦敦版	1936 年牛津版
3. Effects of a treaty of peace	21. Personal Exemption extending to his Family, Secretaries, Servants, &c
4. *Uti possidetis* the basis of every treaty of peace unless the contrary be expressed	22. Exemption of the Minister's House and Property
5. From what time the treaty of peace commences its operation	23. Discussion between United States and Prussia as to Exemption of Public Ministers from Local Jurisdiction
6. In what condition things taken are to be restored	24. Duties and Taxes
7. Breach of the treaty	25. Messengers and Couriers
8. Disputes respecting its breach, hoe adjusted	26. Public Minister passing through the Territory of another State than that to which he is Accredited
	27. Freedomof Religious Worship
	28. Consuls nor entitled to the Peculiar Privileges of Public Ministers
	29. Termination of Public Mission
	30. Letter of Recall
	Chapter II: *Rights of Negotiation and Treaties*
	1. Faculty of Contracting by Treaty, how Limited or Modified
	2. Form of Treaty
	3. Cartels, Truces, and Capitulations
	4. Sponsions
	5. Full-power and Ratification
	6. Justification of Refusal to ratify
	7. When a Treaty becomes binding
	8. The Treaty-making Power dependent on the Municipal Constitution
	9. Auxiliary Legislative Measure, how far necessary to the Validity of a Treaty
	10. Freedom of Consent, how far necessary to theValidity of Treaties
	11. Transitory Conventions Perpetual in their Nature

续表

1836 年伦敦版	1936 年牛津版
	12. Controversy concerning the 'North-eastern Fisheries'
	13. Treaties the operation of which ceases in certain Cases
	14. Treaties Revived and Confirmed on the Renewal of Peace
	15. Treaties of Guaranty
	16. Treaties of Alliance
	17. Distinction between General Alliance and Treaties of Limited Succor and Subsidy
	18. *Casus foederis* of a Defensive Alliance
	19. Divers Examples of Defensive Alliance
	20. Hostages for the Execution of Treaties
	21. Interpretation of Treaties
	22. Mediation
	23. Diplomatic History
	Part Fourth: International Rights of States in Their Hostile Relations
	Chapter I: *Commencement of War and its Immediate Effects*
	1. Redress by Forcible Means between Nations
	2. Reprisals
	3. Effect of Reprisals
	4. Embargo previous to Declaration of Hostilities
	5. Right of making War, in whom vested
	6. Public or Solemn War
	7. Perfect and Imperfect War
	8. Declaration of War, how far necessary
	9. Enemy's Property found in the Territory on the Commencement of War, how far liable to Confiscation
	10. Rule of Reciprocity

续表

1836 年伦敦版	1936 年牛津版
	11. Droits of Admiralty
	12. Seizure of Enemy's Property found within the Territorial Limits of the Belligerent State on the Declaration of War
	13. Opinion of the Supreme Court in Brown *v.* United States
	14. Debts due to the Enemy
	15. Trading with the Common Enemy by Subjects of the Belligerent State unlawful
	16. Trade with the Common Enemy unlawful on the Part of Allied Subjects
	17. Contracts with the Enemy prohibited
	18，Persons domiciled in the Enemy's Country liable to Reprisals
	19. Species of Residence constituting Domicil
	20. The Native Character easily reverts
	21. Case of *The Diana*
	22. Persons removing from the Enemy's Country on the Breaking-out of War（Case of *the Ocean*）
	23. Decision of the American Courts（*The Venus*）
	24. Merchants residing in the East
	25. House of Trade in the Enemy's Country
	26. Converse of the Rule
	27. Produce of the Enemy's Territory considered as Hostile，so long as it belongsto the Owner of the Soil，whatever may be his National Character or Personal Domicil
	28. National Character of Ships
	29. Sailing under the Enemy's License
	Chapter II：*Rights of War as between Enemies*
	1. Rights of War against an Enemy
	2. Limits to the Rights of War against the Person of an Enemy

续表

1836 年伦敦版	1936 年牛津版
	3. Exchange of Prisoners of War
	4. Persons exempt from Acts of Hostility
	5. Enemy's Property, how far subject to Capture and Confiscation
	6. Ravaging of the Enemy's Territory, when lawful
	7. The Burning of Washington
	8. Restitution of the Works of Art taken from the Louvre
	9. Distiction between Private Property taken at Sea and on Land
	10. What Person are authorized to engage in Hostilities against the Enemy
	11. Non-commissioned Captors
	12. Privateers
	13. Title to Property Captured in War
	14. Recaptures and Salvage
	15. Recaptures from Pirates
	16. Recapture of Neutral Property
	17. Recapture from an Enemy
	18. Recapture of Property of Allies
	19. Laws of different Countries as to Recaptures
	20. What constitutes a 'Setting-forth as a Vessel of War'
	21. Recapture by a Non-commissioned Vessel
	22. Military Salvage for Recapture
	23. Salvage on a Second Recapture, a Rescue, or a Restitution
	24. Rate of Salvage
	25. Validity of Maritime Capturesdetermined in the Courts of the Captor's Country
	26. Condemnation of Property lying in the Ports of an Ally

续表

1836 年伦敦版	1936 年牛津版
	27. Property carried into a Neutral Port
	28. How far the Jurisdiction of the Captor's Courts is Exclusive
	29. Condemnation by a Consular Tribunnal in a Neutral Country
	30. Responsibility of the Captor's Government for the Acts of its Commissioned Cruisers and Courts
	31. Unjiust Sentence of a Foreign Court is Ground for Reprisal
	32. Distinction between Municipal Tribunals and Courts of Prize
	33. Report on the Silesian Loan Causes
	34. Mixed Commissions
	35. Danish Indemnities under Treaty of March 28, 1830
	36. Title to Real Property, how Tranaferred in War. *Jus Postliminii*
	37. Good Faith toards Enemies
	38. Truce or Armistic
	39. Power to conclude an Armistice
	40. Period of its OPERATION
	41. Rules for Interpreting Conventions of Truce
	42. Capitulations for the Surrender of Troops and Fortresses
	43. Convention of the Caudine Forks
	44. The Armistice of Closter-Seven
	45. Passports, Safe-conducts, and Licenses
	46. Licenses to trade with the Enemy
	47. Authority to grant Licenses
	48. Ransom of Caotured Property
	Chapter III: *Rights of War as to Neutrals*
	1. Definition of Neutrality

续表

1836年伦敦版	1936年牛津版
	2. Different Species of Neutrality
	3. Perfect Neutrality
	4. Imperfect Neutrality
	5. Neutrality of the Swiss-Confederation
	6. Neutrality of Switzerland during the Warsof the French Revolution
	7. Neutrlity of Belgium
	8. Neutrality of Cracow
	9. Conventional or Gurranteed Neutrality
	10. Neutrality Modified by a Limited Alliance with one of the Belligerent Parties
	11. Qualified Neutrality arising out of anteccedent Treaty Stipulations admitting the Armed Vessels and Prizes of one Belligerent into the Neutral Ports, whilst those of the other are exclued
	12. Hostilities within the Territory of a Neutral State
	13. Passage through Neutral Territory
	14. Captures within the Maritime Territoyial Jurisdiction or by Vessels stayioned within it, or hovering on the Coasts
	15. Vessels chased into the Neutral Territory, and there captured
	16. Claim on the Ground of the Violation of Neutral Territory must be sanctioned by the Neutral State
	17. Restitution, by the Neutral State, of Property captured within its Jurisdiction, or otherwise in Violation of its Neutrality
	18. Extent of the Neutral Jurisdiction along the Coasts, and within the Neutral State
	19. Limitations of the Neutral Jurisdiction to restore in Cases of Illegal Capture
	20. Right of Asylum in Neutral Ports dependent on the Consent of the Neutral State

续表

1836 年伦敦版	1936 年牛津版
	21. Inwhat Neutral Impartiality consisits
	22. Arming and Equipping Vessels and Enlisting Men within Neutral Territory, by either Belligerent, unlawful
	23. United States Neutrality Acts
	24. British Foreign-Enlistment Act
	25. Immunity of the Neutral Territory, how far extended to Neutral Vessels on the High Seas
	26. Distinction between Public and Private Vessels
	27. Usage of Nations subjecting Enemy. s Goods in Neutral Vessels to Caoture
	28. Neutral Vessels laden with Enemy's Goods subject to Confiscation bythe Ordinances of some States
	29. Goods of a Friend on board the Ships of an Enemy
	30. The Two Maxims of 'Free Ships, Free Goods' and 'Enemy Ships, Enemy Goods,' not necessarily connected
	31. Conventional Law as to 'Free Ships, Free Goods'
	32. Treaties on this Subject
	33. Armed Neutrality of 1789
	34. The proposed Renewal by Treaty of the Doctrines, 'Free Ships, Free Goods' and 'Enemy Ships, Enemy Goods'
	35. Rules disregarded in the Wars of the French Revolution
	36. Armed Neutrality of 1800
	37. International Law of Europe adopted by America, and Modified by Treaty
	38. Prize Courts of the United States condemn Enemy's Goods in Neutral Ships

续表

1836 年伦敦版	1936 年牛津版
	39. Treaties of the United States with the South American Republics on this subject
	40. A Neutral Ship attempting to cover Enemy. s Goods by False Papers, &c
	41. The Rule of 'Enemy Ships, Enemy Goods,' not applicable to Goods shipped before the War
	42. The Two Maxims in later Treaties
	43. Contraband of War
	44. Articles *ancipitis usus*, —Provision and Stores
	45. Transportation of Military Persons and Despatches in the Enemy's Service
	46. Fraudulent Conveying of Hostile Despatches
	47. Carrying Displomatic Despatches
	48. Penalty for the Carrying of Contraband
	49. Must be taken *in delicto*
	50. Rule of the War of 1756
	51. Breach of Blockade
	52. Besieged and Blockaded Ports
	53. Violation of Blockade
	54. Actual Presence of Blockading Force required
	55. Temporary Interruption to Blockade
	56. Knowledge of Existence of Blockade
	57. Constructive or Presumed knowledge
	58. Treaty Stipulations as to Notification of Blockade
	59. Re-establishment of Blockade
	60. Breach of Blockade
	61. Purchase in a Blockaded Port
	62. Effect of Blockade on Inland Navigation
	63. Duration of the Delictum in Breach of Blockade
	64. Right of Visitation and Search
	65. How affected by Neutral Convoy

续表

1836年伦敦版	1936年牛津版
	66. Armed Neutrality of 1800
	67. Forcible Resistance by an Enemy Master
	68. Right of a Neutral to carry his Goods in an Armed Enemy Vessel
	69. Neutral Vessels under Enemy's Convoy liable to Capture
	Chapter IV：*Treaty of Peace*
	1. Power of making Peace dependent on the Municipal Constitution
	2. Power of making Treaties of Peace limited in its Extent
	3. Indemnity to Individuals for Losses by Public Cessions
	4. Dismemberment of States by Treaty
	5. Treaty-making power in Great Britain
	6. Treaty-making power in Confederacies
	7. Effects of a Treaty of Peace
	8. *Uti possidetis* the Basis of every Treaty of Peace, unless the contrary be expressed
	9. Effect of Restoration of Territory bya Treaty of Peace
	10. From what Time the Treaty of Peace takes effect
	11. Cessation of Hostilities after Treaty
	12. In what Condition Things taken are to be restored
	13. Breach of the Treaty
	14. Disputes respecting its Brech, how adjusted

二 "局势对这种书的需求早已引起我的注意。"——丁韪良翻译《万国公法》的原因

丁韪良本想通过上层路线扩大基督教在中国的影响，但他的这一愿望最终落空。不过，他的这一指导思想却促成了中国第一部国际法

译著——《万国公法》的问世。早在《天津条约》谈判过程中，丁韪良就意识到国际法著作"可以对我自己的事业，以及中、英这两个帝国产生一定程度的影响。其实，局势对这种书的需求早已引起我的注意。"① 他发现清政府与西方列强的某些冲突源于清政府对国际法知识尤其是两国间交往的国际礼节一无所知：

> 他（耆英）建议列先生预先要排练一下接旨的仪式，但列先生拒绝了。耆英补充说："您得下跪受书。"列先生回答："不行，我只在上帝面前下跪！""但皇上就是上帝！"耆英说。②

丁韪良希望国际法的引入，能够改变清政府对西方的印象："可以让中国人看看西方国家也有'道理'可讲。他们也是按照道理行事的，武力并非他们唯一的法则。"③ 董恂在给《万国公法》作的序文中也说：

> 涂山之会，执玉帛者万国，维时某氏宅某土，其祥弗可得闻已。顾或疑史氏侈词，不则通九州外之国林立矣，不有法以维之，其何以国？此丁韪良教师《万国公法》之所由译也。

国际法对于国家的重要性，丁韪良在《公法便览·自序》中也有明确表述：

> 邦国局势既有变迁，地球图式亦异。囊昔兼之名家著作代出，公使大会叠见，而大国争端每延友邦调处，以免兵戈，公法因之益重。审是，则将公法新书刊译华文，不得谓非急务矣。

与此同时，经历了两次鸦片战争之后的清政府，也正为不懂国际

---

① 丁韪良著，沈弘等译：《花甲记忆》，广西师范大学出版社2002年版，第150页。
② 丁韪良著，沈弘等译：《花甲记忆》，广西师范大学出版社2002年版，第116页。
③ ［美］丁韪良：《花甲记忆》，沈弘等译，广西师范大学出版社2002年版，第159页。

交往规则，担心遭人欺蒙而苦闷：

> 窃查中国语言文字，外国人无不留心学习，其中之尤为狡黠者，更于中国书籍，潜心探索，往往辩论事件，援据中国典制律例相难。臣等每欲借彼国事例以破其说，无如外国条例，俱系洋字，苦不能识，而同文馆学生，通晓尚须时日。臣等因于各该国互相非毁之际，乘间探访，知有《万国律例》一书，然欲径向索取，并托翻译，又恐秘而不宣。①

总理衙门说它想了解国际法的动机是"每欲借彼国事例以破其说"，了解国际法的方式则是"于各该国彼此互相非毁之际，乘间探访"，并且担心对方"秘而不宣"。这些词语十分真实地反映了清朝政府的心态，十分自然，也十分真实。1863年11月，文祥得知丁韪良翻译了《万国公法》后，十分高兴：

> "我把自己还没有翻译完的惠顿氏法律著作放在案头，尽管中国的办事大臣对其本质和内容知之甚少，他们还是非常高兴。——他（文祥）说：'派遣驻外公使时，此书可供吾等参考。'我解释道，我还没有翻译完，不过我会尽快完成的。"②

最后，文祥不仅答应由清政府出资印刷，而且派遣何师孟、李大文、张炜、曹景荣，对该书润色、修改。

丁韪良翻译《万国公法》有一个目的，就是想借献书之际扬名，以取得清朝政府的信任，扩大自己的影响。总理衙门在奏疏中就称："臣等窥其意，一则夸耀外国亦有政令，一则文士欲效从前利玛窦等，在中国立名。"③

此外，丁韪良将《万国公法》介绍到中国还有更深层考虑，他希

---

① 李书源整理：《筹办洋务始末》（同治朝）卷27，中华书局1979年版。
② ［美］丁韪良：《花甲记忆》，沈弘等译，广西师范大学出版社2002年版，第159页。
③ 李书源整理：《筹办洋务始末》（同治朝）卷27，中华书局1979年版。

望人们在接受国际法的同时，渐渐地皈依基督教。因为19世纪欧洲国际法理论强调国际法是基督教文明的产物，"或问万国之公法，皆是一法乎？曰：非也。盖此公法，或局于欧罗巴崇耶稣服化诸国，或行于欧罗巴奉教人迁居之处，此外奉此公法者无几，夫欧罗巴之公法，与他处所遵之公法有别。"① 当美国长老会得知丁韪良将大量时间耗费在《万国公法》的翻译上时，决定解聘丁韪良。丁韪良辩称该书可以把"对上帝的承认和他永恒的公正带给这个无神的政府，或许会把一些基督教的精神传给他们。"② 丁韪良在对《万国公法》中的地图作文字说明时，宣扬世界都由上帝主宰："五洲之外，汪洋大海，岛屿甚多。然天下邦国，虽以万计，而人民实本于一派，惟一大主宰，造其端，佑其生，理其事焉。"③

《万国公法》得以问世，蒲安臣④起了很大的作用。1862年，中国与法国之间因为多起教案而屡次交涉，由于双方分歧较大，应清政府的要求，蒲安臣推荐了丁韪良的译著：

> 我乐于告诉你，我已经成功地劝说中国政府采纳和出版惠顿的《万国公法》。此事正值这样的时机：去年夏天，清政府因同法国纠纷而同我商讨，清政府的主要大臣文祥希望我向他们推荐一种为西方国家公认的国际法著作，我当然指定为惠顿的书，并

---

① ［美］惠顿著：《万国公法》，丁韪良译，何勤华点校，中国政法大学出版社2003年版，第17页。
② W. A. P. Martin, *Pioneer of Progress in China*, 第145页，载田涛《国际法输入与晚清中国》，济南出版社2001年版，第48页。
③ ［美］惠顿著：《万国公法》，丁韪良译，何勤华点校，中国政法大学出版社2003年版。
④ 蒲安臣（Anson Burlingame, 1820年11月14日—1870年2月23日）美国著名的律师、政治家和外交家，著名的废奴主义者，1861年，林肯总统任命蒲安臣为美国第十三任驻华公使。1862年7月20日，蒲安臣成为第一批入驻北京的外国公使之一。蒲安臣积极执行美国国务卿西华德提出的对华"合作政策"：开展"公正的"外交活动，以取代"武力外交"。1870年2月23日，蒲安臣因肺炎在圣彼得堡逝世，终年50岁。清朝政府为表彰蒲安臣其担任驻华公使时"和衷商办"及出使期"为国家效力"，授予一品官衔以及抚恤金一万两银子。

德国传教士花之安曾描绘了一幅人们由遵守国际法而皈依基督教的美妙图景："公法有于王国，依之而行，易相和协，惟是人心不一，日久弊生，恐有不协之处，则法不若理之纯备也，惟能以上帝之宏恩，化其心之偏见，各国有难协者，以天国之理协之，心慕于天理之公，自可去人欲之私矣，岂不可复大同之世哉！"——《自西徂东》，第85页，香港中华印务总局光绪十年（1884）版。

第二章 《万国公法》的翻译与出版

答应翻译若干段落。我写信给我们的领事乔治·西华德，他发现美国人丁韪良博士正在翻译此书。我全力鼓励他。当丁韪良博士到达北京后，清政府一反中国固有的习惯，安排了双方的会晤，在阅读了已经翻译的部分章节后，达成了一个使丁氏深感满意的协议，即中国会协助他编译此书，一旦完成，他们会用政府的名义刊印此书。①

蒲安臣为什么对《万国公法》的翻译如此热心呢？这与美国当时的对华政策有关。相对于英、法等老牌殖民主义国家而言，美国在中国问题上处于劣势。为了在中国事务上拥有更大、更多的发言权，美国推行对华合作政策。此时的美国希望在西方列强与清政府之间扮演协调者的角色，因此驻华公使蒲安臣利用清政府急于了解国际法规则的时机，积极地向清政府推荐丁韪良翻译的《万国公法》。同时，清政府接受丁韪良翻译的《万国公法》，也是对蒲安臣外交工作成绩的肯定。蒲安臣对此十分得意，1863年清政府同意采用丁韪良翻译的《万国公法》后，他立即向美国国务卿作了汇报，1865年《万国公法》出版后，他又急切地将该书寄给美国国务卿，并在信中大肆渲染清政府对该书是如何重视：

"中国官员虽未再函告此事，但径直造访我，以表示他们对翻译工作完成的重视。当恭亲王和随从人员高兴地坐在一起照相时，负责指导翻译工作的董恂，提出要手持一本《万国公法》来摄影。②

《万国公法》的出版也有赖于赫德的支持。丁韪良在《万国公法·译者序》中讲：

---

① Burlingame to Secretary of State. October 30, 1863, Norma Farquhar: *W. A. P. Martin and the Westernization of China*, M. A. thesis. Indiana University, 1854, p. 125.
② Mr. Burlingame to Mr. Seward, Shang Hai, April 25, 1865, *Papers Relating to Foreign Affairs of U. S.* 1866, M. A. thesis. Indiana University, 1854, p. 439.

> 在我的致谢名单中,我将帝国海关总税务司赫德放在最后,这只是为了让我可以全面地涉及他所作的重要工作。独立于我的工作之外,他早就寻求让中国政府相信有必要熟悉调节国家之间交往的法律,并且亲自准备了一份摘要说明这个法律的主要原则,供他们使用。由于没有民族偏见(在管理海关时他总是如此表现),他热情地欢迎一个美国教科书,并且发挥他的影响力使它得到赞许和接纳。①

清政府为了准确了解国际交往规则,多方求助在华的不同国家的外国人,除了美国人蒲安臣外,英国人赫德也是他们的求助对象。

> 1863年7月14日,董(恂)、薛(焕)、恒(祺)、崇(纶)来访,他们非常盼望我翻译惠顿的国际法,或者至少翻译能为他们所用的一些部分。与俄国条约中的一个条款的措辞似乎出现了一些困难,但是因为只有一个俄文本与中文比照,我帮不了他们,当天,从卜鲁斯(Bruce)那里借到了惠顿;7月15日,摘录惠顿国际法的第三部分,以翻译成中文;7月23日,将我关于取自惠顿的一些段落的介绍性评论翻译为中文,我打算将这些段落翻译为中文,以启迪衙门;7月26日,攻惠顿,完成使节权;8月3日,今天做了更多的惠顿;8月6日,攻"惠顿";8月17日,董给了我一份我所翻译的惠顿,是相当可观的一大卷。②

赫德选译了美国国际法学家惠顿的《国际法原理》的部分章节,其具体内容不得而知,但从文祥与丁韪良的对话中,可知它有二十四条:"文祥问我:'其中包含二十四款否?'他是指赫德先生为他们编选的条约里的重要章节。"③ 赫德与丁韪良同时选用惠顿的《国际法

---

① 张用心:《〈万国公法〉的几个问题》,《北京大学学报》2005年第3期。
② Bruner, K. F. & Fairbank, J. K. ed, *Entering China's Service*: *Robert Hart's Journal*, 1854 – 1863, Mass: Harved University Press, 1986, p. 295 – 303.
③ [美]丁韪良:《花甲记忆》,沈弘等译,广西师范大学出版社2002年版,第159页。

原理》作为翻译底本，应该是一个巧合，但它有利于清政府接受丁韪良的译作。此外，赫德得知丁韪良在翻译惠顿的《国际法原理》后，鼓励他"保证这本书会被总理衙门接受的。"① 1864年8月17日，当丁韪良向赫德展示了他翻译的《万国公法》首页时，赫德承诺从征收的海关关税中提取白银500两予以支助。

对于是否将国际法知识介绍给清政府，西方列强也有不同的态度，法国临时代办克士可士吉②就说："这个家伙是谁？竟然想让中国人对我们欧洲的国际法了如指掌？杀了他！——掐死他；他会给我们找来无数麻烦的！"③

《万国公法》的问世，还与1863年发生的普、丹大沽口事件有关。1863年普鲁士政府派遣李斯福为驻华公使，4月间，李斯福乘坐兵舰"羚羊号"抵达中国天津大沽口海域，遭遇三艘丹麦商船。当时普、丹正在欧洲因领土问题交战，于是，普鲁士兵舰将三艘丹麦商船拿捕。清政府根据惠顿《万国公法》第2卷第4章第6节："各国所管海面，及澳港长矶所抱之海，此外更有沿海各处，离岸十里之遥，依常例归其辖也。盖炮弹所及之处，国权亦及焉，凡此全属其管辖，他国不与也"，认为普舰在中国洋面拿捕丹麦商船，"显系夺中国之权"。并与普鲁士公使进行了严正交涉，最终迫使普舰释放二艘丹麦商船，并对第三艘予以折款抵偿。这件事让清政府认识到了《万国公法》一书的价值，恭亲王奕䜣在一份奏折中说：

> 臣等查该外国律例一书，衡以中国制度，原不尽合，但其中亦间有可采之处。即如本年布国在天津海口扣留丹国船只一事，臣等暗采该律例中之言，与之辩论，布国公使，即行认错，俯首无词，似亦一证。④

---

① [美]丁韪良：《花甲记忆》，沈弘等译，广西师范大学出版社2002年版，第159页。
② 克士可士吉（Cecile Kleczkowski），法国人，法国驻华代办歌士奇之弟。1861年经过歌士奇推荐为天津第一任税务司。其后历任镇江、厦门等口岸的税务司。
③ [美]丁韪良：《花甲记忆》，沈弘等译，广西师范大学出版社2002年版，第159页。
④ 李书源整理：《筹办夷务始末》（同治朝）卷27，中华书局1979年版。

三 "除了希伯来人之外,世界上没有一个民族曾经从古人那儿继承过这么珍贵的遗产"——丁韪良对中国文化的理解与《万国公法》的翻译

"翻译,作为一种在认识论意义上穿越于不同界限之间的喻说(trop),总是通过一种事物来解说另一种事物。"① 法学作为一门独立的学科,自有其完整的知识体系,也有其专门的术语。19 世纪的中国法学所运用的专门术语与西方法学是大不一样的,如果翻译者对中国文化没有精到的把握,将近代西方法学的一套话语系统用汉语表达出来,将是难以想象的事情。

丁韪良学习中国语言及文化,最初的动机是为了让中国人尽快接受基督教,丁韪良"学土音,习词句,解训诂,讲结构。不数年而音无不正,字无不酌,义无不搜,法无不备。"② 在来到中国仅仅四年之后,便用中文写就了《天道溯源》一书,希望"以道之大原,笔之于书,俾人共信。"③ 但是,丁韪良的传教工作并无多少建树,他勤奋学习中国文化的努力为他日后翻译法学著作奠定了很好的基础。透过《天道溯源》、《中国古世公法论略》、《花甲记忆》等著作,我们可以看到丁氏对中国历史、哲学、宗教以及语言都有较为深刻的把握。

为了尽快掌握汉语,丁韪良以欧洲语言中的元音作为基础,加上其他一些变音符号,编出了一套音标,"每一个音节分为声母和韵母,如把 ning 拼为 n-ing,hang 拼为 h-ing,long 拼为 l-ong。"④ 根据这套拼音系统,丁韪良能够复制从老师嘴唇里说出来的话语,不久便能与人交流。来华 6 个月后,丁韪良已经能够用汉语布道。以现在的标准看,丁韪良创造的这套拼音系统是相当科学的。"当地的中国人看到自己的孩子只学了几天就能够阅读,都感到十分惊奇,因为他们学汉语,往往要经过数年的悬梁苦读才能做到这一点。70 岁的老婆婆和不识字的仆人与劳工在皈依基督教时都发现这种拼音的方法能使自己

---

① 刘禾:《跨语际实践》,生活·读书·新知三联书店 2002 年版,第 1 页。
② [美] 丁韪良:《天道溯源·序言》,伦敦圣教书类社 1880 年版。
③ [美] 丁韪良:《天道溯源·序言》,伦敦圣教书类社 1880 年版。
④ [美] 丁韪良:《花甲记忆》,沈弘等译,广西师范大学出版社 2002 年版,第 30 页。

张开眼睛，用生来就会的母语阅读上帝的圣经。"① 学习汉语一年半之后，丁韪良用汉语撰写了他的第一首赞美诗。

丁韪良对中国文化称赞有加："除了希伯来人之外，世界上没有一个民族曾经从古人那儿继承过这么珍贵的遗产"。② 从1850年到1855年，丁韪良系统学习了《尚书》、《易经》、《诗经》、《春秋》、《周礼》、《论语》、《大学》、《中庸》、《孟子》等儒家经典著作。通过这些著作，丁韪良大大加深了对中国文化的理解。

丁韪良从寓言故事入手，对中国文学很快就有了较深的认识，他称赞中国历代诗人中有不少可以跟古希腊、古罗马的诗人相媲美，而小说家要比西方的同行早了整整一千年。"难道这么一座反映人类最伟大民族之一生活的文学丰碑将来不会在我们知识殿堂中占据一席之地吗？"③ 但他又认为《诗经》虽然在反映中国古代生活和风俗方面具有很高的价值，却很少看到缪斯的激情和想象力。

丁韪良对中国历史有较多的了解。他介绍：

> 《尚书》是由一些（多少经过校改的）残篇所组成，主要讲述夏、商、周这三个中国最早朝代的历史，以及在夏朝之前（公元前2200年）的那个黄金时代，那时候王位的继承是按功劳来决定，并非完全是世袭的——贤明君主会越过自己的子孙来挑选更好的继承人。——《春秋》由孔子本人编纂，并由其后来的追随者左秋明加以润色和扩充。这部书被公认为是史学著作的典范。④

1884年丁韪良出席国际法年会提交的论文《International Law in Ancient China》（汪凤藻将它译为《中国古世公法论略》）一文虽然谈的是法学的问题，但从中可以看出丁韪良对春秋、战国时期历史的熟

---

① ［美］丁韪良：《花甲记忆》，沈弘等译，广西师范大学出版社2002年版，第29页。
② ［美］丁韪良：《花甲记忆》，沈弘等译，广西师范大学出版社2002年版，第32页。
③ ［美］丁韪良：《花甲记忆》，沈弘等译，广西师范大学出版社2002年版，第33页。
④ ［美］丁韪良：《花甲记忆》，沈弘等译，广西师范大学出版社2002年版，第32页。

稔程度。"鲁史僖公九年夏,公会宰周公、齐侯、宋子、卫侯、郑伯、许男、曹伯于葵邱。——如周襄王为国人所逐,出居于外。晋文公以兵纳王,王既复于王城,劳文公以地,辞,请隧。王知所请虽小,而所窥伺者实大,因毅然拒之。——如鲁襄公四年,西北山戎如晋请和,且愿列为附庸。晋侯曰:'戎狄无亲而贪,不如伐之。'其臣立言和戎有五利,晋侯始许盟。"① 此外,丁韪良对大禹治水、三过家门而不入等历史典故也十分熟悉。

对于中国哲学与宗教,丁韪良也有自己的见解。他认为《易经》:

> 是如此的深奥,以至人们普遍认为没有一个外国人(有人甚至认为没有一位中国人)能够真正理解它。尽管我并不公然宣称自己能完全理解它,但我却毫不犹豫地指出,在科学的伪装下,它只不过是一整套荒诞无稽的占卜体系。在用落后的迷信来桎梏中国人心灵方面,它所起的作用要比任何一本其他的书都更为有害。②

对于世界源于金、木、水、火、土五种物质相生相克的中国古代本体论,丁韪良基本肯认:"夫地之为物也,内藏金银铜铁诸类。上生草木禽兽等物,草木遗子于土,雨淋日照得以长成,则系水火土合而成之也。而禽兽则食草木者居多。盐与石本乎金,而金之诸类混于饮食中者不一。此古人所以称金、木、水、火、土为五行。"③ 但他认为"草木固籍三行而成,而又必赖乎风。盖木生叶以吸风之情气,如人之有肺以通呼吸,然此西土古传所以称水、火、风、土为四行也。"④ 因此,物质运动理论中,西方缺少金与东方缺少风,都是不妥当的。

对于儒家文化,丁韪良毁誉参半。他肯定儒家传统是中华文明的

---

① 于宝轩辑:《皇朝蓄艾文编》卷13,上海官书局1903年版,第8册,第23、25、26页。
② [美] 丁韪良:《花甲记忆》,沈弘等译,广西师范大学出版社2002年版,第32页。
③ [美] 丁韪良:《天道溯源》,伦敦圣教书类会社1880年版,第15页。
④ [美] 丁韪良:《天道溯源》,伦敦圣教书类会社1880年版,第16页。

根基，对维系社会秩序、国家一统影响很大。其中《四书》是类似于《犹太教法典》的中国《新约》，而《论语》又是《四书》中最重要的作品：

> 《大学》告诫统治者应该如何做到'新民'。掌权者首先要按照贤明君主的榜样来'洗心革面'。——《中庸》论述有关德行的理论，由圣人孔子的孙子执笔完成。所谓德行，就是在无节制和欠缺这两个极端之间保持中庸，而孔子本人即是这种德行的化身。《孟子》的同名作者堪称儒教中的圣保罗。他要比孔子晚出世180年。是他将儒教的理论发扬光大，并且传播到四面八方。他以圣徒般的热忱来阐释儒教的原理。并以希伯来先知的勇气斥责高官的罪孽。①

但他认为孔子所宣扬的是一种哲学而不是一种宗教，而且对孔子对待来生的说法持严厉的批评态度。对于佛教，丁韪良认为它所包含的信仰唯一神和灵魂不死理论是有价值的内容，但是，佛教不过是大众信仰基督教的一个过渡，它是为人们信仰基督教作准备的。对于道教，丁韪良的认识较为肤浅，他认为道教的根本思想在于相信人具有控制人的肉体的可能性，以便保护人们不至于衰弱和死亡。

丁韪良对中国文化的认识水平尤其是语言表达能力得到了当时中国士大夫的认可。董恂称："韪良能华言，以是书就正。——韪良盖好古多闻之士云。"② 恭亲王奕䜣给丁韪良取了一个雅号"冠西"："当时懂得中国学问的人甚少，所以当恭亲王了解我熟知中国的作家、作品后，立即对我另眼相看，并给我起了一个'冠西'的雅号。此后许多中国人都尊称我为'丁冠西'。"③ 陈兰彬在《公法便览》序文中称丁韪良：

---

① [美]丁韪良：《花甲记忆》，沈弘等译，广西师范大学出版社2002年版，第33页。
② [美]惠顿：《万国公法·序》，[美]丁韪良译，何勤华点校，中国政法大学出版社2003年版。
③ [美]丁韪良：《花甲记忆》，沈弘等译，广西师范大学出版社2002年版，第199页。

"居中土久，口其语言，手其文字，又勤勉善下，与文章学问之士游，浸淫于典雅义理之趋，故深造有得如是。"①王文韶在《公法会通》的序文中称赞："同文馆总教习丁冠西先生为美国好学深思之士。"②

四 《万国公法》的翻译底本问题

1862年，从美国休假归来的丁韪良希望到北方传教。但由于负责上海教会工作的克陛存去世，丁韪良不得不留下来协助处理事务。也就是在这段时间里，丁韪良着手翻译国际法著作。起初，他准备翻译瑞士法学家滑达尔的著作，但考虑到惠顿的著作年代更近，影响更大，最后还是选择了惠顿的 *Elements of International Law*（今译为《国际法原理》）。

Elements of International Law 于1836年初次出版后，先后有多个版本问世，丁韪良据以翻译的底本是哪一个呢？许多研究者对此众说纷纭：何勤华认为：《万国公法》译自"1836年出版的《国际法原理》"③、刘禾认为："丁韪良的中译本采用的是第三版（即1846年费城版）"④、徐中约认为：《万国公法》卷前有一篇2页的短文（描述世界上的各个国家）和2幅地图（东西半球各一），是惠顿原著所没有的，"1836年和1855年的版本都没有"⑤、"《国际法历史学报》发表的一份关于19世纪实在国际法著作的书目也注明，《万国公法》的翻译蓝本是1855年在波士顿出版的《国际法原理》的第6版"⑥、张用心认为："1855年的第6版（1855波士顿版）虽然也参考了1846

---

① [美]丁韪良等：《公法会通·序》，同文馆聚珍版1878年。
② [美]丁韪良等：《公法会通·序》，同文馆聚珍版1880年。
③ 何勤华：《〈万国公法〉与清末国际法》，《法学研究》2001年第5期。
④ 刘禾：《〈万国公法〉与十九世纪国际法的流通》，《视界》第1辑，河北教育出版社2000年版，第78页。
⑤ *China's Entrance into the Family of Nations: The Diplomatic Phase, 1858-1880*, Mass.: Harvard University Press, 1960.
⑥ Macalister-Smith, Peter & Schwietzke, Joachim, "Bibliography of the Textbooks and Comprehensive Treatises on Positive International Law of the 19th Century", *Journal of the History of International Law*, Vol. 3, No. 1, 2001, pp. 75-142.

年的第 3 版（1846 年费城版），却是以 1848 年的第 4 版（1848 年巴黎版）作为蓝本。事实上，1855 年的第 6 版与 1846 年的第 3 版在章节上有所出入：第一部分第一章，第 3 版有 16 小节，而第 6 版只有 12 小节；第一部分第二章，第 3 版有 26 小节，第 6 版只有 25 小节；第二部分第一章，第 3 版有 17 小节，第 6 版只有 16 小节，第二部分第二章，第 3 版有 22 小节，第 6 版只有 21 小节。第 6 版所分小节数目虽较第 3 版少，但是在实际内容上，第 6 版包括了第 3 版之所有，且有第 3 版所没有的新内容，如第一部分第一章第十节题为《赫夫特尔（Heffter）的体系》（《万国公法》第一卷第一章第十节《海［付达］氏大旨》正好对应）。"① 丁韪良的翻译工作开始于 1862 年之前，

Elements of International Law 1855 年波士顿版封一

---

① 张用心：《〈万国公法〉的几个问题》，《北京大学学报》2005 年第 3 期。

因此，他所选用的底本只可能是1857年以前的版本。此外，根据丁韪良放弃瑞士法学家滑达尔的著作、选用惠顿著作的理由："我本打算翻译瓦岱尔（Vattel）（即滑达尔）的作品，但华若翰先生建议我采用惠顿氏的，他的书同样权威，且更现代一些。"① 除了惠顿是美国人之外，他的书距离时代更近，是丁韪良选择惠顿的 Elements of International Law 的重要原因。因此，丁韪良以1836年出版的伦敦版为翻译底本的可能性不大。而此前1848年出版的巴黎版是法文版、1852年出版的莱比锡版是德文版，1854年出版的墨西哥版是西班牙文版，考虑到语言的因素，丁韪良选用的底本应该是1855年出版的波士顿版或1857年重印版。

笔者将1855年劳伦斯（William Beach Lawrence）编辑的波士顿版目录与汉译本《万国公法》目录对照，两者的内容基本相符。

Elements of International Law 1855年波士顿版与《万国公法》目录对比表②：

英语原文	丁韪良译文
Elements of International Law	《万国公法》
Part First：Definition, Sources, and Subjects of International Law	第一卷 释公法之义，明其本源，题其大旨
Chapter I：Definition and Sources of International Law	第一章 释义明源
1. Origin of International Law	第一节 本于公义
2. Natural law defined, by Grotius	第二节 出于天性
3. Natural law identical with the law of God, or divine law	第三节 称为天法
4. Law of nations distinguished from natural law, by Grotius	第四节 公法、性法犹有所别
5. Law of natural and law of nations asserted to be identical, by Hobbes and Puffendorf	第五节 理同名异 常用大例

---

① 丁韪良：《花甲记忆》，沈弘等译，广西师范大学出版社2002年版，第150页。
② ［美］Henry Wheaton, Elements of International Law, Boston：Little, Brown and Company, 1855；［美］惠顿：《万国公法》，［美］丁韪良译，何勤华点校，中国政法大学出版社2003年版。

续表

英语原文	丁韪良译文
6. Law of nations derived from reason and usages	第六节　理、例二源
7. System of Wolf	第七节　性理之一派 分为三种
8. . Difference of Opinion between Grotius and Wolf on the Origin of the Voluntary Law of Nations	第八节　二子所论微异
9. Systems of Vattel	第九节　发氏大旨
10. System of Heffter	第十节　海氏大旨 分为二派 公法精义 公法不一 应否称法 出于同俗、行于他方
11. Definition of international law	第十一节　公法总旨
12 Sources of international law	第十二节　公法源流
Chpter II：Nations and Sovereign State	第二章　论邦国自治、自主之权
1. Subjiects of International Law	第一节　公法所论
2. Definition of a State	第二节　何者为国
3. Sovereign Princes the Subjects of International Law	第三节　君身之私权
4. Individual or Corporations the Subjects of International Law	第四节　民人之私权
5. Sovereign defined	第五节　主权分内外
6. Sovereignty, how acquired	第六节　在内之主权 在外之主权
7. Identity of a state	第七节　不因内变而亡 他国或旁观或相助 争者皆得战权
8. Parties to Civil War entitled to Rights of War against each other	第八节　外敌致变
9. By the Joint Effect of Internal and External Violence confirmed by Treaty	第九节　内变外敌并至

续表

英语原文	丁韪良译文
10. Province or Colony asserting its Independence, how considered by other Foreign States	第十节　省部叛而自立
11. International Effects of a Change in the Person of the Sovereign, or in the Internal Constitution of the State	第十一节　易君变法 于盟国如何 于国债如何 于国土名产如何 如他国被害者如何
12. Sovereign States defined	第十二节　释自主之义
13. Semi-sovereign States	第十三节　释半主之义
14. Tributary and Vassal States	第十四节　进贡藩属所存主权
15. Single or united States	第十五节　或独或合
16. Personal Union under the same Sovereign	第十六节　相合而不失其主权
17. Real Union under the same Sovereign	第十七节　相合而不失其内在之主权
18. Incorporate Union	第十八节　相合而并失其内外之主权
19. Union between Russia and Poland	第十九节　波兰始合于俄 继得国法权利 终则被俄所并
20. Federal Union	第二十节　会盟永合有二
21. Confederated States, each retaining its own Sovereignty	第二十一节　会盟连横
22. Supreme Federal Government, or Compositive State	第二十二节　合盟为一
23. Germanic Confederation	第二十三节　日耳曼系众邦会盟
24. United States of America	第二十四节　美国系众邦合一 上国制法之权 首领行法之权 司法之权 立约之权 各邦所无之权
25. Swiss Confederation	第二十五节　与前二国异同如何

续表

英语原文	丁韪良译文
Part Second: Absolute International Rights of Staes	第二卷 论诸国自然之权
Chapter I: Rights of self—preservation and Independence	第一章 论其自护、自主之权
1. Rights of Sovereign States with respect to one another	第一节 操权二种
2. Right of self—preservation	第二节 自护之权为大 立约改革推让均可
3. Right of Intervention or Interference	第三节 与闻他国政事之例
4. Wars of the French Revolution	第四节 以法国为鉴 五国横连之故
5. Congress of Aix-la-Chapelle, of Troppau, and od Laybach	第五节 三国管制那国，英国驳之
6. Congress of Verona	第六节 四国管制西国，英不许之
7. War between Spain and her American colonies	第七节 四国管制西之叛邦，英、美斥之
8. British Interference in the Affairs of Portugal, in 1826	第八节 葡国有争，英管制之
9. Interfefrence of the Christian powers of Europe in favour of the Greeks	第九节 希腊被虐，三国助之
10. Intreference of Autria, Great Britain, Prussia, and Russia, in the Internal Affairs of the Ottoman Empire, in 1840	第十节 埃及叛土，五国理之
11. Interference of the five Great power in Belgic Revolution of 1830	第十一节 比利时叛土，五国议之
12. Independence of the State in respect to itsInternal Government	第十二节 各国自主其内事
13. Mediation of other foreign States for the settlement of the internal dissensions of a State Treaties of mediation and guarranty	第十三节 他国与闻，或临事相请，或未事有约 盟邦互保

续表

英语原文	丁韪良译文
14. Independence of every State in respect to the Choice of its Rulers	第十四节　立君举官，他国不得与闻
15. Exceptions growing out of compact or other Just right of intervention	第十五节　立君举官而他国可与闻者
16. Quadruple Alliance of 1834, between France, Great Britain, Portugal and Spain	第十六节　西、葡立君，英、法与闻之
Chapter II: Rights of Civil and Criminal Legislation	第二章　论制定律法之权
1. Exclusive power of civil legislation	第一节　制律之权 变通之法
2. Conflict of laws	第二节　变通之法，大纲有二 简要三则 三则合一
3. Lex loci rei site	第三节　植物从物所在之律
4. . Droit d'aubaine	第四节　古禁外人购买植物 昔以外人遗物入公 遗产徙外酌留数分
5. Lex domicilii	第五节　动物从人所在之律
6. Personal status	第六节　内治之权 法行于疆外者 第一种定己民之分位 准外人入籍 制疆内之物 律从写契地方
7. Lex loci contractus	第七节　第二种就事而行于疆外者 其不行者有四 不合于物所在之律则不行 妨碍于他国则不行 遇契据应成于他国则不行
8. Lex fori	第八节　遇案之应由法院条规而断者则不行

续表

英语原文	丁韪良译文
9. A Foreign sovereihn, his ambassador, army, or fleet within the territory of another State	第九节　第三种就人而行于疆外者 因一案覆论三端 君身过疆国权随之 使臣在外国权随之 兵旅过疆国权随之 兵船另归一例 法国接待商船之例 按此例罪分二等 公案二件 不得藉此例而谋为不轨 犯局外之权而捕拿船货进口必归地方管辖
10. Jurisdiction of the State over its public and private vessels on the highSeas	第十节　船只行于大海均归本国管辖 海外犯公法之案各国可行审办 他国之船不可稽查
11. Consular jurisdiction	第十一节　第四种因约而行于疆外者 领事等官
12. Independence of the State as to its judical power	第十二节　审案之权各国自秉
13. Extent of the judical power over criminal offence	第十三节　四等罪案审罚可及 交还逃犯之例
14. Extra-territorial operation of a criminal offences	第十四节　法院定拟旁行于疆外
15. Piracy under the law of nations	第十五节　审断海盗之例 各国或另有海盗之例 公禁贩卖人口
16. . Extent of judicial power as to property within the territory	第十六节　疆内植物之争讼审权可及
17. Distinction between the rule of decision and the rule of of procedure as affecting cases in *rem*	第十七节　疆内动物之争讼审权可及 继遗物之例
18. Conclusiveness of foreign sentences*in rem*	第十八节　以他国法院曾断为准
19. Extent of judicial power over foreigners residing within the territory	第十九节　疆内因人民权利等争端审权可及
20. Distinctionbetween the rules of decision and rule of proceeding in cases of contract	第二十节　断案之法、兴讼之例有别

续表

英语原文	丁韪良译文
21. Conclusiveness of foreign sentences in personal actions	第二十一节　涉身之案他国既断本国从否
Chapter III：Rights of Equality	第三章　论诸国平行之权
1. Natural eqality of States modifiedby compact and usage	第一节　分尊卑出于相许
2. Royal Honors	第二节　得王礼之国
3. Precedence among princes and States enjoying royal honors	第三节　得王礼者分位次
4. Usage of the *alternal*	第四节　互易之方
5. Language used in diplomatic intercourse	第五节　公用之文字
6. Titles of sovereign princes and States	第六节　君国之尊号
7. Maritime ceremonials	第七节　航海礼款
Chapter IV：Rights of Property	第四章　轮各国掌物之权
1. National proprietary *rights*	第一节　掌物之权所由来
2. Public and private property	第二节　民物亦归此权
3. Eminent domain	第三节　民物听命于上权
4. Prescription	第四节　历久为牢固之例
5. Conquest and discovery confirmed by compact and the lapse of time	第五节　权由征服寻觅而来者
6. Maritime territorial jurisdiction	第六节　管沿海近处之权
7. Extent of the term *coasts* or *Shore*	第七节　长滩应随近岸
8. Right of fishery	第八节　捕鱼之权
9. Claims to portions of the sea on the ground of prescription	第九节　管小海之权
10. Controversy respecting the dominion of the seas	第十节　大海不归专管之例
11. Rivers forming part of the territory of the State	第十一节　疆内江湖亦为国土
12. Right of innocent passage of rivers flowing through different States	第十二节　无损可用之例
13. Incidental right to use the banks of the rivers	第十三节　他事随行之例
14. These rights *imperfect* in their nature	第十四节　同上
15. Modification of these rights by compact	第十五节　同享水利之权可让可改
16. . Treaties of Vienna respecting the great European rivers	第十六节　同航大江之例

续表

英语原文	丁韪良译文
17. Navigation of the Rhine	
18. Navigation of the Mississippi	
19. Navigation of the St. Lawrence	
Part Third: International Rights of States in Their Pacific Relations	第三卷　论诸国平时往来之权
Chapter I: Rights of Legation	第一章　论通使之权
1. Usage of permanent diplomatic missions	第一节　钦差驻扎外国
2. Right to send and obligation to receive, public ministers	第二节　可遣可受
3. Rights of legation, to what States belonging	第三节　何等之国可以通使
4. How affected by civil war or Contest for the sovereignty	第四节　国乱通使
5. Conditional reception of foreign ministers	第五节　先议后接
6. Classification of public ministers	第六节　国使等级
7. Letters of credence	第七节　信凭款式
8. Full power	第八节　全权之凭
9. Instructions	第九节　训条之规
10. Passport	第十节　牌票护身
11. Duties of a public minister on arriving at his post	第十一节　莅任之规
12. Audience of the sovereign or chief magistrate	第十二节　延见之规
13. Diplomatic etiquette	第十三节　交好礼款
14. Privileges of a public minister	第十四节　国使权利
15. Exceptions to the general rule of exemption from the local jurisdiction	第十五节　例外之事
16. Personal exemption extending to his family, secretaries, servants, &c	第十六节　家人置权外
17. Exemption of the minister's house and property	第十七节　房屋器具置权外
18. Duties and taxes	第十八节　纳税之规
19. Messengers and couriers	第十九节　寄公信者
20. Public minister passing through the territory of another State than that to which he is accredited	第二十节　路过他国
21. Freedom of religious worship	第二十一节　礼拜不可禁止

续表

英语原文	丁韪良译文
22. Consuls nor entitled to the peculiar privileges of public ministers	第二十二节　领事权利
23. Termination of public mission	第二十三节　国使卸任
24. Letter of recall	第二十四节　召回国使
Chapter II: Rights of Negotiation and Treaties	第二章　论商议立约之权
1. Faculty of contracting by Treaty, how Limited or modified	第一节　限制若何
2. Form of treaty	第二节　盟约款式
3. Cartels, truces, and capitulations	第三节　约据章程
4. Sponsions	第四节　擅约准废
5. Full power and ratifications	第五节　公约准废
6. The Treaty-making power dependent on the municipal constitution	第六节　谁执定约之权
7. Auxiliary legislative measure, how far neceessary to the validity of a treaty	第七节　因约改法
8. Freedom of consent, how far necessary to the validity of treaties	第八节　被逼改法
9. Transitory conventions perpetual in their nature	第九节　恒约不因战废
10. Treaties the operation of which ceases in certain cases	第十节　常约存废
11. Treaties revived and confirmed on the renewal of peace	第十一节　盟约多兼二种
12. Treaties of guaranty	第十二节　保护之约
13. Treaties of alliance	第十三节　合兵之盟
14. Distinction between general alliance and treaties of limited succor and subsidy	第十四节　立约助兵
15. *Casus foederis* of a defensive alliance	第十五节　相互之例
16. Hostages for the execution of treaties	第十六节　交质以坚信
17. Interpretation of treaties	第十七节　解说盟约
18. Mediation	第十八节　中保之例
19. Diplomatic history	第十九节　主持公论之学
Part Fourth: International Rights of States in Their Hostile Relations	第四卷　论交战条规

续表

英语原文	丁韪良译文
Chapter I: Commencement of War and its Immediate Effects	第一章　论战始
1. Redress by forcible means between nations	第一节　用力伸冤
2. Reprisals	第二节　强偿之例
3. Effect of reprisals	第三节　强偿之用
4. Embargo previous to declaration of hostilities	第四节　战前捕物二解
5. Right of making war, in whom vested	第五节　定战之权
6. Public or solemn war	第六节　公战之权
7. Perfect and imperfect war	第七节　战有三等
8. Declaration of war, how far necessary	第八节　宣战之始
9. Enemy's property found in the territory on the commencement of war, how far liable to confiscation	第九节　敌货在我疆内者
10. Rule of reciprocity	第十节　照行而行
11. Droits of admiralty	第十一节　敌物在疆内者不即入公
12. Debts due to the Enemy	第十二节　债欠于敌
13. Trade with the enemy, unlawful on the part of subjects of the belligerent State	第十三节　与敌贸易
14. Trade with the common enemy unlawful on the part of allied Subjects	第十四节　合兵之民通商敌国
15. Contracts with the enemy prohibited	第十五节　不可与敌立契约
16. Persons domiciled in the enemy's country liable to reprisals	第十六节　敌民居于疆内者
17. Species of residence constituting domicil	第十七节　何谓迁往别国 本名易复
18. Merchants residing in the east	第十八节　西人住于东土者
19. House of trade in the enemy's country	第十九节　商行设于敌国
20. Converse of the rule	第二十节　身在敌国行在局外
21. Produce of the enemy's territory considered as hostile, so long as it belongs to the owner of the soil, whatever may be his national character or personal domicil	第二十一节　敌国土产属地主时即为敌货
22. National character of ships	第二十二节　船因船户得名

续表

英语原文	丁韪良译文
23. Sailing under the enemy's license	第二十三节　领照于敌国
Chapter II：Rights of War as between Enemies	第二章　论敌国交战之权
1. Rights of war against an enemy	第一节　害敌有限
2. Limits to the rights of war against the person of an enemy	第二节　害敌之权至何而止
3. Exchange of prisoners of war	第三节　互换俘虏
4. Persons exempt from acts of hostility	第四节　何等人不可杀
5. Enemy's property, how far subject to capture and confiscation	第五节　敌人之产业
6. Ravaging of the enemy's territory, when lawful	第六节　抄掠敌境
7. Distiction between private property taken at sea, or on land	第七节　水陆捕拿不同一例
8. What person are authorized to engage in hostilities against the enemy	第八节　何人可以害敌
9. Non-commissioned captors	第九节　船无战牌而捕获者
10. Privateers	第十节　民船领战牌者
11. Title to property captured inwar	第十一节　被捕之货可讨与否
12. Recaptures and Salvage	第十二节　夺回救货之例
13. Validity of maritime captures determined in the courts of the captor's country	第十三节　审所捕之船归捕者本国之法院
14. Jurisdiction of the coyrts of the captor, how far exclusive	第十四节　局外之法院审案
15. Condemnation by consular tribunnal sitting in the neutral country	第十五节　领事在局外之地者不足断此案
16. Responsibility of the captor's government for the acts of its commissioned cruisers and courts	第十六节　照例所捕在国不在民柱理断案自行理直
17. Title to real property, how tranaferred in war. *Jus postliminii*	第十七节　植物如何还主
18. Good faith toards enemies	第十八节　守信于敌
19. Truce or armistic	第十九节　停兵之约
20. Power to conclude an armistice	第二十节　停兵之权
21. Period of its operation	第二十一节　自何时遵行

续表

英语原文	丁韪良译文
22. Rules for interpreting conventions of truce	第二十二节 解说停兵之约
23. Recommencement of hostilities on the expiration of truce	第二十三节 停兵期满复战
24. Capitulations for the surrender of troops and fortresses	第二十四节 投降款约
25. Passports, safe-conducts, and licenses	第二十五节 护身等票
26. Licenses to trade with the enemy	第二十六节 凭照与敌贸易
27. Authority to grant licenses	第二十七节 何权足以出照
28. Ransom of caotured property	第二十八节 捕获讨赎
Chapter III: Rights of War as to Neutrals	第三章 论战时局外之权
1. Definition of neutrality	第一节 解局外之意
2. Different species of neutrality	第二节 全半二字
3. Perfect neutrality	第三节 局外之全权
4. Imperfect neutrality	第四节 局外之半权
5. Neutrality modified by a limited alliance with one of the belligerent parties	第五节 局外之权被约限制
6. Qualified neutrality arising out of anteccedent treaty stipulations admitting the armed vessels and prizes of one belligerent into the neutral ports, whilst those of the other are exclued	第六节 因前约准此而禁彼
7. Hostilities within the territory of a neutral State	第七节 在局外之地不可行战权
8. Passage through neutral territory	第八节 经过局外之疆
9. Captures within the maritime territoyial jurisdiction or by vessels stayioned within it, or hovering on the coasts	第九节 沿海辖内捕船
10. Vessels chased into the neutral territory, and there captured	第十节 追至局外之地而捕者
11. Claim on the ground of the violation of neutral teritory must be sanctioned by the neutral State	第十一节 局外者讨还
12. Restitution, by the neutral State of property captured within its jurisdiction, or otherwise in violation of its neutrality	第十二节 犯局外之权而捕之货，局外者自必交还赔偿

续表

英语原文	丁韪良译文
13. Limitations of the neutral jurisdiction to restore in cases of illegal capture	第十三节　交还之权有限制
14. Right of asylum in neutral ports dependent on the consent of the neutral State	第十四节　在局外之地避患、买粮、卖赃
15. Neutral impartiality, in what it consists	第十五节　守中有二事
16. Arming and equipping vessels, and enlisting men within neutral territory, by either belligerent, unlawful	第十六节　借局外之地招兵备船即为犯法
17. Prohibition enforced by municipal statutes	第十七节　律法禁之投军别国
18. Immunity of the neutral territory, how far extended to neutral vessels on the high seas	第十八节　局外之船于大海如何
19. Usage of nations subjecting enemy's goods in neutral vessels to caoture	第十九节　捕拿敌货在局外之船者为常事
20. Neutral vessels laden with enemy goods subject to confiscation by the ordinances of some States	第二十节　载敌货之船有时捕为战例
21. Goods of a friend on board the ships of an enemy	第二十一节　捕拿友货在敌国之船有人行之
22. The Two maxims of '*free ships, free goods* and '*enemy ships, enemy goods*,' not necessarily connected	第二十二节　二规非不可相离
23. Conventional law as to *free ships free goods*	第二十三节　局外者装载敌货
24. Contraband of war	第二十四节　战时禁物
25. Transportation of military persons and despatches in the enemy's service	第二十五节　寄信载兵等
26. Penalty for the carrying of contraband	第二十六节　载禁物之干系
27. Rule of the war of 1756	第二十七节　通商战者之属邦
28. Breach of blockade	第二十八节　封港犯封 犯封三问 实势行封 犯者知之 实事犯封
29. Right of visitation and search	第二十九节　往视稽查之权

续表

英语原文	丁韪良译文
30. Forcible resistance by an enemy master	第三十节　敌人为船主而强御者
31. Right of a neutral to carry his goods in an *armed enemy vessel*	第三十一节　局外者借敌人之兵船载货
32. . Neutral vessels under enemy's convoy, liable to capture	第三十二节　局外之船借敌人之保护可捕拿
Chapter IV: Treaty of Peace	第四章　论合约章程
1. Power of making peace dependent on the municipal constitution	第一节　谁执和权惟国法所定
2. Power of making treaties of peace limited in its extent	第二节　立合约之权有限制
3. Effects of a treaty of peace	第三节　合约息争
4. *Uti possidetis* the basis of every treaty of peace, unless the contrary be expressed	第四节　各守所有
5. From what time the treaty of peace commences its operation	第五节　合约自何日为始
6. In what condition things taken are to be restored	第六节　交还之形状当如何
7. Breach of the treaty	第七节　犯条悖约
8. Disputes respecting its brech, how adjusted	第八节　合约争端如何可息
Appendix	
1. Additional note on naturalization, by the editor	
2. Act to remodel the diplomatic and consular systems of United States	
3. Debate on neutral rights, House of Commons, July 4, 1854	
ADDENDA TO THE NOTES	
TABLE OF CASES	
INDEX	

此外，选择 Elements of International Law 1855 年波士顿版第一卷第

二章第十三节与汉译本对照，可以发现两者的内容、句子的顺序都十分一致，区别在于少数内容没有译出。

13. Semi-Sovereign States   States which are thus dependent on other States, in respect to the exercise of certain rights, essential to the perfect external sovereignty, have been termed semi-sovereign States. Thus the city of Cracow, in Poland, with its territory, was declared by the Congress of Vienna to be a perpetually free, independent, and neutral State, under the protection of Russia, Austria, and Prussia. By the final act of the Congress of Vienna, Art. 9, the three great powers, Austria, Russia, and Prussia, mutually engaged to respect, and cause to be respected, at all times, the neutrality of the free city of Cracow and its territory; and they further declared that no armed force should ever be introduced into it under any pretext whatever. It was at the same time reciprocally understood and expressly stipulated that no asylum or protection should be granted in the free city or upon the territory of Cracow to fugitives from justice, or deserters from the dominions of either of the said high powers, and that upon a demand of extradition being made by the competent authorities, such individuals should be arrested and delivered up without delay under sufficient escort to the guard charged to receive them at the frontier. By the convention concluded at Paris on the 5th of November, 1815, between Austria, Great Britain, Prussia, and Russia, it is declared that the islands of Corfu, Cephalonia, Zante, St. Maura, Ithaca, Cerigo and Paxo, with their dependenoies, shall form a single, free, and independent State; under the denomination of the United States of the Ionian Islands. The second article provides that this State shall be placed under the immediate and exclusive protection of His Majesty the King of the United Kingdom of Great Britain and Ireland, his heirs and successors. By the third article it is provided that the United States of the Ionian Islands shall regulate, with the approba-

tion of the protecting power, their interior organization; and to give all parts of this organization the consistency and necessary action, His Britannic Majesty will devote particular attention to the legislation and general administration of those States. He will appoint a Lord High Commissioner who shall be invested with the necessary authority for this purpose. The fourth article declares, that, in order to carry into effect without delay these stipulations, the Lord High Commissioner shall regulate the forms of convoking a legislative assembly, of which he shall direct the operations, in order to frame a new constitutional charter for the State, to be ratified by His Britannic Majesty. The fifth article stipulates, that, in order to secure to the inhabitants of the United States of the Ionian Islands the advantages resulting from the high protection under which they are placed, as well as for the exercise of the rights incident to this protection, His Britannic Majesty. The sixth article provides that a special convention with the government of the United States of the Ionian Islands shall regulate, according to their revenues, the object relating to the maintenance of the fortresses and the payment of the British garrisons, and their numbers in the time of peace. The same convention shall also ascertain the relations which are to subsist between this armed force and the Ionian government. The seventh article declares that the merchant flag of the Ionian Islands shall bear, together with the colors and arms it bore previous to 1807, those which His Britannic Majesty may grant as a sign of the protection under which the United Ionian States are placed; and to give more weight to this protection, all the Ionian ports are declared, as to honorary and military rights, to be under the British jurisdiction, commercial agents only, or consuls charged only with the care of commercial relations, shall be accredited to the United States of the Ionian Islands; and they shall be subject to the same regulations to which consuls and commercial agents are subject in other independent States.①

丁韪良在《万国公法》中将该段翻译为：

> 第十三节　释半主之义：凡国，恃他国以行其权者，人称之为"半主之国"。盖无此全权，即不能全然自主也。即如波兰之戈拉告一城，并其辖下土地。维也纳公使会，公议立为一国，出告示，许其永为自主、自立局外之国，凭俄、奥、普三国之保护也。按公使会第九条，俄、奥、普三国，互相应允，不强犯戈拉告局外之地，并不许他国强犯之。又告诸天下，无论何国兵旅，无论何故，皆不得过戈拉告之疆界。又互相应允，戈拉告城内、城外，皆不准罪犯捕逃藏匿，若他国之有司，追讨捕逃之罪犯，戈拉告之官，立当捕之，护送出疆交还。一千八百十五年间，英、奥、普、俄四国，立约于法国之巴勒莫城，其一条云："以阿尼诸岛，合成一国，自立、自主者，名为以阿尼合邦。"第二条云："此国全赖大英君主并其后代保护。"第三条云："以阿尼合邦，自治其国内之事，当听其护主答应施行，大英君主，亦当鉴察其制法、行法等情。"第四条云："大英钦差，驻扎该国，可聚其法会，以主其议。"第五条云："以阿尼合邦，既蒙此保护，当任大英君主，屯兵于其关口、炮台等处。其合邦之兵，亦归英将之麾下。"第六条云："当另设章程，定护兵之额，与合邦归粮之款。"第七条云："合邦商船，并本国旧旗，亦当统带英旗。"②

今译为：

> 第十三节　半自主国　行使对外主权时，依赖它国的国家称为半自主国。如波兰城市克拉科夫及其所辖区域，维也纳大会宣

---

① Henry Wheaton, *Elements of International Law* Boston：Little, Brown and Company, 1855.
② ［美］惠顿：《万国公法》，［美］丁韪良译，何勤华点校，中国政法大学出版社2003年版，第38页。

布该城为自由、独立、中立的国家，但要接受俄罗斯、奥地利、普鲁士三国保护。根据维也纳会议最终协议第九条，奥地利、俄罗斯、普鲁士三国彼此尊重，始终承认克拉科夫及其所辖区域中立、自由之现状；任何武装力量不得以任何借口进入该地。同时，本着相互理解之精神，明文规定，克拉科夫不得为任何逃犯提供庇护场所，并应主权国引渡逃犯之要求，逮捕逃犯，妥为看押，在边境移交他国。根据1815年11月5日，奥地利、英国、普鲁士、俄国在巴黎所签协议规定：科孚岛、凯法利尼亚岛、赞特岛、圣马拉岛、伊萨卡岛、基西拉岛、帕克斯欧岛组成一个单一、自由、独立的国家，命名为爱奥尼亚联邦。第二条规定，该联邦置于大不列颠及爱尔兰王国陛下及其继承人的保护之下，第三条规定：在保护国的许可下，爱奥尼亚联邦应当管理其内部事务，对各机构施加持续稳定的影响，英国女王陛下对各州的立法和行政将予以特别关注。为此，他将任命一名拥有必要权利的上议院特派员。第四条规定：为了使这些协议尽快付诸实施，该上议院特派员可以规定立法会议的召集形式，他还可以直接采取措施，以便英国女王陛下批准新的宪章。第五条规定：为了保护爱奥尼亚联邦的居民及其利益，英国女王陛下有权派兵占领上述国家的城堡和村镇。他们的军队将听命于英国女王陛下手下的军官。第六条规定，爱奥尼亚联邦政府制定特殊条款，将每年财政收入中的一部分用以支付和平时期维护城堡以及驻扎英军的开销。第七条规定：爱奥尼亚联邦商船悬挂的旗帜颜色及其护卫武装如同1807年前一样，受英国女王陛下的保护。为了增加保护的影响力，所有爱奥尼亚港口在荣誉和军事上仅归属英国司法以及商务官员管理，有时商务关系由得到爱奥尼亚联邦授权的领事处理。他们与派驻其他独立国家的领事一样，按照规则办事。

第三节 《万国公法》的版本及内容

根据张斯桂所作序文时间"时在癸亥端午"推断，丁韪良初步完成《万国公法》翻译的时间应该在 1863 年 5 月之前，因为丁韪良不可能将尚未完成的书稿交给别人作序。由于翻译法学术语的难度较大，丁韪良一直在修改该书稿："适美公使蒲安臣来言，各国有将《大清律例》翻出洋字一书，并言外国有通行之例，近日经文士丁韪良译出汉文，可以观览。旋于上年九月间，带同来见，呈出《万国律例》四本，声称此书凡属有约之国，皆宜寓目，遇有事件亦可参酌引用，惟文义不甚通顺，求为改删，以便刊刻。"① 这是恭亲王奕䜣 1864 年上的奏疏，从中可以看出 1863 年 9 月奕䜣就已经见到了《万国公法》的翻译本，只是仍需修改。1863 年 11 月丁韪良随蒲安臣到总理衙门拜见文祥时，所携带的应是基本完成的稿本，但是还没有最后定稿，最后定稿日期应在 1864 年 9 月以前。1865 年 4 月 25 日蒲安臣写信给西华德："我荣幸地通过最后一班邮程向您寄上丁韪良博士翻译的《万国公法》。——去年九月总理衙门的官员通知我，丁韪良博士在由恭亲王委派的中国学者的帮助下，已经完成了翻译，并已拨款用于该书的印刷。"② 丁韪良匆忙请人作序以及将未定稿带到总理衙门，只不过反映丁韪良急于取得清政府的信任而已。

《万国公法》在中国有多个版本，有刻印本、铅印本、石印本，最早由 1864 年京都崇实馆镌刻出版。《万国公法》在中国出版后，当年就有手抄本传入日本京都。日本开成所（东京大学的前身）在人名、地名旁加上日文字母的读音后，翻刻了中文版《万国公法》。随后又出现了庆应元年（1865 年）、庆应四年（1868 年）、明治四年（1871 年）、明治八年（1875 年）、明治十四年（1881 年）、明治十九年（1886 年）五种翻刻本。日本政府还于明治五年（1872 年）公布的新学制中，将《万国公法》指定为教科书。

根据北京大学图书馆收藏的崇实馆刻本《万国公法》，该书内容依次为：中文版权页、英文版权页、译者序（英文），万国公法序（董恂）和万国公法序（张斯桂）、凡例、地球全图及说明文字、目录、正文。

---

① 李书源整理：《筹办夷务始末》（同治朝）卷 37，中华书局 1979 年版。
② 王维俭：《普丹大沽口船舶事件和西方国际法传入中国》，《学术研究》1985 年第 5 期。

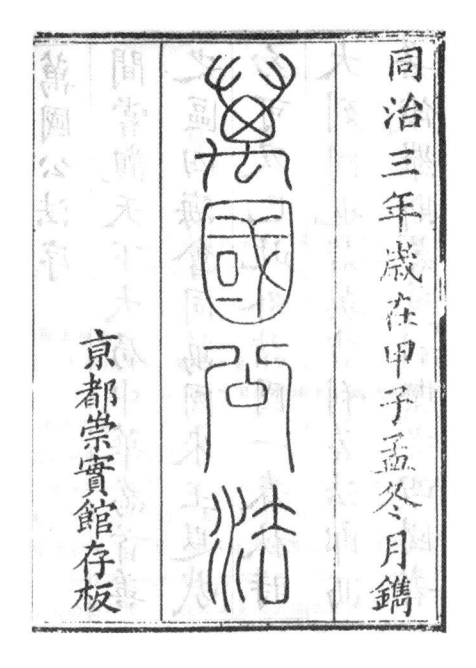

《万国公法》封二

董恂①所写序言为：

> 涂山之会，执玉帛者万国，维时厶（某）氏宅厶（某）土，其详弗可得闻已。顾或疑史氏侈词，不则通九州外数之。今九州外之国林立矣，不有法以维之，其何以国？此丁韪良教师《万国公法》之所由译也。韪良能华言，以是书就正，爰属历城陈钦、

---

① 董恂（1810—1892），江都县邵伯镇人。1840 年（道光二十年）成进士后踏上仕宦之途，至 1882 年（光绪八年）正月，以 76 岁高龄退休罢职，先后历事道光、咸丰、同治、光绪 4 朝，历任户部主事、湖南储运道、直隶清河道、顺天府尹、都察院左都御史及兵、户两部侍郎、尚书。其中户部尚书任期最长，自同治八年六月至光绪八年正月，达 12 年之久。在此期间曾充殿试读卷、会试正副主考官，以及文宗、穆宗二帝实录馆总裁，又曾入总理各国事务衙门，作为全权大臣，奉派与比利时、英国、俄国、美国等国签订通商条约。曾参与处理阿思本舰队问题，并将英文诗歌《长友诗》译为中文，被卫三畏称为中国外交部最有学问、文学造诣最深的人。先后著有《随轺载笔七种》、《楚漕江程》、《江北运程》、《甘棠小志》、《荻芬书屋诗文稿》以及《手订年谱》等近百卷。丁韪良在《花甲记忆》中描述董恂："不仅是严谨的学者，更是谦谦君子。——不仅礼貌待人，而且大度。——总理衙门中，大多数文件都是董起草的，恭亲王文采斐然的国书实际上出于董的文笔。文件中可以明显看出董对进步事业的同情，尤其是那些有关建立同文馆的文件。"

郑州李常华、定远方濬师、大竹毛鸿图，删校一过归之。韪良盖好古多闻之士云。①

张斯桂在序言中分析了英国、法国、俄国、美国的国情及强盛的原因，预言日本即将崛起，但言语之中仍然流露出天朝大国的心态，读来令人深思：

间尝观天下大局，中华为首善之区，四海会同，万国来王，遐哉勿可及已。此外诸国，一春秋时大列国也。若英吉利，若俄罗斯，若美利坚之四国者，强则强矣，要非生而强也。

英吉利，一岛国耳。其君若相，务材训农，通商惠工而财用足；秣马厉兵，修阵固列而兵力强。遂雄长乎西洋。然犹虞土产不丰，易致坐困，乃多设兵船分布天下。暇则遍历山川，有立马绘图之概；急则夺据关隘，有投鞭直渡之强，故越国鄙远不知其雄。

法兰西，制器之巧、用军之精为西国冠。竟与英吉利并驾齐驱，树晋角楚犄之势。

俄罗斯，积弱久矣。自其先君见西洋诸国蒸蒸日上，恐外患之迭乘而内顾之不暇也。乃效赵武灵微服过秦之术，游历诸国，罗奇才而致之幕下，购利器而教之国中，不二十年遂郡县北方诸国，而统苞之舆图几与中国埒。然北地苦寒，无南方通商海口，则地势使然也。

美利坚，初为英之属地，嗣有华盛顿者，悯苛政，倡大义，鏖战八年而国以立，而官天下未家天下，俨然禅让之遗风。且官则选于众，兵则寓于农，内资镇抚而不假人尺寸柄，外扞强御而不贪人尺寸土。华盛顿迈百王哉！

在昔春秋之世，秦并岐丰之地，守关中之险，东面而临诸侯，俄罗斯似之。楚国方城汉水，虽众无用，晋则表里山河，亦

---

① ［美］惠顿：《万国公法·序》，［美］丁韪良译，何勤华点校，中国政法大学出版社2003年版。

必无害，英、法两国似之。齐表东海，富强甲天下，美利坚似之，至若奥地利、普鲁斯，亦欧罗巴洲中两大国，犹鲁、卫之政，兄弟也。土耳其、意大利，犹宋与郑，介于大国之间也。瑞士、比利时，国小而固，足以自守。丹尼、荷兰、西班牙、葡萄牙等国，昔为大国，后渐陵夷，然于会盟、征伐诸事，亦能有恃无恐，而不至疲于奔命。其间蕞尔国，不过如江、黄、州、蓼，降为附庸，夷于邱县，或割地而请和，或要盟以结信，不祀忽诸，可胜道哉？可知不备不虞不可以师，鲜虞不警边，舒、庸不设备，千古有同慨焉。

东方亚细亚洲，内如日本、安南两国，诚能振作有为，休养生息，富强可待也。统观地球上版图，大小不下数十国，其犹有存焉者，则恃其先王之命，载在盟府，世世守之，长享勿替，有渝此盟，神明殛之，即此《万国律例》一书耳。故西洋各国公使、大臣、水陆主帅、领事、翻译、教师、商人，以及税务司等莫不奉为蓍蔡。

今美利坚教师丁韪良翻译此书，其望我中华之曲体其情而俯从其议也。我中华一视同仁，迩言必察，行见越裳献雉、西旅贡獒，凡重译而来者，莫不畏威怀德。则是书亦大有裨于中华，用储之以备筹边之一助云尔。

是为序。①

书中"凡例"对原书作者惠顿作了简要介绍，并指出《万国公法》又名《万国律例》。重点说明书中的"公师"即法理学家："是书所称'公师'，乃各国学士、大臣秉公论办诸国交际之道者，以其剖明义理，不偏袒本国。是以称为诸国之公师焉。"

书中有一幅世界地图，上面标有北极、南极以及亚洲（亚细亚）、欧洲（欧罗巴）、非洲（亚非利加）、美洲（南、北亚美利加）、南极洲（南水洋）、大西洋、印度洋、太平洋（大东洋）、北冰洋（北水

---

① ［美］惠顿：《万国公法·序》，［美］丁韪良译，何勤华点校，中国政法大学出版社2003年版。

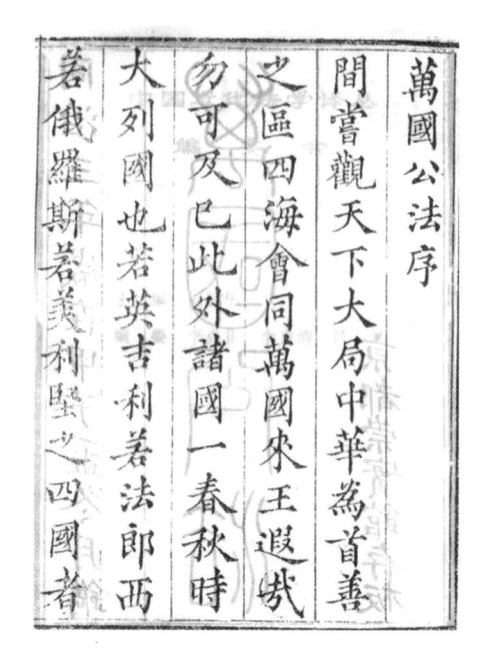

张斯桂为《万国公法》写的序文

洋);从地图上看,中国只是众多国家中的一个。但为了迎合中国人的心态,丁韪良将中国摆在地图的中心位置。

《万国公法》刊印后,最早的阅读群体是与外事有关的官员。曾纪泽出使英国之前,反复阅读该书,充分肯定它的积极作用:"西洋各国以公法相维制,保全小国附庸,俾皆有自立之权,此息兵安民最善之法。"[1] 维新志士谭嗣同高度评价该书:"即如《万国公法》,为西人仁至义尽之书,亦即《公羊春秋》之律。昔中国自己求亡,为外洋所不齿,曾不足列于公法,非法不足恃也。"[2]

《万国公法》共有四卷十二章:

第一卷 "释公法之义,明其本源,题其大旨"。分为二章:"第一章 释义明源;第二章 论邦国自治、自主之权。"

第二卷 "论诸国自然之权"。分为四章:"第一章 论其自护、

---

[1] 曾纪泽:《曾纪泽日记》,岳麓书社1998年版,第859页。
[2] 甘韩:《皇朝经世文新编续集》卷1"通论",上海书局1902年版。

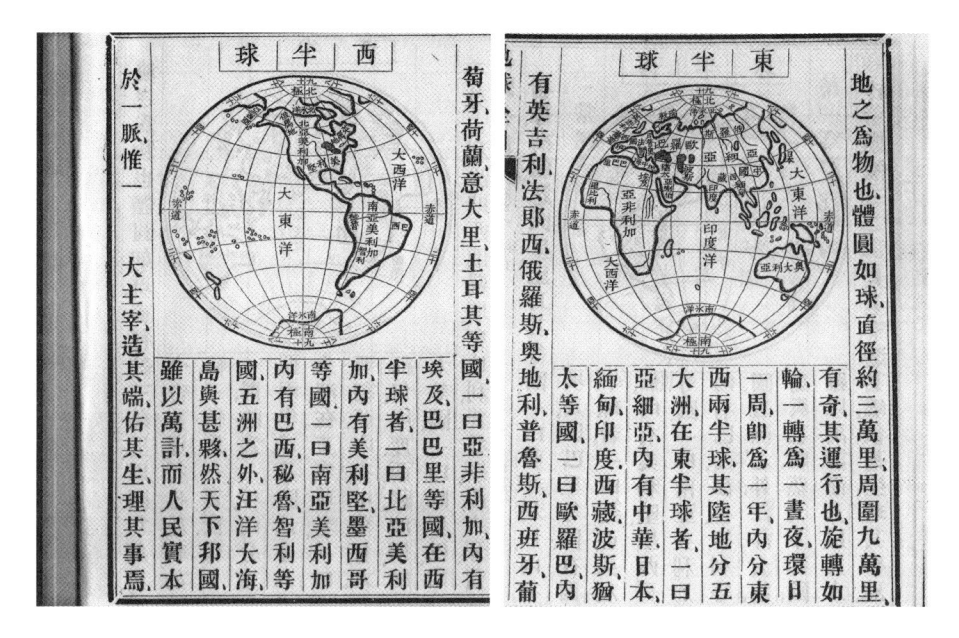

刊于《万国公法》的世界地图

自主之权；第二章　论制定律法之权；第三章　论诸国平行之权；第四章　论各国掌物之权。"

第三卷　"论诸国平时往来之权"。分为二章："第一章　论通使之权；第二章论商议立约之权。"

第四卷　"论交战条规"。分为四章："第一章　论战始；第二章　论敌国交战之权；第三章　论战时局外之权；第四章　论和约章程。"

将《万国公法》与王铁崖主编的《国际法》予以比较，除了"空气空间和外层空间、国际组织、国际经济法、国际争端的解决"等内容外，《万国公法》基本上涵盖了近代西方国际法的大部分内容，即国际法的渊源、主体、条约、外交与领事关系、领土和海洋法、战争法等各项内容。

丁韪良译《万国公法·目录》与王铁崖主编《国际法·目录》目录对比表①

丁韪良译《万国公法》	王铁崖主编《国际法》
第一卷 释公法之义，明其本源，题其大旨	
第一章 释义明源	第一章 导论
第一节 本于公义	第一节 国际法的概念 一 国际关系与国际法 二 国际法是法律的一个特殊体系 三 国际法效力的根源
第二节 出于天性	第二节 国际法的历史发展 一 国际法的来源与发展 二 中国与国际法 三 现代国际法的动向
第三节 称为天法	第三节 国际法的渊源 一 概说 二 国际条约 三 国际习惯 四 一般法律原则 五 确定法律规则的辅助方法
第四节 公法、性法犹有所别	第四节 国际法的编纂 一 国际法的编纂的意义 二 国际法的编纂的发展 三 联合国国际法委员会与国际法的编纂
第五节 理同名异 常用大例	第五节 国际法与国内法的关系 一 关于国际法与国内法关系的理论 二 关于国际法与国内法关系的实践
第六节 理、例二源	第二章 国际法的基本原则
第七节 性理之一派 分为三种	第一节 概说 一 国际法基本原则的概念 二 国际法基本原则与强行法 三 国际法基本原则的历史发展

---

① ［美］惠顿：《万国公法·目录》，［美］丁韪良译，何勤华点校，中国政法大学出版社2003年版；王铁崖主编：《国际法·目录》，法律出版社1981年版。

续表

丁韪良译《万国公法》	王铁崖主编《国际法》
第八节 二子所论微异	第二节 联合国宪章与国际法基本原则 一 联合国宪章与国际法基本原则 二 联合国的其他文件与国际法基本原则 三 联合国与民族自决原则
第九节 发氏大旨	第三节 和平共处五项原则 一 和平共处五项原则的产生和发展 二 互相尊重主权和领土完整 三 互不侵犯 四 互不干涉内政 五 平等互利 六 和平共处 七 和平共处五项原则在国际法基本原则体系中的地位
第十节 海氏大旨 分为二派 公法精义 公法不一 应否称法 出于同俗、行于他方	
第十一节 公法总旨	
第十二节 公法源流	
第二章 论邦国自治、自主之权	第三章 国际法的主体
第一节 公法所论	第一节 主权国家是国际法的基本主体 一 国际法主体的概念 二 国家的要素 三 国家的种类 四 国家的基本权利与义务
第二节 何者为国	第二节 其他的国际法主体 一 争取独立的民族的国际法主体资格 二 国际组织的国际法主体资格 三 关于个人和法人有无国际法主体资格的问题

续表

丁韪良译《万国公法》	王铁崖主编《国际法》
第三节　君身之私权	第三节　国际法上的承认 一　承认的意义和学说 二　国家承认与政府承认 三　交战团体和叛乱团体的承认 四　承认的形式与效果
第四节　民人之私权	第四节　国际法上的继承 一　概说 二　国家的继承 三　政府的继承 四　国际组织的继承
第五节　主权分内外	第五节　国际法上的国家责任 一　国家责任概说 二　国家责任的构成条件 三　国家责任的免除 四　国家责任的形式
第六节　在内之主权 　　　　在外之主权	第四章　国家领土
第七节　不因内变而亡 　　　　他国或旁观或相助 　　　　争者皆得战权	第一节　国家领土与领土主权 一　国家领土的概念 二　领土主权不可侵犯
第八节　外敌致变	第二节　国家领土的组成部分 一　概说 二　内水——河流、运河、湖泊及内海
第九节　内变外敌并至	第三节　国家领土的变更 一　概说 二　领土变更的方式
第十节　省部叛而自立	第四节　领土主权的限制 一　共管 二　租借 三　势力范围 四　国际地役

续表

丁韪良译《万国公法》	王铁崖主编《国际法》
第十一节　易君变法 于盟国如何 于国债如何 于国土名产如何 如他国被害者如何	第五节　国家边界 一　边界的概念 二　划界 三　边界争端 四　边境制度
第十二节　释自主之义	第六节　南北极 一　南极 二　北极
第十三节　释半主之义	
第十四节　进贡藩属所存主权	
第十五节　或独或合	
第十六节　相合而不失其主权	
第十七节　相合而不失其内在之主权	
第十八节　相合而并失其内外之主权	
第十九节　波兰始合于俄 继得国法权利 终则被俄所并	
第二十节　会盟永合有二	
第二十一节　会盟连横	
第二十二节　合盟为一	
第二十三节　日耳曼系众邦会盟	
第二十四节　美国系众邦合一 上国制法之权 首领行法之权 司法之权 立约之权 各邦所无之权	
第二十五节　与前二国异同如何	
第二卷　论诸国自然之权	
第一章　论其自护、自主之权	
第一节　操权二种	
第二节　自护之权为大 立约改革推让均可	

续表

丁韪良译《万国公法》	王铁崖主编《国际法》
第三节 与闻他国政事之例	
第四节 以法国为鉴 五国横连之故	
第五节 三国管制那国，英国驳之	
第六节 四国管制西国，英不许之	
第七节 四国管制西之叛邦，英、美斥之	
第八节 葡国有争，英管制之	
第九节 希腊被虐，三国助之	
第十节 埃及叛土，五国理之	
第十一节 比利时叛土，五国议之	
第十二节 各国自主其内事	
第十三节 他国与闻，或临事相请，或未事有约盟邦互保	
第十四节 立君举官，他国不得与闻	
第十五节 立君举官而他国可与闻者	
第十六节 西、葡立君，英、法与闻之	
第二章 论制定律法之权	第七章 国际法上的居民
第一节 制律之权 变通之法	第一节 国籍问题 一 国籍和国籍法的概念 二 国籍的取得 三 国籍的丧失 四 双重国籍的产生和解决 五 无国籍的产生和解决 六 中华人民共和国的国籍立法和实践
第二节 变通之法，大纲有二 简要三则 三则合一	第二节 外国人的法律地位 一 国家对外国人的管辖权 二 外国人入境、居留和出境的一般原则 三 外国人待遇的一般原则 四 外国人在中华人民共和国的法律地位
第三节 植物从物所在之律	第三节 国际法上的人权问题 一 人权问题的产生与发展 二 人权的国际保护 三 关于人权问题的不同主张

续表

丁韪良译《万国公法》	王铁崖主编《国际法》
第四节 古禁外人购买植物 昔以外人遗物入公 遗产徙外酌留数分	第四节 庇护和引渡 一 庇护 二 引渡
第五节 动物从人所在之律	
第六节 内治之权 法行于疆外者 第一种定己民之分位 准外人入籍 制疆内之物 律从写契地方	
第七节 第二种就事而行于疆外者 其不行者有四 不合于物所在之律则不行 妨碍于他国则不行 遇契据应成于他国则不行	
第八节 遇案之应由法院条规而断者则不行	
第九节 第三种就人而行于疆外者 因一案覆论三端 君身过疆国权随之 使臣在外国权随之 兵旅过疆国权随之 兵船另归一例 法国接待商船之例 按此例罪分二等 公案二件 不得藉此例而谋为不轨 犯局外之权而捕拿船货进口必归地方管辖	
第十节 船只行于大海均归本国管辖 海外犯公法之案各国可行审办 他国之船不可稽查	
第十一节 第四种因约而行于疆外者 领事等官	
第十二节 审案之权各国自秉	

续表

丁韪良译《万国公法》	王铁崖主编《国际法》
第十三节 四等罪案审罚可及 交还逃犯之例	
第十四节 法院定拟旁行于疆外	
第十五节 审断海盗之例 各国或另有海盗之例 公禁贩卖人口	
第十六节 疆内植物之争讼审权可及	
第十七节 疆内动物之争讼审权可及 继遗物之例	
第十八节 以他国法院曾断为准	
第十九节 疆内因人民权利等争端审权可及	
第二十节 断案之法、兴讼之例有别	
第二十一节 涉身之案他国既断本国从否	
第三章 论诸国平行之权	
第一节 分尊卑出于相许	
第二节 得王礼之国	
第三节 得王礼者分位次	
第四节 互易之方	
第五节 公用之文字	
第六节 君国之尊号	
第七节 航海礼款	
第四章 论各国掌物之权	
第一节 掌物之权所由来	
第二节 民物亦归此权	
第三节 民物听命于上权	
第四节 历久为牢固之例	
第五节 权由征服寻觅而来者	
第六节 管沿海近处之权	
第七节 长滩应随近岸	
第八节 捕鱼之权	
第九节 管小海之权	
第十节 大海不归专管之例	

续表

丁韪良译《万国公法》	王铁崖主编《国际法》
第十一节 疆内江湖亦为国土	
第十二节 无损可用之例	
第十三节 他事随行之例	
第十四节 同上	
第十五节 同享水利之权可让可改	
第十六节 同航大江之例	
第三卷 论诸国平时往来之权	
第一章 论通使之权	第八章 外交和领事关系
第一节 钦差驻扎外国	第一节 外交关系法概说 一 国家外交关系机关的体系 二 外交关系法概念
第二节 可遣可受	第二节 国家的中央外交关系机关 一 国家元首 二 政府 三 外交部门
第三节 何等之国可以通使	第三节 使馆及其人员 一 使馆制度的产生 二 外交关系和使馆的建立 三 使馆的职务 四 使馆人员的类别 五 使馆馆长的等级和位次 六 使馆人员的任命 七 外交团 八 使馆人员职务的终止
第四节 国乱通使	第四节 使馆及其人员的特权和豁免 一 外交特权和豁免的根据 二 使馆的特权和豁免 三 外交人员的特权和豁免 四 其他人员的特权和豁免 五 特权和豁免的开始和终止 六 使馆人员及其家属在第三国的地位
第五节 先议后接	第五节 使馆和享有外交特权和豁免人员对接受国的义务

续表

丁韪良译《万国公法》	王铁崖主编《国际法》
第六节 国使等级	第六节 特别使团 一 概说 二 特别使团的派遣 三 特别使团的人员及其任命和召回 四 特别使团及其人员的特权和豁免
第七节 信凭款式	第七节 联合国和联合国各专门机构的特权和豁免 一 概说 二 常驻联合国和联合国各专门机构的使团及其人员的特权和豁免 三 派到联合国和联合国各专门机构的临时性代表团及其人员的特权和豁免 四 联合国和联合国各专门机构及其官员的特权和豁免
第八节 全权之凭	第八节 领事馆及其人员 一 领事制度概说 二 关于领事的条约和公约 三 领事关系和领事馆的建立 四 领事职务 五 历史上的领事裁判权 六 领事馆的人员
第九节 训条之规	第九节 领事特权和豁免 一 领事馆的特权和豁免 二 领事官员和其他人员的特权和豁免 三 特权和豁免的开始和终止 四 领事馆人员及其家属在第三国的地位
第十节 牌票护身	第十节 领事馆和享有领事特权和豁免人员对接受国的义务
第十一节 莅任之规	
第十二节 延见之规	
第十三节 交好礼款	
第十四节 国使权利	
第十五节 例外之事	

续表

丁韪良译《万国公法》	王铁崖主编《国际法》
第十六节 家人置权外	
第十七节 房屋器具置权外	
第十八节 纳税之规	
第十九节 寄公信者	
第二十节 路过他国	
第二十一节 礼拜不可禁止	
第二十二节 领事权利	
第二十三节 国使卸任	
第二十四节 召回国使	
第二章 论商议立约之权	第九章 条约
第一节 限制若何	第一节 概说 一 条约的定义 二 条约的历史 三 条约的编纂 四 条约的种类和名称
第二节 盟约款式	第二节 条约的缔结及生效 一 缔约能力 二 条约的缔结程序 三 条约的加入 四 条约的保留 五 条约的生效 六 条约的有效期
第三节 约据章程	第三节 条约的遵守、适用及解释 一 条约必须遵守 二 条约的适用 三 条约的解释 四 条约与第三国
第四节 擅约准废	第四节 条约的修改及终止 一 条约的修改 二 条约的无效 三 条约的终止及停止实施
第五节 公约准废	第五节 条约的保管和登记 一 条约的保管 二 条约的登记

续表

丁韪良译《万国公法》	王铁崖主编《国际法》
第六节　谁执定约之权	
第七节　因约改法	
第八节　被逼改法	
第九节　恒约不因战废	
第十节　常约存废	
第十一节　盟约多兼二种	
第十二节　保护之约	
第十三节　合兵之盟	
第十四节　立约助兵	
第十五节　相互之例	
第十六节　交质以坚信	
第十七节　解说盟约	
第十八节　中保之例	
第十九节　主持公论之学	
第四卷　论交战条规	
第一章　论战始	第十三章　战争法
第一节　用力伸冤	第一节　战争与国际法 一　战争的概念 二　对所谓的"诉诸战争权"的限制 三　战争的废弃 四　终止非法使用武力
第二节　强偿之例	第二节　战争法的编纂和发展 一　战争法的概念和范围 二　战争法规的编纂 三　关于战争法规的条约的特点
第三节　强偿之用	第三节　战争与武装冲突的开始和结束 一　战争与武装冲突的开始 二　战争与武装冲突的结束及其法律后果
第四节　战前捕物二解	第四节　战争法规（一）——作战手段和方法 一　战争法规的基本原则 二　禁止的作战手段和方法

续表

丁韪良译《万国公法》	王铁崖主编《国际法》
第五节　定战之权	第五节　战争法规（二）——交战者和战争受难者 一　交战者 二　战俘待遇 三　伤病员待遇 四　战时平民地位
第六节　公战之权	第六节　战争法规（三）——海战和空战中的特殊问题 一　海战法规中的某些特殊问题 二　空战法规中的某些特殊问题
第七节　战有三等	第七节　中立 一　中立的概念 二　中立制度的历史发展 三　1907年海牙第五公约和第十三公约对中立国权利、义务的规定 战争的废弃和非法使用武力的禁止与中立 封锁 战时禁制品
第八节　宣战之始	第八节　战争犯罪及其责任 一　战争犯罪的概念 二　第二次世界大战期间要求审判战争犯罪的文件 三　纽伦堡国籍军事法庭宪章及审判 四　远东国际军事法庭宪章及审判 五　纽伦堡、东京审判原则及其重要意义
第九节　敌货在我疆内者	
第十节　照行而行	
第十一节　敌物在疆内者不即入公	
第十二节　债欠于敌	
第十三节　与敌贸易	
第十四节　合兵之民通商敌国	
第十五节　不可与敌立契约	

续表

丁韪良译《万国公法》	王铁崖主编《国际法》
第十六节　敌民居于疆内者	
第十七节　何谓迁往别国本名易复	
第十八节　西人住于东土者	
第十九节　商行设于敌国	
第二十节　身在敌国行在局外	
第二十一节　敌国土产属地主时即为敌货	
第二十二节　船因船户得名	
第二十三节　领照于敌国	
第二章　论敌国交战之权	
第一节　害敌有限	
第二节　害敌之权至何而止	
第三节　互换俘虏	
第四节　何等人不可杀	
第五节　敌人之产业	
第六节　抄掠敌境	
第七节　水陆捕拿不同一例	
第八节　何人可以害敌	
第九节　船无战牌而捕获者	
第十节　民船领战牌者	
第十一节　被捕之货可讨与否	
第十二节　夺回救货之例	
第十三节　审所捕之船归捕者本国之法院	
第十四节　局外之法院审案	
第十五节　领事在局外之地者不足断此案	
第十六节　照例所捕在国不在民枉理断案自行理直	
第十七节　植物如何还主	
第十八节　守信于敌	
第十九节　停兵之约	
第二十节　停兵之权	
第二十一节　自何时遵行	

续表

丁韪良译《万国公法》	王铁崖主编《国际法》
第二十二节 解说停兵之约	
第二十三节 停兵期满复战	
第二十四节 投降款约	
第二十五节 护身等票	
第二十六节 凭照与敌贸易	
第二十七节 何权足以出照	
第二十八节 捕获讨赎	
第三章 论战时局外之权	
第一节 解局外之意	
第二节 全半二字	
第三节 局外之全权	
第四节 局外之半权	
第五节 局外之权被约限制	
第六节 因前约准此而禁彼	
第七节 在局外之地不可行战权	
第八节 经过局外之疆	
第九节 沿海辖内捕船	
第十节 追至局外之地而捕者	
第十一节 局外者讨还	
第十二节 犯局外之权而捕之货，局外者自必交还赔偿	
第十三节 交还之权有限制	
第十四节 在局外之地避患、买粮、卖赃	
第十五节 守中有二事	
第十六节 借局外之地招兵备船即为犯法	
第十七节 律法禁之投军别国	
第十八节 局外之船于大海如何	
第十九节 捕拿敌货在局外之船者为常事	
第二十节 载敌货之船有时捕为战例	
第二十一节 捕拿友货在敌国之船有人行之	
第二十二节 二规非不可相离	

续表

丁韪良译《万国公法》	王铁崖主编《国际法》
第二十三节 局外者装载敌货	
第二十四节 战时禁物	
第二十五节 寄信载兵等	
第二十六节 载禁物之干系	
第二十七节 通商战者之属邦	
第二十八节 封港犯封 犯封三问 实势行封 犯者知之 实事犯封	
第二十九节 往视稽查之权	
第三十节 敌人为船主而强御者	
第三十一节 局外者借敌人之兵船载货	
第三十二节 局外之船借敌人之保护可捕拿	
第四章 论合约章程	
第一节 谁执和权惟国法所定	
第二节 立合约之权有限制	
第三节 合约息争	
第四节 各守所有	
第五节 合约自何日为始	
第六节 交还之形状当如何	
第七节 犯条悖约	
第八节 合约争端如何可息	

国际法是近代欧洲的产物。1625年，格老秀斯的《战争与和平法》问世，1643——1648年的威斯特法利亚公会标志近代国际法的产生。《万国公法》较为全面地译介了国际法的内容：

第一卷 释公法之义，明其本源，题其大旨

第一章 释义明源：

"公法之学，创于荷兰人名虎哥者。虎哥与门人，论公法曾分之为二种。世人若无国君，若无王法，天然同居，究其来往相待之理，应当如何？此乃公法之一种，名为'性法'也。夫诸国之往来，与众人同理，将此性法所定人人相待之分，以明各国交际之义，此乃第二种也。虎哥著书，名曰《平战条规》"①

"布氏门人，以公法之学，为性理之一派，盖视为人人相待之性法，而推及诸国交际之分也。此后，俄拉费以诸国之公法与人人之性法，分门别户。发得耳赞之，谓其有功于公法之学也。"②

"虎哥云：'公法之所以行，或因万国间，多有许之者。盖性法固通行万国。此外，别无所谓通行之法也。固常见此处遵此法，而他处遵他法，此余所以言多有奉之者，而不言人皆奉之也。'宾克舍云：'诸国之公法，即是诸国准情酌理，所遵守也。虽不皆遵之，遵之者，犹过半，且遵之之国，教化最盛焉。'莱本尼子云：'诸国甘服之法，乃其所默许者也。非云，万国万世，皆奉一法。盖欧罗巴与印度，论诸国之公法，多有不同，即吾侪阅世久长，公法亦有变更。'孟德斯鸠著书，名曰《律例精义》，云：'各国自有公法也，即夷狄掳人而食之者，亦有公法。盖互相遣使接使，并有和战条规，岂非有公法乎？惟不本于正理耳'。"③

"万国之公法，其原有六：一、有名之公法师，辩正诸国之常例，褒贬诸国相待之是非，并其随时详辨改革，而共许者也。"④

第二章　论邦国自治、自主之权：

"人成群立国，而邦国交际有事，此公法之所论也。得哩云：

---

① ［美］惠顿：《万国公法》，［美］丁韪良译，何勤华点校，中国政法大学出版社2003年版，第6页。
② ［美］惠顿：《万国公法》，［美］丁韪良译，何勤华点校，中国政法大学出版社2003年版，第12页。
③ ［美］惠顿：《万国公法》，［美］丁韪良译，何勤华点校，中国政法大学出版社2003年版，第18页。
④ ［美］惠顿：《万国公法》，［美］丁韪良译，何勤华点校，中国政法大学出版社2003年版，第22页。

'所谓国者,惟人众相合,协力相护,以同立者也。'今之公师,亦从其说,然犹属未尽,而必限制之者,其端有四:一、当除民间大会凭国权而立者,无论其何故而立也。即如英国,昔有客商大会,奉君命而立也,得国会申命,为通商东印度等处。此商会,前虽行自主之权,在东方或战或和,不待问于君,尚不得称为一国,况后每事必奉君令乎?盖此商会之行权,全凭本国之权,惟交际印度诸国之君民,则商会代本国而行,其于他国所有之事,则本国为之经理。一、盗贼为邦国所置于法外者,虽相依同护得立,亦不得称为一国。一、蛮夷流徙无定所,虽相依同护得立,亦不得称为一国。盖为国之正义,无他,庶人行事,常服君上,居住必有定所,且有地土、疆界,归其自主。此三者缺一,即不为国矣。一、有时同种之民,相护得存,犹不成为国也。盖数种人民,同服一君者有之,即如奥地利、普鲁士、土耳其三国,是也。一种人民,分服数君者有之,即如波兰民,分服奥、普、俄三国,是也。"①

"治国之上权,谓之主权。此上权或行于内,或行于外。行于内,则依各国之法度,或寓于民,或归于君。论此者,尝名之为'内公法',但不如称之为'国法'也。主权行于外者,即本国自主,而不听命于他国也。各国平战、交际,皆凭此权。论此者,尝名之为'外公法',俗称'公法',即此也"。②

"若从前所属之国,尚未认之,且某国若未认之,则某国之法院,并其民人,必须由旧而行。邦国易君主、变国法之时,其于公法如何,可论有四:会盟通商之约,一也;国债,二也;国土民产,三也;他国被害,并他国人民受屈,四也。公师论盟约有二种,曰君约,曰国约。君约者,专指君之身家而言,即如保其身家在位,并和亲等情。若君崩家灭,则此约自废矣。国约

---

① [美]惠顿:《万国公法》,[美]丁韪良译,何勤华点校,中国政法大学出版社2003年版,第25、26页。
② [美]惠顿:《万国公法》,[美]丁韪良译,何勤华点校,中国政法大学出版社2003年版,第27页。

者，专指所议之事而言，在其事，不在其人。虽易君主，变国法，其约仍存而无碍焉。"①

"凡有邦国，无论何等国法，若能自治其事，而不听命于他国，则可谓自主者矣。就公法而论，自主之国，无论其国势大小，皆平行也。"②

"国之合而为一者，即如苏格兰、英吉利、爱尔兰合为大英一国是也。其君位统于一，其制法之会亦归于一，但各国仍有己之律法、己之理治也。各国之主权，无论其行于内者、行于外者，皆归于统一之国也。"③

"若美国之合邦，其合之之法，与日耳曼迥不相同。不惟为自主之国，相连以防御内外强暴，亦是合成之国，秉上权，以制盟内各邦，并直及庶民者也。其合盟有云：此盟为合邦庶民所立，而其所以立之之故，盖欲相合更密，坚公义，保民安，御外暴，聚众庆，且保自主之福，爰及后世。"④

第二卷　论诸国自然之权

第一章　论其自护、自主之权：

"凡自主之国相待，操权有二：曰自有之原权；曰偶有之特权。诸国自有之原权，莫要于自护。此为基而其余诸权皆建于其上。"⑤

"此国遭内乱，彼国前来欲为调处，本为正例。若战者允许，则来者即有权，可主持其间。或此国早有约据，许彼国遇事便可居间保护，则虽此国未请其调处，亦得有权矣。——凡自主之

---

① ［美］惠顿：《万国公法》，［美］丁韪良译，何勤华点校，中国政法大学出版社2003年版，第34页。
② ［美］惠顿：《万国公法》，［美］丁韪良译，何勤华点校，中国政法大学出版社2003年版，第37页。
③ ［美］惠顿：《万国公法》，［美］丁韪良译，何勤华点校，中国政法大学出版社2003年版，第46页。
④ ［美］惠顿：《万国公法》，［美］丁韪良译，何勤华点校，中国政法大学出版社2003年版，第49页。
⑤ ［美］惠顿：《万国公法》，［美］丁韪良译，何勤华点校，中国政法大学出版社2003年版，第57页。

国，就其内政，自执全权，而不依傍于他国。其君主官长，可以自行拣择。其国法，可以自为议定。若君位系世传，则嗣君必依国法而定，或因嗣续而起争端，则本国亦可自理，不必他国居间管理约束也。若民主之国，则公举首领官长，均由自主，一循国法，他国亦不得行权势于其间也。"①

第二章 论制定律法之权：

"凡自主之国，制律定己民之分位、权利等情，并定疆内产业、植物（所谓植物者，即如房屋、田亩，不能移动之类，不独树木然也）、动物，无论属己民、属外人，皆得操其专权。然民或有产业不在本国者，或有在他国立契据、写遗嘱等情，或在他国有亲人死而无遗嘱本身继之。如此，则一民并服二三国之法，其故土，或其所居之地，固服之；其产业所在之地，亦服之；其契据所写所成之地，又服之。其服故土也，则直自始生之日，至弃绝本国而后已。至于产业所在之地，契据所写所成之地，则虽云不尽服其法，但就事而服之也。在外国有产业者，称为不住之地主；在外国写成契据者，称为暂住之人民。"②

"国权既如何定律，则法院断案必当遵之。若本地无律可制其事，则法院或可斟酌其间，仿照他国之律而行之也。至于明许他国之律法，行于疆内者有二：或制法者定议而许之，或公使会他国立约而允之。其默许者亦有二：有司断案，并公师论理，是也。行他国之律于本国中，各国之制法者、审法者、论法者，皆以为情所可为，非分所必为。"③

"自主之国，莫不有内治之权，皆可制律，以限定人民之权利、分位等事，有权可管辖疆内之人，无论本国之民，及外国之民，并审罚其所犯之罪案，此常例也。至地方律法、刑典行于疆

---

① [美]惠顿：《万国公法》，[美]丁韪良译，何勤华点校，中国政法大学出版社2003年版，第71页。

② [美]惠顿：《万国公法》，[美]丁韪良译，何勤华点校，中国政法大学出版社2003年版，第77页。

③ [美]惠顿：《万国公法》，[美]丁韪良译，何勤华点校，中国政法大学出版社2003年版，第79页。

外者,亦有四种。第一种:定己民之分位。第一种乃限定人民之分位、权利也。本国律法制己民之分位、权利者,虽其民徙往他国,亦可随地而制之。"①

"第二种,若有契据写在某国,而后在他国兴讼,则本国之律法,可就事而行于疆外。其不行者有四:(1)不合于物所在之律则不行。——(2)妨害于他国则不行。若于他国之主权、贸易、征税、人民权利、内治、安泰有所妨碍,则不行。——(3)遇契据应成于他国则不行。若立契据者,其契据或由所立地方律法,或由立契者明言应在他国成就,则凡成就之事,必从其国之律法也。——(4)遇案之应由法院条规而断者不行。各国法院审案条规,为各国自定。若有成契之案,当由法院条规而断者,则其立契之地方律法不得行也。"②

"第三种包括三端:(1)此国之君主往彼国者,不归彼国管辖,此乃诸国友谊之常也。(2)钦差等国使,在其所遣往疆内,亦不归地方管辖,一若仍在本国,全属本国管辖者然。(3)兵旅、水师驶行过他国疆域,或屯在他国疆内者,若其君与他国之君和好,则不归地方律法管辖。"③

"自主之国审办犯法之案,尽可自秉其权,不问于他国,此大例也。然若其国与他国有盟约相连,或特立约据,则此权或有所减。④

"凡有罪案在此国,按地方律法审断不能直行于他国,若定其人之罪,不能加刑于其身物在疆外者。即其罪犯系可耻重案,而削其为民之权利,但此议亦不直行于他国之自主者。此国之法院所断,或拟罪、或免罪,犹可旁行于他国者,即其案既在所犯

---

① [美]惠顿:《万国公法》,[美]丁韪良译,何勤华点校,中国政法大学出版社2003年版,第84页。
② [美]惠顿:《万国公法》,[美]丁韪良译,何勤华点校,中国政法大学出版社2003年版,第88、89、90页。
③ [美]惠顿:《万国公法》,[美]丁韪良译,何勤华点校,中国政法大学出版社2003年版,第90、101、106页。
④ [美]惠顿:《万国公法》,[美]丁韪良译,何勤华点校,中国政法大学出版社2003年版,第107页。

之处，或在其人所属之国，循该国律法审断，则他国不可复行追究。但审断若系在他国，非其犯案之处、非其所属之国者，则其所定拟，或坐罪、或释放，皆归于虚，不能循庇其人，使管辖之国不复行追究也。犯公法之案有数种，各国刑权所能及者，如海盗等类是也。"①

"凡人有亏空，按此国律法而得释放，若有植物、动物在他国，其释放之凭能护其物与否，诸国无常例，公师不同意。凡因人之权利约据屈害而起争端，若其人住疆内，无论争由何处，皆为各国审断之权所可及。"②

第三章　论诸国平行之权：

"自主之国，本皆平行均权，其后等级判高低、名号分尊卑、礼款别轻重者，盖有特条明许之，或由常行以为默许之。欧罗巴诸国，按公法有应得王礼、不应得王礼者。"③

"诸国本有平行之权，与他国共议时，俱用己之言语文字，尽可从此例者，不无其国也。但剌丁古文在欧罗巴系通行，而诸国用以共议，前以为便。三百年前，欧罗巴各国莫大于西班牙，连合该管属国众多，故文移事件概从西班牙文字。惟二百年来，诸国文移公论几尽用法国言语文字。若议约通问用本国言语文字，则附以译本，概为各国相待之礼。"④

第四章　论各国掌物之权：

"自主之国各有权掌管己之土地、公物，或由开拓、或由征服、或由推让。历时既久，他国立约认之，其权皆坚固焉。其掌

---

① [美]惠顿：《万国公法》，[美]丁韪良译，何勤华点校，中国政法大学出版社2003年版，第111页。
② [美]惠顿：《万国公法》，[美]丁韪良译，何勤华点校，中国政法大学出版社2003年版，第116页。
③ [美]惠顿：《万国公法》，[美]丁韪良译，何勤华点校，中国政法大学出版社2003年版，第124页。
④ [美]惠顿：《万国公法》，[美]丁韪良译，何勤华点校，中国政法大学出版社2003年版，第127页。

公土、公物之权本无限制，不但他国不得揽越，即己民亦不与焉。"①

"各国疆内所有湖海江河皆为国土，应归其专管也。江河发源于外，顺流过疆者，并其入海之澳湾等处，亦为国土，应归其专管也。至江河夹于二国之间者，则以中流为界，二国同享其水利。若系一国先得而早行专辖，则按理仍当归其专辖也。凡物之为用不穷者，一人不可据为己有而禁他人共用，惟他人用之，应无损于其物之主，所谓无损则可用是也。"②

第三卷　论诸国平时往来之权

第一章　论通使之权：

"古来教化渐行，诸国以礼相待，即有通使之例，惟近今又有钦差驻扎各国之例。缘近二百年内，各国通商、交际更密，每有不明之事，特派钦差以治理之。又恐各国有恃强凌弱，而碍于均势之法，故设驻京钦差以防之也。此万国公法所以立有章程，定通使往来之权。自主之国，若欲互相和好，即有权可遣使、受使，他国不得阻碍。若不愿遣使，他国亦不得相强。惟就常例而论，倘不通使，似近于不和。然通使虽为当行之例，断无必行之势，其行与否，当视其交情厚薄、事务紧要而定。至属国、半主之国，其通使必视所属、所倚之大国秉有何权。"③

"万国公法之初兴，分使臣尊卑，惟因其所任之职而定。后渐有分别，每起衅端，故诸国公议，分别使臣品级，以为款待之制。现今使臣分为四等，第一等使臣系代君行事，其余三等系代国行事。第一等使臣系代君行事，其余三等系代国行事。第一等使臣应以君礼款待，一若其君亲来者。钦差有常任、特使之别，亦有常任兼特使之名者。若以职守分钦差品级，则第一与第二可

---

① ［美］惠顿：《万国公法》，［美］丁韪良译，何勤华点校，中国政法大学出版社2003年版，第131页。
② ［美］惠顿：《万国公法》，［美］丁韪良译，何勤华点校，中国政法大学出版社2003年版，第136页。
③ ［美］惠顿：《万国公法》，［美］丁韪良译，何勤华点校，中国政法大学出版社2003年版，第141页。

为同等,"①

"国使如不寄信凭,则不能以使臣之礼仪权利归之。上三等使臣寄信凭于君,第四等则寄信凭于部臣。其信凭或为密函、或为公函。商议立约全权之据,可在信凭内总括,或另缮一角。其式略如公诰。"②

"国使之妻子及从事员弁、记室、代书、佣工、器具、私衙、公馆皆置权外,他国不得管辖。"③

"国使驻扎他国,若在自己教堂礼拜,可照本国教礼而行。领事官不在使臣之列,各处律例及和约章程或准额外赐以权力,但领事等官不与分王国公法所定国使之权利也。若无和约明言,他国即可不准领事官驻扎其国,故必须所往国君准行方可办事。若有横逆不道之举,准行之凭即可收回,或照律审断,或送交其国,均从地主之便。至有争讼罪案,领事官俱服地方律法,与他国之人民无所异焉。使臣驻扎他国,或派往国使大会,其卸任之故有七:其一,或任满、或代理而正官来。其二,则因事特遣,而其事或成或不成也。其三,则本国召回也。其四,或本国或所驻之国遇君崩及退位等事,则必须再覆信凭。其五,国使或因所驻之国有干犯万国律例之事,或遇不测之大事,自不能辞其责而不卸任也。其六,或国使自有不法之事,或其本国有横行之举,彼国即可不俟其国书,先命回国。其七,则国使品级职任或有升降也。"④

第二章　论商议立约之权:

"凡自主之国,如未经退让本权,或早立盟约限制所为,即可出其自主之权,与他国商议立约。至于商议立约谁主其事,各

---

① [美]惠顿:《万国公法》,[美]丁韪良译,何勤华点校,中国政法大学出版社2003年版,第144页。
② [美]惠顿:《万国公法》,[美]丁韪良译,何勤华点校,中国政法大学出版社2003年版,第146页。
③ [美]惠顿:《万国公法》,[美]丁韪良译,何勤华点校,中国政法大学出版社2003年版,第149页。
④ [美]惠顿:《万国公法》,[美]丁韪良译,何勤华点校,中国政法大学出版社2003年版,第154页。

听国法所定。君主之国则盟约归君掌握,民主之国则首领或国会、或理事部院,均可任其权焉。"①

"约盟既商定画押,谁执准行之权,使必遵守,均听各国律法所定。若君权之无所限制者,则钦差所行之事或准或废,必俟君命而定。倘君权有所限制,则概由定法之部院会议议定后,其君方能施行。民主之国多由长老院同议同准,首领方可代国加用印信。"②

"常约者,随常之约也,即合约会盟、通商、航海各议。约内虽云永远奉行,然或屡废者。"③

"解说约盟与解说别样律法无异,无论何国语言文字,概是书不尽言,言不尽意也。但解其词者不免有害其义,故别有解说约盟之条,遇有疑难即可引用。"④

第四卷 论交战条规

第一章 论战始:

"自主之国遇有争端,若非公议凭中剖明,即无人执权以断其案,所服者惟有一法,乃万国之公法也。此法虽名为律例,不似各国之律法,使民畏刑而始遵也。所以各国倘受欺凌,别无他策以伸其冤,惟有用力以抵御报复耳。"⑤

"将战,不必先行宣知,方为公战。且敌国货物无论何在,既可捕为战利,则其疆内货物与疆外者,或当从一律俱可捕拿也。"⑥

---

① [美]惠顿:《万国公法》,[美]丁韪良译,何勤华点校,中国政法大学出版社2003年版,第158页。
② [美]惠顿:《万国公法》,[美]丁韪良译,何勤华点校,中国政法大学出版社2003年版,第162页。
③ [美]惠顿:《万国公法》,[美]丁韪良译,何勤华点校,中国政法大学出版社2003年版,第165页。
④ [美]惠顿:《万国公法》,[美]丁韪良译,何勤华点校,中国政法大学出版社2003年版,第172页。
⑤ [美]惠顿:《万国公法》,[美]丁韪良译,何勤华点校,中国政法大学出版社2003年版,第177页。
⑥ [美]惠顿:《万国公法》,[美]丁韪良译,何勤华点校,中国政法大学出版社2003年版,第182页。

"既不准与敌贸易往来,若在战时有与敌私立契据等情,皆为犯法。即如保敌货、出钱票、兑换银两、送银票实物于敌国,或宣战后仍与敌国人民合伙,皆为犯此规例。"①

第二章 论敌国交战之权:

"战者于敌可行何权,必视其因何而战,其事未成则尽法以成之,皆属战者之权。"②

"万国所必遵者有数等,房屋、物件战时置于害外,即如敬神庙宇、文职公廨、学堂书房并奇异之名物等类,民间货物在岸上者亦置于战权之外。但于疆场之上夺来货物,或攻入城池而得其货者,则皆不得恃此权利幸免。至破入敌境令其民捐输军费,与例不悖。"③

"既照例宣战,两国人民互相视若仇敌,本系战例,但诸国渐有变易此规者。若奉国权派令以害敌人,无论其令之或明或默,固可竭力以害之,但未曾派令而私以害敌者,即为公法所严禁也。"④

"战者之战权,可相时用宽,即如彼此议立停兵之约等款是也。夫停兵之约,有全有特。全者,则各处停兵,或定多日、或无期限,与讲和略同。"⑤

"停兵约上所限日期已满,自必复战,毋庸另宣矣。然约上若无限定日期,或所约之时长久,即与和约无甚差别,如将再战,必须通知敌国,方与仁义不悖。定款让城池、炮台地方,并以兵投降等事,俱归将帅执权。若有城邑被困,其守土官弁与攻

---

① [美]惠顿:《万国公法》,[美]丁韪良译,何勤华点校,中国政法大学出版社2003年版,第190页。

② [美]惠顿:《万国公法》,[美]丁韪良译,何勤华点校,中国政法大学出版社2003年版,第197页。

③ [美]惠顿:《万国公法》,[美]丁韪良译,何勤华点校,中国政法大学出版社2003年版,第200页。

④ [美]惠顿:《万国公法》,[美]丁韪良译,何勤华点校,中国政法大学出版社2003年版,第204页。

⑤ [美]惠顿:《万国公法》,[美]丁韪良译,何勤华点校,中国政法大学出版社2003年版,第213页。

城将士定款投降，不必俟两国君上允准而后行也。"①

第三章　论战时局外之权：

"局外之权有二：曰全，曰半。凡自主之国，遇他国交战，若无盟约限制，即可置身局外，不与其事，此所谓局外之全权也。在局外者既有权可行，即当有义必守，尤以守中不偏为大。局外之国与两国俱有友谊，即不得厚此薄彼。盖既为局外，即不当助此害彼，此乃无盟约以限制者，故有全权以守局外之分焉。倘与战者早有盟约限制，致必遵行，即谓局外之半权。"②

"战权所行之处有三：战者疆内，一也；海上，二也；无主之地，三也。三者之外，战权即不可行。至局外之国与二战国均系友谊，无分彼此，放在其疆内行战权者，即为干犯公法。调兵马、船只皆属战事，不能行于局外之地。在局外者管辖所及之处，战船捕敌国之船只、货物，不但为犯法，而其事必废，且战船停泊于其港口，以为征战之地步，则其所捕船只、货物亦多不稳。"③

"一千七百九十四年，美之国会定有一法，于一千八百十八年间复申之云：别国有战争时，倘有人民在美国辖内投其兵船者，或招兵往攻我素所和好之国，或招兵丁、水手为他国所用，抑或备船以巡洋助他国行战，皆为犯法，所备之船皆可捕拿入公。倘公法及和约章程所不准船只在美国港口停泊，而竟敢停泊者，首领可以驱逐。盖首领可凭国势、照律法以自保其局外之权也。后英国又定律法，凡英民投军别国，与夫未奉君命而私备战船于英之疆内者，皆禁止之。"④

---

① ［美］惠顿：《万国公法》，［美］丁韪良译，何勤华点校，中国政法大学出版社2003年版，第216页。
② ［美］惠顿：《万国公法》，［美］丁韪良译，何勤华点校，中国政法大学出版社2003年版，第221页。
③ ［美］惠顿：《万国公法》，［美］丁韪良译，何勤华点校，中国政法大学出版社2003年版，第227页。
④ ［美］惠顿：《万国公法》，［美］丁韪良译，何勤华点校，中国政法大学出版社2003年版，第233页。

"为敌国寄公信、载兵弁,皆归运载禁物之列。"①

"宣战之权,谁执其端,必视各国之法度,至议和之权亦然。人能操其一者,大抵亦能操其二。若君权无限之国,其权柄固归君主掌握;即君权有限之国,有时亦并以二者之权柄托于君手。"②

"立约之时,彼此所有之地方,约上若无明言让还,嗣后即各自存守。"

---

① [美]惠顿:《万国公法》,[美]丁韪良译,何勤华点校,中国政法大学出版社2003年版,第239页。
② [美]惠顿:《万国公法》,[美]丁韪良译,何勤华点校,中国政法大学出版社2003年版,第253页。

第三章　京师同文馆翻译的其他国际法著作

第一节　《星轺指掌》①

《星轺指掌》是根据德国外交官马尔顿（Charles De Martens, 1790–1863）的著作 *Guide Diplomatique* 翻译而成的。马尔顿身为外交官，往来于欧洲各国之间，有着丰富的外交经验。其著作深受各国外交官喜爱。马尔顿的著作刊行于世后，著名学者葛福根根据时代的变化，对该书进行了适当的增订与修改，他将一些案例及后来出现的条文附于书后："葛氏所增注解凡三种：引成案以为证据，一也；载条例以示随时之沿革，二也；辩异同以发明其所未详，三也。"②

该书被译为多国文字，《星轺指掌》翻译所据的是法文本。翻译人员为同文馆学生联芳、庆常，后来经贵荣、杜法孟润色，交给丁韪良最后审定：

> 是书原刊以法文，因通行泰西故也。其翻译华文系同文馆学习人员联芳、庆常初稿，而贵荣、杜法孟稍加润色，复经丁总教习为之校核，期免舛错。③

---

① 参见拙文《〈星轺指掌〉与近代西方外交关系法及外交术语的输入》，《惠州学院学报》2010年第2期；[美] 惠顿：《万国公法》，[美] 丁韪良译，何勤华点校，中国政法大学出版社2003年版，第257页。
② [美] 丁韪良等：《星轺指掌·凡例》，光绪二年同文馆聚珍版。
③ [美] 丁韪良等：《星轺指掌·凡例》，光绪二年同文馆聚珍版。

《星軺指掌》封二

董恂为《星軺指掌》写的序文

丁韪良等人在翻译时，对原书的体例作了一些改动。一是将放在书尾的案例改为与正文相间，便于读者明白易懂；二是增译了美国领事则例。

丁韪良在《星轺指掌·凡例》对"公使""邦国"作了简单的解释：

> 邦国藉公使以相见，故通使之例为万国公法之一门也。公法家无不论及，而此书论之特详；书内多见公使名目。夫封疆大吏、因公差遣之人皆得谓之公使，而书中所谓公使，则惟此国之君简派前往彼国者方可称之；公使名目不一，或称钦差大臣，或称钦使，或称国使。若无另添字句以别之，要皆指公使也。故此书从简而称公使及使臣；第四等公使洋语名为沙尔涉大斐尔，除署理全权大臣归四等公使外，更有特简实任之四等公使，故名为办事大臣以别之；邦国二字虽系通用，然书中所称自万乘以至百乘，皆谓之国也。若邦，或偶指自主之国而言，而于屏藩以及数国合一，则以邦名其各国者为常。①

《星轺指掌·凡例》还介绍了世界各国不同的政体形式及其特点：

> 各国政式不一，有君位世传而君权无限者，有君位世传而君权有限者，皆谓君主之国。复有庶民公举国主而其在位限有年数者，是谓民政之国；凡君权有限之国与民政之国，皆公举大臣，会议国政，是谓国会。君位虽尊而权势往往操之于国会也；凡君权无限之国，莫不设有议政院，其大臣皆由国君简派。而君权有限之国及民政之国，所设国会亦以议政院称之；君权有限之国与民政之国，率由国会公议以制法，国君秉权而行法，复有专设法司以执法而审讯不法之事者，此谓之法院或曰法堂。国政既不同，国君之称号亦异。或称皇帝，或称君主，或称王，要皆以国君为通称。虽民政之国主亦可称君，而洋语则以伯理玺天德称之。②

---

① ［美］丁韪良等：《星轺指掌·凡例》，光绪二年同文馆聚珍版。
② ［美］丁韪良等：《星轺指掌·凡例》，光绪二年同文馆聚珍版。

《星轺指掌》同文馆聚珍版，共分元、亨、利、贞四部，于1876年正式出版。

《星轺指掌》言简意赅，一目了然，梁启超在《读西学书法》中称赞该书："言使臣之职掌及派使待使之道，条理粲然。"

曾纪泽任驻英公使期间，反复翻阅《星轺指掌》：

> 初十日，——至三槐堂书店，更衣后，偕松生游隆福寺。回总署，阅《星轺指掌》，批字典。——十七日，茶食后，登楼久坐，看《星轺指掌》。与松生一谈。——二十二日，除早茶及己、酉两餐外，竟日偃卧。看《星轺指掌》二卷。——二十三日，茶食后，在舱中偃卧。看《星轺指掌》末二册。①

董恂为该书作序，赞赏有加：

> 《星轺指掌》序 古者大行人掌大宾之礼，大客之仪，小行人掌邦国宾客之礼，籍达天下之六节，成六瑞，合六币，见于周礼，小者问大者，聘自图事，命使而假道而郊劳，而致馆，而设飧，而致命，而设字，而醴宾，而私觌，而赠送。凡夫展币释币之文，张旃敛旃之制，辞玉受玉之节，垂缫屈缫之宜，见于仪礼。遐想其时，行李往来，春秋时见难容揖让。肆雅歌风，济济翼翼戢戢如也，谓非叔盛典叹。顾是礼也，行于封建之代而不行于郡县之朝，即封建时亦行于九州之中，而不行于四海之外。岂当日之创制显庸，犹有未周焉者乎！抑因革损茧，固视乎其时也。同文馆总教习丁冠西先生明练典故，淹通古今，深有味乎礼从宜、使从俗之意，爰取迩来海外诸国交际事宜，承馆生辈，译以华言，用备星轺之采。士大夫本忠信笃教之训，成约束坚明之举，将片言重于九鼎，一纸书贤于十部，从此俾四海永清，中外禔福，合乎时而不戾乎古，则是书未始非我行人之一助也。光绪丙子夏五之闰邗江董恂拜譔。②

---

① 钟叔河：《出使英法俄国日记》，岳麓书社1985年版，第105页、141页、142页、143页。
② [美]丁韪良等：《星轺指掌·序》，光绪二年同文馆聚珍版。

王韬十分欣赏《星轺指掌》一书，曾为该书作序：

行人之设，肇自古昔，然皆王国下逮侯邦，而诸侯亦各相聘问，藉以讲信修睦。其载于《春秋》者，行人之选，一时綦重。自是以来，折冲坛坫，焜耀敦槃，国家之强弱，国事之安危，胥系乎将命时之一言，必如宣尼所谓"使于四方，不辱君命"，斯可以当之矣。后世疆宇日廓，交际日繁，汉通西域，奉尺一之诏以羁致之阙下者，亦行人职也。于是行人所至，不在九州以内，而在四海之外。宋、元以降，东洋诸岛渐登王会，献琛赆，贡共球，遣使接迹于道，或请命于天朝，锡封颁爵，以星使之临为荣。盖王者镇抚六合，恢宏八荒，俾屏藩乎四境，原非好勤远略也，时为之也。欧洲诸国航海东来，互市于中土，无不立约设官，以权其贸易事宜，而又特简重臣，驻扎京师，诚以其国首重通商，而官即所以卫商也。又其国每以商力裕其兵力，兵力佐其商力，商之所通，兵亦至焉。水师战舰分布称雄，以是官以卫商，兵以卫官，似若有所恃而不恐。如是则其所为使臣者，或不尽在乎雍容辞令矣，而抑知有不然者，则以万国公法为执持也。《星轺指掌》一书，纪海外诸国遣使往来之事特详，凡膺海外皇华之役者，可取资焉。方今我国家提封数万重，恢乎罔外，南至于越南，北至于俄罗斯，东至于朝鲜，西至于印度。以欧洲诸国重译远交，不可不结信讲好，联两国之欢心而永万年之盟誓。此役也，固为我国从来未有之创举矣，然则衔命前往者，宜若何郑重哉。余尝受其书而读之，叹其足为我行人之一助。惟是留心西事者，争欲先睹为快。金陵叶君，爰出资重付剞劂氏为袖珍本，便于舟车携带，以广其传。庶几见是书者，得窥西国遣使命意之所在，而以忠信笃敬临之，礼义恭让持之，然后能要约于无形，战胜于不兵，薄海咸宁，越裳是宾。[①]

---

① 王韬：《弢园文录外编》卷9，中华书局1959年版。

二 《星轺指掌》与近代西方外交关系法

《星轺指掌》共有四卷，二十八章，基本涵盖了近代外交关系法的主要内容。以王铁崖主编、法律出版社1991年出版的《国际法》为例，将"第八章，外交和领事关系"与《星轺指掌》进行比较，我们可以发现，除了《国际法》中第七节有关联合国的内容外，两书的内容基本相同。但《星轺指掌》深深打上了那个时代的烙印，如领事裁判权等。

《星轺指掌》与王铁崖主编《国际法》章节比较表①：

《星轺指掌》	《国际法》
通使总论	第八章第一节　外交关系法概说
第一章　论各国应有专署以理外事	第八章第二节　国家的中央外交关系机关
第二章　论通使之例	第八章第三节　使馆及其人员；
第三章　论使臣等级	第八章第三节之五　使馆馆长的等级和位次
第四章　论使臣职守	
第五章　论出使人员	第八章第三节之四　使馆人员的类别
第六章　论使臣之权利	第八章　使馆及其人员的特权和豁免
第九章　论使臣升降解任等情	第八章第三节之六　使馆人员的任命
第十章　论各国往来礼节	
第十一章　论水师礼节	
第十二章　论领事官之责任；	第八章第八节之四　领事职务；
第十三章　论领事官所任之事分类	
第十四章　论领事官驻扎回部	
续卷第一章　论领事官等级及总领事职守	第八章第八节　领事官及其人员
续卷第二章　论领事等官授职之例	
续卷第三章　论领事等官莅任之例	
续卷第四章　论领事等官凭公法所享之权利；第五章论领事等官凭条约所享之权利	第八章第九节　领事特权和豁免
续卷第六章　论领事官为本国公使所鉴察	

---

① ［美］丁韪良等：《星轺指掌·目录》，光绪二年同文馆聚珍版；王铁崖主编：《国际法·目录》，法律出版社1981年版。

续表

《星轺指掌》	《国际法》
续卷第七章 论领事官与水师官往来事宜	
续卷第八章 论领事各官俸禄	
续卷第九章 论领事官接任事宜	
续卷第十一章 论发给护照事宜	
续卷第十二章 论领事官照料船商事宜	
续卷第十三章 论照料被撤被难水手	
续卷第十四章 论领事官审讯船主与水手人等所有争端	
续卷第十五章 论领事缉拿逃避水手	
续卷第十六章 论捞救难船	
续卷第十七章 论领事界内买船事宜	
续卷第十八章 论美船装载华民事宜	
续卷第十九章 论照料船只难事	
续卷第二十章 论领事官料理遗产事宜	
续卷第二十一章 论供职杂款	
续卷第二十六章 论领事官在东方各国所乘审断之权	第八章第八节之五 历史上的领事裁判权
续卷第二十八章 附公文程式	

外交关系法是关于外交关系的国际法原则和规则的总和，它主要涉及：外交代表机关（使馆、特别使团等）、人员以及派遣程序；外交代表机关、人员的职务；外交代表机关及其人员的特权和豁免；外交礼仪。

第一卷（第一、二、三、四、五章）"通使总论"介绍外交关系、外交机构、外交人员的级别以及职责等：

"通使之例虽繁，其理至简，要之不外准情度宜，而主在办理交涉事务。"①

"渐则事务益烦，关系益重，而各国京师又皆另立衙署，专

---

① ［美］丁韪良等：《星轺指掌》卷1，光绪二年同文馆聚珍版，第1页。

理交涉事务，始而名曰外务部，继而名曰会议部，后则定为总理外国事务衙署。查总理大臣之职，有关国家安危利害，责任非轻。务选才识卓越者，方可膺斯重任，不致有伤国体。否则，办事一有背谬，即可陷本国于不测之害。是以该大臣之职守，有不可不详为申论者。"①

"总理大臣选派公使，须择其阅历较深、才识兼优、名望甚重者，方可信任。"②

"总理大臣寻常接见公使，皆有定期。除定期外，公使若欲会晤，必须专人面询，或函请时日方可，以无碍该大臣政务为要。遇有紧要事件，以及重任公使，亦可随时前往，不得限以常格。总理大臣卸任，亦当仿照接任之时，通知各使，以尽同舟之谊。"③

"查各国执掌部院事务大臣，洋语称密尼司德，其授以文凭，或全权字样。差往外国，办理交涉事务者，按洋文，其职名与部院大臣相同，至该使宠荣优遇之处，载在万国公法。"④

"凡使臣之等级，皆由本国派定。"⑤

"凡公使会议和约立盟等事，皆当携有全权字据。"⑥

"按照使臣等级以定随使人员之多寡。其随使分为两等：一则使臣之参赞协理等官，皆由国君简派，而得与公使之权利；二则使臣之幕友，以及随侍人等，皆归私役。参赞等员皆膺公职。"⑦

第二卷（第六、九、十章，缺七、八章）介绍公使权利及其外交活动：

---

① ［美］丁韪良等：《星轺指掌》卷1，光绪二年同文馆聚珍版，第5页。
② ［美］丁韪良等：《星轺指掌》卷1，光绪二年同文馆聚珍版，第7页。
③ ［美］丁韪良等：《星轺指掌》卷1，光绪二年同文馆聚珍版，第8页。
④ ［美］丁韪良等：《星轺指掌》卷1，光绪二年同文馆聚珍版，第10页。
⑤ ［美］丁韪良等：《星轺指掌》卷1，光绪二年同文馆聚珍版，第16页。
⑥ ［美］丁韪良等：《星轺指掌》卷1，光绪二年同文馆聚珍版，第32页。
⑦ ［美］丁韪良等：《星轺指掌》卷1，光绪二年同文馆聚珍版，第36页。

"凡授以使臣权利,原为其得称职守,无有阻碍。其权利中之最要者,系不得禁锢耳。"①

"使臣公署不得据之屯兵,亦不能令其捐银以资屯费。"②

"使臣应需各等学问以备出使。"③

"使臣驻扎外邦,有保护人民之责。"④

"差期已满,即应交卸回国,毋庸俟本国谕旨。其署任公使遇正使到任,亦当如是;出使若专为庆吊等典,或专办某事,一俟其事或成或败,应即行回国奏明;使臣奉命调回本国者,当即交卸起程;本国之君或驾崩,或退位,使臣例应解任;彼国若干犯公法,侮慢使臣,或别有重大事故,则当酌度情形,解任回国;使臣不知自检,扰乱国政,干犯法禁。则彼国可以发给护照,令该使回国,并勒限出境,不准逗留。如情节甚重,即派兵押解出境;使臣遇有升降,亦宜解任。"⑤

"按公法凡自主之国俱用平行之礼,虽国势强弱不一,其权利并无参差,则均有自主之权也。⑥

第三卷(第十三、十四章)介绍领事的职责、权利以及领事裁判权等:

"查领事官系在驻京公使之先而设也。八、九百年前,回回地方有义、法、日等国城镇各设领事。日耳曼之沿海城镇亦各派绅董以理通商。嗣后贸易渐盛,事务日繁。其遣派领事之权,操之国主,不归郡邑商会。渐则沿海各国市舶云集,彼此互相简派领事,以便办理。"⑦

---

① [美]丁韪良等:《星轺指掌》卷2,光绪二年同文馆聚珍版,第1页。
② [美]丁韪良等:《星轺指掌》卷2,光绪二年同文馆聚珍版,第16页。
③ [美]丁韪良等:《星轺指掌》卷2,光绪二年同文馆聚珍版,第33页。
④ [美]丁韪良等:《星轺指掌》卷2,光绪二年同文馆聚珍版,第40页。
⑤ [美]丁韪良等:《星轺指掌》卷2,光绪二年同文馆聚珍版,第54页。
⑥ [美]丁韪良等:《星轺指掌》卷2,光绪二年同文馆聚珍版,第60页。
⑦ [美]丁韪良等:《星轺指掌》卷3,光绪二年同文馆聚珍版,第1页。

"领事职守系稽查航海通商事务,保护本国人民安居乐业,代办契约字据,代向地方官伸诉冤抑,为本国人民调处争讼等事。"①

"领事首务应保护本国船商,以免受屈。本国人民有控诉地方官者,如果属实,领事即当代为料理。倘本国人民有冤抑情事,地方官不肯查办,即由领事禀知本国公使,转请该国执政大臣查办。"②

"领事应随时保护本国水手人等,遇险当救,有冤代申。有事而请示者,即应指示,至本国人民之身家财产,亦一体保护。若有被屈情事,领事或函请、或面商地方官,代为昭雪。凡船主初到该口,若不熟悉该处法律风俗以及税则章程,应由领事逐件示知。"③

"凡本国人民在领事境内者,领事当随时保护。倘地方官不遵常例,违犯条约,或本国人民受屈,而地方官不肯作主,抑或枉理屈断等情,应由领事设法调处。"④

按照国家主权原则,领事官不得干预他国内政,但西方国家自恃强大国力,以东方国家野蛮、落后为借口,授予领事官更大的权力,此即领事裁判权:

"惟回国法律、风俗与泰西各国大相悬殊,而领事之权利,亦有别也。况各国人民前往土耳其等处贸易游历者,不可胜计,若任凭土国管辖,是交良民于污吏之手耳。——泰西各国与土耳其、埃及、波斯并巴巴里等回国所立条约,大同小异。皆将本国商民、水手人等,专归领事官管辖。遇有彼此不协之处,由领事自行审断。本国人民与回民互起争端及杀伤人口重案,地方官不可自行查办,亦不可自行定案,必须会同领事,带同翻译官,公同审讯,以免屈抑等弊。倘领事及本国商民与别外国领事人等有

---

① [美]丁韪良等:《星轺指掌》卷3,光绪二年同文馆聚珍版,第1页。
② [美]丁韪良等:《星轺指掌》卷3,光绪二年同文馆聚珍版,第11页。
③ [美]丁韪良等:《星轺指掌》卷3,光绪二年同文馆聚珍版,第21页。
④ [美]丁韪良等:《星轺指掌》卷3,光绪二年同文馆聚珍版,第30页。

不协之处，如两造愿呈诉本国驻京公使，皆听之。遇本国人民有杀害命案，被害者若非彼国之民，则领事秉权审办，地方官不得干预。地方官查拿领事本国人民或别外国人民，一经领事收留，则回人不得闯入公署搜捕。"①

"公使、领事等官驻扎回回等国，应有翻译官随从当差。而翻译员缺向由总理大臣奏保，请旨简放。——司库为领事属员之领袖，向由本国简派，然领事亦可保举，而仍由总理大臣批准。——领事请假离任、委员署理，即当行知该处大宪，并传知所属查照办理。——领事卸任，应会同新任或署领事，将公文书籍册档，并署中器具，逐一查点，交该员接收，并写收单字样，以作证据。又应将已卸任及他人接任之事，行知该处大宪，并传知领事属员。领事卸任后，任内经手各项文件不可存留原稿，亦不可抄录刊印。领事在任内病故，所遗财物由属员查点封锁，由护理人员禀明本国公使与本国总理大臣，并行知该处大宪。"②

续卷（第一至二十八章，其中二十二至二十五以及二十七章未译）以美国领事条例为例，详细介绍领事的权利、义务与职责以及领事裁判权以及公文格式等：

"美国领事官有十等：总领事兼理办事大臣、总领事、副总领事、委总领事、正领事、副领事、委办领事、代理领事、通商司、副通商司，更有属员二等，以为帮办。"③

"若无条约明文，则领事官不得视为公使，亦不能代国秉权。即不免于地方官管辖，亦为身家房产邀请公使所享优免之处。"④

"除英、法、意并中华、埃及等国，其总领事驻他国者，皆兼办公使之职。其驻英、法、意并中华等国，总领事皆隶于驻扎

---

① ［美］丁韪良等：《星轺指掌》卷3，光绪二年同文馆聚珍版，第38、39页。
② ［美］丁韪良等：《星轺指掌》卷3，光绪二年同文馆聚珍版，第45、47、48页。
③ ［美］丁韪良等：《星轺指掌》续卷，光绪二年同文馆聚珍版，第1页。
④ ［美］丁韪良等：《星轺指掌》续卷，光绪二年同文馆聚珍版，第7页。

该国公使，与领事之隶于总领事同。"①

"护照应由本国总署发给，或由驻京本国公使发给。若无公使，则由总领事发给。若二者皆无，则由各领事发给亦可。"②

"遇美国船只在外国口岸遭患，若按地方律法，事属可行，领事官应设法捞救，交与原主。若无原主及代办之人在彼，领事官应代为收存。其捞获之物，当详为缮单记载。"③

"遇美国人民在外物故，领事官本无料理遗产之权，然有条约明言，或地方官允许，则事属可行。遇美国人民在领事界内物故，其遗物应由领事官收掌，酌量变卖，以免损坏，而清偿遗债。"④

"公文程式，国书二件。大臣出使各国国书。大清国大皇帝问大某国大君主好。朕寅承天命，中外一家，眷念友邦，永敦和好。特选贤能智士前驻京合众国使臣蒲安臣，熟悉中外情形，于办理两国交涉事宜，可期代达衷曲，并派二品衔志刚、孙家谷同赴大某国，俱膺特简重任大臣，以为真心和好之据，朕知此三臣均忠勤醇谨，必能办理妥协。务望推诚相信，得以永臻友睦，共享升平，谅必深为欢悦也。"⑤

第二节 《公法便览》*

《公法便览》译自美国法学家、耶鲁大学校长吴尔玺（The odore Dwight woolsey, 1801–1889）于1860年出版的著作 *Introduction to the Study of International Law*，刊行于1878年。《万国公法》出版十余年后，世界格局发生了一些变化，签订了一些新的国际条约，为了准确

---

① 参见拙文《〈公法便览〉与战争法及其术语的输入》，《三峡大学学报》2011年第3期；[美] 丁韪良等《星轺指掌》续卷，光绪二年同文馆聚珍版，第12页。
② [美] 丁韪良等：《星轺指掌》续卷，光绪二年同文馆聚珍版，第21页。
③ [美] 丁韪良等：《星轺指掌》续卷，光绪二年同文馆聚珍版，第43页。
④ [美] 丁韪良等：《星轺指掌》续卷，光绪二年同文馆聚珍版，第52页。
⑤ [美] 丁韪良等：《星轺指掌》续卷，光绪二年同文馆聚珍版，第66页。

第三章 京师同文馆翻译的其他国际法著作

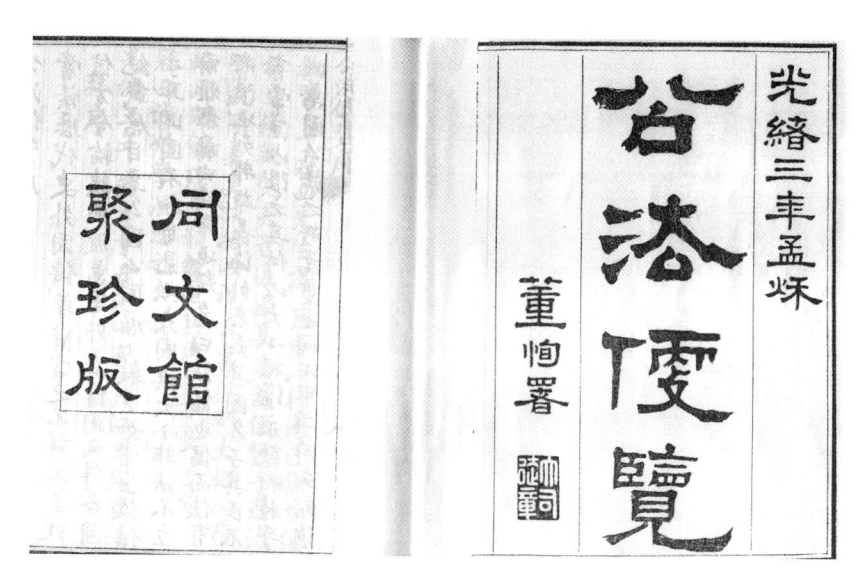

董恂为《公法会通》所署书名

陈兰彬为《公法便览》写的序文

地反映这些变化，丁韪良不避嫌疑，再次选用了美国法学家的著作作为翻译底本，这固然与丁韪良为了维护美国在华利益，帮助美国在华树立良好的形象有关，但吴尔玺本人的声望也是十分重要的原因：

美之公法家向多著名，而其尚在者以吴氏为冠，宜也。缘吴氏学既周备，心亦公正，其条约考略亦包括三百余年之史乘云。观夫英国与美国同文而重刊之，日本与美国异文而翻译之，足知其书为地球东西所推重也。①

丁韪良与吴尔玺相识于十年前，丁韪良为了胜任京师同国文馆的国际法教学工作而赴耶鲁大学学习，听了吴尔玺的课后，丁韪良当时就想将该书引入中国：

余于丁卯年请假回国，曾在雅礼学院得识吴君，观其教法，心甚羡之。复读是书，窃思吴君已用之于本国以课其弟子，曷不可携之于中国而课诸馆生。②

丁韪良介绍吴尔玺：

美之名士也，年近八旬，曾于雅礼学院总理学政，迨以老乞休而专致力于公法，爰著此书以课子弟云。③先生平生以兴学育才为己任，始充古文教习而注释希腊往籍，追先哲于羹墙，继主书院讲坛而提倡当世学风，为儒林之圭臬，终则著是书于一室，传公法于万邦，厥功亦伟矣哉！④

为了避免版权纠纷，他在给吴尔玺的信中解释道：

私拟以先生之书为课，以先生之法为则，实于后学有裨。良旋华时即用原文教课馆生，而外间鲜有能读者，于是翻译华文以期广布，奈未及请命而行，殊深歉仄。然中国向无禁止翻译翻刻

---

① ［美］丁韪良等：《公法便览·自序》，光绪四年同文馆聚珍版。
② ［美］丁韪良等：《公法便览·凡例》，光绪四年同文馆聚珍版。
③ ［美］丁韪良等：《公法便览·凡例》，光绪四年同文馆聚珍版。
④ ［美］丁韪良等：《公法便览·致吴尔玺书》，光绪四年同文馆聚珍版。

之例，且译者又出于公而无所私，区区苦衷，谅邀鉴宥。①

《公法便览》一书的翻译难度颇大：

> 公法既别为一科，则应有专用字样。故原文内偶有汉文所难达之意，因之用字往往似觉勉强。即如一权字，书内不独指有司所操之权，亦指凡人理所应得之分，有时增一利字，如谓庶人本有之权利云云。此等字句，初见多不入目，屡见方知为不得已而用之也。②

此外，丁韪良再次将世界地图刊出，并增加了欧洲地图，配以文字说明：

> 前图因取旧版，地名字样与今少有不合，如普国现作布国，意国现作义国，日耳曼现作德意志是也。书中所载史案，多出于欧洲各国交涉，故另附欧罗巴全图，而邦域之小者，不及备载，各国之京都，以星记之。③

第四卷的最后，是丁韪良译自吴尔玺原著的跋，该跋针砭美国时政，读来令人警醒：

> 公法之学与邦国文教相表里，不独为律法家专门之业，凡读书稽古者，皆当肄习及之。就美国而论，此学尤不可不讲。因美国今日骎骎乎日见富强矣，强则易于骄横而行不义。凡暴戾之习，往往尤而效之。如并吞邻疆，公义者不为，而美之政府则由贿之不可，继以力夺之议，公然高论而不知耻。奸顽聚党，侵扰邻邦，诱助内乱，国法所必惩之。而美国之官宪则约束不力，宽

---

① ［美］丁韪良等：《公法便览·致吴尔玺书》，光绪四年同文馆聚珍版。
② ［美］丁韪良等：《公法便览·凡例》，光绪四年同文馆聚珍版。
③ ［美］丁韪良等：《公法便览·凡例》，光绪四年同文馆聚珍版。

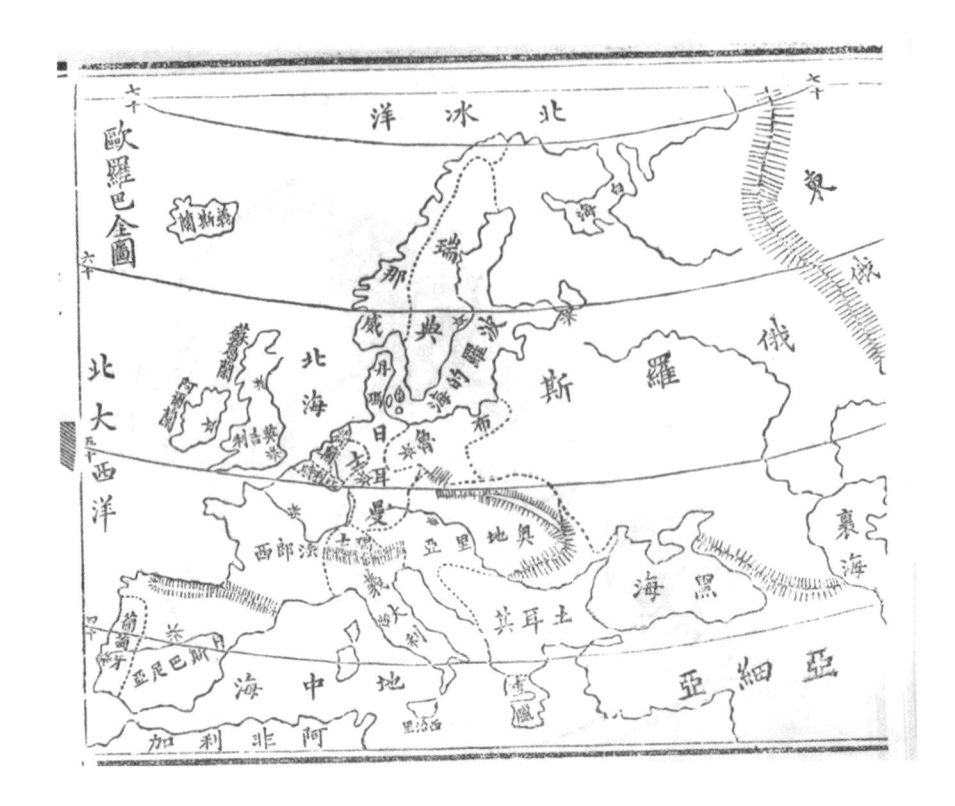

纵养奸，若隐为主谋者然。至于寻衅搆怨，以为争夺之阶，更属不一而足。又如贩卖黑奴一业，美国已禁五十余年，且首先科以海盗罪，诚义举也。乃至今国人犹有谓禁宜驰，业宜复，以是为权利而万无可已者。凡此，皆妄恃天命，惑于利欲，以至义理不明，公道沦丧。非有公法以纠绳其间，使之晓然于义理，而深惕于隐微，势将安所底止哉！则予是书之作，固为学者入门之助，亦期有裨我国家云尔。①

《公法便览》由汪凤藻、凤仪、左秉隆、德明四人历时三年完成，其中"大半出于汪凤藻一手"②。汪凤藻"既具敏才，复精英文。余为之讲解一切，易于领悟，其笔亦足以达之，且能恪遵原本，不减不

---

① ［美］丁韪良等：《公法便览》卷4，光绪四年同文馆聚珍版，第99页。
② ［美］丁韪良等：《公法便览·凡例》，光绪四年同文馆聚珍版。

增，使余省点窜之劳焉"①。最后由桂林、贵荣润色，经过总理各国事务大臣批阅后，蒙命付梓。

清朝太常少卿夏家镐欣然作序：

《公法便览》序：尝读历代史，外国传，率皆言之不详，不足考信。方今轮艘飞渡，万里外若帷闼。又得各国纪载，厝为厶国，厶国历历数之如掌上纹信乎。耳闻固不如目见欤！夫国无大小，非法不立。《尔雅释诂》曰，法，常也。释名曰，偪也，偪而使有所限也。列邦雄长海外，各君其国，各子其民，不有常法以限之，其何以大小相维，永敦辑睦乎！此万国公法之所以为重也。同治甲子同文馆总教习丁冠西先生译其书以行，固已条分缕析，足备观览矣。兹复撮其要为便览一书，汰繁就简，义更赅括。以视前书，彼则大辂之椎轮，此则钁礰之精鍊也。其用心亦良苦矣。冠西诚好学深思之士哉！光绪三年岁在丁丑冬十有一月，江宁夏家镐拜序。②

清朝首任驻美公使陈兰彬亦为该书作序："《公法便览》序：五方不同文，在昔外史氏所掌，即须鞮译，况穷瀛万国。各国文词多异，中国奚从观览哉？然文虽异事，理则一。所译或诘屈聱牙，或铺荼桐达，是在其人诣力之浅深矣。同文馆总教习丁冠西先生，亚墨利加所称博学深思者，初至沪渎，即喜中国书籍而欲达之西书。史无阙格，以便阅习。译有《万国公法》，董醕卿大司农暨张鲁生太守已叙行。今率馆生复译《公法便览》，成属余为序。余取二书反复搜览，觉其笔墨词气进而盖上。譬如造舟车始，而剞木椎轮，继且文茵畅毂也。譬如筑亭台池苑，始而砖石甃甓，垣石堤巩备而已，继且丹漆雕镂，点缀名葩美箭也。质有其文，夫岂偶然哉！盖冠系先生居中土久，口其语言，手其文字，又勤敏善下，与文章学问之士游浸灌于典雅义理之趣，故深造有得如是。余久闻泰西该洽士，流多寄迹香港、

---

① ［美］丁韪良等：《公法便览·自序》，光绪四年同文馆聚珍版。
② ［美］丁韪良等：《公法便览·序》，光绪四年同文馆聚珍版。

上海，间有能殚精研虑于五经四子书者，而且文章赠答。诗歌唱和，综事情而昭文采，积以岁月，当与中国经师学士，著誉艺林不止。如足利之所藏山林，鼎之所述焉。可因译渐精一端，拭目以俟也。光绪三年，岁在丁丑夏六月中浣吴川陈兰彬序。"①

丁韪良在自序中对《公法便览》评价很高：

> 甲子冬，余奉总理各国事务王大臣——兹率馆生复译新书，不惮讥评而仍取诸敝国之作，似当辩之，去岁曾率馆生翻译布国马氏所著《星轺指掌》一书，今岁又译德国步伦氏《公法千章》，且拟陆续增译各国名家著作，俾中华文人学士虽未通习洋文，亦得窥泰西往来交涉之道。庶几对镜参观，不致为一国议论所囿从，可知知四方之公法家所论大同小异。要皆一轨于正诚，不愧夫公法之名焉。至吴氏所长，殆非一端。如欧美二洲，既有重洋之隔，则欧洲诸国之争端，多与美国风马牛不相及。在吴氏议之，无所偏倚，得曰局外论事，固应乃尔。若夫事有关乎美国，吴氏亦能明辨是非，绝无袒护本国之私存乎其间，则非识量过人，曷克臻此？其著书本意专在学院功课，故文义惟求明而易晓，不但小子后生用之以为阶进，即博学通儒读之，亦有裨益。专门家既难讥其浅陋，初学者必不厌其烦琐。又始终有案例相间，使公法得因史案以明，而史案转藉公法以彰。况泰西史乘之译以汉文者不能多见，且他书或专论案牍而胪举太繁，译不胜译，总未若此书之简而能赅。此非余之阿私所好也。吴氏此书在英国重刊者数矣，伦敦新书考曰：吴氏《公法便览》一书问世已十有五载，至今声名颇著，法家视之为权衡准则，而本都书肆重刊已经四次，其所论公而且直，既不徇本国之私，亦不惮斥本国之谬。云又伦敦绘报曰：现今诸国公使屡见会议各国执政研究公法，而学院课读者尤众，则吴氏公法之有新刻，实为幸甚。美之公法家向多著名，而其尚在者，以吴氏为冠宜也。缘吴氏学既周

---

① ［美］丁韪良等：《公法便览·序》，光绪四年同文馆聚珍版。

备，心亦公正。其续卷条约考略，亦包括三百余年之史乘。云观夫英国与美国同文而重刊之，日本与美国异文而翻译之，足知其书为地球东西所推重也。兹译以华文，而词义尚能明晰者，则汪君芝房（凤藻）之力为多。芝房既具敏才，复精英文，余为之讲解一切，易于领悟。其笔亦足以达之，且能恪遵原本，不减不增，使余省点窜之劳焉，故叙及之。旹在光绪丁丑嘉平月，同文馆总教习惠三丁韪良识。①

《公法便览》共有五个部分、十九章。该书介绍了国际法的基本理论、国家、外交等问题，其中有关战争法的内容尤为详细。

《公法便览》与王铁崖主编《国际法》章节比较表②：

《公法便览》	《国际法》
总论　论公法本源	第一章第二节　国际法的历史发展
卷一　论邦国平时之权利与应尽之责守	第三章第一节之四　国家的基本权利与义务
卷一第一章　论邦国自主之权不得互相干预	第四章第一节之二　领土主权不可侵犯
卷一第二章　论邦国辖地掌物之权及水道公用之利	第四章第二节国家领土的组成部分
卷一第三章　邦国相交之权及款待外国人民之例	
卷二　论邦国通使之权利与议约之规例	第八章　外交和领事关系
卷二第一章　论邦国交际之例	第八章第一节　外交关系概说
卷二第二章　论各国通使之例	第八章第三节　使馆及其人员
卷二第三章　论立约权利	第九章　条约
卷三　论交战之例	第十三章　战争法
卷三第一章　论各国自护讨罪等权	第十三章第三节之一　战争与武装冲突的开始
卷三第二章　论陆地交战之例	第十三章第四节　战争法规（一）
卷三第三章　论一国征讨之事	
卷三第四章　论夺据敌物既占据克复之权利	第十三章第四节　战争法规（二）
卷三第五章　论停兵罢兵事宜	第十三章第三节之二　战争与武装冲突的结束及其法律后果

---

① ［美］丁韪良等：《公法便览·序》，光绪四年同文馆聚珍版。
② ［美］丁韪良等：《公法便览·目录》，光绪四年同文馆聚珍版、王铁崖主编：《国际法·目录》，法律出版社1981年版。

续表

《公法便览》	《国际法》
卷四 论战国与局外交际之例	第十三章第三节　中立
卷四第一章　论局外所享之权利与所任之责守；第二章　论局外者与战国通商事宜	第十三章第三节之三 1907 年海牙第五公约和第十三公约对中立国权利、义务的规定
卷三第三章　论战例所禁货物	第十三章第三节之六 战时禁制品
卷三第四章　论封堵海口之例	第十三章第三节之五 封堵
卷三第五章　论盘查船只之权	
卷三第六章　论禁止贩卖人口之例	
卷三第七章　论公法利弊大旨即今日以逆计将来	
续卷第一章　摘录各国盟约大旨	
续卷第二章　证义	

"公法总论"论述国际法的基本原理：

"粤自造物降衷，人之秉性莫不自具应享之权利，应行之责守。二者相辅而不能相离，否则，无以化成。盖理义相待，而化以成矣。是以各国之制法，义与不义，只以人性为准绳。邦国之与庶人所异者，则系自主而不可强制。其与庶人所同者，则系遵理义而行。若悖理义，即为取祸之门。其平行交际，均有不可夺之权利，不可负之理义，无是，则无以成公法也。盖公法之旨，在论定邦国本有之权利，并其会议之条例。"①

"推公法之源，系由渐而行，初迁易而后安定。海氏曰：权利必有以护之者，或借他人保护，或本人以力自护，邦国之权利亦复如是。既他国不能旁贷，其权利本恃己力以护之。至交通邻国，而邻国认之。则彼此难以推诿，而公法于是肇始焉。公法昉自泰西，其故有三：其奉行犹太仁义之教，一也；其承继希腊之性理，与罗马之律法，二也；泰西诸国，界皆毗连，而往来较密，致成例易于通行，三也。至回回各国，虽接壤泰西，道既不

---

① [美]丁韪良等：《公法便览》总论，光绪四年同文馆聚珍版，第1页。

同，久形隔膜，而自置于公法之外。"①

"一千六百五十年，英国阿斯富学院有教习苏志者，著书名曰邦国通法，义即今之公法也。古之罗马国论法学者，尝以各国通行之例，名为诸国通法。然非所谓公法也。"②

"或谓公法之义，一约以蔽之可也。盖人之有约应遵，乃自然之道，且邦国交往，莫不出于约，非立有明条，实系默许者，固皆同为一约耳。欲知现在何为公法，其当究者有二：各国所遵照习行者若何，一也；其所习行者，揆情度理，合与不合，二也。其一若置而不论，则公法凭虚，而无实事以证矣。其二若失于究察，则实事难存，而理义亡矣。公法本于自然之理，一若人民相待之分。"③

"发氏曰：公法分为二种：曰性法，即前所云理法；曰例法，其性法者，系出于自然之理，而世人即秉此天性，有不得不遵守者。例法者，或出于邦国之会议而立，或出于各国之习行而立。其会议而立者，为明许之例法。其习行而立者，为默许之例法，二者不可不遵也。愚按公法分为二种，不如分为三类：其属于义者，一也；其属于仁者，二也；其本与仁义无涉，因而明许或默许竟成定例者，三也。"④

卷一论述国家的权利与义务：

"夫人民居有定界而制有定法，以除暴安良，如是者谓之国。国与国交际有政，惟政府总其治理焉。国之为国，当有孑然独立之形，足以立法于国中，以治民臣，以定政体。"⑤

"国犹人也，不惟有可操之权利，且有当任之责守。国法有变革，而责守常存。责守所系，虽偏端不得或废也。两国相通之

---

① ［美］丁韪良等：《公法便览》总论，光绪四年同文馆聚珍版，第3页。
② ［美］丁韪良等：《公法便览》总论，光绪四年同文馆聚珍版，第6页。
③ ［美］丁韪良等：《公法便览》总论，光绪四年同文馆聚珍版，第8页。
④ ［美］丁韪良等：《公法便览》总论，光绪四年同文馆聚珍版，第16页。
⑤ ［美］丁韪良等：《公法便览》卷1，光绪四年同文馆聚珍版，第1页。

故，若专指保卫当时政式，则遇有兴亡变革，而权利责守遂有变易。此外邦国之权利责守，固不以政变祸乱而遂替也。国政变革而前约可以废弃者，偶亦有之。如叛逆僭国，竟与他国立约借款，或结好以攻其所叛之国。一旦国复正统，其前约概可毁废。"①

"邦国遭内变，或外藩叛立，他国不得助逆以攻其上。盖彼国既认之为自主之国，则其主权国体岂可轻视。或谓依此例，只可助国家而不可助叛民，将见残暴之君。其党皆得肆其权利以虐善良。而仁师义举以除苛政者，转不能借组以制暴也，曰：公法所定，究属不偏之正例，缘无论何等政体之国，无论其叛属为乱民、为义民，皆以一律通行也。"②

"一国必有专辖土地以行其统驭之主权。有土地即有物产，可据民间私产为国家公用，可置产于他国境内而输纳税赋，可贷其财与外国君民，皆属邦国所操之主权也。若就一国而论，国家虽有辖地之权，要不得鬻尺寸以与他国。"③

"以公法主权而论，凡一国与他国交接，其所用章程，当惟本国主裁。推而言之，虽竟拒绝往来，亦无不可。"④

"邦国交接之道，除以上各条不得违背外，凡遇交涉异邦客商一切章程均，由各国主权自定，或立护照以便稽察，或定税则以护土产；或异邦人加之以管束；或通商利益，厚此薄彼。约而言之，无论公道待人，私心为我，一任各国自主。"⑤

"近来东土诸国，有以泰西羁旅之人，免归地方管辖者，盖由其律法风俗与泰西多有殊异。故疑其地方官审断，未必公允。因而为本国人民请免地方管辖也。在土耳其等回回国，外邦羁旅，不止自成部落。无论争端罪案，均归领事官办理，地方官概不与闻。若寻常争讼，领事官审断不服，可以上控本国。至遇罪

---

① [美] 丁韪良等：《公法便览》卷1，光绪四年同文馆聚珍版，第4页。
② [美] 丁韪良等：《公法便览》卷1，光绪四年同文馆聚珍版，第8页。
③ [美] 丁韪良等：《公法便览》卷1，光绪四年同文馆聚珍版，第26页。
④ [美] 丁韪良等：《公法便览》卷1，光绪四年同文馆聚珍版，第37页。
⑤ [美] 丁韪良等：《公法便览》卷1，光绪四年同文馆聚珍版，第39页。

案在罚银以上者，领事只能备录口供，听候本国法司审断。然领事秉权之大小，一惟各国自定之耳。泰西诸国与中国所立条约，率载此例。"①

"各国疆内遇有罪案，无论犯者谁何？皆得按照本国律法审办，自是公理。而邦国中亦有推广其律法，以治人民之在外国犯罪者。此特各国之律法，非万国之公法。"②

卷二涉及公使、领事、领事裁判权以及条约等内容：

"各国交际之礼，粗看虽似具文，善用之则非虚设，所以敦和好而杜衅端也。邦国无不崇尚名誉，他邦宜谨言慎行，不可毁伤国体，亦不可诽谤君主。"③

"使臣既免地方管辖，其公署与什物亦应宽免。公署无论或买或租与驻之国赏赐，均置于地方辖外。"④

"某国设立官员驻扎外国，料理通商事务及本国人民案件者，名为领事官。"⑤

"两国除使臣与随从人等外，外国人率归地方律法管辖。惟不愿己民听候异教地方律法审断，遂与回回等国定款，令本国人民一切争端罪案，皆归本国审断，而本国必藉公使领事等员以管辖之。"⑥

"邦国之约重于庶民者，以其为万民所系也。且立约之时，业经再三筹度，非同造次。亦非为一朝一夕之计，必期行之久远，其国存则其约俱存。邦国条约或与他国立之，或与人民立之，或与民间公会立之，皆可，而立约之权一也。两国或数国订立之约，有盟约、和约、续约之目。按公法，邦国盟约系自主之

---

① ［美］丁韪良等：《公法便览》卷1，光绪四年同文馆聚珍版，第47页。
② ［美］丁韪良等：《公法便览》卷1，光绪四年同文馆聚珍版，第72页。
③ ［美］丁韪良等：《公法便览》卷2，光绪四年同文馆聚珍版，第1页。
④ ［美］丁韪良等：《公法便览》卷2，光绪四年同文馆聚珍版，第18页。
⑤ ［美］丁韪良等：《公法便览》卷2，光绪四年同文馆聚珍版，第32页。
⑥ ［美］丁韪良等：《公法便览》卷2，光绪四年同文馆聚珍版，第34页。

国以为可行，而情愿立之，方有必遵之责。"①

"凡讲解邦国盟约疑义，与讲解民间合同字样，其例相同，葛氏、发氏论之极详。其条例之尤要者有五：一、盟约字句，必照寻常文义讲解。遇字义作常解而大相径庭者，则当别求解析。遇各艺专用之字，则以其艺义解之。二、遇有二义可解而难执一是者，当推究此句此字为谁而设，必择义之无利于彼者而从之。三、若字句不通于理，或其事万不能成，或前后自相矛盾者，必系误解，当另求解法。四、一约之内，当以其明显者解其晦涩者。欲知其意，必因端竟委，以求其事之故，则文义自明。五、遇苛刻不平之约款，必从字义狭隘处解，以示限制，而免无厌之诛求。若公平仁德之款，则义从其广者可也。六、或一约内前后条款，或两国前后盟约，字义不相符合者，其讲解之例有二：前款字句当从后款讲解。因后款所以增入者，大抵为申明前义与两国后及之意耳。推之盟约，亦当以后款解前约；约款字句之间或含混于此而详悉于彼，当从其详细者解之。又或禁于此而详于彼，则从其禁止之条。"②

卷三、卷四论述战争法的相关规定：

"暂时失和而用兵，无论侵扰他邦以趋利，或力行抵御以避害，皆战也。"③

"交战之权若从严而行之，则敌人之在疆内者，皆可以战场生擒之例待之。"④

"蛮夷交战而恒用者，如置毒于水泉、醮毒于兵刃、买人行刺等事，此皆服化之国所耻也。"⑤

"所谓内乱者，非指滋事于一时言之，乃一国分党相攻、旷

---

① ［美］丁韪良等：《公法便览》卷2，光绪四年同文馆聚珍版，第45页。
② ［美］丁韪良等：《公法便览》卷2，光绪四年同文馆聚珍版，第60、61页。
③ ［美］丁韪良等：《公法便览》卷3，光绪四年同文馆聚珍版，第2页。
④ ［美］丁韪良等：《公法便览》卷3，光绪四年同文馆聚珍版，第15页。
⑤ ［美］丁韪良等：《公法便览》卷3，光绪四年同文馆聚珍版，第28页。

第三章 京师同文馆翻译的其他国际法著作

日持久而足以动摇大局者也。凡遇一国内乱，公法所论究者，其征战之合仁义与否，既关涉外国通商交际之权利而已。"①

"夺据民间财产，古世陆战常行之，今则几不复见。至水战，则按照公法，无论敌人货物，或局外货物，皆得夺而据之。"②

"两国战争之际，其可通往来否，必视彼此相信与否。"③

"邦国战争，其不与于事者，谓之局外。"④

"两国搆兵，欲辨民人之为局外否，不问其原籍何国，迁籍何国，但问其居家何国而已。"⑤

"凡局外售货于敌而货专为战阵所用者，谓之禁货。——各国所论禁互有不同，亦代有更替，兹列其要义如左：一、非经公法断定，或两国明立条约，某国不得逞私擅禁一物；二、限定禁货务须详明确当，不可稍涉含混；三、必有何等货物实足资敌军战攻之用者，则在局外贩之，为背义越分，战国始可缉捕入官。"⑥

"凡战国将水陆往来之道阻绝不通，皆谓之封堵。——封堵海口不以虚词而以实事，且其为时也暂，或不终一战而旋封旋罢。"⑦

"战国当封堵敌港之时，恐局外商船之运输禁货以济敌。于是盘查一事，为其应有之权利。"⑧

"贩卖人口一业，虽各国条约多有科以海盗重罪，著为明禁，而公法尚未有此定例。欧洲诸大国迭经互立条约，许彼此协巡，遇各该国商船形迹可疑者，互得拦查，以杜私贩。"⑨

"公法者，乃天地自然之理义，邦国交际之规例。二者相合

---

① [美] 丁韪良等：《公法便览》卷3，光绪四年同文馆聚珍版，第45页。
② [美] 丁韪良等：《公法便览》卷3，光绪四年同文馆聚珍版，第53页。
③ [美] 丁韪良等：《公法便览》卷3，光绪四年同文馆聚珍版，第67页。
④ [美] 丁韪良等：《公法便览》卷4，光绪四年同文馆聚珍版，第1页。
⑤ [美] 丁韪良等：《公法便览》卷4，光绪四年同文馆聚珍版，第18页。
⑥ [美] 丁韪良等：《公法便览》卷4，光绪四年同文馆聚珍版，第42页。
⑦ [美] 丁韪良等：《公法便览》卷4，光绪四年同文馆聚珍版，第60页。
⑧ [美] 丁韪良等：《公法便览》卷4，光绪四年同文馆聚珍版，第69页。
⑨ [美] 丁韪良等：《公法便览》卷4，光绪四年同文馆聚珍版，第77页。

以成之，而听人用舍者也。其行也由渐而广，名家代作，因时加修，其大旨类于国家之宪典。所异者，不强不知者以必从，特最宽恕耳。公法既不强人以必从，而致用又在全权自主之国，其随时增修，各国所见往往不同。理义向背之间，莫衷一是，故至今未能周备。"①

《公法便览》续卷所载为各个时期的条约以及对前四卷的补充：

1648年威司发里之约（即威斯特伐利亚和约）："威司发里之约，其要端分为七段，具述如左，第一段，德瑞分疆，其要端有五：一、瑞国归侵地于德，德以波末拉尼郡北境、虑耿岛暨波郡南境数处予瑞；二、波郡南境之余地，若白兰登堡宗翮乏绝，则并归瑞国，而波郡全境尽属瑞有；三、德复以白里门大镇、兀登郡、威斯马海口予瑞；四、此数处仍名属德国，而瑞君实为地主。因得在德国国会同议政事；五、德以帑银五百万元偿瑞军饷。第二段，德法分疆，其要端有二：一、德以美兹、土尔、兀登三城，暨辟葛纳尔、阿尔塞斯等郡予法；二、许法屯兵于非里拨斯堡要隘。第三段，释罪归地，其要端有二：一、彼此官民有背国助敌者，均赦罪免究；二、彼此侵占之疆土，酌量归还，以复二十四年前情形。第四段，诸侯复位分界，其要端有四：一、巴拉丁公归国，仍辖巴郡之北境；二、其南境暂归巴威利辖治，俟本支绝翮，即归巴公；三、旧例，司公举德国翮皇之诸侯七人，今列入巴公而为八；四、其兀登堡、巴登、那骚等诸侯，各归国复位。第五段，瑞士自立。第六段，限制德皇主权，其要端有四：一、德皇遇关议和议战及制法一切事宜，必询国会而从其众；二、议政诸藩不独彼此可以联盟，亦得与外邦立约；上法院大臣必于新旧二教中择任之，设额相若；三、上法院办案，设因异教不同道，而意见或相歧异，则将原案送交国会，即凭公议定

---

① [美]丁韪良等：《公法便览》卷4，光绪四年同文馆聚珍版，第90页。

夺。第七段，限制奉教权利，其要端有五：一、巴扫及奥格斯堡之和约，已许人崇奉新教，无所禁阻，且与旧教不相统属。兹于本约内复行申明而固持之；二、教堂产业分归新旧二教，应以一千六百二十四年为准；三、设有掌管堂产之教民欲改奉别教，除须遗弃其堂产及本教一切权利外，所有往年已得之利益，准免缴还，并于本人体面声名亦毫无损碍；四、有国者若改奉他教，或得异教之地而君临之，只能于官内率家人自奉其教。不得强民间改奉己教，亦不得以己教之人补充民间教职；五、旧约所指人民改教之款，于本约内申明而固持之，准日耳曼诸藩邦一体照行。"①

"自一千八百六十三年以来，邦国数有立约，互定人民入籍之例者，如一千八百六十八年二月，美国与北日耳曼众邦约，五月，又与巴威利约，二约大略相同，兹述其要款如左：一、凡布国、巴国人民寄居美国，或美国人民寄居布巴等国，有愿呈请入籍者，须以常川居住五年为期。期满方准入籍，与本地居民同。若徒请入籍而并未久居如例者，不准；二、凡已入寄籍之民，偶回本籍。如从前有犯案未经断结者，准由本籍地方官提集到案，按律审断办；三、在布约内，议定一千八百五十二年所立互交逃犯之约，作为美国与日耳曼众邦合立之约，在巴约内，声明一千八百六十三年之约，仍宜彼此遵行；四、凡已寄籍之人旋归故国后，或无意再回寄籍者，即将寄籍注销；五、议定所立款约，自盖印之日起，以十年为期。彼此如有愿停止者，须于限期五个月前行文知照，否则，期满后再加一年。"②

第三节 《公法会通》③

1878年，丁韪良在《公法便览》自序中说：

---

① ［美］丁韪良等：《公法便览》续卷，光绪四年同文馆聚珍版，第7、8、9、10、11页。
② ［美］丁韪良等：《公法便览》续卷，光绪四年同文馆聚珍版，第67页。
③ 参见拙文《〈公法会通〉与近代西方国际法术语及其内涵的输入》，《惠州学院学报》2014年第2期。

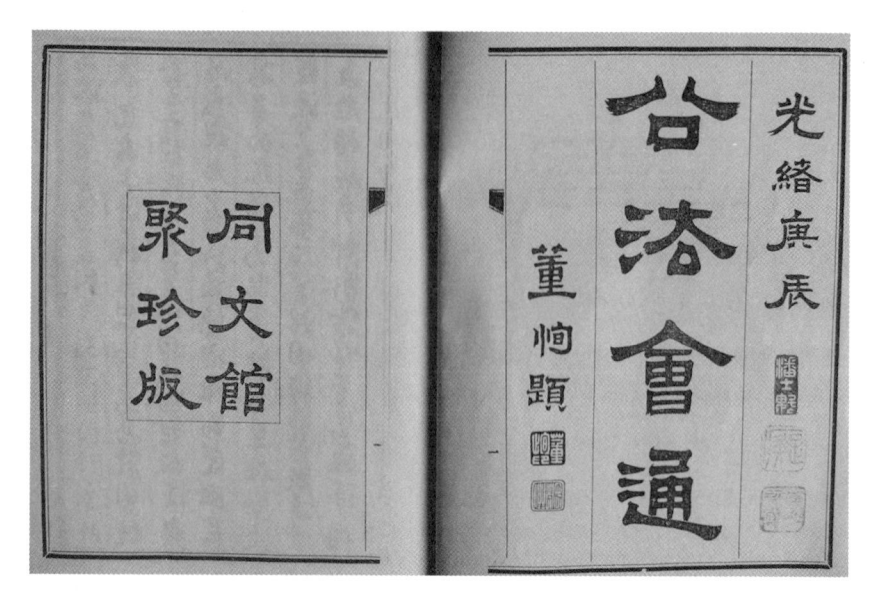

董恂为《公法会通》所题书名

王文韶为《公法会通》写的序文

兹率馆生复译新书，不惮讥评而仍取诸敌国之作，似当辩之，去岁曾率馆生翻译布国马氏所著《星轺指掌》一书，今岁又译德国步伦氏《公法千章》，且拟陆续增译各国名家著作，俾中华文人学士虽未通习洋文，亦得窥泰西往来交涉之道。庶几对镜参观，不致为一国议论所囿从，可知知四方之公法家所论大同小异。要皆一轨于正诚，不愧夫公法之名焉。①

事隔 2 年之后，在丁韪良及同文馆师生的共同努力下，《公法会通》于 1880 年正式刊行。

《公法会通》译自瑞士法学名家（J. C. Bluntschli，1808－1811）的国际法著作，原文为德文，于 1868 年出版，后译为法文 *LeDroit International Codifie*，《公法会通》以法文为翻译底本。步伦乃"瑞士之名士也，年逾七旬，前在本国著作甚多，名播欧洲，因受德国之聘，往海德堡学院充公法教习，乃著《公法会通》一书"②。1881 年，丁韪良游历欧洲时，见到了在海德堡讲学的步伦教授："余至其地竭诚往拜，在此流连三旬，每日乘便造院，听布君讲解公法肯要。"③

1879 年，丁韪良与他人合作将 *LeDroit International Codifie* 译为中文，最初书名为《公法千章》，后采纳总理衙门官员董恂的建议，将《公法千章》更名为《公法会通》，并于 1880 年正式刊行："余督率馆生翻译此书，既将洋文为之讲解于前，复将译稿祥加校阅于后，而鲁鱼亥豕之讹仍恐在所不免。——原书系布文，后译为法文，兹由法文译汉，复与布文核对，以免舛误。前半为法文馆副教习联芳、庆常、联兴翻译，余为余口译，由天文馆副教习贵荣、前同文馆学生桂林笔述，复经贵荣前后逐细校阅，既竣乃呈。"④ 在翻译过程中，丁韪良基本忠实于原著，但新增了一些历史事件来说明原有的法律规定："其文义或有疑难之处，余偶加注释以发明之，或间遇所引史案，每增数字以指定某地某时，而未敢以己意参入正文。"⑤ 丁韪良所增加的部分，主要是《公法会通》原著 1868 年出版后所发生的历史事件。如关于侨民："1871 年，法国发币，赈济居京被难之客民，则不在此

---

① ［美］丁韪良等：《公法便览·自序》，光绪四年同文馆聚珍版。
② ［美］丁韪良等：《公法会通·凡例》，光绪六年同文馆聚珍版。
③ 《续修四库全书·西学考略》，上海古籍出版社 2002 年版，第 695 页。
④ ［美］丁韪良等：《公法会通·凡例》，光绪六年同文馆聚珍版。
⑤ ［美］丁韪良等：《公法会通·凡例》，光绪六年同文馆聚珍版。

例。盖拯困而非赔损，且不独行之于客民，即本国之民，亦同沾此惠。"① 又如关于占领地的管理："1870 年，德法交战之时，德君示谕所踞之地方，将法国募兵之例，全行废弛，并云：如有遵旧例而投军本国者，均应籍没资产充公，本身科以流徙，不准回境。"②

由于牵涉版权问题，丁韪良特意给 J. C. Bluntschli 写了一封信，该信件内容刊于《公法会通》的首页：

> To DR. J. C. BLUNTSCHIL
>
> Professor of Public Law University of Heidelberg Sir
>
> In this translation of your "International Law" I feel bound to insert a prefatory note, not merely as an act of homage to the Author, but by way of apology for what might otherwise be regarded as an infringement of his rights.
>
> In this country copyright is unknown, because authorship is rarely, if ever, a source of emolument. Accordingly, in selecting works for translation into Chinese, the courtesy of applying to theauthor for a formal permission is not always observed. In the case of your valuable work I have to plead guilty to this culpable omission. It was not indeed until I had begun to collate the translation with the original that I remarked the caveat traductor on the title-page, Das recht der ubersetsung ist vorbehatten.
>
> Hoping that you will admit this explanation as an excuse for an apparent trespass, and that you will accept as a sort of indemnification the consciousness of being on the most numerous branch of the human family,
>
> I remain with sentiments of high esteem
>
> Your truly W. A. P. MARTIN, President of the Tung Wen College.
> Peking, 28th April 1880.

---

① ［美］丁韪良等：《公法会通》卷 4，光绪六年同文馆聚珍版，第 9 页。
② ［美］丁韪良等：《公法会通》卷 7，光绪六年同文馆聚珍版，第 10 页。

将其译为中文，即是："值此翻译大作《国际法》之际，插入这篇前言，我深感必要。一者表达我对作者的敬意，同时也藉此向作者道歉，以免有侵犯作者著作权之嫌疑。著作权于该国人而言是一个陌生的概念，因为作者几乎不靠写作维持生计。将他国著作翻译为中文时，人们也不会征求原著者的意见。直到将译作与原著校对时，我才注意到原著扉页上的警告，对此给您带来的损失，我本人难辞其咎。

中国是人类大家庭中人数最多的国度，您的著作将开启他们的心智。如果您能接受此种解释，那将是对侵犯您著作权的一种补偿。"

随后是政务大臣王文韶为该书写的序：

"《公法会通》序：尝观木之为柯叶也，其高者轮囷离奇，至于干霄，亟宙而诋，因根抵之盘深。又观水泉之发源也，始则从幽岩穷兮，首细涓涓而扬其波，竟成江海之钜，浸卷万殊，一本理固循环。惟赖多闻多见，触类引申，期能得其会通耳。同文馆总教习丁冠西先生为美国好学深思之士，督课之作，率馆生翻译各书于公法一首，尤为致意。前经译出惠氏《万国公法》、吴氏《公法便览》两书，刷印成帙。兹复译出瑞士国步伦氏《公法会通》十卷，删繁辑要，理明词达，两书相表里，而更觉融贯。昔者苏眉山之论文词，绚烂之极，归于平淡；韩昌黎之论文词，其皆醇也，然后肆焉！冠西之经译是书，始其选钦，索余序，为缀数语于简号。光绪六年庚辰孟夏仁和王文韶拜譔。"①

丁韪良亦该书作序：

"《公法会通》序：公法者，诸国之通例也。会通者，条分而件系也。夫例之原有三：其出于天理自然，而邦国不得不同然

---

① ［美］丁韪良等：《公法会通·序》，光绪六年同文馆聚珍版。

者,一也;其出于会议相约而立有明文者,二也;其出于习久默许而成者,三也。顾法家所论往往详于义理,略于规条。务于评陟邦国之是非,而仍未指明界限。是以学者必溯其流,始能穷奇源,由其末乃得求其本焉。步伦氏所以著此书,余所以译此书者,职是故耳。步伦氏为德国(原籍瑞士)法学名家,因论辩公法疑案得著。令闻爱编此集,以汇辑公法之同行者。每以一例列为一章,俾阅者易于洞悉,更加注释以解之,引史案以证之。其持论既公而不偏,叙事亦确而有据,缘是经理外政诸大宪多欣赏之,四方译刊问世者已不胫而走矣,兹译以华文于邦国交涉事务,殆不无裨益焉。夫惠吴二氏之作,既已译之于先,而今复译此书者,以其提纲挈领,执简御繁,遇事便于比拟,援引又出于二家之后。凡二家之论所谓及者,步伦氏皆得详之,盖公法非一国所能私。苟遇诸国名家意见如出一辙,即为公法之定例,而无可疑义。故虽译就三家,尚未满志。将来必期博采各家名论,撮要而编辑之,用之印证,则中华士大夫虽未肄习洋文,而于公法之学亦得悉其梗概云。光绪六年岁在庚辰仲春之月,美国丁韪良悳三序。"①

丁韪良评价该书:"爱编此集以汇辑公法之通行者,每以一例列为一章,俾阅者易于洞悉,更加注释以解之,引史案以证之。其持论既公而不偏,叙事亦确而有据。缘是经理外政诸大宪多欣赏之,四方译刊问世者已不胫而走矣。——夫惠、吴二氏之作既已译之于先,而今复译此书,若其提纲挈领、执简御繁,遇事便于比拟援引,又出二家之后,凡二家之论所未及者,步伦氏皆得祥之。"②

政务大臣王文韶称赞该书:"删繁辑要,理明词达。"③

南学会称:"中国所译诸公法书皆不甚畅,惟《公法会通》一书

---

① [美]丁韪良等:《公法会通·序》,光绪六年同文馆聚珍版。
② [美]丁韪良等:《公法会通·凡例》,光绪六年同文馆聚珍版。
③ [美]丁韪良等:《公法会通·序》,光绪六年同文馆聚珍版。

提纲挈领，最为完善。"①

《公法会通》共有十卷："卷一 论公法之源流及邦国之权位；卷二 论代国而行；卷三 辖地之权；卷四 论辖人之权；卷五 论条约；卷六 论邦国启衅皆因违背公法；卷七 论邦国交战；卷八 论邦国水战；卷九 论局外之权利；卷十 美国行军训诫"。内容涉及国际法主体、领土、条约、战争等。

《公法会通》与王铁崖主编《国际法》章节比较表②：

《公法会通》	《国际法》
卷一 论公法之源流及邦国之权位 第一至第十六章 论公法之纲纪 第十七至第六十一章 论公法所辖者 第六十二至第九十四章 论邦国自主之权 第九十五至第一百一十四章 论诸国均势以保大局	导论 第二节 国际法的历史发展 第三章 国际法的主体 第一节 主权国家是国际法的基本主体
卷二 论代国而行 第一百一十五至第一百三十四章 论国主代国之权 第一百三十五至第一百五十三章 论国主公使等游历友邦 第一百五十四至第一百五十八章 论国戚 第一百五十九至第一百六十九章 论邦国交际之责 第一百七十至第二百四十章 论邦国通使之例 第二百四十一至第二百七十五章 论委员 领事等职	第八章 外交和领事关系 第二节 国家的中央外交关系机关 第三节 使馆及其人员 第四节 使馆及其人员的特权和豁免 第五节 使馆和享有外交特权和豁免人员对接受国的义务 第六节 特别使团 第八节 领事官及其人员 第九节 领事特权和豁免 第十节 领事馆和享有领事特权和豁免人员对接受国的义务
卷三 辖地之权 第二百七十六至第二百九十五章 论得地失地之例 第二百九十六至第三百三章 论定界之例 第三百四至第三百五十二章 论江河湖海通用之例 第三百五十三至第三百五十九章 论世累之例	第四章 国家领土 第一节 国家领土与领土主权 第二节 国家领土的组成部分 第五章 海洋法 第二节 内海海域 第三节 领海 第四节 用于国际航行的海峡

---

① 《续修四库全书·西学考略》，上海古籍出版社2002年版，第726页。
② ［美］丁韪良等：《公法会通·目录》，光绪六年同文馆聚珍版；王铁崖主编：《国际法·目录》，法律出版社1981年版。

续表

《公法会通》	《国际法》
卷四 论辖人之权 第三百六十至第三百六十三章 论禁奴之例 第三百六十四至第三百七十四章 论定籍之例 第三百七十五至第三百八十章 论人民侨居异邦而仰赖本国保护之例 第三百八十一至第三百九十三章 论保护客民之例 第三百九十四至第四百一章 论交出逃犯之例	第七章 国际法上的居民 第一节 国籍问题 第二节 外国人的法律地位 第四节 庇护和引渡
卷五 论条约 第四百二至第四百一十六章 论遵约之责 第四百一十七至第四百二十四章 论条约格式 第四百十二至第四百四十六章 论合盟等约 第四百五十至第四百六十一章 论废约之例	第九章 条约 第二节 条约的缔结及生效 第三节 条约的遵守、适用及解释 第四节 条约的修改及终止
卷六 论邦国启衅皆因违背公法 第四百六十二至第四百八十章 论干与他国内政之例 第四百八十一至第四百九十八章 论调处公案之例 第四百九十九至第五百九章 论未战而势逼之例	第十二章 国际争端的解决 第一节 国际争端及其解决办法 第二节 国际争端的政治解决方法
卷七 论邦国交战 第五百一十至第五百二十八章 论交战缘由 第五百二十九至第五百三十六章 论战时事宜 第五百三十七至第五百五十六章 论敌国必遵之权责 第五百五十七至第五百六十七章；论交战违例之事 第五百六十八至第六百二十六章 论宽代敌国并，兵民之例 第六百二十七至第六百四十三章 论处治逃兵奸细暨叛逆之例 第六百四十四至第六百六十三章 论陆战处置敌货之例	第十三章 战争法 第一节 战争与国际法 第三节 战争与武装冲突的开始与结束 第四节 战争法规（一）作战手段与方法 第五节 战争法规（二）交战者和战争受难者

续表

《公法会通》	《国际法》
卷八　论邦国水战 第六百六十四至第六百九十九章　论水战处置敌货之例 第七百至第七百二十六章　论战毕立约之例 第七百二十七至第七百四十一章　论失物复归之例	第十三章　战争法 第六节　战争法规（三）海战和空战中的特殊问题
卷九　论局外之权利 第七百四十二至第七百九十七章　论邦国守局外之权利 第七百九十八至第八百六十二章　论封堵敌国口岸之例	第十三章　战争法 第七节　中立
卷十　美国行军训诫 第一至第三十章　论交战权宜之例 第三十一至第四十七章　论处置敌国公产、私产以及禁止损害敌国人民等例 第四十八至第八十章　论惩罚逃兵擒获人物以及交质等例 第八十一至第八十五章　论处治不按例助战人民之例 第八十六至第一百四章　论给与护照以及处治卖国奸细等例 第一百五至第一百一十八章　论互易俘虏以及执白旗通往来等例 第一百一十九至第一百三十四章　论凭信释放之例 第一百三十五至第一百四十七章　论停兵以及败降等例 第一百四十八章　论行凶之违例 第一百四十九至第一百五十七章　论处治纷争叛逆之例	第十三章　战争法 第一节　战争与国际法 第三节　战争与武装冲突的开始与结束 第四节　战争法规（一）作战手段与方法 第五节　战争法规（二）交战者和战争受难者 第六节　战争法规（三）海战和空战中的特殊问题 第七节　中立

卷一论述国际法源流以及国家基本理论：

"公法者，邦国所以恃以交际者也。谓之公法者，各国恪遵与律法一体。谓之公者，非一国所得而私焉。其制非一国亦非由一世，乃各国之人历代往来，习以为常。各国大宪审断交涉公案，而他国援以为例。明士论定是非，阐明义理而后世悦服。三者相参，公法始成。公法以理义为准绳，而例俗虽未能尽善，亦渐归于纯厚。"①

"邦国之交际，有通例以理之。人民之权利，有通例以卫之。出于理而见于事，邦国赖以联络，人民恃以相安，是为公法。"②

"公法所辖者，乃邦国也。按公法，邦国无论有君无君，君权有限无限，国之大小，法律异同，幅员狭阔，莫不相交以道，相接以礼。普天之下，凡有设官以治民，划野以分疆，而为长久之计者，公法即谓之为国。游牧之民不得谓之邦国，因无城邑以聚之，无定界以限之。"③

"邦国之主权有五：自立政体，一也；自定律例，二也；自行治理。三也；自选臣工，四也；自遣使臣，五也。凡此五者，若行之不违公法，则他国不得擅预。邦国既不愿他国在其疆内行权，如管辖人民、审理词讼、征收饷税等事，即不得行之于彼国。其不在此例者有二：按公法应加优免者，一也；按条约自行退让者，二也。"④

"公法有均势之论，非谓各国幅员无狭阔，势力无强弱，人民无多寡之别。盖邦国之根由各殊，其风化人情不同，而天气地土又复互异，自不能不分为强弱。"⑤

"百余年来，各国每藉均势之名而肆其兼并之欲。俄国既割波兰之地，奥国因求片土于土耳其，布奥战争寻创瓜分波兰之议，即持均势以饰其非。八十年前，德国费克德曾云：日耳曼诸小邦之间，于大国如天平之砝码，此重而加之于彼，彼重而移之于此，以致欧洲各国之势为均。又十数年前，法国因义国渐大，

---

① ［美］丁韪良等：《公法会通·凡例》，光绪六年同文馆聚珍版。
② ［美］丁韪良等：《公法会通》卷1，光绪六年同文馆聚珍版，第1页。
③ ［美］丁韪良等：《公法会通》卷1，光绪六年同文馆聚珍版，第7页。
④ ［美］丁韪良等：《公法会通》卷1，光绪六年同文馆聚珍版，第23页。
⑤ ［美］丁韪良等：《公法会通》卷1，光绪六年同文馆聚珍版，第33页。

乃并赛服、爱尼斯二土，数年前那波伦第二见日耳曼并南方数邦，遂起意兼并比利时，以广其地。按公法均势之论，非谓各国之大小强弱相等，果如此，是遏天下各国自强之机也。"①

卷二论述外交关系：

"邦国外交之权，惟由执政者操之。"②

"公使等既免于管辖，地方官自不可稍行拘束，——则不可征其税项。"③

"邦国遣使，其选择之权，由本国自操之。"④

"领事官之职，在照料本国人民于一方，而无办理两国交际之政，即不得作为公使论。此国设领事官，驻扎彼国城邑口岸，或听之，或阻之，均由彼国操权。"⑤

卷三、卷四论述国家主权：

"邦国之主权就地而论之，谓之辖地之权。邦国辖地之权有二：人民已立为私产，而由图秉上权以辖者，一也；人民未立为私产，而邦国以为公产者，二也。"⑥

"两国以江河为界，其中洲屿，若无条约明言，必归相近之国管辖。如适在水之中央，则两国均分为是。两国若以山岭为界，而无条款指明山麓、山顶，则必以山顶为界。两国若以江河为界，而水面不专归一国者，则必以中央为界，中央恒以船只往来之道而定。"⑦

---

① ［美］丁韪良等：《公法会通》卷1，光绪六年同文馆聚珍版，第34页。
② ［美］丁韪良等：《公法会通》卷2，光绪六年同文馆聚珍版，第1页。
③ ［美］丁韪良等：《公法会通》卷2，光绪六年同文馆聚珍版，第8页。
④ ［美］丁韪良等：《公法会通》卷2，光绪六年同文馆聚珍版，第16页。
⑤ ［美］丁韪良等：《公法会通》卷2，光绪六年同文馆聚珍版，第40页。
⑥ ［美］丁韪良等：《公法会通》卷3，光绪六年同文馆聚珍版，第1页。
⑦ ［美］丁韪良等：《公法会通》卷3，光绪六年同文馆聚珍版，第8页。

"某地遇因立约，而世世应有若干款项归于某国、某家者，即谓之世累。世累或出于条约明文，或出于习久成例，惟需其国认有确据，始无推诿。邦国之主权，无不因世累而受限制，以致己所欲为而不得为，或他人为而己不得禁之。"①

"天下无无国之民，则侨寓某国而无籍者，既在彼立业，或居家已久，即视为某国之民。"②

卷五论述条约：

"议约之人必须操代国之权，无此权，则其约并无必遵之责。"③

卷六、卷七、卷八、卷九论述战争法：

"此国若侵犯彼国之权利，致与之启衅。彼国不但得设防抵御，即力行讨伐以示惩警亦可。"④

"此国与彼国执兵相争，以护其权利者，谓之战。"⑤

"养病伤处所以及行军医院，若实有病伤之人在彼，皆应作为局外，由两国一体保护，惟遇一国设兵护卫，其局外之利益遂失。行军医院之医士、教士人等，专理病伤者，若实有病伤之人在彼资其照料，则皆得置身局外。"⑥

"使者前往敌营，必执白旗，以明其职，方得仰赖公法保护。"⑦

"邦国外无干预他国战事，内有防范己民越分，则谓之局外。

---

① [美]丁韪良等：《公法会通》卷3，光绪六年同文馆聚珍版，第26页。
② [美]丁韪良等：《公法会通》卷4，光绪六年同文馆聚珍版，第4页。
③ [美]丁韪良等：《公法会通》卷5，光绪六年同文馆聚珍版，第1页。
④ [美]丁韪良等：《公法会通》卷6，光绪六年同文馆聚珍版，第2页。
⑤ [美]丁韪良等：《公法会通》卷7，光绪六年同文馆聚珍版，第1页。
⑥ [美]丁韪良等：《公法会通》卷7，光绪六年同文馆聚珍版，第26页。
⑦ [美]丁韪良等：《公法会通》卷8，光绪六年同文馆聚珍版，第7页。

局外之国既不预战，则一切关系军情之举，利于此国而损于彼国者，决不可为。局外者必实无预战之举，方得享局外之权利。"①

卷十为美国军事纪律：

"遇敌兵占据某地，则军例遂行，居民悉归管辖。军例既行，其地方律法遂停。地方官遂撤，人民均归将帅节制。"②

"军旅经过地方，若虐待居民，毁坏房屋、偷窃抢劫、私行杀伤以及侮辱妇女等事，皆为律法所严禁，应察其情节轻重，量加惩治。兵弁有犯此者，该管官禁之不听，则立时杀之可也。"③

"我国人民无论有无职任，若暗通消息于敌者，即不问其如何得知，必以死罪处之。凡奸细罪从重拟，虽只以军情小节通知于敌，亦作奸细论，而以死罪处之。"④

"战者欲缓战，应立停兵特约，系由两国秉大全者为之。议立停兵特约而无明订章程，则军务所在地方，一律停兵。"⑤

第四节 《中国古世公法论略》

1881 年，丁韪良为了参加在柏林举办的东文大会，特意用英文撰写了《中国古世公法论略》一文，该文先后以法文、中文刊行于世。法文刊登于比利时布鲁塞尔《国际法比较法制杂志》（*Revue de Droit in Ternational et de legislation Compare*）。

丁韪良记述此次会议：

余诣布京赴东文大会，各国向有此等文会，迩来复设总会，

---

① [美] 丁韪良等：《公法会通》卷9，光绪六年同文馆聚珍版，第1页。
② [美] 丁韪良等：《公法会通》卷10，光绪六年同文馆聚珍版，第1页。
③ [美] 丁韪良等：《公法会通》卷10，光绪六年同文馆聚珍版，第11页。
④ [美] 丁韪良等：《公法会通》卷10，光绪六年同文馆聚珍版，第21页。
⑤ [美] 丁韪良等：《公法会通》卷10，光绪六年同文馆聚珍版，第30页。

> V.
>
> INTERNATIONAL LAW
> IN
> ANCIENT CHINA.*
>
> THE recent treaties, by which China has been brought into closer relations with the nations of the West, and especially the establishment of intercourse by means of permanent embassies, have led Chinese statesmen to turn their attention to the subject of international law.†
>
> For them, it is a new study, involving conceptions which it would hardly have been possible for their predecessors to form at any time in the course of the last two thousand years; though, as we shall endeavor to show, they possessed something answering to it in their earlier history.
>
> ---
> * Read at Berlin, before the Congress of Orientalists; reprinted from the International Review, January, 1883.
> † The works of Wheaton, Woolsey, Bluntschli, and others, on this subject, have been translated for their use by the author of this Paper.

《中国古世公法论略》英文版

例定每三载广延谙习东土语言文字者互相砥砺。始聚于伦敦，依次聚于法俄义德。会之于义也，国君曾亲幸之。会之于俄也，国君饬廷臣具柬敦请会友，令诣其宫以相见。惟会于伯林，因国君避暑未归，以故未克亲临，谕令学部大臣代尽地主之谊（系兼理教务，职似中国礼部）。先于私第设筵相邀会友面晤，礼不拘泥。客至有二百余人。复于大客寓款待，视前尤优。其花园覆以玻璃凉棚，高五六丈。下列长几三行，每行五十余座。宾主互相庆贺，至文会事务，则集于太学，列为三班，每班另室，每日朝夕两次相会。其东雅细亚一班，以汉文、日文为重，其西雅细亚一班，以犹太、亚剌伯、土耳其等文为重，其南雅细亚一班，以印度文为重。余于斯时所建议者，乃本东周列国往来之例，以示中国早有公法之意。①

梁启超在《读西学书法》中评价该文：

《中国古世公法论略》，丁韪良得意之书。然以西人谈中国古事，大方见之鲜为不笑。中国当封建之世，诸国并立，公法学之昌明，不亚于彼之希腊，若博雅君子而补成之，可得巨帙，西政之合于中国古世者多矣，又宁独公法耶？②

该文以春秋战国时期的中国历史为材料，力图证明国际法及其相关规则在中国古代就已经存在。兹录自序及全文（中、英文）如下：

国无邦交则已，有邦交则不能无公法，其势然也。或谓邦国相交既有条约，则何去何从岂无可据之则？不知条约之款有限，每见一约不足更立一约以补苴之，前约未明复立一约以解释之，虽累至数十百款而终不能括事理之全。往往所值之案出于所备之外，欲援据而无，自将比附而不能。则必以是非公义与交涉之通例断之，此二者即所谓公法之大纲也。是故交际之道莫备于公法，亦莫善于公法，足以为天下公约而举其纲并能正各国之专约而袪其弊。强国不敢肆其贪，弱国得以免于祸。昭示大公，维持全局，胥恃之也。泰西之轮船、铁道、电线不过创于近数十年之间，公法之兴迄今亦止一二百年，然公法之利国实出机器之上。考中国古史春秋列国交际之道，一秉乎礼，即其时之公法。盖中国文教之兴先于泰西，如日之始升于东而后及于西也。不独指南针之作及篆刻之巧见于西国未有文字之前，其公法之学亦肇端于西国未兴之始。余尝以此语西士，西士未之信也。迨光绪八年，余在欧洲著为是篇且于德京东土文会中出而诵之。自是而后，用英法文字屡刊之于欧美二洲，读之者始信余言之有据，盖敬慕中

---

① ［美］丁韪良：《西学考略》卷上，光绪九年同文馆聚珍版（1883），第696、697页。
② 梁启超：《西学书目表》，《时务报》1896年7月。

国之声名文物固自昔而已著也。同文馆副教习汪君凤藻讲求公法有年矣,爰取是作译成汉文。有心时务者试以中国之古法与泰西之今法互证而参观之,将见同者固多而异者亦复不少。如古之使臣因事特遣,今则常川驻扎于外国都城;古之通商止于陆路,今则兼及海道;古无领事之官,今则凡属通商互市之区皆设领事以资治理。而古今之最不同者莫若战例。古之战也获敌人而杀之,虏妇女幼弱则鬻之奴之;今则禁掠平民,有所执获不过拘禁之以待两军互换而已,有负伤者且付医馆与本国军士一体调治,此公法渐进之据也。盖公法萌芽于古之中国、希腊,渐渐扩充至于今日而大备,不啻古人播植之而今人刈获之耳。要之,公法与国法体异而用同,使国有邦交而不讲公法犹人之涉讼狱而不谙国法,未有不失其利者,然则有国者可不知所务哉?"①

"中国自与泰西各国立约通商,交涉之事益烦。近又简派使臣,分驻各国,以通情好。时局为之一变,耳目为之一新。于是执政大臣不得不讲求公法之学,见前人所未见,闻前人所未闻,诚周代以来未有之奇矣。然考诸中国,分封之事、会盟骋伐,史不绝书,则固未尝无公法行其间也。

按中国自秦代至今,历二千余年。其间世变不同,以西史志之,约分为三纲:自罗马与嘉大治之战,迄海道始通印度之年,为第一纲;自此以后,约三百五十年,略有通商交涉之事,为第二纲;自一千八百三十九年鸦片之衅,以迄于今,为第三纲。当第一纲之世,中西隔绝重洋,凡西国一切治乱变故,于中国渺不相涉,盖不啻别居一世界焉。第二纲之世,中国知有欧洲各大国矣。然犹未悉其幅员之大,与风俗政治之要也。至第三纲之世,经英法前后两战,然后知泰西兵力之强。迨凿通苏意士河,而中国益以密迩强邻为虑矣。自是以来,不独讲求武备,整饬边防,亦且乐从事于公法,冀与万国共其利赖。由是三百年来,所习视在藩属之列者,皆得以平等相交,此岂一蹴致之哉!

---

① 李秀清、陈颐主编:《朝阳法科讲义》,上海人民出版社2014年版,第八卷之金保康述,沈康疏《平时国际公法》,第9页。

按亚洲东境诸小国，悉隶中国藩属。其联属之故，或以同教，或以互市。而大半皆出于畏威怀德之诚，尊之如天帝，敬之若神明。以故中国居高临下，大莫与京，如古之罗马然，辄自称其一国为天下也。此小国者，彼此绝少往来，其通贡于中国也，初无报聘之事，中国狃于所见，又安知宇宙固有平行相等，如泰西各国者哉！夫中国重一统之治，建无外之规，于今二千年矣。其间割据纷争，事极罕见，公法之学，固无自而兴。向使欧洲至今犹统于一尊，则亦不能有公法，为其无相需之势也。苟有相需之势，必有公法之学，此出于人心之自然，特行之有盛有不盛耳。相需之势有二：若干自主之国，境壤相接，舟车可通，势不能不讲信修睦，以联邦交，一也；诸国交际往来，各以平行相接，而无上下之分，二也；此二者中国自秦汉以来无之。而当周室分封之世，则明明有之。其时列爵分土，同姓之封数十国，谊亲而分均，文同而化一，虽欲不往来得乎。

昔之希腊，亦有此相需之势。其究至于定条例，以断两国之争，此实公法之滥觞，参之近日欧洲各国会议希腊边界之举，其揆一也。中国古世情形，与希腊相似，而往来交际之盛，且远过之。抑更有不同者，昔希腊诸邦，皆散处之部落，起自蛮夷，初无政教以相系。中国诸侯，则系一王所封建。各遵守天子之法度、礼、乐、刑、政，异派而同源。一如欧洲中古之世，制度文章皆自罗马教皇出也。盛衰兴废之迹，著于周之季世。溯其相当年代，约自索伦氏始生之年，迄雅里三大殁后之百年。其间会盟聘伐之事，盛极一时，历春秋战国而周亡。

盖自武王赐爵，同姓创为封建之制，而列国分争之祸，实根于此。（日本亦沿此制至一千六百六十八年之乱，始变封建为郡县）与日耳曼之楂尔满，无以异也。其制诸侯皆以世及，土地人民，各私所有。未几而干弱枝强，渐起不臣之志。始也天子当阳，诸侯用命。继也王室虽卑，而霸国犹知尊周，往往上告天子以断曲直。及其久也，强弱并吞，遂至显叛其上而不顾，此所谓战国之势也。前乎战国而诸侯犹有好会者，春秋列国之世也。夫以境壤相接之国，而有往来交际之亲，则其间玉帛兵戎，必有成规之可守，而公法之条例，即于是乎存。

今试读春秋战国之史，纵不得竟谓之公法，然其迹有不可泯者。不见夫同文同伦同教之数十国，有交际通商之政乎？不见其遣使往来，有宾客宴享之仪乎？不见其会盟立约，藏之盟府以为信乎？不见其寓均势之法于纵横之中，以御强而保弱乎？不见其约法相循，俨然有局外权利之守乎？且不见夫智谋之士，专事揣摩，以与人家国乎（此辈以游说为主，以纵横为策，与意大利玛施弗力之时风尚略同）。凡此数百年之陈迹，莫非公法之要纲，昔未纂述成书，以传诸后世耳。然使果有其书，恐亦毁于秦火矣。（始皇筑万里长城，功在万世。而焚书之举，千古同恨焉）今所传者，惟散见于孔孟之书、诸子百家之说以及稗官野史之所记。而《周礼》一书，尤足以资考证。

中国于外邦交际之道，日益讲求。或有如葛氏之蒐辑希腊意大利列国公例，未可知也。至于是编，不过择其要者，借引一二端，以证余之所见，且示中国古世实有公法，可考云尔。必欲胪举其事，博采其文，则不独限于篇幅，亦非余立言之本意也。按中国公法，甲寓于封建之初，而显著于春秋之世。自尧舜始建十二州，立十二牧，疆分界划，上应星辰。盖古时分天图为十二方，以国之十二州富之。取每方例宿之名，定各州分野之界。孔子云：为政以德，譬如北辰，居其所而众星拱之，亦以北辰喻天子，以众星喻诸侯也。夫合天文地理之学，以为经理疆域之用。良言美意，计孰有逾于此乎。彼罗马立界神以司疆域，同一神道设教之意，要不若星野立法之善。故数百年间，在西土历巴毕伦波斯希腊之兴亡相继，疆域屡更而中国十二州独持久而不变。本始非法制之善，有以使之也。

迄于周代，众建诸侯，分十二州之地为千有余国。内外相维，小大相制。立政之繁密，与后罗马相类。其命爵则如欧洲中古之世，列为五等，曰公侯伯子男。下此为附庸之国，皆以时朝觐天子，为王室屏藩。春秋之初，诸侯虽强，犹以尊周室攘夷狄为事。而列国会盟，有一举而五等之封咸集者，如鲁史僖公九年夏，公会宰周公齐侯、宋子卫侯、郑伯许男、曹伯于葵邱。古传会于葵邱，寻盟且修好，礼也。按此所谓礼，即当时公法之根据，半皆出于《周礼》一书。是书之作，约在西历纪年前一千一百余年。今所传本，非完璧也。

周礼者，所以定尊卑、别贵贱。举凡朝觐会同之事，冠婚丧祭之仪，设官制禄之经，取赋明刑之典，以至齐权度，一量衡，极于至纤至细而莫不有礼。以此施于泰西，则殊若其繁重，而行之中国古世，则人必以为便，与古犹太人之尊奉摩西律法无异也。故内而王畿，外而列国，朝野上下，一秉周礼。独嬴秦处乎西北，其俗不用周礼，而从殷礼，隐然有弗率之意，而周亦卒亡于秦。秦以外诸国，既秉周礼，则一切政教科条，若合符节，于近世所谓通融律例，自无所用其讲求矣。

盖周礼之作，与封建之制相表里。周礼行而王室之声灵，赖以不坠。侯国之君，属在藩臣。虽其自专国政，一如今日之安南库尔喀等国，不过循数载一朝之典。然其仰望天子，则以为至尊无对。凡礼仪之所在，惟天子之命是从。其尊敬之诚，惟中古罗马教诸国之于教皇，足以拟之。如周襄王为国人所逐，出居于外，晋文公以兵纳王。王既复于王城，（狭小邑居天下之中，是为王城。如罗马之有皇城，近为义国所吞并）劳文公以地，辞，请隧。王知所请虽小，而所窥伺者实大，因毅然拒之。文公遂受地成礼而还。此可见时至春秋，强侯犹不敢违王命也。周之列国，惟同为王室屏藩，故虽时相侵伐，而气类自亲。至其与夷狄化外之国，则攘之恶之，历千百年而风气曾不少易。如鲁襄公四年，西北山戎如晋请和，且愿列为附庸。晋侯曰，戎无亲而贪，不如伐之。其臣魏绛力言和戎有五利，晋侯始许盟，非鄙夷戎狄之明证欤？

春秋之初世，列国尚称辑睦，其往来交际，有合于公法者甚多。即如重商一端，古今亦有同揆。不独孔门之高弟，尝以货殖见称，凡诸侯图治者，亦莫不通商惠之，争相招徕，以为富国之计焉。而其时贸易之盛，尤莫若人才。往往一国之学校，而他国之士，群焉附之。所学既成，即可委贽于异邦之君。故贤人君子文学经济之士，皆历聘四方，传食诸侯，即孔子亦辙迹半天下，以冀一日之用。而及门从学者，大都皆来自远方。后百余年，孟子以仁义之说游历齐梁，亦犹是木铎设教之意也。彼秦之日臻强大，寻至代周而有天下者，独非用贤之效乎！史称秦孝公（西历前三百六十八年）发愤修政，欲以强秦，令中国曰：宾客群臣能有出奇计强秦者，吾且尊官与之分土。公孙鞅卫之庶孙也，好刑名之学，闻孝公令，遂入秦求见。说以富国强兵之术，孝公大悦，举国而听之。鞅下令变法，兵革大强，诸侯畏惧，后百年而遂得兼并天下，商君之力也。始皇时，李斯亦以客为卿。时秦宾客多用事，群臣忌之，因议逐客。李斯上书谏而止。其书首述先世四君，皆用客致强，以见客之有功于秦，末以河海不择细流为喻，使始皇立除逐客之令，信不刊之至论也。

  春秋之世，诸侯朝会之事不一而足。使非诚信相孚，何以至此？虽其间未必猜嫌之尽释，而敦槃玉帛，大率尽礼守信者居多。按定公十年，夹谷之会，孔子相焉。齐侯以莱人从，欲劫鲁君。孔子预修武备，命司马止之，而折齐人以辞。于是齐计不得逞，且返鲁之侵地。此以见两君好会，有文事亦必有武备也。若襄公九年，公送晋侯至于河上。谈谑间晋侯知鲁君尚未受冠礼，因请即日行之，从者以礼乐未具对。时去卫近于鲁，乃请假卫地以成此礼，晋侯曰：诺。公遂冠于卫成公之庙，假钟磬焉，礼也。此则情谊浃洽，纯乎好合者矣。至于会盟立约，修好睦邻之举，则更层见叠出，率以大国主盟，而小国从其后，与今日欧洲之局，遥遥相对，如出一辙。

  更遣使通好，尤属古今之常道。使臣身不可犯，此例古亦有之。然不能无执获杀戮之事者，信不立也。其间杀者，直以使人为间谍，故杀之以示决战。其见执者，或藉口于使臣之过我以达邻国，未先假道。又以其行为图我，故执之以沮其谋。外此，则皆以礼相待，恒视其人或其君之爵命，以定仪文之隆杀焉。若数国之使，会聘于一国，其先后争长之间，亦复据理而断。特不如欧洲维也纳之会所定章程，为简明划一耳。如隐公十一年，滕侯薛侯同朝于鲁，争长。薛侯曰：我先封；滕侯曰：我，周之卜正也。薛，庶姓也，我不可以后之。公使人告以宾有礼，主则择之。周之宗盟，异姓为后，愿以滕君为请，薛侯许之，乃长滕侯。不烦兵甲，以一言而息两国之争，此在欧洲当一千八百一十五年以前，未易觏也。

若夫侮辱使臣，往往为兴戎之阶。如成公元年，有四国之使同时而聘于齐，一秃一眇一跛一偻。齐顷公出以游戏，亦使秃者、眇者、跛者、偻者四人分迎之。惟妇人于台上，窃而笑之，闻于客。客知齐人之戏已也。怒而出，誓必以报。次年，四国遂率师伐齐，齐师败绩。赖有宾媚人之辞令，又致赂以谢，始免于祸。盖侮人适自侮，至此悔之已晚矣。如文公元年冬，叔孙敖如齐，《左传》云，始聘焉，礼也。凡君即位，卿出并聘，践修旧好，要结外援，好事邻国，以卫社稷，忠信卑让之道也。春秋遣使，凡近世所有各种条约，古皆有之。载盟之法，必临之以神，申之以誓，歃血执牛耳以为信。书成则谨藏于深严之地，谓之盟府。其盟约之辞，有可得而举者，如襄公十一年四月，诸侯伐郑，七月，同盟于亳。载书曰：凡我同盟，勿蕴年，毋壅利，毋保奸，毋留匿；救灾患，恤祸乱；同好恶，奖王室。或闻兹命，司慎司盟。名山名川，群神群祀。先王先公七姓十二国之祖，明神之，俾失其民，坠命亡氏，陪其国家，此盖神道设教之意。

亦有不以文以实者，或以子为质，或更使他国作之监，以讨背盟之罪。而尤莫奇于索国君之母以为质。如成公二年，鲁卫曹晋四国伐齐，齐师败绩。齐侯使人致赂以求成，晋人不可，曰：必以萧国叔子为质。而使齐之封内，尽东其亩。齐人谓齐晋匹敌之国，先王所建。晋不顾土宜而使尽东其亩，非先王之命。反先王则不义，何以为盟主。至必欲以君之母为质，则是以不孝令。宁收合余烬，背城借一，以与晋国旋。于是鲁卫为之调停，陈说利害以谏晋，晋人乃许之，受赂以还。

按交质之法，中国古儒皆以为非，谓夫适足启彼此之疑。而成交恶之势耳。西儒亦主此说，而论之之切，未有逾于中国古儒者。人而无信，不知其可也。大车无輗，小车无軏，其何以行之哉！又尝以食、兵、信三者，为国政之要，而信为重。以为去兵与食，国犹可存，去信则国不立矣。若夫行阵之间，则与欧洲古世国，皆舍一国之私例，而从天下之公理。其蹂躏残杀之惨，亦希腊罗马相伯仲。昔希腊君雅里三太尝戒军士弗犯诗人宾氏宅，固见好文敬士之意。然所戒止于是，则其他之得肆荼毒可知，古中国亦然。胜则著其威，败则任其祸。杀掠之患，非有殊恩异数，不能免也。昔者秦攻齐，令有敢去柳下季垄五十步而樵採者，死不赦。而有能得齐王头者，封万户侯，赐千金镒，事正相类。阿契利（希腊名将）尝谓法度非吾辈而设，中国将帅亦持此见。然逞私背义者，古时虽多，而军旅之法度，固自可考。兹约举之如左：

一、军旅所至，民间秋毫毋得犯。考诸史载，凡仁爱者，名誉之所归，残暴者，怨谤之所集。自有征伐以来，其用力少而成功者多，未有不以仁爱胜。故孔子曰：仁不可为众也。孟子曰：仁者无敌。

二、兵必以鼓进，敌未成列者不击。《左传》：宋公及楚人战于泓，楚人未既济，司马请击之，公不可。既济而未成列，又以告，公又不可。既陈而后击之，宋师败绩。国人皆咎公，公曰：君子不重伤，不禽二毛。古之为君也，不以阻隘也。寡人虽亡国之余，不鼓不成列。宋襄公之迂拘若此，后世传为笑柄。而古泰西勇侠之士，以乘敌之危为耻，亦此意也。

三、无故不得兴兵。师出有名一语，为中国谈兵者所诵法。盖师旅之兴，不出于怨，则出于贪，恃有是非之公义以持其间耳。不但此也，义之所在，虽强弱有可弗论者。如古人所云，师直为壮曲为老是矣。西人诗云，兴师以义，三倍其器，意竟与此同。

四、御敌卫弱，恒谓之义。凡遇强敌侵陵，不独被祸之国急于自谋,即远处局外者,亦以发兵救援为义。春秋若此之举,史不绝书,而尤莫著于六国之合纵以御强秦(时在西历纪年前三百二十年)。时六国用苏秦之策,联盟合众,并力拒秦相持二十年之久。其后盟寒约散,卒使强秦得肆其蚕食,六国相继灭亡。而周室八百年之祚,至是遂绝。秦既兼并天下,遂自称为始皇帝,废封建,置郡县,北筑长城,河山统一。自是以来,不独皇帝之号,历代因之,其郡县天下制,亦复亘古不移,屹然与万里长城同其巩固矣。

五、诸侯不得擅灭人国,以弃先王之命,此义战至战国而始湮。春秋之世,诸侯虽相侵伐,犹未敢冒天下之不韪。往往危急存亡之际,赖此义以自全。如齐孝公帅师伐鲁,鲁侯使展喜犒师,冀有以止其军。齐侯曰:鲁人恐乎?对曰:小人恐矣,君子则否。齐侯曰:室如悬磬,野无青草,何恃而不恐?对曰:恃有先王之命。因进详齐鲁受封之始,盟府所载之辞。责之以义,讽之以情,卒使齐侯辞屈而还,此一证也。至若以王国而亦有赖于此者,则如楚子伐陆浑之戎,遂至于雒,观兵于周疆。定王使王孙满劳楚子以审其意,楚子有窥伺神器之心,故以鼎之轻重为问。王孙满不遽答其问,第为之言鼎所自来。始于夏禹,铸鼎象物,使民知神奸。历有殷六百祀而鼎迁于周,遂为王室之重器。终之以周德虽衰,天命未改,鼎之轻重,未可问云云。楚子乃废然而返。此固由辞令之妙,亦由大义之犹在人心耳。

六、局外之国,亦俨有权利之可守。古者希腊诸国,初无局外之说。苟其国所处,有关于战局之重轻,则于彼于此,必使之择一以从。虽欲置身事外,弗可得也。中国则不然,局外之国可以两无所兴,使彼此师旅皆不得越其境。即有假之以道者,亦第弗为之阻而已,他仍无所兴也。且假道,危事也,智者所不为。如僖公五年,晋侯复假道于虞以伐虢。宫之奇谏曰:虢,虞之表也。虢亡,虞必从之,晋不可启,寇不可玩。一之谓甚,其可再乎?虞公弗听,卒假之以道。晋既灭虢,师还,遂并灭虞,其前鉴也。

综观春秋战国时事，有合乎公法者如此其多，则当时或实有其书而不传于后世，未可知也。亦如希腊本有公法，而今所存者，不过篇目而已。要之书之有无不可必，而以其事论之，则古中国实有公共之法，以行于干戈玉帛之间，特行之有盛与不盛耳。周礼三传国语国策等书，皆足以资考证。而尤可为天下万国法者，莫如孔子所修之春秋，综二百四十年之事，悉经笔削而定。往往予夺褒贬，寓于一字。千载而下，更无有能议其后者。所谓一字之褒，荣于华衮。一字之诛，严于斧钺是也。

今中国执政者，亦谓欧洲大小各国境壤相接，强弱相维，有似于春秋列国。而考之籍载，觉其事其文其义，亦复与今之公法相印合，故中国亦乐从泰西公法，以与各国交际。由此观之，则谓公法一书，必有一日焉，为天下万国所遵守，而遂以立斯世和平之准也，夫岂托诸梦想已哉！"①

"INTERNATIONAL LAW
IN
ANCIENT CHINA

The recent treaties, by which China has been brought into closer relations with the nations of the West, and especially the establishment of intercourse by means of permanent embassies, have led Chinese statesmen to turn attention to the subject of international law.

For them, it is a new study, involving conceptions whichit would hardly have been possible for their predecrssors to form at any time in the course of the last two thousand years; though, as we shall endeavor to show, they possessed something answering to it in their earlier history.

Their modern history commences two centuries befor the Christian era; for our purpose, it may be divided into three periods. The first, extending from the epoch of the Punic wars down to the discovery of the

---

① 于宝轩辑：《皇朝蓄艾文编》卷13，上海官书局印1903年版，第8册，第19—29页。

route to the Indies by the Cape of Good Hope; the second, comprehending three centuries and a half of restricted commercial intercourse; and the third, commencing with the so-called 'opium war', in 1839, and covering the forty years of treaty relations.

During the first, the Chinese were as little affected by the convulsions that shook the western would as if they had belonged to another planet. During the second, they became aware of the existence of the principal State s of modern Europe; but the light that reached them was not yet sufficient to reveal the magnitude and importance of those far-off powers. Within the last period, the rude experiences of two wars have made them acquainted with the military strength of European nations; and the opening of the Suez Canal has brought them into what they regard as a dangerous proximity to formidable neghbors.

These unwelcome discoveries have led them, not only to push forward their defensive armaments, but to seek in fact, if not in form, to put themselves as much as possible under the aegis of what fairly be called the public law of the civilized world. such are the steps by which China has been led to accept intercourse on a footing of equality with nations which, for three centuries, she had been accustomed to class with her own tributaries.

Her tributaries included all the petty States of Eastern Asia. Attracted partly by commercial interest, but more, perhaps, by the moral effect of her national greatness, they rendered a voluntary homage to the master of a realm so vast that, like Rome of old, it has always called itself by a title equivalent to *orbis terrarum*. These vassal States had few relations with each other, and it was not to be expected that China, acknowledging nothing like reciprocity in her intercourse with them, should learn from them the idea of a community of nations possessed of equal rights.

For twenty centuries she had presented to her own people, as well as to her dependent neighbors, the imposing spectacle of an empire unrivaled in extent, whose unity had been broken only by rare intervals of revolution or anarchy. During this long period, it was no more possible that an international code should spring up in China than it would have been for such a thing to appear in Europe, had the Rome empire remained undivided until the present day. The requisite conditions were wanting. Where they exist, a code based upon usage, and more or less developed, comes into being by the necessities of the human mind.

These conditions are: —

1st. —The existence of a group of independent States, so situated as to require or favor the maintennance of friendly intercourse;

2nd. —That those States should be so related as to conduct their intercourse on a basis of equality.

If these condition were conspicuously absent under the consolidated empire, they were no less obviously present in the preceding period, accompanied by every circumstance that could favor the development of an international code.

The vast domain of China proper was at that epoch divided between a number of independent principalities, whose people were of one blood, posseessors of a common civilization already much advanced, and united by the additional bond of a common language.

These conditions concurred in ancient Greece, and the result was a rudimentary code, culminating in the Amphictyonic Council, —a provision for settling international disputes, which suggests comparison with the concert of European powers recently employed in settling the question of the Greek frontier.

In ancient China, the conditions are similar, but the scale of Operation is vastly more extended. There is, moreover, another important difference; and, with reference to the object of the present eassay, it desrves to be marked with special emphasis. The Chinese States were not, like those of Greece, a cluster of detached tribes who had together emerged from barbarism, without any well-defined political connection; they were the fragments of a disintegrated empire, inheriting its laws and civilization, as the States of modern Europe inherited those of Rome.

The period during which they rose and fell was the latter half of the dynasty of Cheo, pretty nearly corresponding to that exteding from the birth of Solon to the close of the first century after the death of Alexander, which in China, as in Greece, was an age of intense political avtivity. The normal form of government for the empire was the feudal, the archetype of that which prevailed in Japan until swept away by the revolution of 1868. The several States were created by the voluntary subdivision of the national domain by the founder of the dynasty, who, like Charlemagne, by this arrangement planter within it the seeds of its destruction.

The throne of each State being hereditary, a feeling of independence soon began to spring up. The emperors were at first able to preserve order by force; and, even when shorn of their power, their court, like that of the Holy See in the Middle Ages, continued for a long time to serve as a court of appeal for the adjustment of international difficulties. But at length, losing all respect for authority, the feudal princes threw off the semblance of subjection, and pursued without restraint the objects of their private ambtion. This age is called by the native historians *chan-kuo*, or that of the "warring States"   and that which preceded it, characterized by ordery and pacific intercourse, is described as *Lie-kuo*, or the family of "co-ordinated States."

A family of States, with such an arena and such antecedents, could hardly fail to develop, in the intercourse of peace and war, a system of usages which might be regarded as constituting for them a body of international laws.

Accordingly, if we turn to the history of the period, in quest of such an indigenous system, we shallfind, if not the system itself, at least the evidence of its existence. We find, as we have said, a family of States, many of them as extensive as the great States of western Europe, united by the ties of race, literature, and religion, carrying on an active intercourse, commercial and political, which, without some recognized *Jus gentlium*, would have been impracticable. We find the interchange of embassies, with forms of courtesy, indictive of an elaborate civilization. We find treaties solemnly drawn up and deposited for safe keeping in a sacred place called *meng-fu*. We find a balance of power studied and practised, leading to combinations to check the aggressions of the strong and to protect the rights of the weak. We find the rights of neutrals to a certain extent recognized and respected. Finally, we find a class of men devoted to diplomacy as a profession, though, to say the truth, their diplomacy was not unlike that which was practised by the States of Italy in the days of Machiavelli.

No formal text-book, containing the rules which for so many centuries controlled this complicated intercourse, has come down to our times. If such writings ever existed, they probably perished in the 'conflagration of the books,' which sheds such a lurid light on the memory of the builder of the Great Wall. The *membra disjecta* of the such an international code as we have supposed are, however, to be found profusely scattered over the literature of those times, —in the writings of Confucius and Meneius; in those of other philosophers of the last five centuries B. C; in various historical records; and particularly in the *Cheo-li*, or *Book of Rites*, of the dynasty of Chow.

The day may perhaps come when some Chinese Grotius will gather up these desultory hints as carefully as the illustrious Hollander did the traces of international usages in Greece and Italy. To make even a partial collection of the passages in Chinese writers relating to this subject, would neither come within the scope nor the compass of the present Paper. All that I propose to myself, in addition to indicating, as I have done, the existence between the States of ancient China of a peculiar system of consuetudinary law, is to make a few citations confirmactory of the views expressed, and throwing light on some of the more interesting of the topics to which I have adverted.

The clearest view of the public law which was acknowledged by this group of States, after they became independent, is undoubtedly to be sought for in their relations to each other while subject to a common suzerain.

The greater States were tewlve in number, and for ages that distribution of territory was regarded as no less permanent than the order of the heavenly bodies. It was consecrated by the science of astrnomy as it then existed, and an ancient map of the heavens gives us a duodecimal division, with the stars of each portion formally set apart to preside over the destinies of a corresponding portion of the empire.

Confucius appears to allude to this in a beautiful passage in which he compares the emperor, or the wisw man—for the words have a double sense—to the polar sar, which sits unmoved on its central throne, while allthe constellations revolve around it. Could anything be devised more effectual than this superstitious alliance of geography and astronomy, to place the territorial rights of the several States under the safeguard of religion? More picturesque than the Rome method of placing the boundaries under the care of a special divinity, it was probably more efficacious, and contributed in no small degree to maitain the eqilbrium of a naturally unstable system, during a period which, in the West, witnessed the rise and fall of the Babylonian, Persian, and Greek empires, entailing the complete obliteration of most of their minor divisions.

These twelve States had a great number of lesser principalities dependent on them, the whole constituting a political organization as multifarious and complex as that which exusted in Germany under the sway of the 'Holy Roman Empire.' As in mediaval Europe, the chiefs of these States were ranked with respect to nobility in five orders, answering to duke, marquis, earl, viscount, and baron, the inferior depending on the superior, but all paying homage to the Son of Heaven, a title which was even at that early period applied to the Emperor, who had a right, for the common good, to command the service of all. In the annals of Lu, we find the following curious entry: —

'In the ninth year of his reihn, the Duke met in conference at Kwe-chiu the Duke of Cheo, the Marquis of Chi, the Viscount of song, the Marquis of Wei, the Earl of cheng, the Baron of Hu, and the Earl of Tsao'

We note here the presence of all the five orders. The commentary of Tso, we may add, states the object of the meeting as 'the formation of a league and the promotion of friendly relatios in accordance with *authorized usage.*'

The authorized usages here referred to constituted the basis of the international law of the time. They were contained in part in the *Cheo-li*, or *Book of Rites* of the Cheo dynasty, published by imperial authority about 1100 B. C, and, in a somewhat mutilated form, extant at the present day. This Code defines the orders of nobility; prescribes a sumptuary law for each, extending even to their rites of sepulture; regulates the part of each in the public sacrifices; and lays down a form of etiquette to be observed in all their public meetings. It gives in detail the hierarchy of officers, civil and military; indicates their functions; fixes the weights and measures, the mode of collecting the revenue, and the modes of punishment; and all this mixed up with an infinitude of ceremonial detail which to us appears the reverse of business-like, but which was no doubt as well adapted to the character of the ancient Chinese as was the ritualistic legislation of Moses to that of the Hebrews.

Primarily obligatory on the immediate subjects of the imperial house, this Code was secondarily blinding on all the vassals of the empire, by all of whom it was adopted in the minutest particulars, with the single exception of the State of Chin, in the extreme noethwest, a State which obstinately adhered to the ritual and etiquette of the earlier dynasty of Shang, and, cherishing a spirit of alienation, became the secret foe and ultimately the destroyer of the imperial house.

With this exception, the laws and usages of the several States were so uniform—all being copied from a common model—that there was little occasion for the cultivation of that branch of international jurisprudence, which in modern times has become so prominent under the title of the 'conflict of laws.'

Ideas derived from the feudal system were so interwoven with every part of this complicated legislation that its general acceptance formed the mainstray of the imperial throne. The great princes styled themselves vassals; though as independent as Annam and Nepaul are at the present day, and like these latter, paying formal homage only once in five years. They accordingly looked up to the emperor as the founction of honor, and the supreme authority in all questions of ceremony, if not in questions of right.

Of this moral ascendency, for which we can find no parallel better than the veneration which, in the Middle Ages See, we have a remarkable example in the *Kuo-yu*. The emperor, Siang-wang, 651 B. C., being driven by a domestic revolt from his territories—a small district in the center of the empire, which may be compared to the Pontifical States recently absorbed by the kingdom of Italy—was restorted to his throne by the powerful intervention of the Doke of Tsin. In recompense for such a signal service, the emperor offered him a slice of land. The duke declined it, and asked, instead, that he might be permitted to construct his tomb after the model of the imperial mausoleum. The emperor, viewing this apparently modest request as a dangerous assumption, promptly refused it, and the duke was compelled to abide by the recognized Code of Rites.

The possession of this common Code, originating in the will of a common suzerain, contributed to maintain for nearly a thousand years among the States of China, discordant and belligerent as they often were, a bond of sympathy in strong contrast with the feeling they manifested toward all nations not comprehended within the pale of yheir own civilization. When, for instance, the Tartars of the north—west presented themselves at the court of Tsin, requesting a treaty of peace and amity, and humbly offering to submit to be treated as vassals of the more enlightened power, — 'Amity' exclaimed the prince, 'what do they know of amity? The barbarous savages! Give them war as the portion due to our natural enemies.' Nor was it until his minister had produced five solid reasons for a pacific policy that the hayghty prince consented to accept them as vassals.

In the history of those times, the curtain rises on a scene of peaceful intercourse which, in many ways, implies a basis of public law. Merchants are held in esteem, one of the most distinguished of the disciplesof Confucius belonging to that class; and a rivalry subsisits between the several princes in attracting merchants to their States. Their wares are subjected to tolls and customs; but the object is revenue, not protection.

The commerce of mond reveals relations of a still more intimate character. The schools of one State are often largely frequented by students from another; and those who make the greatest proficiency are readily taken into the service of foreign princes. Philosophers and political reformers travel from court to court, in quest of patrnage. Confucius himself wanders over half the empire, and draws disciples from all the leading States.

A century later, Mencius, with the spirit of a Hebrew prophet, proclaims in more than one capital his great message that the only toundation of national prosperity is justice and charity.

It was to this kind of intercourse that Ch'in, the rising power of the North-west, was indebted for the ascendency which it slowly acquired in affairs of the empire, and which eventually placed its princes in possession of the inmperial throne.

The Duke Hiao (368 B. C), conscious of the backward stateof his people, made proclamation to the effect that any man, native or foreign, who should be able to devise a new method for promoting the prosperity of his dominions, would be rewarded by a grant of land and a patent of nobility. Shang-yang, a native of a neighboring State, a young man of noble family, who, the historian says, 'had given much attention to legal studies,' presented himself, and requested an audience. The duke, charmed by the clearness and originality of his ideas, gave him *carle blanche* for putting them in practice. The reforms effected were of the most thorough character, and the seed was then sown of triumphs achieved a century later. Further on we find Li-sze, another foreigner, at the helm, in the same principality. At this time, so great was the influx of strangers that the natives, as in other lands, became jealous, and made a movement to expel them. The prince was disposed to yield, when the minister averted the blow by laying before the throne a masterly plea for freedom of intercourse. This notable document, whose good effect did not cease with the emergency that gave it birth, begins by showing that the ancestors of the prince had for four generatuons admitted foreign statesmen to the rank of confidential counsellors, and concludes by comparing their policy with their own majestc river, the Hoang-ho, which owes its greatness to the rivulets that combine to swell its volume.

The personal intercourse of sovereign princes forms a striking feature in the history of those times. Their frequent interchange of visits indicates a degree of mutual confidence which speaks volumes for the public sentiment. Confidence was, indeed, sometimes abused, as it has been in other countries; but such intercourse was always characterized by courtesy, and mostly by good faith.

On one occasion, when a powerful price came with a great retinue to visit the Duke of Lu, Confucius, who was Minister of Foreign Affairs, adopted such precautions, and conducted the interviews with such adroitness, that he not only averted what was believed to be a danger, but induced the foreign prince to restore a territory which he had unjustly appropriated.

A visit of the Duke of Tsin to the Duke of Lu may be mentioned, as illustrating the freedom and familiarity which sometimes marked this princely intercourse. The host accompanied his guest as far as the Yellow River. The later, learning during a parting entertainment that the former had not yet received the *Kwan-li*—a rite answering somewhat to the conferring of knighthood—offered, them and there, to confer it. It was objected, then and there, to confer it. It was objected that the means were wanting for performing the ceremony with due solemnity; and the capital of Wei being nearer than his own, the Duke of Lu proposed to proceed thither for the purpose. They did so, and the rite was celebrated with suitable pomp in a temple borrowed for the occasion.

General meetings of the princes for the purpose of forming or renewing treaties of alliance were of frequent occurrence. Embracing what were then regaded as all the leading powers of the earth, these meeting present a distant, but not faint, parallel to the great congress of European soverigns.

The more usual form of friendly intercourse between the States of China was, as elsewhere, bymeans of envoys.

The person of an envoy was sacred; but instances are not wanting of their arrest and execution. In the latter case, they were regarded as spies, and the punishment inflicted on them was consided as a declaration or act of war. In the former, the violence was sometimes defended on the ground that the envoy had undertaken to pass through the territory into a neighboring State without having first obtained a passport, his visit being at the same time held to have a hostile object. Ordinarily, an envoy was treated with according to his own rank, or that of his sovereign. Questions of precedence, which often arose, were decided according to settled principles; but the rules were by no means as clear and simple as those enacted by the Congress of Vienna.

A dispute of this kind arising between the envoys of two duchies at the court of Lu, one claimed precedence on the ground that his State was more ancient than the other. The minister of the latter replied that his sovereign was more nearly allied to the imperial family. The difficulty was happily terminated without bloodshed, which was not always the case with such quarrels in Europe prior to 1815, The master of ceremonies reminded the litigants that the placing of guests belongs to the host, and gave preference to the kinsman of the emperor.

Insults to envoys were not unfrequently avenged by an appeal to arms. Of this, a notable instance was an insult given by the Prince of Chi, at one and the same time, to the representatives of four powers.

These envoys arriving simultaneously, it was observed by some wag (the court fool, perhaps) that each was marked by a blemish or deformity in his personal appearance. One was blind of an eye; a second was bald; another was lame; and the last was a dwarf. It was suggested to the duke that a little innocent amusement might be made out the hint, appointed as attendant or introducteur to each ambassador an officer who suffered from the same defect. The court ladies, who, comcealed by curtains of thin gauze, witnessed the ceremony of introduction and the subsequent banquet, laughed aloud when they saw the blind leading the blind, and the dwarfs, the bald, and the lame, walking in pairs. The envoys, hearing the merriment, became aware that they had been made involuntary actors in a comedy. They retired, vowing vengeance, and the next year saw the capital of Chi beleagured by the combined forces of the four powers, which were only induced to withdraw by the most humiliating cincessions on the part of the young prince, who, too late, repented his indecent levity.

In the history of Tso, we find a rule for the sending of envoys, which has its parallel in the diplomatic usage of modern nations. Speaking of a mission to a neighboring Stae, he adds: — 'This was in accordance with usage. In all cases where a new prince comes to the throne, envoys are sent to the neighboring States to confirm and extend the friendly relations maintained by predecessor.'

The highest function of an envoy was the negotiation of a treaty. Treaties of all kinds known to modern diplomacy were in use in ancient China. Signed with solemn formalities, and confirmed by an oath, —the parties mingling their blood in a cup of wine, or laying their hands on the head of an ox to be offered in sacrifice, —such documents were carefully treasured up in a sacred place called *Meng-fu*, the 'Palace of Treaties.'

We are able to give, by way of specimen, the outlines of a treaty between the Prince of Cheng and a coalition of princes who invaded his territories in 544 B. C.

PREAMBLE: —The parties to the present Treaty agree to the following Articles:

Article 1. —The exportation of corn shall not be prohibited.

Article 2. —One party shall not monopolize trade to the disadvantage of others.

Article 3. —No one shall give protection to conspiracies diected against the others.

Article 4. —Fugitives from justice shall be surrendered.

Article 5. —Mutual succor shall be given in case of famine.

Article 6. ——Mutual and shall be given in case of insurrection.

Article 7. ——The contracting powers shall have the same friends and the same enimies.

Article 8. ——We all engage to support the Imperial House.

CONCLUSION: ——We engage to inviolate the terms of the foregoing Agreement. May the gods of the hills and rives, the spirits of former emperors and dukes, and the abcestors of our seven tribes and twelve states, watch over its fulfillment. If any one prove unfaithful, may the all-seeing gods smite him, so that his people shall forsake him, his life be lost, and his posterity be cut off.

The outline of a similar convention is given by Mencius. On this occasion, the great barons were called together by Siao-po, Prince of Ch'i, for the purpose of effevting needful reforms in 651 B. C. Being a century earlier than the other, it is instructive to compare the two documents. While in that of later date the Imperial authority is so far gone that the barons engage to uphold the Impwrial House, in this the authority of the Suzerain is fully recognized, ——each article of the convention being styled an 'Ordinance' of the Emperor.

That his hold on his vassals was already much weakened is, however, evident from the provisions that they are not to exercise certain powers of sovereignty in the way of rewards and punishments without at least formal reference to the 'Son of Heaven.'

The stipulations are partly in favor of good morals, and partly to facilitate intercourse, and to raise the character of the official hierarchy.

Article 1. ——To punish the unfilial; not to change the succession to the throne (of each state); and not to raise a concubine to be a wife.

Article 2. ——To respect the virtuous and cherish talent.

Article 3. ——To honor the aged and to be kind to the young, and not to neglect strangers.

Article 4. ——Officers not to be hereditary; proxies not to be permitted. Suitable men to be sought and found. Death not to be inflicted on nobles without reference to the Emperor.

Article 5. —Not to divert water-courses, not obstruct the transport of grain. Not to grant land in fief without reference to the Emperor.

CONCLUSION: —All we who are parties to this Covenant agree to be at peace with each other.

'These five rules, adds the philosopher,' are openly violated by the nobles of our day.

In addition to the rites of religion by which such engagements were ratified, they were usually secured by sanctions of less sentimental character. As in the West, hostages or other material guarantees were given in pledge; sometimes also they were guaranteed by third parties, who, directly or indirectly interested, engaged to punish a breach of faith. We have, for instance, one prince, demanding the mother of another as a hostage. The case is instructive in more than one of its aspects. The Prince of Tsin, calling on the Prince of Chi to recognize him as his chief, and to surrender his mother as a pledge of submission, the latter replies that his State was created the peer of the other by the will of the former Emperors, and that one who would despise the patent of an Emperor was not fit to be the head of League. As to the demand for his mother as a hostage, that was a proposition so monstrous that, rather than submit to it, he would meet the enemy under the walls of his last fortress.

At this point, the affair takes a turn which serves to illustrate a procedure of frequent occurrence in the history of those times. The princes in the history of those times. The princes of two neighboring States come forward as mediators. and bring about an accommodation on less oppressive conditions.

The more enlightened writers of Chinese antiquity condemn the practice of exchanging hostages, as tending to keep up a state of *quasi* hostility and mutual mistrust; and no writers of any nation have been more emphatic in insisting on good faith as a cardinal virtue in all international transactions.

Says Confusions: — 'A man without faith is like a wagon without a coupling-pole to connect the wheels.' Speaking of a State, he says: — 'Of the three essentials, the greatest is good faith. Without a revenue and without an army, a State may still exist; but it cannot exist without good faith.'

It remains to speak of the intercourse of war. '*Inter hostes scripta jura non valero at valere non scripta*' —is a principle that was as well understood in ancient China as among the ancient nations of the Western world; and war in China was, to say the least, not more brutal than among the Greeks and Romans.

The command of Alexander to spare the house of the poet Pindar, if it shows a degree of literary culture, indicates, on the other hand, that moral barbarism which asserts a right to the spoils of the conquered. In China, we find the same state of things; *vae victis* is the sad undertone in every narrative of military glory, relieved, indeed, by brilliant instances of generosity and mercy. We find an invading chief enjoining, under penalty of death, respect for the very trees that overshadow the tomb of a philosopher, and at the same time setting a price on the head of a rival prince.

Every military leader proclaims, like Achilles, that 'laws are not made for him;' yet we do not despair of being able to show that laws existed in war as well as in peace, even though they were systematically trampled on. With this view, we shall call attention to the following facts: —

First: —In the conduct of war, the persons and property of non—combatants were reqired to be respected.

This we infer from the praise bestowed on humane leaders, and the reprobation meted out to the cruel. In Chinese history, the example of those who have achieved the easiest and most permanent conquests is always on the side of humanity.

second: — In legitimate warfare, the rule was not to attack an enemy without first sounding the drum, and giving him time to prepare for defense.

The following instances beyond this requirement, and reminds us of the code chivalry which made it infamous to take advantage of an antagonist. The Prince of Sung declined to engage a hostile force while they were crossing a stream, and waited for them to advance. He was beaten, and, when reproached by his officers, he justified himself by appealing to ancient usage. 'The true soldier,' said he, 'never strikes a wounded foe, and always leat the gray-headed go free; and in ancient times it was forbidden to assail an enemy who was not in a state to resist. I have come near losing my kingdom, but I would scorn to command an attack without first sounding the drum.'

We are not surprised to learn that the captains of that age 'laughed at the simplicity of the unfortunate prince'.

Third: —A war was not to be undertaken without at least a decent pretext.

These words, in fact, are almost a translation of an oft-quoted maxim, *She ch'uh yiu ming*, 'For war you must have a cause,' which indicates that passion and cupidity were held in check by public opinion pronouncing its judgment in conformity with an acknowledged stangard of right.

Another maxim, equally well known, makes the justice of the cause a source of moral power which goes far to compensate the inequality of physical force.

'Soldiers are weak in a bad cause, but strong in a good one,' saidthe ancient Chinese, assigning as high a place to the moral element as our own poet, when he says, — 'Thrice is he armed who hath his quarrel just.'

Fourth: —A cause always recognized as just was the preservation of the balance of power.

This principlecalled to arms not merely the States immediately thretened, but those also which, by their situation, appeared to be remote from danger.

Not to speak of combinations to resist the aggressions of other disturbers of the public peace, we find, 320B. C, six States brought into line to repress the ambition of Chin. This powerful coalition, the fruit of twenty years' toil on the part of one man, who is immortalized as the type of the successful negotiator, was, we may add, after all destined to fail of its object. The common enemysucceeded in detaching the members of the league, and in overcoming them one after another. The arch of States which protected the throne of their suzerain being destroyed, the conqueror swept away the last vestige of the house of Cheo, which for eight hundred years had exercised a feudal supremacy over the princes of China. Proclaiming himself instead, under the title of ShuHwang-ti, the 'first of the universal sovereihns,' he abolished the feudal constitution of the empire, at the same time that he completed the Great Wall. His successor to the present day are called *Hwang-ti*, and the system of centralized government which he inaugurated is as firmly established as the Great Wall itself.

Fifth: —The right of existence, prior to the revolution just noticed, was, in general, held sacred for the greater States which held in fief from the Imperial Throne.

This right is often appealed to, and proves effectual in the direst extremity; *e. g*—the prince of Chi, at the head of a strongforce, enters Lu, with an evidently hostile intent. Chan-hi, a minister of Lu, is aent to meet him, in the hope of arresting his progress. 'The people of Lu appear to be very much alarmed at my approachy,' said the prince. 'True,' replied the minister, 'the people are alarmed, but the ruler is not.' when his troops are in disorder, and his magazines as empty as a bell? On what does he repose his confidence that he should affect to be superior to fear?

'He rests on the grant which his fathers received from the ancient emperors,' said the minister, He then proceeded to vindicate the rignts of his master, under what was recognized as the traditional law of the empire, with such force that the prince desisted from his purpose, and withdrew without any further act of violence.

A similsr instance, it will be remembered, has been cited already in another connection, —the case in which a prince, after urging in vain this same plea, —the sacredness of the imperial grant was saved from humiliation or extinct by the mediation of neighboring power, who recognized and were determined to uphold the principle.

A third example of the kind is one in which the existence of the now feeble remnant of the imperial domain was itself at stake. The Prince of Chu, after a victorious campaign against other foes, crossed the Rubicon and entered the territories of the house of Cheo, with the evident intention of seizing the imperial throne. The emperor, unable to oppose armed resistance, dispatched Wang Sun-man, one of his ministers, to cinvey a supply of provisions to the invading army, and to ascertain the designs of its leader. The latter veiled his purpose in figurative language, asking to be informed as to the 'weight of the nine tripods,' —insinuating that if not too heavy he intended to carry them away. The minister, without answering directly, gave the history of the yripods, relating how they had been cast in bronze by Ta Yu, the founder of the first great dynasty, and emblazoned with a chart of the empire in relief; how for fifteen centuries they had been preserved as emblems of the imperial dignity; and, exposing in a masterly manner the necessity of respect for that venerable power to the order of othe several States, he concluded by saying— 'All this being true, why should Your Highness ask the weight of the tripods'?

The chief, struck by the force of his arguments, which, like the most effective on such occasions, were purely historical, renounced his nefarious purpose, and retried to his own dominions.

Sixth: —Finally, the rights of neutrals were admitted, and to a certain extent respected.

It has been remarked that, in the wars of Greece, there were no neutrals; those who desired to be such, if they were so situated as to be of any weight in the conflict, being always compelled todeclare themselves on one side or the other. This was not the case in China. The neutral frequently rejected the overtures of both parties, and his territories interposed an effectual barrier in the way of the belligerents. We have numerous instances of passage being granted to troops without further participation in the conflict, and one case in which a wise statesman warns his master against the danger of such an imprudent concession. 'In a former war,' said he, 'you granted it to your detriment; if you do so again, it will be to your ruin.' His chief failed to profit by the warning; and the prince thus unjustly favored, after destroying his antagonist, turned about and took possession of the territory of his friend.

CONCLUSION

It is, as we have intimated, quite possible that text-books on the subject of international relations may have existed in ancient China, without coming down to our times, just as the Greeks had books on that subject, of which nothing now survives but their titles, Whether this conjecture be well founded or otherwise, enough remains, as we have ahown, to prove that *the States of ancient China had a Law written or unwritten, and more or less developed, which they recognized in peace and war.* The Book of Rites and the histories of the period attest this.

Of these histories, one was acknowledged as constituting in itself a kind of international code, I allude to the *Spring and Autumn Annals*, edited by Confucius, and extending over two centuries and a half. Native authors affirm that the awards of praise and blame expressed in that work, often in a single word, were accepted as judgments from which there was no appeal, and exercised a restraining influence more potent than that of armies and navies.

Chinese statesmen have pointed out the analogy of their own country at that epoch with the political divisions of modern Europe. In their own records they find usages, words, and ideas, corresponding to the terms of our mordern international law; and they are by that fact the more disposed to accept the international code of Christendom, which it is no utopian vision to believe will one day become a bond of peace and justice between all the nations of the earth."①

第五节 《陆地战例新选》

《陆地战例新选》（*Manual of the Law of War on Land*）是丁韪良1883年翻译的一部战时法规。全书由原序、丁韪良序、陈兰彬序以及正文八十六条战时规则组成。该书曾由国际法学会②于1897年编辑、出版。现将全书抄录如下：

《陆地战例新选》原序为：

粤籍史乘，战争古来常有，即将来亦在所不免。盖邦国欲自主而久存者，不得不有力以自护。然邦国多尚仁义，民俗亦较前

---

① W. A. P. Martin, D. D., Lld. Hanlin Papers——Essays on the History, Philosophy, and Religion of the Chinese. ShangHai: Kelly Walsh The Tientsin press, 1894, pp. 111 – 141.

② 国际法学会是一个民间机构，它规定："一、本会之意专在兴公法之学，并非奉官而设，乃众友心志相同。按时聚集，互相砥砺；二、会友不得逾六十之数，系由诸国而选之，其有功于公法之学者方能膺选。

第三章 京师同文馆翻译的其他国际法著作

《陆地战例新选》封一

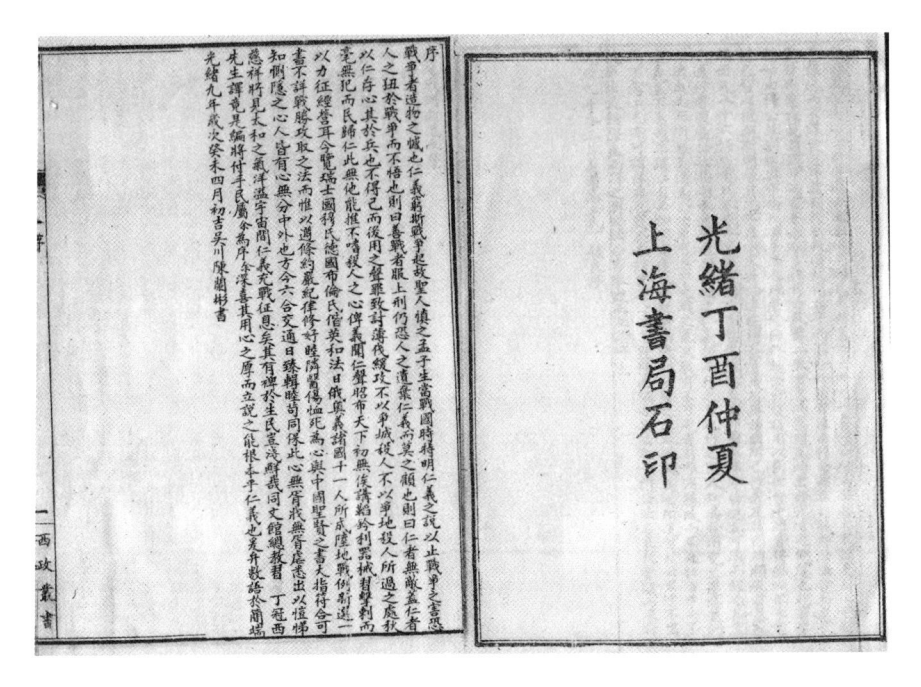

上海书局石印《陆地战例新选》（1897年）

归厚，则战争应有定例可遵，以免肆行残忍。一千八百七十四年，诸国于比国京都会议，其议虽未成，足征早有同心。公法固有战例，惟揆之人心民俗，尚可增添，以补旧章之所缺。诸国之会于比京，由俄皇创议，专为此事。今我公法会刊刻此书，亦此意也。前议未成，今则时逾六载。时势少为变更，故再四等划，通融立论，则本会所议或可冀其有成，所拟款目八十六条，皆不涉于新奇，均以顺时势、合实用为要，且不期诸国骤能以之入盟约，惟管见所及，恭献于执政者，以资采择而已。此书系本会派人纂辑，复经众友聚于鄂斯甫，逐款评论，莫不深许，方为付梓。其原派纂辑者，德之布伦氏、瑞士之穆尼耶，更有英和法日俄奥义等国十一人参议，共襄斯举。其有益于邦交者，阅者当然谅之。是为序。①

丁韪良所写序言为：

余前岁经过瑞士国，得识公法家穆尼耶，见惠《新选公法条例》一书。穆公以法学著名家称，素封心好行善，谋道而不谋食。近年诸国设法救济被伤兵卒，而不分畛域者，系由穆公诸君创议。即公法会新选交战条例，意在范围战争而免荼毒，亦多赖穆公鼓舞。二举事异而意同，盖均出于方寸之恻隐也。此书原稿始由穆公草创，继与布伦氏等十三人琢磨修饰，终经全会复议，用以问世。会中虽皆博学鸿儒，未尝恃己智以擅拟新例。缘其志不在撰文著论，专在博察远搜，务得诸国所已行者及诸国所愿行者，纂入编册，凡八十六条，皆有所本。或本交战常例，或本历代盟约，或本邦国军律，要视其可法而录之。其业已通行者，固属公法。其尚未通行者，邦国揆之仁义，择而行之可也。行之既久，知其合用，竟至遵为通例，公法由此而渐臻美备。马公法原有息争免战之策，然战有不可免者。则邦国扬威而不失仁，力争而不忘义，岂不美哉！非谓仁者必如宋襄公，俟敌军既济而成列始击之。其取败而为世所笑，然所云君子不重伤，不禽二毛，亦可谓厚非也。窃思本馆曾译公法书数种，此编亦公法之一门。公

---

① ［美］丁韪良等编译：《陆地战例新选》，上海书局石印1897年版，第2页。

法名家既会议而深许，故率法文馆学生而译之，与公法各书参观而互证可也。光绪九年春三月，美国惠三氏丁韪良序。①

陈兰彬所写序言为："战争者，造物之憾也。仁义穷，斯战争起。故圣人慎之。孟子生当战国时，特明仁义之说，以止战争之害。恐人狃于战争而不悟也。则曰，善战者服上刑。仍恐人之遗弃仁义而莫之顾也，则曰，仁者无敌。盖仁者，以仁存心，其于兵也，不得已而后用之。声罪致讨，薄伐缓攻。不以争城杀人，不以争地杀人。所过之处，秋毫无犯，而民归仁。此无他，能推不嗜杀人之心，俾义闻仁声昭布天下。初无俟讲韬钤、利器械、习击刺，而以力征经营耳。今览瑞士国穆氏、德国布伦氏，偕英和法日俄奥义诸国十一人，所成《陆地战例新选》一书，不详战胜攻取之法，而惟以遵条约、严纪律、修好睦邻、医伤恤死为心，与中国圣贤之书大旨符合。可知恻隐之心人皆有，心无分中外也。方今六合交通，日臻辑睦。苟同保此心，无胥戕，无胥虐，悉出以恺悌慈祥，将见太和之气洋溢宇宙间，仁义充，战争息矣。其有裨于生民，岂浅鲜哉！同文馆教习丁冠西先生译竟是编，将付手民，嘱余为序。余深喜其用心之厚，而立说之能根本乎仁义也。爰弁数语于简端。光绪九年岁次癸未四月初吉，吴川陈兰彬书。"②

《陆地战例新选》涉及战斗人员、武器、战俘、伤员、战时医院、战时占领等规定，共有八十六条：

第一条　交战乃战国军旅持械互掣而已，凡人民之不属军旅者，不得越俎而干预战争（按此条兵民有别，故下文遂将军旅二字辨明）。

第二条　所谓属军旅者，凡有四等：练军义勇，一也；民间团防，二也；水师战船，三也；民之未经团练而执兵自卫者，四

---

① ［美］丁韪良等编译：《陆地战例新选》，上海书局石印1897年版，第2页。
② ［美］丁韪良等编译：《陆地战例新选》，上海书局石印1897年版，第1页。

也。民间团防必须统以员弁，以专责成，穿有号衣，以资区别。所用军械，尤须明而不暗，三者缺一不可。

第三条　交战时，军旅兵卒必当遵照公法之战例。

第四条　按公法，害敌之方有合例，有不合例者。凡无济于事而徒害敌人之举，不可为之。凡背理违义以及残暴不仁之举，亦均不可为之（按彼德堡一千六百六十八年之条约，战国意在破败敌国兵势而已，此外若互相戕害，非正也）。

第五条　战时议立条约如休兵、投降等款，必当谨遵勿背。

第六条　此国若占踞必国地方，只可视为暂行管辖。两国未和以前，不得作为己有。

第七条　交战既属军旅之事，则民之循分无过者，毋得伤害之。

第八条　交战既有定例，则一切毒物概不得使用。不得设奸诈之谋以害敌命（如买人行刺，或佯为投降等事），不得冒敌国旗帜、号衣以攻不备。并不得假冒会议白旗以及各国条约所设护身、记号，均不得设诈使用。

第九条　交战既不宜徒害于人，即不得故意设法以伤害之，致令痛楚难医（如不及三两重之炸炮，内含火药，触物即发者等类）。凡敌人之业已投降，或不预战事者，毋得戕伤之。未战以前，不得以不受投降宣示。盖己虽不邀投降之例（有决意就死而弗降者），而仍须以之待敌焉。

第十条　凡病伤兵弁，无论所属何国，均应收留而善为调剂（自此条至下文第十八条，皆论病伤者及照料医药之人，俱应免于战场之险）。

第十一条　凡敌兵受伤而被执者，当时送交敌国，任其自行调剂可也。惟须揆度情形，实属可行，或两国业已允准，方得行之。

第十二条　凡专为收看病伤之公所，以及供事之人，均作为局外而恃以保护。

第十三条　诸医士、教士以及看管医所之人，运载照料病伤者，并各善会所派料理病伤人等，均按前条作为局外，一俟无病伤可看顾者而后已。

第十四条　如地方被敌占踞而医所仍有伤病者，应按上条所论医士、教士等，照常供职可也。

第十五条　此等人如呈请退境，该敌国带兵官应指定启程日期，非军务不得已，不可迟延而强留。

第十六条　如地方被据而此等人被敌国执留者，应酌给膳食养赡之资。

第十七条　因照料病伤而作为局外者，应以带红色十字之白布一条，缠膊为记。此等记号，统由将帅发给。

第十八条　战国之将帅应晓谕居民人等，照料被伤兵卒，并示以因此得邀何等利益。如遇居民前来供是役者，胥免损害。

第十九条　战场死尸皆不可剥去衣服，戕伤体骨。

第二十条　敌兵尸骸未及埋葬，应先查取所带之书籍、信件，以备考证姓氏，而免于混失。此等证据，宜交所属军营，或送交该国可也。

第二十一条　凡属军营之人，若被敌执，按第六十一款以战时被俘待之（凡明寄公文者，并乘气球而通信窥探等人，均归此类）。

第二十二条　至随从军旅而不属于军者，即如新报馆所派访事之人，并买办等，若被敌执，应行释放。非军务不得已，切弗延迟而强留。

第二十三条　凡疑为奸细而被执者，看待皆不得邀以战场俘虏之例。

第二十四条　敌军之将弁兵卒，遇有入境探听消息而衣冠无所假装者，不得以奸细待之。至明寄公文之人，与乘气球而探消息者，皆不得视为奸细（见上文二十一条）。

第二十五条　因疑为奸细而被执之人，未经照例审断者，不得擅行治罪（战时被执之人，恒有以奸细诬告者。即应谨遵此条，以免罪及无辜）。

第二十六条　遇奸细探听消息，业已出境而复经被执者，不可因前案而加罪焉。

第二十七条　凡奉官执白旗前来会议者，均作为公使论，以免伤害。

第二十八条　该公使跟随人等，如吹号筒、击鼓、张旗以及通言向导之人（各一人），均免伤害（此例出于不得已，且减祸有益。但彼国不得藉以为攻敌之计）。

第二十九条　遇有执白旗前来者，应否接纳，均由将帅揆度情形而定。

第三十条　来使既已接，待将帅亦须设法以备不预（该使并其随从之人，既蒙接待，即当谨遵条例，不可乘机谋害地主）。

第三十一条　如将帅疑此等公使有谋为不轨者，即可暂行拘留。若查实有用其公使之利益，以图奸害，则所享之处概行革除，而不以公使待之可也。

第三十二条　凡残忍无济于事之举既不可行，则城镇之被陷，断不得纵兵抢劫。非军务不得已，则房产无论公私，概不得肆行毁坏。城镇无人抵御，断不可无故开炮轰击。

第三十三条　凡城垣处所有守兵抵御者，虽例得轰击，仍应谨慎而行，以免殃及池鱼。是以将帅若非攻其不备，宜于未经开炮，先行设法知照地方官可也。

第三十四条　如轰击城垣，应设法以免损坏教堂、庙宇、书院等公所。惟此等公所，不得用之以资抵御，方得邀免。其被围者应于此等处所竖立旗号，并知照敌军方妥。

第三十五条　如有拯救病伤，而无保护医院之例，既难期有成效。是以按照冉奈发之条约，凡军营应需医所，均作为局外论。战国彼此加以保护，俟在彼不复有病伤者而后已。

第三十六条　民间房屋暂充医所以便安置病伤之人，亦皆作为局外论。

第三十七条　凡医院等所，若设兵保护，即不作为局外论。然巡街兵役看顾之，即与上条无妨。

第三十八条　医所有恒暂之别。其恒者，按照战例，统归胜者管辖。而医士人等虽得退出，除其私物外，一切物件，概不得携带。其暂者，不从此条。所有物件，俱可随人迁移无阻，故谓之行军医院。

第三十九条　凡行军应用医所以及房屋或暂充此用，或随军挪移，均作为行军医院论。

第四十条　凡医院等所，一体竖立白旗、带以红色十字，用示记号。而仍应竖国旗于其上以示谁属。

第四十一条　遇彼国军旅闯入此国地方，该地方官或逃遁，或号令不行，而彼国军旅有力以安民，即谓之占踞。其占踞境界之广狭、时日之久暂，皆由是而断。

第四十二条　客军占踞地方，既暂为管辖，即应先行晓谕居民，俾知秉以何权，并所据之境界广狭如何。

第十四三条　客军应竭力设法俾地方民众乐业安居，照常生理。

第四十四条　客军应令民等仍遵向来律例，非出于不得已，不可革除而更易之。

第四十五条　该地方大小官员等，有情愿照旧供职者，即当仰赖客军保护。惟客军有权以废之，官员亦有权以辞退。地方官若非寝职，或用之奸害客军，即不可以他故问罪。

第四十六条　客军得以揆度情形，而令地方绅士相助安民。

第四十七条　遇地方被敌国占踞，居民既未成为敌国之民，敌国即不得勒令降服。但居民如有执械抵御者，即可问罪。

第四十八条　地方既被占踞，而居民有不愿听受敌国号令者，敌国虽勒令遵照可也。然不得勒令充队以攻击本国，亦不得勒令在军营操作，如筑城、掘地等工（见第四条）。

第四十九条　不可无故伤害人命，亦不可肆行无忌，败人名节。其敬神修福之礼，概应准其遵行，断不可搅扰而阻碍之。

第五十条　客军虽代敌国暂行管辖，其未经和约，仍不得视其地为己有。惟该敌国之银库、军器库、仓房以及敌国所用以资争战者，均归客军充用。

第五十一条　敌国之舟车用以运载电线，用以通信，亦皆归客军充用。非军务不得已，不可毁坏。俟两国和约后，该地方交还此等公物，应照原来体式归之。

第五十二条　至敌国之公所，如宫殿、衙署树林以及公地，只归客军暂行调摄，仍宜谨加保护，以免损伤。

第五十三条　民之公产、公所，以及教会、善会、一切房产并庠序、学校、博物院等处，均免充公。此等处所并塔标、牌坊等，非军务不得已而擅行毁坏，均为严禁。

第五十四条　客军既不得擅据敌国之公产，其敌民之私产尤不得擅据之。故民之私产无论属一人，属众人，应加意保护。

第五十五条　舟车、电线、军器、火炮，无论属一人、属公司，均听客军据之。惟和约后，应照数交还，或偿以物价。

第五十六条　客军令军民捐输军需，应量民力而定之。非有急需，亦不可行也。凡此等勒捐，系由客军之统领而定，各将弁不得擅举。

第五十七条　至客军征税于国，课定例外，不应征以分文，且当用之以资治理如彼国无异。

第五十八条　遇客军征税，该居民有延不交纳者，则以银两罚之可也，但不得另设税课而征之。至勒令居民捐输银两，非有境内之文武大宪特谕而自任之，则不可行也。其摊派捐项之轻重，应照向来之国课办理。

第五十九条　凡遇摊牌款项以备兵卒之居住，或捐输粮草，若民间向有乐于照料病伤之人者，则应酌免之。

第六十条　遇捐输米谷以及各项军饷，应发给收条。因此等收条所系匪轻，即宜谨慎而行，弗可草率。

第六十一条　因禁俘虏原无治罪报仇之意，惟将其人拘留之，以免干预战事。至俘虏应如何看待，如何防范，则详见下文。战时被俘之人皆归俘之之国管辖，将弁于此不得擅权。

第六十二条　俘之之国军旅向有之例，该俘虏应一体遵行。

第六十三条　看待俘虏弗可暴虐不仁。

第六十四条　该俘虏除兵器外，一切私物仍为己有。

第六十五条　俘虏遇彼国询问姓名、品级等事，即应吐实不讳。倘有隐瞒情弊，则较他人处治稍严，以示惩警可也。

第六十六条　俘虏令居某城、某营、某境，禁其越界则可。惟关锁、囹圄，非万不得已，则不可行也。

第六十七条　俘虏如有不顺服之举，即从严惩治，不为违例。

第六十八条　遇俘虏脱逃而尾追之，应先令其止步。如违，虽以枪击之可也。如尚未越境，或未及本国军营，复被擒拿，可从严看守，以示薄惩，但不可视同罪犯。其业经出境，或已入本国营垒而后被执，则前案置若罔闻，不得追究。然该俘虏若已立誓不逃，后又背誓而潜逸，即革其俘虏之利益，以为惩罚可已。

第六十九条　某国若擒人为俘虏，即应给以养赡之资。若两国未经议立特款，则俘虏养赡之资即当与该国不出战之兵卒等。

第七十条　不得勉强俘虏以令助战，虽事之稍涉于战者，亦不可令其干预，不得勒令出具口供而泄本国之密机。

第七十一条　凡工作不直涉于战事者，若非异常劳苦，亦不为凌辱（其事之有无耻辱，自应揆度其人之出身而定），即令其操作可也。

第七十二条　该俘虏如准其为民间佣工操作者，其工价应由上司收储，或用之以资供给，或存之以俟释放时，再行发给可也。

第七十三条　两国业经讲和，彼此所擒之俘虏俱应释放，盖不复有拘禁之故也。然如何释放之处，均由两国妥议而行。

第七十四条　两国业经讲和，彼此所擒之俘虏，俱应释放。盖不复有拘禁之故也。然如何释放之处，均由两国妥议而行。

第七十五条　战事未毕，两国将帅会议互换俘虏亦可。①

---

① ［美］丁韪良等编译：《陆地战例新选》，上海书局石印1897年版，第1—7页。

第七十六条　两国虽无互换俘虏之举，若律法无所禁阻，将帅将其所擒获者，令之立誓不复充兵而释放之，可也。如遇俘虏立誓得以自由，所许者应详细注册，该俘虏亦当谨遵弗违。既归本国，该国不应令其干预战事，以致背信。

第七十七条　俘虏有不愿立誓以得释放者，断不可勒令立誓。其俘虏之请立誓而得释放者，该国准否，皆听自便。

第七十八条　遇俘虏立誓而得释放者，若充兵而复攻释放之国，一经被执，则不予以俘虏之利益可也。惟其既经释放，而后有登名于互换册者，则所立之誓作为销除，虽当兵而被执者，亦不失其利益焉。

第七十九条　局外之国遇战国败兵逃避入境，应将该败兵择地而划界以居之。俾与战场远隔，以免干预战争。如遇战国之人借局外之地，以加害敌国，该局外之国亦应谨防而阻止之（局外之国若有稍助于战国者，即涉于偏袒。至听战国借地，尤当谨防。然遇战国败兵逃避入境，以期免死，倘该国拒而不纳，是为不仁之甚）。

第八十条　凡此等人（指败兵越境求护者）除划地而禁之，令居营寨或城垣，均无不可（宜斟酌便宜而行也）。至将弁令其立誓，不出国而稍听自由，以示优待亦可。

第八十一条　至于此等拘禁之兵，其养瞻之资，若条约未及言明如何办理之处，则一切所需者，均仰给于局外之国。其所携带兵器、炮火等件，皆由局外之国收存。两国和后，或未和以前，该败兵等所属之本国，应将其资费照数归还，以免累及友国。

第八十二条　至病伤者以及料理病伤之医士等人，并避入局外之境者，其如何办理之处，均应遵照冉奈发一千八百六十四年所立之条约（第十条至第十八条、第三十五条至第四十条、第五十九条至第七十四等条）。

第八十三条　假道局外之国，以便运载病伤兵卒，虽未为俘虏，亦无所妨碍。惟携带物件，应为病伤所需，非为战者所需也。该局外之过亦应一路加意保护，以免有违例之举。

第八十四条　遇人擅犯以上诸条，敌国若力所能为者，即可惩治。惟须详细审问，而准被告者自行辨明，以便定断。人之违犯军例者，按各国之刑典惩治亦可。然本人若已远飏，断难加罪，则报复于敌国，以警不法，未为不可。至报复之例，罪及无辜，在所不免。故心怀仁义者，决不可轻行之。如用之，应以下文两条节之。

第八十五条　若敌国之人有违例加害之举，而后日行赔补者，断不可以报复。

第八十六条　若不得已而行报复，则所加之害，不可甚于敌国之所为。非将帅允准，亦不可行之。虽行报复，总不得有违于仁义。

第四章 《法国律例》的翻译与出版

第一节 《法国律例》

《法国律例》成书于1880年,由毕利干口译,时雨化笔述。目前国内所见的版本为"同文馆聚珍版",该版本6函46卷。其编排顺序及卷数依次为:《刑名定范》4卷、《刑律》4卷、《贸易定律》6卷、《园林则律》2卷、《民律》22卷、《民律指掌》8卷。《法国律例》先后出版了湖北官书局本、上海点石斋石印本、求富强斋石印本等多个版本。传入日本后,明治十五年(1882年)出版了由郑永宁训点的版本。其编排顺序与卷数与"同文馆聚珍版"不尽相同:

篇名	卷	法条	页
刑名定范	2	643	347
刑律	4	484	271
民律	3(部)	2281	1399
民律指掌	5	1041	545
贸易定律	4	648	418
园林则律		226	65

王文韶为该书作有序言,在对毕利干褒奖一番后说:该书"缕析条分,秩然璨然。夫中外风俗各殊,自有不必从同之处。而以备博采周知,则是书之翻译,未始非留心律例者所宜浏览也"[①]。

---

① [法]毕利干:《法国律例·序》,日本司法省1894年版。

日本司法省1894年出版的《法国律例》

关于这六部书的内容，毕利干在《凡例序》中介绍该书：

> 翻译《法国律例》之设，实为本国四民一切行止动作，划一界限，使之有所率循，不致或获于罪也。盖其创设之律例，皆出于至正。至公至当，无可迁就，无可更易。合乎天理，准乎人情，而为一确乎不移知权衡也。其合乎天理者，即如由天所生之律例，系人生自然而然，包含于人性之中者。如父母者于其子女，自具一慈爱之心。为子女者于其父母，应有孝顺之情，实为不能不遵循之律例。不惟于一方应行遵循，即推诸东西南北，或遐或迩制地，亦未有或可改易也。故曰，由天所生之律例，其准乎人情者，即为自然天生。律例以外由人所加增，使人于一切遇事交涉之际，亦如划一界限，使之有所率循而不得少有所违也。但其所制律例，未能一道同风，寔因各地风化习俗有异。因此，律例亦不能推行利，应即按各地习俗与其处人民事业之盛衰，而制以各项殊异之律例。并定以应赏应罚之定制，使人遇事有所率

循。虽系由人所加增，而确为国政人事，至公至当，未可稍易之权衡也。故曰：由人所加增之律例，其于通共所制律例之中，复分为六类：一曰《刑律》、一曰《刑名定范》、一曰《贸易定律》、一曰《园林则律》、一曰《民律》、一曰《民律指掌》。《刑律》系分明解说，指定如干某例，即获某罪，并应科以何刑。其所制《刑名定范》，系陈明某项罪案，应归某官员所管，该官应选某例而科定其罪也。其所制《贸易定律》，系陈明一切商贸交易之事，并于一切运载各货，或系雇贷市船，并市夫水手及铺户、生意赔累、倒行打账等事，均归《贸易定律》，因案按例衡之。其所制《园林则律》，实为国家之要务。不仅可取其材，及于风雨之调顺，地势之通畅。并所有园林，有属之于官，亦有属之于民者，遇事均宜按例遵行。而仍有大关于农务者，向已议设农工之例，附入幅后，尚未刊行。其所制之《民律》，系制定民间一切私利之事业。而此《民律》，夫分为三纲，共计二千二百八十一条。其一纲论人，二纲论资财，三纲论以何法能或赀财利益，并互相有勉行应尽之责。其所制《民律指掌》，系制定各项围范，以便人人行其所执之权也。一遇因事到官考其所执之权，是否切实。如无异议，则其所执之权，系为牢不可破之权，应令照权遵行。兹译原书开首例序，有如是者。

由于汉语水平的限制，与丁韪良等人翻译的国际法著作相比较，毕利干主持翻译的《法国律例》显得晦涩难懂，梁启超曾在1896年发表的《变法通议》中说："中国旧译，惟同文馆本多法家言。——然彼时受笔者，皆馆中新学诸生，未受专门，不能深知其义，故义多闇。即如《法国律例》一书，欧洲亦以为善本，而馆译之本，往往不能达其意，且常有一字一句之颠倒漏略，至与原文相反者。"尽管如此，《法国律例》还是在一定范围内产生了影响。康有为曾系统阅读过《法国律例》，他不仅对弟子讲授其内容，还熟练地在文章中引述："今按《法国律例》民律第一条云，此律例系由国王颁行，凡列名于法国版图中者，无一人不应钦尊谨守。第十八条云，凡形同叛逆，欲行谋害国王者,照弑父大逆重案科罪。此条在论治叛逆,与不论尊卑僭分干犯国王及宗室一条内,皆道名分者,不能悉数。"① 梁启超曾将《法国律例》列为湖南时务学堂的必修科目,并在《西学书目表》中提醒读者:"《法国律例》名为'律例',实则拿破仑治国之规模在焉,不得以刑书读也。"

《法国律例》所包含的六部法典,就是今天的《刑事诉讼法》、《刑法》、《民法》、《民事诉讼法》、《海商法》(《公司法》)、《森林法》。

第二节 《法国律例·民律》②

《法国律例·民律》分为三部分:(一)"论举国生众,并论有可得例应,系法人分中可获者",划分为"论于一切之人有应享受例应与有禁止享受例应者"等十一类。(二)"论一切家资财产之事以及名下所属各类之物",划分为"论各项家资财产之区别"等四类。(三)"论以何法而致有操持物主之权,试将其事约略而陈其情",划分为"论相继接产"等二十类。

毕利干译《法国律例·民律》与林纪东等主编《民法》目录对比表③

毕利干译《法国律例·民律》	林纪东等主编《民法》
第一卷 论举国生众并论有可得例应,系法人分中可获者	第一编 总则
第一类 论于一切之人有应享受例应于有禁止享受例应者	第一章 法例
第一章 论人有应享受之例应系于法人分中可获得者	第二章 人
第二章 论人有禁止享受一切都会土著可得之例应者	第一节 自然人

---

① 康有为:《康子内外篇》,中华书局1988年版,第170页。
② 参见拙文《〈法国律例·民律〉与近代西方民法及其术语的输入》,《惠州学院学报》2015年第2期。
③ [法]毕利干:《法国律例·民律·目录》,日本司法省1894年版;林纪东等主编:《民法·目录》,五南图书出版公司1986年版。

续表

毕利干译《法国律例·民律》		林纪东等主编《民法》	
第一节	论人禁止其享受都会土著可得之例应者。因其虽为法国之人，而因事已失其本国可邀之分力，则自应禁止享受一切福泽利益矣	第二节	法人
第二节	论有禁止享受法国可邀之例应者，系因其人曾经因罪而被该管官有科断之罪	第三章	物
第二类	论众民所立婚丧产育之合同	法律行为	
第一章	论所立合同大致情形	第一节	通则
第二章	论产育之合同	第二节	行为能力
第三章	论办理一切婚姻之合同	第三节	意思表示
第四章	论办理一切丧事之合同	第四节	条件及期限
第五章	论婚姻产育丧事之合同，而子系兵弁于法国境界外者	第五节	代理
第六章	论呈请更正各项合同之事	第六节	无效及撤销
第三类	论人所弃居址地	期日及期间	
第四类	论其人现时不在场者	消灭时效	
第一章	论尚未得确据，亦无实在把握而悬揣其人或不在场者	第二编	债
第二章	论已经报明周知其人实系不在场者	第一章	通则
第三章	论有人不在场者之所关系	第一节	债之发生
第一节	论不在场者之所关系，系其所有房产土地等项者	第二节	债之标的
第二节	论不在场者之所关系，系关于将来偶尔能得与否，而有例应可享受其遗产者	第三节	债之效力
第三节	论不在场者之所关系婚姻之事者	第四节	多数债务人及债权人
第四章	论应者某人现时不在场者，其所出后嗣弱冠孩童之例	第五节	债之转移
第五类	论结联婚姻之理	第六节	债之消灭
第一章	论查其势分并课强受物之情，以便乾坤两造而结联婚姻之事	第二章	各种之债
第二章	论办理结联婚姻事宜，一切礼节仪文之条例	第一节	买卖
第三章	论于一切结联婚姻之事，而有例应能以遏阻者之条例	第二节	互易
第四章	论于一切婚姻事件，有应呈请注销者	第三节	交互计算
第五章	论于婚姻事中有应尽之责者	第四节	赠与
第六章	论男女两造所携例例应于其人彼此应行之本分	第五节	租赁
第七章	论将既结之婚遇事而灭绝者	第六节	借贷

第四章 《法国律例》的翻译与出版

续表

毕利干译《法国律例·民律》		林纪东等主编《民法》	
第八章	论续娶而兴转嫁之事	第七节	雇佣
第六类	论婚姻应行离异之例	第八节	承揽
第一章	论缘何离异之由	第九节	出版
第二章	论缔结婚姻事宜有特定缘由	第十节	委任
第一节	论特定之缘由与离异之围范	第十一节	经理人及代办商
第二节	论有一切应行离异事件,既经接据其呈,应暂时接办其案中要件	第十二节	居间
第三节	论凡有离异之请而揆之于例应不允其所请者	第十三节	行纪
第三章	论夫妇因事离异,实系两造互相情愿者	第十四节	寄托
第四章	论夫妇离异者之所关系	第十五节	仓库
第五章	论夫妇两造因事有关夫妇异居者	第十六节	运送营业
第七类	论为父者之势分,与其所应领属,并论其一脉正根子女辈所接替之事	第十七节	承揽运送
第一章	论所生后嗣,系按例结婚时事中所出,名正言顺之正根者	第十八节	合伙
第二章	论倚恃何等约据而知所生子女系一脉正根亲身之子女者	第十九节	隐名合伙
第三章	论非按例婚姻时事中所生子女而系私出者	第二十节	指示证券
第一节	论以私出之子女而冒充正根子女者之例	第二十一节	无记名证券
第二节	论办理私出之子女应行识志之例	第二十二节	终身定期金
第八类	论一切过继子女之理,并论充当义父系其人自行情甘充当者	第二十三节	和解
第一章	论一切过继子女之理	第二十四节	保证
第一节	论过继子女与其理中所有之关系	第三编	物权
第二节	论办理过继事务之围范	第一章	通则
第二章	论办理过继事务并论情甘充当养父之责者	第二章	所有权
第九类	论为父者所执之威权,独有关于其子女者	第一节	通则
第十类	论弱冠子女之事,并论为义父者应有栽培训诲之事,并准其自主事业之事	第二节	不动产所有权
第一章	论人于弱冠之时	第三节	动产所有权
第二章	论栽培训诲之事	第四节	共有
第一节	论为父母者,于其子女有应充当养父之责	第三章	地上权
第二节	论为父母者,应寄托何人办理一切栽培训诲之事	第四章	永佃权

续表

毕利干译《法国律例·民律》	林纪东等主编《民法》
第三节 论栽培训诲之事,系其尊长辈经理者	第五章 地役权
第四节 论栽培训诲之事,出自其家亲会议所寄托者	第六章 抵押权
第五节 论为副义父之事	第七章 质权
第六节 论宽免办理栽培训诲之事,其所以宽免之原由	第八章 典权
第七节 论办理栽培训诲之事,其人之才有不能胜任者,并论未善其事,有应驱逐其人者有应将其人驳斥者	第九章 留置权
第八节 论为义父者,经手所宜办理之事	第十章 占有
第九节 论为义父者,于办理一切栽培训导事中出入款项若干,作何交代章程	第四编 亲属
第三章 论一切弱冠者,年至准其自理事业之事	第一章 通则
第十一类 论已冠者、被禁者,应由家亲会议禁止其人等料理一切私事及须佐之,以详为代办者	第二章 婚姻
第一章 论人为已冠者	第一节 婚约
第二章 论人为被禁者之事	第二节 结婚
第三章 论详为代办者	第三节 婚姻之普遍效力
第二部 论一切家资财产之事,以及名下所属各类之物	第四节 夫妻财产制
第一类 论各项家资财产之区别	第五节 离婚
第一章 论房产、土地等项为定资者	第三章 父母子女
第二章 论各类动资质物	第四章 监护
第三章 论人所有一切产物而有干系于本物者	第一节 未成年人之监护
第二类 论人于一切物件而有操持物主之权者	第二节 禁治产人之监护
第一章 论一切生物而有操持物主之权者	第五章 扶养
第二章 论有操持之权,系于物之本质相合而为一质者	第六章 家
第一节 论有操持物主之权而于一切定资质物者	第七章 亲属会议
第二节 论有操持物主之权而于动资项上者	第五编 继承
第三类 论享受沾利代守之事,与使用一切物件及居处其地之权者	第一章 遗产继承人
第一章 论有例应享受沾利代守之业者	第二章 遗产之继承
第一节 论沾利代守者所挟制例应	第一节 效力
第二节 论沾利代守者有勉应尽之责	第二节 限定之继承
第三节 论沾利代收之事,合意即为其事告终之时	第三节 遗产之分割
第二章 论语一切事物所以使用之例应,并与所居处之例应	第四节 继承之抛弃

续表

毕利干译《法国律例·民律》	林纪东等主编《民法》
第四类　论有借益于人及关径借益之事	第五节　无人承认之继承
第一章　论借益之事，系因其天然地之形势而然者	第三章　遗嘱
第二章　论借益之事，系因律例拟定而设者	第一节　通则
第一节　论两益之墙与两益之沟洫	第二节　方式
第二节　论两主人所占房基相距之数，并建立护垣之事	第三节　效力
第三节　论凿壁偷光于邻院者	第四节　执行
第四节　论一切房屋之房脊，并滴檐以及通流水路、天沟之事	第五节　撤销
第五节　论来往路径之例应	第六节　特留分
第三章　论有关涉人之原由而设立借益之事者	
第一节　论于各项产物、土地而有借益之事者	
第二节　论以何法而能设立借益之事	
第三节　论收受借益事务之主人所可得之一切例应	
第四节　论何如情形即致将借益之事息绝者	
第三部　论以何法而致有操持物主之权，试将其事约略而陈其情	
第一类　论相继接产之事	
第一章　论相继接产之事，并有承受遗产之人所得一切利益之事	
第二章　论有何等势分始可由相继接产之事	
第三章　论一切分应相继接产之次序	
第一节　论相继接产之事大略情形	
第二节　论有权能以相代承受父业者	
第三节　论相继接产之事应归给其后辈者	
第四节　论相继接产之事应归给长辈者	
第五节　论相继接产之事应归给于旁族者	
第四章　论相继接产之事系出于循分之外而得之者	
第一节　论私生子女于其父母产业之例应，并私子死亡而无嗣可承此遗产之例应者	
第二节　论夫妇之中，其现时生存之或夫或妇，并论遗产吾人承受，应归于公者之例应	
第五章　论收留相继接产之事，并论推辞相继接产之事	
第一节　论收留相继接产之事	
第二节　论推辞相继接产之事	
第三节　论所收留系有盈无亏之遗产，并其事中之关系与收留者应尽之责	

续表

毕利干译《法国律例·民律》	林纪东等主编《民法》
第四节　论虚悬相继接产之事	
第六章　论分析遗产之围范，并论事先所授之产物，今经分析，复将所授者取出，以敷分数之不足者	
第一节　论分析遗产之围范	
第二节　论事先曾有收受之物，今经分析遗产，应即将原物取出，以敷其分析数之不足者	
第三节　论于分析遗产，分中而有欠负之端，应发给银两照数清偿者	
第四节　论分析遗产事中之所关系，并论各同受遗产之人，于其事中有互相保护之理	
第五节　论遗产既经分析，而其事中尚有未能尽美尽善之处，应行复为分析之事者	
第二类　论人有生前付物者之情，并论曾有遗书之事者	
第一章　论其事之大略情形	
第二章　论将物件有给予于人之权，并论有收受物件之权者，盖缘事中曾有生前付物之情，或有遗书之命者	
第三章　论有任便给付之产之事，并论于其事中有提取所逾之数，于其数种量加减除之事	
第一节　论任便给付之产，并论其数目多寡之事	
第二节　论于给付之物件，或俾以遗念之物，而以任便给付之产之数，计其所逾之数，量加减除提取之事	
第四章　论有生前付物者之事	
第一节　论生前付物者之围范	
第二节　论有生前付物之情，系按例其事定而不移者，亦有时应行破以成格者	
第五章　论凡立具遗书者，其所具一切情形之事	
第一节　论立具遗书者，其事中大旨围范	
第二节　论致志专备数条之例，而为立具遗书者之围范	
第三节　论指挥某人可以为相继接产之人，并论有人可以给以遗念之物者	
第四节　论给以遗念之物，系有普权齐备之情者	
第五节　论于普权齐备之中，系抽分给之者	

续表

毕利干译《法国律例·民律》	林纪东等主编《民法》
第六节 论有特给遗念之物者	
第七节 论有监收之人而于遗书项上者	
第八节 论于遗书而有翻悔成议,并论所立遗书系衰迈不合时者	
第六章 论例准承受之事及其孙子女,并其侄儿女、甥儿女辈者	
第七章 论各辈尊长而将产业分晰,各授于其子女及其后嗣者	
第八章 论给付物件之事,而于立具婚嫁资产契之时,并论给付物件而于夫妇两造之中,及其子女者	
第九章 论夫妇两造互相给予物件之情,或系按照婚嫁资产契而为者,或于结亲后即立合同,互相给之一物者	
第三类 论立具合同,并一切盟约契券之事	
第一章 论合同盟约契券等事,初基之大略	
第二章 论所具合同其中一切紧要情节,委系结实可靠与否	
第一节 论于合同而有甘心遵允之事者	
第二节 论于立具合同者,其人是否能有办理其事之权	
第三节 论于合同中所载之物,即如合同之本质,而究之系为何事所立具者	
第四节 论立具合同之缘由	
第三章 论应尽之责事中之所关系	
第一节 论事中大略情形	
第二节 论应尽之责而于给付物件项上者	
第三节 论于应尽之责或于一事应为,或于一事系不应为者	
第四节 论有赔补安慰之需,系因于所应尽之责有不遵照而为者	
第五节 论于合同、契约等件,而有应讲解文义者	
第六节 论契约之中所具各项关系,系向之于他人者	
第四章 论于应尽之责,其事中之等类	
第一节 论应尽之责而有课程受物之情者	
第二节 论应尽之责,而于将来之事而指定异日某时者	
第三节 论应尽之责,系选给两益酬报者	
第四节 论应尽之责,而事中彼此有承担之责者	
第五节 论应尽之责,或系能分晰而为者,或系不能分晰而为者	
第六节 论于应尽之责,系有惩罚之情者	
第五章 论以何事而于应尽之责即为灭而绝之	

续表

毕利干译《法国律例·民律》	林纪东等主编《民法》
第一节　论以资补债即可无事	
第二节　论向所约据者，而今则有更易从新之事	
第三节　论债主于所还补欠款而有宽免交纳者	
第四节　论冲折欠款以为还补者	
第五节　论以其两造之权可以相消而等于无者	
第六节　论于所欠之物事竟有遗失情者	
第七节　论有将所立合同而销毁者，并有减撤之情者	
第六章　论于应尽之责，而呈有切确不移之据，并论于还补欠款而呈有切实之凭据者	
第一节　论以书信字据而以之为凭者	
第二节　论以事中见证人所语言而以之为执者	
第三节　论凭虚逆料，由此事而推及于彼事中之所关系者	
第四节　论在事之人，有识认真确之情者	
第五节　论矢誓之事	
第四类　论因事相及遵照而行，却系并未立有契约者	
第一章　论类似立有契约者	
第二章　论所行事有干于罪者，并类似近似于罪者	
第五类　论婚嫁资产契，并一切夫妇两造所挟之例应者	
第一章　论其事之大略情形	
第二章　论合资营生者之围范	
第一节　论合资营生事中所含一切物件，系关于所出之款及所储之项者	
第二节　论经理合资营生事务，并该夫妇两造所行之事，而有关系于合资营生事中者	
第三节　论灭绝合资营生事务，而有数项关系者	
第四节　论收留合资营生，并?联合资营生之事，及与此二事而有课程受物之情者	
第五节　论有分晰合资营生之事，而于收留之后者	
第六节　论推辞合资营生之事，并论其事中之所关系者	
第二项　论合资营生系二人合心共意而为者，并论其合心共意立具文约，能以将第一项按照定例而为者，所定事宜，更易其事，或将其事销撤不存者	

第四章 《法国律例》的翻译与出版

续表

毕利干译《法国律例·民律》	林纪东等主编《民法》
第一节 论合资营生事务,惟有应得之一物者	
第二节 论有一项情形,系于动资之物,或为统共之数,或为一分之数而为合资营生事务以外之物者	
第三节 论将定资之物入于合资营生事中,而变易其情,等于动资之物者	
第四节 论将欠款而有分晰之情形	
第五节 论为妇者,将其随嫁之资提取收回,而即为了结无干,并即为减免一切费用之情者	
第六节 论预沾其惠系立有约据者	
第七节 论所办事务情形,系为酌定于合资营生事中所得之分数有不相等者	
第八节 论合资营生事务系关普享其利者	
第九节 论所立一切情节,系出于合资营生事外者	
第三章 论事有只享其利而不能亏其原本者,其事中之围范	
第一节 论设立随嫁之赀事中一切情形	
第二节 论为夫者所挟之例应,而有于随嫁之赀者,并此赀根底系牢固而不能撼移者	
第三节 论随嫁之赀事中而有偿补之情者	
第四节 论有定动之赀,系逾乎随嫁定动赀以外者	
第六类 论售卖物件之例	
第一章 论售卖者所行之事,并其事之情形及其事之围范	
第二章 论何为售卖者,并论何以为赔买者	
第三章 论例准能以售卖之物	
第四章 论售卖物件者应尽之责	
第一节 论总论售卖事中大略情形	
第二节 论发交所售物件之事	
第三节 论保质物件之理	
第五章 论于购买者,其所应尽之责	
第六章 论售卖之事,有化为无有情事者,并有解散其交易情事者	
第一节 论执有售而复购之权者	
第二节 论售卖物件之事,而有减撤之情,系因所售之物而有损伤,关涉为价过廉者	

续表

毕利干译《法国律例·民律》	林纪东等主编《民法》
第七章 论未易分晰之物,而有数物主应按合总喝卖之事行之者	
第八章 论于债欠之事,而有自此转移于彼之情者,并于无关质之例应,而亦有自此转移于彼之情者	
第七类 论以一物而还补一物之事	
第八类 论事关雇赁所立之合同	
第一章 论其事之大约情形	
第二章 论雇赁物件之事	
第一节 论所立章程,系为公同于房产,并于土地、庄田项上,而有立具租券者	
第二节 论租赁房屋契约而有特定之章程	
第三节 论因庄田所立租券而有特定章程	
第三章 论雇赁之事于人工艺业项上者	
第一节 论雇赁之事系于仆隶匠役者	
第二节 论车夫而与船户之遄行,或系由旱路者,或系由水路者	
第三节 论论工酌价,并议价事宜	
第四章 论包收分滋利之契	
第一节 论其事之大略情形	
第二节 论包收分滋利契,系按寻常之规而立具者	
第三节 论所立包收分滋利契系按均分者	
第四节 论所立包收分滋利契,系由本物主给与包收分滋利契者,或给以庄田,或给以招垦之事者	
第五节 论所立 包收分滋利契,而竟有谬称强谓为包收分滋利契之类	
第九类 论社会中所立合同之例	
第一章 论事之大略情形	
第二章 论各项社会之事	
第一节 论所立之社会,系有普全齐备之情者	
第二节 论所立社会系独指某项情事者	
第三章 论众会友彼此勉行遵契而为,并有关于局外他人者	
第一节 论勉行遵契而为,系于会友中者	
第二节 论会友勉行遵契而为,系于局外他人者	
第四章 论有何等一切情势,始可致社会至于灭绝之时	
第十类 论各项借贷物件之理	

第四章 《法国律例》的翻译与出版　211

续表

毕利干译《法国律例·民律》	林纪东等主编《民法》
第一章　论借贷于使用之物者	
第一节　论借贷于使用之物，系循其事之围范者	
第二节　论借贷物件者，其所遵契而行之事，系为其人应尽之责	
第三节　论借物于人，遵契而行，系为其所应尽之责	
第二章　论所借贷之物，系关乎食饮之物者，或仅言借贷者	
第一节　论所借贷之物，其使用系循其事之围范者	
第二节　论以物借之于人者，其有所应尽之责	
第三节　论借贷物件者，其所应尽之责	
第三章　论有利息之借贷者	
第十一类　论储留物件而与押质物件之事	
第一章　论储留物件大略情形，并其事有分为数类者	
第二章　论物件仅为储留而已者	
第一节　论储留物件文约之本意	
第二节　论心甘储留物件之事	
第三节　论为人储留物件者，其所应尽之责	
第四节　论欲行储留物件者，其所应尽之责	
第五节　论实需储留诸物之事者	
第三章　论一切押质之事	
第一节　论押质等类之事者	
第二节　论押质之事，系由人自行立具者	
第三节　论押质之事系由官谕而立具者	
第十二类　论所立之文约，系利言听命，由天而为遇事恃运者	
第一章　论各项赌博与打赌之事	
第二章　论所设议定之资，系至死方休者	
第一节　论一切议立文约情节，其事中所应有者而尽有之，则其文约始为结实可据	
第二节　论所立文约系有关系而于在事之众者	
第十三类　论立具文约系为一事，命人代操其权者	
第一章　论命人代操其权其事中之情形并其事之一切围范	
第二章　论为人代操其权者应尽之责	
第三章　论命人代操其权者应尽之责	
第四章　论待操其权，系致有何等情势，即可至于灭绝之时	

续表

毕利干译《法国律例·民律》	林纪东等主编《民法》
第十四类　论因事而有备质之银	
第一章　论备质之事而有巨细轻重之别,并其情形或质之一银,或有保质之事者	
第二章　论为保质者,其事中所有之关系	
第一节　论为保质者之干系,系于债主与保质之本身者	
第二节　论为保质者之关系,系在欠债者而与为保质者	
第三节　论保质之关系,系于数为保质者	
第三章　论所设保质之情势,至有灭绝之事者	
第四章　论保质之事有二项情形,一系遇事循例而自有者,一系因词讼经官所定拟者	
第十五类　论减数相就而理之事者	
第十六类　论拘勒其身而乃关涉于民例者	
第十七类　论一切备质之事	
第一章　论备质之事而于动资之物者	
第二章　论所备质之物系以定资之物者	
第十八类　论倚势沾光并指物沾利之事	
第一章　论其事之大略情形	
第二章　论倚势沾光之事	
第一节　论于动赀项上而有倚势沾光之事者	
第二节　论倚势沾光之事,系关于定赀之物者	
第三节　论倚势沾光之事,系兼关于定、动二资项上者	
第四节　论以何法能以维持存留倚势沾光之权	
第三章　论各项指物沾利之事	
第一节　论由律例生发而有然者指物沾利之事	
第二节　论由官所定而应然者之指物沾利之事	
第三节　论两造互相议定而当然者指物沾利之事	
第四节　论指物沾利字次序	
第四章　论指物沾利一切情事而诣官注册之法要	
第五章　论于指物沾利事中而有删减之情,或于所余者而有减撤之事	
第六章　论指物沾利并倚势沾光之事,关系于接受其事者之他人	
第七章　关于指物沾利并倚势沾光而有灭绝之情	

续表

毕利干译《法国律例·民律》	林纪东等主编《民法》
第八章　论指物沾利并倚势沾光之事，而具有疏通其事之行者	
第九章　论有妇之夫，与为弱冠之义父者，其所有定资之物原有指物沾利之权，未经注于官册，则以何法而疏通之	
第十章　论掌册簿之官，其责应令众人周知，以便悉知其实者	
第十九类　论勒撤物主之权，并非物主情甘及各债主例应之次序	
第一章　论勒撤其物主之权者	
第二章　论为债主者，其于分拨售物价值，其事中先后之次序	
第二十类　论例准援免之事	
第一章　论其事之大略情形	
第二章　论于物而有操持之权者之理	
第三章　论遇一切事故，而致有阻止其例准援免之事者	
第四章　论于一切事故，有能以隔断例准援免之事者，亦有能以暂时悬系例准援免之事者	
第一节　论有事故系能隔断例准援免之事者	
第二节　论一切事故系能暂时悬系例准援免之事者	
第五章　论所得之时光足敷行其例准援免之事	
第一节　论事之大略情形	
第二节　论例准援免之事系以三十年为止者	
第三节　论例准援免之事，或以十年为止者，或以二十年为止者	
第四节　论例准援免之事，系由特意而破以成格者	

毕利干译《民律》① 与《中华人民共和国民法典》目录对比表

毕利干译《法国律例·民律》	《中华人民共和国民法典》
第一卷　论举国生众并论有可得例应，系法人分中可获者	第一编　总则
第一类　论于一切之人有应享受例应于有禁止享受例应者	第一章　法例
第一章　论人有应享受之例应系于法人分中可获得者	第二章　自然人

---

① [法] 毕利干：《法国律例·民律·目录》，日本司法省1894年版；《中华人民共和国民法典·目录》。

续表

毕利干译《法国律例·民律》	《中华人民共和国民法典》
第二章 论人有禁止享受一切都会土著可得之例应者	第一节 民事权利能力与民事行为能力
第一节 论人禁止其享受都会土著可得之例应者。因其虽为法国之人，而因事已失其本国可邀之分力，则自应禁止享受一切福泽利益矣	第二节 监护
第二节 论有禁止享受法国可邀之例应者，系因其人曾经因罪而被该管官有科断之罪。	第三节 宣告失踪和宣告死亡
第二类 论众民所立婚丧产育之合同	第四节 个体工商户和农村承包经营者
第一章 论所立合同大致情形	第三章 法人
第二章 论产育之合同	第一节 一般规定
第三章 论办理一切婚姻之合同	第二节 营利法人
第四章 论办理一切丧事之合同	第三节 非营利法人
第五章 论婚姻产育丧事之合同，而子系兵弁于法国境界外者	第四节 特别法人
第六章 论呈请更正各项合同之事	第四章 非法人组织
第三类 论人所弃居址地	第五章 民事权利
第四类 论其人现时不在场者	第六章 民事法律行为
第一章 论尚未得确据，亦无实在把握而悬揣其人或不在场者	第一节 一般规定
第二章 论已经报明周知其人实系不在场者	第二节 意思表示
第三章 论有人不在场者之所关系	第三节 民事法律行为的效力
第一节 论不在场者之所关系，系其所有房产土地等项者	第四节 民事法律行为的附条件和附期限
第二节 论不在场者之所关系，系关于将来偶尔能得与否，而有例应可享受其遗产者	第七章 代理
第三节 论不在场者之所关系婚姻之事者	第一节 一般规定
第四章 论应者某人现时不在场者，其所出后嗣弱冠孩童之例	第二节 委托代理
第五类 论结联婚姻之理	第三节 代理终止
第一章 论查其势分并课强受物之情，以便乾坤两造而结联婚姻之事	第八章 民事责任
第二章 论办理结联婚姻事宜，一切礼节仪文之条例	第九章 诉讼时效
第三章 论于一切结联婚姻之事，而有例应能以遏阻者之条例	第十章 期间计算

第四章 《法国律例》的翻译与出版

续表

毕利干译《法国律例·民律》	《中华人民共和国民法典》
第四章 论于一切婚姻事件，有应呈请注销者	第二编 物权
第五章 论于婚姻事中有应尽之责者	第一分编 通则
第六章 论男女两造所携例例应于其人彼此应行之本分	第一章 一般规定
第七章 论将既结之婚遇事而灭绝者	第二章 物权的设立、变更、转让和消灭
第八章 论续娶而兴转嫁之事	第一节 不动产登记
第六类 论婚姻应行离异之例	第二节 动产交付
第一章 论缘何离异之由	第三节 其他规定
第二章 论缔结婚姻事宜有特定缘由	第三章 物权的保护
第一节 论特定之缘由与离异之围范	第二分编 所有权
第二节 论有一切应行离异事件，既经接据其呈，应暂时接办其案中要件	第四章 一般规定
第三节 论凡有离异之请而揆之于例应不允其所请者	第五章 国家所有权和集体所有权、私人所有权
第三章 论夫妇因事离异，实系两造互相情愿者	第六章 业主的建筑物区分所有权
第四章 论夫妇离异者之所关系	第七章 相邻关系
第五章 论夫妇两造因事有关夫妇异居者	第八章 共有
第七类 论为父者之势分，与其所应领属，并论其一脉正根子女辈所接替之事	第九章 所有权取得的特别规定
第一章 论所生后嗣，系按例结婚时事中所出，名正言顺之正根者	第三分编 用益物权
第二章 论倚恃何等约据而知所生子女系一脉正根亲身之子女者	第十章 一般规定
第三章 论非按例婚姻时事中所生子女而系私出者	第十一章 土地承包经营权
第一节 论以私出之子女而冒充正根子女者之例	第十二章 建设用地使用权
第二节 论办理私出之子女应行识志之例	第十三章 宅基地使用权
第八类 论一切过继子女之理，并论充当义父系其人自行情甘充当者	第十四章 居住权
第一章 论一切过继子女之理	第十五章 地役权
第一节 论过继子女与其理中所有之关系	第四分编 担保物权
第二节 论办理过继事务之围范	第十六章 一般规定
第二章 论办理过继事务并论情甘充当养父之责者	第十七章 抵押权

续表

毕利干译《法国律例·民律》	《中华人民共和国民法典》
第九类　论为父者所执之威权，独有关于其子女者	第一节　一般抵押权
第十类　论弱冠子女之事，并论为义父者应有栽培训诲之事，并准其自主事业之事	第二节　最高额抵押权
第一章　论人于弱冠之时	第十八章　质权
第二章　论栽培训诲之事	第一节　动产质权
第一节　论为父母者，于其子女有应充当养父之责	第二节　权利质权
第二节　论为父母者，应寄托何人办理一切栽培训诲之事	第十九章　留置权
第三节　论栽培训诲之事，系其尊长辈经理者	第五分编　占有
第四节　论栽培训诲之事，出自其家亲会议所寄托者	第一分编　通则
第五节　论为副义父之事	第一章　一般规定
第六节　论宽免办理栽培训诲之事，其所以宽免之原由	第二章　合同的订立
第七节　论办理栽培训诲之事，其人之才有不能胜任者，并论未善其事，有应驱逐其人者于有应将其人驳斥者	第三章　合同的效力
第八节　论为义父者，经手所宜办理之事	第四章　合同的履行
第九节　论为义父者，于办理一切栽培训导事中出入款项若干，作何交代章程	第五章　合同的保全
第三章　论一切弱冠者，年至准其自理事业之事	第六章　合同的变更和转让
第十一类　论已冠者、被禁者，应由家亲会议禁止其人等料理一切私事及须佐之，以详为代办者	第七章　合同的权利义务终止
第一章　论人为已冠者	第八章　违约责任
第二章　论人为被禁者之事	第二分编　典型合同
第三章　论详为代办者	第九章　买卖合同
第二部　论一切家资财产之事，以及名下所属各类之物	第十章　供用电、水、气、热力合同
第一类　论各项家资财产之区别	第十一章　赠与合同
第一章　论房产、土地等项为定资者	第十二章　借款合同
第二章　论各类动资质物	第十三章　保证合同
第三章　论人所有一切产物而有干系于本物者	第一节　一般规定
第二类　论人于一切物件而有操持物主之权者	第二节　保证责任
第一章　论一切生物而有操持物主之权者	第十四章　租赁合同

续表

毕利干译《法国律例·民律》	《中华人民共和国民法典》
第二章 论有操持之权，系于物之本质相合而为一质者	第十五章 融资租赁合同
第一节 论有操持物主之权而于一切定资质物者	第十六章 保理合同
第二节 论有操持物主之权而于动资项上者	第十七章 承揽合同
第三类 论享受沾利代守之事，与使用一切物件及居处其地之权者	第十八章 建设工程合同
第一章 论有例应享受沾利代守之业者	第十九章 运输合同
第一节 论沾利代守者所挟制例应	第一节 一般规定
第二节 论沾利代守者有勉行应尽之责	第二节 客运合同
第三节 论沾利代收之事，合意即为其事告终之时	第三节 货运合同
第二章 论语一切事物所以使用之例应，并与所居处之例应	第四节 多式联运合同
第四类 论有借益于人及关径借益之事	第二十章 技术合同
第一章 论借益之事，系因其天然地之形势而然者	第一节 一般规定
第二章 论借益之事，系因律例拟定而设者	第二节 技术开发合同
第一节 论两益之墙与两益之沟洫	第三节 技术转让合同和技术许可合同
第二节 论两主人所占房基相距之数，并建立护垣之事	第四节 技术咨询合同和技术服务合同
第三节 论凿壁偷光于邻院者	第二十一章 保管合同
第四节 论一切房屋之房脊，并滴檐以及通流水路、天沟之事	第二十二章 仓储合同
第五节 论来往路径之例应	第二十三章 委托合同
第三章 论有关涉人之原由而设立借益之事者	第二十四章 物业服务合同
第一节 论于各项产物、土地而有借益之事者	第二十五章 行纪合同
第二节 论以何法而能设立借益之事	第二十六章 中介合同
第三节 论收受借益事务之主人所可得之一切例应	第二十七章 合伙合同
第四节 论何如情形即致将借益之事息绝者	第三分编 准合同
第三部 论以何法而致有操持物主之权，试将其事约略而陈其情	第二十八章 无因管理
第一类 论相继接产之事	第二十九章 不当得利
第一章 论相继接产之事，并有承受遗产之人所得一切利益之事	第四编 人格权

续表

毕利干译《法国律例·民律》	《中华人民共和国民法典》
第二章 论有何等势分始可由相继接产之事	第一章 一般规定
第三章 论一切应相继接产之次序	第二章 生命权、身体权和健康权
第一节 论相继接产之事大略情形	第三章 姓名权和名称权
第二节 论有权能以相代承受父业者	第四章 肖像权
第三节 论相继接产之事应归给其后辈者	第五章 名誉权和荣誉权
第四节 论相继接产之事应归给长辈者	第六章 隐私权和个人信息保护
第五节 论相继接产之事应归给于旁族者	第五编 婚姻家庭
第四章 论相继接产之事系出于循分之外而得之者	第一章 一般规定
第一节 论私生子女于其父母产业之例应,并私子死亡而无嗣可承此遗产之例应者	第二章 结婚
第二节 论夫妇之中,其现时生存之或夫或妇,并论遗产吾人承受,应归于公者之例应	第三章 家庭关系
第五章 论收留相继接产之事,并论推辞相继接产之事	第一节 夫妻关系
第一节 论收留相继接产之事	第二节 父母子女关系和其他近亲属关系
第二节 论推辞相继接产之事	第四章 离婚
第三节 论所收留者系有盈无亏之遗产,并其事中之关系与收留者应尽之责	第五章 收养
第四节 论虚悬相继接产之事	第一节 收养关系的成立
第六章 论分晰遗产之围范,并论事先所授之产物,今经分晰,复将所授者取出,以敷分数之不足者	第二节 收养的效力
第一节 论分晰遗产之围范	第三节 收养关系的解除
第二节 论事先曾有收受之物,今经分晰遗产,应即将原物取出,以敷其分晰数之不足者	第六编 继承
第三节 论于分晰遗产,分中而有欠负之端,应发给银两照数清偿者	第一章 一般规定
第四节 论分晰遗产事中之所关系,并论各同受遗产之人,于其事中有互相保护之理	第二章 法定继承
第五节 论遗产既经分析,而其事中尚有未能尽美尽善之处,应行复为分析之事者	第三章 遗嘱继承和遗赠
第二类 论人有生前付物者之情,并论曾有遗书之事者	第四章 遗产的处理

续表

毕利干译《法国律例·民律》	《中华人民共和国民法典》
第一章　论其事之大略情形	第七编　侵权责任
第二章　论将物件有给予于人之权，并论有收受物件之权者，盖缘事中曾有生前付物之情，或有遗书之命者	第一章　一般规定
第三章　论有任便给付之产之事，并论于其事中有提取所逾之数，于其数种量加减除之事	第二章　法定继承
第一节　论任便给付之产，并论其数目多寡之事	第三章　责任主体的特殊规定
第二节　论于给付之物件，或俾以遗念之物，而以任便给付之产之数，计其所逾之数，量加减除提取之事	第四章　产品责任
第四章　论有生前付物者之事	第五章　机动车交通事故责任
第一节　论生前付物者之围范	第六章　医疗损害责任
第二节　论有生前付物之情，系按例其事定而不移者，亦有时应行破以成格者	第七章　环境污染和生态破坏责任
第五章　论凡立具遗书者，其所具一切情形之事	第八章　高度危险责任
第一节　论立具遗书者，其事中大旨围范	第九章　饲养动物损害责任
第二节　论致志专备数条之例，而为立具遗书者之围范	第十章　建筑物和物件损害责任
第三节　论指挥某人可以为相继接产之人，并论有人可以给以遗念之物者	附则
第四节　论给以遗念之物，系有普权齐备之情者	
第五节　论于普权齐备之中，系抽分给之者	
第六节　论有特给遗念之物者	
第七节　论有监收之人而于遗书项上者	
第八节　论于遗书而有翻悔成议，并论所立遗书系衰迈不合时者	
第六章　论例准承受之事及其孙子女，并其侄儿女、甥儿女辈者	
第七章　论各辈尊长而将产业分晰，各授于其子女及其后嗣者	
第八章　论给付物件之事，而于立具婚嫁资产契之时，并论给付物件而于夫妇两造之中，及其子女者	

续表

毕利干译《法国律例·民律》	《中华人民共和国民法典》
第九章 论夫妇两造互相给予物件之情，或系按照婚嫁资产契约而为者，或于结亲后即立合同，互相给之一物者	
第三类 论立具合同，并一切盟约契券之事	
第一章 论合同盟约契券等事，初基之大略	
第二章 论所具合同其中一切紧要情节，委系结实可靠与否	
第一节 论于合同而有甘心遵允之事者	
第二节 论于立具合同者，其人是否能有办理其事之权	
第三节 论于合同中所载之物，即如合同之本质，而究之系为何事所立具者	
第四节 论立具合同之缘由	
第三章 论应尽之责事中之所关系	
第一节 论事中大略情形	
第二节 论应尽之责而于给付物件项上者	
第三节 论于应尽之责或于一事应为，或于一事系不应为者	
第四节 论有赔补安慰之需，系因于所应尽之责有不遵照而为者	
第五节 论于合同、契约等件，而有应讲解文义者	
第六节 论契约之中所具各项关系，系向之于他人者	
第四章 论于应尽之责，其事中之等类	
第一节 论应尽之责而有课程受物之情者	
第二节 论应尽之责，而于将来之事而指定异日某时者	
第三节 论应尽之责，系选给两益酬报者	
第四节 论应尽之责，而事中彼此有承担之责者	
第五节 论应尽之责，或系能分晰而为者，或系不能分晰而为者	
第六节 论于应尽之责，系有惩罚之情者	
第五章 论以何事而于应尽之责即为灭而绝之	

第四章 《法国律例》的翻译与出版

续表

	毕利干译《法国律例·民律》	《中华人民共和国民法典》
第一节	论以资补债即可无事	
第二节	论向所约据者,而今则有更易从新之事	
第三节	论债主于所还补欠款而有宽免交纳者	
第四节	论冲折欠款以为还补者	
第五节	论以其两造之权可以相消而等于无者	
第六节	论于所欠之物事竟有遗失情事者	
第七节	论有将所立合同而销毁者,并有减撤之情者	
第六章	论于应尽之责,而呈有切确不移之据,并论于还补欠款而呈有切实之凭据者	
第一节	论以书信字据而以之为凭者	
第二节	论以事中见证人所语言而以之为执者	
第三节	论凭虚逆料,由此事而推及于彼事中之所关系者	
第四节	论在事之人,有识认真确之情者	
第五节	论矢誓之事	
第四类	论因事相及遵照而行,却系并未立有契约者	
第一章	论类似立有契约者	
第二章	论所行事有干于罪者,并类似近似于罪者	
第五类	论婚嫁资产契,并一切夫妇两造所挟之例应者	
第一章	论其事之大略情形	
第二章	论合资营生者之围范	
第一节	论合资营生事中所含一切物件,系关于所出之款及所储之项者	
第二节	论经理合资营生事务,并该夫妇两造所行之事,而有关于合资营生事中者	
第三节	论灭绝合资营生事务,而有数项关系者	
第四节	论收留合资营生,并?联合资营生之事,及与此二事而有课程受之情者	
第五节	论有分晰合资营生之事,而于收留之后者	
第六节	论推辞合资营生之事,并论其事中之所关系者	

续表

毕利干译《法国律例·民律》	《中华人民共和国民法典》
第二项 论合资营生系二人合心共意而为者，并论其合心共意立具文约，能以将第一项按照定例而为者，所定事宜，更易其事，或将其事销撤不存者	
第一节 论合资营生事务，惟有应得之一物者	
第二节 论有一项情形，系于动资之物，或为统共之数，或为一分之数而为合资营生事务以外之物者	
第三节 论将定资之物入于合资营生事中，而变易其情，等于动资之物者	
第四节 论将欠款而有分晰之情形	
第五节 论为妇者，将其随嫁之资提取收回，而即为了结无干，并即为减免一切费用之情者	
第六节 论预沾其惠系立有约据者	
第七节 论所办事务情形，系为酌定于合资营生事中所得之分数有不相等者	
第八节 论合资营生事务系关普享其利者	
第九节 论所立一切情节，系出于合资营生事外者	
第三章 论事有只享其利而不能亏其原本者，其事中之围范	
第一节 论设立随嫁之赀事中一切情形	
第二节 论为夫者所挟之例应，而有于随嫁之赀者，并此赀根底系牢固而不能撼移者	
第三节 论随嫁之赀事中而有偿补之情者	
第四节 论有定动之赀，系逾乎随嫁定动赀以外者	
第六类 论售卖物件之例	
第一章 论售卖者所行之事，并其事之情形及其事之围范	
第二章 论何为售卖者，并论何以为赔买者	
第三章 论例准能以售卖之物	
第四章 论售卖物件者应尽之责	
第一节 论总论售卖事中大略情形	
第二节 论发交所售物件之事	
第三节 论保质物件之理	

续表

毕利干译《法国律例·民律》	《中华人民共和国民法典》
第五章 论于购买者,其所应尽之责	
第六章 论售卖之事,有化为无有情事者,并有解散其交易情事者	
第一节 论执有售而复购之权者	
第二节 论售卖物件之事,而有减撤之情,系因所售之物而有损伤,关涉为价过廉	
第七章 论未易分晰之物,而有数物主应按合总喝卖之事行之者	
第八章 论于债欠之事,而有自此转移于彼之情者,并于无关质之例应,而亦有自此转移于彼之情者	
第七类 论以一物而还补一物之事	
第八类 论事关雇赁所立之合同	
第一章 论其事之大约情形	
第二章 论雇赁物件之事	
第一节 论所立章程,系为公同于房产,并于土地、庄田项上,而有立具租券者	
第二节 论租赁房屋契约而有特定之章程	
第三节 论因庄田所立租券而有特定章程	
第三章 论雇赁之事于人工艺业项上者	
第一节 论雇赁之事系于仆隶匠役者	
第二节 论车夫而与船户之遄行,或系由旱路者,或系由水路者	
第三节 论论工酬价,并议价事宜	
第四章 论包收分滋利之契	
第一节 论其事之大略情形	
第二节 论包收分滋利契,系按寻常之规而立具者	
第三节 论所立包收分滋利契系按均分者	
第四节 论所立包收分滋利契,系由本物主给与包收分滋利契者,或给以庄田,或给以招垦之事者	
第五节 论所立包收分滋利契,而竟有谬称强谓为包收分滋利契之类	
第九类 论社会中所立合同之例	

续表

毕利干译《法国律例·民律》	《中华人民共和国民法典》
第一章　论事之大略情形	
第二章　论各项社会之事	
第一节　论所立之社会,系有普全齐备之情者	
第二节　论所立社会系独指某项情事者	
第三章　论众会友彼此勉行遵契而为,并有关于局外他人者	
第一节　论勉行遵契而为,系于会友中者	
第二节　论会友勉行遵契而为,系于局外他人者	
第四章　论有何等一切情势,始可致社会至于灭绝之时	
第十类　论各项借贷物件之理	
第一章　论借贷于使用之物者	
第一节　论借贷于使用之物,系循其事之围范者	
第二节　论借贷物件者,其所遵契而行之事,系为其人应尽之责	
第三节　论借物于人,遵契而行,系为其所应尽之责	
第二章　论所借贷之物,系关乎食饮之物者,或仅言借贷者	
第一节　论所借贷之物,其使用系循其事之围范者	
第二节　论以物借之于人者,其有所应尽之责	
第三节　论借贷物件者,其所应尽之责	
第三章　论有利息之借贷者	
第十一类　论储留物件而与押质物件之事	
第一章　论储留物件大略情形,并其事有分为数类者	
第二章　论物件仅为储留而已者	
第一节　论储留物件文约之本意	
第二节　论心甘储留物件之事	
第三节　论为人储留物件者,其所应尽之责	
第四节　论欲行储留物件者,其所应尽之责	
第五节　论实需储留诸物之事者	
第三章　论一切押质之事	
第一节　论押质等类之者	

续表

毕利干译《法国律例·民律》	《中华人民共和国民法典》
第二节　论押质之事，系由人自行立具者	
第三节　论押质之事系由官谕而立具者	
第十二类　论所立之文约，系利言听命，由天而为遇事恃运者	
第一章　论各项赌博与打赌之事	
第二章　论所设议定之资，系至死方休者	
第一节　论一切议立文约情节，其事中所应有者而尽有之，则其文约始为结实可据	
第二节　论所立文约系有关系而于在事之众者	
第十三类　论立具文约系为一事，命人代操其权者	
第一章　论命人代操其权其事中之情形并其事之一切围范	
第二章　论为人代操其权者应尽之责	
第三章　论命人代操其权者应尽之责	
第四章　论待操其权，系致有何等情势，即可至于灭绝之时	
第十四类　论因事而有备质之银	
第一章　论备质之事而有巨细轻重之别，并其情形或质之一银，或有保质之事者	
第二章　论为保质者，其事中所有之关系	
第一节　论为保质者之干系，系于债主而与保质之本身者	
第二节　论为保质者之关系，系在欠债者而与为保质者	
第三节　论保质之关系，系于数为保质者	
第三章　论所设保质之情势，至有灭绝之事者	
第四章　论保质之事有二项情形，一系遇事循例而自有者，一系因词讼经官所定拟者	
第十五类　论减数相就而理之事者	
第十六类　论拘勒其身而乃关涉于民例者	
第十七类　论一切备质之事	
第一章　论备质之事而于动资之物者	

续表

毕利干译《法国律例·民律》	《中华人民共和国民法典》
第二章　论所备质之物系以定资之物者	
第十八类　论倚势沾光并指物沾利之事	
第一章　论其事之大略情形	
第二章　论倚势沾光之事	
第一节　论于动赀项上而有倚势沾光之事者	
第二节　论倚势沾光之事，系关于定赀之物者	
第三节　论倚势沾光之事，系兼关于定、动二赀项上者	
第四节　论以何法能以维持存留倚势沾光之权	
第三章　论各项指物沾利之事	
第一节　论由律例生发而有然者指物沾利之事	
第二节　论由官所定而应然者之指物沾利之事	
第三节　论两造互相议定而当然者指物沾利之事	
第四节　论指物沾利字次序	
第四章　论指物沾利一切情事而诣官注册之法要	
第五章　论于指物沾利事中而有删减之情，或于所余者而有减撤之事	
第六章　论指物沾利并倚势沾光之事，关系于接受其事者之他人	
第七章　关于指物沾利并倚势沾光而有灭绝之情	
第八章　论指物沾利并倚势沾光之事，而具有疏通其事之行者	
第九章　论有妇之夫，与为弱冠之义父者，其所有定赀之物原有指物沾利之权，未经注于官册，则以何法而疏通之	
第十章　论掌册簿之官，其责应令众人周知，以便悉知其实者	
第十九类　论勒撤物主之权，并非物主情甘及各债主例应之次序	
第一章　论勒撤其物主之权者	
第二章　论为债主者，其于分拨售物价值，其事中先后之次序	

续表

毕利干译《法国律例·民律》	《中华人民共和国民法典》
第二十类　论例准援免之事	
第一章　论其事之大略情形	
第二章　论于物而有操持之权者之理	
第三章　论遇一切事故，而致有阻止其例准援免之事者	
第四章　论于一切事故，有能以隔断例准援免之事者，亦有能以暂时悬系例准援免之事者	
第一节　论有事故系能隔断例准援免之事者	
第二节　论一切事故系能暂时悬系例准援免之事者	
第五章　论所得之时光足敷行其例准援免之事	
第一节　论事之大略情形	
第二节　论例准援免之事系以三十年为止者	
第三节　论例准援免之事，或以十年为止者，或以二十年为止者	
第四节　论例准援免之事，系由特意而破以成格者	

民法是调整平等主体的公民之间、法人之间以及公民与法人之间的财产关系和人身关系的法律规范的总称。

《法国律例·民律》是西方输入中国的第一部民法典，基本涵盖了财产所有权、财产继承权、合同等近代西方民法的主要内容。

1. 关于民事权利与民事责任：

"第七条　凡人无论曾否系属都会、土著，均可邀得分中之例应，而惟不能并享在官之分力。

第八条　凡无论何项法国之人，均可身沾分中可获之例应

第十条　凡幼小孩童之父，系原籍法国人而产其子于外国者，子应仍为法国之人。设其父曾经因事自失其本国可享之例应者，而其所生之子，仍可复邀其法国各项享受之例应。然惟须遵照第九条所载之例照例而为，方为准行。

第二十条　凡如法国之人，既经因事失其本国可得之例应，

嗣后复按照第十、第十八、第十九等条所载之情，而有能复邀各项例应者，亦不能以复邀例应自为可恃。须将诸条中所载课程受物之情均能办理裕如，然后则可为复邀其例应之利益。

第二十八条　凡所科断之案，系照脱身稽传而科者。倘于五年限内，或于一、二年，竟能复行投首，则即以其投首以前之时日为止，将其人可邀之例应，概行停止。或既逃脱后，而于限内被官跴缉，其时或系一、二年，或系三、四年者，则即以其跴缉以前之时日为始，概行停止其所可邀之例应。至其人所有房产、土地及一切可邀之例应，亦有人代为经理。其所有产业，即照如不在其名下者之事，照例办理。"①

2. 关于婚姻家庭：

"第三十四条　凡如所立合同，系关婚丧产育等事者，应注明某年月日。今于某日，接到欲行立具之事，仍应于合同上注明。其在合同上之人系某人，其人姓名、籍贯、居址，并以何业为生，均应逐一注明。

第四十条　凡婚丧产育之合同，于每处街巷之中，如有人欲行立具者，应将其事照抄一册簿之上，并将此册簿依样照抄，共二分，以备稽考。"②

"第五十五条　凡遇有产育之事，须于产后三日内，将其产育之事报明该处之该管官。并将所产婴孩抱赴该管官前查验，以辨虚实真伪。

第五十六条　凡呈报产育之事，应由所产婴孩之父前往呈报。设其无父，或由经管产育医家，或由收生婆，或由在侧护持产务之人前往该管官前呈报。倘该产妇现在不在本处居住者，则应由所居之处主人前往呈报。既经呈报，应即立具合同，仍应有

---

① ［法］毕利干：《法国律例·民律》上卷，日本司法省1894年版，第5、6、11、18页。
② ［法］毕利干：《法国律例·民律》上卷，日本司法省1894年版，第23、26页。

证见二人，当堂跟同立具。"①

"第六十三条　凡因婚姻之事，应于立具合同之先，将其事中一切情形，由官宣扬二次。既宣扬初次毕，则间以八日，再为宣扬。仍应将所宣扬之事开具清单。注明两造姓名、居址、以何为业。除欲联婚夫妇外，并应将该两造父母姓名、居址及以何为业为生，其本人年纪、既冠、未冠，并此合同于某处、某月、某日、某时，曾经宣扬，均应详细一一注明。惟既经宣扬之后，即将此项合同照抄一册簿之上，每页须按照第四十一条之例，由官画具花押，并于每年将此宣扬之事，所立之册，率交理事坊之检收处，以备考核。

第六十五条　凡有婚姻之事，既经宣扬以后，竟至一年外尚未将其事议成者，须从新再为宣扬，即如未经宣扬其事者等。"②

"第七十七条　凡一切人既经死亡，不能私自竟行下葬，须由该管官批准下葬，始得下葬。其批即用行常素纸，以免呈缴费用，惟于批准之先，须令官医至该死者之前，认真相验，而其批准字样须报到某人已死于二十四点钟以后，方可施行。除有关涉众人不和，与一切非命而死者以外，始得如此办理。

第七十九条　凡因人死立具合同，应将死者之姓名、居址，并以何业为生，今于某年月日时身故，均应注明。倘死者如夫妇中有一人死亡，则未亡之夫或未亡之妇，须将其人姓名、年纪、居址、以何业为生，今于某年月日时身故，并事中证见人之姓名、年纪、以何业为生，其证见人与死者系何亲属，或系尊长，其辈数如何，均宜逐一注明至此合同上，如能知该死者之父母姓名、居址、以何业为生，并该死者其产育之时，于某处，亦应一并注明。"③

"第一百四十四条　凡男子于十八岁之先，女子于十五岁之先，均不得愿情办理婚姻之事。

---

① ［法］毕利干：《法国律例·民律》上卷，日本司法省1894年版，第36页。
② ［法］毕利干：《法国律例·民律》上卷，日本司法省1894年版，第42、43页。
③ ［法］毕利干：《法国律例·民律》上卷，日本司法省1894年版，第52、53页。

第一百四十六条　凡一切婚姻之事，如该乾坤两造之父母，于此结婚之事，有未甘心允准两造宜乎婚姻者，或该两造本人未能情甘，不愿依允者，则均不得妄即为可以婚姻，妄为嫁娶。"①

"第一百六十五条　凡办理结联婚姻事宜，须于大庭广众之前，管理民例之官当面。设该男女两造不在一处相居者，不拘两造中何人，须有一该管其人之官当面，始可办理。惟按定章而论，须于坤造所居之处该管之官当面，尤属合宜。

第一百六十七条　凡如上文所载，应于那女所居之处二次宣扬，设该男女于某处只暂居有六月之久者，则仍应于该男女等原先久居之处，该管官署中，再为宣扬，以便周知。"②

"第一百七十三条　凡无父而有母者，则其母有可遏阻结婚之权。如其并无者，则其祖父母亦有遏阻结婚之权。纵为之孙及为之孙女者，虽年已逾二十五与二十一者，在其祖父母亦有可以遏阻结婚之权。

第一百七十五条　凡如上条所载二项情形，倘其事中之人，或为义父者，或详为代办者，于此结联婚姻之事，不能动为遏阻，除经家亲会议议准其可遏阻者，始可遏阻，以昭限制。"③

"第一百八十条　凡结联婚姻之事，设其男女两造中，彼此未能情甘协意，或两造中而有一人未能情甘协意，则不论或男或女而准有呈请注销其妇之权，或其事中实有错误，而实有害于其本身者，亦准被害者有呈请注销其婚之权。

第一百八十二条　凡有结婚孩子事，或无其父母允准之命，或无其祖父母允准之命，或于其家亲会议亦无有允准之命，则此嫁娶之事，既未奉其尊长之命，设已结婚，而复欲呈请注销者，则惟准其以前许其结婚之尊长等，能有呈请注销之权。或其两造本人年未及时可以遇事自主，须奉命于其亲者，亦能有此注销其

---

① [法] 毕利干：《法国律例·民律》上卷，日本司法省1894年版，第97、99页。
② [法] 毕利干：《法国律例·民律》上卷，日本司法省1894年版，第111、112页。
③ [法] 毕利干：《法国律例·民律》上卷，日本司法省1894年版，第115、116页。

婚之权。"①

"第二百零三条　凡如夫妇两造结婚，其事中有自然而然应尽之责，有如其所生之子女，该夫妇两造等，须为之栽培训诲，此系婚姻事中自然而然该夫妇应尽之责也。

第二百零六条　凡女婿与出嫁之女，倘值其岳父母贫而无力，不能以自度日者，即宜备资以养赡之，然亦有二项情形，即可不照定章而为也。其一情形，倘为其岳母者，既嫁而复转嫁，可以不劳养赡矣，其二情形，倘与其切近骨肉相关之人，业已物故，并其所生之子，又复死亡者，则亦不劳其养赡矣。"②

"第二百一十二条　凡夫妇两造，彼此应互相为爱，遇事不分彼此，两相扶持，护佑襄助力。

第二百一十四条　凡为妇者，应随其夫一地而居，倘其夫竟有欲行迁移居处之事，则其妇亦应随之前往，而为之夫者，亦应收留其妇，并应酌给其妇一切需用之物与资财等项。其所应给数之多寡，以其家资之丰啬，计其轻重而予之。"③

"第二百二十七条　凡何以即应灭绝既结之婚，下文详为陈明。其一如男女两造中有一死亡者，则应灭绝其婚；其二，因事曾经该管官按例科以离异者，则应灭绝其婚；其三，如男女两造中，有一获罪，系关科以灭绝福泽者，则亦应灭绝其婚。

第二百二十八条　凡一切妇人，如有再醮之事，须其初结之婚既经灭绝而于十月以后，始能复有再醮之事。"④

"第二百二十九条　凡一切男子能以禀请该管之官办理离异之事。设其妇与人实有奸私者，即应如此办理。

第二百三十一条　凡夫妇两造均能请官科办离异之事。惟须有重大情由，或因嫖赌奸淫，或因殴伤诅詈，均准男女等禀请离异。"⑤

---

① ［法］毕利干：《法国律例·民律》上卷，日本司法省1894年版，第121、122页。
② ［法］毕利干：《法国律例·民律》上卷，日本司法省1894年版，第136、137页。
③ ［法］毕利干：《法国律例·民律》上卷，日本司法省1894年版，第142、143页。
④ ［法］毕利干：《法国律例·民律》上卷，日本司法省1894年版，第151、152页。
⑤ ［法］毕利干：《法国律例·民律》上卷，日本司法省1894年版，第153、154页。

"第二百三十六条　凡递禀呈请官议办夫妇离异案件者,其原呈上须详细注明事中一切实在情形,并其缘由。无论两造中系由何人呈递,惟应亲身赴署呈递于该管衙门之首领官,并其案中卷宗、书约、物件等项,均须一并呈交。倘首领官未在署中,即应呈交于代理承审官。如该递呈者一时抱病,未能亲身赴署呈递,应?有医生二人结称其人确系实病,并非托故。即恳请该承审官至递呈者之家,以便将所欲递禀呈及卷宗、书约物件等项,由在案原告当面呈缴。

第二百四十七条　凡离异之呈,既经实收所请后,该衙门即可备具文移之情,并监审官所拟情意,深悉其案中一切底蕴,应准者即可批准照行。倘其案中情节甚?支离,未能瞭然者,则该递禀之人,令其如有的确证据,并于被禀之人设有执证,均可呈缴前来,以资借证。"①

"第二百七十五条　凡男子未至二十五岁,其妇亦当青年,未至二十一岁者,虽属两造互相情愿离异者,亦不能准如所请。

第二百七十七条　凡一切夫妇既经结婚二十年者,则不准其有离异之请。更如其妇年已四十五岁者,亦不准其有离异之请,以示限制。"②

"第二百九十五条　凡一切夫妇既经当官办过离异之案,嗣后不论有何事故,不准该夫妇再为聚首。

第二百九十七条　凡夫妇有关离异者,系两造彼此相愿者,则在两造中,不论男女某人,均不准有续娶再嫁之事。"③

"第三百零九条　凡在案男子因其妇既已犯奸获罪,该男子可以自具主见,禀请该管官免罚其妇,甚至欲将其妇照旧领回相处,则该管官亦可从宽令其承领。

第三百一十一条　凡如有干夫妇异居之案,则其所有资财应

---

① [法] 毕利干:《法国律例·民律》上卷,日本司法省1894年版,第157、163页。
② [法] 毕利干:《法国律例·民律》上卷,日本司法省1894年版,第179页。
③ [法] 毕利干:《法国律例·民律》上卷,日本司法省1894年版,第190、192页。

即一并分析开交,各自经理,以免牵混。"①

"第三百一十二条 凡如所生之子女,而其受气成形之始,系于其父母结联婚姻时事中者,则按例该子女等均应归于为之父者??承管。倘如夫妇两造中,该为夫者谓为所生子女实有切据,而以其产生后计之,于其未经出世三百日之内,往前推计一百八十日以前,该夫妇或因伤病事故,未能两造合房者,则例准可以不认为亲生之子。

第三百一十四条 凡夫妇既经结婚,而却在结婚后,计期则在一百八十日以先,而乃生有子女者,则在该夫亦竟有不能不认其子女之事,如下文所载各情,实有不能不认之处。其一情,倘于结婚之先,明知该妇已经身孕者,事属先知,则不能不认;其二情,所立生育子女合同之上,曾有夫亲手自画之押,或经陈明委系不能画押,则亦不能不认;其三情,倘于所生子女,其夫因其形迹明知其胎气不足,产后即可死亡者,则亦可不得不认。"②

"第三百二十八条 凡如为子女者,而有索讨之情,系欲索其应行承受而与其应有势分者,则不能归于例准援免,至限即行灭绝之情。

第三百三十条 凡如有人欲行申诉其子嗣应受之利益者,而其族中分应沾润遗产之人,亦可接纳办理此等事件。然亦不能?办,除以先欲行申诉之人,原欲办而复不欲办者,或于着手办后而复不欲办者,则即不准分应沾润遗产之人,接续办理其事。"③

"第三百三十二条 凡如有人系其父母私出而冒充为正出之子女者,乃其本人或已死亡而乃生有子女者,则已死亡而乃生有子女者,则在其子女亦可请官核办,承受其父所遗,以私冒充正出子女者所应得之利益。

第三百三十三条 凡以私出而冒充嫡亲子嗣者,在其父母既经结婚,而此冒充嫡亲之子女一切应得之利益,则与婚姻例中亲

---

① [法] 毕利干:《法国律例·民律》上卷,日本司法省1894年版,第198、200页。
② [法] 毕利干:《法国律例·民律》上卷,日本司法省1894年版,第201、203页。
③ [法] 毕利干:《法国律例·民律》上卷,日本司法省1894年版,第213页。

生之子女无异。"①

"第三百四十九条　凡一切为子女者之职分,自应由以奉养其父母,则办过继者与被过继者,虽属过继,究属名分攸关,自应按照子女奉养其父母之之职分,一例比拟办理。

第三百五十条　凡被过继之人,不能与办过继者之父母名分上妄有可邀之利益,然而惟能与办过继者婚姻例中所生嫡亲子女一律承受利益。倘办过继者于既过继之后,乃生有嫡亲子嗣者,则被过继者,能与其后来亲生子女事同一律。"②

"第三百六十二条　凡夫妇两造不能自主充当义父之责,须其二人中有一愿充者,有一准其充当者,则始可充当。

第三百六十三条　凡应管属此项弱冠子女之息讼官,于其愿充义父者之势分衔名,及一切应行索讨之件,该管官应为之立具清单,以资办理。"③

"第三百七十三条　凡如夫妇两造,其于结联婚姻之时,惟为其父者,有可施措所挟之权。

第三百七十四条　凡为子女者,不能自主擅离其父母之家,除有父命令其前往某处者,则始可挪移,倘在男子,其年已过十八,而自行情愿充当兵丁者,则可不遵其父之命矣。除此以外,其余无论何情,须以父命是遵。"④

"第三百八十八条　凡一切人不论或男或女,但其年未满二十一者,则即为弱冠之人。

第三百九十二条　凡派人经理栽培训诲之事,其应如何拣派之处,下文陈明。其一情,其父曾有遗书,或将其情已经禀明于该管息讼官,当面并在侧曾有书史一人,或有理事绅宦二人当面辨者,均为例准拣派之事。除此以外,其余各情均属不能。

第三百九十三条　凡为夫者,于既死亡之后,其妇曾已身怀

---

① [法] 毕利干:《法国律例·民律》上卷,日本司法省1894年版,第215、216页。
② [法] 毕利干:《法国律例·民律》上卷,日本司法省1894年版,第225页。
③ [法] 毕利干:《法国律例·民律》上卷,日本司法省1894年版,第232页。
④ [法] 毕利干:《法国律例·民律》上卷,日本司法省1894年版,第237页。

有孕，则应由家亲会议拣派一人，为之保护其胎，一至产育之时，则其母即可为义母矣。而此保护胎产之人，则应名之为副义父。"①

"第四百七十六条　凡为弱冠者，既至可以结联婚姻之时，按例即可以准其自理事业之时。

第四百七十七条　凡为弱冠者，如尚未至结婚之时，亦间有可以准其自理事业之事者。惟应听命于其父。如其无父，则听命于其母。然尤须其年已满十五岁者则然。至欲准其自理事业之事，如何办理，应由其父或由其母，将准其经理事业情由，呈明于该管息讼官，并须有书吏等在侧，由官批准，方为可行。"②

"第四百八十八条　凡为已冠之人，自已冠以至二十一岁为满，除有干涉结婚之事以外，其余一切事件，均可自行料理。

第五百零七条　凡为妇者，亦能为其夫之义母，惟此项情事，须由家亲会议先给该妇照何办理章程，倘该妇于其事中颇有不满心志之处，亦准该妇有诣官控诉之权。

第五百零八条　凡无论何人，除为夫妇、长辈、晚辈外，不能勒令一切之人办理栽培训诲之事，而竟逾于十载者，一至其期，即由义父禀请该管之官，另易一人前往接办其事。"③

3. 关于物权：

"第五百一十六条　凡如家资财产分为二类。一为动资，一为定资。如系各项家具等类为动资，如系房产、土地等类者，即为定资。

第五百二十一条　凡应砍伐之树木，其应命之为动资者，系为一经砍伐之树木而言。

第五百二十二条　凡如牲畜，因随地所用者，即为定资。倘

---

① ［法］毕利干：《法国律例·民律》上卷，日本司法省1894年版，第244、246、247页。
② ［法］毕利干：《法国律例·民律》上卷，日本司法省1894年版，第296、297页。
③ ［法］毕利干：《法国律例·民律》上卷，日本司法省1894年版，第304、313、314页。

牲畜被人游牧者，即为动资。"①

"第五百三十条　凡如按照永远岁定之资，而售以定资之物者，嗣后亦可酌付以资，将此岁定之货购回。惟此事而为债主者，亦可酌定其赎回之情形如何，并准该翟准向之追索。然虽准该翟准追索赎回，而实不能遽尔追索，惟须以三十年而为赎回之定律。

第五百三十一条　凡有过渡载重艨艟，内载有磨碾？堂在内者，因此物浮于船中，或一切器具而无柱脚者，即为动资。或有留物备抵之物件，而其重大形迹，与其船之船之轻重相等，则别有措办章程，即于民律定范文中详言之矣。"②

"第五百三十七条　凡人于自由之家资财产，可以自具识见，措办一切，然须遵照律例所制一切定章而为。如其家资财产中，或有事业物件等，不属私产，而属官产，及会中公产者，则此项家资财产，应即按照定章，以便遵办。

第五百三十八条　凡一切周道路径，都归国家管理。并各处江河，能行船只，及排筏等类，能浮送各类物件，各处海滨，人可居止之处，各处海口、埠头等处，均应属官管理，而不归于私产例中。"③

"第五百四十四条　凡人于一切物件有有主管之权，何以言之，盖于其物有措置之例应，并可随己之意，不拘将所有之物作何措置，均可任己之意，或将其物出售于人，或将其物给予于人，其于随意措置之时，惟须遵照律例而行，除于措置之时，设有不按照律例者，则不准其所行。

第五百四十五条　凡不论何人，均不能勒令某人将某人之物给予于人。然如其物实于公众之中大有裨益者，亦可勒令使其给予。惟须将所给与之物该值若干，存以公道之心如数补还，以免

---

① ［法］毕利干：《法国律例·民律》上卷，日本司法省1894年版，第319、321、322页。
② ［法］毕利干：《法国律例·民律》上卷，日本司法省1894年版，第326、327页。
③ ［法］毕利干：《法国律例·民律》上卷，日本司法省1894年版，第330页。

亏累。"①

"第五百四十七条　凡一切果实之类，或属天性生产而得，或属人力栽培而生。并如房产租息、田地租息，岁定之资所出利息，牲畜蕃滋之利益，均宜归其本物之主，则此项可邀之例应，该物主均有操持物主之权。

第五百四十八条　凡一切众物所滋之利益，既皆应归本物之主，则此项可邀之例应，该物主均有操持物主之权。"②

"第五百五十八条　凡如湖泊与池塘，不得按照上文之例，一例办理。其湖泊与池塘之主，倘遇水势涨溢，浸占旱地，该湖泊、池塘之主自不得占据，视为自有。

第五百五十九条　凡或江或河，不论其水能行船与否，倘因水势涨溢，竟致淹没冲刷一甚长地基，则该本地之主可以前往识认地基，与之索讨。然此索讨之例应，须于既刷其地一年内者，始有此索讨之例应。倘有逾限，则不准如所行。然虽如此，若逾一年，而该收得冲刷出地之地主，竟未有地主之权者，则原地主人可索讨。"③

"第五百七十八条　凡何以为享受沾利代守之事，有如一人享受一物，而实非为该物之主，惟既享受其物应有负荷之责，而宜护持该物。

第五百七十九条　凡享受沾利代守之事者，其所以能享受之处，或系被律例制定，或由人意拟准，故能有享受之权。"④

"第六百二十五条　凡使用之例应与居处之例应，倘竟欲行销撤者，应即仿照办理沾利代守之事一例办理。

第六百二十六条　凡如沾利代守之例应，亦不能骤即获其事中利益，除其事中或有结保，或有留质之银，并备有查物底单之事，则始可以享受其利益。"⑤

---

① ［法］毕利干：《法国律例·民律》上卷，日本司法省1894年版，第334、335页。
② ［法］毕利干：《法国律例·民律》上卷，日本司法省1894年版，第336页。
③ ［法］毕利干：《法国律例·民律》上卷，日本司法省1894年版，第343、344页。
④ ［法］毕利干：《法国律例·民律》上卷，日本司法省1894年版，第353、354页。
⑤ ［法］毕利干：《法国律例·民律》上卷，日本司法省1894年版，第384页。

"第六百三十七条　凡借益于人,与关径益人之事,何以言之,有如一人令某一人而负荷之情,使之与其人有不便者,竟可通融,无有不便,此之谓借益之事也。

第六百三十八条　凡如借益之事,不能以其人之事业,而与他人之事业有崇卑之等级,不过以其与人有未便者,而使之借益,以图有便于人。"①

"第六百七十五条　凡无论何人,不能将两益之墙,有钻孔开窗,以及既已钉固之窗而复开启等事,除该邻人准其所为者,则始可行。

第六百七十六条　凡一切寻常墙壁,而与邻人之墙院相接者,该墙主可以于此墙间有钻孔开窗等事,惟须于钻孔开窗之处,外护以铁栅铜丝窗网,钉固之玻璃等物,始为可行。"②

"第六百九十七条　凡如有收受借益之人,而其人于所借益事中一切工程,均宜自尽其责,则可以保护其借益事中所可使用之例应也。

第六百九十八条　凡人既经获有借益之事,并应有工作之情,则其事中花费,自应归诸妻本身备具,除于立具文约之时言明而有别项情形者,则为格外之事。"③

"第一千四百零二条　凡如一切定资之物,系合资营生事中者,或系由合资营生事中而得者,除事经执有切实之凭,谓为所有定资之物,或系夫妇两造中,为某一造自有者,或系由相继接产事中而得者以外,而其余所有定资之物,均应归入合资营生事中。

第一千四百零三条　凡如伐木之事,并石窖、金矿所生之利息,如系执有沾利代守之例应者,均宜归入于合资营生事中,并应按照第二部第三类所载之情,一例遵照办理。惟按照此例,原应有伐木之事生有利益,系可两造均分,而乃竟无者,则两造中

---

① [法]毕利干:《法国律例·民律》上卷,日本司法省1894年版,第389、390页。
② [法]毕利干:《法国律例·民律》上卷,日本司法省1894年版,第410、411页。
③ [法]毕利干:《法国律例·民律》上卷,日本司法省1894年版,第422页。

之某一造，非为园林之主者，则不能获其染指余润，而于其人，应备有安慰之需，或及于其本身，或及于其身后，分应承受遗产者，至如石窑金矿中所有事务，而于结联婚姻时，而有开启情事者，则其事中所生一切利息，即须归于合资营生事中，应以之先为赔补两造中抱歉者应行赔补之人。"①

"第一千五百三十条　凡如有立具文约，系夫妇两造而于结婚时，并无合资营生情事者，则为之妇者，即无有权可以为主，而于所有资财及资比果等类利息项上，而此等财资比果、利息等，应即归之于为夫者所管理，即可以为其家中一切用度、花费之需。

第一千五百三十一条　凡如为夫者而有存留经管其妇所有定、动二资之权者，则该妇随嫁之资所有动资之物，并其结婚以后，该妇所得动资之物，亦均归之于其夫管理，然而一至婚姻灭绝之时，或至分晰产业之时，仍应将原物还之于其本人。"②

"第一千五百六十六条　凡如随嫁之资，而有动资之物系归妇人操有物主之情者，设因使用该物致有损伤消耗之情，而并非由其夫所致之故者，则该为之夫者，应于还补其物之时，即以其物现为何等情形，按其本色还之。虽如此言，而在为妇者，例准将其自用中衣、外衣及一切零用什物提取备用。然此等衣服等，如已估有定价，而一至该夫还补其物之时，即于还补总数之中扣除该衣服等所值之数，以昭公允。

第一千五百六十七条　凡如随嫁之资事中，或系为预定数票，或系为岁定之资，而立有约据者，倘有遗失、抽减、损折之情，系非为夫者所致之故，亦不能令其有赔补之情，应由该夫将其原票依旧缴回，即为克尽其责。"③

"第一千五百八十八条　凡如所欲售卖之物，其事遇有应行试用之情者，则其事中自然含有应暂行缓办而宜有课程受物

---

① ［法］毕利干：《法国律例·民律》下卷，日本司法省1894年版，第12、13页。
② ［法］毕利干：《法国律例·民律》下卷，日本司法省1894年版，第110页。
③ ［法］毕利干：《法国律例·民律》下卷，日本司法省1894年版，第131、132页。

之情。

第一千五百九十四条 凡勿论何等人，惟其人系非为律例所禁约者之人，均可为售卖物件而与购买物件之人者。"①

"第一千五百九十九条 凡如所售之物，系不出于本物主而为他人所有之物者，则此售卖之事，亦惟置之不议。倘在购物者并不知悉为他人之物，而该为置买者，则亦或有安慰之需。

第一千六百零三条 凡为售物者，其有紧要应尽之责，有如于既经议或售卖之物，应将该物发交购买本主，而并于此物有为保作证之情。

第一千六百三十四条 凡如所售之物，而在购买者或有修理及有增美之费，并其所为系为合宜者，则此等所需之费，或由售物者亲自还之于购物者，或勒令强却其权者，还之于购物者，均无不可。"②

"第一千六百五十条 凡为购买物件者，其所应尽之责事之最要者，有如给与该购买物件之价，而于其所定交给之日，或于其所定交给之处，即为其责之至要者。

第一千六百六十二条 凡售卖者缘由售而复购之权，然此售而复购之事，亦有制定之限。如在定限之中，该售物者倘未举办此复购之事，则在买物者，即于所购之物而有牢不可破为其物主之权。"③

"第一千六百八十七条 凡为数物主者，均挟有权，令事外人前来经手，理此售卖之事，倘此数物主中，而有一为弱冠者，则尤须请事外人前来，理此售卖之事。

第一千六百九十三条 凡有以债欠之事，及无体质之例应，而出售于人者，纵其事中无须有保质之情，然亦须保质其当初原购此项权利之时，其所关涉一切例应，委系生机活泼而毫无废弛

---

① ［法］毕利干：《法国律例·民律》下卷，日本司法省1894年版，第144、147页。
② ［法］毕利干：《法国律例·民律》下卷，日本司法省1894年版，第150、153、168页。
③ ［法］毕利干：《法国律例·民律》下卷，日本司法省1894年版，第175、182页。

之情者。"①

"第一千七百零二条　凡如所谓以物而还补一物之事者，其事即如立有文约而以此物还补其所得之彼物也。

第一千七百零八条　凡如立具雇赁之合同，其事中有二项情形，一系于一切物件项上者，一系于一切工作项上者。

第一千七百一十四条　凡有行其雇赁之事者，或见诸语言，或形诸字迹，以为雇赁者，均为例所准行。"②

"第一千七百八十条　凡如工匠、仆役及各项手艺人等，按例不得属于一人所役用，在雇赁时，须定有期限，或以一项工程而以为成论。

第一千七百八十七条　凡欲有人而欲一人工作，应即议有工作给付工价之情，并应议有供给所需物料之事。"③

"第一千八百条　凡何以为包收分滋利契，即如立具合同，因某人将其自由生物付于伊恩，令其管守豢养，而其在事之二人，因而即有立具约据之事矣。

第一千八百零二条　凡如一切生物，能以蕃滋畅茂而得有利益者，或其事归之于农工，或其事归之于商贸者，均能归包收分滋契一律视之。"④

"第二千九十二条　凡无论何人，其于己身勉行自尽之责，于一切应尽事宜，均宜悉心毕尽其事，而于定、动二资项上，或属现时所有，并将来所有者，均与之有所干涉。

第二千九十四条　凡何以为于某人而有独应归给之情，盖因数人中而乃有一人挟有倚势沾光，或指物沾利之权者，即可由独应归给情事。"⑤

"第二千九十六条　凡如有数债主，而俱挟有倚势沾光之权者，则何以定其独应归给于某一债主，而以定其次序之先后，应

---

① ［法］毕利干：《法国律例·民律》下卷，日本司法省1894年版，第197、202页。
② ［法］毕利干：《法国律例·民律》下卷，日本司法省1894年版，第208、211、214页。
③ ［法］毕利干：《法国律例·民律》下卷，日本司法省1894年版，第253、256页。
④ ［法］毕利干：《法国律例·民律》下卷，日本司法省1894年版，第264页。
⑤ ［法］毕利干：《法国律例·民律》下卷，日本司法省1894年版，第426、427页。

即以其倚势沾光之事，其情势之巨细、缓急、轻重，即可以定其次序之先后矣。

第二千九十九条　凡如倚势沾光之事，例准于定、动二资项上，因事而设立者。"①

"第二千一百一十五条　凡如欲挟有指物沾利之权者，惟须遵照律例所定一切围范，始克挟有指物沾利之权，否则不能。

第二千一百一十六条　凡如指物沾利之事，须有三项情形。或系由律例生发而有然者，或系由该管官所定而应然者，或系由在事两造互相议立而当然者。"②

"第二千一百四十七条　凡如有数项债主，而同于一日之中，将其挟有指物沾利之权，诣官注册者，则在该债主等不得谓为有先后次序之别与早晚时候之辨，则在该经历此事之该管官而欲以到官先后，分其等第者，亦不能行。

第二千一百四十九条　凡如注册系关定资之物，而有指物沾利之情，乃该本物主现已物故者，即应按照上文第二情律例所载一切围范，遵照注明，勿庸另有他议。"③

"第二千一百五十七条　凡何以将指物沾利事中之物删去，或系由在事两造均能以自主之人而当面议订明确允行者，或系由该管之官拟议，其情委为牢不可破而发有示谕者，均可奉守遵行。

第二千一百五十八条　凡如上文所载二项情形，其在欲删去指物沾利之事者，须于经理此项册簿之官，将所议定依允照抄之合同，或由官指定照抄之示谕当堂呈验，始为可凭。"④

"第二千一百六十八条　凡如上文所言之情，其在接受其物者，于此情事，惟有所应尽之责，则于事中原欠本利，或系备资按数清还于债主，或系将所指沾利之物抛弃，如此即可。谓为清

---

① ［法］毕利干：《法国律例·民律》下卷，日本司法省1894年版，第428、429页。
② ［法］毕利干：《法国律例·民律》下卷，日本司法省1894年版，第445、446页。
③ ［法］毕利干：《法国律例·民律》下卷，日本司法省1894年版，第463、465页。
④ ［法］毕利干：《法国律例·民律》下卷，日本司法省1894年版，第470页。

结其债矣。

第二千一百七十二条　凡在接受其物者，其于所指沾利物中，而有欲抛弃其物之情，须视其人于此欠款中，委无其人应尽之责，而并挟有能以过权之权者，始可有抛弃之事。

第二千一百八十条　凡如指物沾利并倚势沾光之情，何以即至于其事灭绝之时，下文胪列陈明。其一情，其为指物沾利事中之欠债者，其所应尽之责。倘能毕尽其责，即可谓灭绝之时。其二情，其为指物沾利与倚势沾光事中之为债主者，竟致推辞，不愿承受其事者，亦即可谓灭绝之时。其三情，其在接受其物者，能将指物沾利与倚势沾光事中一切未便之处，疏通而行之，亦可谓为灭绝之时。其四情，如其指物沾利与倚势沾光之情，已至例准援免之日，亦可谓为灭绝之时。然论此援免之事，其在欠债者于所指定资之物，何以即至例准援免之时。该因其事中原行立具文约，其所可挟例应既至灭绝之时，即可为例准援免之日。而如论于接受其物者之他人，其何以至例准援免之时，应于所挟物主之权已满之时，即可获有例准援免之益。惟此项例准援免之事，须立有切实字据，即以该字据注入官册之日为始计之，而为援免之时。并该为债主者，如以所挟一切之权，亦欲注入官册之中者，则与例准援免之事毫无所伤。"①

"第二千一百八十二条　凡如欲有照录定资之物，传递物主之权，注于官册之中者，则其事实不足，即可谓已疏通指物沾利与倚势沾光之事业。盖因原本物主于此等定资之物，原有被人可执之权。今虽将物传递于人，而该物仍实带有可挟之权，故不足以为疏通之事。

第二千一百八十四条　凡为接受其物者，应持以前所立字据，前往报知指物沾利者之债主，谓为现欲刻即清还欠款。惟须还以接受其物者原定之价，如价还之。亦不拘至于还补之期与否，实为可行。"②

---

① ［法］毕利干：《法国律例·民律》下卷，日本司法省1894年版，第476、478、482页。
② ［法］毕利干：《法国律例·民律》下卷，日本司法省1894年版，第485、486页。

"第二千一百九十三条　凡如有妇之夫与为义父者，其所有定资之物，或因其妇，或因弱冠者已有指物沾利之情，而未注入官册者。倘有人欲于此等定资之物而有他项指物沾利之情者，则设以何法而疏通之。

第二千一百九十六条　凡护持管守册簿之官，倘经有人呈请，将册簿中所注文约字据等件，欲行照抄一分者，该管官应即准其照抄。盖在指物沾利之事，其已诣官注册者，固应准其抄录。设竟未诣官将其事实注册者，则该管经手理此事务之官，应行缮具字据，谓为此事实系未经前来注册，以便将所给字据可以为凭。"①

4. 关于继承：

"第七百一十八条　凡何以即为开首兴办相继接产之事，有如本业主现时死亡，或其人未亡，而系灭绝祖泽者，则即可以开首兴办相继接产之事矣。

第七百一十九条　凡开首兴办相继接产之事，如因系被官科断灭绝福泽者，即以科断之日为始计之。倘其事关本例第二章第二节享用福泽，或阻止福泽等项作载之情者，即可为开首兴办相继接产之事。"②

"第七百二十九条　凡承受相继接产之人，既为忘恩负义之徒，自应驱逐，使其不能妄邀相继接产之事，倘其人以先曾有幸得利益之处，即自开办相继接产之日，如数缴回。

第七百三十条　凡如忘恩负义之人，绝不得享获其父母所有之利益，惟至忘恩负义之子女，而始可递相承受相继接产事中之利益，而该忘恩负义之人，更不能于其子女享获利益之关系，而有可以续获之例应。"③

---

① 〔法〕毕利干：《法国律例·民律》下卷，日本司法省1894年版，第493、496页。
② 〔法〕毕利干：《法国律例·民律》中卷，日本司法省1894年版，第6、7页。
③ 〔法〕毕利干：《法国律例·民律》中卷，日本司法省1894年版，第13页。

"第七百三十五条　凡以何法即知道其人为相连切近应行承受遗产之人，应以其位分所居之代数计之，其所谓一代者，则为一级。

第七百三十六条　凡一级相连之人为一脉，而一脉之中分为二族，一族直论以族，旁支直族者，递次相贯而下，使为晚辈。若旁族者，虽非同亲所生，则为开原一祖而来。至论直族，亦有所别，有为晚辈者，有为长辈者，盖如自直族举重，由某辈为止而论，或由以上而论，或由以下而论，上者，则与其长辈相连之人，下者，则与其晚辈相连之人也。"①

"第七百五十八条　凡如私子之父母，若无相连切近之亲谊，可以照例承受此等遗产，则为私子者，始可幸得其父母身后所遗之产。

第七百五十九条　凡如遗产之事，倘为私子者，竟致死亡，而其所生之子女，亦可前来援照上条所定章程，索讨其所得遗产之例应。"②

"第七百七十四条　凡遇相继接产之事，有因理直事顺，宜乎收留者，或有因系有盈无亏之遗产而收留者。

第七百七十五条　凡无论何人，于此相继接产之事，均不准勒令某人令其收留相继接产之情，或系收留，或系推辞，均可任便自主。"③

"第八百一十六条　凡如遗产事中而有同受遗产之人，自行割据其分，而其余众同受遗产者，仍可请官为之分晰。倘竟未经立具分晰之合同，或其人亦未至例准援免之限，如欲分晰此项遗产，亦能呈请分晰之权。

第八百一十七条　凡有分应同受遗产之人，而其人系弱冠者，或系被禁者，如遇分晰之事，须由为其义父者代操其权，而此义父得以干预此事，实由该遗产事中家亲会议而来，始为可

---

① ［法］毕利干：《法国律例·民律》中卷，日本司法省1894年版，第17页。
② ［法］毕利干：《法国律例·民律》中卷，日本司法省1894年版，第30、31页。
③ ［法］毕利干：《法国律例·民律》中卷，日本司法省1894年版，第39页。

行。设遇分晰遗产之事而应承受之人，现时经未在场者，则其所委代其操权之人，自可代为分晰，以便承受。"①

"第八百九十四条　凡何以及为生前将产物给付于人，如其事中曾经立具合同，系某一人将其自有之物给予一人，而在给予者，则自给予之日起，其自有而已给人之物，即永不归其管属矣。而在收受者，亦即于此日起，于人所给之物，实有收受管属之权。

第八百九十五条　凡何人即为奉有遗书之情，有如事先曾经立具合同，议准某人身故之后，将该故者所有产物，或一切或一分给予一人，届期即可持书承领，此所谓奉有遗书之情。惟此项遗书，事前曾经议准如何给予情形。倘嗣后仍有未能洽心满志之处，亦可将所议定遗书拆割改易，再为议定给予情形，即至该给予者至已去世为止。"②

"第九百零二条　凡除例载某人有不能自主之权者以外，其余一切之人，均有可以给予物件，与收受物件之权。

第九百零三条　凡为弱冠之人，倘其年纪未及十六岁者，不能有将物件任便给人之权，除本例第九章所载以外者，皆不能有任便给人物件之权。"③

"第九百二十条　凡如有生前付物之情，或系有遗书之情，如其所给之数，竟有逾于任便给付之产之数者，则应于开办相继接产之时，准有提取所逾之数情事。

第九百二十一条　凡如有生前付物之情，倘其所给之数，竟逾于任便给付之产之数者，则分应提取此项所逾之数者为何等人，应由例准保护事中权利之人，或系其本人，或系其身后承受遗产之人，均无不行。而若论及于收受给付物件之人，与承受遗念物件之人，并该遗产身故者之债主等，均不能有此提取之权，

---

① ［法］毕利干：《法国律例·民律》中卷，日本司法省1894年版，第61页。
② ［法］毕利干：《法国律例·民律》中卷，日本司法省1894年版，第109、110页。
③ ［法］毕利干：《法国律例·民律》中卷，日本司法省1894年版，第115页。

并其事中一切利益,亦均不能妄相享受。"①

"第九百三十一条 凡欲立具合同,系因有生前付物之情者,则立此项合同须于理事绅宦当面,并应按照所定一切围范而行,尤须将此合同原稿寄存于该绅宦之手,否则虽有所议,亦惟置之不行。

第九百三十二条 凡有生前付物之情者,其事中所有之关系,即自收受者与给予者,因事言明据有此物,自此实归收受者之手中为始,而有关系。并该收受之情,其事中所有关系即由该收受者,于给予者报明此物今已收留,则其事中之关系,即以此日为始,而立此收受之合同,无论何时均可,惟须给予者在世之时,则无不行。并其所立之合同,惟应存于公所之中。"②

"第九百九十条 凡无论系属何情,而欲立具遗书者,须有二纸原稿,以备移交收存。

第九百九十一条 凡如船抵外国口岸,而其口中乃驻有法国领事官者,其所立遗书原稿,应将一分严行封固,呈交于法国领事官,由该官转交于管理水师事务衙门堂官,再由该堂官递交于立此遗书者其人所居本处息讼官署中检收处,以便收存。"③

"第一千四十八条 凡如为父母者,而于任便给付之产,可以任便给于其子女一人,或数人,或给一分,或数分,惟须于立具遗书之时,言明此项任便给付之产,今既给予为子女者承受,而相传以下,尤须由子女传给其孙子女,以便承受。

第一千七十五条 凡为父母尊长等,均能将已有之产业,分于其儿女及孙儿女者。

第一千八十八条 凡如给付产物之事,系因婚嫁事务而始给付者,倘其所议婚姻之事,竟未克成。则因此而为给付之事,亦属衰迈不宜于时者而不能行之例一例论之。"④

---

① [法] 毕利干:《法国律例·民律》中卷,日本司法省1894年版,第129、130页。
② [法] 毕利干:《法国律例·民律》中卷,日本司法省1894年版,第135、136页。
③ [法] 毕利干:《法国律例·民律》中卷,日本司法省1894年版,第171页。
④ [法] 毕利干:《法国律例·民律》中卷,日本司法省1894年版,第210、225、234页。

5. 关于债与合同：

"第一千一百零一条　凡何以谓为合同盟约、契券等类，系与一人或与数人，因事立一证据，或欲为谋一事，或不欲为某一事，有此可以为据，此之谓立具合同、盟约、契券之事业。

第一千一百零九条　凡于合同所载者，虽为应行遵允之事，乃于其应行遵允事中，而误有错谬之处，均不能即为遵允，或如应行遵允之事，而其事中实有强逼勒派之情，亦不能为应遵允之事，而皆为未为结实可靠。

第一千一百三十五条　凡如合同中一切应行遵照事宜，不但于所载各项情由，即其事中所有各项关系，亦须遵照而行，即如有关定例者，应行率循及其地习俗，并应秉公处置一切事宜，均须遵照而行。"①

"第一千一百八十五条　凡如指定异日某时，而与课程受物者，其情亦何有别，盖所谓指定异日某时者，则于其事不能有停止之情，不过可以稍为迟延其所应尽之责而已。

第一千一百八十七条　凡如有指定异日某时情事，大约逆料可与欠负之人有所利益之处，除事经言明其事中情形，系与债主有所利益者，则始不归此例一律论之。"②

"第一千二百八十二条　凡如所立文约而有信押之情，该为债主者，而乃以此等约据付之于欠债之人，而为子撤销者，则此事即等于还欠无异也。

第一千二百八十三条　凡如有将原行约据照抄一分，给于欠债之人者，则此事不过足可以令人逆料，而有宽免交纳之情也。除事经另立有切实约据，执之以为凭者，则此所给照抄之文约，自不足以为据矣。"③

"第一千三百五十二条　凡如按照律例所设尔有凭虚逆料之

---

① ［法］毕利干：《法国律例·民律》中卷，日本司法省1894年版，第243、248、263页。
② ［法］毕利干：《法国律例·民律》中卷，日本司法省1894年版，第290、291页。
③ ［法］毕利干：《法国律例·民律》中卷，日本司法省1894年版，第350、351页。

情，设其事中所有利益，如其归之于某人者，则此人勿庸执有别项凭据，而即以此可以为凭。倘经按照律例而有凭虚逆料之情，而乃有人谓为别有可凭之处，则为例不准行。或有凭虚逆料之事，而于所立文约，谓为仍有所凭，而其人竟与此拟料之事，有相抗衡者，则亦为例不准行。除经于其事之先曾已呈明，系或为律例中格外之事，或具有矢誓之情，或经官有识认之事，则始为可行。

第一千三百五十七条　凡如矢誓之事，亦有二项情形，有如甲谓乙令其矢誓，即可定其所判断者而结案，此之谓结局之矢誓。其二情，有由该官于定案之时，于两造之中，命其一人矢之以誓，即可定案，此之谓定案之矢誓。"①

"第一千三百七十一条　凡如所谓类似立有契约者，有如某人所行之事，系其人情甘所行，而因之相因而及生发，有遵议而行之情，或所行事向之于他人者，或所行事向之于两造中之一人，系彼此均有关系者。

第一千三百八十五条　凡如豢养各种牲畜之主，与使用各种牲畜之人，如其所有牲畜竟致人有损害情事，则无论该牲畜等或系于管束之时，或系于散放之际，该豢养之主而与使用之人，应于被其损害者均有应禁之责。"②

"第一千八百三十二条　凡何以为社会之事，即如立一合同，或系二人，或系数人，将所有众物聚集一处，令其滋生利益，而此二人或数人均有可以享用之权。

第一千八百三十三条　凡如所谓社会之事，在设立者其所希图可享之例应，自应于例理毫无所违，而与风俗教化均无所伤，至固结此等社会之事，原应与在此社会之人，公同均有所裨益之处，惟每会友，均应代入资财，或土地，或本人自有才能，始可享获其利。"③

---

① ［法］毕利干：《法国律例·民律》中卷，日本司法省1894年版，第404、408页。
② ［法］毕利干：《法国律例·民律》中卷，日本司法省1894年版，第416、426页。
③ ［法］毕利干：《法国律例·民律》下卷，日本司法省1894年版，第280、281页。

"第一千八百六十二条　凡于贸易事务以外设立社会之事者，该会中之会友等，其于会中之欠款实无按名摊赔之责，并众会友等彼此亦无互相勒令按名承担之责，除事经执有可以勒令摊赔之权者，始为格外之事。

第一千八百六十三条　凡如众会友而于社会中之债主，均有分应承担之责，而即按照均分其数之事，照例行之。即其人所入社会中之股分较小者，亦应均分补赔，除事经于立具文约之时，言明遇有价补债欠之事，而在股分较小之会友，实照所入股分较大之会友，其承担之责有异者，在需格外之事。"①

"第一千八百七十五条　凡何以为借贷于使用之物，有如立具文约，将某一人所有之物而乃出借于人，则在借之者，其所应尽之责，应于该物一经使用既毕，即将原物归还本主，此即可谓尽责。

第一千八百七十六条　凡如所谓借贷之事，其事中系无望酬思报之情者。"②

"第一千九百零五条　凡如制定之例，原准于借贷事务，或为资财，或为食饮之物，或为一切动资之物，均应因其借贷而即计其利息，实为例所准行。

第一千九百零六条　凡为借贷者，其于所立文约之中，并为因事计及其利，而乃自甘备给利息缴还者，设日后致有翻悔之情，则不能向已物借之于人者，而有索回已缴利息之情，亦不能于所借贷原本之上，而有抽扣利息之数之情。"③

"第一千九百五十五条　凡所谓押质之事，或有由二人自行立具文约而押质者，或有由该管官谕令立具文约押质者。

第一千九百五十七条　凡所谓押质物件之事，亦能有望酬思报之情者。"④

---

① ［法］毕利干：《法国律例·民律》下卷，日本司法省1894年版，第298页。
② ［法］毕利干：《法国律例·民律》下卷，日本司法省1894年版，第307页。
③ ［法］毕利干：《法国律例·民律》下卷，日本司法省1894年版，第318、319页。
④ ［法］毕利干：《法国律例·民律》下卷，日本司法省1894年版，第317、318页。

"第一千九百八十一条　凡如所议给与岁定之资，不能不归之于他人，而有扣留情事，惟其事中并无望酬思报之情者，则始为格外之事。

第一千九百八十二条　凡如议给岁定之资，不能因有灭绝福泽之情，妄为阻碍之端。纵其人因事致有灭绝福泽之情，亦与议给岁定之资毫无干涉。"①

"第一千九百八十四条　凡何以谓命人代操其权，即如一人给与某一人之权，命其代为办理某项之事，并何以为其事之已成，即在被命代操其权者，诸凡允如所言而行，即可谓其事之已成矣。

第一千九百八十七条　凡如命人代操其权之事，其所议定者，或系有命其特办一事，或系有普全齐备之情，而命其统办诸事者。"②

"第一千九百九十一条　凡如被命代操其权之人，其于应尽之责，应即遵照，命代操其权者所定一切章程而为。倘竟不遵照而为，如其事中有关配比安慰之需，则惟向该代操其权者是问，并如该命其代操其权者其人竟尔物故，则该被命代操其权者，如于其所司之事而起有废弛之情，则亟应妥为经管料理，总以至其事之已成，方可为止。

第一千九百九十三条　凡如被委代操其权者，须将其所司之事，而于该命其代操其权者，有汇总禀报之情，并其人凡于所立文约之中，曾经命之者给以其权，而以其权所得之物，自应如其物汇总禀报，即非以其权而得之物，自亦为命之者之物，亦应入其物报明。"③

"第二千条　凡如被委代操其权者，倘于其所应尽之责，致有亏累损耗之端，并非由其人涉险之故致有然者，则在命人代操其权者，按理而言，应即有安慰赔补之需。

---

① ［法］毕利干：《法国律例·民律》下卷，日本司法省1894年版，第361页。
② ［法］毕利干：《法国律例·民律》下卷，日本司法省1894年版，第362、364页。
③ ［法］毕利干：《法国律例·民律》下卷，日本司法省1894年版，第366、367页。

第二千零一条　凡为代操契券者，其于所代操应尽之责，设有欲行垫付资财情事，则在命人代操其权者，自应按本兼利一并给还，然以何日为始计算之，即自议定有垫付之情之日为始而计算之。"①

"第二千一十一条　凡如委人欲其尽卖一事，而在委之者，未能宽放其心，乃复命为保者，以为尽责者之保，则在应尽其责者，倘竟未能尽责，则该为保者，应即代尽其责矣。

第二千一十二条　凡如为保质者，不得率尔为人之保质，须其所保质之事系何例而为，结实可靠者，始为可行。虽如此言，而于为保质者，经其人所保质之事，亦准间有可以销毁之情，盖因尽责者，或于其人有所未宜，而于他人则无不合，故有能销毁之情。"②

"第二千二十一条　凡如为保质者，倘遇欠债之人，竟不能清还其债，以致为保质者有代还债欠之事，须于该原欠债者讨其所有定、动之资，委为不能以之还债者，始为可行。除事经为保质者曾经辞其于欠债者，核计其人所有定、动之资能否可以还债，或该为保质者而于原欠债者曾有公摊赔补之责者，则为格外之事，而惟一遇有此情事，即应按照相摊赔补债欠之责，一例论之。

第二千二十二条　凡为债主者，而于欠债之人，倘经其未能还账而转迫索于为保质者，欲其代为赔补，则在为保质者，须令债主将该欠债者所有定、动之资，尽数查验，果系能以抵补债欠与否，而一经有此情事，则在为债主者，即应将欠债者所有定、动之资，详为查验，以便该欠款终有着落。"③

"第二千三十四条　凡如其所应尽之责系为保质之事者，倘其事竟至于灭绝之时，则亦应与一切他项勉尽其责至于灭绝者一律论之。

---

① ［法］毕利干：《法国律例·民律》下卷，日本司法省1894年版，第373页。
② ［法］毕利干：《法国律例·民律》下卷，日本司法省1894年版，第379页。
③ ［法］毕利干：《法国律例·民律》下卷，日本司法省1894年版，第385页。

第二千三十五条　凡如欠债者，而有一人为之保质，复有一人为保质者之保质，倘在欠债者而与为保质者有结联一气，相消至于灭绝，并有相继接产之情者，则其事中原债主即与复为保质者之保质者，而有索讨原债之权。"①

"第二千四十一条　凡无论何人，未能自行寻觅有人为之保质，惟应备具一物，以为备质之需，而尤须该物所值之数足以敷其原欠之数者，始为可行。

第二千四十二条　凡如为保质者，倘系由该管之官所指名拣委者，则该为保质者不能挟有先事查验该欠债者所有定、动之资，果系能以还债与否。"②

"第二千四十六条　凡如有干过失例禁，因而甚至有干涉刑律之案，倘其于民律案中有应行安慰之处，既经安慰，因将民律之案已销者，而实不足即将其有干刑律之案，亦一并概行注销。

第二千四十七条　凡如既经减数相就而理，乃其事中竟有不行遵照而为者，则于其事中亦可酌增一议，拟以作如何惩办之处者，亦为例所准行。"③

"第二千六十四条　凡如所立文约字据等项，须即为例之所准行者，倘其欲施拘勒其身之事，系施之于弱冠者，则亦为例不准行。

第二千六十五条　凡如事中所关之资财，而一核计其数，有未至三百夫浪者，则亦不能有拘勒其身之事。"④

"第二千七十一条　凡何以为备质之事，有如立具文约，指出一物，由欠债者将该物交付债主者之手，而以为押质其所欠负之款。

第二千七十二条　凡如备质之事，亦分有二项情形，其一相则有以动资之物而为备质者，其二项则有以定资之物而为备

---

① ［法］毕利干：《法国律例·民律》下卷，日本司法省1894年版，第393页。
② ［法］毕利干：《法国律例·民律》下卷，日本司法省1894年版，第397页。
③ ［法］毕利干：《法国律例·民律》下卷，日本司法省1894年版，第400页。
④ ［法］毕利干：《法国律例·民律》下卷，日本司法省1894年版，第410页。

质者。"①

"第二千七十三条　凡如备质之物，系以动资之物者，则以此物既经付于债主者之手，而在债主较之他项债主，因此即可有挟持之权，其权为何，即于此项备质动资项上而有倚势沾光之情。

第二千七十六条　凡如备质动资之物，何以即有倚势沾光之情，惟应将其动资之物交付清楚于债主者之手，或由欠债者而与债主者两造亲身议定，将所欲行备质动资之物，交付于某一人之手者，则始可以有倚势沾光之情。

第二千八十九条　凡如事经欠债者与债主者两造议定明确，议以欠债者所欠之利息，而以其所备质之物生发果子、利息，以之两数相抵而相销，或为统共之数，或为若干之数，均属与例相符，而为准行之事。"②

"第二千二百零四条　凡为债主者，而于欠债者之人所有定资，并其相随杂件及其所有之物，而该债主实挟有例应，能以撤其物主之权，并于沾利代守定资项上，而亦有追索之权，实为例所准行。

第二千二百零九条　凡如为债主者，而于欠债人所有一项定资之上，乃有指物沾利之情，则不能向欠债者其余他项定资之上，指一索讨其债，除事经原行指物沾利之物，委不足以清还其债者，则始可及于其余所有定资之物，以示限制。

第二千二百一十八条　凡为债主者，其于分拨售物价值，其事中次序之先后，而给付于各债主者，其一切应行事宜及各项应遵围范，均宜遵照民律指掌中所定围范，遵照而行。"③

"第二千二百一十九条　凡何以即为例准援免之事，即如遵一法则，可以得其物主之权，并可宽释其己身一切应尽之责，及有一切获益之处。然惟须于制定期限之中，遵服各项章程而行。

---

① ［法］毕利干：《法国律例·民律》下卷，日本司法省1894年版，第414页。
② ［法］毕利干：《法国律例·民律》下卷，日本司法省1894年版，第415、417、425页。
③ ［法］毕利干：《法国律例·民律》下卷，日本司法省1894年版，第501、505、510页。

第二千二百二十条　凡如一切之人，实不准于未得例准援免之先，而有欲推辞其可获例准援免之益。惟于既得例准援免之益以后者，始可准其有推辞之事。"①

"第二千二百二十八条　凡何以于物而有操持之权，有如或于一物，或于一例应，或经其人亲手主持，或经其委人代为管守，而于其人或可器便其物，或可享用其利，此即可为操持之权也。

第二千二百二十九条　凡如得有例准援免之权者，须于其事由能主持之情，历经三十年之久，而实有物主之权，并于其事委系安善，一切他项事务，实无与之相抗，而众人皆知实有此事，委为真实可据。其人犹之乎持有物主之权者，然后始得有此例准援免之事。"②

"第二千二百三十七条　凡如上文所言之人，其所挟之例应，既不得妄有牵混，即其身后相继接产之人，亦不能妄邀有例准援免之事。

第二千二百三十八条　凡虽如此而言，其在第二千二百三十六、第二千二百三十七等条所载农夫人等，设此人等所执之文约，设有更易、改变情事，亦不论其致事情节为何，惟系此项人等，始可行其有例准援免之权。"③

"第二千二百四十二条　凡如例准援免之事，有能隔断之情者，而其致事之由，或有因事出于自然而然者，或有事关民律中所载案情而然者。

第二千二百四十三条　凡何以为事出自然而然，将例准援免之事隔断者。有如一人曾执有于是事操持之权，而其事业经年余之久，乃竟由本物主，或由他人将其所操持事中，有可享用之权屏去者，则即可为隔断其例准援免之事矣。"④

---

① ［法］毕利干：《法国律例·民律》下卷，日本司法省1894年版，第511页。
② ［法］毕利干：《法国律例·民律》下卷，日本司法省1894年版，第514、515页。
③ ［法］毕利干：《法国律例·民律》下卷，日本司法省1894年版，第519页。
④ ［法］毕利干：《法国律例·民律》下卷，日本司法省1894年版，第522、523页。

"第二千二百六十条 凡如欲计例准援免之事,须不以时,让以何法计之,盖欲核计其事,则应论日不论时。

第二千二百六十一条 凡如按照期限所定之日,而于其临末之日已成,即可得例准援免之时。"①

第三节 《法国律例·刑律》

《法国律例·刑律》共四卷。第一卷"论治犯法与治犯过之罪以及其关系";第二卷"论治犯法与犯过之案,或宜惩办,或宜宽宥以及应行惩办案中有承担之责者之例";第三卷"论犯法与过失之罪并其应行如何科断之例";第四卷"论一切越理之案应归正,尤应所管属者并其因案应科之罪"。

毕利干译《法国律例·刑律》与林纪东等主编《刑法》目录对比表②

毕利干译《法国律例·刑律》	林纪东等主编《刑法》
论刑律大略 卷一 论治犯法与治犯过之罪以及其关系	第一编 总则
第一章 论一切犯法之案应科以重罪者	第一章 法例
第二章 论治犯过之罪名	第二章 刑事责任
第三章 论治犯过与犯法之罪	第三章 未遂犯
第四章 论治复行犯法与复行犯过之罪	第四章 共犯
卷二 论治犯法与犯过之案,或宜惩办,或宜宽宥以及应行惩办案中有承担之责者之例	第三章 刑
卷三 论犯法与过失之罪并其应行如何科断之例	第四章 累犯
第一类 论所犯之案有干于国计民生者	第七章 数罪并罚
第一章 论治煽惑扰乱于国家君民之罪	第八章 刑之酌科及加减
第一节 治在边疆处所谋为不轨,扰乱于国者之罪	第九章 缓刑
第二节 论在国境之内谋为不轨扰乱于国者之罪	第十章 假释

---

① [法]毕利干:《法国律例·民律》下卷,日本司法省1894年版,第533页。
② [法]毕利干:《法国律例·刑律·目录》,日本司法省1894年版;林纪东等主编:《刑法·目录》,五南图书出版公司1986年版。

续表

毕利干译《法国律例·刑律》	林纪东等主编《刑法》
第三节 论有关国计民生之要务，或不应泄露者而为之泄露，或不应隐匿者而为之隐匿者之罪	第十一章 时效
第二章 论治违犯国法之罪	第十二章 保安处分
第一节 论治干犯有经理公私事务之权者之罪	第二编 分则
第二节 论治干犯妄行自恃有可以自主之权者	第一章 内乱罪
第三节 论治官员通同舞弊之例	第二章 外患罪
第四节 论各项职守之官，而于其本职之外，竟有能越俎妄行干预庶政之例	第三章 妨害国交罪
第三章 论治案犯有关于民生之罪	第四章 渎职罪
第一节 论治诸凡伪造之罪	第五章 妨害公务罪
第二节 论治官员在任内干犯罪过，有不忠于君而失其职守之罪	第六章 妨害投票罪
第三节 论治掌教之士，于其本责一切应为之事而竟紊乱，未合围范者之罪	第七章 妨害秩序罪
第四节 论治于官场一切政治，胆敢有不遵循而抗拒违悖者之罪	第八章 脱逃罪
第五节 论治凶恶棍徒与流民并乞丐，而敢结党成群，滋生事端者之罪	第九章 藏匿人犯及湮灭证据罪
第六节 论治干犯过失与越理之事，并非自口致罪，系以书籍画谱，并此等书籍画谱亦未注明著作印刷者系何名姓之罪	第十章 伪证及诬告罪
第七节 论治未奉明文，未合于例，擅敢聚众会议事件之例	第十一章 公共危险罪
第二类 论治干犯各项罪案，有碍于民生者之例	第十二章 伪造货币罪
第一章 论治所干之罪有碍于民生者之罪	第十三章 伪造有价证券罪
第一节 论之一切杀伤人命之案，并一切有关死罪者，系一语言威吓，欲杀其人之命者之罪	第十四章 伪造度量衡罪
第二节 论治有心殴伤于人及干一切罪过之案，不得归于故杀一律论者之例	第十五章 伪造文书印文罪
第三节 论治误伤人命、误致殴伤而其致罪之情，有可以原谅者，有无可以原谅者，并误伤人命与误致殴伤之案，有不能科之以罪者	第十六章 妨害风化罪

续表

毕利干译《法国律例·刑律》	林纪东等主编《刑法》
第四节 论治于风俗教化有伤者	第十七章 妨害婚姻及家庭罪
第五节 论治任意妄拿无辜以及私行押禁无辜之例	第十八章 亵渎祀典及侵害坟墓尸体罪
第六节 论治获过与罪,系于婴孩归原之生育合同,或胆敢该易,或行销毁,并偷窃子女,或与子女生命有伤及于葬殓之事有干罪者	第十九章 妨害农工商罪
第七节 论治伪为质证、诬指有罪,或有意牵引、诬为报告,或欺凌于人,或于人,或发其一切机秘之事者	第二十章 鸦片罪
第二章 论治所干罪过之案,有碍于物产者之例	第二十一章 赌博罪
第一节 论治窃盗之例	第二十二章 杀人罪
第二节 论一切铺户设局诓骗并欺诈公私资财及一切?诈骗之事	第二十三章 伤害罪
第三节 论治人毁坏缺损损坏一切诸物者之例 论汇总诸务可以遵行章程	第二十四章 堕胎罪
卷四 论一切越理之案应归正,尤应所管属者并其因案应科之罪	第二十五章 遗弃罪
第一章 论正尤?应科之罪	第二十六章 妨害自由罪
第二章 论治干犯越理之案并应如何科断之例	第二十七章 妨害名誉及信用罪
	第二十八章 妨害秘密罪
	第二十九章 窃盗罪
	第三十章 抢夺强盗及海盗罪
	第三十一章 侵占罪
	第三十二章 诈欺背信及重利罪
	第三十三章 恐吓及掳人勒赎罪
	第三十四章 赃物罪
	第三十五章 毁弃损坏罪

毕利干译《法国律例·刑律》与《中华人民共和国刑法》目录对比表①

毕利干译《法国律例·刑律》	《中华人民共和国刑法》
论刑律大略 卷一 论治犯法与犯过之罪以及其关系	第一编 总则

---

① [法]毕利干:《法国律例·刑律·目录》,日本司法省 1894 年版;《中华人民共和国刑法·目录》。

续表

毕利干译《法国律例·刑律》	《中华人民共和国刑法》
第一章 论一切犯法之案应科以重罪者	第一章 刑法的任务、基本原则和适用范围
第二章 论治犯过之罪名	第二章 犯罪
第三章 论治犯过与犯法之罪	第一节 犯罪和刑事责任
第四章 论治复行犯法与复行犯过之罪	第二节 犯罪的预备、未遂和中止
卷二 论治犯法与犯过之案，或宜惩办，或宜宽赦以及应行惩办案中，有承担之责者之例	第三节 共同犯罪
卷三 论犯法与过失之罪，并其应行如何科断之例	第四节 单位犯罪
第一类 论所犯之案有干于国计民生者	第三章 刑罚
第一章 论治煽惑扰乱于国家君民者之罪	第一节 刑罚的种类
第一节 治在边疆处所谋为不轨，扰乱于国者之罪	第二节 管制
第二节 论在国境之内谋为不轨扰乱于国者之罪	第三节 拘役
第三节 论有关国计民生之要务，或不应泄露者而为之泄露，或不应隐匿者而为之隐匿者之罪。	第四节 有期徒刑、无期徒刑
第二章 论治违犯国法之罪	第五节 死刑
第一节 论治干犯有经理公私事务之权者之罪	第六节 罚金
第二节 论治干犯妄行自恃有可以自主之权者	第七节 剥夺政治权利
第三节 论治官员通同舞弊之例	第八节 没收财产
第四节 论各项职守之官，而于其本职之外，竟有能越俎妄行干预庶政之例	第四章 刑罚的具体运用
第三章 论案犯有关于民生之罪	第一节 量刑
第一节 论治诸凡伪造之罪	第二节 累犯
第二节 论治官员在任内干犯罪过，有不忠于君而失其职守之罪	第三节 自首和立功
第三节 论治掌教之士，于其本责一切应为之事而竟紊乱，未合围范者之罪	第四节 数罪并罚
第四节 论治于官场一切政治，胆敢有不遵循而抗拒违悖者之罪	第五节 缓刑
第五节 论治凶恶棍徒与流民并乞丐，而敢结党成群，滋生事端者之罪	第六节 减刑
第六节 论治干犯过失与越理之事，并非自口致罪，系以书籍画谱，并此等书籍画谱亦未注明著作印刷者系何名姓之罪	第七节 假释

续表

毕利干译《法国律例·刑律》		《中华人民共和国刑法》	
第七节	论治未奉明文，未合于例，擅敢聚众会议事件之例	第八节	时效
第二类	论治干犯各项罪案，有碍于民生者之例	第五章	其他规定
第一章	论治所干之罪有碍于民生者之罪	第二编	分则
第一节	论之一切杀伤人命之案，并一切有关死罪者，系一语言威吓，欲杀其人之命者之罪	第一章	危害国家安全罪
第二节	论治有心殴伤于人及干一切罪过之案，不得归于故杀一律论者之例	第二章	危害公共安全罪
第三节	论治误伤人命、误致殴伤而其致罪之情，有可以原谅者，有无可以原谅者，并误伤人命与误致殴伤之案，有不能科之以罪者	第三章	破坏社会主义市场经济秩序罪
第四节	论治于风俗教化有伤者	第一节	生产、销售伪劣商品罪
第五节	论治任意妄拿无辜以及私行押禁无辜之例	第二节	走私罪
第六节	论治获过与罪，系于婴孩归原之生育合同，或胆敢该易，或行销毁，并偷窃子女，或与子女生命有伤及于葬殓之事有干罪者	第三节	妨害对公司、企业的管理秩序罪
第七节	论治伪为质证、诬指有罪，或有意牵引、诬为报告，或欺凌于人，或于人，或发其一切机秘之事者	第四节	破坏金融管理秩序罪
第二章	论治所干罪过之案，有碍于物产者之例	第五节	金融诈骗罪
第一节	论治窃盗之例	第六节	危害税收征管罪
第二节	论一切铺户设局诓骗并欺诈公私资财及一切？诈骗之事	第七节	侵犯知识产权罪
第三节	论治人毁坏缺损损坏一切诸物者之例　论汇总诸务可以遵行章程	第八节	扰乱市场秩序罪
第四卷	论一切越理之案应归正，尤应所管属者，并其因案应科之罪	第四章	侵犯公民人身权利、民主权利罪
第一章	论正尤？应科之罪	第五章	侵犯财产罪
第二章	论治干犯越理之案并应如何科断之例	第六章	妨害社会管理秩序罪
		第一节	扰乱公共秩序罪
		第二节	妨害司法罪
		第三节	妨害国（边）境管理罪

第四章 《法国律例》的翻译与出版

续表

毕利干译《法国律例·刑律》	《中华人民共和国刑法》
	第四节 妨害文物管理罪
	第五节 危害公共卫生罪
	第六节 破坏环境资源保护罪
	第七节 走私、贩卖、运输、制造毒品罪
	第八节 组织、强迫、引诱、容留、介绍卖淫罪
	第九节 制作、贩卖、传播淫秽物品罪
	第七章 危害国防利益罪
	第八章 贪污贿赂罪
	第九章 渎职罪
	第十章 军人违反职责罪
	附则

《法国律例·刑律》是掌握政权的集团以国家名义颁布的关于什么行为是犯罪和如何惩罚犯罪的法律。《法国律例·刑律》对刑法基本原则、犯罪概念、犯罪原因、刑罚的种类、犯罪的分类等均有涉及：

关于犯罪：

第一条 "凡犯罪有三等，即越礼过失犯法，其罪案归正尤厅拟办者，皆为越礼之案。而案归于惩儆司理事坊拟办者，皆为过失之案。至于有干羞辱之罪，与有干各项重罪者，皆为犯法之案。

第二条 凡有意犯法，欲成未成者，如始而已动其恶念，继而欲行其恶事，而乃忽然转念终止，或因被阻未成，或其事出意外，未遂其愿，因而未成，而其形迹已属昭然，皆应以已成者论，照例惩办。

第三条 凡有意犯过，而一查实情，除所致之案有关例载，按例应以已成者照论外，其余各项犯过案件，自应以未成者置论。"①

关于刑罚及其具体运用：

"第十七条　凡有干犯充军之罪者，应将该犯照例发往到配，并令其永远居住配所。倘该犯胆敢逃回，应从重治以永作缧绁苦工之罪。设该犯所逃之地，在本国界外有法兵驻扎之所，即将该犯发往本处配所。如国家并未设此等充军配所，即将该犯永远监禁，或在本国监内，或在法国所属边外监内，由承审官拟定发往。设至配所道路阻梗，即将该犯暂行监禁在本国。

第十八条　凡案犯永远缧绁作工与充军等罪者，则其人亦即为灭绝福泽之人。然虽如此，亦有案犯充军之罪，倘准办理公私事件者，或予以全权，或仅予以微权，以示有别。

第十九条　凡案犯限定年月缧绁作工之罪者，其期限至少五年，至多二十年。"②

关于危害国家安全罪：

"论治在边疆处所谋为不轨，扰乱于国者之罪：

第七十五条　凡有持执军器私助敌国而反于本国倒戈抗逆者，著照例科以斩罪。

第七十七条　凡遇谋为不轨，心向敌国，作为敌国向导，或将城池、炮台、险要关隘以及海口停泊船只、军中支应局、军需局投献敌国，或惑乱本国水陆各军军心，以致军心散漫，使敌国得以获胜，或于本国之武职、兵弁、水手人等，离间、散漫其忠君爱国之心，以上诸罪，均科以斩罪。

第七十八条　凡与敌国投递信函，于本国机密、军机事务以

---

① ［法］毕利干：《法国律例》之《刑律》，日本司法省1894年版，第1、2页。
② ［法］毕利干：《法国律例》之《刑律》，日本司法省1894年版，第6、7页。

及本国之友邦有关系窒碍之处，虽不犯以上诸款所列之罪，又无谋为不轨真情实据大罪，而其所递信函，在敌国即可借此得其事中利益，或其人更敢私递信函，借以传其侦探之事者，则尤应从重科以应得之罪。

第七十九条　凡有谋为不轨，私通敌国，竟敢将本国之友邦机密事务，而泄露于两国之敌国者，均照第七十六条、七十七条之例，一例惩办。

第八十条　凡大小文武职官，以及在官应役人等，如其职能以与闻机密军机事务，有如兴师动众等事，而竟敢将此等事私泄于邻国与敌国者，均应照第七十六条之例，一例办理。

第八十一条　凡大小文武官员，其职应行守护本国炮台、军需局、海口、马头等处地图文式者，而乃监守自盗，竟敢将此等图式献与敌国，或献与敌国大员之手，无论多寡，一经事犯到官，即科以斩罪。若将此等图式呈献现时无所交涉事务之邻国，或友国者，一经查出，即应科以监禁之罪。

第八十三条　凡无论军民人等，遇有明知某人为敌国侦探，或敌国哨马，而竟徇隐不举，反为之寻觅窝处容留者，一经查出，即拟以斩罪。

第九十二条　凡未奉有国家明文，或不遵军令，擅自调动兵马，或私自使人兴师，或私自招募勇丁，或以兵马、军装、器械等件，私自予之于人者，均著科以斩罪。

第九十三条　凡僭越非分，并无明文，亦无军令，擅自无故统带水陆各军，或于要隘、汛地、海口、城池诸处所，亦未奉有明文，妄自驻扎管辖，或已解其兵权，而仍恋栈把持，或曾经遣撤之兵，而仍含混容留在伍者，均科以斩罪。

第九十四条　凡遇国家按律招兵之时，其有统辖兵丁之责者，倘敢从中阻扰，玩泄众心，遏止众人不得充当兵弁，即或得以充当，而迫以权势牵掣阻扰，使众人不得稍伸其气者，即科以斩罪。若其事未能如愿，即按其事未成之例，科以重罪。"①

关于伪造国家货币罪：

"论治私造国家印信，并官场设立银行兑票、银票以及各色物件、印证并盖用印花、空白纸票之罪：

第一百三十二条　凡假造及改造金银钱文，希冀在本国境内含混行用者，其伙同行使之人，与明知其为私造钱文而由他处带入法国者，均科以永远缧絏苦工之罪。其假造或改造铜钱，希图在本国境内含混行用者，其伙同行使之人，与明知其为私造铜钱而由他处带入法国者，均科限以年月缧絏苦工之罪。

第一百三十三条　凡在法国境内或私造他国钱文，或同某人行使，或由他处将私钱带入法国者，均科限以年月苦工之罪。

第一百三十四条　凡本国与他国通行国宝，如有照式配用药料颜色伪造假冒，或以铜冒充银钱，或以银冒充金钱；或在本国境内行使，或帮同一人在他处私造假冒带入法国者，以致真伪难分，一经查出，均科以监收之罪。少则六月，多则三年。其帮同行使与伙同伪造假冒之人，以及将伪造之钱由他处带入法国者，均科以一体同罪。"②

关于危害公共安全罪：

"第九十一条　凡有人首先倡率为乱，致使民间互相争斗，或肆行抢掠，或妄行杀伤为盗等罪者，均著科以斩罪。或有意谋叛而尚未逆迹昭著者，即应查其案情之轻重，援照第八十九条之例一例惩办。

第二类　论治干犯各项罪案，有碍于民生者之例。

---

① ［法］毕利干：《法国律例·刑律》，日本司法省1894年版，第32、33、34、35、36、40、41页。
② ［法］毕利干：《法国律例·刑律》，日本司法省1894年版，第59、60页。

第一章 论治所干之罪有碍于民生者之罪。

第一节 论治一切杀伤人命之案,并一切有关死罪者,系一语言威吓,欲杀其人之命者之罪。

第一段 论治灭伦重案,并误伤人命,故杀、谋杀、杀害婴孩及一切毒杀人命之例。

第二百九十五条 凡有致伤人命之事,而一核实情由,系于当时情甘杀伤人命者,则应将其案归于故杀者一律置论。

第二百九十六条 凡有于致事之先,已伏杀伤恶念,或预设圈套,诱之以计,因而诱杀者,应即按照谋杀人命者之案,一例科断。

第二百九十七条

凡如谋杀人命之事,其致事之由,系有等于课程受物,如不能为即行杀伤致命者,倘遇此等案情,即应归于有心谋杀者一律置论。"①

"第二节 论治有心殴伤于人及干一切罪过之案,不得归于故杀一律论者之例

第三百零九条 凡有情甘殴伤于人,或用强横欺凌因而被殴之人,气忿成疾。或其被殴致伤,而于二十日以外,尚不能动作诸工者,一经查获,著将该情甘殴伤于人之犯,科以监收之罪,少则二年,多则五年,并令罚缴银两,少则十六个夫浪,多则二千夫浪。俟监收期满之日,能以援照第四十二条所设之例,禁止该犯经理公私事件,少则五年,多则十年,倘该犯用强殴伤,竟将被伤之人肢体毁伤,或单双目失明,当时成为残废之人。抑或因伤医治不效,渐成残废者,均将该犯科以监禁之罪。若该犯虽属有意殴伤,而其本愿亦不欲其人即至殒命,而被其所伤者,竟致内伤殒命,一核其案中情节,著将该犯科限以年月缧绁苦工之罪。

第三百一十条 凡人有意谋伤于人,或诱之以计,使其人自

---

① [法]毕利干:《法国律例·刑律》,日本司法省1894年版,第40、146、147页。

落圈套，以便殴伤可以泄忿。而被其所伤之人竟致因伤殒命者，一经查出，著将该犯科以永远缧绁苦工之罪。其次，或因殴伤致成残废，并双单目失明及遍体伤痕甚重者，著将该犯科限以年月缧绁苦工之罪。倘其案中情节有干犯第三百零九条所载之事者，著将该犯科以监禁之罪。"①

关于妨害社会管理秩序罪：

"第三百三十条　凡人于大庭广众之间，胆敢不顾廉耻，故作各种形态，实属有伤风化，一经拏获，即将该犯科以监收之罪，少则三个月，多则二年，并令罚缴银两，少则十六个夫浪，多则二百夫浪。

第三百三十一条　凡未及十三岁之幼童弱女，本属年幼无知。倘有一时愚昧，被人欺骗，致有失节之类，无论其案已成未成，查其案中情形，尚无？强逼威吓等情者，著将该起意致人失节之犯，科以监禁之罪。至同族一姓之人，设有长辈，无论男女，敢有与晚辈竟有淫荡邪秽之情，而其所属意之人尚在髫龄，未至准其自理事业之时，或其年已逾十三，而犹未能准其自理事业者，著将该行止不端、有灭伦常之长辈，科以监禁之罪。

第三百三十二条　凡遇有案关强奸之罪者，著将该犯即科限以年月缧绁苦工之罪。如所奸之人系十五岁以上之幼女，著将该犯从重科限以年月缧绁苦工之罪。至有倚强逼迫，令人含垢蒙羞，有意致人失节，无论男女，亦无论其案已成未成，即将该犯科以监禁之罪。倘干此罪之犯，其所属意者，系十五岁以上之人，著将该犯科限以年月缧绁苦工之罪。

第三百三十三条　凡遇有案关上文所载情形，其致罪者系出于与被其奸污者有栽培训诲之责之人，并各掌教士、各项仆役暨其尊长等所用之仆役，而乃敢与该晚辈幼孩，竟有奸污邪秽之

---

① ［法］毕利干：《法国律例·刑律》，日本司法省1894年版，第153、154页。

情，则无论其案系一人自犯之罪，或恐事不如愿，因？人串通？助，以致同人共犯之罪，实系大伤风化，致如干犯第三百三十一条头一段情形者，一经访获，即将该犯科限以年月缧絏苦工之罪，如此等之人设有干犯第三百三十二条所载强奸等事者，将该犯即科以永远缧絏苦工之罪。

第三百三十四条 凡有伤风化之事，有如于二十岁以上之男女，倘敢调唆愚憨，或代为引领路径，或代为帮助，竟致该男女一时愚昧，被其所惑，因而被人污秽者，一经查出，著将该犯科以监收之罪，少则六个月，多则两年，并罚缴银两，少则五十夫浪，多则五百夫浪。至如有调唆等情之人，系该男女之父母及一切由栽培训诲之责之人，更属罪不容？，著即从重科以监收之罪，少则二年，多则五年，并罚缴银两少则三百夫浪，多则一千夫浪。

第三百三十五条 凡有干犯第三百三十四条所载案情者，著即禁止该犯经理栽培训诲、详为代办及家亲会议等事。至如有干此罪者，系关第三百三十四条首一段案情者，其禁止经理栽培训诲等事期限，少则二年，多则五年。至有干犯此罪者，系关第三百三十四条二段情形，其禁止经理栽培训诲等事期限，少则十年，多则二十年。至为父母者，若干此罪，除照例惩办外，仍应查照民例之第一卷第九类所载，为父母者能以享用子女所有之利益即行禁止享用，并干此罪者，无论系属何情，亦能将该犯交巡捕厅约束，其约束之限，即照禁止之期限，照数计之。"①

关于贪污、受贿罪：

"论一切官员及一切在官人役，并经征赋则之官及一切应役之人，敢有枉法贪污、诈赃、受贿情事者：

第一百七十四条 凡治理国家诸政之官，并经理征收一切钱

---

① ［法］毕利干：《法国律例·刑律》，日本司法省1894年版，第167、168、169、170页。

粮，诸凡应交官项银两之人及应役人等，而于所司之事，敢有枉法贪污、诈赃受贿，或逾额浮征，或越量勒索，而于国家应征应缴各项银两实有耗伤者。查其数若在三百夫浪以下，其官员科以监禁之罪，其在官应役人等科以监收之罪，少则二年，多则五年。若其银数在三百夫浪以上者，其官员则科以监收之罪，少则二年，多则五年。其在官应役人等，亦科以监收之罪，少则一年，多则四年。不论官员人役，其有意欲犯此罪，而其事虽未成者，即照已成者论，照例惩办。其科以监收之犯，能以随时查照第四十二条之例，再为惩治。即以其案万释放之日为始计算，少则五年，多则十年。一俟限满之后，亦能酌核案由轻重，交巡捕厅，按照该犯监收之日数，再为严加约束。其有案犯此例之罪者，无论系何情节，除照例惩办外，亦能罚缴银两，其罚缴之数，即照案中应交赔补安慰之银归总，酌核多寡之数，多则四分之一，少则十二分之一，再行追罚。其各部院衙署，并理事绅宦与理非之绅等项人者，设有经手银财事故，而有干上项之情者，亦惟按照科治职官之罪一例惩办。"①

对于司法部门的贪污、受贿行为，《刑律》规定从重处罚：

"第一百七十七条　凡治理诸政之官及一切办理刑名事务之官，欲其本责应为事中，或由己追索，或因人祈请而有收受请托、收受贿赂情弊，其迹甚可令人指摘者，一经查出，著即科以禁止经理公私事件之罪，并查委系有赃，即按原赃之数，加倍勒罚。即以所罚之数，至少而论，亦不得在二百夫浪以下。倘此等劣员因得贿嘱，胆敢于其本责应为之件，故意迟延而不为者，亦照此例惩办。至由官派充与公众特举之人，堪为经纪验匠等类者，不敢收受贿嘱，意存偏袒，竟敢颠倒是非，指鹿为马者，亦惟照此例一例惩办。

第一百七十八条　凡如上文所载贪污之职官，倘其获罪情形科以禁止经理公私事件之罪，尤觉轻纵者，著即从重严为科断。

---

① ［法］毕利干：《法国律例·刑律》，日本司法省1894年版，第81页。

第一百八十一条　凡承审、监审之官并秉公议论词讼之绅，倘有枉法营私、贪污受贿，因而办案之时畸轻畸重，故为出入者，一经查出，应即援照第一百七十七条之例，令其罚缴银两。而于此外，仍宜科以监禁之罪。"①

关于渎职罪：

"论一切官员等有越分妄为，于其职守之外，凡一切不应为者而乃越分妄为，竟致有干涉商贾贸易之事者：

第一百七十五条　凡大小官员以及公使之人，或竟直言，或徇隐不言，或令人冒名顶替，而乃有收受请托行贿之事于其所应管属之件，以图营私获利者。如于出具合同字据等类，或故为因循缓办，或率尔包揽结局。无论事属与人公办，或由己私办，或属一力承办，或于事中仅办一分者。一经查出，均著科以监收之罪，少则六个月，多则两年，并令罚缴银两，但其所罚之数，即以安慰银两之数比拟罚之，须至四分之一，然亦不得不及十二分之一。至大小官员于其任中经手出发各项银两，须先发有示谕始能出发。倘于结算清釐各项帑饷之中，竟有从中染指情弊者，亦惟照比例一例惩办。

第7段论未到任及已离任之官，而竟妄权施行诸事者

第一百九十六条　凡大小职官于未发誓到任之先，倘其身系职官预行妄权施行诸事者，一经查出，著科以罚缴银两，少则十六个夫浪，多则一百五十夫浪。

第一百九十七条　凡官员于已奉有明文，或属任满，或应休致，或已革职，而仍贪恋好爵，恋栈不去者，著科以监收之罪，少则六个月，多则二年，并令罚缴银两，少则一百夫浪，多则五百夫浪。俟监收期满之日，再为禁止经理公私事件。即以出监之日为始计算年月，少则五年，多则十年。至武职之员，设有干犯

---

① ［法］毕利干：《法国律例·刑律》，日本司法省1894年版，第84页。

律例,如地九十三条之罪者,亦惟从重惩办。"①

关于保护儿童:

"第三百四十九条　凡有人将年未及七岁之幼孩、弱女,弃置荒寂处所者,或系该犯自获此罪,或系委之于人代干此罪,倘其事已成者,惟应将该犯科以监收之罪,少则十六日,多则二年,并令罚缴银两,少则十六夫浪,多则二百夫浪。

第三百五十条　凡如上条作载之事,倘有人干此案者,无论男女,或系该幼童、弱女之义父、义母,有照料抚育之责者,或系教习,有栽培训诲该幼童、弱女之责者,均著科以监收之罪,少则二年,多则五年,并令罚缴银两,少则五十夫浪,多则四百夫浪。

第三百五十一条　凡第三百四十九条、第三百五十二条二条所载案情,设有干此等罪案者,一查其弃置之孩童,或系有伤,或因伤成癫,或已亡故,均应将该犯按有意殴伤,与有意殴杀之例,一例办理。

第三百五十二条　凡有人将未及七岁之幼孩弃置于人烟丛集之处者,一经访获,著将该犯科以监收之罪,少则三个月,多则一年,并令罚缴银两,少则十六个夫浪,多则一百夫浪。

第三百五十三条　凡如上条所载案情,倘有致干此罪者,系该幼孩之义父,或该幼孩之教习等类者,更属罪难宽纵。著将该犯等从重科以监收之罪,少则六个月,多则二年,并令罚缴银两,少则二十五个夫浪,多则二百夫浪。

第2段论治诱拐引诱年幼子女,有关淫邪之事者

第三百五十四条　凡如有人或以诱骗,或竟用强,或竟引诱,以致将该弱冠子女窃去者,或其人本有照料、抚养幼孩之责,而乃将该应抚养之子女,本宜安置于此处者,而竟移于彼

---

① [法]毕利干:《法国律例·刑律》,日本司法省1894年版,第82、95、96页。

处，或该犯自知不便下此毒手，而乃转请他人代行其奸谋者，似此实属大干例禁，一经访获，无论事属本人自之罪，或系代人故干此罪，并将其案中主谋之人查出，均著科以监禁之罪。

第三百五十五条　凡如上条所载案情，倘其诱骗窃去弱冠之子女，其年在十六岁以上者，著将该犯科限以年月日缧绁苦工之罪。

第三百五十六条　凡十六岁以上之幼女，倘有被人诱骗窃去之事，而该幼女竟自情愿跟随逃走者，一查该诱骗窃去幼女之犯年纪已及二十一岁，或已逾二十一岁，著将该犯科限以年月缧绁苦工之罪。倘该犯尚未及二十一岁，著从轻科以监收之罪，少则二年，多则五年。

第三百五十七条　凡如上条所载之幼女，或系被人诱骗，或系被人窃去，而竟与诱骗窃去幼女之犯成为夫妇者，倘查照民例所载之情，除经两造之父母先将二人婚姻之据销毁者以外，其余一切他人不得于此事妄行干预，倘该两造之父母欲行究办此事者，亦须先将该夫妇婚姻之据销毁，然后始可究办。"①

关于丧葬：

"第三段　论事关葬殓者之例

第三百五十八条　凡如有人未奉该管官之命，而乃擅将私人埋葬者，著即科以监收之罪，少则六日，多则二月，并罚缴银两，少则十六个夫浪，多则五十夫浪，而于此外，如仍有他项不法之情，则尤须格外罚惩，至无论系有何项情形，而于葬殓定限未至其期，而竟埋葬者，著亦照上文之例，科以同罪。

第三百五十九条　凡有杀害尸身与伤毙尸身，倘有人胆敢窃留隐匿者，一经访获，著将该犯科以监收之罪，少则六月，多则二年，并令罚缴银两，少则五十夫浪，多则四百夫浪。倘查于此

---

① ［法］毕利干：《法国律例·刑律》，日本司法省1894年版，第179、180、182、182页。

案中，更有别项致罪之情，须再酌其案节轻重，斟酌惩办。

第三百六十条 凡有胆敢掘挖坟墓，或窃取坟墓所用之祭器，或于坟墓之前诸般放肆傲慢不恭者，一经查出，均著科以监收之罪，少则三个月，多则一年，并令罚缴银两，少则十六个夫浪，多则二百夫浪。倘于此等案情之外，更有别项致罪之情者，著即斟酌案由轻重，比拟科断。"①

关于重罪：

"第四百七十六条 凡如上条所载之事，除照例将该犯等罚缴银两之外，倘其情节较重，尤应科以监收之罪，至多则不过三日。如上条所论车夫干犯之罪，与于茶酒等物搅合假物之罪，以及砖石秽物之罪，均须于罚缴银两之外，仍应科以监收之罪，惟其数不得过三日。

第四百七十七条 凡如第四百七十五条所载，有人胆敢在街巷之间，人烟聚集之处，开场聚赌，以及拈阄?会等类者，一经事犯到官，著将该犯局中所用之家具、器皿等类以及在场赌博人之银钱物件，全行查抄入官。至有人于吸饮之物，如茶酒等类，胆敢搀合假物，一经查出，即将该犯所卖搀假之茶酒等类，尽行□弃，至于有伤风化自己邪词淫册，或系描画，或系刊刻、刷印，一经拿获，即将其物全行销毁，至有贩卖一切食物，竟致气味臭恶，物质溃坏者，一经查出，即将该犯所卖之物，勒令全行抛掷，不准到处贩卖。

第四百七十八条 凡如第四百七十五条所载各案情形，设有人于各案中干犯一罪，除照例惩办外，而日后仍然复犯者，著将该犯科以监收之罪，至多则五日。至如第四百七十五条其五所载罪案情形，设有人已犯而复犯者，即于研讯属实后，将该犯科以监收之罪，少则六日，多则一个月，并令罚缴银两，少则十六个

---

① ［法］毕利干：《法国律例·刑律》，日本司法省1894年版，第183、184页。

夫浪，多则二百夫浪。

第四百七十九条　凡论一切获罪情形，较之第四百七十五条所载各罪情形，稍形重大者，其各犯等因案应罚之银，应自十一个夫浪至十五个夫浪为止。今将各案情形开载备查，其一，凡有干犯罪案情形，尚不至如第四百三十四至第四百六十二条所列罪案之情形者，而其案中情节系任意伤损拆毁他人之一切动资、器具、物件者；其二，或系无执御之才，而乃不审货物分两之重轻，将车任意装载者，或无因无故任意将车马驱驰，或遇有疯癫病症之人，而有拘束之责之人，竟任其在外闲游，不为赶紧安置处所，或放凶猛??而有驱逐之责者，不为赶紧驱逐，以致伤害他人一切牲畜；其三，或开放火枪等物，或抛掷砖石等物，虽非有心将他人饲养牲畜伤害，而乃失于小心，误致将他人之牲畜伤害；其四，一切房屋墙垣等项，年久亏朽，而该房主竟不赶紧修葺，致因坍塌，误伤人命，或临一切房屋基址之地，不按制定界限，竟尔任意挖掘坑井之类，以致房屋墙垣受伤倾圮，致将人命伤害；其五，凡一切铺户，竟敢有违定制，使用私造之升斗、砝码、尺丈等类之物，固属罪有应得。其有知其为私造之升斗等类者，而竟准其任意使用，尤属罪难轻纵。一经查出，著由该管衙门查核案中情形，治以应得之罪。其六，倘有胆敢仍行使用复制之升斗、砝码、尺寸等类，以冀获利者，并卖假售与卖肉之人，竟不遵照市价营私售卖者；其七，口出无稽之谈，煽惑众人，以为可以求福避祸及推算命运，圆解梦寐之事；其八，倘有胆敢于寅夜之时，大声疾呼，以致人心惊异，似有十分危急之事者，一经缉获，著不论首从，照例科以应得之罪；其九，遇有顽梗不法之徒，胆敢负气，将奉官张贴告谕文示撕毁者；其十，凡他人之田地及有花草之地、葡萄园、柳树行，并一切橄榄、石榴、橘柚，并一切人力栽培小树秧，竟有将各牲畜在该等处牧放行走者；其十一，凡一切官街大道，竟敢有作践拆毁者，并侵占官街者；其十二，私起官街之土石，并青草等类，并于村堡镇店中之土石，除执有使用之权者之外，而竟敢私起土石者，均直照例科之以罪。

第四百八十条 凡如上条所载一切罪案情形，而其中所载有意伤害他人之牲畜，或使用私造之砝码、升斗、尺寸等类，或使用非现时制定之砝码、升斗、尺寸等类，或卖假售与卖肉人，挽假营私，到处售卖或谣言惑众，圆解梦寐之事，或于寅夜大声疾呼，使众人心惊，似有十分危急之事者，以上各罪案，均应于罚缴银两之外，再行酌夺案中各情，将该犯科以监收之罪，惟至多不逾五日。

第四百八十一条 凡如上条所谕，使用私造之砝码、升斗、尺丈以及使用不按现时制定之砝码、升斗、尺丈，并圆解梦寐，谣言惑众，伪为可以求福避祸，并用一切干犯例禁器具及妄取各种异样服饰，一经事犯到官，均应将各案中之赃物，全行查抄入官。

第四百八十二条 凡如第四百七十九条所载之罪案，倘有人一时愚昧，致干其罪，既经惩办之后，而竟敢仍然复犯者，著将该犯罚缴银两之外，仍应科以五日收监之罪。

第四百八十三条 凡何以即为复犯之罪，如有人于一年之内，因事曾干一罪，而于此一年内，又干一罪，即可谓为复犯之罪。

第四百八十四条 凡遇一切案件，如详查本例，并无作何科断专条，其情系出于本例格外者，则经手办理其案之官，应于他项律例章程，详为比拟，遵照办理。"①

关于伪证：

"第七节 论治伪为质证、诬指有罪，或有意牵引、诬为报告，或欺凌于人，或于人，或发其一切机秘之事者

第一段 论治伪为质证之例

---

① ［法］毕利干：《法国律例·刑律》，日本司法省1894年版，第265、266、267、268、269、270、271页。

第三百六十一条　凡有案关犯法，其情甚重者，而乃有人为之避重就轻，甘为袒护，竟敢伪为质证，或致被告之犯，因而可以释罪，亦或因而可以增罪。似此类颠倒是非，混淆曲直，所关甚重。一经查出，著将该伪为质证之犯，科以监禁之罪。倘伪为质证者，于被告之犯，胆敢诬为屈抑，若按其所指情节，可使被告所获之罪，较之科以监禁之罪，尤应从重者，其伪为质证之犯，更关肆行无忌，一经研讯得实，著将该伪为质证之犯，与本案被告应得之罪，一例科断。

第三百六十三条　凡有干犯民律之案，系小民一切争讼之案者，倘于研讯之时，胆敢有人伪为质证，或诬为屈抑，或巧为开脱，实属有意颠倒是非，混淆曲直。一经审讯得实，著将该伪为质证之犯，科以监收之罪，少则二年，多则五年，并令罚缴银两，少则五十夫浪，多则二千夫浪。亦能随时酌照第四十二条之例，斟酌罚惩。

第二段　论治诬为报告，或欺凌于人，或于人，或发其一切机秘之事者

第三百七十三条　凡有书写呈词、禀函，设意株连，或于案中诬扳一人，或诬扳多人，而竟敢于执政理刑等官之前，妄行呈递者，实属异常狡猾。一经查出，著将该犯科以监收之罪。少则一个月，多则一年，并令罚缴银两，少则一百夫浪，多则三千夫浪。

第三百七十六条　凡有于人妄行欺辱凌虐者，而查其情形，尚非十分重大，亦非于耳目众多之前，著将该犯姑从末减，应照干犯过失之案，归正尤应科办者之例，比拟科断。"①

妨害婚姻家庭罪：

"第一百九十二条　凡婚丧嫁娶以及生辰之合同册档，其理民之官本宜按册详书以备稽考者，乃有应行添注者，反舍弃应书之册，而随便拾纸登载者，即科以监收之罪，少则一个月，多则

---

① ［法］毕利干：《法国律例·刑律》，日本司法省1894年版，第185、187、190、191页。

三个月,并令罚缴银两,少则十六夫浪,多则二百夫浪。

第一百九十三条 凡婚嫁之事,原宜有父母之命始可结亲,而该理民之官竟不问其有无父母之命,而率行给予结亲之据者,著将该官科以监收之罪,少则六个月,多则一年,并令罚缴银两,少则十六个夫浪,多则三百个夫浪。

第一百九十四条 凡理民之官,于民律二百二十八条所设妇人再醮定限之先,擅许妇人再醮者,著罚缴银两,少则十六个夫浪,多则三百个夫浪。

第一百九十五条 凡如上文所载该官应得之罪,而其所发未合之文据凭约,纵在领者尚无阻止注销之情,而该官应得之罪,仍宜照例科罪,而于此本罪外,或仍有干涉民律第一本第五类罪情者,尤应格外追罚。"①

关于宗教活动:

"第三节 论治掌教之士,于其本责一切应为之事而竟紊乱,未合围范者之例。

第一段 论治掌教之士于其本责,应司婚丧嫁娶及生产等事,致有窒碍未合者之例。

第一百九十九条 凡掌教士遇于教会中行祝婚之礼者,宜本那女两造先有理民官发给宜婚之据,而后教中始行此礼也。倘该掌教士不先查其曾有宜婚之据与否,而竟率然行此礼者,一经查出,若系初犯,著令其罚缴银两,少则十六个夫浪,多则一百夫浪。

第二百条 凡如上条所载,擅行祝婚之礼,倘查该掌教士曾经干犯此案,而今系第二次复犯者,著从重科以监收之罪。少则二年,多则五年。若至第三次复犯者,则应从重科以监禁之罪。

第二段 论掌教之士于大庭广众之中,宣讲教中道义之时,

---

① [法]毕利干:《法国律例·刑律》,日本司法省1894年版,第93、94页。

语涉排贬国政，或恃掌教之势，而妄为规正国政，或竟乱言煽惑国政之罪。

第二百零一条 凡掌教之士于大庭广众之中，宣讲教道，语忽旁涉，以此喻彼，竟尔讥刺国政，并排贬国家律例，及一切由官所定示谕文稿等件者，著即科以监收之罪，少则三个月，多则二年。

第二百零二条 凡掌教士，其于宣讲教道之时，倘敢藉讲道为名，怂恿众人违悖国家律例，及一切应遵公令，甚或煽惑人心，致无知小民起衅构怨，因而互相争斗者，一经查出，倘事尚属未成，著科以监收之罪，少则二年。多则五年。其煽惑众心，致违公令，幸而不及为乱者，著将该掌教士科以徒罪。"①

第四节 《法国律例·民律指掌》

《法国律例·民律指掌》一共有五卷。第一卷"论息讼官署"；第二卷"论各项微末职官之衙署"；第三卷"论所上控者之官署"；第四卷"论非按照寻常法要而有推究于所发之示谕者"；第五卷"论有示谕应照而为之事者"。此外，还有杂律三卷。

毕利干译《法国律例·民律指掌》与林纪东等主编《民事诉讼法》目录对比表②

毕利干译《法国律例·民律指掌》	林纪东等主编《民事诉讼法》
第一集 论一切控诉案件，而有推敲追比之情系在官署之中	第一编 总则
第一卷 论息讼官署	第一章 法院
第一类 论传案票之类	第一节 管辖
第二类 论息讼官当堂拟办词讼之事，并案中原被到案之事	第二节 法院职员之回避

---

① ［法］毕利干：《法国律例·刑律》，日本司法省1894年版，第97、98、99页。
② ［法］毕利干：《法国律例·民律指掌·目录》，日本司法省1894年版；林纪东等主编：《刑法·目录》，五南图书出版公司1986年版。

续表

毕利干译《法国律例·民律指掌》		林纪东等主编《民事诉讼法》	
第三类	论所拟发示谕系因脱身稽传而于事有阻止之情者	第二章	当事人
第四类	论所拟示谕系关词讼于物主之权者	第一节	当事人能力及诉讼能力
第五类	论所拟示谕系非牢不可破者，并谕其遵照而为之事	第二节	共同诉讼
第六类	论为保之人而有牵连其身置于案中者	第三节	诉讼参与
第七类	论于案中而有研究查验之事	第四节	诉讼代理人及辅佐人
第八类	论于致事地方而有周阅巡视之情，并衡量其事合理与否	第三章	诉讼费用
第九类	论息讼官遇事有应回避之情	第一节	诉讼费用之负担
第二卷	论各项微末职官之衙署	第二节	诉讼费用之担保
第一类	论因事说和以息争端	第三节	诉讼救助
第二类	论案情而有展限易日之情者	第四章	诉讼程序
第三类	论于晰讼之绅而拣选一人，以为驳辨原被告所呈约据者	第一节	当事人书状
第四类	论案中所有一切之情，按例应报之于监审官者	第二节	送达
第五类	论当堂办理案件，应于大庭广众之前，并论当官务宜静谧　整饬者之事	第三节	期日及期间
第六类	论于各案而有衡酌之情，并其研究之情系书之于字者	第四节	诉讼程序之停止
第七类	论出发拟结案件之示谕	第五节	言词辩论
第八类	论所发示谕系脱身稽传或有阻止之情者	第六节	裁判
第九类	论因案有应破以成格之情者	第七节	诉讼卷宗
第十类	论所缮录文约而有校对真伪之事	第二编	第一审程序
第十一类	论捏造妄书各项字据而有关于民律指情者	第一章	通常诉讼程序
第十二类	论悉心查验之事	第一节	起诉
第十三类	论查验之官系由亲临行其查验之事	第二节	言词辩论之准备
第十四类	论为经纪者因事所覆之语言	第三节	证据
第十五类	论于各项案情而有审讯之情者	第四节	和解
第十六类	论于案情而有节外生枝之情者	第五节	判决
第十七类	论有续讼而复委晰讼之绅者	第二章	调解程序
第十八类	论于案情而有不相识认之事者	第三章	简易诉讼程序

续表

毕利干译《法国律例·民律指掌》		林纪东等主编《民事诉讼法》	
第十九类	论案关应归数项衙门,而终归于何署办理者	第三编	上诉审程序
第二十类	论案经转移别项衙门拟办,因承审官与讼者有亲谊之情者	第一章	第二审程序
第二十一类	论遇案情而有回避之情者	第三章	第三审程序
第二十二类	论词讼之事致有已兴中辍而息绝者	第四编	抗告程序
第二十三类	论已讼而有悔讼者之情者	第五编	再审程序
第二十四类	论轻掌易理之事	第六编	督促程序
第二十五类	论与词讼之案而有关于通商事务之衙门者	第七编	保全程序
第三卷	论所上控者之官署	第八编	公示催告程序
独指一类	论上控之事,并论上控而有研讯之情者	第九编	人事诉讼程序
第四卷	论非按照寻常法要而有推究于所发之示谕者	第一章	婚姻事件程序
第一类	论于示谕而有推究之情,系因两造外而仍有波及之人者	第二章	亲子关系事件程序
第二类	论所具秉呈系关民律中所生者	第三章	禁治产事件程序
第三类	论于拟案未合而有牵涉办此本案之官者	第四章	宣告死亡事件程序
第五卷	论有示谕应照而为之事者		
第一类	论收受为保与备质银两之理		
第二类	论于安慰之银应行清理备办者		
第三类	论清理各项果子之理		
第四类	论于数目而有汇总核算之事		
第五类	论清理支销费用之事		
第六类	论大约围范蒋合同示谕文约等件应行遵照而为者		
第七类	论扣执停行并有关阻止之事		
第八类	论兴办扣执停行之事者		
第九类	论插标识记之事,系果实而植于地中者		
第十类	论扣执停行之事,而于岁定之资系?于民间者		
第十一类	论按分分成均分拨还欠款者		
第十二类	论有关扣留物件之事而于定资项上者		
第十三类	论于所扣定资项上而有节外生枝之情		
第十四类	论清还债欠而于其先后之次序		
第十五类	论一切罪干监收者之事		

续表

毕利干译《法国律例·民律指掌》	林纪东等主编《民事诉讼法》
第十六类 论？官核定之事	
杂律	
第一卷	
第一类 论奉具资财清还债务,并奉具存储资财之事	
第二类 论房屋主人之例应,而于住户、庄田并衣服及果实项上者	
第三类 论所扣留之物,系有挽回物主之权者	
第四类 论格外增值于乐购之分于情甘过？之事	
第五类 论于合同欲缮一分,系遵何项法则,或遵照某法则而有变易合同之情者	
第六类 论有围范系为不在场者之定资,而有人请官权且接手得其物主之权者	
第七类 论有夫之妇遇事到官而有允准之事者	
第八类 论夫妇？业之事	
第九类 论异居离居之理	
第十类 论家亲之所议论者	
第十一类 论被禁者之事	
第十二类 论扣给定资物件而以为清偿者	
第二卷 论一切围范系开办相继接产之事者	
第一类 论人至物故后而有关防赌物之事	
第二类 论有阻止之情而于关防之事者	
第三类 论于关防之事而有启手指情者	
第四类 论立具查物底单之事	
第五类 论将动资之物出售者	
第六类 论售卖定资之物系于弱冠者	
第七类 论定资之物有应剖分各据,并有应难分变价各得者	
第八类 论有盈无亏者之遗产	
第九类 论推辞合资营生与相继接产之理,并出售随嫁定资之事	
第十类 论详为代办者,其于相继接产之事,而有虚？其事之情者	
第三卷 论独指一类系于调处说和之事者	

毕利干译《法国律例·民律指掌》与《中华人民共和国民事诉讼法》目录对比表①

毕利干译《法国律例·民律指掌》	《中华人民共和国民事诉讼法》
第一集 论一切控诉案件,而有推敲追比之情系在官署之中	第一编 总则
第一卷 论息讼官署	第一章 任务、适用范围
第一类 论传案票之类	第二章 管辖
第二类 论息讼官当堂拟办词讼之事,并案中原被到案之事	第三章 审判组织
第三类 论所拟发示谕系因脱身稽传而于事有阻止之情者	第四章 回避
第四类 论所拟示谕关词讼于物主之权者	第五章 诉讼参加人
第五类 论所拟示谕系非牢不可破者,并谕其遵照而为之事	第六章 证据
第六类 论为保之人而有牵连其身置于案中者	第七章 期间 送达
第七类 论于案中而有研究查验之事	第八章 调解
第八类 论于致事地方而有周阅巡视之情,并衡量其事合理与否	第九章 保全和先予执行
第九类 论息讼官遇事有应回避之情	第十章 对妨害民事诉讼的强制措施
第二卷 论各项微末职官之衙署	第十一章 诉讼费用
第一类 论因事说和以息争端	第二编 审判程序
第二类 论案情而有展限易日之情者	第十二章 第一审普通程序
第三类 论于晰讼之绅而拣选一人,以为驳辨原被告所呈约据者	第十三章 简易程序
第四类 论案中所有一切之情,按例应报之于监审官者	第十四章 第二审程序
第五类 论当堂办理案件,应于大庭广众之前,并论当官务宜静谧 整饬者之事	第十五章 特别程序
第六类 论于各案而有衡酌之情,并其研究之情系书于字者	第十六章 审判监督程序
第七类 论出发拟结案件之示谕	第十七章 督促程序
第八类 论所发示谕系脱身稽传或有阻止之情者	第十八章 公示催告程序
第九类 论因案有应破以成格之情者	第三编 执行程序
第十类 论所缮录文约而有校对真伪之事	第十九章 一般规定
第十一类 论捏造妄书各项字据而有关于民律指情者	第二十章 执行的申请
第十二类 论悉心查验之事	第二十一章 执行措施
第十三类 论查验之官系由亲临行其查验之事	第二十二章 执行中止
第十四类 论为经纪者因事所覆之语言	第四编 涉外民事诉讼程序的特别规定

---

① [法]毕利干:《法国律例·民律指掌·目录》,日本司法省1894年版;《中华人民共和国民事诉讼法·目录》。

续表

毕利干译《法国律例·民律指掌》	《中华人民共和国民事诉讼法》
第十五类　论于各项案情而有审讯之情者	第二十三章　一般原则
第十六类　论于案情而有节外生枝之情者	第二十四章　特别管辖
第十七类　论有续讼而复委晰讼之绅者	第二十五章　送达、期间
第十八类　论于案情而有不相识认之事者	第二十六章　仲裁
第十九类　论案关应归数项衙门，而终归于何署办理者	第二十七章　司法协助
第二十类　论案经转移别项衙门拟办，因承审官与讼者有亲谊之情者	
第二十一类　论遇案情而有回避之情者	
第二十二类　论词讼之事致有已兴中辍而息绝者	
第二十三类　论已讼而有悔讼者之情者	
第二十四类　论轻掌易理之事	
第二十五类　论与词讼之案而有关于通商事务之衙门者	
第三卷　论所上控者之官署	
独指一类　论上控之事，并论上控而有研讯之情者	
第四卷　论非按照寻常法要而有推究于所发之示谕者	
第一类　论于示谕而有推究之情，系因两造外而仍有波及之人者	
第二类　论所具秉呈系关民律中所生者	
第三类　论于拟案未合而有牵涉办此本案之官者	
第五卷　论有示谕应照而为之事者	
第一类　论收受为保与备质银两之理	
第二类　论于安慰之银应行清理备办者	
第三类　论清理各项果子之理	
第四类　论于数目而有汇总核算之事	
第五类　论清理支销费用之事	
第六类　论大约围范蒋合同示谕文约等件应行遵照而为者	
第七类　论扣执停行并有关阻止之事	
第八类　论兴办扣执停行之事者	
第九类　论插标识记之事，系实而植于地中者	
第十类　论扣执停行之事，而于岁定之资系？于民间者	
第十一类　论按分分成均分拨还欠款者	
第十二类　论有关扣留物件之事而于定资项上者	

续表

毕利干译《法国律例·民律指掌》	《中华人民共和国民事诉讼法》
第十三类　论于所扣定资项上而有节外生枝之情	
第十四类　论清还债欠而于其先后之次序	
第十五类　论一切罪干监收者之事	
第十六类　论？官核定之事	
杂律	
第一卷	
第一类　论奉具资财清还债务，并奉具存储资财之事	
第二类　论房屋主人之例应，而于住户、庄田并衣服及果实项上者	
第三类　论所扣留之物，系有挽回物主之权者	
第四类　论格外增值于乐购之分于情甘过？之事	
第五类　论于合同欲缮一分，系遵何项法则，或遵照某法则而有变易合同之情者	
第六类　论有围范系为不在场者之定资，而有人请官权且接手得其物主之权者	
第七类　论有夫之妇遇事到官而有允准之事者	
第八类　论夫妇？业之事	
第九类　论异居离居之理	
第十类　论家亲之所议论者	
第十一类　论被禁者之事	
第十二类　论扣给定资物件而以为清偿者	
第二卷　论一切围范系开办相继接产之事者	
第一类　论人至物故后而有关防睹物之事	
第二类　论有阻止之情而于关防之事者	
第三类　论于关防之事而有启手指情者	
第四类　论立具查物底单之事	
第五类　论将动资之物出售者	
第六类　论售卖定资之物系于弱冠者	
第七类　论定资之物有应剖分各据，并有应难分变价各得者	
第八类　论有盈无亏者之遗产	
第九类　论推辞合资营生与相继接产之理，并出售随嫁定资之事	

续表

毕利干译《法国律例·民律指掌》	《中华人民共和国民事诉讼法》
第十类 论详为代办者,其于相继接产之事,而有虚？其事之情者	
第三卷 论独指一类系于调处说和之事者	

《法国律例·民律指掌》是调整民事诉讼活动以及确定民事诉讼活动中诉讼法律关系的法律规范,如:

1. 关于案件管辖:

"第一条 凡传案票,系传人至息讼官衙署出发该禀,须注明行于某年月日,原告者系何姓名、居址,现以何业为营生,并须注明事中理非之绅,系何姓名、居址,被告人之姓名、居址。尤须注明在原告者系因何等情由,持有何项约据,倚恃何项条例,而有此控告情事,并须注明拟办此案息讼官,系何姓名,及知名应于何时日应即前来到案。

第二条 凡一切案情,倘系关涉本身以及动资之物者,则其票中所注拟办此案之息讼官,该官应为管属彼告所居之本处官。

第三条 凡如息讼之官,其于出发传案之票,应于该地方实为于其本物而有管属之责者,其所发传票之情,须有四项情形。其一情:或如于田地事中而有所损;或如于资比果等类而有所伤;或如收获谷实而有所碍。有此等情,应于管属该本物者之息讼官为之拟办。其二情:或有挪移界石、侵占地基、私移树木篱墙及侵占园垣沟洫,而其所干之罪,系在本年干犯者;或如流水之泉及各水泽之主而有所伤碍者。有此等情,应于管属该本物者之息讼官为之拟办。其三情:或其涉讼之情,系关租赁房屋而议定有零修碎补之情者,应于管属本地之息讼官为之拟办。其四情:或系租种庄田而在租种之人,其于庄田所享裨益致与本地有伤,而并不能阻其所挟之例应者;或系租赁房屋,该住户竟于所租之房有所伤损。有此等情,应于管属本地之息讼官为之拟办。

第四条 凡如传案之票,系由何人所发出,于案中被告所居本处之息讼官，委令本处理非之绅前往报送。倘该本处理非之绅不能前往，则由该息讼官特委理非之绅前往报之。无论系由何绅，惟须将该传案之票依文照录，给于被告之人。倘该传案票一经报到，而该被告者竟不在其家中，其家复无他人，则须将该票转交于被告所居本处之总甲官，或副总甲官。一经将该照录之票交付该总甲官或副总甲官，仍应于作发原票幅末注明，曾经查阅，画押其上，并此等情事亦无需费。至该理非之绅倘系该案中原、被告两造亲戚友谊之人，则不应妄为理此报之情事。"①

2. 关于证人、证言：

"第一百二十一条　凡如矢誓之事，须其人本身当堂矢誓，倘该矢誓之人，委有万难脱身前来一切阻碍情事者，则亦可于承审官当面，惟该官系由该官衙门委令前往矢誓之人所居处所，并有书吏一人在侧者，始为可行。——尤须令其陈明于某年月日而有矢誓情事。

第一百二十二条　凡如该管衙门遇有应行展限之情，以便在事之人能以遵照而为者，则惟须出发示谕，注明所以展限之故。

第一百二十三条　凡如展限之事，如原、被均为在场者，则应自出发示谕之日为始计之。倘在事者如有脱身稽传情事，则应自报知之日为始计之。

第一百三十条　凡在事之人，如其为讼负者之人，则应令其备具事中一切讼费之数。

第一百三十一条　凡如事中所需费用，亦能分列均分其数，各为承认。有如或夫而与货妇者，或有位居尊长而与或为晚辈者，或有如弟兄、姊妹等，或系亲谊戚友系一级者，或有案关在事之人应缴之费，或在讼胜者有数分，而在讼负者亦有数分，则此共数之中，须两造均分承认，以免偏怙。

---

① ［法］毕利干：《法国律例·民律指掌》，日本司法省1894年版，第1、23、4页。

第一百三十二条 凡如晰讼之绅、理非之绅，如有妄权情事，并义父详为代办者，并有盈无亏之相继接产者，及一切在事有所司事之人，而乃于其所司之事，致有损伤之处，其所需之费，则惟其人是问，并仍应有罚缴安慰之银，而于此外，在该晰讼之绅，并理非之绅等，应即罢斥其责，至论于义父及详为代办者，遇有干涉前文情事，亦可禁其应行司事之责，不使置身于所司事中。

第一百四十九条 凡如案中被告或未议倩其人，或已议倩，而至应行当堂之日，竟不前来者，应即将其案情按照脱身稽传之例，一例办理。

第一百五十条 凡如案情之中，如应声明现有脱身稽传情事，须于当堂之时声明，一经有此情形，则在原告所具一切呈词文据等件，如经该管之官阅之，尚属理直者，则应按其所具情词拟议，虽如此言，然惟应将所具文约禀呈，置于公案之上，以俟下次当堂在为究办。

第二百六十七条 凡如各为证见之人者，倘该查验之官不能一日之中一并取其供辞者，则该官应即谕令异日待办，而其所定之时日，即由该查验官自行酌定，不需再行出发传案之票于为证见者及案中原被两造之人。

第二百六十八条 凡不论何人，如于案中或原或被两造之中，系有骨肉亲谊之人，其谱系系直族，或为原、被两造中之夫，或为其妇，不论系同居而或系析业者，均不准为案中证见之人。"①

3. 关于第一审普通程序

"第十五类 论于各项案情而有审讯之情者

第三百二十四条 凡一切在事之人，例准能以无论如何案

---

① ［法］毕利干：《法国律例·民律指掌》，日本司法省1894年版，第67、68、71、72、80、142页。

情，彼此恳请该管之官，审讯于以情或数项情事，而实于案情有相关者。然惟不应于该官办此案情及所拟发示谕，而乃有谓为迟延稽缓之情。

第三百二十五条　凡因案审讯之事，系由在事者递具禀呈，申明现有某项案情经该管官出发示谕，拟定某日而有当堂审讯之事，惟此项审讯之事，或于总承审官当面，或由其所拣委之官当面，均无不行。

第三百二十六条　凡如递具禀呈之人所居之处较远者，则须由总承审官委令该处理事坊之总承审官，或其处息讼官为之就近审讯，均无不行。

第三百二十七条　凡如被委之承审官，应将总承审官所札文移幅末，注明今于某月日时，而有当堂审讯之情，不必由该官另备传饬之谕，而该在事者，届期即应前来。

第三百二十八条　凡经传饬审讯之人，至期竟不前来，而一查其情，委系不克来者，则该官例准前往该造所居之处而审讯之。

第三百二十九条　凡被审讯之人，须于二十四点钟之先，将该官审讯所发示谕之情，报其知之。即如有某造经总承审官派委某官，现定于某月日而有前往审讯之情者，亦应由理非之绅先期前往报知，以便候讯。

第三百三十六条　凡如各项公所、官所之中，如遇有应行查讯之事，而既经查讯，应由该所之中委官一员代为复以回情，并申明所以查讯之事。而所复者，应均确实。如不遵此定例而为者，则所查讯之事，即等于事已承招无异。其于查询之件以外，设有关涉于所委之员本身情事者，亦为例准其行。

第十六类　论于案情而有节外生枝之情者

第1段论于节外生枝项上而有索讨之情者

第三百三十七条　凡如案关有节外生枝索讨情事者，其以何情而举发之，惟此事须有字据，即注明所以索讨之由，并其归终主见及其可凭之字据，在该被索讨者，即由检收处发给阅看，并须复以回单一纸。惟控此节外生枝之人，应取彼造所据之字据，而与所复之回音，以便执以为凭。

第三百三十八条　凡如案关节外生枝而有数项索讨之情者，应即一并供出。倘于数情中未能一并申诉，而复有续出之情者，将其续出之情而乃悉于以前之情，而同供者，则其应交讼费，责令自行备出。除事经已供，而仍有应供者，则为格外之事。至其原案情节有应录于禀呈之上者，则其节外生枝一切情事，亦应一并附载，呈于当堂，以俟该管官定拟如何。

第2段论有情甘置身其间者之事

第三百三十九条　凡有情甘置身其间者，须递禀呈言明其所施行，并其归终主见如何。而此等情事应即照抄一分，并其事中可以为据之约券、卷宗等件，亦应照抄一分，以便执行。

第三百四十条　凡如原案所办情形，既经拟议妥协，则不得因有置身其间之情，而有稽缓其原案应为情事。

第三百四十一条　凡如原案中之情事，有应缮录者，倘置身其间有关口角之情，应将其情呈至当堂，以便该管官因案定拟如何。"①

4. 关于第二审程序：

"第十七类　论有续讼而复委晰讼之绅者

第三百四十二条　凡有一案情形，而已拟议齐备，则其所发拟议之示谕，不能暂行停止。纵其案中在事者，有改易情势之情者，或有在事者而有不司其职之事，或该两造中而有事故及有被禁者，均不得有所停止其案之情。

第三百四十三条　凡何以为办理一案，而为齐备之时，应于有驳辩剖析之情。而为齐备之时，并何以为驳辩剖析之言妥协之时，应于两造中某造而有归终主见之时，即为齐备之时。倘其当

---

① ［法］毕利干：《法国律例·民律指掌》，日本司法省1894年版，第167、168、169、171、172、173、174页。

堂研讯之时，系落于缉拿者，则一经讯有端倪，则为齐备之时，或在此造而有询问之定期，而在彼造亦有复以回音之定期。惟至其所定之期一满，则亦为齐备之时。

第三百四十四条　凡如案件而于办理未经齐备之时，该原、被两造乃有一造物故者，则其案中一切应行报知该故者之情事，均可置之不听。如两造之中，而此造所偕晰讼之绅，致有物故，与不司其职及有关被禁、革斥之情者，则其以先所拟一切情事，亦惟置之不议。除非事经此造而有续偕晰讼之绅者，则为格外之事。

第三百四十五条　凡如案中在事者，而有改易势分之事，或不理以先所应官属之事者，则此等情不足可以停止其案中应行之件。虽如此言，倘在原告并未改易势分，与亦未不理其以先应管之事，并未尝？雇有晰讼之绅者，则于其案仍有可追讨之情，即应传令该造于八日之内前来，以便定拟其归终主见如何。

第三百四十六条　凡如案关传令某造前来为续讼之事，或为续雇晰讼之绅情事，则其传饬之情，应按本卷第二类所载定限而行之，并应指明在先为晰讼之绅者，系何姓名及承办此案之官系何姓名，均应指明。

第三百四十七条　凡如续讼之事，以何法行之，惟应由此造为其晰讼之绅者，报于彼造为其晰讼之绅者，而其报知之事，系以字据行之者。

第三百四十八条　凡如续讼案中，而其应行被传之人，设有口角之端，则应将其致事大概情形，按照轻举易理之例，一例为之。

第三百四十九条　凡如例定之限一满，而被传之人竟未到案者，即应出发示谕，言明现有续讼情事，并此示谕之上，仍须言明应按照前情遵照办理，不能再为展限。

第三百五十条　凡如出发示谕系关脱身稽传之情，而有续讼情事者，则此示谕应由理非之绅前往报知所指向之人，为其晰讼之绅者，并此报知之事，须注明办此案者之承审官系何姓名。

第三百五十一条　凡于上文所载此项示谕，而有阻止之情者，应将其情呈于当堂，即其案应呈于办此案件之官者，亦应呈于当堂。

第十八类　论于案情而有不相识之事者

第三百五十二条　凡有奉献之情，或有识认之情，或有允许之情，而此等事不得徒托空言，须出有切实之凭，始为可行，否则等于未相识认，而与允许者一律。

第三百五十三条　凡遇由不相识认之情，应将此情呈于办理此案衙门中检收处。然此事何以行之，须由该造立一文约，即由该造画押，或由代操其权者画押，并此文约中，须言明所以不相识认之缘由，与其所以归终主见，而仍须议立一晰讼之绅，以资办理。

第三百五十四条　凡不相识认之事，系于办此案情之时而致者，则应由此造晰讼之绅，前往报知彼造晰讼之绅知之，并此报知之事，即足可以令彼造护持其所行为之事。

第三百五十五条　凡如晰讼之绅，倘有不司其职者，则此报知之事，应报之于其本人所居之本处。倘其人系已物故者，则此不相识认之事，应报知于其相继接产者知之，并须出发传唤之情，由办此案件之该管衙门，尤须将此案情报知于在事人，即由此造为其晰讼之绅者前往，报知于彼造为其晰讼之绅者知之。

第三百五十六条　凡不相识认之情，应报知于何项衙门，应报知于原于此不相识认事务所属之衙门，并此不相识认之情，亦应报知于不相识认之人前来，以便办此不相识认之事。

第三百五十七条　凡如原案中因情所发示谕，即应暂行停办。一俟不相识认之情拟议已竣，再行照原案所发示谕办理。倘不遵此定章而为者，则其虽有所为，亦惟置之不议。然虽如此而言，亦可饬令不相识认之人，拟定期限，将此不相识认之情拟办告竣，否则即惟照该管官所拟定者，遵照而行之。"①

---

① ［法］毕利干：《法国律例·民律指掌》，日本司法省1894年版，第175、176、177、178、179、180、181页。

5. 关于回避：

"第三百七十九条　凡如承审官而与在事人之义父，或详为代办者，或办理公所社会之事者，而与其人等系有亲戚之谊者，则不足即可致有应行回避之事。除事经与该义父详为代办者及经理公所社会事中而有所株连牵涉之情者，则始可照例回避。

第三百八十条　凡为承审官者，倘遇有应行回避之情，应将其情咨明于本衙门中之总议厅，以便众官酌议其情果应回避与否。

第三百八十四条　凡何以行其回避之事，须立一文移交于本署检收处。惟须注明其所以回避孩子缘由，而此所立文移，须由申呈者画押，或代操其权者画押，并代操其权者所执之凭，亦应粘附于文移之上。

第三百八十五条　凡如有备具回避之文移，该署书吏须照抄一分，呈于本衙门之总承审官于二十四点钟。而该总承审官于二十四点钟之内，须听该监审官于此事归终主见如何，而递交于该管衙门之承审官。倘此回避之情，须出发示谕，委系无理应行驳斥者，或其情系能实收者，则须饬令按照下文所载之情，将此回避文移呈于管属回避事务之承审官，以便将其情事分晰如何，而于例定期限之中，或将此回避文移传观于监审官，并委一承审官办理其事，惟须汇总禀报所办情形如何。

第三百九十条　凡如递具申呈，欲行回避之事者，倘该衙门以为未合应行驳斥者，则其应科罚缴银两之事，其数不下一百夫浪。而于此外，仍于该管承审官有宜备具安慰之需，惟该官一经索取此项安慰之需，即不得复充为承审官之职矣。

第三百九十一条　凡如出发示谕系关回避，而有上控之情者，倘案中在事者具呈申明，委有急迫之情，难以俟上控案情办竣，再行拟办原案者，则该衙门亦可酌拟为之主办，即另委一员，以代应行回避之官。

第三百九十三条　凡如欲行回避之文约，应照抄一分，其承审官之归终主见如何，与事中示谕字据等件，及有无上控之情，一切均应由检收处之书吏，将此等情转移于该管之衙门中之书吏接受，而其所需费用，即由欲上控者之原告备出。

第三百九十四条　凡接收各项情事之书吏，应将所接文约字据等件，于三日内详明。管理上控本衙门之该管官，应出发示谕，现委有承审官查办，然虽经查办其情，仍须俟监审官于此案归终主见如何，以便汇总禀报，惟该衙门定拟其事，所出示谕其情如何，勿庸饬知案中原被两造。

第三百九十五条　凡经出发示谕之后，而于二十四点钟之内，该接收上控情词之书吏，应将所接文书字据等件，转还于原办此案理事坊中之书吏。"①

6. 关于简易程序：

"第二十四类　论轻举易理之事

第四百零四条　凡如下文所载一切轻举易理之事者，下文条缕陈明，有如于息讼官所发之示谕，而致上控之情者，或其索讨有关银两，而其数若干，均有字据之可凭，而此字据不能由为债主者为之驳斥，或其索讨之情，而其的确数目不得逾乎一千夫浪者，并其所索讨之情，系暂时之情，或有缓急之情者，均应速为拟办，其所索讨之情，或系索取房屋租息与田地利息，及岁定之资者，均宜归此例一例比拟办理。

第四百零五条　凡如轻举易理之事，其事中应行之示谕，须于当堂出发，仍须于传案之票其期已满之时，始为可行。惟此等示谕究以何法行之，应即备具文书，并不需遵照一切他项围范，即为可行。

第四百零六条　凡如案关有节外生枝与置身其间者之情，则惟应由晰讼之绅行之。而其所具之呈，不过申明其归终主见，并

---

①　［法］毕利干：《法国律例·民律指掌》，日本司法省1894年版，第194、196、199、200、201页。

其事之缘由。

第四百零七条 凡如有关查验之事,而其所发示谕之上,须言明其查验之事,并其事之所以然,然而尤须酌定于某月日时,收取为证见者之口供而于当堂之上。"①

7. 关于案件执行:

"第五百五十八条 凡如事中之为债主者,并无字据,该债主可以禀请该欠债者所居之处该管之官,或为该欠债者,有欠其人之款之人,其人所在之处该管之官,令该欠债者之欠款人,不使议财物还给于原欠债者,则为例所准行。

第五百五十九条 凡如扣执停行之文据,或与阻止之文书,系依恃此等文据而行,以之为凭者,须于所立文约上注明事中之钱财,系若干数目。倘此文约等系由官立定者,亦须注明钱财之数,尤须将承审官应行饬令之情形注明。惟此扣执停行之情,系由官所行。而其事中之资财系非国宝源流者,则该管之官须于所立文书之上,注明有物抵债,可得价值若干。倘此扣执停行之文书,系该债主而与欠负者,实未尝一同居处于某处,则惟应由欠负者选择某一地而居之。倘不遵此定章而为者,设有所为,亦惟置之不议。"②

"第六百二十九条 凡如售卖之事须有宣扬之情,而何以行之,须于售卖八日之先宣扬、粘贴、张挂,以便周知。而此张挂、粘贴之事,须于被扣执者之门前、该处总甲官之门前、总市会处,或无市会须于相近市会之处,并息讼官门前,均宜粘贴张挂,以便宣扬。

第六百三十条 凡如粘贴张挂之事,须注明售卖之时日,并须注明欲行扣执停行之人与被扣执停行之人姓名、居址,并须注明其所扣执停行之田,系何基址,其所生果实系何等类及其地系

---

① [法]毕利干:《法国律例·民律指掌》,日本司法省1894年版,第206、207页。
② [法]毕利干:《法国律例·民律指掌》,日本司法省1894年版,第278页。

归何处管辖者,均须逐一注写清楚。"①

"第六百七十六条　凡如上文所言立具清单之事,惟应依文照录,注明于管理此项事务官册之中,而于此事之先,须将此项清单呈于管理此项定资地方之总甲官批阅。倘该定资之物系不归于一总甲官所属者,则须将各应管属之总甲官概行批阅,始为可行。

第六百七十七条　凡如扣留物件之事,自应报之于被扣留物件之人,惟此事亦有制定之限。即自立具清单已竣十五日内,即应前往报之。倘该被扣留物件之人所居之地,与该管此等事务之衙门相距较远者,则每多七十里,例准展限一日。其报知扣留之字据,须于管理其处之总甲官批阅,始为可行。

第六百七十八条　凡扣留物件与报知有扣留物件字据,应一并注明于管理指物沾利事务官册之中。而其注册期限,则以十五日。惟其限自何为始,即自报知有扣留之情,而于被扣留物件者之日为始计之。

第六百七十九条　凡如管理此项扣留字据之官,既经接到此等扣留字据,与其情事,而乃诿为无暇,未能当面刻即注入官批中者,则该管应于原呈字据之上,注明此项字据系于某年月日时所接到者。倘于接据此项字据之日,而其时恰有相同呈递此项字据者,则以何人所呈字据为先呈者,须以其时先为呈递者,即为第一先呈字据之人,而照例注于官册之中。

第六百八十条　凡如扣留物件之字据,欲行注入于官册中者,而该管理此等事务之官,适于此项官册之中,已有注入此项情事,而未能再为注入所递字据者,应即有推辞之情,而究以何情推辞之,应于次来注册原字据幅侧,注明系于某年月日已有接据此项注册之字据,并行此扣留者,系何等之人,该案应归何项衙门管理,并申明行此扣留物件者,系现雇某晰讼之绅,其缮写此项字据,系于某年月日时,均应逐情注明。

---

① [法]毕利干:《法国律例·民律指掌》,日本司法省1894年版,第311、312页。

第六百八十一条　凡如其所扣留者，系为数定资之物，并此定资系未被人所租赁者，则该被扣留物件之人，即可以此项定资之物，暂为该欲行扣留者所按捺之物，并须按照官定押质之物之例而为，以至于出售此项定资物件之日为止。除事经有数债主，其于应管此项事务之总承审官，呈明事中另有别项情节者，则为格外之事。虽如此言，而该为债主者，亦能呈请该管承审官，呈明其人能以令人将此吾人所租或系田地、房屋中所滋生果子、谷实，或植之于地者，或垂挂于枝间者，使人收获，呈明总承审官允准，不论按照何等情形，为之售卖而于承审官所拟定期限之中，并其所得售物之价，即行注纳于公注赀财署中，以备拨发欠款。

第六百八十二条　凡如一切果子利益，或为天工果，或为人力果，系由扣留物件所滋生者，并其所得系于扣留字据，既经注入官册之后者，则此项果子之利益，或为该物本质，或为售价，均应聚集一处，而以定资之物一律视之。然后即将此项果子与所扣留定资之物，一并出售，归给不债主。并应按照指物沾利之次序，按次发交。

第六百八十三条　凡被扣留物件之人，其所有之物如系树林者，则不能擅自砍伐，即如他项亦不能有损坏之情。倘竟有违乎律例情事，亦可至有安慰之需，并于缴此安慰之项，至有延迟之情者，尤可至有拘勒其身，令其呈缴安慰赔补之款。除此情以外，倘仍有违例之端，应即援照制定刑律第四百条与第四百三十四条之例，从重惩罚。"①

"第六百八十四条　凡如被扣留物件之人，其于报之欲行扣留物件之先，其所有定资之物，原无契券，并亦尚无定限者，倘嗣后为债主者，与该乐购之人，以为此项定资之物，实不足以为凭者，亦可呈请于官为之注册，以便为凭。

第六百八十五条　凡如房租与田租，自扣留注于官册之后，

---

① ［法］毕利干：《法国律例·民律指掌》，日本司法省1894年版，第337、338、339、340、341页。

应将其租聚集一处，即归于定资一类出售得价，一并发交于应收受者之债主。惟拨发之事，缘由次序可循，即按指物沾利之次序而拨发之。倘该欲扣留之债主，或他项债主，而于被扣留者租赁房田人，于其所应拨发之租息，乃有阻止 之端者，则此等情事，即按捺之端者，则此等情事，即相等于扣留其资贴，而于租赁房田之人者之手。该租赁房田人亦有所应尽之责。其责何以尽之，即于管理此项事务之官，恳请将该租赁之资呈交该管之官，以便拨发各债主，或呈请将此等租资存储公注资财署中。至该为债主者，倘于此资并无阻止按捺之情，而该租赁房田人，乃将租资交于被扣留物件者，则论于租赁房田人所交之资，固为结实可靠，而论于被扣留物件者，如已收得其租息，亦不过相等于有押质之情，而惟于众债主等，亦须有汇总禀报之情。

　　第六百八十六条　凡为被扣留物件者，不能以所扣留定资之物而有过权于人情事，并即自有扣留物件之事而注于官册之中为始计之。倘竟不行遵照而有违者，则其所为过权情事，系自然而然归于置之不议者之案视之，并不需恳请该管官于此事特发示谕，即为准行。

　　第六百八十七条　凡如上文虽如此言，其于扣留之物不能有过权情事，然亦有时可以行者。倘为购物者于其所购之物，而实出有乐购之分，乃将其购价储留，足可敷其各债主等应还之款者，则于此事，该债主亦未为不行。惟须将其所售之价若干，先为报明于各债主等知之，并须先备有若干资财，足敷事中之欠款及各费用者，始为可行。

　　第六百八十八条　凡如购买者，其所储留之赀，系特借贷于他人者，则在此他人自于所扣留之物项上，而有倚事沾光之权，然其所挟之权较之各为债主者，其权稍差。

　　第六百八十九条　凡于售卖物件之先，而未能预呈赀财若干为之储留者，则实能有宽展储留之期限。"①

---

①　［法］毕利干：《法国律例·民律指掌》，日本司法省1894年版，第342、343、344、345页。

"第七百零五条　凡如呈明得有乐购之分情事，须出晰讼之绅于该管官当堂呈明，惟既经初次得有乐购之分，须刻烛燃烧俟时为律。其烛一枝燃烧时刻不过时之一分，有如初经得有乐购之分，即烧烛以待。嗣复有人续增其价，复呈一乐购之分，则不论二次续呈乐购之分事能成交与否，而在先所呈乐购之分之人即为无干。

第七百零六条　凡何以为乐购之分定局之时，即视其所燃之烛相连三枝俱届时告尽之时，即可以末次所得之价而定其所得乐购之分。盖如所呈乐购之分三烛已尽，而并无复有钜重之价，则以末次所得之价，即为乐购之分之定价。其在初呈乐购之分者，既经燃其烛一枚，嗣复有人续呈以乐购之分，而以后并无再为增值呈有乐购之分者，其续行燃烧三烛已尽，则其公平至善之价，即为在（再）次呈有乐购之分者是归。"①

"第一千三十三条　凡如传案之票而有展限之情，以及一切词讼，系关立具合同之事，原有立定期限，惟其期限之为首为尾不计外，总以扣足其日为定限。倘其事中按例须有展限之情者，亦照此例一例办理。惟所展之限，亦有定章。按例如每加远七十里，准令展限一日。倘于七十里以外，仍有奇零之数，如系加多二十里，则例不计议。如系加多至三十里，则例准再为展限一日，以示限制。

第一千三十四条　凡如传案之票，系关经纪等核估，而有汇总禀报之情者，则须令在事者亲身在侧，视其拟办。倘经初次传唤后，而其事乃未办竣，必须续行下次接办者，则不需再发传案之票，以免烦扰。

第一千三十五条　凡如案关收受原被两造矢誓之情，或系欲核之事，或系有为保与备质之情，或欲查明案件的确情事，或欲究诘某项情事，倘该应行管属之衙门相距较远，则该管原衙门可以咨请与之就近之衙门为之拟办，以昭简便。

---

① ［法］毕利干：《法国律例·民律指掌》，日本司法省1894年版，第357、358页。

第一千三十六条　凡如该管衙门于一切所管案情，其事中所有字据、书函等件，系与人有诬赖讪谤之情者，能以销撤不存，或于其诬赖讪谤之情明显指出者，则在该管衙门于此案情所发示谕，或于各处黏贴，或刷印于新闻纸上，均为例所准行。

第一千三十七条　凡如饬令传知及各示谕，应遵照而为之事，亦有定期。盖自十月初一日，以至三月三十一日为止，不得于早间六点钟及晚间六点钟之后，而有饬令传知之情。又自四月初一日以至九月三十日，其早间四点钟以先，晚间至九点钟以后，而有行此饬令传知之情，并诸般庆贺之日，及安息之日，亦不准行，除有燃眉之急，应行迅速办理之事，须由官所准者，则可施行。

第一千三十八条　凡如词讼案件之中，其有晰讼之绅，原于其案经手办理，由该管衙门出有示谕，系为牢不可破者，则此绅即宜仍旧经理其事，不须复发示谕，令其遵行办理，亦不须再俾以权，惟行此事，须于发示谕本年则行，倘致迟延日久，则即不行。

第一千三十九条　凡如传报之情，系干于官者，该管应即接收其情，并于其清单之上批阅其事，须无所需花费者。倘该官竟尔推辞不为接收者，即可由就近理事坊监审官批阅。然该推辞不接之官，亦可有关罚缴银两之事，即应随其案情之轻重，以定其罚款之巨细，惟至少不得不及五个夫浪，尤须采取监审官于此案意见如何，以资办理。

第一千四十条　凡如接收字据之官，于所应办之件，有如立具合同字据清单之事，须于其本衙门、本处为之。惟须有一吏襄助而为。该吏应将所立合同字据原稿收存，如有欲行照抄其事者，即由该吏给发在事人照抄。然其事中如有急迫之情，亦可于该官私第迅为定拟。惟究须有？官核定之事，则始可行。

第一千四十一条　凡如本例所载一切章程应行遵照而为之日，何为其日之始，即自一千八百零七年正月元旦之日为始，以后凡一切词讼案件，均宜遵照而行。其以先所定章程与其地方习俗，即应注销不议。

第一千四十二条　凡如未至一千八百零七年以前，其一切词讼案件之情，有关费用情事者，须由该管官立具章程，由国会批准，确以为然者，则以为可行。"①

第五节　《法国律例·刑名定范》

《法国律例·刑名定范》共二卷：第一卷"办理各项刑名因案科断之例"；第二卷"论治事执公平衡之义"。

毕利干译《法国律例·刑名定范》与林纪东等主编《刑事诉讼法》目录对比表②

毕利干译《法国律例·刑名定范》		林纪东等主编《刑事诉讼法》	
第一卷	论办理各项刑名，因案科断之例	第一编	总则
第一章	论办理刑名之事务	第一章	法例
第二章	论各处正副总印官，并各处巡捕应首领官之职守	第二章	法院之管辖
第三章	论坚守树林并守护贵苗之兵役之责	第三章	法院职员之回避
第四章	论正副监审官	第四章	辩护人辅佐人及代理人
第一节	论正副监审官遇于一切刑名事务以及其职守应尽事宜	第五章	文书
第二节	论正副监审官执事一切围范	第六章	送达
第五章	论有襄赞监审官之责者之官	第七章	期日及期间
第六章	论督理信谳官之职守	第八章	被告之传唤及拘提
第一节	论督理信谳官	第九章	被告之讯问
第二节	论督理信谳官之职守	第十章	被告之羁押
第七章	论传唤票以及代案收禁监禁等票	第十一章	搜索及扣押
第八章	论一切案中人犯可以暂行释放与取保作质事宜	第十二章	证据

---

① ［法］毕利干：《法国律例·民律指掌》，日本司法省1894年版，第541、542、543、544、545、546页。

② ［法］毕利干：《法国律例·刑名定范》，日本司法省1894年版；林纪东等主编：《刑事诉讼法》，五南图书出版公司1986年版。

续表

毕利干译《法国律例·刑名定范》	林纪东等主编《刑事诉讼法》
第九章 论督理信谳官于一切案中，既经讯有端倪，应拟如何办理之处，具文咨呈，？办之例	第一节 通则
第二卷 论治事执公平衡之义	第二节 人证
第一类 论惩忿司衙门所理之事	第三节 鉴定及通译
第一章 论正尤应即办一切越理之署	第四节 勘验
第一节 论息讼官于其本质外，兼有理惩忿之责	第十三章 裁判
第二节 论正副总甲官于其本责外，兼有办理越理案件之责	第二编 第一审
第三节 论越理之案致有上控者	第一章 公诉
第二章 论惩忿司衙门所理之事	第一节 侦查
第二类 论一切词讼案件，应归于秉公议论词讼之署中，照案办理者	第二节 起诉
第一章 论究办一切案件而以某人命为案中实系被告者	第三节 审判
第二章 论议设定谳处之围范	第二章 自诉
第三章 论定谳处办理各项案件围范	第三编 上诉
第四章 论详查一切案件于定拟各项案件，以及案已拟定后，照所科断而行之事	第一章 通则
第一节 论详查一切案件之例	第二章 第二审
第二节 论一切词讼案件于各案拟定后，因案照例施行者	第三章 第三审
第五章 论秉公议论词讼之署	第四编 抗告
第一节 论秉公议论词讼之绅	第五编 再审
第二节 论会集秉公议论词讼之绅之围范	第六编 非常上诉
第三类 论呈请注销一切之条例	第七编 简易程序
第一章 论审理一切案件及已拟定之案所发示谕，其间有可呈请应行视以不足据者	第八编 执行
第一节 论有获罪其案情校钜者	第九编 附带民事诉讼
第二节 论过失与越理之案，应行注销之条例	
第三节 论以下所载之例与上两节所定之例，有可比拟实行者	
第二章 论一切案件呈请注销覆勘者	
第三章 论例应磨勘一切大小案件之例	

续表

毕利干译《法国律例·刑名定范》	林纪东等主编《刑事诉讼法》
第四类 论于办理寻常案件之外，而仍有超众应行拟办之案之例	
第一章 论办理捏造不实一切公文字据等项置例	
第二章 论治负罪逃犯之例	
第三章 论各承审官干犯制定律例之罪。其干犯情形，分为两项：其一项有于其职守中而干犯律例者，系公罪；一项有于其职守外而干犯律例者，系私罪	
第一节 论各承审官所干犯律例之罪，而于其职守外者，应行拟办之例	
第二节 论总核庶务衙门，总司刑曹衙门，总定？处之总承审官以外，而论及于各项衙门之承审官，于其职守之中而有干犯律例者	
第四章 论一切例应尊敬之官长，而乃竟有干犯之事之例	
第五章 论干犯各项案件，或属过失，或属较重之罪，系尊爵近？宗室王爵王眷属、御前内大臣及各卿？等官，以何体制授其所具亲供	
第六章 论逃逸罪犯复被拘缉，当场？？，应以何法始？办其是否	
第七章 论一切已结未结之案卷宗示谕等件，而原文竟致有伤毁过失，或被人抢窃等事者，应以何法再为办理	
第五类 论如一项案情内？三四官署应行科办者，而其案？应归于其衙门拟办，以专责成，并有接到一切案情，而其案却非该署应？理者，应即转移于应管制衙门，以资科办	
第一章 论有案关三、四官署应办之件，而其案究竟应归于某承审官拟办者之例	
第二章 论一切案件有关？文转移之事	
第六类 论特建异案官署之事	
第七类 论有数件条例而特与？家眷民有所关涉，并关涉一切休戚之事者	
第一章 论储藏一切各项案件示谕之例	

续表

毕利干译《法国律例·刑名定范》	林纪东等主编《刑事诉讼法》
第二章　论各处监视于暂押班房并？抑制所之例	
第三章　论设法禁止一切官役及各项人有无故不按例载，胆敢私押私收者	
第四章　论一切获罪之人，既经因案科断之后，而乃有呈请洗冤者，与事后竟克涤垢自新者之事	
第五章　论例准援免并论满限销权之事	

毕利干译《法国律例·刑名定范》与《中华人民共和国刑事诉讼法》目录对比表①

毕利干译《法国律例·刑名定范》	《中华人民共和国刑事诉讼法》
第一卷　论办理各项刑名，因案科断之例	第一编　总则
第一章　论办理刑名之事务	第一章　任务和基本原则
第二章　论各处正副总印官，并各处巡捕应首领官之职守	第二章　管辖
第三章　论坚守树林并守护贵苗之兵役之责	第三章　回避
第四章　论正副监审官	第四章　辩护与代理
第一节　论正副监审官遇于一切刑名事务以及其职守应尽事宜	第五章　证据
第二节　论正副监审官执事一切围范	第六章　强制措施
第五章　论有襄赞监审官之责者之官	第七章　附带民事诉讼
第六章　论督理信谳官之职守	第八章　期间、送达
第一节　论督理信谳官	第九章　其他规定
第二节　论督理信谳官之职守	第二编　立案、侦查和提起公诉
第七章　论传唤票以及代案收禁监禁等票	第一章　立案
第八章　论一切案中人犯可以暂行释放与取保作质事宜	第二章　侦查
第九章　论督理信谳官于一切案中，既经讯有端倪，应拟如何办理之处，具文咨呈，？办之例	第一节　一般规定
第二卷　论治事执公平衡之义	第二节　讯问犯罪嫌疑人
第一类　论惩愆司衙门所理之事	第三节　询问证人
第一章　论正尤应即办一切越理之署	第四节　勘验、检查

---

① ［法］毕利干：《法国律例·刑名定范·目录》，日本司法省1894年版；《中华人民共和国刑事诉讼法·目录》。

续表

	毕利干译《法国律例·刑名定范》		《中华人民共和国刑事诉讼法》
第一节	论息讼官于其本质外，兼有理惩愆之责	第五节	搜查
第二节	论正副总甲官于其本责外，兼有办理越理案件之责	第六节	查封、扣押物证、书证
第三节	论越理之案致有上控者	第七节	鉴定
第二章	论惩愆司衙门所理之事	第八节	技术侦查措施
第二类	论一切词讼案件，应归于秉公议论词讼之署中，照案办理者	第九节	通缉
第一章	论究办一切案件而以某人命为案中实系被告者	第十节	侦查终结
第二章	论议设定谳处之围范	第十一节	人民检察院对直接受理的案件的侦查
第三章	论定谳处办理各项案件围范	第三章	提起公诉
第四章	论详查一切案件于定拟各项案件，以及案已拟定后，照所科断而行之事	第三编	审判
第一节	论详查一切案件之例	第一章	审判组织
第二节	论一切词讼案件于各案拟定后，因案照例施行者	第二章	第一审程序
第五章	论秉公议论词讼之署	第一节	公诉案件
第一节	论秉公议论词讼之绅	第二节	自诉案件
第二节	论会集秉公议论词讼之绅之围范	第三节	简易程序
第三类	论呈请注销一切之条例	第四节	速裁程序
第一章	论审理一切案件及已拟定之案所发示谕，其间有可呈请应行视以不足据者	第三章	第二审程序
第一节	论有获罪其案情校钜者	第四章	死刑复核程序
第二节	论过失与越理之案，应行注销之条例	第五章	审判监督程序
第三节	论以下所载之例与上两节所定之例，有可比拟实行者	第四编	执行
第二章	论一切案件呈请注销覆勘者	第一章	未成年人刑事案件诉讼程序
第三章	论例应磨勘一切大小案件之例	第二章	当事人和解的公诉案件诉讼程序
第四类	论于办理寻常案件之外，而仍有超众应行拟办之案之例	第三章	缺席审判程序
第一章	论办理捏造不实一切公文字据等项置例	第四章	犯罪嫌疑人、被告人逃匿、死亡案件违法所得的没收程序

续表

毕利干译《法国律例·刑名定范》	《中华人民共和国刑事诉讼法》
第二章 论治负罪逃犯之例	第五章 依法不负刑事责任的精神病人的强制医疗程序
第三章 论各承审官干犯制定律例之罪。其干犯情形，分为两项：其一项有于其职守中而干犯律例者，系公罪；一项有于其职守外而干犯律例者，系私罪	附则
第一节 论各承审官所干犯律例之罪，而于其职守外者，应行拟办之例	
第二节 论总核庶务衙门，总司刑曹衙门，总定？处之总承审官以外，而论及于各项衙门之承审官，于其职守之中而有干犯律例者	
第四章 论一切例应尊敬之官长，而乃竟有干犯之事之例	
第五章 论干犯各项案件，或属过失，或属较重之罪，系尊爵近？宗室王爵王眷属、御前内大臣及各卿？等官，以何体制授其所具亲供	
第六章 论逃逸罪犯复被拘缉，当场？？，应以何法始？办其是否	
第七章 论一切已结未结之案卷宗示谕等件，而原文竟致有伤毁过失，或被人抢窃等事者，应以何法再为办理	
第五类 论如一项案情内？三四官署应行科办者，而其案？应归于其衙门拟办，以专责成，并有接到一切案情，而其案却非该署应？理者，应即转移于应管制衙门，以资科办	
第一章 论有案关三、四官署应办之件，而其案究竟应归于某承审官拟办者之例	
第二章 论一切案件有关？文转移之事	
第六类 论特建异案官署之事	
第七类 论有数件条例而特与？家眷民有所关涉，并关涉一切休戚之事者	
第一章 论储藏一切各项案件示谕之例	
第二章 论各处监视于暂押班房并？抑制所之例	
第三章 论设法禁止一切官役及各项人有无故不按例载，胆敢私押私收者	

续表

毕利干译《法国律例·刑名定范》	《中华人民共和国刑事诉讼法》
第四章 论一切获罪之人，既经因案科断之后，而乃有呈请洗冤者，与事后竟克涤垢自新者之事	
第五章 论例准援免并论满限销权之事	

《法国律例·刑名定范》是规定刑事案件处理程序的法律，如：关于法院任务：

"第一章 论有巡缉一切干犯例禁之责者，以及各营官员之职守

第十条 凡各府城太守之官及巴里京师军门堂官，其于一切干犯例禁之人，均可自行巡缉，亦可转令上项所列各官认真巡缉有无犯法犯过越理等事，否则如有此等情事，即应将案中一切情节，或有证质，或有赃据，并该犯一并呈交该管之官，以便因案照例究办。

第二章 论各处正副总甲官及各处巡捕厅首领官之职守

第十一条 凡如村镇之处，倘无设立巡捕厅首领之官，其一切应行巡缉之件，由该处总甲官兼司其事。设该总甲官别有要差，即由该处副总甲官兼司其事。至若守护青苗之人与监守树株之人，虽有巡缉专责，而遇有干犯青苗树株之犯，而在该处总甲官更较本管官，尤有巡缉督办之责。至该监审官如遇接到一切禀呈揭报供词等件，即行开具清单，以便将一切干犯例禁之人，并一切欲涉词讼之人，其案中一切详细情节，事中原委，并案中一切证质确据，及该犯于某处某时起事情由，逐一缮清，以便办理。

第十二条 凡村镇之处，截分段落，按段设立巡捕厅，其在村镇境内，设有一切干犯例禁之人，即由该处巡捕厅首领官巡缉究办。其该首领等官遇有应行巡缉之件，不得意存彼疆此界，互相推诿。惟应不分彼此，一体认真协办，不得谓为此事非在本厅属下，即行置之不问。倘遇有应行巡缉之事，虽不在该听所辖境

内，亦应一体协办。其所以分为段落界址者，原以各厅首领官易于梭巡，以昭严密而专责成。

第十三条　凡如所分某段落之巡捕厅首领官，倘一时或有别项要差，而又有应行巡缉之件，其同责之官，例应代办，以免将巡缉一切干犯例禁之责，稍有疏忽。其同责等官亦不得以此厅与彼厅并非紧邻，竟以推诿之？意存观望。

第十四条　凡有村镇之处，倘其地方较小，仅止设立巡捕厅首领官一员者，设有应行巡缉之件，而该首领官实非有意怠忽，系有所阻，万难分身之事，则该处总甲官或别总甲官，亦应兼司其责，以免应行巡缉之件，或有延误，俟该厅首领官可以自行视事之时，再为交替。

第十五条　凡正副总甲官接到一切案件卷宗，当即于三日内将其案中一切情节，转行咨明管理监审官之责之官，由该官查阅究办。"①

关于立案：

"第二卷　论治事执公平衡之义

第一类　论惩惩司衙门所理之事

第1章论正尤应即查办一切越理者之署

第一百三十七条　凡有案关刑例第四卷所载之事，其案中应罚之银数，不过十五夫浪者，即应将该被告科以监收之罪，亦不得有逾五日，并无论其案中有无查抄入官之物，亦无论其所应查抄物件价值若干，凡遇此等案件，均应以偶尔越礼过失之案，照例科断。

第一百三十八条　凡遇越礼与过失之案，均应归息讼官与总甲官按照下条所载之例，分别照例惩办。

第1段论息讼官于其本职外，兼有办理惩惩之责。

---

① ［法］毕利干：《法国律例·刑名定范》，日本司法省1894年版，第7、8、9、10、11页。

第一百三十九条　凡息讼官应行专办之案，惟有七则：一、凡该员所属境内本邑之中，或敢有越理之人，应归该员惩处；二、凡在该员所属境内本邑之外，有人致有越理情事，系属无可疑义之外，而其人不于该员所驻之地本邑之中居住，而亦非在该员所属境内浮居者，则其所干越理情事，亦应归该员惩处。或于某案中切要为证之人，不于该员所驻之地本邑之中居住者，而亦非在该员所属境内浮居者，亦应归该员惩处；三、凡有越理之案，而其案中原告呈请令被告赔补银两者，或未定其数，或其数逾十五夫浪者，亦应归该员惩处；四、凡有于树林致干例禁者，经该员治下之人禀请查办前来，亦应归该员惩处；五、凡有人胆敢肆行，向人辱骂、讪谤者，应归该员惩处；六、凡有张贴各种淫邪告白、物事式单以及各种邪书淫像，有伤风化者，应归该员惩处；七、凡有案关代人测字圆梦，妄言祸福等情者，均应归该员惩处。

第一百四十条　凡除息讼官专办案情以外，其余一切越礼情事，应归该员等管理者，而该处总甲官亦能一体办理。

第一百四十一条　凡市镇之区，若独设息讼官一员者，其办理一切越理情事之案，惟应自行核办。至该衙门书吏人等，于一切越礼情事之案，亦应随同该员一体兼办。

第一百四十二条　凡市镇较阔之区，若设有息讼官二员或数员分司其事者，该员等于兼办一切越礼之案，须择其年长者为之先导，余则更番轮流该值。倘仍有鞭长莫及之势，除应有书吏外，须专派书吏一员专司办理一切越礼案件、文移稿案，庶无疏忽之虞。

第一百四十三条　如上所论兼办一切越礼案件情形，倘或事紧，亦可于该息讼官中，分设两股，每一股中即设息讼官一员兼司其事，随同有书吏一人，专办一切。设派该息讼官二员者，应于书吏一人之外，再派书吏一人作为副襄办，仍须该书吏实心矢誓，以便从公。

第一百四十四条　凡于一切越礼案件，应由监审官所司之责者，始可办理裕如，而其处并未设有监审官之职，应将其责假之于本处总巡捕厅首领官，委令代办。设其处并未设立巡捕厅官，或设有其官，于其本责外，不能兼顾者，即于该处总甲官或副总甲官委令代办。设其地原设有巡捕官职员者，应由总甲官于职员中酌派一员或数员一体办理一切越礼之案。

第一百四十五条　凡遇有越礼之案，应由监审官具衔饬发传唤之票，或经该案中原告呈请该管官饬传该越礼者到案究办。其饬发该票之时，即派书吏一人持票前往传知，并将原票依文照式抄录一分，交给该案中被告之人收□。倘被告一时未能？面，即将该票交于该被告切近家属之人代领。

第一百四十六条　凡遇出发传唤票，将案中被告传唤到案者，须于出票后至少须逾二十四点钟以外，则须到案。倘该被告所居之处较远者，每以七十里而论，可再展限一倍。倘该管官不俟到案定限届满，即行率尔谓为该案中被告，势将脱身稽传，？？将案预先竟行定拟，则其所定拟之案，实不足为信凭，应即注销，置之勿论，不得即行照办。设该案中被告，因所定拟情形，欲行申诉阻止者，亦应于该管官升堂之际，即行辨明。至有紧要案件情节甚重者，则该管官于例定传唤到案定限酌量加紧。即由息讼官饬发传唤票，限定于某日某刻该案中原被两造，赶即到案，以便究办。

第一百四十七条　凡案中原被两造，一经得有欲行传唤到案之知？而尚未发有传唤票者，亦能自行投首，不俟既发传唤票，亦可准其自行到案。

第一百四十八条　凡遇案件于息讼官未经过堂以前，其案中情形有关亲身查验之事，该息讼官或奉有监审官札饬，或接案中原告禀呈，即可亲往查验受累情形轻重，或委人代查亦可。或自开犯单，或委人代开亦可。至有一切紧要事件，须查其情形，或自行亲身拟办，或委人代办均可，总期案无稽迟，妥速办理。

第一百四十九条　凡于一切案中应行传唤之人，倘于原票定例定期刻，竟不遵照到案者，应即援照脱身稽传之例，将该案预行定拟。

第一百五十条　凡遇案案中应行传唤之人，竟不组照例定期刻到案，即应照脱身稽传之例，先将案中情形定拟者，除以下各条所载，应准上控之例以外，倘该案应传之人，更不遵照下条所载之例，照限亲自到案者，其于拟定之案，即不准其妄行阻止。

第一百五十一条　凡照脱身稽传之例，应将该案预行定拟者，而该案中之人致有阻止情形，应于传唤票幅末注明，或自接到传唤票之日起，计三日之内，另具亲供，投递该管之官。倘该应传之人居处较远，应仍照每以七十里为度，再行予限一日，以便究办。至有因案预行定拟，而该案中之人欲有阻止之事，应由该管之官将该被告再为传唤过堂究办，而所发传唤之票，仍应遵照例定期限。倘该被告竟不到案者，则虽有阻止之事，应即勿庸置议。

第一百五十二条　凡应传唤到案之人，或本人自行遵照到案，或遣有执守证据之人，代为申诉，均无不可。

第一百五十三条　凡于审办一切案件之时，例准案外无干之人，环立视听。除于一切不令人周知之案，另行密办外，其于一切各项案件，倘于审讯之时，并未经众人视听，则其所审办之案，实不足为？谳，应不得照议拟结。至每案于审办之时，尤须遵照例定办理先后次序，如某案中既有犯单，须先令书吏照单朗诵一遍，如监审官饬传案中有可作证之人，或案中原告当堂禀请饬传作证之人，既经传唤到案，应即将该作证人先行逐一审讯，嗣令原告供明本意此案欲作如何办结，然后始可令该案中被告恳请准其申诉剖辩，以免有所屈抑。至传到为该被告作证之人，与同该被告前来作证之人，应援照下条所载之例，查该作证之人可以准其到案者，始可令其到案。至该管官于定拟其案，应于既经过堂审讯后，即行定拟。设尚未经定拟，即至迟亦须于下次过堂审办后，即行拟结，不得稍事稽迟，以免拖累。

第一百五十四条　凡遇办理越礼之案，须有切实凭据，或如有该管官所？犯单，或有某人据实禀揭，或有的确证见，均可执以为凭。倘无犯单禀揭等件，仅有的确证见之人，亦可据其所证者究办。至该管官原系由律例制定为各案中经理犯单事务，是其专责。除经有人竟敢指实证明所开犯单实有虚诬之处，则自勿庸遵照。若其所开者并无稍涉虚诬之处，则自应执为切实之据，不准案中为证者任意妄行分辨。至于他项职官，既非律例定准经理犯单是其专责，或尽其实，或有虚诬，自应仍需查办。至有所开不合之犯单，该证见人应以其所证所据——指实，分晰辨别，或具禀呈投递，或当堂口供，仍应由该衙门核准，方可遵行。

第一百五十五条 凡一切案中作证之人，于欲为证见之时，须当堂先为实心矢誓。如谓所供实无虚伪，必将所知事实合盘托出，即由书吏照所矢誓之语注册备核。倘该作证人并不实心矢誓，则所供词不得？以为据。至该作证人履历、籍贯以及作何生理，并所供紧要情节，一并注册存案备核。

第一百五十六条 凡被告人之尊长、晚辈、兄弟姐妹并其戚？等辈，以及被告之妻室，无论曾否析业者，均不得传唤到案，借伊等情辞，或可得其案中头绪。然于传唤时，须该案中原、被两造并无阻止情事，始可传唤。嗣经该案拟结，其原、被两造不得以作证人并非例准之人，希冀借口翻案。

第一百五十七条 凡遇案中作证之人，一经传唤，竟不遵照到案者，倘该案中情形实属紧要，则该管官即可勒令该作证人赶即到案，并按照监审官批示，于过堂之日，照初次脱身稽传之例，议以罚缴银两。倘二次仍不遵照到案，即可将该人证押解到案，以便究办。"①

关于侦查：

"第三百一十条 凡一切案犯于过堂审讯之时，无庸束缚其身。须有兵役等相随卫守，以防脱逃之事。即由总承审官询明该

---

① ［法］毕利干：《法国律例·刑名定范》，日本司法省1894年版，第81、82、83、84、85、86、87、88、89页。

犯名姓、年岁、籍贯，及平素以何事务营生等情，均须一一询明。

第三百一十一条　凡案中护屈伸冤之人，于过堂办案之时，应由总承审官先行示谕，令其不可有昧天良而出言。有与定例背谬者，惟需据实直陈、和平允协，详言一切。

第三百一十二条　凡总承审官向秉公议论词讼之绅立言之时，该绅需免冠敬礼。其总承审官辞曰，令尔一秉大公，此心可以上鉴乎昊天，下无愧乎世众，推诚布公，倾心矢誓，务将某人现在被控各情，悉心详核。勿使两造或有畸轻畸重之偏。其于该案未经拟结之先，切勿轻与局外人动言局中一切事务。而于案中两造据事直陈，万勿挟仇嫌而藉以报复，万勿或念旧谊而意存袒护，勿留惨忍之心，勿生畏葸之命，尔其当堂将被告被控之情与该犯自招之供既已洞悉而无遗，即应倾心秉公而直语。其总承审官言毕一切，将秉公议论词讼之绅指名而呼。设能如此，公道昭明，斯案中自无屈抑之事也。则各秉公议论词讼之绅应举手而应曰，遵如是命，必当秉公而言，从心矢誓。倘有不如此办理者，则所科之案应不准行。

第三百一十三条　凡如上文所载之情既经办毕，该总承审官应令该犯细听。案下书吏将该案发交总司刑曹衙门，由该衙门所出示谕，将该犯所以命为被告之人，与由定谳处所拟办谕文，并该案中一切情状当堂朗诵一遍，以昭核实。

第三百一十四条　凡如书吏既将谕帖并案犯罪状宣读毕，应由总承审官将该犯罪状所控各情，逐一再言，即向该犯曰，此即尔被控致罪一切情形也。现今将尔所以被控各情均可细听，依所质据并人证等历历言之，以辨无所扳诬。

第三百一十五条　凡总监审官应将该犯被控一切罪状详述一遍，并将该案中应行传唤到案人证等开具名单，当堂呈出。而该人证，或系该员酌核指传者，或系两造中请传者，均应按名附入单内，以免遗漏，仍应将其名单令书吏按名朗诵一遍。至所开具人证名单，应于未经临案研讯二十四点钟以前，该总监审官与案中原告所指、所请应行传唤人证之名姓、住址，及素以何等事业谋生一切情由，该总监审官逐细开单，一一传令该犯知悉。而该犯所请提传之人证，亦应于二十四点钟以前按名呈明总监审官，以资查核。倘不遵此而为，则一切他人不得滥入名单，作为证见。

　　第三百一十六条　凡总承审官既经传唤人证到案，应令其在班房内听候提审取供。其各人证等于未过堂取供以前，总承审官应酌拟案中一切情节，设法防范该人证等彼此议论案中情由，勾串合供，以杜弊端。

　　第三百二十八条　凡于升堂审讯案件之时，其秉公议论词讼之绅与总监审官及各项承审官，于该案人证所具供词并该案犯剖辩之处。设该犯证等所供，实有紧要言词，准令该员等将所供词注册存记，但不得藉此稽延，暂停质审此案。"①

关于陪审：

　　"第五章之第一节　论秉公议论词讼之署
　　第二节　论会集秉公议论词讼之绅之围范
　　第三百九十八条　凡秉公议论词讼之绅进署供职，倘其所司之事尚未办竣，而竟敢无故擅离其责者，应即查照第三百九十六条所载之例，照例办理。如委因有事，并非无故擅离其责者，亦由定谳处查明，分别办理。

　　第三百九十九条　凡每于办理各案之时，以及会审案件之期，应于未过堂以前，将众秉公议论词讼之绅中未经止?者，及未?宽免此差者齐集到署，在总监审官与该案被告面前，?验众名，即将众名各?一签，留于尊内，以便抽取十二员名，充当秉公议论词讼之差。至该案中被告与被告所?护屈伸冤者，及办理此案之总监审官，如查某绅揆之于例，有未尽符之处，似不应充

---

①　［法］毕利干：《法国律例·刑名定范》，日本司法省1894年版，第169、170、171、172、173、181页。

当此差者，应即摈斥其人，并指名恳请该管官将其名扣除，但除下文所载按例作何分别以外，始得摈斥其人。盖既经该被告呈请之后，而为总监审官者亦有摈斥其绅之权，并该员与案中被告及该被告所？护屈伸冤者，如有欲行恳请扣除某绅，其因何恳请扣除之故，不得声叙清楚，至应充此选之众绅，既经签掣十二员名，其额已足，即可各供其职。

第四百条　凡于签掣众秉公议论词讼之绅之时，倘该绅等仅足十二员名之职，则总监审官与该被告等，有以为未协者，即不得率行恳请扣除，以符体制。

第四百零一条　凡按定例，总监审官与该案中被告，于秉公议论词讼之绅，如有以为未协，应准恳请扣除若干名，其余不扣除之绅，计其人数，则属单数。则此单数以双数比之，自多一人，即以单数之绅归？该案被告，以资案情明晰。

第四百零二条　凡一案中而有被告数人者，如欲联名恳请扣除某绅，亦无不可。或一人独请扣除某绅，亦无不可。总之无论数人联名，或一人独请，惟不得违上条所载定章一切应遵事宜。

第四百零三条　凡如案中被告有不愿联名恳请扣除某绅之事者，则须拈阄，计其孰应在先，孰应在后，以定其恳请扣除先后之次序。其被告中，若有一恳请扣除某绅之事者，即如众被告恳请无异，一俟拣派足额，即不能再为更易。

第四百零四条　凡案中被告等，如有愿欲商同一齐于一班中恳请扣除秉公议论词讼之绅数员者，亦准所行。而其所余众绅等，若该被告有欲恳请扣除某绅者，须按以前签掣前后次序，按次恳请扣除。

第四百零五条　凡拣派秉公议论词讼之绅，既经拣派足额，应即将该被告过堂讯办。

第四百零六条　凡遇定谳处因有别项紧要事故，将案犯单所载各项罪名，或一单而载有数罪者，无暇究办，移于下次会审时再为研讯，应即将秉公议论词讼之绅，另行缮具名单，查明有无可以扣除之处，照以上各条所载定章，另行签掣十二员，以资查办。若不遵此而为，则其案虽经科断，亦惟置之不议。"①

关于第二审程序：

"第三类　论呈请注销一切案件之条例

第一章　论审理一切案件及已拟定之案所发示谕，其间有可呈请应行视以为不足据者。

第四百零七条　凡遇获罪与过失越理三项之案，倘该管官所定之案，所发之谕以及审办捕拿一切事宜，竟有与定例未符之处，准其援照下条所载各情，照例比拟，呈请视以不足为据。

第一节　论有获罪其案情较巨者

第四百零八条　凡遇案中被告，既经获罪，嗣经总司刑曹衙门将该犯解交定谳处会审者，而其所发示谕，或其该管衙门原拟之罪，或该定谳处所科之罪，竟有于例未能尽合者，且遇有承审官等于某案事件，原无办理之权，而竟越俎妄?，或有案中被告请示之事，而竟置之不答，或竟忘怀，漏未答复，甚或于总监审官呈请例准之事，而该承审官竟置之不答，或竟忘怀，漏未答复者，则该监审官与被告所请示之事，揆之于例，内虽未载有若不答复，即将此案注销明文，亦惟按照此条之例，即行注销。

第四百零九条　凡有案中被告，经该管衙门拟将该被告释放，免其置议者，设总监审官以为原拟开释免究所发一切示谕，于例未宜，呈请注销原案，而于定例，实有更正合宜之处者，既经查明，即可具呈申请，但不得与开释免究之人有所干涉亏累之处。

第四百一十条　凡一切案件，既经定拟，而其所拟之罪，竟有与例不符，或所援引之例，竟有错误等情者，则该办案之总监审官与该被罪之人，均可照例，请将所定之罪以及出发示谕等项，即行注销。至各承审官判断各案，应得罪名，本有定例可

---

① ［法］毕利干：《法国律例·刑名定范》，日本司法省1894年版，第229、230、231、232、233页。

遵，而或竟以某案应得之罪未载？例，而乃？援第三百六十四条之例，率行拟以赦免者，该总监审官一经查知，应即将所出赦免示谕呈请注销，以杜轻纵之弊。

第四百一十一条　凡承审官于定拟各案罪名，系比拟定例，实无故为出入，甚属妥善者，则不得以其所发拟结示谕幅末抄录所援之例，妄为错误，呈请将所定之案视以不足为据。

第四百一十二条　凡案中被告系照例应行免究赦免者，则该案原告断不准将该管官所定免究与赦免等项示谕，呈请注销。然而遇有该管官所拟案中，原告应缴安慰赔补等项银两者，而其所拟之银数，较之该被告合请之数，反有加增之处，则应准该原告将此应缴安慰之银一事，呈请注销复核，以昭公允。

第二节　论过失与越礼之案，应行呈请注销之条例

第四百一十三条　凡如第四百零九条所载，呈请注销案件之事，倘遇有越理与过失之案，将案拟结之时，无论或系拟以罚款，或系拟以免究，设与定例有相违悖之处，则该总监审官并该案中原被两造均应准其呈请，将案注销。然该管官如有将案判令免究，业经声明后，则在案之人亦不得以尚有别项情节应行研究托故，将所定免究之案，呈请视以不足为据。

第四百一十四条　凡遇越理及过失之案，至拟结之时，应如何办理以及所发示谕等项，均应援照第四百一十一条之例，照例办理。

第三节　论以下所载之例与上两节所载之例有可比拟施行者

第四百一十五条　凡总核事务衙门或总司刑曹衙门，查出某案原先拟办于例不符，应行注销，将其案复勘者，其复勘之一切费用应由该衙门视其案情，酌核轻重数目，向原先拟办错误之督理信谳官，或其本处该管官勒令呈缴。然虽如此办理，亦须实有大过者，仍须自颁发此例之日为始计之。俟二年后，设有犯大过者，方可如此办理。

第二章　论一切案件呈请注销复堪者

第四百一十六条　凡有呈请注销某案，以祈复勘者，无论于

其案拟议作何发落之先,或于其案既经拟定之际,须俟其案业经拟定后,始可呈请注销复勘。至有案件业经拟定,已准作何发落而施行者,则在欲行呈请注销原案之人,仍有可挟之权。至有呈请注销以祈复勘者,因其案于该衙门实无管理之权,则不得援照此条之例比拟办理,自有别项定章可以遵循。

第四百一十七条 凡被议获罪之人,遇有呈请将案注销者,应赴检收处投递禀呈,并同该检收处书吏公同画押其上。设具呈之人不能画押或不欲画押,由该书吏注册存案。倘该被议获罪者,或所遣护屈伸冤者,或遣及他人代为投递禀呈,亦可一例照办,但必须系某人前来递呈。其有此权力之处,则载于禀呈之上。至此项禀呈当于检收处注册存案,并无论何人,皆准看视,仍准自祈该处书吏照录,自行收执。

第四百一十八条 凡办理重罪与过失越理等案,至其案经拟定应作如何科断,作发结案批示等件,倘该案中原告及总监审官,以为此案所办未协,呈请将所定之案注销复核者,除照上条所载照例先行注册外,即当于三日之内,将递禀呈欲行注销复勘之情,通知被控之人,设被控之人此时尚在监中收禁,即由书吏将所欲递注销此案禀呈朗诵一遍,令先后一切情辞逐一知悉,并令其于此禀呈上画具花押。倘该被告不能画押,或不欲画押,亦由该书吏将未画押之处注明禀呈之上。如被控之人现在业经开释,应由该呈请注销此案之人,往情理非之绅,或觌面通知其人,或于其所择待?小寓之处,详细通知,均无不可。设其所居小寓之处,地方较远,循例每多七十里之遥,于例限外展限一日,以资措办。"①

关于减刑:

"第六百三十三条 凡如执有信牌者,应即呈于酌夺此案应

---

① [法] 毕利干:《法国律例·刑名定范》,日本司法省1894年版,第234、235、236、237、238、239、240、241页。

允所请与否，与之居处相近之衙门，然后仍应将此信牌照抄一分，呈于原拟结此案之该管衙门，以资查核。而所照抄之信牌，仍应照录于该署册簿之中。

第六百三十四条　凡有应准其洗冤者，则将其以前所科禁止办理一切公私事件之罪，自涤垢自新以后，诸应禁止之处，即行开免。然此等情事，亦有区别。如以前所科禁止之事，系按贸易章程第六百一十二条所载之事者，则亦不能？行开免。至有已被罪后而复干犯一罪，则纵有呈请洗冤之事，而亦不准其所请矣。倘有被罪者既邀洗冤之后，而乃复干一罪者，则因准其洗冤所得一切利益之处，均著一概注销。

第五章　论例准援免并论满限销权之事

第六百三十五条　凡原案所科治罪示谕，系干犯较重之罪者，应过二十年则始得准其有例准援免之事，惟其期限应自原案拟结之日为始计算。至被罪之人，虽应由例准援免之事，而该犯所居之处，不准在其原案犯事地方，并不准其在该案中原告者所居之处，与该原告所继承受遗产者所居之处，在此等处居住。而于此等情以外，在国家亦能饬令该被罪者，指地迁居某处，以资愧悔。

第六百三十六条　凡已拟结之案，而其获罪情形较轻者，则过五年后，可以有例准援免之事。惟五年之限，则应自原案拟结之日起为始计算。如该管衙门将案已拟结，系属牢不可破，并不至有上控之事者，则自其拟结已定之日起为始计算。如该管衙门将案，而尚有可以上控之事者，则自上控之限已满之日为始计算，始得呈请例准援免之事。

第六百三十七条　凡被罪者原案所获之罪，系关死罪与羞辱重罪者，则应行追迫其罪之事。倘于十年内，在国家与该案原告竟未？及按例追迫，今已十年，则亦勿庸苛求，即准该犯有呈请例准援免之事。倘该犯于十年内，其案情未能一一研讯属实，实不能将其案刻即拟结者，则应自援例酌拟此案未定之末日起为始计算，于十年后，可以有例准援免之事。倘该案中系有同谋之人，自应按例科办，而其例定援免之限，亦可一例拟办。

第六百三十八条　凡如以上所载两项情形之中，设有案系干犯过失越理之案，则于三年后，可以准其有例准援免之事。

第六百三十九条　凡如干犯越理之案，则其应得之罪过二年后，可以准其有例准援免之事，惟其定限应自出具示谕，不致复有上控之事，而其案已拟结之日起为始计算。倘该被罪者执有上控之权，则应自准其上控定限已逾之时为始计算。

第六百四十条　凡如干犯越理之案，虽其罪既经研讯属实，而尚未拟结者，则过一年后，可以准有例准援免之事。倘该原案在该管衙门既已拟结，而乃有人上控者，则自传知案中在事者有上控之事之日起一年后，即可例准援免之事。

第六百四十一条　凡无论何项案情，该犯既经科罪，或属脱身稽传，或系负罪逃犯，虽原案所获之罪照例有例准援免之事，亦惟不准有涤垢自新与呈请洗冤之事。

第六百四十二条　凡因案拟结所发示谕，系按刑名之例拟议，而其案情仍有干涉民例之事，则被罪者有可例准援免之限，亦即按民例所载者，一例办理。

第六百四十三条　凡本例所备之款，其中所载不应重论之案，如干越理过失等事者，则亦有制定专条，而并与本例所列他款无不相符，可以比拟"①

第六节　《法国律例·贸易定律》

《法国律例·贸易定律》共三卷。第一卷"论总赅贸易情形"；第二卷"论沿海通商之条例"；第三卷"论各项商人亏累，情出无奈不得已而打账者，及事属有心，故意闭门逃走者，应行办理之条例"；

---

① ［法］毕利干：《法国律例·刑名定范》，日本司法省1894年版，第341、342、343、344、345、346、347页。

毕利干译《法国律例·贸易定律》与林纪东等主编《公司法》、《海商法》目录对比表①

毕利干译《法国律例·贸易定律》	林纪东等主编《公司法》、《海商法》
第一卷　论总该贸易情形	《公司法》 第一章　总则
第一类　论一切商贾贸易之人	第二章　无限公司
第二类　论一切商贾贸易所立各项册簿之事	第一节　设立
第三类　论一切商贸市会之事	第二节　公司之内部关系
第一节　论一切商会之名及其一切围范	第三节　公司之对外关系
第二节　论各会中商友遇有口角争执之端，则以何法为之调处而排遣之	第四节　退股
第四类　论夫妇析业之例	第五节　解散、合并及变更组织
第五类　论市馆中公局商总暨船师及各项经纪人等之事	第六节　清算
第一节　论市馆之例	第三章　有限公司
第二节　论公局、商总暨经纪人等之条例	第四章　两合公司
第六类　论以各项物件留以备质，并论充当代购诸物之商者	第五章　股份有限公司
第一节　论以各项物件留以备质者	第一节　设立
第二节　论代购诸物商人之例	第二节　股分
第三节　论水陆中一切代购诸物之商	第三节　股东会
第四节　论车夫条例	第四节　董事及董事会
第七类　论一切买卖产物之例	第五节　监察人
第八类　论兑票并传使票及至限例准援免职事	第六节　会计
第一节　论兑票之事	第七节　公司债
第二节　论相传代还禀之例	第八节　发行新股
第三节　论例准援免之例	第九节　变更章程
第二卷　论沿海通商之条例	第十节　公司重整
第一类　论各项海船之条例	第十一节　解散及合并
第二类　论扣留船只售卖以补所亏之事	第十二节　清算
第三类　论船主一切事宜	第六章　删除
第四类　论舟师与艇长应尽事宜	第七章　外国公司
第五类　论雇请船中舟师水手暨一切应役人等之条例	第八章　公司之登记及认许

---

① ［法］毕利干：《法国律例·贸易定律》，日本司法省1894年版；林纪东等主编：《公司法》、《海商法》，五南图书出版公司1986年版。

续表

毕利干译《法国律例·贸易定律》	林纪东等主编《公司法》、《海商法》
第六类　论雇赁船只立具合同之例	第一节　申请
第七类　论各项货物名色之单条例	第二节　规费
第八类　论搭附雇觅运载船只之例	第九章　附则
第九类　论凭天债格立具合同之条例	
第十类　论保险之事	《海商法》 第一章　通则
第一节　论立保险合同并其样式及其用处之事	第二章　船舶
第二节　论保险人与被保险者，其本分应为之事	第一节　船舶所有权
第三节　论于所有之物遇有事出无奈万不得已，致将其物弃置者	第二节　优先权及抵押权
第十一类　论于货物船只有所亏折之事	第三章　船长
第十二类　论弃置物件以资济险轻舟，并论公摊之事	第四章　海员
第十三类　论例准援免之例	第五章　运送契约
第十四类　论遇有却其所请之情者	第一节　货物运送
第三卷　论各项商人亏累，情出无奈不得已而打账者，及事关有心、故意闭门逃走者，应行办理之条例	第二节　旅客运送
第一类　论情出无奈不得已而打账者之例 此章系总统约略计之	第三节　船舶拖带
第一章　论遇有呈报到官之事，系因打账之人欲行打账，而有所关系之条例	第六章　船舶碰撞
第二章　论由官拣委经理打账事务绅董之条例	第七章　救助及捞救
第三章　论奉官指明为打账之商者，于其诸物应先盖用关防，并一切应为紧要事件	第八章　共同海损
第四章　论暂时权且拣委充当公举首事之人，并论复易实办公举首事者之事	第九章　海上保险
第五章　论公举首事者，其责任中应行措办之事	第十章　附则
第一节　论将其事如何办理大略情形总而言之	
第二节　论开启已盖关防，并立具查物底单之事	
第三节　论售卖货物家具等项，并论凭票兑资之事	
第四节　论所行之事系为护持事中一切所有例应之处	
第五节　论查验各项欠款数目多寡，并检查其事虚实之条例	

第四章 《法国律例》的翻译与出版

续表

毕利干译《法国律例·贸易定律》	林纪东等主编《公司法》、《海商法》
第六章 论公予宽减之事，并论打账者与各债主有和议之事	
第一节 论召会一切债主者，并论各债主前来会晤之事	
第二节 论公予宽减之事	
第三节 论停议公予宽减之事，系因资财不足者	
第四节 论各债主会集一处之事	
第七章 论一切债主各分等类，并于打账事务有例应之处	
第一节 论负债者于其事中有所关涉，同应承担之责者，并论及事中为中保之人者	
第二节 论有押账之债主，并应沾光于动资项上之债主	
第三节 论有指物沾利之债主，并论其于定资、动资项上独有沾光之权者	
第四节 论商者之妇所挟之例	
第八章 论分拨银两于各债主，并论于各项定资、动资之物项上有理应变价者之权	
第九章 论出售定资各物之为打账者	
第十章 论有索讨收回原物之权者	
第十一章 论打账事务已经拟结而复有上控者	
第二类 论事属有心故意闭门逃走者	
第一章 论有情近有心故意闭门逃走者	
第二章 论有心欺骗者	
第三章 论打账事中，致有干犯一切罪案系在事之他人干犯者	
第四章 论办理一切有心诓骗闭门逃走之案，其事中所有定资、动资等项之物者	
第三类 论一切涤垢自新之事	
第四卷 论其所司之事有经管一切贸易之权者	
第一类 论建设督商司之官署	
第二类 论督商司衙门各项职役应尽事宜	
第三类 论案至督商司衙门案前应办一切围范	
第四类 论案至一切总司刑曹衙门案前惩办一切围范	

毕利干译《法国律例·贸易定律》与《中华人民共和国公司法》、
《中华人民共和国海商法》目录对比表①

毕利干译《法国律例·贸易定律》	《中华人民共和国公司法》、《中华人民共和国海商法》
第一卷　论总该贸易情形	《中华人民共和国公司法》 第一章　总则
第一类　论一切商贾贸易之人	第二章　有限责任公司的设立和组织机构
第二类　论一切商贾贸易所立各项册簿之事	第一节　设立
第三类　论一切商贸市会之事	第二节　组织机构
第一节　论一切商会之名及其一切围范	第三节　一人有限责任公司的特别规定
第二节　论各会中商友遇有口角争执之端，则以何法为之调处而排遣之	第四节　国有独资公司的特别规定
第四类　论夫妇析业之例	第三章　有限责任公司的股权转让
第五类　论市馆中公局商总暨船师及各项经纪人等之事	第四章　股分有限公司的设立和组织机构
第一节　论市馆之例	第一节　设立
第二节　论公局、商总暨经纪人等之条例	第二节　股东大会
第六类　论以各项物件留以备质，并论充当代购诸物之商者	第三节　董事会、经理
第一节　论以各项物件留以备质者	第五节　上市公司组织机构的特别规定
第二节　论代购诸物商人之例	第五章　股分有限公司的股份发行和转让
第三节　论水陆中一切代购诸物之商	第一节　股份发行
第四节　论车夫条例	第二节　股份转让
第七类　论一切买卖产物之例	第六章　公司董事、监事、高级管理人员的资格和义务
第八类　论兑票并传使票及至限例准援免职事	第七章　公司债券
第一节　论兑票之事	第八章　公司财务、会计
第二节　论相传代还禀之例	第九章　公司合并、分立、增资、减资
第三节　论例准援免之例	第十章　公司解散、清算
第二卷　论沿海通商之条例	第十一章　外国公司的分支机构
第一类　论各项海船之条例	第十二章　法律责任

---

① ［法］毕利干：《法国律例·贸易定律·目录》，日本司法省 1894 年版；《中华人民共和国公司法·目录》、《中华人民共和国海商法·目录》。

续表

毕利干译《法国律例·贸易定律》	《中华人民共和国公司法》、《中华人民共和国海商法》
第二类　论扣留船只售卖以补所亏之事	第十三章　附则
第三类　论船主一切事宜	
第四类　论舟师与艇长应尽事宜	《中华人民共和国海商法》 第一章　总则
第五类　论雇请船中舟师水手暨一切应役人等之条例	第二章　船舶
第六类　论雇赁船只立具合同之例	第三章　船员
第七类　论各项货物名色之单条例	第四章　海上货物运输合同
第八类　论搭附雇觅运载船只之例	第一节　一般规定
第九类　论凭天债格立具合同之条例	第二节　承运人的责任
第十类　论保险之事	第三节　托运人的责任
第一节　论立保险合同并其样式及其用处之事	第四节　运输单证
第二节　论保险人与被保险者，其本分应为之事	第五节　货物交付
第三节　论于所有之物遇有事出无奈万不得已，致将其物弃置者	第六节　合同的解除
第十一类　论于货物船只有所亏折之事	第七节　航次租船合同的特别规定
第十二类　论弃置物件以资济险轻舟，并论公摊之事	第八节　多式联运合同的特别规定
第十三类　论例准援免之例	第五章　海上旅客运输合同
第十四类　论遇有却其所请之情者	第六章　船舶租用合同
第三卷　论各项商人亏累，情出无奈不得已而打账者，及事关有心、故意闭门逃走者，应行办理之条例	第一节　一般规定
第一类　论情出无奈不得已而打账者之例 此章系总统约略计之	第二节　定期租船合同
第一章　论遇有呈报到官之事，系因打账之人欲行打账，而有所关系之条例	第三节　光船租赁合同
第二章　论由官拣委经理打账事务绅董之条例	第七章　海上拖船合同
第三章　论奉官指明为打账之商者，于其诸物应先盖用关防，并一切应为紧要事件	第八章　船舶碰撞
第四章　论暂时权且拣委充当公举首事之人，并论复易实办公举首事者之事	第九章　海难救助

续表

毕利干译《法国律例·贸易定律》	《中华人民共和国公司法》、《中华人民共和国海商法》
第五章 论公举首事者，其责任中应行措办之事	第十章 共同海损
第一节 论将其事如何办理大略情形总而言之	第十一章 海事赔偿责任限制
第二节 论开启已盖关防，并立具查物底单之事	第十二章 海上保险合同
第三节 论售卖货物家具等项，并论凭票兑资之事	第十三章 时效
第四节 论所行之事系为护持事中一切所有例应之处	第十四章 涉外关系的法律运用
第五节 论查验各项欠款数目多寡，并检查其事虚实之条例	第十五章 附则
第六章 论公予宽减之事，并论打账者与各债主有和议之事	
第一节 论召会一切债主者，并论各债主前来会晤之事	
第二节 论公予宽减之事	
第三节 论停议公予宽减之事，系因资财不足者	
第四节 论各债主会集一处之事	
第七章 论一切债主各分等类，并于打账事务有例应之处	
第一节 论负债者于其事中有所关涉，同应承担之责者，并论及事中为中保之人者	
第二节 论有押账之债主，并应沾光于动资项上之债主	
第三节 论有指物沾利之债主，并论其于定资、动资项上独有沾光之权者	
第四节 论商者之妇所挟之例应	
第八章 论分拨银两于各债主，并论于各项定资、动资之物项上有理应变价者之权	
第九章 论出售定资各物之为打账者	
第十章 论有索讨收回原物之权者	
第十一章 论打账事务已经拟结而复有上控者	
第二类 论事属有心故意闭门逃走者	

续表

毕利干译《法国律例·贸易定律》	《中华人民共和国公司法》、《中华人民共和国海商法》
第一章 论有情近有心故意闭门逃走者	
第二章 论有心欺骗者	
第三章 论打账事中，致有干犯一切罪案系在事之他人干犯者	
第四章 论办理一切有心诓骗闭门逃走之案，其事中所有定资、动资等项之物者	
第三类 论一切滌垢自新之事	
第四卷 论其所司之事有经管一切贸易之权者	
第一类 论建设督商司之官署	
第二类 论督商司衙门各项职役应尽事宜	
第三类 论案至督商司衙门案前应办一切围范	
第四类 论案至一切总司刑曹衙门案前惩办一切围范	

《法国律例·贸易定律》包含《公司法》与《海商法》，它是以商事关系（一定社会中通过市场经营活动而形成的社会关系，主要包括商事组织关系和商事交易关系）为调整对象的法律规范的总称。

1. 关于商人及贸易活动

"第一条 凡何以即可谓为贸易之人，有如其人平素经营于生意之间者，即可谓为贸易之人。

第8条凡贸易为商之人，每日须立有日记，登载出入两项账目，如其所借之款，与其所亏之项，并一切关涉商贸之事。如汇票、传？票，或系受之于人者，或系授之于人者，及其家中一切费用均应逐一详细著明，此等情形，系为商者应为之要件。而于此外，如案贸易习俗，亦有将干涉一切贸易事件而登载于他项账簿中者，则为格外之事。至其所收于人者之信函，应件件汇集一处，其给于人者之信函，则须将原文照抄于一簿之中。

第二十一条 凡聚名协资之会者，其会中所起之字号，即用在会商友或一人或数人,以其人姓名定为该会之字号。

第七十条　凡自经本国酌中准理定成例,有明条之后,而于一年内,凡两造结婚,该夫妇无论或系析业而居者,或系带有随嫁之资,可以借之滋生利益,不能亏损其原产者,均应于定成例有明条之日起,设该夫妇中有一人欲为商贸易者,即应将所结婚姻合同,照例呈报该管之官,以便照例办理。倘有胆敢不遵者,惟应科同前罪。

第七十一条　凡所谓市馆者,系公局商总,并各船师及各项经纪人等,会集酌议各行行情,各物市价之处也。其事系属国家准行,并其一切所为,均系奉守国家制定章程者。"①

2. 关于票据

"第一百一十条　凡兑票者,系以一票出此处,寄至彼处,见票如数兑银也。惟其票上须注明系某年月日时、至某处见票兑银;其兑发银两者,系何姓名;此票系于某处某时领取,以先接此兑票之时,曾经给以兑换之银,或者给以相等之货,或见票系包总兑发清完,或系汇总核算清款。其持此票取银者,系奉某人之命,或即系取银之本人,或系非本人而出于他人。其兑票上系何号头次序,如首票未兑银两,则以所备二票兑银,如此等情,均应详细注明于该票之上。

第一百一十一条　凡如以兑票欲兑银两之时,而非于其应兑银者本人所居之处、系于他人处所者,则为例所准行之事,并此等兑票,亦有系由他人命其前往兑银者,则亦为例所准行之事。

第一百一十二条　凡如兑票之上所具姓名而有虚诈不实之情者,或于票上原注姓名,与其本人姓名、职役并所居地方不符,而有冒名顶替之情者,则此兑票不足执以为据,只可等于'允许不实,用以塞责,而随便允许人财物者之事一例论之'。

---

① ［法］毕利干:《法国律例·贸易定律》,日本司法省1894年版,第1、5、11、36、37页。

第一百一十三条　凡如兑票之上所具花押，或出于有夫之妇，或系未嫁之女而并非为商者，则此兑票亦不足以为据，只可等于'允许不实，用以塞责，而随便允许人财物者之事一例论之'。"①

"第三节　论售卖货物家具等项，并论凭票兑资之事。

第四百八十四条　凡将查无底单既经办毕，其所有一切货物、家具、现银、兑票、传使票及册簿、约据、衣服等类，即交公举首事者验明，将此项物件等收讫，则该公举首事者，应于查无底单幅末注明该物现已收到。

第四百八十五条　凡公举首事者所办凭票兑资之事，应由在事绅董查其所办如何。

第四百八十六条　凡绅董能以？听指名列为打账者之言，准其将货物、器具等件交付公举首事者，令其变卖，惟其变卖之事，仍应由该绅董定拟，或由买卖两造相议售卖，或由他项绅董将货售卖。如该绅董谓为应由某绅宦出售，即由公举首事者，将所指谓令其售卖之绅宦中，拣择一人前来，为之售卖。

第四百八十七条　凡属公举首事者，于办理其事，能以有减数和事之权，然须有二项情形，须由在事绅董准如所为，或有口角之端，须将该打账者唤之前来，如其口角之情，不因动资之物而致，系因定资之物而起者，则该公举首事者亦有此减数和事之权。倘其口角之情，系因欲售之物未将实价定准，或其所售之物，其值过三百夫浪者，则公举首事者，应将其情禀明督商司衙门，由该衙门批准确以为然，始可减数和事。至其所售之物，如系动资者，应即禀于督商司衙门，如其物系定资者，应即禀于理事坊衙门，俟该衙门批准确以为然，即可将该打账者唤之前来，办此减数和事之事。如该打账者有以为未宜之处，亦准有阻止之事。倘其所售之物，系一定资之物者，须其组织之情，足可以将此事置之不议者，始可阻止。

---

① ［法］毕利干：《法国律例·贸易定律》，日本司法省1894年版，第61、62、64页。

第四百八十八条　凡打账之人，果属邀免将其人拘禁，或给有任便护照，则公举首事者，亦可令其人在局帮同办理打账之事，以便其人可以发明事中一切事实，惟须由绅董拟定其人，准其前来者，则始可来助办，并间有酬劳之款。

第四百八十九条　凡因打账事务，以物所售之钱及以票兑取所收之钱，应由现在钱财中，除去因事所需之费，其下余之资，即于三日内交公注资财署收存备用。而其事中需费若干，即由在事绅董酌定其数，该署既经收到此项资财，应于三日内给予该绅董业已收到回头一纸，以为依据。倘有延迟情事，竟迟至三日以外，尚未的有回头之据者，则应罚该公举首事者，令其按照应交存若干资财，能滋之利若干，如数追罚。至将此项资财收存公注资财署之事，或由公举首事者解交该署，或由他人解交该署。如欲自署复将此项提出，须有绅董之命，始准提出。倘于提取此项资财之先，而竟有阻止之事者，"①

3. 关于保险

"第三百三十二条　凡因保险事物而立具合同，应将事中议定一切情节逐一注明，不得稍有遗误。其所应注明者，有如于某年月日时，立此合同，或立此合同系按照画具信押办理者，并缮写此等合同，须将文义联珠鱼贯而书，不得间断留有空白余纸地步；其保险人之姓名、居址，被保险者系何人氏，或即为货物之主，或为代购货物之主；其所载货之船系何名号，该船舟师系何姓名；其所装载者系何等货物；现从某口开行至何口岸停泊；其所保险者系何货物名色，并其价值；其保险之期限自何时起至何时止，并其保险之价若干。设于事中因事或至有口角之端，亦预为议定，应请某谙练调处人为之调处。凡以上如此等情，均应详细逐一注明于合同之中。

---

① [法] 毕利干：《法国律例·贸易定律》，日本司法省1894年版，第307、308、309、310、311、312页。

第三百四十八条　凡如保险之事而于立具合同之时，未将应道之言尽情吐露，系虚报不实者，或其所言者，而与货物名色竟有殊异不符者，盖以此诡诈之情，希冀令人深恐，借此欲减少保险之价。一遇有此等情，则其所立之合同，可以置之不议，不足视为可据。纵即按其诡诈之言立具合同，幸而于程途中竟未遇有意外非常之变故者，则其所立之合同，亦不足视为可据。

第三百五十条　凡既载于保险合同中之一切物件，设有遗失损坏、遭风相触，或改易程途，致船搁浅礁石、沉陷、失火、被劫、被困，或遇仇敌报复被毁，或因事将物抛掷于水及海面中一切意外危险，而其船适逢其难者，其所有损坏遗失之物，均归保险人一力承担。"①

4. 关于海运

"第一百九十条　凡一切航海船只，如以遇事而论，实可归为动资一类之物，因其系动资之物，而于售卖者，如有欠负之端，则即可以之为押账之物，至论于账目中而操有倚势沾光之权者，则以此等动资之物赔债累，尤为至要之物。

第二百二十三条　凡一切船中应需人夫、水手、舵工等项，该舟师、艇长实有经理之责。所以雇觅时，应由该舟师与艇长自行找寻。如使该船主所居不远者，则该舟师与艇长应会同一齐寻觅雇募也。

第二百七十五条　凡雇赁船只系按月包雇者，倘未立有合同，则其船脚价即由该船开行之日为始计算。

第二百七十六条　凡一切船只于开行之先，其所欲往之口岸适值有禁止通商之事者，则其所立合同应即作为废纸，并不得讨索安慰银两，而其装卸货物之费，仍须由货主备出。

第二百八十五条　凡代办商人及寄收货物之人，其照单收货

---

① ［法］毕利干：《法国律例·贸易定律》，日本司法省1894年版，第193、204、206页。

之时，须将收到货物名色之单交于舟师查收，并由舟师付以收到回字，则始可行。否则遇有未协之处，应需一切费用、安慰、赔补及多延时日各项银两，均应令其备出。"①

5. 关于贸易纠纷

"第一百八十九条　凡有词讼案件，系干涉兑票及相传代还票之事，其在立此票者，出自商贾，因贸易之事而开写者，或由银行中之人，因事开写，或不拘何人，因买卖之事而开写着，如论至例准援免之限，均系五年，而其期限为始之日，须自立具理非之券之日为始计算，或自其事已致经官涉讼，而案未拟结之日为始计算，至遇此等事件，该债主须请该管之官，将该负债者传至当堂，令其从心据实矢誓，自谓是否曾系欠负某人之财。倘竟公然谓为不有所负，则即可将此欠款置之不议可耳。倘该负债之人业已物故，须令其孀妇亲子当堂言由衷出。设竟言大略约计，此项欠款曾若赔还，则此事亦只置之不议。

第六百四十四条　凡遇有上控之案，因其案既经拟结，而复有上控情事者，应将其案交于总司刑曹衙门所管属之衙门，以便究办。

第六百四十五条　凡遇有上控之案，其案既经拟结，而复有上控情事者，则准其上控定限，应自其案？拟结，当堂示知案中原、被两造之日起，限以两月为期。如中在事者，有关脱身稽传之情，则自定限告满之日起，限以两月。倘自拟定其案之日，即欲有上控情事者，亦无不行。"②

第七节　《法国律例·园林则律》

《法国律例·园林则律》即《森林法》。它是关于森林、林木、林地使用权流转的法律规范，共分十五类。

---

① [法] 毕利干：《法国律例·贸易定律》，日本司法省1894年版，第105、130、158、164页。
② [法] 毕利干：《法国律例·贸易定律》，日本司法省1894年版，第103、415、416页。

毕利干译《法国律例·园林则律》与林纪东等主编《森林法施行细则》目录对比表①

毕利干译《法国律例·园林则例》		林纪东等主编《森林法施行细则》	
第一类	论护持管守一切园林之法则	第一章	通则
第二类	论护持管守园林之要范	第二章	国有林、公有林、私有林
第三类	论于国家所有园林或为平林或为遥林者	第三章	保安林
第一节	论分疆立界之章程，并论及界桩界石之类	第四章	森林土地之使用
第二节	论调养栽培园林之定法	第五章	监督
第三节	论获有乐购之分，于己砍伐之木者	第六章	保护
第四节	论修治滋养园林，使之可以滋生利益之法	第七章	奖励及承领
第五节	论复行丈量查得长短宽窄之势，合数与否	第八章	附则
第六节	论因放牧猪豕之收乐值者，准其用橡实饲养猪豕，并有权准其将猪豕牧放于林中		
第七节	论于国家所属之园林，而有材物酌提，独归置于某项事务之所需者		
第八节	论有例应能以使用于国家所有之平林、遥林者		
第四类	论一切平林、遥林，系归于御林者		
第五类	论获有御颁、御赏园林之权者，而此项园林究应归于国家，系赐之令其世传长子，承袭其利，而至其终究系属于国者		
第六类	论平林、遥林属于村堡镇店，及一切公所之中者		
第七类	论一切平林、遥林均？护持管守园林要范一律论之，而未分晰各据者		
第八类	论平林、遥林系属于民者		
第九类	论于木料独置一用，系备国家所需者		
第一节	论于木料独置一用，系备水师事务所需者		
第二节	论于木料系备桥梁、壩？所需者		
第十类	论有护持管属平林、遥林者之例		
第一节	论总理园林之事务		
第二节	论此例所设系专归园林围范，遇事可以比拟办理者		

---

① ［法］毕利干：《法国律例·园林则律》，日本司法省 1894 年版；林纪东等主编：《森林法施行细则》，五南图书出版公司 1986 年版。

续表

毕利干译《法国律例·园林则例》	林纪东等主编《森林法施行细则》
第十一类　论有干犯越理过失之事，而该管官应科惩以赔补银两者	
第一节　论科惩越理过失案情于平林、遥林，系归园林围范者	
第二节　论园林中而有越理过失之？而其园林系不归国家园林围范一例论者	
第十二类　论获罪而与科罪或施之于其身，或施之于其事，系于一切园林内者	
第十三类　论案经拟结，应即照其所拟而施行者	
第一节　论照所拟结而施行，系归围范而论之园林，而有越理过失之事者	
第二节　论案经理结，应照所拟施行，系干越过失之案，于平林、遥林不归围范之园林者	
第十四类　论汇总核定一切章程	
第十五类　论属于民人之园林，而乃有擅伐树株，欲为改易平原之事	

毕利干译《法国律例·园林则律》与《中华人民共和国森林保护法》目录对比表①

毕利干译《法国律例·园林则例》	《中华人民共和国森林法》
第一类　论护持管守一切园林之法则	第一章　总则
第二类　论护持管守园林之要范	第二章　森林权属
第三类　论于国家所有园林或为平林或为遥林者	第三章　发展规划
第一节　论分疆立界之章程，并论及界椿界石之类	第四章　森林保护
第二节　论调养栽培园林之定法	第五章　造林绿化
第三节　论获有乐购之分，于己砍伐之木者	第六章　经营管理
第四节　论修治滋养园林，使之可以滋生利益之法	第七章　监督检查
第五节　论复行丈量查得长短宽窄之势，合数与否	第八章　法律责任

---

①　［法］毕利干：《法国律例·园林则律》，日本司法省1894年版；林纪东等主编：《中华人民共和国森林法》。

续表

毕利干译《法国律例·园林则例》	《中华人民共和国森林法》
第六节　论因放牧猪豕之收乐值者，准其用橡实饲养猪豕，并有权准其将猪豕牧放于林中	第九章　附则
第七节　论于国家所属之园林，而有材物酌提，独归置于某项事务之所需者	
第八节　论有例应能以使用于国家所有之平林、遥林者	
第四类　论一切平林、遥林，系归于御林者	
第五类　论获有御颁、御赏园林之权者，而此项园林究应归于国家，系赐之令其世传长子，承袭其利，而至其终究系属于国者	
第六类　论平林、遥林属于村堡镇店，及一切公所之中者	
第七类　论一切平林、遥林均？护持管守园林要范一律论之，而未分晰各据者	
第八类　论平林、遥林系属于民者	
第九类　论于木料独置一用，系备国家所需者	
第一节　论于木料独置一用，系备水师事务所需者	
第二节　论于木料系备桥梁、壩？所需者	
第十类　论有护持管属平林、遥林者之例	
第一节　论总理园林之事务	
第二节　论此例所设系专归园林围范，遇事可以比拟办理者	
第十一类　论有干犯越理过失之事，而该管官应科惩以赔补银两者	
第一节　论科惩越理过失案情于平林、遥林，系归园林围范者	
第二节　论园林中而有越理过失之？而其园林系不归国家园林围范一例论者	
第十二类　论获罪而与科罪或施之于其身，或施之于其事，系于一切园林内者	
第十三类　论案经拟结，应即照其所拟而施行者	
第一节　论照所拟结而施行，系归围范而论之园林，而有越理过失之事者	
第二节　论案经理结，应照所拟施行，系干越理过失之案，于平林、遥林不归围范之园林者	
第十四类　论汇总核定一切章程	

续表

毕利干译《法国律例·园林则例》	《中华人民共和国森林法》
第十五类 论属于民人之园林，而乃有擅伐树株，欲为改易平原之事	

关于森林保护人员的职责：

"第三条 凡不论何人，必须其人年逾二十五者，始可任以护持管守园林之责。然虽如此而言，倘为肄业生徒，系出自习学园林事务之学馆者，虽其人未及二十五之年，亦可破以成格，令其充当护持管守园林之务。

第五条 凡如大小职官既经充任护持管守园林之责，须实心矢誓于其所属理事坊官员当面，并将其所执执照、文凭及其所矢誓之语，一一照录于其所任事之处、该管衙门之检收处。倘嗣后升迁他处，仍为护持管守园林之责者，即可免其再行矢誓矣。

第六条 凡为监守园林兵役，倘于其所司事中，竟有越理伤损妄行之事，则为该监守之兵役是问。至有事关罚缴安慰银两之事，而该兵役等竟未能查明者，亦惟该兵役是问。"①

关于森林砍伐与售卖：

"第十六条 凡属国家所有平林遥林，除按照定法及时砍伐外，不能有破成格格外砍伐之事，惟除事经奉有国君特旨，令其另行砍伐者，则始可行，否则不能。倘无特旨，竟行破格砍伐，希图售卖者，则其售卖之事，实不足以为据。即有成约，亦惟置之不议。而于欲行购买木料之人，或未能知其并未奉有特旨，如有亏累之情，则于准行售卖木料之官，或准行砍伐木料之官，均有可以索讨之权。其因此事国君所出特旨，即归于朱批廷谕一类论之。

---

① ［法］毕利干：《法国律例·园林则律》，日本司法省1894年版。

第十七条　凡交易之情于已伐之木，其木系属国家所有平林遥林，或系寻常按时买卖，或系奉有特旨售卖，均应按照国家平林遥林，作为采货照章喝卖。而此喝卖之事，须于十五日已前，将此情由宣扬告白于众，咸使知之。并将其宣扬告白之情，粘贴于卖此木料之处。该处知府城中，并此木料园林系何地方所属，即在其地并此园林本处沿边村落，一并粘贴宣扬告白，便众咸知。

第十八条　凡如一切售卖木料之事，倘不按照众采货指物喝卖章程售卖者，即将此售卖之人以走私者置论。而其事中所议交易之情，实不足以为据。而承办此项事务之官以及人役等，能以令此售卖木料之人，与经手为之售卖之人，同为罚缴银两三千夫浪之数，至多则六千夫浪之数。并于此外将事中买木之人，亦按所买价之数比拟其数，令其人认罚。"①

关于森林保护与法律责任：

"第十五类　论属于民人之园林而乃有擅伐树株，欲为改易平原之事

第二百二十条　凡有欲伐木而改易平原者，其该管官有应阻止之情，则有六项情形：其一项情形，有如由田之间存留树木，可以护障其田，及侧势之地，有木乃可护田；其二项情形，有如地近河流，恐被侵占冲刷者，则存留树木，实可护障其地；其三项情形，存留树木，即可护守泉源流水；其四项情形，存留树木，即可护循海沿海侵地界、砂占地基；其五项情形，存留树木，即如国家之障蔽，并可以保护国家地土之多寡，立树即可定界；其六项情形，存留树木，可以致国众身体健壮无伤，无树则于人有所未宜。有此六情，始可照例阻止。

第二百二十一条　凡于第二百一十九条所载制定之例，而竟

---

① ［法］毕利干：《法国律例·园林则律》，日本司法省1894年版。

敢有违者，则应将该园林本主科以罚缴银两之罪。其数之多寡，则以已被更改变易之地计之，？有一亩，至少则罚五百夫浪，多则应罚一千五百夫浪，而于此外，亦能被户部堂官饬令，将所改易之地，使之仍复原势之事，不得有逾三年。

  第二百二十二条　凡于园林之主，倘不遵照饬定期限，将地仍复原势，未能依限补种树木者，则该管守园林之官，即可代其兴办。然须由该管之知府准行，则即可行。并其应缴费用之数，亦由该知府酌定。"①

---

① ［法］毕利干：《法国律例·园林则律》，日本司法省1894年版。

附录一

ADVERTISEMENT[1]

The object of the Author in the following attempt to collect the the rules and principles which govern, or are supposed to govern, the conduct of States in their mutual intercourse in peace and in war, and which have therefore received the name of International Law, has been to compile an elementary work for the use of persons engaged in diplomatic and other forms of public life, rather than for mere technical lawyers, although he ventures to hope that it may not be found wholly useless even to the latter. The great body of the rules and principles which compose this Law is commonly deduced from examples of what has occurred, or been decided in the practice and intercourse of nations. These examples have been greatly multiplied in number and interest during the long period which has elapsed since the publication of Vattel's highly appreciated work: a portion of human history abounding in fearful transgressions of that Law, (more properly called the Law of God,) and at the same time rich in instructive discussions in cabinets, courts of justice, and legislative assemblies, respecting the nature and extent of the obligations between the independent societies of men called States. The principal aim of

---

[1] [美] Henry Wheaton, *Elements of International Law*, London: B. Fellowes, Ludgate Street, 1836.

the Author has been to glean from these sources the general principles which may fairly be considered to have received the assent of most civilized and christian nations, If not as invariable rules of conduct, at lest as rules which they cannot disregard without general obloquy and the hazard of provoking the hostility of other communities who may be injured by their violation. Experience shows that these motives, even in the worst times, do really afford a considerable security for the observance of justice between States, if they do not furnish the perfect sanction annexed by the lawgiver to the observance of the municipal code of any particular State. The knowledge of this science has, consequently, been justly regarded as of the highest importance to all who take an interest in political affairs. The Author cherishes the hope that the following attempt to illustrate it will be received with indulgence, if not with favour, by those who know the difficulties of the undertaking. Berlin, *Jan.* 1, 1836.

附录二

SKETCH of THE HISTORY OF INTERNATIONAL LAW.[①]

The classic nations of antiquity had very imperfect notions of international justice. With the Greeks and Romans '*foreigner*' and '*barbarian*,' or '*enemy*,' were synonymous in language and in fact. By their rude theory of public law, the persons of aliens were doomed to slavery, and their property to confiscation, the moment they passed the bounds of one petty state and touched the confines of another. Nothing but some positive compact gave them any exemption from this unsocial principle. Piracy was unblushingly practised by the most civilized nations which then existed. The peaceful merchant was liable to be plundered both on sea and land, by men with whom he and his country had no quarrel; and even the philosopher, who visited foreign countries to enrich his native land with the merchandize of science and art, was exposed to be captured and sold as a slave to some barbarian master. As to these barbarians themselves, the acutest of the Grecian philosophers gravely asserts that they were intended by nature to be the slaves of the Greeks, and that it was lawful to make them so by all possible means. Thucydides has cor-

---

① [美] Henry Wheaton, *Elements of International Law*, London: B. Fellowes, Ludgate Street, 1836.

rectly stated the leading political maxim of his countrymen, — "that to a king or commonwealth, nothing is openly avowed by the Athenians, in their reply to the people of Melos. Aristides distinguished in this respect between public and private morality, holding that the rules of justice were to be sacredly observed between individuals, but as to public and political affairs, a very different conduct was to be followed. He accordingly scrupled not to invoke upon his own head the guilt and punishment of a breach of faith, which he advised the people to commit in order to promote their national interest.

If such were what may be called the *pacific* relations of the Grecian states with each other, and with the rest of mankind, we may easily imagine that the rights of *war* must have been exerted with extreme rigour, To reduce to slavery prisoners taken in war, was the universal practice of the ancient world. But the cold-blooded cruelty with which the Athenians could deliberately devote, by a public decree, to mutilation or death those whom they ought, even in compliance with their own national prejudices, to have regarded as brethren, is a striking proof how lamentably deficient was their theory and practice of international justice. The institutions of Lycurgus imparted a still more stern and unrelenting character to the savage people for whom he undertook to legislate. The Lace-demonian government was the patron of the aristocratic faction throughout all Greece; and as the popular interests in the different republics naturally looked up to the all democracy of Athens for support. And there was no supreme federal authority adequate to check and control them, these rival powers kept every other state in continual commotion and furious disorders, which reduced them to misery, and thinned their population by proscriptions, banishments, and massacres.

Cicero's theory of justice in the intercourse of states seems to have been more liberal than that of the Grecian statesmen and philosophers, though the practice of his countrymen varied as much from that theory as their religious notions differed from his sublime conception of the Divine attributes. But neither had any correct or adequate notion of a science of international law, as understood in modern times. The intercourse of the Romans with foreign nations was but too conformable with their domestic discipline. Their ill-adjusted constitution fluctuated in perpetual mutations, but always preserved the character impressed upon it by Rome's martial founder of a state, the very law of whose being was perpetual war, and whose unceasing occupation was the conquest and colonization of foreign countries. For more than seven centuries the Romans pursued a scheme of aggrandizement, conceived in deep policy, and prosecuted with inflexible pride and pertinacity, at the expense of all the useful pursuits and charities of private life. All solicitude for the fate of their fellow-citizens made captive in war was disdained by their stern and crafty policy.

"Hoc caverat mens provida Reguli
Dissentientis conditionibus
Fadis, et exemplo trahenti
Perniciem veniens in avum,
Si non periret immiserabilis
Captiva pubes.

The institution of the Fecial law, with a college of heralds to expound it, which they borrowed from the Etruscans, is the only symptom of a recognition by these *Barbarians*, as the Greeks called them, of an international code, distinct from their own municipal law. This mere formal institution strongly contrasts with their oppressive conduct towards their allies, and their unjust and cruel treatment of their vanquished enemies. "VICTORY," in their expressive, metaphorical language, "made even the *sacred* things of enemy *profane*;" confiscated all his property, movable and immovable, public and private; doomed him and his posterity to perpetual slavery; and dragged his kings and generals at the chariotwheels of the conqueror.

Though the Romans had a very imperfect knowledge of international law as a science, and little regard for it as a practical rule of justice between states, yet their municipal code has essentially contributed to construct the edifice of public law in modern Europe. The stern spirit of the Stoic philosophy was breathed into the Roman law, and contributed to form the character of the most highly gifted, virtuous, and accomplished aristocracy the world ever saw. There is a calm and placid dignity in the pictures drawn by the classic writers of the private manners of the Roman patrician, strongly contrasting with the harsher features of their public conduct, but which blended together to form a character admirably fitting them to perform the dignified office of consultation in the laws.

"Romaa dulce diu et solemne, reclusa

Mane domo vigilare, clienti promere jura."

Theirs was for a long time the exclusive prerogative of administering justice. The usage insensibly grew up of certain families devoting their peculiar attention to the study and practice of jurisprudence, and transmitting the knowledge thus gained, as a private inheritance and most valuable instrument of political power. These circumstances essentially contributed to the perfection of the science in a state, where any other liberal pursuit, except the study of philosophy, was for a long time thought unworthy of its ingenuous citizens. In performing the duty of interpreting the laws to their clients and fellow-citizens, they invented a sort of judicial legislation, which was improved from age to age by the long line of jurisconsults, following each other in regular and unbroken succession from the foundation of the republic to the fall of the empire. The consequence was, that civil law, which seems never to have grown up to be a science in any of the Gecian republics, became one very early at Rome, and was thence diffused over the civilized world. The mighty fame and fortune of the Roman people, in this respect, cannot be contemplated without emotion. Its martial glory has long since departed, but the "Eternal City" still continues to rule the greatest part of the civilized and christian world, through the powerful influence of her civil codes. The acute research and unrivalled sagacity of an illustrious German civilian of the present day, have laboriously collected and happily combined the multiplied proofs, scattered in many a worm-eaten volume, that the Roman law, so far from having been buried in the ruins of the Roman empire, survived throughout the middle age, and continued to form an integral portion of European legislation long before the period of the pretended discovery of the Pandects of Justinian at Amalfi, in the beginning of the twelfth century. The vanquished Roman provincials were neither extirpated nor deprived of their personal freedom, nor was their entire property confiscated, by the Gotheic invagers, as we are commonly taught to believe. The conquered people were not only permitted to retain a large portion of their lands, and the personal laws by which they had been previously governed; but the municipal constitutions of the Roman cities were preserved, so that the study and practice of the Roman law could never have been entirely abandoned, even during what has been called the midnight darkness of the middle age. Accordingly, we find that in every civilized country of Europe, the Scandinavian nations and England excepted, the Roman civil law either formed the original basis of the municipal jurisprudence, or constitutes a suppletory code of "written reason," appealed to where the local legislation is silent, or imperfect, or requires the aid of interpretation to explain its ambiguities.

The foundation of the modern science of international law may be traced to a period nearly coincident to that memorable epoch in the history of mankind—the revival of letters, the discovery of the new world, and the reformation of religion. The Roman law infused its spirit into the ecclesiastical code of the Romish Church; and it may be considered a favourable circumstance for the revival of civilization in Europe, that the interests of the priesthood, in whom all the moral power and knowledge of the age were concentrated, induced them to cherish a certain respect for the immutable rules of justice. The spiritual monarchy of the Roman pontiffs was founded upon the want of some moral power to temper the rude disorders of society during the middle age. The influence of the papal authority was them felt as a blessing to mankind: it rescued Europe from total barbarism; it afforded the only shelter from feudal oppression. The compilation of the canon law, under the patronage of Pope Gregory IX., contributed to diffuse a knowledge of the rules of justice among the Catholic clergy; whilst the art of casuistry, invented by them to aid in performing the duties of auricular confession, opened a wide field for speculation, and brought them in view of the true science of ethics. The universities of Italy and Spain produced, in the sixteenth century, a succession of labourers in this new field. Among these was Francis de Victoria, who flourished as a professor at Salamanca about 1546, and Dominic Scoto, who was the pipil and successor of Victoria at the same seat of learning, (which Johnson said he loved for its nobles decision upon the Spanish conquests in America.) and published, in 1560, an elaborate treatise "Of Justice and Law," the subject-matter of his lectures delivered there, which he dedicated to the unfortunately celebrated, Don Carlos, Both Victoria and Soto condemned, with honest boldness and independence, the cruel wars of avarice carried on by their countrymen in the new world, under the pretext of propagating what was called Christianity in that age. Soto was the arbiter appointed by the emperor Charles V. to decide between Sepulveda, the advocate of the Spanish-American colonists, and Las Casas, the champion of the unhappy natives, as to the lawfulness of enslaving the latter. The edict of reform of 1543 was founded upon his decision in their favour. It is said that Soto didi not stop here, but condemned in the most unmeasured terms the African slave-trade, then beginning to be carried on by the Portuguese. But I do not understand that Soto reprobated slavery in general, or even the slave-trade itself, so long as it was confined to that unfortunate portion of the inhabitants of Africa who had been doomed to servitude from time immemorial, or had been enslaved by conquest in war, in that age universally regarded as giving a legitimate title to property in human beings *jure gentium*; but only that he condemned that system of kidnapping, by which the Portuguese trader seduced the natives to the coast, under fraudulent pretences, and forced them by violence on board their slave-ships.

Long before the appearance of them labourers in the new field of natural jurisprudence, the genius of commerce, ever favourable to the improvement and happiness of mankind, had reduced to a written text the long-established customs and usages of the maritime nations bordering on the shores of the Mediterranean Sea. Spain and Italy mutually contest with each other the honour of compiling the *Consolato de Mare*. This code embraces a great mass of civil commercial regulations, with a few chapters on the subject of maritime captures in war, which show that the leading principles of prize-law, as since practised by the maritime sates of Europe, had been settled and generally adopted at this early period. The first printed edition of this curious monument of commercial legislation is nearly coveval with the art of printing itself, and was published in the Catalonian dialect, at Barcelona, in 1494. There is no question that it was collected long previous to that period; but at which particular epoch, and by which of the numerous commercial republics with which the Mediterranean coasts were studded during the middle age, is matter of great uncertainty. The question of its origin has exercised the learning and ingenuity of various critics, whose zeal in exploring this dark recess of legal antiquities has been stimulated by national vanity and rivalship. Many of the provisions of this antique code have been incorporated into the more modern ordinances of the different European states, and especially into that beautiful model of legislation, the marine ordinance of Louis XIV. Its decisions are in general dictated by a spirit of justice and equity which recommends them to adoption, even at the present day; and they unquestionably attest the general sense of Christian Europe at the period when they were collected, respecting the commercial relations of its different states.

Albericus Gentilis was the forerunner of Grotius in the science whose history we are reviewing. He was born in the March of Ancona, about the middle of the sixteenth century, of an ancient illustrious family. His father, being one of the few Italians who openly embraced the doctrines of the Reformation, was compelled to fly with his family into Germany, whence he sent his son *Al*-

berico to England, where he found, not only freedom of conscience, but patronage and favour, and was elected to fill the chair of jurisprudence at Oxford. He did not confine his attention to the Roman law, the only system then thought worthy of being taught in a scientific manner, (the municipal code being abandoned to the barbarous discipline of the inns of court, of which Sir Henry Spelman has left us so feeling an account;) but investigated the principles of natural jurisprudence, and of the consuetudinary law then governing the intercourse of christian nations. His attention was especially directed to this last, by the circumstance of his being retained as the advocate of Spanish claimants in the English courts of prize. The fruits of his professional labours were given to the world in the earliest eports of judicial decisions on maritime law published in Europe. His more scholastic and academical studies produced the first regular treatise upon the law of war, considered as a branch of international law, which appeared in modern times. This work served as a light to guide the path of the illustrious Grotius, when he entered upon and pursued the same track of investigation in the following century.

Grentilis also wrote a treatise on embassies, which he dedicated to his friend and patron, the gallant and accomplished Sir Philip Sidney, whose "high thoughts were seated in a heart of courtesy," who was the generous protector of persecuted genius in that stormy and tumultuous age. In this work, Gentilis defends the moral tendency of Machiavelli's *Prince*, commonly supposed to have been intended as a manual of tyranny, but which he insists is a disguised satire upon the vices of princes, and a full and calm exposition of the arts of tyrants, for the admonition and instruction of the people; written by a man always actually engaged on the popular side in the factions of his own country, and almost a fanatical admirer of the ancient republicans and regicides. Whatever may be thought of this long-disputed question as to Machiavelli's motives in writing, his work certainly presents to us a gloomy picture of the state of public law and European society in the beginning of the sixteenth century: —one mass of dissimulation, crime, and corruption, which called loudly for a great teacher and reformer to arise, who should speak the unambiguous language of truth and justice to princes and people, and stay the ravages of this moral Pestilence.

Such a teacher and reformer was Hugo Grotius, who was born in the latter part of the same century, and flourished in the beginning of the seventeenth. That age was peculiarly fruitful in great men, but produced no one more remarkable for genius and for variety of talents and knowledge, or for the important influence his labours exercised upon the subsequent opinions and conduct of mankind. Almost equally distingished as a scholar and man of business, he was at the same time an eloquent advocate, a scientific lawyer, classical historian, patriotic statesman, and learned theologian. His was one of those powerful minds which have paid the tribute of their assent to the truth of Christianity. His great abilities were devoted to the service of his country, and of mankind. He vindicated the freedom of the seas, as the common property of all nations, against the extravagant pretensions of Great Britain and Portugal. His ungrateful country rewarded his virtues and services with exile, and would have extended her injustice to perpetual imprisonment or death, but for the courageous contrivance and self-devotion of his wife. Involved in the persecution of the Pensionary Barnevelt and the other Arminians, he was shut up in the fortress of Louvestein, in the year 1619. He was, however, allowed the society of his books, and of his accomplished and heroic wife, who contrived to deceive his guards, and induce them to carry him out in a chest, while she remained thus voluntarily exposed to the vengeance of his enemies. Grotius escaped into France, and in his banishment returned good for evil by rendering the most important services to his countrymen; and even his persecutor, Prince Maurice of Nassau, is treated with perfect fairness and impartiality in his Belgic history. In an age peculiarly infected with party animosity, Grotius preserved himself pure from the taint of bigotry; and though actively engaged in the contention between the religious factions of the Gomarists and Arminains, his expansive toleration embraced every sect, whether

Catholic or Protestant; —a degree of liberality almost unexampled in those times. When he could no longer be useful in active life, he laboured to win men to the love of peace and justice by the publication of his great work, which made a deep impression upon all the liberal-minded princes and ministers of that day, and contributed essentially to influence their public conduct. Alexander carried the Iliad of Homer in a golden casket, to inflame his love of conquest; whilst Guetavus Adolphus slept with the Treatise on the Laws of War and Peace under his pillow, in that heroic war which he waged in Germany for the liberties of Protestant Europe. It is difficult to decide which presents the most striking contrast—the poet of Greece and the philosopher of Holland, or the two heroes who imbibed such different and opposite sentiments from their pages.

Nor was this the only immediate practical effect of this publication. Its enlightened and benevolent doctrines so forcibly struck the mind of that liberal sovereign, the Elector Palatine, Charles Lewis, that he founded at Heidelberg the first professorship of the law of nature and nations instituted in Europe, and bestowed the chair upon the celebrated Puffendorf, who used the treatise of Grotius as his text-book. Grotius thus became the creator of a new school of political philosophy, which laid the foundation for all those important improvements in the science of government, political economy, and legislation, which have marked the two last centuries as an ara in the progress of mankind. His work was illustrated by a crowd of commentators in the universities of Holland and Germany, and within forty years after his death obtained an honour which had been exclusively reserved, by the learned world, for the classical writers of antiquity: it was edited *cum commentariis variorum.* His Latin style is sometimes obscured by an imitation of the sententious brevity of Tacitus; and the work sins against the prevailing taste of present age, in being adorned with profusion of illustrations from the writers of sacred and heathen antiquity. Yet it should be remembered, that these are so many different witnesses summoned to attest the concurring sentiments and usages of mankind among all ages and nations, and that their testimony was much more revered by the contemporaries of Grotius than the unsupported authority or reasonings of any individual writer of their own time.

The great treatise of Grotius on the *Law of Peace and War*, defective as it confessedly is in scientific arrangement and distinctiveness of aim, produced a wonderful impression on the public mind of christian Europe, and gradually wrought a most salutary change in the practical intercourse of nations in faxour of humanity and justice. This new science of natural jurisprudence, developed by the disciples of Grotius, and applied in the first instance to ascertain those rules of justice which ought to regulate the conduct of individuals in the social state, was subsequently adopted to determine the like rules which govern, or ought to govern, the conduct of independent nations and states, considered as moral beings living in a social state, independent of positive human institution. This gave rise to the mixed science of the law of nature and nations, which soon came to form an indispensable part of liberal education all over Europe. Whatever defects may have been justly imputed to the works of the more eminent publicists, considered as scientific, expository treatises, it would be difficult to name any writers who have contributed so much to promote the progress of civilization as "these illustrious authors---these friends of human nature—these kind instructors of human errors and frailties—these benevolent spirits, who held up the torch of science to a benighted world." If the internatioanl intercourse of Europe, and the nations of European descent, has been since marked by superior humanity, justice, and liberality, in comparison with the usage of the other members of the human family, they are mainly indebted for this glorious superiority to these private teachers of justice, to whose moral authority sovereigns and states are often compelled to bow, and whom they acknowledge as the ultimate arbiters of their controversies in peace; whilst the same authority contributes to give laws even to war itself—mitigating its ferocity, and limiting the range of its operations within the narrowest possible bounds, consistent with its purposes and objects.

Protestant Germany was the field where the science of natural and international jurisprudencewas first cultivated with most assiduity and success. The scientific writers of that intellectual land had not yet learned to use freely their native Teutonic tongue. That rich, copious, and expressive dialect—for scientific purposes clearly and decidedly superior to any other, except Greek alone—was almost entirely neglected by her scholars and men of science. They wrote in the dead language of Rome, to instruct the living men of their own age and country. In Germany more than any other country, (and *then* even more than *now*,) scientific and active life stand detached from each other like two separate worlds. Their mutual intercourse, at this period, was kept up through the medium of the learned or fashionable language, common to both. Leibnitz wrote mostly in Latin or French, and Wolf, his disciple, almost exclusively in Latin. Leibnitz, so justly compared by Gibbon to those conquerors whose empire has been lost in the ambition of universal conquest, comprised both the philosophy of law and the details of practical jurisprudence within the vast circle of his attainment. Wolf gleaned after Puffendorf in the field of natural jurisprudence; he entitled himself to the credit of first separating the law which prevails, or ought to prevail, between nations, from that part of the science which teaches the duties of individuals; and of reducing the law of nations to a full and systematic form, as derived from a suitable application of the rules of natural justice to the conduct of independent sovereigns and states. The slumber of his once celebrated work, in nine ponderous tomes, is probably not now often disturbed; especially as all that is really valuable in their contents has been incorporated into the treatise of Vattel—"a diffuse, unscientific, and superficial, but clear and liberal writer, whose work still maintains its place as the most convenient abridgment of a part of knowledge which," in the words of Mackintosh, "calls for the skill of a new builder."

Previously to these writers, Bynkershoek had selected for discussion the particular questions deemed the most important, and of most frequent occurrence in the practical intercourse of nations, instead of undertakinf, after the example of his predecessors in the school of Grotius, an entire system of natural and public law. In precision and practical utility, he excels all the other publicists. It should be observed, however, as detracting not a little from his merits, that his pages are stained with ferocious sentiments respecting the rights of war, unworthy of a writer who flourished in the commencement of the eighteenth century: holding every thing lawful against an enemy—that he may be destroyed, though unarmed and defenceless, and even by poison, or any kind of weapons. It might be supposed that an author who sets out with such notions as these would write a very compendious treatise upon the laws of war: yet Bynkershoek proceeds to unfold, in a very clear and arrogant style, the principles of this branch of the science; from which we learn that there are many modes of hostility which the mitigated usage of nations, operating with the force of law, has prohibited between enemies, and in which the respective rights of belligerents and neutrals are expounded in a more critical and satisfactory manner than by any other elementary writer.

附录三

Preface to The Third Edition[①]

Since the publication of the two former editions of the present Treatise, the Author has submitted to the public judgment another work connected with the same subject, andentitled 'History of the Law of Nations in Europe and America, from the earliest Times to the Treaty of Washington, 1842.' In the present edition of the 'Elements of International Law,' constant reference has been had to this historical deduction, in which the Author endeavored to trace the origin and progress of those rules of international justice so long acknowledged to exist, and which have been more or less perfectly observed by the Christian nations of modern Europe; which have been adopted by their descendants in the New World, from the first planting of European colonies on the American Continents; and have been more recently applied to regulate the relations of the European and American nations with the Mohammedan and Pagan races of the other quarters of the globe.

The law of nations acknowledged by the ancient Greeks and Romans was exclusively founded on religion. The laws of peace and war, the inviolability of heralds and ambassadors, the right of asylum, and the obligation of trea-

---

① [美] Henry Wheaton, *Elements of International Law*, Oxford: At The Clarendon Press. London: Humphrey Milford, 1936.

ties, were all consecrated by religious principles and rites. Ambassodors, heralds, and fugitives who took refuge in the temples, or on the household hearth, were deemed inviolable, because they were invested with a sacred character and the symbols of religion. Treaties were sanctioned with solemn oaths, the violation of which it was believed must be followed by the vengeance of the gods. War between nations of the same race and religion was declared with sacred rites and ceremonies. The heralds proclaimed its existence by devoting the enemy to the infernal deities. 'Eternal war against the Barbarians,' was the Shibboleth of the most civilized and enlightened people of antiquity. Among the Romans 'stranger' and 'enemy' were synonymous. *Adversus hostem aterna auctoritas esto* was the maxim of the Twelve Tables, and Justinian considered all nations as enemies unless they were the allies of Rome. More permanent relations could exist only between nations of the same origin, and professing the religious faith common to the entire race. Such were the Hellenic tribes represented in the great Amphictyonic council of Greece, which was rather a religious than a political institution. But even the purest moralists hardly admitted any other duties between the Greeks themselves than such as were founded on positive compact.

The introduction of Christianity tended to abolish the Pagan precept: 'Thou shalt hate thine enemy,' and to substitute for it the benevolent command: 'Love your enemies,' which could not be reconciled with perpetual hostility between the different races of men. But this milder dispensation long struggled in vain against the secular enmity of the different nations of the ancient world, and that spirit of blind intolerance which darkened the ages succeeding the fall of the Roman Empire. During the Middle Ages the Christian States of Europe began to unite, and to acknowledge the obligation of an international law common to all who professed the same religious faith. This law was founded mainly upon the following circumstances: —

First: The union of the Latin Church under one spiritual heard, whose authority was often invoked as the supreme arbiter between sovereigns and between nations. Under the auspices of Pope Gregory IX, the canon law was reduced into a code, which served as the rule to guide the decisions of the Church in public as well as private controversies.

Second: The revival of the study of the Roman law, and the adoption of this system of jurisprudence by nearly all the nations of Christendom, either as the basis of their municipal codes, or as private controversies.

The origin of the law of nations in modern Europe may thus be traced to these two principal sources, ---the canon law and the Roman civil law. The proofs of this double origin may be distinctly discovered in the writings of the Spanish casuists and the professors of the celebrated University of Bologna. Each general council of the Catholic Church was a European Congress, which not only deliberated on ecclesiastical affairs, but also decided the controversies between the different States of Christendom. The professors of the Roman law were the public jurists and diplomatic negotiators of the age. The writers on the law of nations before the time of Grotius, such as Francis de Victoria, Balthazar Ayala, Cobrad Brunus, and Albericus Gentilis, fortified their reasonings by the authority of the Roman civilians and the canonists. The great religious revolution of the sixteenth century undermined one of the bases of this universal jurisprudence: but the public jurists of the Protestant school, whilst they renounced the authority of the Church of Rome and the canon law, still continued to appeal to the Roman civil law, as constituting the general code of civilized nations.

The establishment of the system of a balance ofpower among the European States also contributed to form the international law recognized by them. The idea of this system, though not wholly unknown to the statesman of antiquity, had never been practically applied to secure the independence of nations against the ambition of the great military monarchies by which the civilized world was successively subdued. The modern system of the balance of power was first developed among the States of Italy during the latter part of the fifteenth century, and was applied, in the first instance, in order to maintain their mutual independence, and, subsequently, to unite them against the invasions of the transalpine nations. Such was the policy of the Republic of Florence under Cosmo and Lorenzo de Medici, and such was the object of Machiavelli in writing his celebrated treatise of the *Prince*. Unfortunately for his own fame, and for the permanent interests of mankind, this masterly writer, in his patriotic anxiety to secure his country against the dangers with which it was meanaced from the *Barbarians*, did not hesitate to resort to those atrocious means already too familiar to the domestic tyrants of Italy. The violent remedies he sought to apply for her restoration to pristine greatness were poisons, and his book became the manual of despotism, in which Philip II. of Spain, and Catherine de Medici found their detestable maxims of policy. But policy can never authorized a resort to such measures as are prohibited by the law of nations, founded on the principles of eternal justice; and, on the other hand, the law of nations ought not to prohibit that which sound policy dictates as necessary to the security of any State. 'Justice,' says Burke, 'is the great standing policy of civil society, and any eminent departure from it, under any circumstances, lies under the suspicion of being no policy at all.'

Whatever may be thought of the long-disputed question as to the motives of Machiavelli in writing, his work certainly reflects the image of that dark and gloomy period of European society, presenting one mass of dissimulation, crime, and corruption, which called loudly for a great teacher and reformer to arise, who should stay the ravages of this moral pestilence, and speak the unambiguous language of truth and justice to princes, and people. Such a teacher and reformer was Hugo Grotius, whose treatise on the *Laws of Peace and War*, produced a strong impression on the public mind of Christian Europe, and gradually wrought a most salutary change in the practical intercourse of nations in favor of humanity and justice. Whatever defects may be justly imputed to the works of Grotius, and the public jurists formed in his school, considered as scientific, expository treatises, it would be difficult to name any class of writers which has contributed more to promote the progress of civilization than ' these illustrious authors---these friends of human nature---these kind instructors of human errors and frailties---these benevolent spirits who held up the torch of science to a benighted world'. If the international intercourse of Europe, and the nations of European descent, has been since marked by superior humanity, justice, and liberality, in comparison with the usage of the other branches of the human family, this glorious superiority must be mainly attributed to these private teachers of justice, to whose moral authority Sovereigns and States are often compelled to bpw, and whom they acknowledge as the ultimate arbiters of their controversies in peace; whilst the same authority contributes to give laws even to war itself, by limiting the range of its operations within the narrowest possible bounds consistent with its purposes and objects.

It has been observed by Sir James Mackintosh, that, without overrating the authority of this class of writers, or without considering authority in any case as a substitute for reason, the public jurists may justly be considered as entitled to great weight as impartial witnesses bearing testimony to the general sentiments and usages of civilized nations. Their testimony receives additional confirmation every time their authority is invoked by statesmen, and from the lapse of every successive year in which the current of this authority is uninterrupted by the avowal and practice of contrary principles and usages. Add to which, that their judgments are usually appealed to by the weak, and are seldom rejected except by those who are strong enough to disregard all the principles and rules of international morality. ' The opinions of these eminent men, 'says Mr. Fox, ' formed without prejudice upon subjects which they have carefully studied, cannot but be considered as entitled to the highest respect, The maxims laid down by them are uninfluenced by national prejudices or particular interests; they reason upon great principles and with enlarged views of the welfare of nations; and by comparing the results of their own reflections with the lessons taught by the experience of preceding ages, they have established that system which they considered as of the greatest utility and of the most general application. '

The rules of international morality recognized by these writers are found on the supposition, that the conduct which is observed by one nation towards another, in conformity with these rules, will be reciprocally observed by other nations towards it. The duties which are imposed by these rules are enforced by moral sanctions, by apprehension on the part of sovereigns and nations of incurring the hostility of other States, in case they should violate maxims generally received and respected by the civilized world. These maxims may, indeed, be violated by those who choose to suffer the consequences of that hostility; but they cannot be violated with impunity, nor without incurring general obloquy. The science which teaches the reciprocal duties of sovereign States is not, therefore, a vain and useless study, as some have pretended. If it were so, the same thing might be affirmed of the science of private morality, the duties inculcated by which are frequently destitute of the sanction of positive law, and are enforced merely by conscience and social opinion. As the very existence of social intercourse in private life depends upon the observance of these duties, so the existence of that mutual intercourse among nations, which is so essential to their happiness and prosperity, depends upon the rules which have generally been adopted by the great society of nations to regulate that intercourse.

In prefor the press the present edition of the Elements of International Law, the work has been subjected to a careful revision, and has been considerably augmented. The Author has endeavored to avail himself of the most recent questions which have occurred in the intercourse of States, the discussion and decision of which have contributed to throw new light upon that system of rules by which all civilized nationa profess to be bound in their mutual intercourse. He has especially sought for those sources of information in the diplomatic correspondence and judicial decisions of our own country, which form a rich collection of instructive examples, arising out of the peculiar position of the United States during the wars of the French Revolution, and during the war declared by them against Great Britain, in 1812. That international law, common to all civilized and Christian nations, which our ancestors brought with them from Europe, and which was obligatory upon us whilst we continued to form a part of the British Empire, did not cease to be so when we declared our independence of the parent country. Its obligation was acknowledged by the Continental Congress, in the mean time, the United States had recognized, in their treaty of alliance with France, those principles respecting the rights of neutral commerce and navigation which subsequently became the basis of the armed neutrality of the northern powers of Europe. The American government has ever since constantly recognized and respected the same principles towards those maritime States by whom they are reciprocally recognized and respected and respected. As to all others, it continues to observe the pre-existing rules of the ancient law of nations, whilst it has ever shown itself ready to adopt measures for mitigating the practices of war, and rending them more conformable to the spirit of an enlightened age.

The Author has also endeavored to justify the confidence with which he has been so long honored by his country in the different diplomatic missions confided to him, by availing himself of the peculiar opportunities, and the means of information thus afforded, for a closer examination of the different questions of public law which have occurred in the international intercourse of Europe and America, since the publication of the first edition of the present work. Among these questions are those relating to the exercise of the right of search for the suppression of the African slave-trade, and to the interference of the five great European powers in the internal affairs of the Ottoman Empire. The former of these questions had already been discussed by the Author, in a separate treatise, published in 1841, in which the immunity of the national flag from every species and purpose of search, by the armed vessels of another State, in time of peace, except in virtue of a special compact, was maintained by an appeal to the oracles of public law both of Great Britain and the United States, and has since been solemnly sanctioned by the treaty of Washington, 1842, and by the convention concluded, during the present year, between France and Great Britain, for the suppression of the mutual right of search conceded by former treaties. He indulges the hope that these additions to the work may be found to render it more useful to the reader, and make it more worthy of the favor with which the previous editions have been received.

BERLIN,

November, 1845.

附录四

IntroductoryRemarks[①]

The position, which Mr. Wheaton occupied in the world of letters, and the space, which he fills in the legal and diplomatic annals of his own country, would give interest to the most ample details connected with his biography. These the Editor hopes to be able to present, at a future day, with a selection from those miscellaneous writings, —the results of the favorable opportunities for the cultivation of the elegant arts, as well as for investigations more particularly appertaining to his peculiar pursuits, which his long residence in different capitals of Europe afforded. His public despatches, and the correspondence which he carried on with many of the most eminent of his contemporaries, both at home and abroad, on subjects which have entered into the permanent history of the world, or which tend to elucidate questions of constitutional or international law, will likewise impart additional value to "The Life of Henry Wheaton."

The pagesallotted to an Editorial Notice will not admit of any extended remarks, not immediately applicable to treatise of which it forms the Introduction. The rank, however, which is accorded to the "Elements of International

---

① [美] Henry Wheaton, *Elements of International Law*, Boston:: Little Brown And Company, 1855.

Law," in the cabinets of Christendom, where it has replaced the elegant treatise of Vattal, whose summary long formed a substitute for the more elaborates works of Grotius and Wolf, and the consideration which it enjoys, not only among diplomatists, but in legislative assemblies and in the tribunals administering the common jurisprudence of nations, seem to render it proper, in offering to the public the first American edition of his great work, that has appeared since Mr. Wheaton's death, to furnish a brief sketch of his public career and preliminary pursuits. Those who are acquiring from his labors the fundamental principles of that science, of which he was not only a teacher, but which he successfully applied to the service of his country, may well desire a personal acquaintance with the author. It will, it is believed, at least, tend to dispel the illusion, that eminence in diplomacy is attainable by different means from those which are required in other pursuits of life, and show that a minister, worthy of the name, is no more to be created by an executive fiat than a general or an admiral.

Henry Wheaton was born at Providence, in the State of Rhode Island, on the 27th of November, 1785. He was descended from a family identified with that Commomwealth from its earliest colonization. His father, Seth Wheaton, acquired, by commerce and navigation, a fortune sufficient to enable him to afford to his son those advantages of liberal culture and early foreign travel, that so eminently contributed to his success in the subsequent pursuits of life. The elder Mr. Wheaton maintained, during a long business career, a distinguished position among his fellow-citizens; and he held, at the time of his death, the Presidency of the Rhode Island Branch of the Bank of the United States, a station which, from the controlling influence possessed by the parent institution over the currency of the country, till its fatal contest with the government of the Union, in President Jackson's administration, was regarded as the most honorable distinction that could be conferred on a retired merchant.

Mr. Wheaton's mother is represented to have been a woman of strong intellect and of rare delicacy and refinement; and it was by the intercourse with her brother, Dr. Levi Wheaton, not only eminent as a physician, but his father-in-law, that our author's early taste for knowledge was stimulated and encouraged.

Mr. Wheaton, after receiving the ordinary preliminary instruction, graduated at the College og his native State, now Brown University, in 1802. During the ensuing three years he prepared himself, in the office of Nathaniel Searle, then among the prominent practitioners at Providence, for admission to the bar. His studies were, from his earliest days, of a character appropriate to the education of a publicist. Besides his proficiency in the classical and mathematical departments, he was particularly distinguished, at school and college, for his fondness for general literature, and especially for historical research and the investigation of the political annals of nations.

In the spring of 1805, he went to Europe, and though his desire for intellectual improvement and his sound moral principles would, probably, have proved an adequate protection against all improper temptations, it was, perhaps, well for his future success that his father's moderate views of expense did not permit him, at once, to luxuriate in a great metropolis. He established himself at Poitiers, where there was a school of law. His object seems to have been to acquire a familiarity with the use of the French language, in which he had been early instructed; while he availed himself of the opportunity to frequent the tribunals and study the civil law. Indeed, in this branch of jurisprudence, Mr. Wheaton might almost be deemed a pioneer among his countrymen. Even Pothier, whose works contributed so largely to the Napoleon Code, had not then been made accessible to the American lawyer. Nor had Kent and Story, whose decisions derive so much value from their abundant stores of continental lore, and both of whom had repeated occasion to appreciate the early studies of Mr. Wheaton, then assumed their places in the tribunals, which they subsequently illustrated—the one as Chancellor of New York, the other as a member of the Supreme Federal Judiciary.

At the time of Mr. Wheaton's residence in France, the legislation, substituting a uniform system for the somewhat diversifed modifications of the civil law, existing before the Revolution in the several provinces, had only been a year in operation. He was thus induced, at an early day, to study the codes which had not then been rendered into English, and of which he made a translation, the publication of which was only prevented by the accidental destruction of the manuscript. A witness of the transition from the *droit coutumier*, and from a system composed of the Roman civil law and of royal ordinances and local regulations, to a uniform written law, he was preparing himself to exercise an enlightened judgment on codification—a subject which, as a Commissioner of New York, under the first law passed by any State of the Union, for the liberal revision of its statutes, he had, twenty years afterwards, occasion to discuss, with a view to its practical application.

After visiting Paris, where General Armstrong, with whom he was in after life brought into intimate relations, represented the United States, he went to London. He was very kindly received there by our minister, Mr. Monroe, subsequently President of the United States, and he passed six months in that metropolis. As he was in England during the change of Ministry, when Mr. Fox came into power, and during the proceedings against Lord Melville, in which the judicial authority of the House of Lords was exercised, on the presentation of the Commons, as the grand inquest of the nation, he had a favorable opportunity of studying the constitutional system of our mother country, the knowledge of which is so essential to the thorough understanding of our own. He was, also, enabled to compare the practical working of the common law, in the country to which we refer its origin, with the administration of the civil law, whose tribunals he had just quitted.

But it was not merely by the study of the constitutional and municipal jurisprudence of what were then the two greatest nations of Europe, that his foreign residence was beneficial to the future diplomatist. Paris was the centre of all that was attractive, of all that was interesting on the Continent of Europe.

THe Italian campaigns had already embellished her palaces and her museums with the *chefs d'auvre* of art, which centuries had accumulated in the capital of the ancient world, and in the most favored cities of the Republics of the Middle Ages. The territorial arrangements, which the Treaty of Utrecht was supposed to have settled on a firm basis, were, despite the successive coalitions to uphold the obsolete fabric of European organization, at an end. Even Ebgland had recognized, in 1802, by the short-lived peace of Amiens, concluded with the First Consul, the new order of things, to which every other power had previously given its adhesion. The French Revolution itself had been, it was supposed, brought to a close by the assumption, on 18th of May, 1804, with the almost unanimous approbation of the people, of the sceptre by Napoleon, and by his coronation, under circumstances of peculiar solemnity, on the 2d of December following, as Emperor of the French.

It was while the American student was still at Poitiers, that, by the battle of Austerlitz, the undisputed sway of the Continent, and which was scarcely affected by the untoward movements of Prussia, terminating in the Treaty of Presburg and the affiliation of the French and Russian Emperors, became the property of Napoleon. On the other hand, by the battle of Trafalgar, contemporaneous with the capitulation of Ulm, the dominion of the sea was secured to England.

A state of war is emphatically the relations of his country towards the great European powers, which divided the supremacy of the world, were well calculated to lead an inquisitive mind to the investigations on which Mr. Wheaton's lasting fame reposes. The accession of Mr. Fox, who was understood not to coincide, as to many points affecting neutral rights, with the administration which had preceded him, inspired at Washington new confidence of a settlement of all pending difficuties. THis expectation was, also, strengthened by the prospect of a general European pacification, as the members of the new government, when out of office, had been opposed to the policy that had prevailed in reference to the French Revolution. These hopes, however, were destined to an early disappointment.

The Treaty of 1794 with England, objectionable as it was in other respects, had established a joint commission to ascertain the amount of damages sustained by citizens of the United States, for irregular and illegal captures and condemnations, under color of British authority, and for which adequate compensation could not be obtained in the ordinary course of judicial proceedings. Between 1793 and 1800 serious injuries had, also, been inflicted on our commerce, by the capture and condemnation of our vessels and the seizure of our property by France, in violation of the law of nations and existing treaties. All demands for redress were, however, met by counter claims of that power, growing out of the alleged infraction, on our part, of the stipulations of the treaties of alliance and of commerce, of 1778, and of the consular convention of 1788. After hostile measures, extending even to what our author terms an imperfect war, had been resorted to by the United States, the respective pretensions of the two parties, not specially reserved, were abrogated by the operation of the treaty of peace, of September 30, 1800, or were renounced with its ratification. Reclamations, which had been reserved by that traty, or such as were, at the time, deemed to be valid by the plenipotentiaries of the two powers, were provided for by one of the conventions, concluded on the 30th of April, 1803, for the purchase of Louisiana.

The Berlin and Milan decrees, the commencement of that system which had for its object the exclusion of English produce and manufactures from the whole European Continent, had not, with the Orders in Council professed to be based on them, then been issued. But, the practice of paper blockades was begun, and an apology for those decrees and other obnoxious imperial ordinances, which laid the foundation for claims that occupied our diplomacy for more than a quarter of a century, and until their liquidation under President Jackson, had, according to that belligerent code which considered the spoliation of one enemy a just ground for an equivalent violation of neutral property by the other, already been afforded. The practice of impressing seamen from our merchantmen, when visited by British men-of-war, under the belligerent plea of the right of search for contraband, or, according to the rule that then prevailed, for enemy's property, which had been a ground of complaint from the earliest days of the French Revolution, and which, at all events, had no pretension of retaliation, founded on enemy's proceedings, to support it, had been resumed on the termination of the peace, established by the Treaty of Amiens. Not only had the rule of the war of '56——never asserted in the intervening one of the American Revolution, and for captures under which compensation had been made, in pursuance of the Treaty of 1794, been revived; but, instead of its being confined to a prohibition of the direct trade between the enemy's colonies and the mother country, colonial produce, though reexported from the United States, in accordance with the rule, as announced by Lord Hawkesbury to the American Minister, Mr. Rufus King, in 1801, was captured and condemned in the Courts of Admiralty.

What was well calculated to increase the offensive character of the British proceedings was, while they excluded all neutral vessels from the trade assumed to be open them in war but not in peace, that is to say, from the enemy's colonial and coasting trade, a communication with the enemy's colonies was encouraged, by licenses and other means. Thus, by the Act of 45 Geo. III. C. 57, 2 (27th of june, 1805,) free ports were established in the English West India island, and an intercourse formed between therein mentioned, being the growth, produce, or manufacture of any of the colonies or plantations in America, belonging to any European State, were allowed to be imported, from any of those colonies or plantations, into the enumerated ports, in any foreign vessel whatever, not having more than one deck, and owned and navigated by persons inhabiting those colonies or plantations. Tobacco was especially permitted to be exported from those countries to the enumerated ports, and from thence to the United Kingdom. The exportation from those ports to any of the colonies or plantations in America, belonging to or under the dominion of any foreign European sovereign, in any vessel in which importations were authorized, of "rum, the produce of any British island, and also" (in order, it would seem, to encourage the British navigation engaged in the slave-trade,) "of negroes, which shall have been brought into the said island in British-built ships, owned, navigated, and registered according to law," was particularly favored. All other articles, except those specially prohibited, might likewise have been thus exported. Goods, also, from any port of Europe, were allowed to be, in the same way, brought into the British islands, and from thence to be exported in a British vessel to any British colony in America or the West Indies, and Order in Council, of the 5th of August, 1805, prohibited, under the penalty of confiscation of the vessel and cargo, all intercourse of neutrals with the enemy's colonies, except through the free ports.

The same course was subsequently pursued, in reference to the trade with the Continent of Europe, after the blockade of the French coast. By the Act of 48 Geo. III. c, 37, 1 (14th April, 1808,) the king was empowered by an Order in Council to permit, during hostilities, goods to be imported into any port of Great British or Ireland, from any port or place from which the British flag was excluded, in any ship or vessel belonging to any country, whether in amity with England or not. And it is stated that, while all regular neutral commerce was interdicted, 8000 English licenses were granted in 1811, and in 1808 and 1809 the system had been carried to a still greater extent. Thus English vessels had been authorized by their own government to violate a blockade, which this same government had been obliged, according to their own declaration, to establish for the purpose of legitimate defence, and which it so vigorously maintained against neutrals.

It was the seizure, in 1805-6, of a large number of vessels, whose cargoes had been landed and the duties on them paid, which it had been previously declared would be deemed to break the continuity of the voyage, that, in connection with the subject of impressment, induced President Jefferson, in April, 1806, to until Mr. Pinkney with Mr. Monroe in that mission, which led to the conclussion, *sub spe rati*, of the treaty with Lord Holland and Lord Auckland, that failed to meet the approbation of the Executive. The absence of any provision with regard to impressment would have been sufficient to have prevented its submission to the Senate. The official note, which the American Plenipotentiaries had received from the British Commissioners, pledging their government to caution in the exercise of the practice, so far from being deemed a substitute for an express stipulation, might have been regarded to as a recognition of the pretension; while a proposed reservation, at the moment of signing the treaty, and which was intended to justify the retaliatory measures that might be founded on the French decree of November 21st, 1806, and control our proceedings towards a third party, for the vindication of our neutral rights, would alone have rendered a ratification, on our part, inadmissible. By the British it was expressly declared, that their ratification would not be given, unless the FRench either withdrew the Berlin decree or the United States gave their government assurances that they would not submit to it.

On Mr. Wheaton's return to America, he entered on the practice of his profession in his native town, but the character of the business, usually instrusted to a yong lawyer in a provincial capital, is not such as was calculated to call into exercise the particular attainments of our aythor. There was, however, in the condition of the world ample scope for the talents of a yong American, conversant by practical observation with the events that characterized the first part of the nineteenth century. The seven years from 1806 to 1813, which comprise the period that elapsed between Mr. Wheaton's return home and his final removal from his native State, were precisely those during which the neutral powers were exposed to the alternate aggressions of the two great belligerents; "the conduct of both of whom," in the language of Mr. Madison, when Secretary of State, "displayed theri mutual efforts to draw the United States into a war with their adversary;" and among maritime States, Ameruca, after the gross violation of the law of nations by England towards Denmark, in 1807, stood alone.

Mr. Wheaton, whose nearest relatives were of the school of Jefferson, and whose republican sentiments were unavoidably strengthened by his European residence, was, during these years of comparative leisure, an efficient supporter, by his contributions to tyhe periodical press, of the administrations of Jerfferson and Madison. THe Rhode Island Phonix, afterwards The Rhode Island Patriot, copies of which are still presrved in the HIstirical Society of the State, contain many papers from his pen. Among his fellow laborers of that period of that period were the present venerable Judge Pitman, of the United States District Court, and the late Governor Fenner, both of whom belonged to the Republican party, as the friends of the administration were then termed, while its opponents, according to the political nomenclature of the day, were called Federalists. Jonathan Russell was also associated with him in the task of instructing the public mind of New England, as to the wrongs with their country was receiving at the hands of the European belligerents; and with him, while the diplomatic representative of the United States, successively in Paris and London, in 1810, 1811, 1812, as well as during his residence adroad, as a Commissioner at Ghent, and our first Minister to Sweden, he carried on a continued correspondence, which would elucidate many details connected with that eventful period of our diplomacy.

The letters addressed to Mr. Wheaton, at this time, from distinguished citizens in different sections of the Union, show, that his reputation was already being established beyond the limited bounds of his native State, and it would seem that his appointment as Secretary of Legation, either to Paries or London, was then contemplated. Among his correspondence of 1811 there is a letter from one of the Heads of Department, enclosing a communication, which he fully endorses, from the editors of the National Inteligencer, not only the ablest journal at the seat of government, but then, as it was understood, the exponent of the views of the Administration, thanking him in strong terms for a political article, which he had furnished, and inviting further contributions.

While yet resident at Providence, he delivered, on the 4th of July, 1810, an oration before his townamen, in acknowledging the receipt of which Mr. Jefferson says: "he rejoices over every publication wherein such sentiments are expressed. While these prevail all is safe."

In 1811, Mr. Wheaton married his cousin Catharine, the daughter of Dr. Wheaton, to whome he had been attached from tudes of fortune, at home and abrad, still survives her irreparable loss. He appears, at this period, to have sought a wider field than his native places affored for his talents, and to have intended to exercise his profession in the State of New York. This, however, was prevented by the old system of apprenticeship or clerkship, only fully abrogated by the Constitution of 1846. It, at the time referred to, required a novitiation of at least three years, which, Judge Spencer wrote to his father in law, could not then be dispensed with, even in the case of a practitioner from another State, or in consequence of attainments however extensive.

Towards the close of 1812, and some months after the declaration of the war with England, Mr. Wheaton was induced to take charge of a paper in New York, established under the title of the National Advocate, as the organ of the Republican party, in the city. The editorship of a daily newspaper at that time presented no flattering position. With the exception of the National Intelligencer, and of a few other cases, the newspapers of the United States, forty years ago, instead of being the vehicles of sound political intelligence and the means of diffusing correct information among the people, on the great topics of public interest, were the mere conduties of personal invective and party acerbity.

The establishment of the National Advocate constitutes a new epoch in the history of the newspaper press of the country. At the conclusion of the first year, the Editor remarks: "Our ideas of the manner in which a free press should be conducted were developed in the Prospectus, and we contracted the obligation that this print should be conducted in conformity to them. We promised that it should never wound the feelings of viryue; never infringe the laws of decorum; and never spare the vices of political turpitude. It is for our readers to determine how far we have performed our engagements."

In the Advocate were discussed, with the pen of a gentleman and scholar, the great questions of violated neutral rights, which had given rise to the belligerent position of the country. The new duties which war had created, on the part of our country, towards other nations, and the rights which it gave us, as well as the obligations of the several State governments to Federal government, and the paramount allegiance of the citizens of the different States to the United States, were elucidated with the learning of an accomplished publicist.

The period was one well calculated to arouse the patriotism of a republican editor. War had been declared when there had been a refusal to make an adjustment on the subject of impressment, and after it had been officially announced to the American government, that the obnoxious Orders in Council would not be repealed, without a repeal of internal measures of France, which, not violating any neutral rights, we regarde to which England, therefore, had no excuse for asking us to interpose, even if one belligerent could make it a ground of offence towards a friendly power, that it had neglected to exact from the other all that its neutral rights would authorize. Great Britain, after first requiring us to obtain the repeal of the Berlin and Milan decrees to induce an abandonment of the Orders in Council, was not satisfied with their abrogation, as regarded the United States, but demanded that their repeal should be general, and should extend to the removal of the prohibition of English produce and manufactures from the continent of Europe, where they operated as internal and municipal regulations not contravening any rights of neutrality.

The diplomatic papers of the American government, indeed, show that there was ground enough for a resort to extreme measures against both the great European belligerents, especially after the case of The Horizon, in 1807. The effect of such an anomalous condition of things would scarcely have changed the actual position of the parties, inasmuch as the navy of Great Britain, by driving from the ocean not only the military, but mercantile, marine of France, had left her unassailable by us, in a maritime war, ——the only species of hostilities that we could carry on against a strictly European power. Moreover, the avowed withdrawal of her hostile decrees, by France, in 1810, though the indemnity for past spoliations was deferred, had, already, induced a distinction in her favor as to our retaliatory interdicts on commercial intercourse. And the conviction, which circumstances subsequently confirmed, that the savages had been, while peace with the mother country still continued, excited by her provincial authorities, to carry the horrors of barbarous warfare into our frontier settlements, and that a secret agency had been instituted to separate the New England States from the Union, was deemed to justify a difference of conduct towards the two nations. War was consequently declared, on the 18th Of June, 1812, against England alone.

At this day, looking not only to the causes of the war—the utter disregard of our flag in the impressment of our seamen, aggravated, even so early as June, 1807, by the act of a British admiral, scarcely disavowed and most inadequately atoned for, in wresting, after the loss of several lives, four of the crew from a ship of war of the United States, and the condemnation of our vessels, in pursuance of Orders in Council, which even the British courts of admiralty did not venture to assert were consistent with the law of nations, but to the manner in which it was conducted—subjecting to conflagration edifices consecrated to legislation, setting at naught the ties of a common origin and introducing the tomahawk of the Indian among the weapons of British warfare, it is scarcely possible to believe that those, to whom the Constitution confided the conduct of our foreign affairs, did not receive the unanimous support of the American people and of the State authorities.

Such, however, was not the fact. It is true that some of the most illustrious, in the annnals of federalism, merged all party considerations in theirpatriotic obligations, —that the coadjutor of Jefferson in the declaration of Independence and his great rival, at the origin of the government, the Ex-President Adams, exclaimed, "How it is possible that a rational, social, or moral creature can say that the war is unjust, is to me utterly incomprehensible. I have thought it both just and necessary for five or six years." Such, also, were the often reiterated opinions of Oliver Wolcott, Secreatary of the Treasury under the administrations of Washington and Adams. Samuel Dexter, another memeber of the last cabinet of the federal party, whose political reputation was merged in his forensic fame, and Rufus KIng, deservedly esteemed one of the most enlightened statesmen among the founders of the government, and who was looked to as the individual, on whom alone President Madison's opponents could consistently rally for the chief magistracy, though not approving the war in advance, achiexed for themselves an eternal claim to the gratitude of their country, by sustaining the administration, when menaced by foreign armies and internal foes.

Not only were the energies of the government shackled by local legislatures denying, in the very midst of hostilities, the sufficiency of the causes of the war, and justifying theacts of Great Britain as being retaliatory of those of France, while enen the victories achieved by our own infant navy were availed of to repudiate their glorious exploits, as unbecoming the approbation of a moral and religious people; but the federal authorities were, in 1813, brought into direct collision with those of Massachusetts and Connecticut. THe Governors of those States assumed the right of determining for themselves the exigencies, which authorized the calling out of the militia, even in time of war, and refused to allow them to be placed in any case under the orders of the officer of the United States, commanding the regular troops within the military department. The unconstitutionality of these pretensions, which it was obvious would have defeated the main object for which the federal government was formed, and which, as pronounced by the Supreme Court of the United

States, it was one of his last acts, when connected with that tribunal, to report, was, at the time, ably exposed by Mr. Wheaton in the columns of his journal. It was, also, his duty to point out the highly objectionable nature of the convention of delegates from some of the New England States, held at Hartford, in 1814, for the purpose of considering their sectional interests; but which the news of peace, arriving almost simultaneously with their adjournmnet, rendered wholly innocuous.

Among the articles of the Advocate, which appropriately belong to the Advocate, which appropriately belong to the department of international law, was a vindication on the authority of Vattel and Bynkershoek, of the right of expatriation, in answer to Gouverneur Morris, an eminent statesman and diplomatist of the Anti-Republican party. Nor was this subject then a mere theoretical question. Great excitement had prevailed, in consequence of the menaces of the enemy to excute the naturalized citizens of British origin, who might be taken prisoners of war, the barbarity of which was not a little increased by the fact that military service was exacted from natives of the United States domiciled in Canada. The retaliatory measures of the American government, in selecting as hostages British prisoners to double the number of the individuals whose lives were in jeopardy, seems to have prevented a perseverance in the threat. Questions of maritime law were frequently discussed, and in the columns of his friend's paper first appeared Judge Story's opinion, deciding the illegality of enemy's licenses—a subject which, from the extent to which they were then used in order to supply with provisions the British armies in the Spanish Peninsula, attracted great attention.

Enjoying, as Mr. Wheaton did, the confidence of the members of the Cabinet, the Advocate was frequently selected as a medium through which to acquaint the people with the views of the administration. Such was the case, as regards the statement of the reasons, which, at an eventful period of the war, induced the removal of Generals Wilkinson and Hampton, with which he was furnished by the Secretary of War, General Armstrong. He received, after the conclusion of peace, through the Attorney-General, Mr. Pinkney, an expression of the obligations of all his colleagues for the abl support which he had rendered to the government, with a special commendation of the papers published by him on the treaty, and which that eminent jurist declared to be "as well as could be wished."

Of an oration pronounced on 4th of July, 1814, and while the war still continued, a notice remains in a letter of the gentleman who succeeded Mr. Pinkney as Attorney-General. He says: "I have read it with equal attention and pleasure. It is filed with correct, enlarged, patriotic, forcible thoughts, purely expressed, and oftentimes with energy and eloquence. I am glad to see the reponlican mind getting roused to the assertion of our great principles in times like these, when the aristocracy of the other hemisphere is so boldly attacking them. I am particularly delighted with the manner in which you have handled the European question."

It was not merely to American affairs that the discussions of the Advocate were confined. His knowledge of Europe. with his intercourse with those most faniliar with passing events, including the French Minister, Mr. Serurier, of whom he was a correspondent, enabled its editor to present the different aspects of the great pending contest, which was destined to change the whole fabric of European organization. His sagacity anticipated the permanent predominance, which Alexander was already achieving for Russia in the affairs of Europe; while the Emperor's accordance with us in maritime questions is shown to have been the reason, why, though united with him in an alliance, for continental matters, on which the destinies of both seemed to depend, Great Britain refused his proffered mediation, in the war with the United States.

While engaged in his editorial avocations, Mr. Wheaton received the commission of Division Judge-Advocate of the army. THe unanimous confirmation of the appointment, on the 26th of October, 1814, was announced to him not only by letters from two distinguished Senators, but the venturable

Vice-President Gerry made it subject of a congratulatory communication; in which he says: — "Your appointment was not only unanimous, but the voice of the Senate was expressed with cordiality." This was the more flattering, as General Armstrong had already quitted the War Office, and the National Advocate had continued, in opposition to popular prejudice, excited against him on account of the disastrous affair of Washington, to suport and sustain him, as "entitled to the gratitude of the nation, for having put out of the way the superannuated generals, and for bringing forward a set of generals, (Brown and Scott,) who refused our country from eternal disgrace."

In May, 1815, Mr. Wheaton left the National Advocate, on being appointed one of the Justices of the Marine Court, —a tribunal of limited jurisdiction, and which is now shorn of much of its former consideration; though in presiding over it, some of those, who were afterwards distinguished as the most eminent at the bar, passed a portion of their professional novitiate. Whilst occupying a seat in this court, which he continued to fill till July, 1819, he had occasion to vindicate the paramount treaty-making power of the Federal Government. The case arouse in 1816, under the commercial convention with Grerat Britain of the preceding year, and the question was, whether the reciprocity provision extended to the exemption of British vessels from the discriminating charges imposed by a local law of the State on foreign vessels.

In 1815, under the modest title of a "Digest of the Law of Maritime Captures or P rizes," Mr. Wheatom published his first systematic treatise. This was a subject to which he appears to have directed his attention from the period when, by the declaration of war by the United States against England, the admiralty jurisdiction became a matter of serious attention to the members of the legal profession, resident in the seaports. But, though its preparation was induced by th want of a work, for the daily reference of the practising lawyer, its utility was far from being limited to the circumstances out of which it arouse. The "Digest" is not a mere index, but presents an exposition of the law of nations, as then understood and administered; and though the language of the orignal authorities, to insure accuracy, is properly employed in preference to his own, no position is stated, the full effect of which is not appreciated by the writer.

Indended as a practical treatise, Mr. Wheaton gives a full analysis of the adjudications of the tribunals of different countries, and especially of England and the United States, on questions of prize, and which necessarily involved a review of all those debateable points of maritime law, which had been the subjects of our diplomatic discussions. The opinions on which the reputation of Sir William Scott (Lord Stowell) is based, had already been promulgated, with his views of the influence which the instructions of his government ought ti have even over tribunals professedly acting as the exponents of the law of nations. And if any important additions have since been made to the authorities, on which reposes the law, deduced from the decisions of Admiralty Courts, as it was understood prior to the commencement of the present war, it is mainly in the reports of that tribunal, with which Mr. Wheaton's name is indissolubly connected, that they are to be found.

In reference to this work, Judge Story wrote to the author, on 13th of December, 1815: — "You have honorably discharged that duty, which every man owes to his profession, and I am persuaded that your labors will ultimately obtain the rewards which learning and talents cannot fail to secure." At the same time, the Attorney-General of the United States, Mr. Rush, who was subsequently Minister, at different periods, to Ebgland and France, informed him that he had made his book the basis of a work on the state of American jurisprudence.

Thirty years after its publication, an English writer, a high authority on international law, declared the work on captures to be, "in point of learning and methodical arrangement, very superior to any treatise on this department of the law, which had previously appeared in the English language." Nor has it been superseded by the other books of Mr. Wheaton. It embraces a department of public law not discussed, or at most only incidentally touched on, in the more general treatises with which he has enriched the science of international jurisprudence. Though intended as an exposition of the existing state of prize law, as administered in our tribunals, nowhere else can so clear and accurate a view of the English and French edicts against neutral commerce be found; and in no other publication are they so ably brought to the test of the universal law of nations.

Mr. Wheaton also prepared, in 1815, abankrupt law, and endeavored to procure its through Congress. This measure was, at that time, deemed the more important, as the constitutionality of the State Insolvent Laws began to be questioned, and it was believed that the power delegated to the General Government could alone meet the provisions on this subject, supposed to be required in a commercial community.

He also published, after the peace of Ghent, "An Essay on the Means of Maintaining the Commercial and Naval Interests of the United States." He advocated, as called for by the restrictive policy then existing in Europe, a navigation act, giving special advantages to our vessels, and excluding all foreign sailors from our merchant marine. The former measure has been rendered inapplicable, in a great degree, in consequence of the arrangements since made with most maritime States by our reciprocity treaties, or by means of the acts of Congress, proffering to all nations a mutual abrogation of the discriminating duties on the tonnage of their respective vessels, and on the produce, manufactures, and merchandise imported in them.

The exclusion of alien seamen was repeatedly proposed by the Executive, not, however, on politico-economical considerations, but in connection with an arrangement with the British government on the impressment question, but without result. Though we cannot distinguish between native citizens and those who are already entitled by naturalization to the same rights, save in the exceptional cases expressed in the Constitution; yet it was supposed that the Act of 1813, requiring a continuous residence during the probationary tern, which is wholly incompatible with the nature of the sea-faring life, might have been received by England, as a practical exclusion from the commercial service of all foreign-born seamen. That provision was repealed in 1848; and the Act of March 27, 1804, denationalizing any American vessel, the owner of which, in whole or in part, if a naturalized citizen, shall reside more than a year in the country from which he originated, or more than two years in any foreign country, which still remains in force, would seem to be only discrimination now known to our laws between native and naturalized citizens.

In 1816, Mr. Wheaton became Reporter of the Supreme Court of the United States, in which capacity he continued till 1827. Twelve volumes of Reports, containing, as it is well termed in a German notice of our author, "the golden book of American law," permanently connect his name with the jurisprudence of the Union. Already familiar with the languages and literature of Europe, and with her legal systems, he was called on to record the application of every branch of public and municipal law to the diversified objects of international and federal relations, as well as of private rights. It was his fortune to be associated with that high tribunal during the period when the Prize Code, which he had already traced, as far as it was then established, was completed by the subsequent adjudications of the cases growing out of the recent war. In his time, also, the power intrusted to the Court, and which is peculiar to institutions like ours, of bringing to the test of the Constitution the validity of all the proceedings of Congress and of the State legislatures, was exercised to such an extent, as to leave little room for the further interpretation of our organic law.

In a review by Mr. Wheaton of one of the volumes of the Reports of Judge Story's Circuit decisions, and which includes many prize cases, he thus gives a history of prize law to the time of the late war: "Among the leading principles of law, developed and settled during the war of the Revolution, and which have ever since been recognized as a part of the prize code of this country, are the following: —The exclusive jurisdiction of the Court of Admiralty over all the incidents of prize and its right to entertain a supplemental libel for distribution of the prize proceeds after condemnation. That an ally is bound by the capitulation made by another ally with the inhabitants of a conquered country, by which their property is exempted from capture. But that an ally is not bound by a mere voluntary suspension of the rights of war against a part of the enemy's dominions, by a co-belligerent, not growing out of a capitulation. The distinction between a perfect war and an imperfect war, or partial hostilities. That in a perfect war nothing but a treaty of peace can restore the neutral character of any of the belligerent parties; and consequently that the British proclamation of 1781, exempting from capture all Dutch ships carrying the produce of Dominica according to the capitulation by which that island had surrendered to the French, did not restore back to a Dutch ship her original neutral character, so as to protect her cargo from capture by American cruisers under the ordinance of Congress of April 1, 1781, by which the United States temporarily adopted the principles of the armed neutrality, which had been formed in Europe the preceding year. That the rule recognized by this ordinance of *free ships free goods*, did not extend to the case of a fraudulent attempt by neutrals, to combine with British subjects to wrest from the United States and France the advantages they had obtained over Great Britain by the rights of war in the capitulation of Dominica, by which all commercial intercourse between that island and Great Britain was prohibited. That Congress didi not mean by their ordinance to ascertain in what cases the rights of neutrality should be forfeited in exclusion of all other cases; for the instances not mentioned were as flagrant as the cases particularized. That the papers which a vessel is directed to sail with, by the municipal law of her own country, are the documents which a prize court has a right to look for as evidence of proprietary interest; though not conclusive evidence. The fraudulent blending of enemy's and neutral property in the same claim involves both in the same condemnation. The domicile of a party is conclusive as to his national character in a prize court. The municipal laws of any particular country cannot change the law of nations: as between captor and captured, the property is divested in-stantly on the capture; but a neutral claimant is not barred until a final condemnation in a competent prize court. All other municipal regulations of salvage extend only to the citizens of the country making those regulations. The authority of the prize court to make distribution of the prize proceeds where there is no agreement between the owners, officers, and crew of the capturing vessel. And its authority to decree a sale where the *res* in litigation is perishable. The conclusiveness of sentences of condemnation upon the papers found on board, and the examination of the captured persons. That the omission of the captors to bring in all the captured persons and papers will not forfeit their rights of prize, unless a fraudulent omission. All lastly, the illegality of trade by a citizen with the enemy. "

Mr. Wheaton very happily contrasts our system of admiralty courts, as at present organized, with those of other countries. "The subjects of foreign States have had reason to rejoice that the decision of their rights have been vested in the same pure hands, with which the people of this country have intrusted their dearest privileges. Nor does the experience of other countries give us or them any reason to regret that our prize jurisdiction is not placed in a cabinet council, or judges removable at the pleasure of such a council. Even that highly gifted and accomplished man, (Sir W. Scott,) has been compelled to avow that he was bound by the king's instruction; and we know that his decrees are liable to be reversed by the privy council, from which those instructions emanate. So, also, in France, both under the royal and imperial governments, the prize jurisdiction has been almost constantly vested in the Council of Prizes, —a board composed of members removable at the pleasure of the crown—a mere commission created at the breaking out of every war, and dissolved on its termination. During the anarchy of the Revolution, it was exercised by judges, many of whom were notoriously concerned in privateers, the fruits of whose plunder from innocent neutrals they were to adjudge. The rapacity and injustice of the French and British courts of vice-admiralty in the colonies, are notorious. "

Even while the United State, after the achievement of their independence, were at peace with all the world, controversies between the assured and the underwriters presented questions requiring the application of the principles of the law of nations, and in that way the law of blockade, of commercial domicile, and other points affecting the international code, as well as the innovations which the belligerents were attempting to introduce into maritime law, were judicially considered. The court, also, in the decision of the cases, growing out of the war of 1812, reported before Mr. Wheaton's connection with them, had declared that, as the United States at one time formed a component part of the British Empire, their prize law was, as understood at the time of the separation, the prize law of the United States, though no recent rules of the British courts were entitled to more respect than those of other countries; yet tah, where there were no reasons to the contrary, they should regard the decisions of the English courts of admiralty.

In the case of The Nereide, they had not only affirmed the rule, that the goods of an enemy in the vessel of a friend were prize of war, and that those of a friend in the vessel of an enemy were to be restored, to be a part of the law of nations, but they also decided that the stipulation in the treaty of 1795, with Spain, that "free ships shall make free goods," does not imply the converse proposition that "enemy ships shall make enemy goods." In the same case, they differed from Sir William Scott, and recognized the right of a neutral to carry his goods in an armed vessel of enemy. And in the case of The Adeline, it was decided, that the law of France denying restitution upon salvage after twenty-four hours possession by the enemy, the property of persons domiciled in France should be condemned as prize by our courts, on recaption, after being in possession of the enemy that length of time.

The volumes of Wheaton contain decisions, declaring the property of a citizen engaged in trade with the enemy liable to capture and confiscation as prize of war, under whatever circumstances it might be carried, whether between an enemy's ports and the United States or between such port and any foreign country; that the sailing under an enemy's license was sufficient of itself to subject to confiscation without regard to the object of the voyage or port of destination; that a citizen of the United States, who had acquired a domicile abroad, but had returned to the United States and become a redintegrated American citizen could not, *flagrante bello*, acquire a neutral domicile, by again emigrating to his adopted country; that the stipulation in a treaty, "free ships make free goods," although they should belong to enemies, contraband excepted, does not exempt the goods belonging to citizens of the captor's country engaged in trade with an enemy; that the property of a house of trade in an enemy's country is confiscable, notwithstanding the neutral domicile of one or more of the partners; that there can be no restitution, on payment of salvage to the original owner, where a vessel captured and condemned, was recaptured by an American privateer, the original title being extinguished by the condemnation.

The Supreme Court also decided that it is the exclusive right of governments to acknowledge new States arising in the revolutions of the world, and until such recognition by our government, or that to which the new State belonged, courts of justice are bound to consider the ancient order of things as remaining unchanged; that in case of the Spanish American governments, the governments of the United States having recognized the existence of a civil war between Spain and her colonies, the courts of the United States were bound to consider as lawful those acts, which were authorized by the law of nations, and which the new governments may direct against their enemies, and their captures were to be regarded as other captures *jure belli*, the legality of which cannot be determined in the courts of a neutral country.

The court likewise decided, in reference to the acts declaring the slave-trade piracy, passed by the United States and Great Britain, that the right of visitation and search did not exist in time of peace, and that a vessel engaged in the slave-trade, though it was prohibited by the country to which it belonged, could not be seized on the high seas and brought in for adjudication in the courts of another country.

But, it is by the important adjudications, defining the limits of the federal and state jurisdictions, that the judicial administration of Marshall, who presided during the whole period, was distinguished. That the repeal or alteration, by a State, of the charter of a private corporation, which a college was declared to be, was a violation of the constitutional prohibition to pass any law impairing the obligations of contracts—that it was competent for Congress to establish a national bank, which could not be taxed by any individual State—and that no State could grant a right for the exclusive use of its navigable waters, nor pass a bankrupt or insolvent law, affecting preexisting contracts, or contracts between citizens of different States, are among the decisions to be found in Wheaton's Reports; while, —what connects these adjudications immediately with the treatise to which these remarks are introductory, —the faith of international obligations was upheld, not only by establishing the appellate jurisdiction of the Supreme Court, in a case where the validity of a State law was called in question, as repugnant to a treaty of the United States, but by asserting, what is the distinguishing feature between our existing institutions and those of the old confederacy, the power to carry into full effect the judgment, without the aid of the State Court.

The character, which Mr. Wheaton at once acquired as a reporter, was unrivalled. He didi not confine himself to a summary of the able arguments by which the cases were elucidated, but there is scarcely a proposition on any of the diversified subjects to which the jurisdiction of the court extends, that might give rise to serious doubts in the profession, that is not explained, not merely by a citation of the authorities adduced by counsel, but copious notes present the views which the publicists and civilians have taken of the question. Not only are Pothier and the civil code constantly quoted, and their conclusions compared with those of the common law; but, on the introduction of a case from Louisiana, we have an explanation of the jurisprudence, which prevailed in that colony at the time of its annexation, showing how far the

French and Spanish laws respectively, were in force.

The value of some of the more extended notes, as well as the general character of the reports, we can have no better means of estimating than by the contemporaneous remarks, in reference to the first volume, of the learned Judge of the Court, to whose correspondence with the author we have already adverted. Judge Story says: "I received yesterday your obliging favor, accompanied with a copy of your reports. I have read the whole volume through hastily, but con amore. I am extremely pleased with the execution of the work. The arguments are reported with brevity, force, and accuracy; and the notes have all your clear, discriminating, and pointed learning. They are truly a most valuable addition to the text, and at once illustrate and improve it. I particularly admire those notes, which bring into view the civil and continental law, a path as yet but little explored by our lawyers, but full of excellent sense and judicial acuteness. In my judgment there is no more fair or honorable road to permanent fame than by the breathing over our municipal code the spirit of other ages. In my judgement your reports are the very best in manner of any taht have ever been published in our country, and I should be surprised, if the whole profession do not pay you this voluntary homage. Respecting the note on the rule of 1756, I have already written my opinion; it is the best comment that the rule has ever received. The kind notice of our friend, Dexter, in the preface, is delightful to us all; and on turning to the argument in Martin v. Hunter, I perceive the splendid paragraph preserved in its original brightness." The work, also, received the approbation of all the other members of the court, and among other commendations, from judicial authorities, of the manner in which Mr. Wheaton's task was performed we may refer to that of the great English admiralty judge, Sir William Scott.

Judge Story's letter renders unnecessary the insertion of the equally strong testimony of the merits of the reports by William Pinkney, whose note lies before us. Danied Webster, to whom the North American Review was indebted for an article on one of the early volumes, says: "We wish to express our high opinion of the general manner in which the Reporter has executed his duty in the volume before us. Mr. Wheaton has not only recorded the decisions with accuracy, but has greatly added to the value of the volume by the extent and excellence of his notes. In this particular his merits are, in a great degree, peculiar. No reporter in modern times, as far as we know, has inserted so much and so valuable matter of his own. Those notes are not dry references to cases, of no merit, but as they save trouble of research. They are an enlightened adaptation to the case reported of the principles and rules of other systems of jurisprudence, or a connected view of decisions on the principal points, after exhibiting the subject with great perspicuity and in a manner to be highly useful to the reader. Mr. Wheaton's annotations evince a liberal and extensive acquaintance with his profession. His quotations from the treatises of the continental lawyers are numerous and well selected. This is a branch of learning not much cultivated among us. Mr. Wheaton appears to have pursued it to some extent and to good purpose. It enables him to give a peculiar interest to his volume, nor is there a better mode in which he could communicate his own acquisitions of this sort to the profession than by judicious and appropriate notes to reported cases." Ina notice of the subsequent volumes, the writer, in suggesting a work on the admiralty jurisdiction exercised by our courts, before and since the adoption of the Federal Constitution, remarks, "A work embracing this and its cognate topics is a desideratum; and we know no man who could accomplish it with greater facility or talent than Mr. Wheaton. We will hazard a suggestion that when he shall publish another edition of this valuable treatise on prize law, he will greatly enhance the the obligation of the profession, by adding an historical sketch of the kind we have above mentioned. Let us not be supposed, however, to have overlooked his excellent notes on the prize jurisdiction and practice appended to the two first volumes of his reports. There is no systematic treatise on the jurisdiction of the admiralty in England, or here, that is accurate and thorough. True and lasting fame awaits the jurist who shall produce one."

Mr. Duponceau, the jurist, as well as philologist, and whose annotations of Bynkershoek, in common withthe original treatise, are cited in the "Elements," among the authorities on which international law is based, names the notes of Mr. Wheaton, giving comparative views of the laws of different countries on the various subjects treated of the body of the work, among the most valuable contributions made to the science of law; while he alludes to the treatise on captures, in connection with Judge Story's and Chancellor Kent's works, as being "the fruits of the cultivation of the branches of the jurisprudence not accessible to ordinary lawyers."

And we may here venture the hope that in the improved condition of judicial science, it may not be by the piratical abridgment, to which we shall have occasion to refer, that the decisions of the Supreme Court during itsmost glorious days are to be known to posterity. The adjudications of that tribunal, explanatory as they are of the fundamental principles of our Constitution, would lose much of their value, if they are hereafter to go forth, unaccompanied by the commentaries of the eminent advocates and statesmen—of Pinkney and his contemporaries and successors in forensic fame, Dexter, Harper, Wirt, Emmett, Hunter, Edward Livingston, Ingersoll, Clay, and Webster, who constituted a bar worthy of Marshall, Washington, Livingston, Story, and Thompson.

It was not only as the medium of communication with the public that Mr. Wheaton was connected with the Supreme Court. Associated with the jurists of historical fame, to whom we have just alluded, in the argument of causes, the decisions of which he reported, we find his contributions to the common stock of legal learning, combined with theirs in every volume to which his name is attached. The law of real property, the principles regulating commercial contracts, as well as those relating to that department of jurisprudence, prize law, with which he had shown a peculiar acquaintance, were discussed by him in the character of counsel.

Nor did he omit to take an efficient part in those questions on which the interpretation of ourorganic law is based. IN the great case which settled the limits of the sate and federal legislation, in reference to bankruptcy and insolvency, and which, first argued in 1824, was held under advisement and not finally disposed of till after a second argument, in 1827, he was throughout the sole associate of Daniel Webster; while there were, at different times, arrayed against them Mr. Clay, Mr. Ogden, Mr. Haines, Mr. Wirt, (Attorney-General,) Mr. Edward Livingston, Mr. Jones, and Mr. Sampson, most of whom are known in the political as well as the legal annals of our country. Indeed, such was the position which Mr. Wheaton's industry and learning had acquired for him, that, on the death of Judge Liveingston, in 1823, he was, already, prominently brought forward to fill the vacancy on the bench of the Supreme Court, an appointment which, it is understood, that he would have received, had it not been conferred, by President Monroe, on a member of his cabinet.

IN 1821, Mr. Wheaton was elected a delegate from the city of New York to the convention for forming a new constitution for the State. The original constitution, adopted in 1777, was objected to on account of the restrictions on the right of suffrage, a freehold qualification being required from the electors of the Governor and Senate, and the payment of a tax, with the renting of a tenement of, at least, the specified annual value, from every one who voted for members of the lower house. Exception was, also, taken to the provision, which blended the judicial, executive and legislative powers in the Council of Revision, composed of the Governor, Chancellor, and Justices of the Supreme Court, to whom a veto on the acts of the two houses was accorded, as well as to the irresponsible nature of the appointing power vested, with a concurrent right of nomination in all the members, in a council, consisting of the Governor and one Senator, chosen by the lower house, from each of the four senatorial districts of the State.

In the law providing for the election of delegates, the principle was recognized that whatever restrictions might exist for ordinary legislation, the whole people had a right to participate in the formation of their organic law, and the convention was chosen according to a rule intended to approximate, as near as practicable, to universal suffrage. The members were selected from among the most eminent citizens, and in some degree, without reference to party designation or local residence. Among them were the two eminent citizens, and in some degree, without reference to party designation or local residence. Among them were the two Senators in CONGRESS, Rufus King and Martin Van Buren, since President of the United States, who represented a country where he did not live, as well as the actual Vice-President, Daniel D. Tompkins. The Chancellor, Kent, and Chief Justice, Spencer, were delegates from Albany; while Mr. Wheaton had as an immediate colleague Nathan Sanford, the successor of Chancellor Kent, in his judicial office, and, both before and subsequent to this period, a Senator of the United States.

In this assembly Mr. Wheaton bore a conspicuous part. Among the propositions which he introduced was one rendering it the duty of the legislature to pass general laws on the subject of private corporations, and prohibiting their establishment by special acts. The importance of such a measure was then particularly apparent, inasmuch as private banking was interdicted and the business regarded as a legislative franchise. The obtaining of bank charters had given rise to an extended system of corruption, from the suspicion of which, even the judges, through their connection with the legislation of the State, as members of the Council of Revision, were not wholly exempt. Though the article was not adopted, its wisdom was recognized, when the constitution was again remodelled in 1846, and it now forms a portion of the fundamental law of the State. He also proposed a constitutional provision, making it the duty of the legislature to cause the cities and towns to raise the sums necessary, in addition to the amounts received from the common school find, to maintain public schools in every town for the instruction of all the children.

On the subject of the Judiciary, for the independence of which he was a strenuous advocate, opposing the provision to make the Judges removable by the joint resolution of the two houses of the legislature, he contributed valuable suggestions.

In the canvass for the Presidential term, to commence on the 4th of March, 1825, though following the second election of Mr. Monroe, which had been made with entire unanimity, there seemed to be no concurrence of opinion. Mr. Crawford, the Secretary of the Treasury, who had been designated by the caucus, as the meeting of the republican members of Congress for that purpose was denominated, according to the system which had prevailed at several previous elections, was opposed by all the other aspirants for the station, however much they might differ among themselves. These candidates were John Quincy Adams, Secretary of State, Mr. Calhoun, Secretary of War, Mr. Clay, Speaker of the House of Representatives, and Andrew Jackson, whose administration of the government during two subsequent terms forms so memorable a portion of our history. Though the last named was then known to the nation at large only by his military fame, as having with far inferior forces, composed mainly of militia, triumphantly repelled the veteran legions of England, in their attempted invasion of Louisiana, his course, during the canvass, was already such as to disarm the opposition of many, who had entertained apprehension from the elevation of a successful general to the highest civil office. "Jackson," siad one of the most eminent of his associates in the Senate, and to whom we have before had occasion to refer, as rising above the dictates of party in the war of 1812, "conducts himself in a most unexceptionable manner, and so as to remove prejudices, which may be entertained to his disadvantage."

As the distinctive appellation of "People's Party," assumed by those to whom Mr. Wheaton attached himself, implied, he was opposed to the candidate of the caucus; and while Mr. Calhoun remained before the public for the chief magistracy he was his confidential correspondent. To advance the pretensions of the Carolina statesman to the highest office was Mr. Wheaton's motive, in permitting himself to be elected a member of the New York State Assembly, in November, 1823; and it is not a little remarkable, when we look to the views which Mr. Calhoun subsequently took of our system of government, that our author's original preference for him was induced by a concurrence of sentiment on the subject of the Federal Judiciary. To preserve to the Supreme Court the exposition of the Constitution, in the last resort, was then deemed by Mr. Calhoun, as his letters of that period show, an object of primary importance. And it may well incline us to regard with indulgence the changes which inferior minds undergo, when we find one afterwards so eminent in the liberal school of political economy, and whose integrity of purpose and purity of life are unassailable, writing to his friends in the legislature of New York, to suggest "the propriety of adopting some resolutions not to support any one not known to be openly in favor of domestic manufactures and internal improvements." "The adoption of such," he added, "would go far to prostrate the hopes of the radicals, at once, in your State."

The immediate object, aimed at by Mr. Wheaton and those who voted with him, was theelection of Presidential electors by the people, instead of their being chosen, as had been previously the usage in New York, by the two houses of the legislature. In this effort, notwithstanding the Governor was induced to call an extra meeting to consider the matter, after its failure at the regular session, they were not successful. But, in the final result, only four electors favorable to Mr. Crawford, though he was sustained by the friends of Mr., afterwards President, Van Buren, were chosen, while the remainder were divided between Mr. Adams and Mr. Clay, in the proportion of eighteen for the former and fourteen for the latter. As the loss of the greatest part of the New York votes, though Mr. Crawford was still returned as the third on the list, and therefore eligible to be chosen by the House of Representatives, was deemed fatal to the caucus party, our author received from the most eminent of their opponents, from, among others, John Quincy Adams, Mr. Calhoun, (who was chosen Vice-President by the joint vote of General Jackson's and Mr. Adams's friends,) and Rufus King, the strongest congratulations on the happy result of his labors, in, what the warmth of partisan feeling characterized as, a "struggle for the cause of the people." Mr. Adams's letter thus concludes: "Your share in the legislative labors of the year have been great and conspicuous. I trust it has been introductory for you to movements on a yet wider field; and observe with pleasure your name among those of the candidates for a seat in the United States Senate." Mr. Calhoun writes: — "Never, in this country, has there been a more important political contest. The whole train of future events depended on the result. The part which you have individually taken has been important and honorable to you, and will, Itrust, be held in remembrance to your advantage. You have acted under circumstances of great complication, and of relations apparently contradictory, and if you have erred at all on any point, such error may be traced to a firm and virtuous tone of character."

Divisions in the party, which had achieved the victory in the legislature, were occasioned before the termination of the political year by the removal of De Witt Clinton, to whom the successful issue of the New York system of internal improvements was ascribed, from the place of Canal Commissioner, and which led to his subsequent election as Governor, an office that he had previously filled. In the resolution, respecting Mr. Clinton, Mr. Wheaton voted with the majority. Whatever his merits as a citizen of the State, his course, though avowedly a Republican, in permitting himself to be the candidate of the Federalists for the Presidency during the war, and in opposition to Mr. Madison, could not readily be forgotten by one who had taken an active and zealous part in support of the administration of 1812. These circumstances not only prevented the fulfilment of the suggestions to which Mr. Adams refers, and defeated Mr. Wheaton's election to the House of Representatives, foe which he was nominated in the city of New York, but caused those public proofs of confidence from the administration which, on the election of Mr. Adams, he had a right to anticipate, to be deferred.

As, however, in matters purely of a professional character, no partizan qualities can serve as a substitute for learning, Mr. Wheaton was, in 1825, associated with Mr. Benjamin F. Butler, afterwards Attorney-General of the United States, and Mr. John Duer, now an eminent member of the New York Judiciary, in a commission for revising the statute law of New York. Though the plan in view was a recompilation of the statutes, and not a codification of the commissioners that they should not confine themselves to merely bringing together the laws referring to the same subject, but that they should collate and revise all public acts in force, in such a manner as they should deem most useful and proper to render the acts more plain ane easy to be made in the phraseology or distribution of the sections of any statute, that had been the subject of judicial decision, by which its construction could be affected.

These labors were of a character particularly agrreeable to the taste of Mr. Wheaton. Not merely for the improvement of the existing statutes, but for the preparation of a code of a more comprehensive character, had one been contemplated, he possessed peculiar qualifications, through his varied knowledge of jurisprudence, which included, as has been shown, a familiarity, almost from their origin, with the French codes become, with slight alterations, the law of most of the States of continental Europe.

Applying himself to his new duties, while continuing his professional business and his functions as Reporter of the Supreme Court of United States, he united with his colleagues in a report to the legislature, at the session of 1826, in which they state the arrangements, which they had made for the classification of the statutes, and submit, as a specimen, a portion of the revision, embracing the constitutional and administrative law of the State, together with their views as to the general execution of the work. He also zealously engaged in carrying the plan, which the legislature sanctioned, into execution, and a portion of the revision, as completed, was presented for adoption at the session of 1827; but other duties called him away from the country, before the whole work, as perfected by his associates and Mr. John C. Spencer, eminent as a jurist, and well known as having filled some of the highest stations in his State and in the Union, who had been appointed to succeed him, was enacted as a law.

In his letter of resignation he says: "I cannot refrain from expressing the grateful sense I feel at the proof of confidence which has been reposed in me by the legislature of the State, in associating my name with a work of such magnitude and interest. There is, in my view, no public employment of more permanent dignity and importance; and though considerations, not necessary to be adverted to, have induced me, after mature deliberation, to relinquish it, I feel very great regret in quitting a work, in which I have labored with a zeal disproportioned to my faculties, and which I deem closely connected with the reputation and prosperity of the State of New York."

Mr. Wheaton, at all times, combined the general cultivation of letters with the pursuits more especially connected with his chosen profession; and his right to be enrolled among the *litterateurs* of the country was recognized by his alma mater, as early as 1819, by cinferring on him the degree of Doctor of Laws, in which she was followed, some years afterwards, by Hamilton College and Harvard University at Cambridge. Of the literary societies, that existed in New York during his residence there, he was, of course an honored member. As such the Anniversary Address, before the Historical Society in 1820, was pronounced by him. He selected, as his subject, "The Science of Public or International Law;" and as this essay contain the germ of his great works on the law of nations, it will not be deviating from the proper scope of an introductory notice to refer to the reception which it met with, at the time of its publication, from those of his countrymen most competent to appreciate it.

The venerable John Adams said: "I have read this discourse with uncommon interest and peculiar delight. It is the production of great reading, profound reflection, a discriminating mind, and a our taste. I have never read any discourse produced in America relative to the science of public law with so much satisfaction. Had I read such a discourse sixty-five years ago, it would have given a different and more respectable cast to my whole life."

Mr. Jefferson writes: "I thank you for the very able discourse you have been so kind as to send me on international law. I concur much in its doctrines, and very particularly in its estimate of the Lacedamonian chracter. How such a tribe of savages ever acquired the admiration of the world has always been beyond my comprehension. I can view them but on a level with our American Indians, and I see in Logan, Tecumsech and the LIttle Turtle fair parallels for their Brasidas, Agesilaus, &c. The difficulty is so conceive that such a horde of barbarians could so long remain unimproved, in the neighborhood of a people so polished as the Athenians; to whom they owe altogether that their name is now known to the world. All the good that can be said of them is, that they were as brave as bull-dogs."

Chief Justice Marshall, in a letter in reference to the reports, says: "I did not thank you while in Washington for your anniversary discourse, delivered before the Historical Society of New York, nor for your digest of the decisions of the Supreme Court, because I had not leisure, while at that place, to look into either. Since my return to this place, I have read the first with a great deal of pleasure, and have glanced over the digest with much satisfaction.

"However preeminent the ancients may have been in some of the fine arts, they were, I think you very clearly show, much inferior to us, or a great way behind us, in the more solid and more interesting principles of international law; a law which contributes more to the happiness of the human race than all the statues which ever came from the hands of the sculptor, or all the paintings that were ever placed on canvas. I do not, by this, mean to lessen tha value of the arts. I subscribe to their importance, and admit that they improve as well as embellish human life and manners; but they yield in magnitude to those moral rules which regulate the connection of man with man.

"Old Hugo Grotius is indebted to you for your defence of him and his quotations. You have raised in him my estimation to the rank he deserves."

Chancellor Kent, who, on occasion of the decision of a case in which Mr. Wheaton was counsel, and which rested on the French law of marriage, had acknowledged in the strongest terms his obligations for the elucidation of the nuptial community of goods which his argument afforded, and which he, alone of the bar, was capable of furnishing, thus addressed him, on the receipt of this pamphlet: — "Be pleased to accept my thanks for your very interesting and able discourse on the History of International Law, delivered before the Historical Society. There is no person (unless it be our mutual friend and great master of jurisprudence, Judge Story) who could have handled the subject with so much erudition and enlightened judgement. It is a subject very much to my taste, and awakens the deepest interest. Be assured, my dear Sir, that I feel with full force the great obligations we are all under to you, for your professional efforts and illustrious attainments."

It will be recollected, in this connection, that the Law of Nations forms a branch of those: "Commentaries on American Law," which now occupy with every student of the science the place formerly allotted to Blackstone; which the name of Kent is associated with that of Wheaton, both at home and abroad, as an authority on International Law.

Another occasional discourse, by Mr. Wheaton, was an address delivered at the opening of the New York Athenaum, in 1825, which is thus alluded to by Mr. Madison, in a letter expressing his disappointment that the author's occupations would not permit his undertaking a work that had been proposed to him: — "I shall not be singular in regretting that it could not be executed by the pen, which furnished such a specimen of judicious and interesting observations, as distinguished the elegant address at the opening of the New York Athenaum." In that discourse, Mr. Wheaton took a rapid survey of what had been accomplished in American literature; and pointing out the connection between the principles on which the ancient republics were founded and the rapid growth of the arts and sciences to which they gave encouragement—tracing analogies and causes in a manner which indicated deep reflection on the nature, spirit, and tendencies of our government—he presented an interesting view of the intellectual prospects of the country.

To the periodical literature, and which received no inconsiderable elevation in the respect and consideration of the community, from the extensive attainments and personal reputation of the conductors of the Reviews established at Boston and Philadelphia, he was a large contributor. Accomplished scholars, such as Edward Everett, Jared Sparks, and Robert Walsh, were able to command the assistance, as *collaborateurs*, of many of the United States, at once period, would have favorably compared with the first periodicals of Europe.

Mr. Wheaton's numerous essays in other journals cannot be accurately traced, but in almost every volume of the North American, commencing with the first number, in May, 1815, may be found papers emanating from his pen, or his name is introduced in connection with notices of his works. His earliest article was a patriotic defence of the United States against the illiberal attacks of the British press; whose virulence, increased by the war, had been holding us up to the derision of Europe, because in our infancy our literature had not attained the ripeness of adolescence, and that while all our efforts were required for the creation of the necessaries, we were wanting in some of the refinements, which belong to nations where a favored class have the leisure to devote themselves to the elegancies of life.

Among the reviews furnished by him, while yet at New York, is the exposition of the early Prize Code of the United States, already noticed, and he availed himself of the publication of Mr. Cushing's translation of Pothier on Maritime Contracts, the work by which the present Attorney-General of the United States marked his legal novitiate, to aid in making his countrymen acquainted with the merits of that most learned lawyer, by whose introduction to the English bar Sir William Jones deemed that he had, in some measure, paid the debt that every man owes to his profession. But he was not, as a jurist, exclusively absorbed in the civil and international law. His learning in the old Common Law appeared not only in his own Reports, but in the notice which he gave of Mr. Metcalf's edition of Yelverton, and by the numerous authorities cited in his edition of Selwyn's Nisi Prius; while in making his readers acquainted with what he terms, in a letter to his friend, Mr. Butler, "Verplanck's beautiful speculation on the theory of the Law of Contracts, as to price," and in which he contends for absolute equality in contracts, as binding *foro conscientia*, he had an opportunity of considering how far the doctrines of law and equity, as expounded by the courts, accorded with the rules of natural justice.

The review of a trial for manslaughter, which, arising from the killing of a counsellor-at-law, in an affray growing out of the occurrences at a trial, excted intense interest at the time, contains a learned disquisition on the distinctions between the criminal law of the Continent and that of England, especially in reference to the regard which the former pays, in certain offences, to the intent rather than to the events, as constituting the criminality.

On the other hand, not only had Mr. Wheaton Daniel Webster as the reviewer to whom the "Reports" were assigned, but Edward Everett was himself the author of the learned notice which the Historical Address received.

The last labor in which Mr. Wheaton engaged, while still in the United States, out of the regular performance of his professional duties, and disconnected with the offices which he held as Reporter and Revisor, was the preparation of the Life of William Pinkney; if, indeed, writing the biography of the most eminent member of the profession to which he belonged, and who was also among the most distinguished in the one on which he was about to enter, could be deemed a deviation from his appropriate pursuits.

If this enterprise had had no other effect than to elicit from President Madison two letters, explanatory of the events connected with the adoption of our restrictive system, and of the immediate circumstances that caused the declaration of war, at the time that it occurred, it would have been the means of adding valuable materials to history. In his letter, of the 18th of July, 1824, Mr. Madison says that the President was unofficially possessed of the Order in Council of November 11, 1807, when the message to Congress, of December 11, 1807, recommending an embargo, was sent, and this fact is corroborated by a note to him from Mr. Jefferson, confirming his recollections. He also vindicates the efficiency of the restrictive measures, by referring to the fact, that the repeal of the obnoxious British orders, which took place on the 23d JUne, 1812, was induced by the influence of the manufactures, before it was known in Europe that war had been actually declared by us. The letter of 26th February, 1827, states that the declaration of war was recommended, in consequence of the peremptory statement of Lord Castlereagh, made officially through the minister at Washington, that the British orders would not be repealed, without a repeal of internal measures of France which didi not violate our neutral rights. "The cause of the war lay, therefore, entirely on the British side. Had the repeal of the orders been substituted for the declaration that they would not be repealed, or had they been repealed but a few weeks sooner, our declaration of war, as proceeding from that cause, would have been stayed; and negotiations on the subject of impressment, the other great cause, would have been pursued with fresh vigor and hopes, under the auspices of success in the case of the Orders in Council."

The late President Monroe, the colleague of Mr. Pinkney in the negotiations at London in 1806, and his associate in the cabinet of Madison, placed at Mr. Wheaton's disposition the correspondence which had passed between them at the eventful period of their political connection; and, on his subsequent departure for Europe, he expressed in strong language his satisfaction at his appointment abroad, and sent to him a letter of introduction to Lord Holland, one of the English plenipotentiaries with whom those negotiations were conducted.

It was not till two years after the commencement of Mr. Adams's administration that Mr. Wheaton received, in the spring of 1827, without any previous intimation to him or his friends, an evidence of the confidence of the Federal Government, in his appointment as Charge d affaires to Denmark. The title was the one by which, at that time, all our diplomatic agents in Europe were designated, except in the few cases, limited to the principal courts, at which envoys extraordinary and ministers plenipotentiary were employed. The antecedents of Mr. Wheaton, as the cursory notice of his previous life will have shown, had fully prepared him for the service on which he was about to enter, and might, with propriety, have induced his employment in the highest rank known to our diplomacy. Those places have, however, under our government, been usually accorded to those who have been prominent in local politics, rather than as the results of special attainments; and we have laready adverted to the divisions in "The People's Party," which deprived Mr. Wheaton of the benefit of claims, derived from the distinguished part which he had, in New York, borne in the presidential election.

In going abroad, the new diplomatist was not entering on a world with whose habits and usageshe was unacquainted. Besides his early European experience, the advantage which he possessed over most of his fellow-citizens, however distinguished in other respects, in having a knowledge of the languages and literature, as well as an acquaintance with the legal and political institutions of other countries, had caused his society, at all times, to be sought by enlightened foreigners. With many of those whom the downfall of Napoleon compelled to leave France, General Lallemand, Real, St. Jean d'Angelly, General Bernard, all historical personages, he was on terms of intimacy. With the last named his acquaintance was, to the advantage of his country, renewed in Paris, where General Bernard, after many years' service in the United States, terminated his career under Louis Philippe, whose Minister of War he was.

Mr. Wheaton sailed for England, with his family, in July, 1827. Among the acquaintances which he formed in London were the philosopher of Queen Square Place and his literary executor, Dr. (now Sir John) Bowring, since conspicuous in the parliamentary history of his country and in her East Indian diplomacy, but then distinguished as well for his radical politics, as for his researches in the dialects of Europe least familiar to his countrymen, and for his contributions to English literature from the Russian, Polish, Dutch and Spanish anthologies, to which he had just added translations from the popular Servian poetry. This association of a congenial character was continued under agreeable circumstances, as his investigations of the language and literature of Finland brought Dr. Bowring to Copenhagen, while Mr. Wheaton was occupying his own leisure in the study of whatever appertained to Scandinavia or its adjacent regions. To Jeremy Bentham, whose works, despite the peculiarities of the language, contain an exhaustless mine of intellectual ore, and whose denomination of "International Law," as applicable to the subject of the accompanying treatise, our author has adopted, he was particularly attached, as the prime apostle in the cause of legal reform to which his own attention had been so recently directed. Repeatedly partaking of his hospitality, at those dinners which, never extending beyond a single guest, were literally *tete-a-tete*, and which were the sole occasions that Mr. Bentham devoted to conversation on the great topics that occupied his mind, he found him "a charming old man, less dogmatical than he expected, who criticized the specimens of the New York Revised Laws that had been sent him, in a tone of great politeness, expressing himself satisfied with what the revisors had done, as far as they had attempted to go."

Mr. Wheaton arrived at Copenhagen on 19th September, 1827, as the first regular diplomatic agent from the United States to Denmark. The only minister who had preceded him was Mr. George W. Erving, who, in 1811, was appointed on a special mission, in reference to those seizures and condemnations of American vessels and their cargoes, which constituted the particular matters now confined to him.

Count Schimmelmann, a venerable statesman, who had been for more than fifty years in the public service, was Minister of Foreign Affairs, and by him Mr. Wheaton was very graciously received. He presented him to the king and royal family, by whom he was, at all times during his eight years' residence, treated with a consideration, which attached rather to his distinguished attainments and personal character, than to the diplomatic rank with which he was invested, and which scarcely indicated his true representative character. This was the more flattering, in consequence of the nature of the reclamations which he was making, and which, as it will appear, were not all of a description to preclude discussion.

The government of Denmark was, at that time, absolute, without any restriction on the power of the monarch; but the rectitude of the king, Frederick VI., was universally admitted. He had entered on the administration as Crown Prince, in 1784. Count Schimmelmann, at their first interview, spoke of the king's paternal character; adding, "*mais il a ete tres malheureux.*" Both he and the King of Saxony, the most virtuous sovereigns in Europe, have been despoiled of their dominions. Alluding to the Court, Mr. Wheaton says; — "The king's character for *bonte* is uncontested. He enters into all the minutia of government, which, indeed, is no very hard task in a little kingdom like this. But he is any thing but *a roi faineant*. The army is his hobby. The peasantry, though no longer serfs, are subject to military duty; every farmer's son, of mature ago, being liable to serve six years. In the towns, all must serve in some corps; either the regular troops, or the burgher guard, or fire companies. In short, Denmark is Prussia in miniature. The king gives audience to *all* his subjects every Monday, when every man, woman, or child may present a memorial to him in person, or speak to him. They build a ship of the line, or one or two frigates, every year."

In writing, soon after his arrival, to the Editor, who was then in London, he says: — "I have made the acquaintance of several literary men, and have seen Professor Schlegel, among others, who, you will recollect, wrote in 1799 against Sir W. Scott's celebrated judgement in the case of the

Swedish conveoy. He appears to be a man of extensive learning in his profession. He is a judge (or rather assessor) in the High Court, and, at the same time, a professor in the University, and the head of the Law Faculty. He has written in Danish on the history of legislation. There are here some men who are unknown, if not in the rest of Europe, at least with us, that deserve to be known; and, in general, the attainments of their *savans* are much more profound in what they pretend to a knowledge of, than with us; and I suspect generally, even in England, they do not go to work so doggedly and so perseveringly."

Among his associates will be found not only the names familiar to the literary and scientific world, —Rask, Oersted, and the poet Ohlensclager, who made him the subject of some complimentary verses, —but others, whose fame less extended elsewhere, is equally eminent in their own country. The friendly communications of this period, besides those of the individuals already named, which accident has preserved, embrace letters from Munter, Bishop of Zealand, and his sisiter, Madame Frederiks Brun; whose country-seat of Fredericksdal was the resort of all the distinguished of Denmark, —of Muller, the successor of Munter, Rafn, and Magnusen.

His diplomas, as a member of the Scandinavian Society and of the Icelandic Literary Society, as the sequel fully shows, implied no mere honorary distinctions. A letter from Schlegel, dated March 15, 1830, states his election to the former association to have been on his nomination, and at an extraordinary meeting held for the purpose. He adds: — "Tous les members reconnurent votre merite et le aele avec lequel vous aveztravaille a repandre la connaissance des ouvrages Danois et de L' ancienne litterature du Nord dans les Etats-Unis d'Amerique."

The election to the Icelandic Society is communicated in a note from Rask, of the 22d of November of the same year; and it is even then placed on the ground of "his knowledge of the Northern History, his proficiency in the language, and his zeal in promoting the literature of Scandinavia."

Immediately on his arrival, he resumed those literary pursuits. Which with him were always more or less connected with the study of his favorite science, now become a professional avocation. He imparted to his countrymen, through the pages of the North American Review, the first results of his investigations in the history, mythelogy, and jurisprudence of the Scandinavian nations. The article on the Public law of Denmark, purporting to be a notice of work of Schlegel, already adverted to as being written in Danish, and which appeared in America, when he had only resident at Copenhagen for a twelvemonth, is no slight evidence of his having omitted no opportunity to prepare himself, by a knowledge of the language and institutions of the country to which he was accredited, for an efficient performance of his diplomatic functions.

In this paper not only are the institutions of Denmark—the *lex regic*, which regulated the succession to the throne, and conferred on the king the whole executive and legislative power, as well as the circumstances which went to limit the theoretical despotism of the monarchy through the *Hoiests Rett*, explained, but the political connection with the kingdom of the duchies of Schleswig, Holstein, and Lauenburg, a subject which, several years afterwards, menaced the peace of Europe, is pointed out. Into the philology of the Danish language he had so far entered at an early day, as to present, among his contributions, a notice of Professor Rask's grammar.

The Publio Law of Denmark was soon followed by an Essay on the Scandinavian Mythology, Poetry, and History, in which the sources of the materials, for the early history of the Gothic or Teutonic kingdoms of Norway, Sweden, and Denmark, are indicated. These articles, with the subsequent ones, in reference to the ancient laws of Iceland and the Anglo-Saxon language and literature, with a glance at the antiquities of a widely different region and people, disclosed to the world in the unravelling of the Egyptian hieroglyphics, through the discoveries of Champollion, and on which his friend, Professor Rask, had aided in throwing light, formed the suitable preludes to the classic work which, under the title of the "History of the Northmen, from the Earliest Times to the Conquest of England by William of Normandy," appeared in London and Philadelphia, in 1831. It was, on its publication, noticed with the highest commendation in the principal periodicals of Europe and America. The review of it in the North American is from the pen of Washington Irving.

This book at once took a place among the standard works of the language, and after being enriched by the further investigations of Mr. Wheaton, for which the publication in Denmark of the Icelandic Sagas and the labors of Magnusen afforded new materials, it was introduced, in 1844, though the translation of M. Guillot, to continental readers. This edition, which received the particular notice of the French Academy, and which Mr. Wheaton, at the time of this death, was preparing for publication in English, was rendered specially interesting to the scholars of the United States, by the new light which it sheds on the Scandinavian discoveries in America, the authenticity of which it establishes.

In noticing the French edition, M. de la Nourais remarks: — "Mr. Wheaton is not only an historian, but in his Scandinavian researches he did no lose signt of the main avocation of his life, public law. It is as a publicist that he has investigated, interpreted, and almost always with a rare sagacity, the ancient monuments of the Scandinavian law; at the side of historical events he has known how to place the legislation of the people whose annals he recounts. It is principally in this point of view that we consider the work of Mr. Wheaton within the scope of our labors. He makes known the laws and judicial customs of the people of whom he has rendered himself the historian."

An English contemporaneous notice says: — "Among the forest of those who, in our own days, have furnished important contributions to our stock of Scandinavian literature, stands the name of Dr. Wheaton, a gentleman no less distinguished as a lawyer and statesman than for his historical and antiquarian attainments. The 'Histoire des Peuples du Nord' is less a translation than a new edition of his 'History of the Northmen;' it has been made under the eye of the author, and enriched by him with many notes and illustrations, and with an entirely by him with many notes and illustrations, and with an entirely new chapter, carrying on the History of the Northmen to the extinction of the Norman dynasty in the south of Italy."

Baron Humboldt, the philosopher and traveller, to whom we shall hereafter have occasion to refer as the personal friend and intimate associate of the King of Prussia, as well as of our author, wrote to the translator: — "'L' Histoire des Peuples du Nord' est devenue, grace aux importances additions de l'auteur, comme grace a vos soins et a votre penetration, un ouvrage bien different de celui qui deja, dans sa forme primitive, avait obtenu le succes le plus merite. C'est un spectacle digne du philosophe, que cette civilisation refugiee, abritee, noblement agrandie dans un reduit du monde polaire, —set asoect d'une colonie insulaire etendue sur un continent voisin, si differen parsa nature et des colonies Helleniques et de celles qui se rattachent aux besoins un peu prosaiqyes des siecles industriels. Jemets un double prix au don que vous avez daigne me faire, Monsieur, a l'interet qu'inspirent des recherches, dont vous avez expose la valeur dans la preface de l'ouvrage avec autant de gout que de sagacite, ou l'importance historique se joint a la haute estime que dans ce pays on professe a la cour et dans les cercles litteraires, pour l'habile et vertueux diplomate que je suis fier de compter parmi mes amis les plus intimes. Citoyen de l'Amerique tropicale je peux m'enorgueillir de l'amitie d'un grand citeyen des Etats-Unis. Cette profession de foi est permise sur la colline tres monarchique et tres historique que j'habite." And at the same time, ina note to Mr. Wheaton, he said: — "Votre excellent ouvrage historique, augments de votre 'Scandinavie,' aura aupres du Roi tout l'attrait et le succes de la nouveaute. Je desire vivement que le roi offer au traducteur son image dans la grande medaille d'or destinee aux travaux meritoires dans les sciences et les arts."

Further fruits of his historical studies at Copenhagen also appeared after he had quitted Denmark. The History of Scandinavia was published in 1838, in connection with Dr. Crichton. It contains what was intended by him as a sequel to the History of the Northmen, bringing down the history of Denmark and Norway from the extinction of the Anglo-Danish dynasty, in 1402, to the Revolution of 1660, including the affairs of Sweden, under the union of Colmar. It is proper to add, that, for the other portions of the work, Mr. Wheaton, the extent of whose contributions are pointed out in the Preface, is in no wise responsible. And so late as 1844, there was an essay from his pen in the Review of French and Foreign Law, at Paris, of which he was a regular contributor, on the ancient legislation of Iceland.

Nor was it to these subjects, in addition to the preparation of the works more strictly connected with his public pursuits, and which were not completed till his transfer to another mission, that the leisure which the intervals of business afforded was exclusively applied.

Mr. Wheaton had scarcely been established at at Corpenhagen, before he directed his attention to arevision of the Life of Pinkney, a new edition of which was published in Sparks's American Biography. The American Quarterly, at Philadephia, to which he sent, in October, 1828, an Essay on Scandinavia Literature, and a review of Depping's History of the Normans, as well as the European journals, participated with the North American ib his contributions to the periodical press. Among other papers, an Essay on the Danish Constitution was, in 1833, inserted in the Foreign Quarterly Review.

The special subject confided to Mr. Wheaton was the obtaining of an indemnity for the alleged spoliations on our commerce by Denmark, during the latter years of the European war. At peace with all the world for eighty years, except a slight difficulty with Sweden; one of the parties to the convention of 1789 for the maintenance of the armed neutrality; and placed geographically at a distance from the contending belligerents, the participation of Denmark, in the hostilities growing out of the French Revolution, was, on her part, no voluntary act. Indeed, she had been, at the commencement of these wars, a common sufferer with the United States and other neutral powers, from the aggressions of the respective belligerents. The unprovoked violation of the law of nations, by Great Britain towards Denmark, in 1800 and 1807, by the bombardment of her capital and the seizure of her fleet in times of peace, when the only crime that could be alleged against her was the maintenance of an impartial neutrality, constitute two of the most wanton acts of flagrant injury, inflicted by a stronger on a weaker power, to be found in the annals of history.

Compelled by her conduct to assume the offensive towards England, and deprived, in a great measure, of her national marine, Denmark had recourse, mainly through private armed vessels to reprisals against the commerce of her enemy; and though the Berlin and Milan decrees and other edicts of Napoleon were never formally adopted, yet the execution of the instructions against British commerce, between 1807 and 1811, led to the seizure and condemnation of numerous American vessels. In the latter year, a special mission was intrusted to Mr. George W. Erving, who was measurably successful in arresting further condemnation. As regards past transactions, the effort was without avail, but an intimation was given that when the maritime war was terminated, the subject might be resumed. To prevent those matters passing into oblivion, on two occasions, —in 1818 and 1825, the attention of the Danish government was called to the cases, and in exchanging, in 1826, the ratification of the commercial treaty, a note was addressed by the Secretary of State to the Danish Minister, to preclude all idea of indemnity being abandoned by the United States.

The reclamations were respectfully entertained, though at first met by a plea of poverty. Writing to the Secretary of State, November 20, 1827, Mr. Wheaton says: — "You can hardly have an adequate notion how this country was impoverished by the war brought upon it by the unjust aggressions of England, and followed by the dismemberment of the kingdom, at the peace. If they had remained neutral, their commerce and navigation must have sensibly declined at the latter epoch. But when we consider that they lost, at a single blow, their navigation and all their capital engaged in commerce; that they made immense pecuniary sacrifices to the faithful observance of their alliance with France; that the kingdom, with its diminished territory, population, and resources, is now staggering under a debt of upwards of fifty millions of dollars, we cannot wonder at their reluctance to enter into new engagements. They have no means of replacing the capital thus lost. France, after repeated evasions, has, at last, peremptorily refused to repay them a debt of the most sacred character, being for supplies furnished the French troops, beyond the stipulations of the alliance. This is their condition, although the king ia a man of very simple habits, and observes the most praiseworthy economy in his household, and in other respects, except the army, which has been his hobby from his youth. But the former condition of the kingdom has entailed upon him a numerous pension list, and the burden of supporting establishments quite disproportionate to its diminished resources."

Partial indemnity, satisfactory to the claimants, for a class of the cases, was accorded at the close of 1827, and within two months of Mr. Wheaton's arrival. In January, 1829, the Minister of Justice, M. de Stemann, was united with Count Schimmelmann, to discuss with the American Plenipotentiary the means of an amicable adjustment of all the matters in controversy. This measure had been preceded by a declaration of the king's desire "to use every means to reduce the losses to which some American citizens had been subjected, by negecting, without an intention on their part, those forms which would have served to protect their navigation and their strictly neutral transactions," and by putting Mr. Wheaton in possession of the register of sentences, with the grounds on which they were supported by the competent tribunals, from the year 1807 to 1812.

The appointment of the Danish Plenipotentiaries was made on the eve of the termination of the administration of President Adams; but, fortunately for the country, President Jackson, who was inaugurated in the following

March, "did not," to use the language of an experienced senator, in reference to this transaction, "change the negotiator—didi not substitute a raw for an experienced minister."

Mr. Wheaton was met, as Mr. Erving had been at the outset, with the pretension, that the final decrees of the highest tribunal could not be reexamined, and that it would be a reflection on their character to suppose that they were not in conformity with the law of nations. It was no difficult task to show, that though the decrees were conclusive *in rem*, as regards the title of the property and as respects the sublects of Denmark, they could not be deemed so as between nations; but that, on the contrary, the right of a foreign government to demand redress against an illegal capture only arose after the failure to obtain justice, in the ordinary course, from the courts.

The alleged grounds, on which the American vessels had been condemned, were, principally: 1. For having simulated papers; 2. For having French consular certificates, which the Danish government had been informed by that of France could only have been issued to vessels going direct to that country; and, S. For being found under English convoy.

1. So far as respects simulated papers, it was a question of fact in each individual case, and involved no discussion of principles.

2. On the second point, besides the answer that a French consular certificate was a document not known to the law of nations, and which American vessels, certainly so far as regards Denmark, were not required to have, it was satisfactorily proved that the instructions to the French consuls to confine them exclusively to vessels going directly to France, was not received in America till after the date of the sailing of the vessels in question.

3. The sailing under English convoy presented a subject of consideration noy so readily to be disposed of. And Mr. Wheaton, in giving, in the appropriate place in this work, the substance of the argument, by which he succeeded in accomplishing the object of his instructions, does not affirm as a principle, but presents as a proposition to be discussed, the liability to cap-

ture of neutral vessels sailing under enemy's convoy. He had, indeed, himself, as counsel in the Supreme Court of the United States, contended, in 1821, as appeared in his Reports, that sailing under enemy's convoy was cause for the condemnation both of vessel and cargo; and he had, then, referred to the correspondence with the Danish government by Mr. Erving, who, he said, admits the extreme difficulty of upholding the contrary doctrine, and only seeks to escape from it by contending that the rule could not be extended to vessels forced into convoy, or accidentally involved in the enemy's fleet. "And this," he adds, "may be readily admitted, without at all weakening the general rule."

It was denied by the Denes, that our claims came within the exceptional cases. On the contrary, they contended that: "the convoy was a matter of preconcert; that the American vessels being employed to procure naval stored from Russia, for the use of England, they first submitted to an examination before they were received under convoy, declined to submit to search by the other belligerent, and were defended by the convoy if of superior force, or endeavored to escape during the contest. If worsted, they still claimed their neutrality."

The naked question, of the effect of sailing under enemy's convoy, has never been passed on in the United States' Courts, except so far as it may be supposed to be involved in the decisions respecting the liability to capture of neutral property, on board of an armed vessel of the enemy, as to which, as we have seen, there were conflicting decisions in the British and American Admiralty Courts. But, it is proper to notice, that in his dissenting opinion, in the case of The Nereide, Judge Story lays down in strong language the liability to capture of all vessels under enemy's convoy, and supports himself by a decision of the Lords of Appeal in England; while in the case of The Atalanta, in which the previous decision, allowing neutral goods to be shipped on board of an armed vessel of the enemy, is affirmed, Judge Johnson distinguishes between such a case and that of sailing under enemy's convoy.

The settlement of the claims, by a gross sum to be distributed by the American government itself, precluded any further investigation of the facts by a tribunal, whose authority was recognized by both parties; but it is understood that thoseconvoy cases, which were admitted by the American Commissioners, were proved to have fallen within the exceptional classes, as stated by Mr. Erving, and that their being under British protection was the result of superior force. While the success of Mr. Wheaton, unaided by any hostile menaces, is enhanced by the doubt which attached to a portion of the reclamations, the general result affords the highest proof of the zeal and ability with which his functions were discharged. Indeed, it is only due to the truth of history to record, that without a minister, holding towards the king and the members of the Danish government the relations which Mr. Wheaton maintained, there would never have been an opportunity for those free discussions, to which, and not to any formal conferences, the fortunate termination of the business is to be ascribed. Such is the testimony borne by the agent, who represented the principal claimants, and on that account visited Copenhagen. Count Schimmelmann repeatedly told him, that he considered that "the American government had paid them quite a compliment, in sending them such a representative as Mr. Wheaton." And of the position which he occupied there, as well as of the friendly form which the negotiations assumed, no better proof can be given than is furnished by the following note, taken from among those from the Danish Minister of Foreign Affairs, which their daily intercourse induced: — "Je suis desole, Monsieur, que votre indisposition me prove aujourd'hui de l' avantage de vous voir; ce n' etoit pas des communications officielles que j' etois charge de vous faire, mais je voulois aviser avec vous, Monsieur, sur le meilleur moyen de pouvoir les faire sans retard, et avec l' espoir d'un favorable resultat. J' ai averti le ministre, M. de Stemann, de ce qu' une indisposition vous empeche de sortir, et ce ministre est intentionne de se rendre aujourd'hui chez vous, pour pouvoir vous ebtretenir sur l' objet en question."

Afurther evidence of this view of the case is to be found in the declarations of subsequent text-writers. Mr. Manning, one of the most recent of them among the English, in commenting on this negotiation, considers that the Danish instructions, under which the captures were made, were justified. Ortolan, friendly as he is to neutrals, declares that, apart from the circumstances which occasioned the complete success of the American negotiator, it cannot be said that fact of a neutral vessel sailing under the convoy of a belligerent is not an irregular and illegal act; and Hautefeuille notices the remarkable character of the transaction which, while it accords an indemnity, stipulates that the Convention, it having no other object than to terminate all claims, "can never hereafter be invoked by one party or the other, as a precedent or rule for the future."

The Treaty of Indemnity was signed on the 28th of March, 1830. By it, including what was paid in 1827-8, on account of the seizure, in 1810, of certain vessels at Kiel, (on the cargoes of which, though they were liberated, a duty in kind of fifity per cent. Was imposed during the pendency of the proceedings,) and the renunciation of claims against the United States, about three quarters of a million of dollars were secured for our merchants. This was one fifth more than the American Minister was instructed to insist on. But, what was infinitely more important, Mr. Wheaton's treaty was the pioneer of the conventions with France and Napoles. From those treaties millions were obtained for our citizens, and our right to redress was established for violations of neutral commerce, whose sole palliation was the illegal acts of the opposing belligerents. And, in these last cases, it was also shown that, as long as a nation maintains the forms of external sovereignty, neither a change in the reigning dynasty, nor the plea of the preponderating influence of a powerful ally, can relieve it from its accountability to foreign States.

Besides calling the attention of his government, at an early period of his residence, to the duties imposed by Denmark on the vessels of all countries, in passing the Sound and Belts, Mr. Wheaton was, in other respects, able to make his remote mission beneficial to American commerce. He was successful in obtaining some modifications of the quarantine regulations on vessels from America, which were in 1831-2, more strictly enforced on account of the cholera, and as to which the decision of Denmark was particularly important, in consequence of her acting as the sanitary police for the several Baltic States. In this matter he was enabled, through his personal relations with him, to obtain the efficient cooperation of the Russian Minister at Copenhagen, Baron Nicolay.

In 1830, the Governor-General of the Danish Islands, Von Scholten, was deputed on a special mission to Washington, with a view to the arrangement of a treaty, as respected the trade between those colonies and the United States, to be based on a mutual reduction of duties. Mr. Wheaton's efforts were exerted to promote the objects of the mission, advantageous alike to the country which he represented and to that to which he was accredited. With a view to the adjustment of such propositions as were likely to be acceptable, many preliminary conferences as were, by the invitation of the Danish Minister of Foreign Affairs, held by him with Governor Von Scholten.

Of the matters in Europe intersting to the United States, whether connected or not with his own legation, he was an attentive observer; and his suggestions, as well to his colleagues as to his government, were, at all times, valuable. The subject of our trade with the West Indies, which, on his entering on his duties, was a leading topic of discussion between us and Great Britain, has, by the recognition of the most liberal principles by that power in relation to her colonies, ceased to have the interest of a pending controversy. But it is, even at this day, worthy of notice that the Danish government, though urged by the British to accept the terms of the Act of Parliament of 1825, the noncompliance with which led to the temporary interruption of our intercourse with the West India Islands, declined to do so. The conditions proposed to powers having colonial possessions were much more favorable than those offered to the United States. It was only required of them, in order to participate in that trade, that they should grant to British ships the like privileges of trading with their colonies, as were granted to their ships of trading with the British possessions abroad; whereas it was made a condition that we, as having no colonies, should place the commerce and navigation of Great Britain, and of her possessions abroad, upon the footing of the most favored nation. The Danish government, nevertheless, refused the proposition, not knowing what might be the consequence of giving to the English the direct trade to Europe in their colonial produce, and fearing that such an absolute reciprocity might be very injurious to their navigation.

It is satisfactory to learn, that the common sentiment of Europe approved of the decision of President Jackson, in treating as null the recommendation of the King of the Netherlands, which he had substituted for an award, in reference to the Northeastern Boundary line. The despatch of the Danish Minister at that court, which announced the royal decision, and which is stated to have surprised every one there, was sent to Mr. Wheaton for perusal by Count Schimmelmann. The Danish Envoy expresses the opinion, as being that generally entertained at the Hague, that Mr. Preble's protest was suited to the occasion, and quite temperate and dignified.

Though our claims were then still subjects of discussion, on the occasion of the selection of an arbiter, in conformity to the Convention of 1827, the King of Denmark was, after our first choice the Emperor Nicholas, the sovereign to whom the United States desired, in preference to all others, to submit the controversy. Nor can it be doubted that the knowledge possessed at Washington of the superior fitness of the Minister at Copenhagen, to conduct the reference on our part, was among the motives for placing Denmark second on the list.

In the instructions, given on that occasion, it is said: — "If the late Emperor of Russia was still living and on the throne, there would have been a great repugnance against a second application to him, to act as arbitrator between the parties, after he had once assumed the trouble of officiating in that character. But that objection does not apply to the Emperor Nicholas, who may possibly regard as a compliment the manifestation of the same high confidence in him which was entertained for his illustrious brother. It is probable, therefore, that he may accept the office. No well-grounded objection, on the part of Great Britain, can be anticipated. If, as now appears to us, at this distance to be highly probable from recent information, hostilities have been commenced with Turkey, the fact of Great Britain and Russia being allies, in the prosecution of that war, might render somewhat doubtful the expediency of our agreeing to the choice of the Emperor Nicholas as an arbiter. But, whilst that fact ought to prevent any objection to him on the part of Great Britain, it does not shake the confidence which the President would have in the impartiality and uprightness of his decision, if he should consent to serve." And in a subsequent despatch, in answer to one from the American Charge d'Affaires at London, stating objections, which subsequent events fully sustained, to the KIng of the Netherlands, on account of the comparatively dependent relation in which he stood to England, even before the division of the kingdom, and asking permission to substitute the King of Prussia as our third choice, the Secretary says: — "We are very desirous to learn whether you have come to an agreement for the designation of a sovereign arbitrator, I have nothing to add to former instructions on that subject. It is most desirable that the Emperor of Russia shall be agreed upon. And the King of Denmark would be our second choice. The President weighed all the considerations you have suggested, respecting the King of the Netherlands. They did not seem to him to overrule the confidence which he has in the intelligence and personal character of that monarch. As to the King of Prussia, the circumstance of our having no representative near him, was not without its influence on the omission of his name."

In May, 1830, Mr. Wheaton visited Paris with his family, passing through the Hague, where he attended the deliberations of the States-General. He was very kindly received by the Minister of Foreign Affairs, the Baron

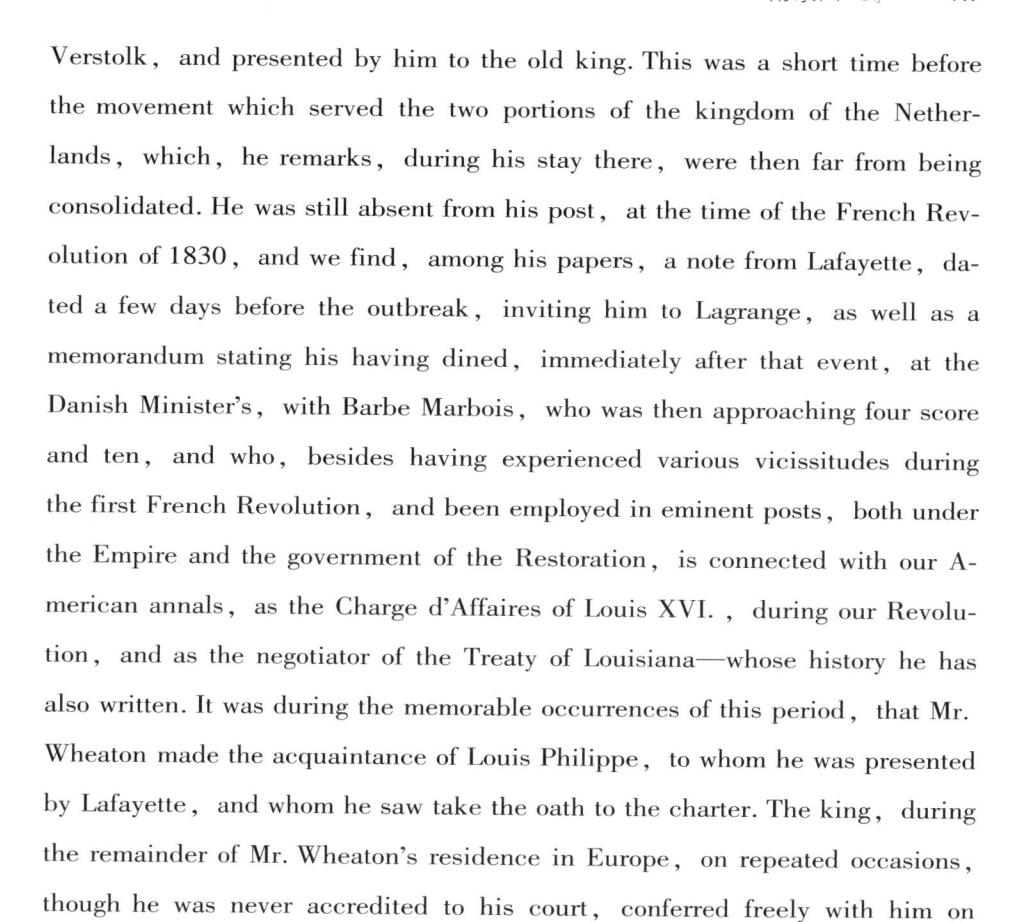

Verstolk, and presented by him to the old king. This was a short time before the movement which served the two portions of the kingdom of the Netherlands, which, he remarks, during his stay there, were then far from being consolidated. He was still absent from his post, at the time of the French Revolution of 1830, and we find, among his papers, a note from Lafayette, dated a few days before the outbreak, inviting him to Lagrange, as well as a memorandum stating his having dined, immediately after that event, at the Danish Minister's, with Barbe Marbois, who was then approaching four score and ten, and who, besides having experienced various vicissitudes during the first French Revolution, and been employed in eminent posts, both under the Empire and the government of the Restoration, is connected with our American annals, as the Charge d'Affaires of Louis XVI., during our Revolution, and as the negotiator of the Treaty of Louisiana—whose history he has also written. It was during the memorable occurrences of this period, that Mr. Wheaton made the acquaintance of Louis Philippe, to whom he was presented by Lafayette, and whom he saw take the oath to the charter. The king, during the remainder of Mr. Wheaton's residence in Europe, on repeated occasions, though he was never accredited to his court, conferred freely with him on matters of state and government. With Guizot, Thiers, and the ther distinguished men of the Orleans dynasty, who added the official rank of ministers to the highest eminence in the literary world, he was, by congeniality of pursuits, brought into association. With the Duke de Broglie he was on terms of the most friendly intercourse, as he was,, also, with the historian Mignet, the Perpetual Secretary of the Institute for the Class of Moral and Political Sciences, and with most of the other celebrities, whose society contributes so much to the intellectual attractions of the French metropolis.

In 1831, Mr. Wheaton visited London by direction of his government, in reference to matters connected with the Danish indemnity. While in England, he not only availed himself of the opportunity of making the acquaintance of the Ministers of State and other public men, as well as of the diplomatic corps, to many of whom he was already known, but he was, at once, recognized as a member of their own fraternity by the most eminent in literature and law.

Among the statesmen by whom he was particularly distinguished on this and the other occasions of his visiting the British capital, were Lord Aberdeen, Lord John Russell, Sir Robert Peel, and Lord Palmerston, and especially the Marquis of Lansdowne. With Sir James Mackintosh, whose judicial independence, when presiding in the Vice-Admiralty Court of a distant possession, contrasted so favorably with the ministerial subserviency of Sir William Scott, and who, in so many way was a congenial spirit, he was well acquainted.

Senior, who, by his able paper in the Edinburgh Review, afterwards contributed to place his merits, as a publicist, properly before the world, was one with whom he was on terms of intimate association, as he was also with Palgrave, Hallam, Hayward, Mr. and Mrs. Austin, and others of like fame. It was at this period that the History of the Northmen was published, and the consideration which its author enjoyed in the literary circles of the metropolis, is the best test of its appreciation. He was, likewise, as a learned juriconsult, requested to furnish answers to the queries of the common-law commission then in session, and who were occupied with the same investigations to which his own attention, as a commissioner at New York, had been directed.

In the autumn of 1833, Mr. Wheaton visited the United States. At New York, he was invited, by a committee of the most influential citizens, at the head of which was the mayor of the city, as "a mark of their respect for his successful efforts, as a scholar and diplomatist, to sustain the reputation and interests of the country abroad," to partake of a public dinner.

He was also requested by "The New York Law Institute," an association composed of his old professional brethren and of those who had, during his absence, been called to the bar, to pronounce a discourse before them, at their anniversary, in May, 1834. Engagements, at Washington, prevented the delivery of the address, which was, however, prepared and subsequently published. The subject selected, as furnishing some of the fruits of his studies abroad, was the progress of the science of law in Europe, since the independence of the United States. After tracing what had been previously done on the continent, and giving a rapid analysis of the great quarrel in Germany, between the historical and philosophical schools, on occasion of the introduction, into the conquered countries, of the French codes, he concludes by awarding to Bentham the title of the greatest legal reformer of modern times.

The principal object of Mr. Wheaton's visit was the prosecution of a suit, which had reached the court of ultimate resort, against his successor in the office of Reporter of the Supreme Court of the United States, who, by the publication of an abridged edition of his Reports, threatened to deprive him of the fruits of twelve years of arduous labor, on which—in accepting an appointment abroad, the compensation of which, it was well understood, would scarcely suffice for his current expenditure—he had relied as a future provision for himself and family. It is seldom that among literary men questions arise rendering necessary a reference to the technical provisions of the copyright act, and among publishers, even in case for which the law does not provide, there is a respect generally paid to priority of possession. It was reserved for a counsellor at law, vested with the confidence of the highest tribunal of the country, in the absence, in a foreign land, of a professional brother, to whose voluntary resignation he owed his place, to disregard all these honorable obligations.

The legal points involved will befound discussed in Peters's Reports. The Court decided that there was no copyright by the common law in Pennsylvania, where the publication was alleged to have been made, especially since Congress had acted on the subject under the Constitution, and that the opinion of the Judges, as published by the Reporter of the Court, were not susceptible of being made private property; and, entertaining doubts, whether there had been a strict compliance with the requisitions of the statute, they remanded the case to the Circuit Court to ascertain the facts. The decision, however, of a majority of the Judges, on the points of law, by reducing the claim of Mr. Wheaton merely to a copyright in the marginal notes and arguments of counsel, and making all indemnity, even on account of them, dependent on affirmative proof of the technical performance of certain specified requirements, of which the public offices in those days sffored but imperfect means of furnishing the evidence, was a most severe blow to our author. The unsatisfactory result of the suit was, moreover, aggravated by the circumstance that this controversy led to the severance, for ever, of those friendly ties which had so long existed between him and Judge Story.

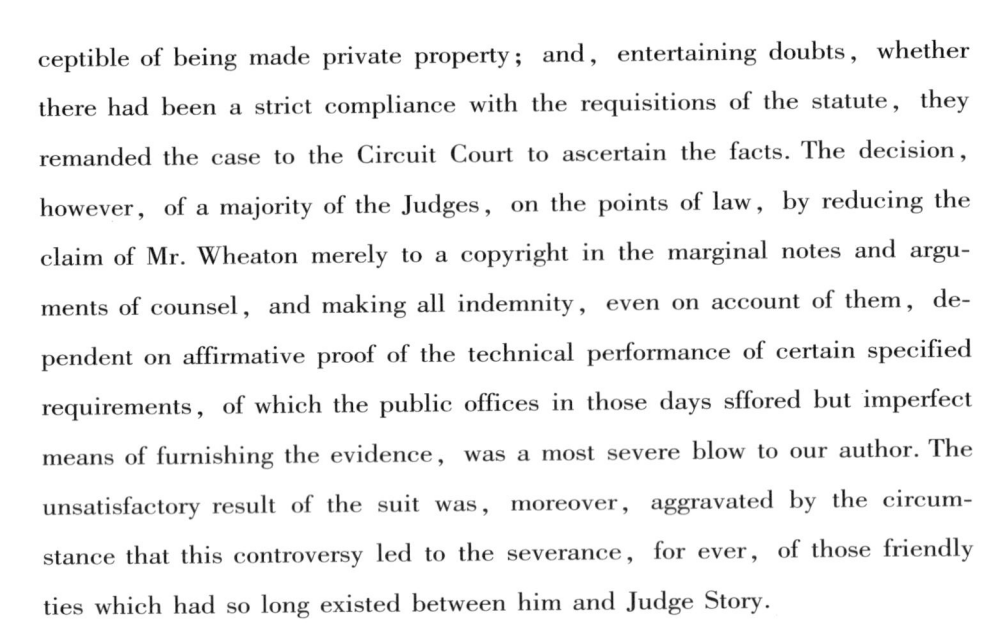

Mr. Wheaton returned, in August, 1834, to Copenhagen, and he refers, in a despatch of the 29th of November, to the accession, by Denmark, to the treaties of 1831 and 1833, between England and France, for the suppression of the slave-trade. He also states, that instructions had been given to the Governor-General to ameliorate the condition of the slaves in the West Indies; that any slave should be permitted to buy his freedom, whenever he was able to do so from the fruits of his labor, during the intervals allowed him for that purpose; and that any slave, who was discontented with his master, and could find a purchaser who was willing to buy him, might, in that way, change his master.

Though Mr. Wheaton's residence at Copenhagen was not at a capital where the earliest intelligence could be commanded; yet as the European governments are in the habit of furnishing their agents abroad, from time to time, with an analysis of the reports which they require to be made to them from all their legations, together with their own views of the pending occurrences, probably nowhere could he have had a better opportunity than at one of the northern courts, removed from the influence of the immediate actors, of studying the politics of the world, and of forming a sound judgment respecting the future course of international relations. The correspondence of Mr. Wheaton during the twenty years of his foreign residence, pointing out, as it does, the causes of events which are yet, in many cases, cabinet secrets, would afford historical annals inferior in interest to no contemporaneous memoirs. A large portion of it for the first part of his Danish mission, was addressed, in the form of private or confidential communications, to the President and Secretary of State. So early as December, 1827, he appreciated the true position of Turkey, when, after the battle of Navarino, he writes: "I think we have only, as yet, the opening scene of a great drama, which is to be enacted in the Eastern world; and how the *denouement* is to brought about without a partition of the Ottoman Empire, I am at a loss to conjecture."

In a private letter to President J. Q. Adams, soon afterwards, (January 5, 1828,) he says: "Mr. Middleton has doubtless sent you a copy of the Russian circular, written after the battle of Navarino, in which the views of that court as to the affairs of the East are developed, That paper certainly looks to the probability of his Imperial Majesty being compelled (however reluctantly) to occupy the principalities of Moldavia and Wallachia, if not to advance further on the road to 'Byzantium.' But the evident interest of the other European States to oppose the territorial aggrandizement of Russia, and to support the support the tottering fabric of the Turkish power, induces a strong belief that some means will yet be found to induce the Porte to listen to the remonstrance of its 'friends.' If the Christian powers had acknowledged the independence of the Greeks three years ago, and labored in good faith to consolidate a real Grecian State to take the place of the Ottoman Empire in the balance of power, they would have adopted a much more sensible course than this their tardy interference, which will probably redound to the advantage of Russia only. But such a course would not have suited the views of Prince Metternich or of Mr. Canning, the latter dreading the creation of a new maritime power, which might rival that of England in the Mediterranean, as much as the former feared the example of successful resistance to oppression and the approximation of the Russian Colossus. "

The circumstances, also, which were leading to a change in the internal constitution of Denmark, in accordance with the promises made at the period of the Congress of Vienna, but which only began to be redeemed in Mr. Wheaton's time, as well as the commencement of the difficulties in the Duchies, which afterwards menaced such fatal consequences to the integrity of the Danish States, are fully appreciated and explained.

At the early date of this letter to the President, he thus adverts to the sentiments of the people on that subject:— "In the *kingdom*, the natural desire of constitutional securities, now felt by every civilized people, is cheeked by the personal good character of the reigning sovereign and the mildness of his administration. In the Duchy of *Holstein* (which you will recollect forms a part of the Germanic Confederation,) there was, four or five years ago, a movement towards innovation, or rather towards a restoration of the former order of things in that country; the prelates and nobles having demanded the convocation of their ancient States. The king, not having complied with their demand, they made application to the Diet at Frankfort; but that body advised them to wait patiently for the constitution which his Majeasty was preparing for them. Nothing has been heard of it since, and the *people* take the less interest in it because they consider it merely a selfish attempt on the part of the privileged orders to secure their feudal immunities, which are still very considerable. In conversation with a resident of the Duchy, on this subject, he observed that they might have a constitution of States if they would— 'mais quel besoin des Etats, quand nous avons un si bon roi?' "

In his correspondence with President Adams, who himself united in a remarkable degree thepuesuit of science and the cultivation of letters with his public duties, he entered into ample details of what the Danish government, notwithstanding its pecuniary embarrassments, was effecting for the advancement of knowledge in that remote corner of the globe. He described the steps taking for the *cadastre* or grand survey of the kingdom, the geometrical part of which, so far as related to Holstein, was under the direction of the celebrated astronomer, Schumacher.

During the whole period of his mission to Denmark, the United States, were not represented in Austria, Prussia, or any other part of Germany. As a resident at the court of a sovereign who, on account of Holstein, was a member of the Germanic Confederation, his attention was necessarily drawn to that important portion of Europe. His despatches not only speak of the political concerns of the Confederation and of the action of the Diet, but he gives us the origin of that commercial league, with which his subsequent career was, for so many years, connected.

Before leaving Denmark, on his visit to the United States, he had received from his Prussian colleague at that court, Count Raczynski, (to whom, as the historian of the Arts in Germany, we shall, in the sequel, have occasion to refer,) a communication, which his government had directed him to deliver to the American Charge d'Affaires, with a view to its transmission to Washington. It expressed a desire for the restoration of diplomatic intercourse between the United States and Prussia, as well as intimated a wish that Mr. Wheaton, whose reputation was already established there, should be sent to Berlin. This appointment was, however, not made till the spring of 1835, when he was commissioned as Charge d'Affaires to Prussia, by President Jackson.

A year before Mr. Wheaton's transfer, Mr. Buchanan, subsequently Secretary of State under President Polk, at the request of President Jackson, expressed to him his views of the proposed nomination. The following is an extract from his letter: "During my residence in St. Petersburg I had frequent opportunities of learning the character and standing of Mr. Wheaton at Copenhagen, and it is but justice to say, that they were such as to make a decided impression in favor both of himself and his country. Baron Nicolay, the Russian Minister at that court, told me there was no member of the diplomatic corps who stood higher in public esteem. His character as an author is, I am inclined to believe, more justly appreciated abroad than at home, and would be the best introduction he could have at Berlin. Besides, he is well acquainted with German literature, and speaks the German language—two great recommendations among a people so proud of their origin as the Germans."

There had been no American Minister at Berlin since John Quincy Adams, whose nomination was made in 1797. An appointment was now proper, not only as a matter of reciprocal courtesy, but the increased political importance of Prussia, and more especially the controlling influence which she exercised over the commercial interests of a great part of Germany through the Zollverein, required that the United States should omit no suitable opportunity of cultivating with her relations of mutual interest.

Mr. Wheaton arrived in Berlin, in June, 1835. The Minister of Foreign Affairs, Mr. Ancillon, at their first interview, requested him to suggest by what means our commercial connections with them might be extended. The articles of the Germanic Confederation, as established by the Congress of Vienna, in 1815, contemplated the regulation, by the Diet, of commercial intercourse among the States, as well as the free navigation of the great rivers; but nothing was ever done towards effecting the former object. The customhouse barriers had, however, been broken down between the individual States, by means of Customs' Unions, of which there existed at the time of Mr. Wheaton's arrival two, the Zollverein, at the head of which Prussia was, and which embraced most of the States of Germany, except the Austrian dominions, the Hanseatic Towns, the duchies of Holstein and Lauenburg, (belonging to the King of Denmark) Mecklenburg, Oldenburg, the kingdom of Hanover, and the duchy of Brunswick, which two last formed, in 1834, a separate commercial league, called the Stuerverein, with which, soon after, Oldenburg was united. AS the principles, on which theses associations were established, were a uniform tariff, the duties from which were to be collected by the frontier States, and divided among the different members according to their population, it was with the leagues rather than their individual members that negotiations were to be conducted. They were represented, so far as respected diplomatic discussions with foreign nations, by Prussia and Hanover respectively; and Mr. Ancillon early intimated his desire to the American Minister, that he should not attempt to approach the Zollverein with any overtures for commercial negotiations, except through Prussia, its founder and natural head.

By his original instructions from the Secretary of State, Mr. Forsyth, his attention was specially directed to an establishment of commercial relations with Germany, found on the new order of things, and also to the removal— for which the connections of many of the States with Prussia, through the Zollverein, would afford facilities—of the obstructions imposed on emigration by the existence of the droit d'aubaine et droit de detraction.

Soon after Mr. Wheaton's arrival, he availed himself of the suspension of diplomatic business to make, in July and August, a tour through a portion of Germany. Proceeding by the way of Lubeck, Hamburg, and Hanover, to the Prussian provinces of Westphalia and of the Rhine, he collected a good deal of useful information respecting the commercial and other resources of those provinces, and of the intermediate States, as well as of Nassau, Hesse-Darmstadt, and Baden. He was furnished by Mr. Ancillon with introductions to the local authorities, who afforded him every facility for the prosecution of his inquiries. On his return to Berlin, Mr. Whaeton suggested to the American government separate negotiations with Prussia and her league, and with Hanover and her associated States; and he was in consequence instructed to inquire whether Prussia and the other German States upon their mutual commercial relations, with a view to an arrangement consistent with the great leading principles upon which our intercourse with foreign and additional stipulations as the peculiar nature of the commercial union might render necessary.

Before any serious step was taken in the course of these negotiations, Mr. Wheaton was promoted, by President Van Buren, to the rank of Envoy

Extraordinary and Minister Plenipotentiary. And contrasted as it it was with the ordinary practice in such cases, to which we have alluded, and which afterwards governed his recall, it is here proper to refer to the magnanimity of the President in making this appointment, as well as to the obligations which the United States are under to Mr. Wheaton's old friend and associate, Benjamin F. Butler, a member of the Cabinet of Jackson, and always a confidential adviser of Van Buren, for his aid in securing to the country the continued services of our distinguished diplomatist.

It was, at the close of the session, immediately precedingthe inauguration of President Van Buren, that an appropriation was made for the outfit and salary of a full minister to Prussia, instead of the salary of a charge d'affaires, thereby rendering a new nomination for Berlin necessary. Mr. Wheaton had been, as we have seen, the pioneer in obtaining, under very peculiar circumstances, indemnity for reclamations from foreign States; and his treaty had been followed by eminent success in other negotiations. With his qualifications as a minister Mr. Van Buren had had the means of being well acquainted, both as Secretary of State and while his colleague abroad, and in London he had had full opportunity to know the advantage which our country derived from his literary character and special attainments in the profession of diplomacy. On the other hand, not only were there, as usual, on the accession of a new President, many individuals, having pretensions from local influence and partizan exertions, who, not supposing a knowledge of public law or of the language and usage of diplomacy a necessary qualification on the part of those who are entrusted with our international inter course claimed all the patronage at the command of the Executive; but Mr. Van Buren had been the acknowledged leader in New York of that party which, in the contest of 1824, Mr. Wheaton had been so instrumental in the contest of 1824, Mr. Wheaton had been so instrumental in defeating. It so happened, however, that the "Elements of International law" had just been published, and though the work had not then acquired the celebrity which it now commands, it had attracted the attention of the Attorney-General, with whose peculiar duties the subject was directly connected. In the interchange of sentiment, which took place between Mr. Van Buren and Mr. Wheaton, alone of all those who, from the commencement of the government of the United States, had been employed in its diplomacy, had made a permanent contribution to the science of international law, and resting his claims on his personal qualifications, and on his eminent services in the negotiation of the Danish treaty, Mr. Butler urged the new President to disregard the clamors of ephemeral politicians, and while rendering justice to an experienced public officer, to di an act which would confer lasting honor on his administration. "All the respectable and intelligent portion of the community," he declared, "all whose good opinions are worth possessing will, at once, sanction your course, and all parties will soon approve of it." In this advice he was earnestly second by the venerable chief who was about retiring from the government, and who had early manifested his own independence of action, by first retaining Mr. Wheaton at Copenhagen, and then transferring him to the more important post at Berlin. It is needless to add, that the counsel of his best and most disinterested friends, in which Mr. Van Buren readily concurred, meets no dissent in what may already be deemed the judgment of posterity.

Mr. Wheaton received his letters of credence, and his commission in his new capacity, in March, 1837; though owing to the vacancy in the department of Foreign Affairs, intervening between the death of Mr. Ancillon and the appointment of Baron de Werther, and the annual visit of his Majesty to the baths of Toeplitz, where he was accompanied by the new minister, he did not deliver his letter to the king till September. He thought that he could not better employ the interval than by making another journey through the Prussian provinces, with a view to complete his former examination of their commercial resources, especially with respect to the question of the tobacco duties, to which his attention had been particularly directed, and the natural and artificial communications, by which the States of Germany associated in the Commercial Union are connected with the North Sea, and the channels opened for our commerce, in common with that of other nations, through the ports of Belgium and Holland, into the interior of the continent. Leaving his Secretary of Legartion in charge of the current affairs of the mission, he proceeded through the province of Brandenburg, which he had not before explored, to Cassel, the capital of Electoral Hesse; and he not only visited the States of Western Germany, but extended his tour through Belgium, where he had occasion to remark the improvements which had occurred under the new government since he first passed through it, in 1830, as well as to notice the intimate connection between the commercial interests of the United States and those of the Rhenish provinces, whose manufactures, in their diminished exports, were experiencing the effects of the monetary crisis, then prevailing in England and America.

The same instructions which conveyed to Mr. Wheaton his appointment, as Envoy Extraordinary and Minister Plenipotentiary, inclosed the report of a Select Committee of the House of Representatives, on the high duties imposed by foreign governments on tobacco; one half of the exports of which, from the United States, were consumed in Germany. Congress, also, had evinced the interest which they took in this trade, by making an appropriation for the compensation of special agents, to be employed for the express purpose of effecting a reduction of the tariff on this article; and it was understood that the rank of the Prussian mission was raised, with special reference to this subject. In the following year, (June, 1838,) a similar resolution was passed, requesting the President to instruct our diplomatic agents in Germany, to procure a reduction of the duties on American rice imported into the States of Germany, especially those associated in the Commercial and Customs' Union. Soon after the transmission of his commission, in June, 1837, Mr. Wheaton received a full power, with instructions from Mr. Forsyth, though preferring a relaxation of the duties by legislative or internal regulation, to conclude, if necessary, a treaty with the Zollverein, —an object which he ever zealously pursued for the ensuing six years. At this time, however, he was not authorized to stipulate for a preference in the ports of the United States of the productions of the German States, over similar articles imported from other countries, as an equivalent for the diminution of the duties or charges on tobacco; but if any such proposition was made, he was to transmit it to his government.

The earlier instructions of Mr. Forsyth were, it should be mentioned, opposed to according any preference, even for a full equivalent, to the productions of Germany, lest we might thereby be embarrassed with those nations, with which we had treaties of reciprocity; and he referred to the difficulties which had, in consequence of such a provision, grown out of the convention for the purchase of Louisiana. That treaty not only contained a stipulation placing the vessels of France and Spain, laden with the productions of their respective countries, for a limited period, on the same footing as those of the United States in the ports of Louisiana, but provided that the vessels of France should be forever thereafter treated in those ports on the footing of the most favored nation. It was, Mr. Forsyth said, to get rid of obligations, which might be deemed to contravene the Constitution of the United, that the preference accorded to French wins was inserted in the Treaty of 1831.

As to the construction to be given to the term, "most favored nation," when used as in the Louisiana Treaty—whether it entitles a power, with which such a treaty exists, on the concession of advantages, for a consideration, to another, to enjoy them gratuitously, it may be remarked that the subject was fully, and, as it is believed, unanswerably argued, in 1817, on the American side, by Mr. Adams, in the controversy with respect to the very treaty referred to; and the same views were always contended for by Mr. Wheaton, in his correspondence with the Department of State.

Mr. Wheaton attended, under the instructions of his government, the Congress of the Zollverein at Dresden, in July, 1838. He presented to them a memoir, embodying all the statistical data and economical reasonings, which could tend to induce the introduction of a liberal policy. The importance to the Germanic Confederacy of the trade with the United States is fully explained, by a reference to facts as well as to general principles. Statistical details do not enter into the plan of this notice, but how satisfactorily to those most deeply interested in the results, this branch of Mr. Wheaton's duties was performed, may be learned by the strong approbation with which it is alluded to in the report of a committee of the House of Representatives on the tobacco trade, and of which Mr. Jenifer, who was appointed, at the special request of the planters, Minister to Vienna, was chairman. The committee say, that "they cannot omit to notice the very able and argumentative memoir, presented to the Congress of Deputies of the German Commercial and Customs' Association, assembled at Dresden, in June last, by our zealous and talented minister, Henry Wheaton; in which he takes an enlarged view of the policy which should be adopted in relation to the products of the Southern States, and submits a project for their consideration, which the committee insert."

Though Mr. Wheaton was not immediately successful, as regards the duties on tobacco, the consideration of which was adjourned to a Congress to bbe held the next year, he obtained a report in favor of the reduction of the duty on rice, which, on being referred to the respective governments of the States comprising the association, was confirmed bt them. The only foreign relations considered at the Congress were those of the United States, arising out of Mr. Wheaton memoir; and the favor which was accorded to his representations may be ascribed to the personal consideration which he commanded, and to the opportunities which his familiarity with the language of the members, as well as his thorough knowledge of the matters which he discussed, afforded him. By the ministers of state, as well as by their sovereigns, he was everywhere received as the honored representative of a great and powerful nation.

A confidential despatch gives an account of his interview with the King of Saxony, with whom he dined, on the 6th July, at Pilnitz: — "His Majesty, who is extremely well informed on all matters connected with the public administration, turned the conversation to the subject of our negotiations with the commercial association. He stated that Saxony had no particular interest in the Question, as to the proposed reduction of the duties on American tobacco, either as to revenue or the cultivation of the native plant, whilst he admits that she had a deep interest in the preservation of a vast and increasing market for German manufactures. At the same time, the king did not disguise from me the difficulties we must expect to encounter, in endeavoring to reconcile so many conflicting interests, as are involved in any change of the present tariff. His remarks were conveyed in the kindest and most conciliatory terms towards our country, with whose resources he is perfectly acquainted, and for whose welfare he expresses the warmest interest, and with an earnest desire to cultivate the most amicable relations."

IN the commercial treaty, of 1815, with Great Britain, reciprocity was established, so far only as regarded the trade between the United States and the British possessions in Europe, in the productions of the respective countries; but in the case of the treaties with the Hanseatic Republics, negotiated in 1827, and of the treaty with Prussia, in 1828, an unlimited right of importing, on equal terms into the respective countries, whatever might be imported therein in their own vessels, was reciprocally accorded. In the Prussian treaty it was specially declared, that the stipulations as to reciprocity shall apply, whether the vessels clear directly from the country to which they respectively belong, or from the ports of any other foreign country.

This liberality, though it was only in accordance with the proffer made to all nations by our reciprocity acts, and of which several powers had availed themselves, had been deemed to operate very disadvantageously to American navigation in the case of the Hanse towns. This was supposed to be especially the case with regard to the importation of tobacco, which was made, to a great extent, though the port of Bremen, for Germany. It was stated that, from there being a great preponderance, in the tobacco trade alone was six to one against our mercantile marine. This point was brought prominently to view in the report, which accompanied the resolution of the House of Representatives, on the subject of the tobacco trade, in 1837. And it induced, in the treaty of commerce which Mr. Wheaton negotiated with Hanover, in 1840, a less extended reciprocity than had been adopted in the previous German treaties. The abolition of the discriminating duties, instead of applying universally, was confined, on the one side, to the productions of the United States and the American Continent and the West Indies, and on the other, to the productions of Hanover, of Prussia, and of the States belonging to the Germanic Confederation. THis arrangement was in accordance with a suggestion made in a private letter of Mr. Wheaton to the President, in February, 1838, explaining the operation of the provision. The treaty was made with Hanover alone, the government of that kingdom having declined to negotiate conjointly with their commercial allies, as at first proposed.

Mr. Wheaton gives the following view of our commercial relations in the North of Europe, on the conclusion of the treaty of 1840: — "The principal seaport of the kingdom of Hanover is Embden, which formerly carried on a considerable foreign commerce, so long as the province of East Friesland belonged to Prussia, and so long as the Prussian flag enjoyed the privileges and advantages of neutrality, during the wars of the American and French Revolutions. The imports and exports of the kingdom of Hanover are principally made through the ports of the Hanseatic Republics of Bremen and Hamburg, the former of which is *enclave* within the Hanoverian territory. As the duties of import and export payable in those places are trifling, and as the transit duty across the Hanoverian territory, whether by land, or by the Eems, the West, and the Elbe, to and from the countries united in the great Prussian Association of Commerce and Customs, is very moderate, the facilities of foreign commerce with the interior of Germany are proportionally great. The participation of the United States in this commerce, on terms of reciprocity, will now be secured by treaties with Denmark, Prussia, the Hanseatic Towns,

Hanover, and the Netherlands, placing their navigation and commerce on a footing with the national navigation and commerce, in all the ports of the North Sea, from the mouths of the Rhine to Tonningen, and of the Baltic, from Memel to Kiel, ecepting those of Oldenburg and Mecklenburg-Schwerin, in which it still rests on the President's proclamation, issued under the Act of 1828."

At the extra session of the Congress of the United States, in May, 1841, a report from the Secretary of State, Mr. Webster, respecting our commercial relations with the Zollverein, was laid before the two houses with the President's message. The materials from which it was compiled were furnished by the despatches of the Mr. Wheaton, as were also those used on the subject of the Sound duties, which was embraced in the same report, and the information concerning which had been communicated by him from Copenhagen and Berlin. In this document the suggestion is distinctly made, of entering into commercial treatise with the States united in the commercial league, as well with a view to the extension of our trade with them, as of abrogating the taxes in the character of droit d'aubaine and droit de detraction, which existed in many of them.

In 1842, Mr. Wheaton again attended a meeting of the Congress of the Zollverein, which was held at Stutgard, where he was presented, on the 15th of July, to the king, an enlightened sovereign, who was duly sensible of the importance of cultivating commercial relations with the United States, and with whom he had a very interesting interview on that subject. On that occasion, he also visited Munich, and had several conferences with Baron de Gise, the Minister of Foreign Affairs of his Bavarian majesty, in relation to the commercial interests of Germany, and of its intercourse with the United States. IN the discussions at Stutgard, he found, as had been the case on the former occasion, that the Deputies were unwilling to make any changes in the tariff, unless accompanied by corresponding reductions in the United States, on the productions and manufactures of Germany; insisting that their tariffs on tobacco were not higer than those of other countries, while cotton was admitted free of duty, and other American imports at a moderate rate. Tobacco was not, they said, a monopoly, as in France, and the duties laid on it are not equal to the one twelfth of those imposed in England. They all expected to receive from us some advantages for their manufactures, in exchange for the facilities they accorded to us; and it had been early objected, that our Treaty of 1831, as regarded French wins in the United States, interfered with the consumption of those of Germany.

After the adjournment of the Congress, the embarrassments to making a treaty were increased by the serious augmentation, in the American tariff of 1842, of the duties on articles usually imported into the United States from Germany, and for which retaliatory measures had been suggested. Indeed Mr. Wheaton writes, under the date of 16th of November, 1842: — "Baron Bulow has recently stated to me that the Prussian cabinet had been invited, by some of its allies in the Germanic Customs' Association, to concur in measures of retaliation against our tariff, which is much complained of as too fiscal, and even pro hibitive, of many German commodities. He intimated that Prussia was not disposed, at present, at least, to take such a step, but would await the result of the deliberations of our Congress, at the ensuing session, to determine the course of policy which the association ought to pursue."

THe Congress of the Commercial Union held a session at Berlin, in September, 1843, and during it Mr. Wheaton was given to understand that a convention could be made for the reduction of duties on tobacco, based upon equivalent reductions in the American tariff on German products and manufactures, and which might be selected from those articles which did not come in competition with the manufactures of the United States. These views were embodied in official notes between him and Baron Bulow, of the 9th and 10th of October. He takes occasion, in his despatch of 11th October, 1843, transmitting these notes, to refer to former despatches, in which he refutes the idea that any reduction of duties made for equivalent reductions by the Zollverein, would accrue gratuitously to the benefit of those countries who have treaties with the United States, stipulating to place them on the footing of "the most favored nation." At the same time, he stated that there was no obligation, on our part, not to make the proposed reductions in duties applicable to imports from other countries as well as Germany.

The assent of the Secretary of State, Mr. Upshur, was immediately accorded to the proposed course, and Mr. Wheaton was directed to proceed with the preliminary arrangements, "bearing always in mind, that the sanction of Congress, as well as of the Executive, will be indispensably required, before we accomplish the object in contemplation." IN a despatch of December, 1843, Mr. Upshur says: — "It gives me pleasure to say that the President entirely approves of the preliminary steps which you have taken, as stated in your communication of the 11th of October, to make the commercial arrangement with the German Customs' Union; and I now transmit, by his direction, a full power, authorizing you to proceed with the negotiations." Again, on 2d January, 1844, he adds: — "It is now the wish of the President that you should, without loss of time, bring these negotiations to a conclusion, on the basis of the notes of 9th and 10th of October last, which passed between you and Baron Bulow. As to the mode in which these arrangements are to be carried out, whether by agreement, convention, or treaty, the President has such confidence in your judgement, that he leaves it to you to adopt that which, in your opinion, will be likely to effect the object, in a manner most acceptable to both countries; the earnest wish of the President being to place the commerce between the United States and Germany, as speedily as possible, on the most favorable footing for both countries."

Before the last of these instructions were given, the President (Mr. Tyler) had, in his annual message to Congress, at the session of 1843-4, referred, with satisfaction, to these negotiations with the Zollverein, then embracing more than twenty German States, and 27,000,000 of people, and especially to the reduction of the duty on rice, and to the strong disposition evinced to reduce the duty on tobacco. "This," he says, "being the first intimation of a concession on this interesting subject, ever made by any European power, I cannot but regard it as well calculated to remove the only impediment, which has so far existed to the most liberal commercial intercourse between us and them. In this view our minister at Berlin, who has heretofore industriously pursued the subject, has been instructed to enter on the negotiation of a commercial treaty, which, while it will open new advantages to the agricultural interests of the United States, and a freer and more expanded field for commercial operations, will affect injuriously no existing interests of the Union." Accompanying the message was a report of the Secretary of States, to which were annexed the notes of Mr. Wheaton and Baron Bulow, giving the outline of the proposed arrangement, and in which Mr. Upshur states that "the basis of a treaty had been agreed upon, and submitted for the consideration and action of our givernment, which would effect the long-cherished object of procuring the reduction of the present duty on our tobacco, secure the continued admission of our cotton free of all duty, and prevent the imposition of any higher duty on rice. For these vast advantages, the conditional arrangement proposes that the United States shall give the Customs' Union proper equivalents, by reducing the heavy duties of the present tariff upon silks, looking-glass plates, toys, lines, and such other articles, as are not of the growth or manufacture of the United States."

The treaty was signed on the 25th of March, 1844. Its peculiar provisions were reciprocal stipulations, with regard to the rate of duties on various articles, therein enumerated. The United States, on their part, agreed not to impose on certain articles, the produce or manufacture of the States of the Germanic Confederacy, duties exceeding 15 per cent., and on a third class they were not to be more than 10per cent. They further agreed not to increase the present duties on the wines of Prussia nor to impose higher duties on the wins of the other States of the Confederation than on those of Prussia. The

Zollverein were, on their side, to reduce the duties to a stipulated rate on tobacco and lard, and not to raise the present duties on rice, and not to impose any duty on unmanufactured cotton. These reductions of duties were only to apply to goods, laden on board of the vessels of one of the contracting parties, or of vessels placed on the footing of national vessels by the laws or treaties, respectively, of the contracting parties, and imported directly from the ports of the one party into the ports of the other. But the States of the Germanic Association of Customs and Commerce reserved the right to consider the ports between the mouths of the Elbe and Scheldt, inclusive, as ports of the association. The conclusion of the treaty induced, at once, the most flattering congratulations from Mr. Wheaton's colleagues at St. Petersburg, Copenhagen, and London.

Mr. Erwin, in apprising Mr. Wheaton from Copenhagen, in a letter of March 1, 1844, of the efforts by England to prevent Hanover from joining the Zollverein, says: "The conventional commercial arrangement made by you with the King of Prussia, on behalf of the Zollverein, has excited deep interest here as well as elsewhere throughout Europe. The achievement being truly regarded as among the most important of modern times, may naturally be supposed to have aroused the jealously of those powers with whose interests it might seem to conflict; —a jealousy that would scarcely be diminished by the announcement in Mr. Upshur's able report of the probable accession to the union of Hanover and the smaller States of the north, by which an addition of more than three millions would be included in your beneficial arrangement."

Mr. Everett writes from London, on the 9th of April, 1844: "I repeat my congratulations on this brilliant result of your labors. Whatever may be the action of the Senate and House of Representatives as to ratifying and carrying it into effect, there can be but one feeling as to the ability with which you have conducted the negotiation." He at the same time, advised him of the jealously entertained by the British government of the result of the negotiation and of the construction which Lord Aberdeen was attempting to give as to its effect on our treaty with England, by claiming under it a participation in the advantages stipulated to the Zollverien, without rendering any correspondent equivalent.

On the 29ty of April, 1844, the President transmitted the treaty to the Senate, and in his message be declares that he "cannot but anticipate from its ratification important benefits to the great agricultural, commercial, and navigating interests of the United States."

The subject was referred, in the Senate, to the Committee of Foreign Affairs, who, after it had been once recommitted to them, reported against it; and it was on the 15th of June, ordered to lie on the table, which, at that period of the session, and with the provision that the ratifications should be exchanged at Berlin within four months from the signature, was equivalent to a rejection. This was effected by a strictly party vote of twenty-six to eighteen. The objections made to the treaty are thus summarily stated: "In the judgement of the committee, the Legislature is the deoartment of government by which commerce should be regulated and laws of revenue passed. The Constitution in terms communicates the power to regulate commerce it in terms to no other. Without engaging at all in an examination of the extent, limits, and objects of the power to make treaties, the committee believe that the general rule of our system is, indisputably, that the control of trade and the function of taxing belong, without abridgment or participation, to Congress. Upon this single ground, then, the committee recommend that the treaty be rejected." They then proceed to deny the importance of the stipulated concessions, in comparison with the equivalent considerations.

Before the conclusionof the treaty, a vacancy had occurred in the Department of State, by the death of Mr. Upshur, who, together with the Secretary of War and other distinguished citizens, was, on the 28th of February, while on board of the steam frigate Princeton, killed by the explosion of a Paixhan gun, to test which was the object of the excursion. This event was of more importance to Mr. Wheaton than the mere severance of official relations, as it was understood that, had the Secretary lived, he would have gone to Berlin, and that Mr. Wheaton would have been transferred to Paris, on the conclusion of the Zollverein negotiation.

John C. Calhoun, the distinguished statesman of South Carolina, and between whom and Mr. Wheaton, twenty years previously, as we have seen, the most intimate relations had subsisted, was appointed in Mr. Upshur's place. The public despatch of Mr. Calhoun, cited in our notes, meets the objections, which had been interposed in the Senate to the ratification of the Zollverein Convention, showing the uniform practice to be otherwise than as stated by the committee, (of which, indeed, the late reciprocity treaty, in relation to our intercourse with the British provinces, is a further illustration,) and that the only question that ever was made, on this point, was whether an act of Congress to sanction and carry into effect the stipulation of such a treaty was necessary; while a private letter, written a few days subsequently, sufficiently explains the true cause of the proceedings of that body. It was found among the papers of Mr. Wheaton, and the time which has elapsed, together with the death of all the parties to be affected by it, renders it, it is conceived, a proper contribution to the history of the period.

"[Private.]"　　Washington, 28th June, 1844.

"My Dear Sir,

"The omission of the Senate to act finally on the treaty with the Zollverein States is at once a subject of deep regret and mortification; —regret on account of the advantages it promised to both parties, and which it is feared may be lost, and mortification on account of the effects it may have on the standing of the government abroad. The cause, to which it is to be attributed, is doubtless the same as that to which the defeat of the Texas treaty may be, excepting in the former the operation of the protecting interest. But, I do not think that, of itself, would have been sufficient. You will see that it is not even alluded to in the report of the committee. The true cause in both cases I believe to be, the bearing which it was feared it would have on the Presidential election. Mr. Clay's friends, who are a decided majority in the Senate, felt confident of his election, under the old issue, as it stood when Congress met; and were averse to admit any new question to enter the issue. The attempt to prevent it has been in vain; and will prove unwise, even in a party point of view. The Texas question has entered deeply into the issue, and Ihave no doubt that questions growing out of the Zollverein treaty will also. Nor would I be surprised, if he should be beaten, in consequence of the part Which his friends in the Senate have acted, as weak, personally, as the candidate opposed to him is comparatively.

"I cannot but hope that the treaty would be sanctioned by the Senate, should the time be prolonged to the next session, when the Presidential election will be over, and the party motives that have led to laying the treaty on the table, shall have passed away. I am strengthened in this opinion from the very inconclusive reasons assigned by the committee on foreign relations for its rejection, and which I feel confident the Senate will never sanction, whatever may be the fate of the treaty.

"Under this impression you have been instructed to have the time so extended as to afford the Senate an opportunity, at the next session, to act finally on the treaty, unless there should be a decided disinclination on the part of Prussia and other Zollverein States to the extension, which I fear may be the case. If such should be the fact, it strikes me that cit would be very indelicate, on our part, to press it. It would be doubly mortifying to us, and still more offensive to Prussia and the other States of the league, if it should be rejected, should we press against their inclination, the extension of the time for the exchange of ratifications.

"Let what may be the fate of the treaty, you can lose no reputation, as an able and successful negotiator. In making the treaty, you have effected what could have been accomplished by few, and what, if it should be consummated, would constitute an era in our commercial history. I cannot doubt it would tend, by its consequences, to other and great changes in the commerce of the civilized world, and lay a solid foundation for an intimate and close commercial and political union between the United States and Germany, which I greatly desire, and which Ido not doubt would be for the mutual advantage of both.

With great respect,
Yours truly,
10. C. Calhoun."

"Hon. Henry Wheaton."

The attempt to extend the time for the ratification was, as might have been expected, unsuccessful. And the administration which, in the ensuing March, succeeded that of President Tyler, refrained from any further proposition to altar, by treaty, the provisions of the tariff. The last meeting of the Zollverein Congress, during Mr. Wheaton's mission. Was held at Carlsruhe, in October, 1845, without making any alteration in their tariff, and without any questions arising as to the commercial relations with the United States.

Before the fate of the Zollverein treaty was known, an overture was made by the Hanoverian Minister, at Berlin, foe a negotiation for the admission of our tobacco and other agricultural products, on the most favorable footing, inreturn for a reduction of duty on linens alone.

Mr. Wheaton's view of the impolicy of the Senate's action is thus succinctly given, in a private letter of December, 1844: — "I still continue impressed with the idea that the only safe and advantageous mode of arriving at a modification of the present tariff—which must inevitably take a place during the ensuing administration, is by reciprocal concessions, to be stipulated with other nations—in which we should 'gain both by what we give and by what we get,' as it has been well expressed. The consequence of not ratifying the treaty at the last session is, that the European States are now looking for a gratuitous reduction of our tariff, by which their fabrics will be relieved from the present exorbitant duties, and our agricultural products will still continue to be subjected to the present heavy imposition in the European markets. This,

I know, to be the impression in London, Paris, and Berlin. The two former cabinets would have been prepared to enter on similar negotiations with us had the Zollverein treaty been ratified."

The union, which has been effected between the States of the Zollverein and Steuerverein, has increased the population subject to the Zollverein to thirty = five millions, which, with the treaty stipulayions between the Prussian league and Austria and her associates, all of whom, at no distant period, are likely to be dependent on the mutable policy of legislation, but by an international convention, a market, with seventy millions of people, for our cotton free of duty, for our rice at the most reduced rates, and for our tobacco on terms that would have greatly increase its consumption.

All this might have been obtained in return for merely nominal changed in our tariff, while the augmented transactions between the United States and these seventy millions would have tended further to favor the emigration of a frugal and industrious people for the settlement of the almost indefinite territory, which still aeaits cultivation and civilization, as well as to strengthen friendly intercourse between us and the great Federal empire, not unlikely, despite the abortive efforts at Frankfort, in 1848—9, the rivalry between Austria and Prussia, and the intervention of other powers, to grow out of the Commercial Unions. Such a confederacy, however differing from us in its internal or municipal institutions, must resemble the United States, and have sympathy with them, from the analogous federal relations, connecting the several parts.

Besides the improvement of our commercial relations generally, Mr. Wheaton's original instructions contemplated the abolition of the *droit d'aubaine* and *droit de detraction*, as operating most injuriously on emigration to the United States. With Prussia the arrangement had been made, by the Treaty of 1828, and the same provision was introduced in the treaty of commerce with Hanover, in 1840; but the full power which had been given in 1836, to conclude seperate conventions with the several States of Germany, was withdrawn, soon after it was granted, in consequence of the refusal of the Senate to ratify a similar one with Switzerkand; and it was not till Mr. Upshur was charged with the State Department, that, by instructions of November 18, 1843, it was renewed, Treaties were made, in pursuance of these instructions, with Wurtembeurg, Hesse Cassel, Saxony, Nassau, and Bavaria. Baden declined making any, in consequence of the vested interest which some of her subjects had in these duties. All these conventions abolish the droit de detraction. In transmitting one of them, Mr. Wheaton says: — "The tax imposed on the funds removed by emigrants, who leave this country, amounts, in Saxony and most of the German States, to ten percentum on the capital thus transferred. This amount is so much clear gain to us, in the capital thus brought into the country by the rich peasants and others, who sell their real property here, and emigrate in great numbers to the United States." The *droit d'aubaine* is equally oppressive, subjecting to a like duty all property, which emigrants to the United States might derive, on the death of relatives in the country of their origin; and the duty imposed in such cases is also, in general, ten per cent. On the capital.

The local law of most of the States of the American Union, being based on the feudal principles of the English common law, is less favorable to foreigners becoming land-owners than that of France, and other countries of the continent of Europe, where aliens are permitted to hold real estate, and to take, *ab intestato* and by will, as native subjects. The treaties referred to only provide, like the previous one with Prissia, would descend to a citizen or subject of the other, were he not disqualified by alienage, he shall have two years, at least, (which is substituted for the indefinite term, *reasonable time*, in the treaty with Prussia,) in which to dispose of it; and, in the treaty with Saxony, this provision is made to apply to those who take by devise, as well as by descent. The general power, however, of disposing of property by will, donation, or otherwise, by the citizens or subjects of the one country, in favor of those of the other, is confined to personal property;

and when, in the treaty with Bavaria, it was attempted to apply it also to "real estate," the Senate refused their ratification, unless these words were stricken out.

IN the despatch from which we have already quoted, the impolicy of preventing aliens from purchasing real estate is discussed, and its effect, in withholding investments of German capital, shown; but this subject has been generally regarded in the United States as a matter for State legislation. Indeed, it is not always easy to reconcile the exclusive authority of the federal government, through the treaty-making power, to enter into agreements with foreign States, in case in which the concurrence of the latter is essential, with the control reserved by the States over all affairs of internal or municipal cognizance. And when, in the Treaty of the 30th of April, 1853, with France, it was proposed to remove the disability on French subjects holding land, the stipulation, on the part of the United States, (probably on account of a doubt of the authority of the general government to go further,) only extended to an engagement that the President would recommend to the several States to pass the laws necessary to secure a reciprocity.

Another important subject for international regulation is the extradition to foreign States of fugitives from justice. Though the Chief Justice, with whom three of the other Judges concurred, declared, in 1840, that "the exercise of this power by the States is totally contrary to the power granted to the United States, and repugnant to the Federal Constitution," the question was left, by the decision of the Supreme Court, an open one. There was, at that time, no subsisting conventional arrangement on the subject, the only previous provision of the kind having been contained in the Treaty of 1794, with England, which expired long before the last war. The present stipulation with Great Nritain on that subject, arose from the Treaty of the 9th of August, 1842; and the Extradition Treaty with France was concluded on the 9th of November, 1843.

A convention for the same object was made with Prussia, on her own behalf and that of seceral other German States, on the 29ᵗʰ of April, 1845; but it differed from the preceding ones, in that each power excepted the extradition of its own subjects. The preliminary note from Baron Bulow, on which the negotiations were opened, had contained the two following conditions: — 1. Qu' aucune de parties contractantes ne sera tenue a livrer *ses propres sujets*. Une pareille extradition a des tribunaux etrangers serait apparement aussi peu compatible avec la legislation des Etats Unis qu avec celle de la Prusseet des autres Etats Allemands; 2. Que quand un criminel fugitif a commis un nouveau avoir lieu que lorsque I' information, pour ce nouveau crim, sera terminee et que le condamne aura subi sa peine.

THe instructions under which it was negotiated were given by Mr. Calhoun, but, before it was received in this country, the administration was changed, and Mr. Buchanan had become Secretary of State. President Polk, in submitting it to the Senate, called their attention to the difference in question; and it is presumed that it was on that ground that the treaty was not ratified. The fact was probably not adverted to, that the proposed exception, which was a *sine qua non* with Prussia, grew out of the difference between the systems of criminal jurisdiction, which prevail on the continent of Europe and in England and the United States. It is not necessary, in most European States, that the offence should be committed within the jurisdiction of the country, in which the accused is tried, but he is justiciable by his sovereign, wherever the crime occurred. The treaty of extradition between Russia and Prussia, concluded in 1844, and which was transmitted by Mr. Wheaton to the Department of State, fully explains this view. It provides that, "if the accused is a subject of the sovereign of the country where he has sought refuge, after having committed a criminal offence in the country of the other sovereign, he shall not be delivered up, but the sovereign of whom he is a subject shall cause justice to be promptly and strictly administered against him, according to the laws of country. But if any individual whatever has been arrested in the country where he has committed a criminal offence, or any misconduct whatever. (*exces quelconque*,) the sovereign of the country where the arrest takes place shall cause justice to be administered against him, and the punishment he incurred to be inflicted upon him, even if such individual be a subject of the other sovereign."

The treaty Prussia and her associated States, which had been rejected when made by Mr. Wheaton, was negotiated anew by Mr. Webster and Baron Gerolt, at Washington, in 1852, and to it several States, not included originally therein, Wurtemberg, Mecklenburg-Schwerin, Oldenburg, and Schaumburg-Lippe. And while this work has been passing through the press, a treaty concluded on the 12th of September, 1853, between the American and Bavarian ministers at London, Mr. Buchanan and Baron de Cetto, to the like effect, has been promulgated. It contains the same provision with the Prussian treaty, that none of the contracting parties shall be bound to deliver up its own citizens or subjects, for which it recites, in common with the other treaty, a constitutional objection on the part of the German powers; and it applies to the same crimes as that treaty does.

Among other subjects which were intrusted to Mr. Wheaton, was that of procuring the assent of the Prussian government to act in the arbitration, provided for under the Convention of April 11, 1839, between the United States and Mexico, for the adjustment of American claims against the latter Republic. He was successful in inducing the acceptance of the office, which had been at first declined, and to his suggestion was the choice of Baron Von Roenne mainly owing. He, however, failed, in the application which he made, by direction of his government to that of Prussia, to obtain the contributions to the science of public law, which the promulgation of the opinions, on which the judgments of the arbiter were based, would have afforded.

A matter not arising in the Prussian dominions, in which the interposition of Mr. Wheaton was asked, was that of the arrest, by the Hanoverian authorities, of the officers of an American merchant ship, charged with the commission of a homicide within their waters. Without raising the question, as to the amenability to a State of the persons on board of a merchant vessel, which comes voluntarily within its jurisdiction, he asked on the grounds of national courtesy, inasmuch as the offence charged grew out of the maintenance of the ship's discipline, as it in nowise injured any Hanoverian subject, or affected the tranquillity and good order of the country, and that the parties were amenable to the tribunals of their own country, that the accused might be delivered to the consul, to be sent home to the United States. The request thus made was complied with, on the payment of the costs of the criminal proceedings, to the time of the extradition.

He had, also, occasion to consider the effect of the return of a naturalized American citizen to the country of his original allegiance, and to refuse him his interposition, on the ground, that, so long as he remained in the country of his birth, his native domicile and national character reverted, and that he was bound, in all respects, to obey the laws, as if had never emigrated.

The subject of the Sound duties at Elsinore, the examination of which was commenced at Copenhagen, was continued at Berlin. IN one of his later despatches he says: — "The most recent project brought forward has in view the redemption of the duties by the other three maritime powers of the Baltic—Russia, Sweden, and Prussia; who might afterwards collect in their ports an amount of tonnage duties, or duties on the importation or exportation of merchandise, equal to the interest of the capital advanced by them for this purpose, and thus the inconvenience, delay, and expense of collecting the duties at Elsinore, might be avoided." But, in a subsequent communication, he announced a new treaty between Prussia and Denmark, regulating the payment of these duties by the former power till 1851, when, he added, "the Convention of 1841, between Great British, Sweden, and Denmark, for regulating the tariff of the Second duties, will expire, and the whole matter will necessarily become subject to revision between Denmark and all other powers interested in the question." To the influence of the Emperor Nicholas, who was actuated therein by political and not commercial considerations, Mr. Wheaton ascribes the continuance of these tolls. His object seems to have been, through the essential support which he afforded to Denmark, for the maintenance of these claims against her neighbors, to secure a protectorate over that power, which held to him on the side of the Baltic the same relation that Turkey did on that Black Sea.

An analogous subject, which likewise received Mr. Wheaton's continued attention, was the duties levied by the Hanoverian government at State, on the goods of all nations passing up the Elbe, except those belonging to citizens of Hamburgh, and the origin of which, as founded on a title going back to an original grant from the Emperor Conrad, in 1038, is historically traced. These duties were not abolished by the Congress of Vienna, or included in the provisions in relation to the rivers of German, because they were considered sea, and not river, tolls. Their importance may be judged of by the fact, that even in 1834, 1835, and 1836, one hundred and forty-five American vessels passing up the Elbe paid, on the cargoes of each, about seven hundred marks banco; and that, in 1840, there were imported int Germany, though the port of Bremen, staple productions of the United States, to the amount of fifteen millions of marks banco, besides an increased amount of colonial produce.

The attention of the American government having been attracted to this subject, in its bearing on the commerce of the United States, by the various communications of Mr. Wheaton, a provision placing American vessels on the same footing with Hanoverian was inserted in the Treaty of 1846.

Nor was the attention of the Minister at Berlin limited to matters which affected the interests of the United States in Prussia, or even in Germany. It will hereafter be amply shown that he lost no opportunity of creating a sound public opinion in Europe, respecting the political course of the United States. He thus alludes to a conversation which he had with the king, Frederick Willian III., at one of the royal entertainments: — "His Majesty expressed the warmest wishers for the prosperity of our Republic, and his satisfaction at the measures taken by the President to preserve our neutrality, in respect to the troubles of Canada, which in their consequences might affect our interests. I ventured to assure his Majesty that in no possible event would the United States swerve from their fixed principles of non-interference in the internal affairs of their neighbors, so long as their own national rights and interests were not injuriously affected."

Mr. Wheaton had also been enabled, though the confidence resposed in him by the Baron de Werther, the Minister of Foreign Affairs, who read to him a despatch from the Prissian Minister in London, to communicate to his government the real sentiments entertained in England, and expressed to the Ministers of other powers, as to our good faith with respect to Canadians affairs.

One of Mr. Wheaton's last official acts was to communicate to the government of Prussia the circumstances which led to the declaration of war against Mexico and the blockade instituted in consequence thereof. "He stated that the blockade intended to be established would not give any just ground of complaint to neutral powers, since it would not be what is called 'a paper blockade,' but would be carried into effect by an actual investment of the ports in question by adequate naval forces. That we professed the same principles, in respect to neutral rights, which had been professed and maintained by Prussia, ever since the reign of Frederick the Great, and should be anxious to preserve our consistency in that respect, by meting out to others the same measure of international justice as belligerents, which we claimed from them when neutrals." Annexed to the despatch, which reported his proceedings in this matter, were extracts from Reddie's "Researches on Maritime International Law," by Ortolan, —works to which repeated reference has been made in these remarks and in our notes, and which were the latest English and French authorities on these points of maritime law.

A matter deeply interesting to the American people, on which Mr.

Wheaton's talents were exercised, grew out of a negotiation to which Prussia was a party, though the United States were not. And he had the satisfaction of communicating to the Secretary of State the assurances of Baron Bulow, that what ever might have been views of England, it was never intended by the other contracting parties, to the Quintuple treaty of 1841, for the suppression of the slave-trade, that it should be executed in any other manner than by searching each other's ships; and that for its application to those of other nations, the British government were alone responsible. The Minister for Foreign Affairs, moreover, expressed his conviction of the difficulty, if not impossibility, of the American government adhering to the principle, which formed the basis of the treaty between the five European powers. Mr. Wheaton was also informed by him, pending the discussions in ukase of the 26th March, (7th April) 1842, for carrying it into effect, that it was not the intention of the Prussian government to adopt, at that time, any similar measure, or to publish the treaty as a public law of the kingdom, as they did not consider it existing, so far as France was concerned, until ratified by that power.

It may not be irrelevant here to state that assurances were given to the same effect, by M. Guizot to General Cass, as to the views of the French government of its bearing on other nations, in the event of the ratification of the treaty by France. IN his leteer of 26th May, 1842, to the American Minister at Paris, M. Guizot says: "I ne m' appartient pas de discuter la valeur des inductions que vous tirez, par rapport aux vues parculieres du cabinet de Londres, de certains passages des depeches ecrites par Lord Palmerston et par Lord Aberdeen Mr. Stevenson; mais je n' hesiterai pas a dire quelle est la pensee du gouvernement du roi sur la grave question que vous soulevez. Le traite du 20 December, 1841, quelles que puissent etre a I' avenir ses destinees, n' est pas fonde sur un autre principe que les Conventions de 1831 et 1833. Les stipulations de ces conventions n' engageaient que la France et I' Angleterre: le traite du 20 Decenber les etend a I' Autriche, a la Prusse et a la Russie, en y apportant quelques changements plus ou moins graves, mais qui n'en alterent pas la nature. Pour qu'on put en faire decouler l'intention, fort extraordinaire, d'imposer aux autres etats l'obligation de s'y soumettre, il faudrait que cette intention, que n'indique en aucune facon l'acte du 20 Decembre, resultat des conventions anterieures. Jamais nous ne les avons entendues, jamais nous n'avons pu les enterdre ainsi."

In directing the public mind of Europe on this subject, Mr. Wheaton was particularly happy. To his "Inquiry into the Validity of the British Claim to a Right of Visitation and Search of American Vessels, suspected to be engaged in the African Slave-Trade," and to the Essay of General Cass, with his letter to M. Guizot, in the nature of a protest against the Quintuple Alliance, the answer to which has been noticed, may, in a great degree, be ascribed the refusal of France to ratify that treaty. How able a coadjutor in the defence of the maritime rights of nations, he was regarded by his eminent colleague at Paris, may be inferred from the following note of General Cass, acknowledging the receipt of Mr. Wheaton's Essay: "I have read your work on the right of search with the greatest pleasure, and I may add, with much profit. I thought I knew the whole history of this question, but I find that Ihad deceived myself, and that I had much to learn, which I have now learned."

"Your historical narrative is most satisfactory, and you put the *Argumentum ad homines* to our friends the English, on the existence of slavery in the United States, with equal good temper and good sense. How they will get out of the dilemma in which you have placed them as the authors of the evil, I do not see."

"Your general deductions are not less convincing; and I think you may safely consider the pretension to search our ships, in time of peace, as a question of right, forever disposed of. I am glad to see you make so good a case of a decision of the Supreme Court."

"On the whole, I congratulate you upon the success of your labors. They will do our country good everywhere, and cannot fail to be useful to yourself, and increase the literary reputation you have already so justly acquired."

The publication which has been referred to received, as it were, an official sanction from Mr. Legare, on his assuming the seals of the State Department. In his earliest instructions he said: "I avail myself of the first opportunity afforded by our new official relations, to express to you my hearty satisfaction at the part you took, with Geberal Cass, in the discussion of 'the Right of Search', and the manner you acquitted yourself of it. I read your pamphlet with entire assent. From the first miment that I was made acquainted with the provisions of the Quintuple Treaty, as they were interpreted by English journalists, and would, there is too much reason to be feared, have been executed by English naval officers, I was deeply impressed with the vital importance of the occasion. The law of nations, like all other laws, shifts with the current of popular opinion and feeling; and in it, as in all other laws, the maxim of wisdom is *obsta principiis*. England, as you know, has over and over again attempted to interpolate, and so far as the practice of her prize courts could effect it, has actualli interpolated new principles into that body of jurisprudence, not only without the assent, but against the unanimous protest of other powers. 'The rule of 56—the blockade of coasts—the confiscation of vessels, *bona fide* destined, in the hope of a free entry, for ports not under blockade at the time of their departure—the granting salvage for neutral vessels taken out of the hands of French captors, even when there was no possible ground of condemnation against them, —these are examples of the spirit of innovation which she has manifested. Were she any other power than one aemed with little less than a maritime despotism, such encroachments would not excite a very anxious jealousy. But in contemplation of any possible resistance to the the practical abuses, which would inevitably flow from the admission in theory of her pretensions to a legal right, as such, in this particular, it is absolutely essential to subject those pretensions to a searching and thorough scrutiny, soas to demonstrate to the conviction of all unprejudiced minds that there is no choice but resistance, I have no idea that war ever ought to be undertaken in a popular government, constituted as this is, unless the great body of the people be fully satisfied that their cause is just, and their wrongs worth the coast of adjusting them by force. It is, at the same time, due to the civilization of the age, and the power of opinion, even over the most arbitrary governments, that every encroachment on the rights of nations should become the subject of immediate censure and denunciation. One great object of permanent missions is to establish a censorship of this kind, and to render by means of it the appeals of the injured to the sympathies of mankind, through diplomatic organs, at once more easy, more direct, and more effective."

It was in acknowledging the foregoing despatch, that, after referring to the discussions, growing out of the construction of the Ashburton Treaty, Mr. Wheaton thus proceeds: — "The right claimed (by the English) comes to this—a right to seize and send in for adjudication, before the court of the captor's country, subject to the payment of costs and damages, in case of seizure without reasonable cause."

"I do not know what Lord Aberdeen and Sir Robert Peel's admiralty lawyers may have told them; but I defy them to show a single passage of any institutional writer on public law, or the judgment of any court by which that law is administered, either in Europe or America, which will justify the exercise of such a right on the high seas in time of peace."

And he shows that the British claim is not be confounded with the case of the seizure of vessels hovering on the coast, to violate the revenue laws of a country: — "The distinction now set up, between a right of *visitation* and a right of *search*, is nowhere alluded to by any public jurist, as being founded on the law of nations. The technical term of 'visitation and search,' used by the English civilians, is exactly synonymous with the *droit de visits* of the continental civilians. The right of seizure for a breach of the revenue laws, or laws of trade and navigation, of a particular nation, is quite different. The utmost length, to which the exercise of this right on the high seas has ever been carried, in respect to the vessels of another nation, has been carried, in respect to the vessels of another nation, has been to justify seizing them within the territorial jurisdiction of the State against whose laws they offend, and pursuing them, in case of flight, beyond that limit, seizing them upon the ocean, and bringing them in for adjudication before the tribunals of that State. 'This, however, 'says the Supreme Court of the United States, in the case of The Mariana Flora, 'has never been supposed to draw after it any right of visitation or search. The party, in such case, seizes at his peril. If he establishes the forfeiture, he is justified.'"

"The treaties between Great Britain and several other European powers have not only stipulated for the mutual exercise of the right of search, but have provided that the vessels seized should be carried, not into the ports of the capturing power, but before the courts of that country under whose flag the captured vessel is sailing. But the Treaty of Washington contains no such provision; and if we were to yield in practice to the British pretension, we should be in a worse situation than if we had actually acceded to the Quintuple Treaty of 1841."

Another discussion, in which Mr. Wheaton was engaged, which excited great interest among the members of the diplomatic corps throughout Europe, and likewise obtained the sanction of Mr. Legare, involved the immunities of foreign ministers, and their exemption from local jurisdiction. It will be found inserted, at large, in the body of the work.

Among others of what may be deemed Mr. Wheaton's semiofficial labors, were two papaers, which he published in 1842, in the Revue Etrangere et Francoise, at Paris. THe one related to the violation of American territory, during the civil war or insurrection in Canada in 1837, during which the steamer Caroline was burnt and one of her crew killed, at Schlosser, in the State of New York, and to the subsequent arrest of a person, named Mcleod, accused of having been engaged in the enterprise. The courts of New York refused to discharge him, though the British government admitted the act to have been committed by its authority, the judges holding that a subject of Great Britain, who, under directions from the local authorities of Canada, commits homicide in the State of New York, may be prosecuted in its courts as a murderer, even though his sovereign subsequently approves his conduct, by avowing the directions under which he did it, as a lawful act of government.

This case involved two very grave points; the one—the right, on the part of the British authorities, to go into American territory, and to take possession, by force, of a vessel belonging to a citizen of the United States—the other, the right of the tribunals of the country to try, as an offence against its criminal jurisdiction, an act committed under the authority of a foreign government.

Though the latter point had been practically settled by the verdict of acquittal, Mr. Wheaton took occasion to present it to the publicists of Europe, in connection with our complex system, which prevented the federal government, which alone conducts our foreign relations, from interfering effectually and promptly with the proceedings of the State judiciary. In this case, however, the difficulty did not arise from any defect in the organic law, which extends the power of the federal judiciary to such cases, but from an omission in the Judiciary Act of 1789, which was subsequently supplied by the Act of the 29th of August, 1842. As the law at the time stood, the case would have been brought to the Supreme Court of the United States, but only after a final decision of he highest court of the State, had McLeod been willing, instead of going to trial, on the question of fact, to have submitted to a succession of appeals. In the event of an unfavorable verdict on his trial, he might have obtained an arrest of judgment from the court on the question of international law involved; and had the courts of New York decided against him, he might have taken an appeal to the Supreme Court of the United Sates, and, according to the true principles of public law, it could only have been, on the failure of the central government to interfere, after the decision in the last resort, that the English government could have had recourse to reprisals. This is according to the opinion given by Lord Mansfield, when Solicitor-Gerneral, and the other law officers of the Crown, in the celebrated case of the Silesian loan. In the various demands that our government has made for indemnity, it has ever been distinctly admitted that it was only after a condemnation by the highest court, or where the uniform course of proceeding was such as to make a condemnation morally certain, that the government of the United States was justified in making reclamations, on account of their citizens, for illegal seizures. Mr. Wheaton remarks that in all free countries governed by representative constitutions, the courts are independent of the immediate action pf the executive power, though, in England, where the prosecution may be terminated in *limine* by the intervention of the Crown, authorizing the Attorney-General to enter a *nolle prosequi*, the responsibility of the government would commence on its refusal to arrest a proceeding against a foreign subject, of which the government of the latter had just reason to complain.

As to the other point—the United States could not admit that, though The Caroline might have been a piratical vessel, the whole American nation had become pirates. ON the contrary, it was maintained that the United States had, as far as possible, fulfilled their duties as a neutral State, which, we have seen, the British government itself admitted, in its communications with other foreign powers; and it was shown that all that England could contend for, in her contest with the insurgents of Canada, was to have the rights that a sovereign may exercise towards his subjects who had rebelled, and those which are allowed to a belligerent, in time of war, with reference to neutral States. It is an incontestible principle that no act of hostility can be exercised by belligerents within the limits of neutral territories. Nor did the case fall within the very doubtful exception, suggested by Bynkershoek, of an attack commenced out of the territory, and continued, *dum fervet opus*, within it, and which, even in such a case, according to the publicists, was always subject to the condition that they any injury that might accrue from it, either to person or property, was to be regarded as an act of aggression. The conditions here annexed to the exercise of the right are scarcely compatible with its existence, but in the case of The Caroline the contingency did not arise. It was not the continuation of a pursuit into an enemy's territory, but a premeditated attack of the military authorities of the Province of Upper Canada, executed during the night, against an American vessel at anchor in a harbor of the United States, on the shores of the Niagara Strait, which separates the respective territories of the two countries. All the writers on public law, especially the English, agree in forbidding such an act of hostility within neutral territory, even against an enemy.

The subject of the other article, which, as well as the case of The Caroline, was discussed between Mr. Webster and Lord Ashburton, was the affair of The Creole. The facts were these. An American planter sailed from Richmond, Virginia, on board of this vessel, with 135 slaves belonging to him, whom he was carrying to New Orleans. IN the straits, between Florida and the Bahama Islands, the negroes revolted, killed their master, put the captain in irons, and wounded several of the crew, and then took possession of the vessel and carried her into Nassau. The governor arrested nineteen of the slaves concerned in the revolt and assassination, and set the others at liberty. As to the prisoners, he asked the direction of his government.

The case arose before the extradition treaty with Great Britain, but subsequent to the abolition of slavery in the West Indies. Theinquiry is preceded by an exposition of the law of nations, in reference to extradition, substantially the same as is given in the "Elements," which work was, indeed, quoted in this very matter, by Lord Campbell, during a debate in the House of Lord, in which he, as well as Lord Brougham, Lord Denman, and Lord Lyndhurst, took part. Mr. Wheaton then remarks that slavery has existed, as a fact, among the most civilized nations; and that though the slave-trade has been abolished by all the powers of Europe and America, its fruits still remain in the United States, Brazils, and the Spanish colonies, the British emancipation act never having been followed in those countries. The independence of every nation in this matter must be respected; and it was to attribute an immense and unheard of power to the legislation of a single nation, to accord to it the right of changing the laws which control the property of all nations. Until Sommersett's case, in1771, slavery was recognized in England, and slaves were publicly sold at the Exchange. Even so late as 1827, Lord Stowell decided that, though slaves arriving in England were free while they remained there, and their masters could not send them out of the country, yet if they returned to the colonies, no matter by what means, their ancient condition was restored. The laws of France formerly preserved, to a greater or less extent, the control of the master over the slaves brought with him from the colonies; but since 1791, the slave who voluntarily seeks an asylum in France, under ordinary circumstances, may claim the protection of the maxim which frees whomever touches the soil; but the French ports cannot become a refuge for robbers, to find succor and impunity for crimes committed against the persons and property of a friendly nation.

Mr. Wheaton shows that, though in the Netherlands, in the middle ages, foreign slaves were free on touching the soil, a distinction was made in favor of masters arriving from the colonies, accompanied by their slaves. In Denmark, a slave from the colonies may be reclaimed by his master. In Prussia, masters travelling with their slaves preserve their rights over them; and in Russia, and other countries where slavery still exists, extradition by the authorities of the country to which the serf escapes prevails; while in Spain and Portugal, masters bringing their slaves from the colonies preserve their property in them. Hence he concludes that the nations of Europe have not established it, as an invariable rule, having the force of a moral law, that an individual, a slave in the country from whence he departs, becomes free when he touches European soil; and if they had, it would not follow that it applied to the case of The Creole.

The only remaining question was, whether the particular circumstances, connected with the arrival of The Creole in the port of Nassau, constituted such an exception to the general rule as to authorize the American government to ask any satisfaction of the English government.

Mr. Wheaton regards the affairs of The Creoleneither as a case of the extradition of the offenders by the government of the country, where they have committed a crime, nor as the ordinary one of slaves seeking an asylum in a country where slavery is not tolerated. The general principle is undoubted, that the vessels of a country, on the ocean, and beyond the territorial limits of any other nation, are subject to its exclusive jurisdiction, and that they only pass under the jurisdiction of a foreign State when they voluntarily enter its ports. The Creole never ceased to be subject exclusively to American jurisdiction. Entering into a friendly port, against the will of the owner and captain, and in consequence of a crime on the high seas, cognizable only by the courts of the United States, The Creole continued to enjoy the rights of her flag, and the captain had a claim for the assistance of the local authorities to regain possession of his vessel. The negroes could not be considered as mixed with the inhabitants; and whatever the generality of its expression, the law could not be taken to be applicable to slaves arriving in the country in consequence of crime, and against the will of their owners.

It may not be irrelevant to state that, by the decision of umpire, a full indemnity was accorded for the value of the slaves on board of The Creole, by the joint commission, under the convention of February 8, 1853, between the United States and Great Britain, for the settlement of claims against either government, by the citizens or subjects of the other, arising subsequent to the treaty of Ghent. The principles contended for by the American government, and discussed in the preceding argument of Mr. Wheaton, were thereby recognized and sustained. Similar adjudications were also rendered in several other cases.

Of an analogous character with the preceding papers was an article published by Mr. Wheaton on the Constitution of the United States, in the Staata-

Zeitung, the official gazette of Prussia, on the 27th of March, 1843. The object of it was, to show the distinction between the debts of the individual States and that of the Union. It appeared at a time when the repudiation of their obligations by some of the States was materially affecting the American reputation abroad; and the occasion was taken to point out the fact, that neither the general government nor the other members of the Confederacy were in any wise connected with the transactions, which were the subject of complaint. While he shows that "the American federal government has always fulfilled, with the most conscientious fidelity, its engagements towards its foreign as well as its domestic creditors," he denies that the suspension of the regular payment of interest on their public debt, by some of the States, where it concerns foreign creditors, contains within itself *a casus belli*, on the part of those powers whose subjects suffer from it; and he refers to the fact, that the federal government had not the constitutional power to compel the States to comply with these obligations. As to its being, in any case, *a casue belli*, he remarks: "This deduction proceeds from the supposition, that where a sovereign State fails to fulfil its agreement with the subjects of a foreign State, it becomes a ground of reprisals on the part of the latter. Such a supposition is nowhere supported by the publicists, and this idea has always been set aside by the British government, in the different claims which it has made in favor of British creditors in Spain, Portugal, and the South American republics." Writing to a friend, about the same period, he says: — "A great deal of my time and attention is occupied in refuting the misrepresentations of our national character and conduct, which are constantly appearing in the German papers, *from no friendly source*, concerning slavery, the slave-trade, State credits, Lynch-law, &c. &c. &c. I hold it to be the duty of a public minister, to take care of the honor of his country abroad."

The revolutions produced in the international policy of China, consequent on the peace of the 26th of August, 1842, with the cession of Hong Kong to England, and the probable opening, through the British treaty, of her ports to the commerce of the world, led, in Germany, to a very through examination of the resources of that great empire, including as well its overland trade with Russia, as its relations with the maritime States of Europe and America, and its internal condition under the Mandschu dynasty, which succeeded, in 1644, to the ancient sovereigns of the country. Not only on account of the commerce from Germany, that passed through Russia, but to promote a maritime intercourse by the Cape of Good Hope, Prussia was preparing, in connection with the States of the Zollverein, though at her own expense, a mission to China, where an American Plenipotentiary Commissioner had already gone. Mr. Wheaton drew up, in August, 1843, from the materials accessible to him, a paper in relation to the recent military and diplomatic transactions of Great Britain in that quarter, and the measures being adopted in Europe to secure the Chinese trade, and which Mr. Upshur directed to be transcribed and forwarded to Mr. Cushing.

He also prepared about the same time, and transmitted to the Department of State, an argument in support of the claim of the representatives of Commodore Paul Jones, against Denmark, on account of prizes sent into Norway, and delivered up by the Danish government to the English, during our revolutionary war. In this paper, after premising that the case was not included in the Treaty of March 28, 1830, and which was confined, in terms, to claims growing out of the last maritime war of Denmark, he examines the relations which the united States held, during the period in question, towards other governments which had not recognized their independence, and shows that, in case of a revolution in a sovereign Empire, by a province or colony shaking off the dominion of the mother country, and whilst the civil war continues, if a foreign power does not acknowledge the independence of the new State, and form treaties of amity and commerce with it, though still remaining neutral, as it may do, or join in an alliance with one party against the other, thus rendering that other its enemy, it must, while continuing passive, allow to both the contending parties all the rights, which public war gives to independent sovereigns. That, in 1779, our case was not that of an ordinary revolt in the bosom of a State, but a civil war entitling both parties to the rights of war, was acknowledged by the parent State itself, in the solemn exchange of prisoners by regular cartels, in the respect shown to conventions of capitulation concluded by British generals, and in the exercise of the other *commercia belli*, usually recognized between civilized States. In the absence of any treaty with England, to exclude the prizes of her enemy, and of any previous prohibition to the United States, by either of which means their prizes might have been refused admission without any violation of neutrality, they had the right to presume the assent od Denmark to send them into her ports; the more especially had they such a right, when based, as in the actual case, on necessity, from stress of weather. When once arrived in the port, the neutral government of Denmark was bound to respect the military right of possession, lawfully acquired through war, by capture on the high seas, and continued in the port to which the prize was brought. He added, that there was no ground for the application of the *jus postliminii*, which could only take place between subjects of the same State or of allies in the war, a neutral State having only a right to interfere to deprive the captor of his possession, when the capture has been made in violation of neutral sovereignty, within the limits of the neutral State, or by a vessel equipped there.

In further accordance with the course, which Mr. Wheaton had adopted, of communicating whatever intelligence he supposed might advance the interests or promote the prosperity of his country, he addressed, at the close of 1845, an elaborate despatch to the Secretary of State, on the importance of reopening the ancient water communication between Europe and the East Indies, by Egypt and the Red Sea and of opening a new route from the United States and Europe to the East INdies, by a ship canal between the Atlantic and Pacific, across the Isthmus connecting North and South America; thus avoiding the immense *detours*, by which the continents of Africa and America are terminated in the southern hemisphere. With the former enterpriser he proposed to connect a line of steamers, not only as mail packets, and for passengers, but for the conveyance of the finer fabrics and of valuable merchandise from the United States to the British Channel and German Sea, touching at Cowes or Havre, and proceeding to Bremen or Hanburg, from whence an intercourse was already established towards the East Indies by hydraulic works, parallel with the railroad route between the Adriatic and the German Sea, and forming a continuous communication between the waters failing into the German Ocean and those that emptied into the Black Sea. The obstacles to the navigation of the Danube had been removed, by the Treaty of 1840, between Austria and Russia, the advantages of which were accorded to all nations that had the right to navigate the Black Sea; while the common use of the rivers of Germany had been previously stipulated that the views above expressed, with regard to the patronage of the government to postal steamers, preceded any action of Congress on the subject; the first appropriation for that object, which was for the Bremen line, having been made June 19, 1846.

The suggestions with reference to the communication by the Isthmus of Panama, besides our author's having the benefit of all the learning on the subject then attainable in Europe, were made on consultation with the venerable Humboldt, who, on all matters connected with this Interoceanic Canal, has, since his travels, been deemed the highest authority. Mr. Wheaton incorporated, in his despatch, the last views of the great traveller, on the practical accomplishment of a work, the value of which to the United States, at its date, was principally estimated by the saving of 10000 miles, in the voyage, by Cape Horn and the North-west coast of America, to China; attention being then particularly attracted to the trade of that country, —an increased intercourse with which it was supposed would be effected by the treaty, recently concluded by Mr. Cushing, with the Celestial Empire. The immense accessions subsequently made to our commercial facilities in the Indian Ocean, with the prospect of opening, through our means, to the trade of the world the Empire of Japan, have added greatly to the contemplated benefits of the proposed route, which, as well as the one through the Isthmus of Suez, it was suggested to put under the common guarantee of all the maritime powers, as part of the great thoroughfare of nations. But though only some nine years have elapsed since Mr. Wheaton wrote, our title to Oregpn had not then been admitted; the war with Mexico had not yet commenced; much less had California been ceded to us, and the foundations laid of a State on the Pacific, which already rivals, in wealth and commerce, the most flourishing of the Atlantic Commonwealths. The prosperity of theses newly acquired regions has justly diverted the attention of the American people from a communication through foreign territory, with guarantees depending on the good faith of maritime and commercial rivals, and the very attempt to from which has occasioned serious diplomatic embarrassments, to direct routes across the continent, wherever convenience may dictate, wholly within our own sovereignty, and binding together, with bolts of iron, the confederated States, extending over the immense tract separating the two oceans.

The close scrutiny, which the long pending negotiations with the Zollverein rendered necessary, into the economical policy of the German States, induced the Minister to acquaint himself with all the conventional arrangements of that nature, which Prussia and her associate States were contracting with other powers, in and out of Germany. We have thus the objections of Prussia to any member of the Confederation entering into a commercial union with a State foreign to Germany, while in the refusal of the King of Holland to ratify a treaty for the union of Luxemburg with the Zollverein, we have an examination of the right of a sovereign to withhold his ratification, though the treaty has been made in strict conformity to instructions and in virtue of a full power.

Reference ia made, in connection with the mission to China, set on foot by Prussia for the purpose of promoting the general commercial interests of Germany, to the project, which was one of the objects of the short-lived Germanic Empire, —the establishment of a national unity, as regards the navigation interests, by the adoption of a system, which might do for shipping what the Zollverein had proposed for commerce. "For this purpose, a plan had been prepared by Dr. Smidt, Senator, Senator and Burgomaster, at Bremen, (who governs that town as Pericles governed Athens, with authority almost absolute, at the same time preserving the forms of a free State,) to eastablish a general union of all the maritime States of Germany, (including Austris,) for the purpose of protecting the common navigation interests of the entire Germanic Confederation. This *Schiff-fahrts Verein*, as it was to have been called, was to have been authorized to make treaties of navigation with foreign powers, for the purpose of securing to German shipping reciprocal advantages in foreign ports, to appoint consuls in those ports, and to adopt a common national flag."

The anomalous position of a government, where religion is an affair of State, but where the sovereign and thepeople belong to different creeds, is presented in the case of the difficulties which arose between the King of Prussia and the ecclesiastical authorities of the Rhenish provinces, where the Catholic religion predominates. The dispute with the Archbishop of Cologne, in 1837-8, for refusing to submit to the king's views as to mixed marriages, and other questions regarded as matters exclusively of ecclesiastical cognizance, and which became almost a subject of European discussion, made the Prussian Cabinet anxious to oppose to the ultra-montane or Jesuit party of Germany the united force of the Protestant community. A very favorite measure of the king to bring about this object was the blending of the Lutheran and Reformed Churches in one communion, to which effect, indeed, a decree was issued so far back as 1817. We have a notice of a conference of ecclesiastical and lay deputies, representing the different Protestant governments of Germany, assembled at Berlin, at the beginning od 1846, for the purpose of promoting unity of faith, discipline, and worship. The disappointment, however, which began to be felt at rhe evasions of the long deferred promise, made by Frederick William III., of a constitutional charter, did not aid the ecclesiastical projects of his successor; and, as Mr. Wheaton remarks, "under these circumstances a measure, which is intended to promote uniformity of faith and worship in the established national church, finds but little favor in public opinion, which tends more and more to tolerate dissent in religious matters, and to demand constitutional securities in political concerns."

Mr. Wheaton's mission terminated, even before the promulgation of the edict of February, 1847, for convoking the Prussian Diet, and by which it was attempted, most imperfectly, to fulfil the promises made under the edict of the 26th of October, 1810, and the declaration of the 25th of May, 1815, of a constitution founded on popular representation. Consequently the revolutionary movements of the succeeding year are not within the particular scope of this notice.

The old king, Frederick William III., who died in June, 1840, though not wanting in that personal courage which has ever distinguished the princes of the House of Brandenburg, had very little of that self-reliance which suggests and executes great revolutions. From his inveterate habits of self-indulgence and procrastination, he ever suffered the most urgent and important business to be neglected. As he frequently consulted, though he was the minister of the great rival of Prussia, Prince Metternich, whom he saw every year at the Baths of Toeplitz, on the affairs of his own kingdom, as well as on matters of foreign policy, it was not extraordinary that nothing was effected towards political reform in his life-time. The present sovereign, Frederick William IV., was described, on his accession to the throne, as "a man of exemplary morals, and a highly educated and accomplished prince."

In a notice of this nature it is impossible to present even an analysis of the despatches from Berlin, on the general questions of European politics. When his mission there began, the agitation consequent on the French Revolution of 1830 had not yet ceased; while in the premature insurrection of Poland, in the movements in Prussia and the other States of Germany, and in the attempts of the sovereigns to satisfy by the smallest concessions possible the popular demands, we have the germ of those demonstrations throughout Europe, to which subsequent events gave vitality. The severance of the KIngdom of the Netherlands, —the creation of the Congress of Vienna, with the separation of Belgium from Holland, —the result of the Revolution of Brussels, the miniature edition of that of Paris, obstinately resisted by the King of Holland, and the controversy respecting it, including the questions connected with the dismemberment of Luxemburg, in which the Diet of the Germanic Confederation claimed the right to intervene, were not fully terminated till 1839. During the intermediate period, there were continued conferences of the Ministers of the five great powers, who, referring to the Protocol of Aix-la-Chapelle, of 1818, as an authority for the perpetual existence of the alliance, undertook, as early as 1831, to make a treaty for Holland and Belgium.

The nationality of Poland was one of the measures supposed to be secured, even when its territory was parcelled out at Vienna. The assurances, however, on that subject, which were without any effective guarantee, were destined to be illusory. In 1832, The Kingdom of Poland had become politically merged in the Russian Empire. The ultimate fate of Cracow, by which the existence of the Republic was annihilated, was not finally settled till after the date of Mr. Wheaton's last despatches; but we learn from them that, in 1836, the Minister of Foreign Affairs of Prussia would scarcely permit to be read to him the protests of England and France against the continued occupation of that free city. And to the application of the Provincial Diet of the Grand Duchy of Posen, embracing that part of Poland occupied on the final partition by Prussia, for the political institutions stipulated for in the treaties of annexation, the king stated that the promise, contained in the declaration of 22d May, 1815, was not obligatory on him, inasmuch as his late royal father, who had substituted for it the edict of the 12ty of June, 1823, had declared that its fulfilment was not binding on him, as not consistent with the welfare of his people. And in one of his last despatches Mr. Wheaton remarked, that

Prussia was gradually blending the Grand Duchy of Posen with the German provinces of her dominions. The affairs of the Peninsula, including the operations of the Quadruple Alliance, concluded in 1834, between England, and France, and Spain and Portugal, for the termination of the civil wars in the two latter countries, are within the scope of these papers, as well as the mediation of France between Naples and Great Britain, in 1840, the importance of which consisted in the settlement of the dispute without the intervention of Austria.

To the Emperor Nicholas, he was presented on occasion of his visit to Berlin, in 1838, and he again met him, the same year, at the Baths of Toeplitz. He had early said of him that "he had elevation of character to feel that to become the legislator of more than fifity millions, of so many various nations, tongues, and religions, is a far more noble object of ambition than a few barren trophies on the banks of the Danube. But in this, as in other respects, he had been obliged to yield to the genius of his nation." We have referred to the views which Mr. Wheaton conceived, at the commencement of his mission at Copenhagen, with regard to the ultimate fate of Turkey. And writing, soon after arrival at Berlin, he says, what commands new interest from recent occurrences: "If I am not wholly misinformed, the Emperor of Russia is not disposed much longer to postpone the execution of those designs upon Turkey, which he has inherited from the traditionary policy of his predecessors—a policy, in the actual nature of things, requiring the possession of Constantinople and the Dardanelles, in order to give complete development to the natural resources of Russia, and to enable her to advance in the career of civilization, in which she is now impeded for want of the complete command of this channel of communication with the Mediterranean, and its rich coasts and islands. It is therefore believed that the Emperor Nicholas has reserved the conquest of Constantinople as the crowning glory of his active reign, and that circumstances alone will determine the choice of the moment for executing this project." On the same occasion he alludes to an opportunity, that he had

had of inspecting the documents found in the cabinet of the Grand Duke Constantine, at the breaking out of the Polish Insurrection in 1830, and from which it appeared that preparations had been made to threaten Austria with an insurrection of the Slavonic population of Hungary and Gallicia, had she attempted, in the campaign of the preceding year, which was terminated by the treaty of Adrianople, to disturb the Russian army in their march towards Constantinople. He also refers to propositions made by Russia to Austria, in 1835, and rejected by her, for an ample share in the partition of Turkey as well as to negotiations, arising out of their failure, with Prussia, by which the latter power was urged to hold herself in readiness to attack Austria in the rear on the Bohemian frontier, and to hold France in check by a military demonstration on the Rhine, while Russia moved on Constantinople by land and by sea. Mr. Wheaton, in the despatch from which we have already quoted, further remarked, that "so long as the treaty of Unkiar Skelessi remains in force, —so long as Russia keeps what the Emperor Alexander called the *keys of his house*, —it is plain that France and England alone, with the utmost exertion of Their power and resources, could not prevent the occupation of Constantinople and the Bosphorus by a Russian fleet and army; and it is perhaps even doubtful whether, with the aid of Autria, they could prevent the accomplishment of this design, whenever the favorable moment arrives for its consummation."

The various negotiations, from those of 1827, for the pacificationof Greece, to the treaty of 1841, recognizing the closing to foreign ships of war, in time of peace, of the waters connecting the Mediterranean and the Black Sea, and which, while it shuts other nations out of the latter sea, also excludes the Russian navy from the former, will be found cited in the "Elements," and will illustrate the international relations between Christian Europe and its Mohammedan State, anterior to the pending controversy. England, in connection with one or more of the other great powers, by participating with Russia in her interference with the internal affairs of Turkey, constantly endeavored to prevent the exclusive protectorate of the Czar, (which seemed to have been permanently secured, in 1833, by the alliance of Unkiar Skelessi,) and to protection of her East INdian possessions, as well as a means to prevent the establishment of a great maritime State, for which the Sultan's dominions in Europe present such facilities. Apprehensions of the separate intervention of Russia, also, induced the other powers to take into their own hands the negotiations between Mohamet Ali and the Porte. And though France, a party to the subsequent treaty of 1841, refused, on account of the terms offered to the pasha being less favorable than she deemed proper, to join in that of 1840, and which was therefore confined to Russia, Great Britain, Austria, and Prussia, the French Minister of Foreign Affairs, (M. Guizot,) expressly states at the time, that, if the execution of the treaty should be landed in Asia Minor, so as to produce a new complication, endangering the European balance of power, France resumed the right of acting as her honor and interest might ultimately dictate.

In 1836, the "Elements of International Law" were published at London. The same year an edition appeared in Philadelphia, and a third one, in English, at the same place in 1844. An edition prepared by the author, with his latest emendations, was published, in French, by Brockhaus, at Leipzig and Paris, in 1848, and another edition was issued from the same press, in 852-3.

The "Elements" were, at once, not only in the author's own country, but by the periodical press of England, France, and Germany, recognized as a standard treatise. They were introduced to the American student of public law by a gentleman known as a scholar, and experienced as a diplomatist, who, after having served his country at different courts of Europe, was lost to the cause of literary and historical research, at the moment when, as the fruits of a new mission to the East, the world was expecting to have unfolded to them the arcana of the Celestial Empire. The able French journal, devoted to juridical science, recommended the work to the young French diplomacy, and urged its immediate translation. It does justice to the frankness with which Mr. Wheaton met the discussion of new and interesting matters, on which his predecessors had maintained silence; particularly on that delicate question, the right of intervention by one power in the affairs of another, which our author has, elsewhere, declared to be an "undefined and undefinable exception to the mutual independence of nations."

The first edition of a Prize Essay, prepared for the Institute of France, under the title of "Histoire des progres du droit des gens en Europe, depuis la paix de Westphalie jusqu' au Congres de Vienne," was published at Leipzig, in 1841; and another edition, much enlarged, appeared there and at Paris, in 1846. A third one was also published by Brockaus, in 1853-4. This work, whose object is to trace the progress which the law of nations has made since the treaty of Westphalis, occupies a place never before filled in the literature of the English language, or in that of any other. All students of jurisprudence, all students of history, who, not content with descriptions of wars and battles, rise to the grand principles, which are the sources of events, will regard this book as not less important than the Elements. An English translation appeared at New York, on 1845, under the title of the "History of the Law of Nations, in Europe and America, from the earliest times to the treaty of Washington, in1842." Among the suggested ameliorations in the law of nations, which Mr. Wheaton discuss, was that of the establishment of perpetual peace, by the settlement of national disputes without resort to hostilities. Schemes have been, at different times, devised by philanthropists for the purpose of putting an end to all war; and he gives us in detail the plans of St. Pierre and Rousseau, of Bentham and Kant, for effecting this object. In some shape or other they are all referable to the principle of a general council of nations, which may serve as a great tribunal, whose jurisdiction all States are to acknowledge. The events of the last few years have not removed the objections that heretofore suggested themselves to the propositions for an Amphictyonic Council, which our author narrates historically. As stated in a review at the time, "this project cannot be deemed a wholly untried experiment. The Holy Alliance, when it parcelled put kingdoms at Vienna, sacrificing Poland to Russia, the greater part of Saxony to Prussia, and the ancient republics of Genoa and Venice to Sardinia and Austria; and when it met at Troppan and Laybach, to sustain the rights of sovereigns against their subjects, was exercising, under the most solemn sanctions of religion, that general superintendence over the affairs of Europe, which the philanthropists propose to vest in a general council. Great as have been the calamities of war, it may well be doubted whether they ought not to be encountered, in preference to a system which would divest every small State of the perfect independence which belongs to all sovereignties."

The compte rendu of the original work, for the *Revue Etrangere*, was prepared by Pinheiro Ferreira, an eminent publicist, formerly the Minister of Foreign Affairs of Portugal, and who had been the editor both of Vatted and Martens. It declares that "it bears evidence of the vast erudition of the author, showing that nothing which had been done or written that was remarkable was unknown to him; and that if there were defects in it, they were to ascribed to the circumstances under which it was written, and with had prevented the author from giving to it the form that he would have adopted, could he have been allowed to follow the inspirations of his clear and methodical mind." And in a subsequent volume, in which the American edition is announced, it is declared to have supplied all preceding omissions, and to have rendered the work a necessary compliment to the "Elements."

A paper in the Edinburgh Review, from the pen of the jurist and political economist, Senior, under the head of the historical treatise, as it originally appeared in the French language, while it presents the difficulty of reducing to any general rules the practice of nations, and contests the author's views on the right of visit in time of peace, does justice to his preeminent fitness for his task. "few men," it remarks, "are better qualified to write a history of the law of nations than Mr. Wheaton. Alawyer, a history of the law of nations than Mr. Wheaton. A lawyer, a historian, and he is the author of one of the best treatises on the actual state of that law, of which in the essay, the subject of this article, he is the historian." And in expressing the hope that Mr. Wheaton would translate it into English, he adds, "It would form an excellent supplements to his great work on international law. There are many persons in his own country and in ours, to whom it is inaccessible in its present form; and he must be anxious that his field of utility and of fame should be co-extensive with the English language."

The German periodicals were not less decided in their commendation of Mr. Wheaton's treatises than those of England and France; though, as was remarked in the Leipziger Blatter fur Literarischen Unterhaltung, the public attention had, in Germany, been long exclusively drawn to those questions of internal public law, which is supposed to regulate their international relations, had been somewhat neglected. THe importance of no longer leaving it as the pursuit of a particular class, but of popularizing the science of international, as that of constitutional law had been, and which would result from the admission of the moral personality of each particular nation, is insisted on. "To effect this requires the development, by such a writer as the enlightened author of the 'Elements of International Law,' of those fundamental principles which constitute the basis of the international law received among the civilized and Christian nations of the earth." M. Ludewig closes his notice, by declaring that "every student of this important science is bound to acknowledge his deep gratitude to the learned author, who, uniting the accomplishments of a public jurist and of a practical diplomat of the school of Franklin and Jefferson, to those of the scholar, already known by his other literary works, has furnished the best commentary on his Elements of International Law."

It is unnecessary to multiply citations from the public press. The references which have been made to the leading periodicals of the principal countries of the world, are only illustrations of what, everywhere, was the expression of enlightened criticism. That these were not mere evanescent marks of commendation, is now established by the fact that all subsequent publicists who have discussed international law, have treated Mr. Wheaton's works as permanent contributions to the science, and as authorities by which their own view are to be modified, and the decisions of cabinets regulated.

Of the systematic treaties which have appeared in England since his time, the most esteemed are those of Manning and Reddie, both of whom discuss the controverted questions of maritime law, and the interpolations attempted to be introduced into it by the imperial decrees and orders in council, when France and England were contending belligerents. Mr. Wheaton had confined himself too much to those branches of the law which had received the adjudication of judicial tribunals, and not dilated sufficiently on the principles which must rest on authority of reason, says: "Dr. Wheaton has written a work professedly elementary, and in which some parts are besides finished in a most instructive manner; he has cultivated the department of the subject which he had selected for his occupation with results that must afford pleasure and information to all who peruse his pages; and no one has a right to complain that he has not chosen a wider fired, or devoted his time to a more laborious production. The interest derivable from his work is not such as merely to concern professional lawyers, but political students of every class will derive satisfaction from his pages. Dr. Wheaton's work is the best elementary treatise on the law of nations that has appeared, and it leaves the impression that the author's abilities might, had he so chosen, have given with advantage a fuller insight into the science which he illustrates."

Mr. Reddie published, in 1842, his "International Law," in which, among the writers on the science, he enumerates the work of "the very able and learned American lawyer, Dr. Henry Wheaton, entitled 'Elements of International law.' Availing himself not merely of the works of the old writers on the law of nations, but also of the more methodical and philosophical treatise of Martens, Schmalz, and Kluber, and of the labors of Martens, in the collection and arrangement of the treaties of the European powers, as constituting the conventional law of civilized nations, Dr. Wheaton has produced an excellent work, which, although not British, is indisputably the best of the kind in the English language." IN his subsequent treatise on "Maritime International Law," a large portion is devoted to an analysis of the principles elucidated by Mr. Wheaton; and he fully redeems the declaration in the introduction, in which he says: "Of that in most respects excellent author's works, his 'Digest of the Law of Maritime Captures,' his 'Elements of International Law,' his 'History of the Progress of the Law of Nations since the Peace of Westphalia,' and his late 'Inquiry into the Right of Visitation and Search, with reference to the Suppression of the African Slave-Trade,' we shall have occasion to speak with the commendation that is justly due to them."

A still later writer, Mr. Polson, though not agreeing with our author as to the title which he has given to his science, unites with the publicists of his country in considering his work the most useful book on the subject extent; while some of the most important positions of Phillimore's "Commentaries of International Law" rest for their authority on Wheaton's Elements. Phillimore, in introducing his work, remarks, that "the history of the progress of international law, has been written by Ompteda, Miruss, and Wheaton, by the last author both in English and French, in a manner which leaves the German, the English, and the French reader but little to desire."

Hautefcuille and Ortolan, whose books were justly esteemed the best exponents of the continental theories on maritime jurisprudence, (the work of the latter, indeed, being intended as a practical guide to the members of the naval profession, to which the author himself belonged,) about in quotations from the treatises of Mr. Wheaton, to whom they unite in assigning the highest rank in science; while the occasional criticisms in which they indulge show that their approbation is not devoid of discrimination. It may be added that the *compte rendu* of the latter's work, in the Review of Mr. Falix, is from Mr.

Wheaton, and that he has not hesitated to adopt in the last edition of his Elements some of Ortolan's suggestions, especially in relation to the jurisdiction over merchant ships in foreign ports.

It may be remarked that the objections made to Mr. Wheaton's works, by the English and French commentators, are of an opposite character. While the former charge him with unfriendly sentiments towards their own country, the latter take exception at his vindication of those principles which our courts equally with those of England have heretofore maintained, in the absence of conventional stipulations, in reference to the conflicting rights of belligerents and neutrals, especially as to the claim of taking enemy's property from neutral vessels. So far as regards any partiality to the prejudice of England, the authority now concede to him by the statesmen and publicists of that country is the best response; and in the great debate, in which the principles of the Queen's declaration of 28th March, 1854, were vindicated by Sir W. Molesworth, on the part of the government, not merely on grounds of temporary expediency, but on considerations of permanent policy, Mr. Wheaton's works were referred to as the highest evidence of the existing law of nations, as well by the Minister of the Crown as by those who sustained the old system.

On the other hand, it is to be remembered that the "Elements" do not purport to be an inquiry into what the law of nations ought to be independently of their usage, but what that law is, as recognized by the practice of nations. That no one would have more heartily rejoiced at the revolution effected by the recent adoption, during a state of war, of those principles which give immunity to neutrals, and which, however often to be found, to a limited extent, in treaties, have always been disregarded after the breaking out of hostilities, is sufficiently apparent from Mr. Wheaton's own writings.

To his extra-official labors in preventing, through the Quintuple treaty of 1841, the application, in time of peace, of the right of search, which, if it exists at all, can only be exercised in war, we have heretofore referred. While Mr. Wheaton's early efforts were directed to the vindication of those rights of neutral commerce, and of the liberty of our fellow-citizens who were taken in derogation of our nationality from our ships, and which ultimately led to the war of 1812, we find, in a publication by him, in 1817, the Treaty of 1794 declared "an indelible disgrace of our national councils, because it sacrificed those rights which it was our bounden duty to maintain, as a member of the community of neutral States."

Among Mr. Wheaton's papers, in the French Review for 1844, is one on the work of Mr. Heffter, Das Europaische Volkerrecht, a book which is repeatedly cited in the first part of the "Elements," where a summary of that writer's system is given.

Mr. Wheaton's old colleague at Copenhagen, Count Raczynski, was not only possessed of one of the best galleries at Berlin, but was the author of a magnificent work, giving an account of the brilliant and rapid progress of the Fine Arts in Germany, since the continental peace of 1815. This book was the subject of successive notices on the appearance of each of the three volumes, presenting in themselves a sketch of the great artists of the different states of Germany, as well as of their productions, and with which Mr. Wheaton's long residence in the country, and his frequent journeys, had made him personally acquainted.

Nor were the fruits of these students confined to the publication of a European period. In 1842, a society was established at Washington, under the title of the National institute, which it was hoped might, from its location at the seat of government, combine in a literary and scientific association those Americans, who were engaged in the cultivation of liberal pursuits, and hereafter take a rank with similar societies in the capitals of the old world. To this association Mr. Wheaton conceived it his duty to communicate whatever information he had collected, that might be useful to his country, and with respect to which he did not correspond with the Depart of State. His letters addressed to his friend, Francis Markoe, Corresponding Secretary of the Society, have never yet been published in a permanent form. They present a most instructive account of the state modern art, as well of architecture as of painting and statuary. In one of them, indeed, we have a description of that recent monument of German nationality, of which Raczynski speak at length, the Walhalla, near the ancient imperial city of Ratishon, where it was intended to unite all these three arts, and in which are brought together the Teutonlc celebrities, going back to Alfred and Egbert, of the Anglo-Saxon race, and foundation of the schools of Munich, Dusseldorf, and Berlin, and in familiarizing his countrymen with the names of Cornelius, Schadow, Wach, as well as with those of the architect Schinkel, and of the sculptor Rauch, and other contemporaries in fame, had he forgotten Thorvaldsen, the Dane, the glory of that country, where so many years of our author's life were passed, and whose death, after his return to the land of his nativity, during the progress of these papers, presented a further occasion for referring to the great works in which he was engaged at Copenhagen, and with his career terminated.

Recondite historical researches, for which his position afforded peculiar facilities, also occupy many columns of the Washington journal, in which the papers of the society appeared. THe physical geography of Humboldt, the writings of Diderot, the geography of Affghanistan, with the war then (1842) raging in Central Asia, and the original object of which, on the part of the British, is described to have been to acquire a predominant control in that region, so as to guard against the contingent danger of Russia agents acquiring such influence among the Affghans as to be hereafter able to wield them, in conjunction with the Persians, as instruments of attack against the British dominions, were among the other topics of these communications.

Ancillon, Werther, and Canitz, successively Ministers of Foreign Affairs, were his personal friends, as well as the Chevalier Bunsen, The distinguished representative of Prussia at London, who, in introducing to him one of the Professors of the University, then engaged in writing a manual on the law of nations, says: "He fully appreciates the importance for him and his science to have access to the one of the greatest European authorities, on many of the most interesting points of international law." He had in the Minister of England, Loed William Russell, the brother of the Minister of State, the Baron Meyendorf, the distinguished representative of Russia, and M. de Bresson, long the representative of France, intimate associates, whose letters, still extant, show that his intercourse with his colleagues of the diplomatic corps was such as exists among enlightened gentlemen, on an equal footing, as regards both attainments and social position. He was also a correspondent of that veteran diplomatist, Sir Rpbert Adair, whose entrance on the public service was coeval with the American Revolution. In transmitting to Mr. Wheaton a copy of the account of his mission to Vienna, in 1806, Sir Robert takes occasion to mention the fact, communicated to him by Mr. Fox himself, that he had only consented to enter the Ministry, which succeeded Lord North's, on the pledge of the immediate unconditional recognition of the independence of the United States; and that his subsequent resignation was induced by the circumstance, that Lord Shelburne, who became Premier on the death of the Marquis of Rockingham, had previously, (on the ground that America was in his department, which, as Home Secretary, then embraced the colonies,) deputed Mr. Oswald to Paris, where Mr. Fox also sent Mr. Grenville.

Mr. Wheaton's despatches contain accounts of interesting interviews with Metternich, whose name was so long synonymous with Austrian diplomacy. In a despatch of the 19th of July, 1838, which is here introduced as one among the many proofs that no opportunity was lost by him of using, for the advantage of his country, (whether or not the matter was embraced within his immediate functions,) the facilities which either his official rank or personal consideration commanded, he says: "I had yesterday a conversation of some length with the Archduke Francis, (who is a member of the council called the *Conference*, by which the government of the Austrian empire is administered,) and with Prince Metternich, (the real sovereign of that empire) both of whom appeared to me attach great importance to the extension of the commercial intercourse between the United States and Austria. I did not fail to seize the occasion for intimating that the main obstacle, which had hitherto restricted that intercourse to a much less amount of exchanges than might have been expected from the great value and variety of the productions of the two countries adapted for exportation to each other, was to be found in the great inequality between their respective tariffs, and especially the discouragements created by the monopolies, lengthened quarantines, and other pernicious restraints on trade existing in the Austrian dominions. I insisted principally on the government monopoly of the trade and manufacture of tobacco, as being almost equivalent to a prohibition of our tobacco, only a small quantity of which is annually purchased by the Austrian *regie* at Bremen, to mix in with the Hungarian and other native tobaccoes."

But his associates were not confined to his professional brethren. Alone of the diplomatic corps, he was elected a foreign member, the number of which is limited to fifteen, of the Royal Academy of Sciences, where he had, as resident confreres, notonly Alexander Von Humboldt, whose unrivalled attainments in physical science are universally recognized, but Ritter, distinguished in geography, Buch and Lichtenstein in natural history, Encke in astronomy, Rose and Mitscherlich in chemistry, Saviguy and Steffens in philosophy, Boeckh in philology, and Bopp in the Sanscrit language and literature.

During the twenty years that Mr. Wheaton had been in diplomacy, he had received the most flattering assurances of the ability with which his duties were discharged, from all the Presidents under whom he had served, including Mr. Adams, Gen. Harrison, and Mr. Tyler; and his course had been equally approved by all those who had had the charge of the Department of State, being, besides Mr. Van Buren, Mr. Clay, Mr. Livingston, (to whom he was also united by kindred pursuits as a scholar and a jurist,) Mr. Mclane, Mr. Forsyth, Mr. Webster, Mr. Legare, Mr. Nelson, Mr. Upshur, and Mr. Calhoun.

It was at the height of his celebrity, and when he might justly have looked fora transfer to one of the great courts of Paris or London, where his experience and peculiar acquirements might have been more useful to his country, that he received an intimation from the Secretary of State, of President Polk's intention to terminate his mission at Berlin, with a view to the appointment of a successor, and the opportunity was afforded him of anticipating his removal by the tender of his resignation. It had been understood that, however general the rule of regarding our foreign missions as transient appointments, the importance of providing against unexpected exigencies would have led to the retaining abroad of at least one experienced diplomatist, through whom the government at Washington might have been advised of what was going on in the cabinets of Europe; and such would seem to have been the policy which, in Mr. Wheaton's case. had governed preceding administrations. Abroad, where our system of rotation in office, and from which, after what occurred in the present case, it cannot be supposed that any services however eminent, any fitness however unquestioned, can create an exception, the recall of Mr. Wheaton seemed scarcely susceptible of explanation. There was not a public journal in Germany that did not express surprise at the course of the American government, while his recall was subject of an elaborate article in the Augsburg Gazette. The only reasons assigned for his removal were such as might well have been regarded as his highest recommendations for continued employment—his great experience and the services that he had already rendered. A distinguished senator and former colleague wrote to him, under the date of June 17, 1846; "I have been somewhat negligent in answering your letter. I should have replied more promptly, if I had had any thing satisfactory to communicate to you. But I had not. I started your wish to remain in Europe, and also your high claims to consideration. But I find while your services and character are appreciated, there was a determination to shorten the terms of service of our diplomatic agents, and that the length of time you had been in

Europe presented an insuperable objection to your transfer to another station."

The King of Prussia not only regretted Mr. Wheaton's departure, but could not conceive it possible that any government could make such a mistake, as voluntarily to deprive itself of such a minister. This we learn not merely from a formal discourse, where it might be regarded as a complimentary phrase, but from the private note of the confidential friend of Frederick William IV., who, on his part, could not regard Mr. Wheaton's recall otherwise than as the prelude to promotion.

"Potsdam, ce 18 Juin, 1846.

Le roi gemit souvent sur votre depart. II sait combien vous nous etiez utile et il ne concoit pas L' erreur d'un gouvernement, qui se priv d'un tel appui. Je suis sur que le roi et la reine seront touches de la delicate attention du voyage de Madame Wheaton. Je ne puis encore me persuader qu' on ne vous destine pas quelque grande place en Europe. Votre nom et celui de Mr. Gallatin resent hautement places, et vous avez L' avantage sur lui d'excellents travaux historiques, c' est une grande et belle conception aussi que celle qui a ouvert la route du Nord des Etats-Unis par Trieate au Levant et dans L' Inde. On vous le doit. Agreez je vous supplie, mon cher et respectable confrere, L' hommage de mon inalterable devouement.

Alex. Humboldt."

The reference of Baron Humboldt is to the plan of communication across Erope, which is traced in one of the despatches, which has been noticed.

That the opinion expressed by Humboldt was no evanescent sentiment, we learn from an account of a visit to him, in Prussia, by our countryman Stephens, who will long be remembered for his graphic description of the monuments of Central America, and by the efforts, to which he sacrificed his life, to carry into effect those interoceanic communications to which the mind of Humboldt had been for so many years directed. "Baron Humboldt inquired about Mr. Wheaton, our late Minister to that country, and what was to be his future career. He said that it was understood at Berlin, that he was to be appointed Minister to France, and expressed his surprise that the United States should be willing to lose the public services of one so long trained in the school of diplomacy, and so well acquainted with the political institutions of Europe."

A despatch of 20th of July, 1846, thus announces the delivery of his letters of recall, on the 18th, at the palace of Charlottenburg: "I was introduced into the king's cabinet, and after delivering to his Majesty my latter of recall, I stated the President's desire to cultivate those amicable relations which had ever existed between the two countries, and which it had been my object to cherish during my long residence at this court. His Majesty was pleased to express his approbation of my zealous efforts to extend the commercial relations between the United States and the German States associated in the Zollverein, accompanied with many expression of regards towards me too flattering to be repeated.

"I had afterwards the honor of dining with the king and queen, and finally took leave, with the repetition, on the part of both their Majesties, of the kindest sentiments towards me."

"My venerable friend, Baron Von Humboldt, had informed me that a copy of the, magnificent edition of the king's expense, would have been offered to me, had it not been that I was not at liberty to accept of any present from his Majesty. I took this occasion, to request, that a copy might be delivered to me for the use of the Liberty of Congress, at Washington. I accordingly this day received from Mr. Olfers, Superintendent General of the Royal Museum, the three first volumes of the work, to be transmitted to the President."

"I shall leave here, with my family, for Paris, on the 23d instant."

On Mr. Wheaton's quitting Berlin, he didi not immediately return to the United States, but remained in Paris till the ensuring year. In that great capital he was no stranger. He had for some years (deeming it the best means of qualifying himself for the discharge of his diplomatic functions to compare the views of the statesmen of different countries,) passed such time there, as his immediate duties in Prussia permitted. His sojourn in Paris was in nowise without direct profit to his country. His European reputation gave him a position with the public men of France, who were there, more than elsewhere, the men of letters and science, which no official rank could command; and a letter of this period, from a gentleman long in our diplomatic service abroad, ascribes to Mr. Wheaton's communications to Washington, written from Paris, the conciliatory tone of President Jackson's message of 1835, and which led to a satisfactory settlement of the difficulty, in reference to the non-fulfilment of the Indemnity Treaty of 1831—a difficulty which had gone so far as to induce the proffer of the mediation of Great Britain. General Bernard was then a member of the king's cabinet, and we have likewise the evidence of his efforts, in the intercourse between him and Mr. Wheaton, founded on ancient associations, to terminate all dissensions between his own country and the one to whose hospitality he had been so long indebted; thus affording another proof, of which the acquisition of Louisiana, half a century ago—adjusted, as the French Plenipotentiary tells us, in friendly intercourse between him and the American Ministers, Mr. Livingston and Mr. Monroe—is a striking illustration, of how much may be effected, towards preserving the peace of the world by an accomplished minister, whose habits and acquirements place him on a footing of social communication with the members of the foreign government.

On several other occasions Mr. Wheaton rendered essential service, in conferring, respecting our policy, with distinguished men, in and out of office—such as Thiers, Mole, De Broglie—with whom his intercourse was based on other than offcial considerations. This was the case not only in 1841-2, when the right of search was a subject of engrossing interest, but in 1844-5, when it was important that our course, as to Texas and Mexico, should be understood. In reference to these subjects, Mr. Calhoun, State, says to him, in a private letter, dated December 26, 1844: — "You need no apology or explanation for your prolonged stay at Paris. I have no doubt that that your time was efficiently and well employed at that great centre of diplomatic relations of the civilized world. To give correct impressions there is all important, in the present state of our relations with England, in reference to Texas, Mexico, and this continent generally. They are, indeed, much needed there. The policy of France is, at present, far from being deep or wise, in reference to the affairs of this continent. It ought to be, on all points, antagonist to that of Great Britain. Should I remain where I am, you may be assured I shall not be indifferent as to what relates to yourself."

In the case of our Oregon difficulties, having a thorough acquaintance with the whole subject, not only were his lucid expositions of importance, in the familiar intercourse which he had with Sir Robert Peel and Lord Aberdeen, but in putting our other representatives abroad in a position in which to vindicate and sustain our country's rights.

In April, 1842, Mr. Wheaton had been elected a corresponding member of the French Institute. Mr. Lackanal, through whom the appointment was communicated, states, that during the forty-seven years that he had been a member, he had never been present at so flattering an election, which was made on the report of M. Berenger, peer of France, seconded by M. Rossi, likewise a peer of France, and who will be remarked by his untimely fate during the revolution at Rome, and by M. de Tocqueville. He adds, that he will undoubtedly be chosen one of the five free academicians, on the occurrence of the first vacancy. At the time of his admission the question was entertained, by the late Baron Degerando, whether he should be received in the section of History or of Jurisprudence. It was to the latter that he was attached.

During his stay in Paris he prepared and read before the Institute his Essay on the Succession to the Crown of Denmark, in which he elucidated from the facts, which his long residence at Copenhagen had made familiar to him, a question which soon thereafter became one of European importance. It was in quoting, after his death, his opinion on this subject, that the London Times say: — "We cannot mention the name of Henry Wheaton without a passing tribute to the character, the learning, and the virtues of a man, who, as a great international lawyer, leaves not his like behind."

Mr. Wheaton finally returned to his country in the spring of 1847. At New York, which had long been his residence, a public dinner was tended to him for the 10th of June, the invitation to which was headed by the names of James Kent and Albert Gallatin, respectively the most eminent citizens in America, in the departments—Law and Diplomacy—with which his own fame was identified. The festival was presided over by the venerable Gallatin, and was attended, without regard to party, by all of the American metropolis who were distinguished in the various professions, or by their political station or social position. And when the Vice-President, Luther Bradish, presented their guest, "Henry Wheaton—we bid him welcome to his home and our hearts," the sentiment was responded to with enthusiasm. John Quincy Adams and Daniel Webster expressed their regret at their inability to participate, in person, in the public testimony of respect and gratitude to a citizen who had long contributed to the honor of our national character, both at home and abroad.

That his involuntary resignstion might cause no stain to his untarnished escutcheon, the Secretary of State, Mr. Buchanan, declared; — "Mr. Wheaton richly merits this token of regard. He has done honor to his country abroad, and deserves to be honored by his countrymen at home. I offer you the following sentiment for the occasion— 'The Author of the Elements of International Law.' While we hail with enthusiasm the victorious general engaged in fighting the battle of his country, our gratitude is due to the learned civilian, who, by clearly expounding the rights and duties of nations, contributes to preserve the peace of the world."

Reuben H. Walworth, then highest legal functionary of the State of New York, and with whom the title of Chancellr expired, says: — "The ability with Mr. Wheaton has discharged his diplomatic duties, during his long absence from his native country, and his valuable contributions to the science of international law, entitle him to this mark of respect from his fellow-citizens of New York." Edward Everett adds to his acknowledgment of an invitation to the dinner, in honor of Mr. Wheaton: — "He is one of those of whom we may well be proud. His public services abroad, for a term of years unusually long in our diplomacy, have been of the most important character. He has enriched the literature of the day, with an excellent work on an interesting and little-explored historical subject, and he has produced the most valuable general compend, which exists in our language, on the great science of international law."

A similar compliment was proffered to him by the most distinguished citizens of Philadelphia, including Mr. Dallas, then Vice-President of the United States. The City Council of Providence, by a formal vote, bade him welcome to the city of his nativity. And he was invited by his old townsman to sit for his portrait, to be placed in the Common Council Chamber.

At the anniversary of his Alma Mater, on 1st of September, in 1847, his last literary discourse was pronounced. It was an Essay on the Progress and Prospects of Germany, and was delivered before the Phi Beta Kappa Society of Brown University. The Preussische Allgemeine Zeitung, published at Berlin, thus closes a notice of this discourse, and bears renewed testimony to the position which Mr. Wheaton held in the estimation of Prussia: — "That there exists in America a sincere wish to soread the knowledge of German life and culture, we find proof in the above-mentioned oration, delivered before a learned assembly in his native town, by one who, during a long residence in this place, had won our affection and respect by his simplicity of character, by his high moral sense, and his extensive knowledge. We refer to Henry Wheaton, well known in the learned and political world by his 'Elements of International Law,' a sketch of the 'Law of Nations from the Peace of Westphalia,' a pamphlet on the 'Right of Search,' and 'a History of the Northmen.' All these works show the profound inquirer, the accomplished statesman, the acute jurist, and, above all, the philosopher, who is capable of taking an enlarged view of things, and discovering the connecting link between cause and effect. The last-mentioned quality is perceptible in this discourse on Germany. Although on some points we do not agree with Mr. Wheaton, and are inclined to attribute a higher meaning and deeper causes to German philosophy and our present religious movement, we cannot but acknowledge the justice of his general conception of our condition, and particularly of our historical development; and we rejoice to find that our national character, our culture, and our progress should be presented in their true light to the people of America."

Mr. Wheaton was to have read, during the ensuing winter, a course of lectures on International Law, before the Law Institute of Harvard UNiversity, preparatory to the establishment of a professorship of that science. The proposed task he was, however, never able to accomplish. While at Washington, where he was accompanied by the writer of these remarks, with a view to the discussion, in the Supreme Court, of the only points connected with his controversy with Mr. Peters, left open by the previous decision, he was attacked by a disease, which, though it did not prevent his return to his family, proved fatal, and he died on the 11th of March, 1848.

The object of this notice has been, to refer to Mr. Wheaton's career as an individual, only so far as it tends to illustrate his works, This, we trust, has been sufficiently done by the mere recital of the events of his life, connected with his literary and diplomatic career. The present is no occasion in which to indulge in giving utterance to sentiments inspired by private friendship; but Mr. Wheaton's unassuming deportment and purity of life may be mentioned, among the characteristics of the accomplished diplomatist; — "From youth to age," to use the words with which Charles Sumner closed his obituary notice, "his career was marked by integrity, temperance, frugality, modesty, and industry. His quiet unostentatious manners were the fit companions of his virtues. His countenance, which is admirably preserved in the portrait of Healy, (taken for the city of Providence,) wore the expression of thoughtfulness and repose. Nor station nor fame made him proud. He stood with serene simplicity in the presence of kings. In the social circle, when he spoke all drew near to listen, sure that what he said would be wise, tolerant, and kind. "

IN closing this notice, it may be proper briefly to advert to transactions affecting the great questions discussed in this work, which have occurred since it underwent the last revision.

The Revolution, which commenced in France, in 1848, became, by subsequent events, like that of 1830, a mere dynastic change. As the resolution of the National Assembly, in May, 1849, recommending "a fraternal compact of Italy," were without result, except as they may have encouraged abortive movements, attended with disastrous consequences to those who placed confidence in the declarations of France; and as, on the other hand, the great powers did not follow the course adopted, in the case of the Revolution of 1789, nor sanction any change in the number or position of the States of Europe, as in the separation of Holland and Belgium, the dethronement of Louis Philippe and of the Orleans branch of the Bourbon family furnishes, of itself, no matter for comment in a treatise of International Law.

The interposition of England and France in the war between Piedmont and Austria, didi not occur till after the contest was virtually decided, and was a mediation in behalf of humanity, in nowise claiming to rest on any right of intervention authorized by the Law of Nations. Emphatically of that character were, also, the good offices proffered by England, in 1853, for the benefit of the Lombards naturalized in Sardinia, after receiving letters of denaturalization from Austria, which freed them from all allegiance, and whose property was, notwithstanding, being confiscated by the latter power, in violation of the treaty between the two States.

The mediation offered by England and France to the Sicilians, on the basis of separate political institutions for the two portions of the kingdom, and declined by them, was not sustained by arms; and the subjugation of the island by the Neapolitans followed.

The occupation of Rome by the French army more properly comes within the cases of intervention, which affect questions of international policy, than any of the preceding transactions; though it was avowedly made on grounds of an exceptional nature, arising from the peculiar character of the Holy Father as the head of the Church. Lamartine said, "AS to Rome, France proposed to meet other Catholics on the subject of the Pontiff;" and "Austria, Spain, and Naples," it was stated by the Prime President as a motive for interference, "were coalescing to restore him to his liberty, but would have the right to give advice."

The case of Hungary, with the right, avowed by the United States, of acknowledging any nation which had established its independence in fact, without awaiting the action of its former masters, is fully elucidated in the correspondence between the American and Austrian governments; and in the instructions to our Minister in Paris, on occasion of the assumption of the Imperial dignity by Napoleon III., the cardinal principle of our policy from the time of Washington, that every nation has a right to govern itself according to its own will, and to change its institutions at its own discretion, is reaffirmed. The effective intervention of Russia, in the war between Hungary and Austria, on the appleal of the latter, was placed by the Czar on the ground of protecting himself against insurrection in Poland.

The never-failing plea of the preservation of the balance of power was invoked, in 1851, by England and France, to preventthe incorporation of the Austrian provinces, out of Germany, into the confederation, and to which Prussia had declared that she would not object, if all governments which wished it should be permitted to enter the Union on the basis of a federal State.

Phillimore, in his recent Commentaries upon International Law, enumerates among the cases of intervention the proposition, in 1852-3, of these same powers to the United States, and which preceded their present hostilities with the Emperor of Russia, to accede to a tripartite treaty, the object of which was to bind the three governments to renounce, both now and hereafter, all intention to appropriate the island of Cuba; or, in other words, as he expresses it, to abide by the *status quo* in the West Indies. And he adds, referring to the instructions of Lord John Russell to Mr. Crampton, of February 16, 1853, "The North American United States refused to be parties to this treaty; but the right of intervention, on the part of England and France, was steadily proclaimed, both on account of their own interests and on account of those friendly States in South America, as to the present ' distribution of power' in the American seas." The inequality of such an arrangement, on the part of the United States, looking to their geographical position, and to the impossibility of their precluding themselves from an acquisition which, in a strategic point of view, might be essential to the defence of all our territory bordering on the Gulf of Mexico, is sufficiently elucidated in the correspondence, which passed between the American Department of State and the French and English ministers at Washington.

Nor can it be deemed otherwise than as a striking illustration of the difference of the principles, by which nation as well as individuals judge of their own conduct and that of their neighbors, that, at the time that England was united with France, in an attempt to arrest the natural development of the resources of the United States, an addition of four or five millions of inhabitants with a territory of proportionate extent, was made to the British Empire in India, by the annexation of Pegu, in Burmah, not only without any protest on the part of any foreign power, but without a word being uttered in Parliament on the subject, except to allude to the fact.

The whole policy which, since Spain by the independence of her continental possessions has ceased to be an important American power, has governed the UNited States, with reference to Cuba, was fully disclosed in the papers communicated by President Fillmore to Congress, in July, 1852, and which comprise the correspondence on that subject, going back to 1822. At that period, England, not apprehending the embarrassments which, since the emancipation of the negroes in her own islands, the character of the population would occasion her, desired the possession of Cuba, to give her the command of the Gulf of Mexico; and it was particularly feared that, should she take the side of Spain, in the war in which the latter was about to be engaged wit France, the price of England interposition might be the cession to her of the two remaining islands of Cuba and Porto Rico. Our policy ever has been that, while we were content that those islands should remain with Spain, and would infringe no obligations of good neighborhood to obtain them, to pass into the hands of any great maritime power. Not only have England and France been constantly that we would not consent to their occupation by either of them, but, in 1826, at the same time that it was officially announced to France, "that the United States could not see with indifference Porto Rico and Cuba pass from Spain into the possession of any other power," we effectually intervened with Mexico and Colombia to suspend an expedition which these republics were fitting out against them. The United States, however, even at that period, explicitly declared to Spain that they could enter into no engagement of guarantee, as such a course was utterly inconsistent with our standing rules of foreign policy. The most recent indications, also, of the views of the American government confirm the preceding statement, and show that, while we deem tha acquisition of Cuba of the highest importance, and would give more than a full equivalent to Spain for a transfer to us of its sovereignty, we will not, without a more imminent necessity than now exists, make her refusal to sell it to us a ground for taking forcible possession of it, as essential to the safety of the Union.

Of the pending contest, which may decide the permanent destiny of that part of Europe now under the dominion of, or subject to, the *suzerainete* of the Porte, so long an excrescence on the European body politic, it is beyond our province to speak, except to record, as has been done in the notes, its ostensible origin; —on the one side, the intervention claimed in pursuance of treaties in favor of the Christian population of Turkey; and on the other, the preservation of the Ottoman Empire, as of essential importance to the balance of power among the States of Europe. Since our annotations were prepared matters have become more complicated, without, however, essentially changing their character. After the failure to substitute for a treaty a diplomatic note or an arrangement to be effected by means of a protocol, signed by the representatives of England, Austria, France, and Prussia, to be assented to simultaneously by Russia and Turkey, war had been declared, on the 4th of October, 1853, by the last-named power, against the Emperor of Russia. On the 28th of March following, England and France had also placed themselves in hostility to the Czar, while Austria and Prussia, parties to the original conferences on the affairs of Turkey, yet continue their diplomatic relations with the Court of St. Petersburg, though in virtue of the Treaty of June 14, 1854, with the Porte, the former occupies the Danubian principalities vacated by Russia; and so early as the 20th of April, of the last year, an alliance was formed between Austria and Prussia, to take effect, in case Russia should incorporate the principalities as well as advance towards the Balkan, and which, by the treaty of the 25th og November, was extended, so that Prussia was to assist Austria if attacked in her own dominions or in the principalities. To these arrangements the Germanic Confederation became a party, by their resolutions of the 28th of July and the 9th of December. On the latter occasion they affirmed the four points hereafter alluded to, which were agreed on in the notes exchanged on the 8th of August, between England and France and Austria, as the necessary basis of peace. But Prussia was no party to the treaty of the 3d of December, by which, in certain contingencies, an alliance offensive and defensive is established between Austria and England and France; and it is understood that the Minister of Frederick William IV., who is supposed to be bound, not only by family ties but by political sympathies with the Emperor of Russia, is with difficultly admitted, though a member of the original conference, to the negotiations for peace to be opened between

Austria, France, and England on the one side, and Russia on the other. Again, the two great German powers are opposed to one another in the Diet; and through the influence of Prussia with the minor States, the proposition of Austria for the mobilisation of the Federal Army has been neutralized; while Sardinia has, by her treaty of the 15th January of the present year, with England and France, not only given her adhesion to the alliance against Russia, but agreed to furnish a military contingent for the war, in which arrangement it is said that other powers are about to follow. And, at the moment that we are closing these sheets, all calculations are set at naught by the intelligence which reaches us of the sudden demise of the Emperor Nicholas, the great master spirit, who seemed prepared, if necessary, to contend singly with coalesced Europe.

In this controversy it is for the publicist to notice, that though England France have embarked in the war to maintain the Ottoman Empire in its present extent, yet that that exclusive internal sovereignty over all the inhabitants of a territory, whether subjects or residents, deemed essential by the public law of Christendom to the independent existence of a State, does not seem to be contemplated for the Porte, by any party. Humanity would forbid the withdrawal of the people of other nationalities from the protection of their diplomatic and consular representatives, a system which distinguishes the international code of the Asiatic family of nations, to which the Turks properly belong, from the European. But there is this marked difference between the Ottoman Empire and the other Mohammedan and Pagan States, that, while in the latter the people of different religions are confined, with comparatively unimportant exceptions, to foreigners engaged in commerce, or to travellers passing through their territory, the great majority of the inhabitants of Turkey in Europe, and in the Danubian principalities the entire population, profess the Christian creed.

Of the utter inability or total disinclination of the government of Turkey, so far, at least, as strangers are concerned, even to maintain an adequate police within its own dominions, sufficient evidence was afforded in the case of Kostza, which, in 1853, formed the subject of a diplomatic discussion between the United States and Austria, Whatever the merits of the controversy, as regards these parties, it cannot be questioned that the territorial sovereignty of the Ottoman Porte was violated, without the slightest interposition of the local authorities, or any subsequent reclamations on the part of the government at Constantinople; and it was assumed in the American argument, that "all parties were in the same condition at Smyrna, in respect to rights and duties, so far as regards that transaction, as they would have been in if it had occurred in their presence in some unappropriated region, lying far beyond the confines of any sovereign State whatever." To the anarchy of which this transaction was an illustration, the leading journal of Great Britain thus alluded at the time: "It is one of the most unfortunate results of the present condition of the Ottoman Empire that the authority of its officers is hardly sufficient to command respect in its own ports, and that the laws of the country and the law of nations are violated with impunity under the very eyes of the Sultan's representatives."

Nor has the anomalous condition of Turkey escaped the notice of English writers. The very recent commentator from whom we have cited, while objecting to the absorption of the Sultan's dominions in any of the existing States, says: "It is not, indeed, true, that Christian Europe requires, as a condition of her security, the existence of a Mahometan power within her boundaries. It is conceivable that Constantinople may again become the seat of a Christian Greek government, capable of maintaining the position and supporting the character of an independent kingdom; and were such an event to occur, the balance of power might be at least as well secured as by the present state of thins."

The propositions made by the other powers to Russia, and which constitute the basis of existing negotiations, do not suggest the emancipation of the Porte from any previousthraldom which it was under to foreign States, but merely the transfer to the five powers, with the right of intervention consequent thereon, of the protectorate of the principalities of Wallachia and Moldavia, where Russia has a concurrent voice in the choice of the Hospodars, and of Servia, where she has the right of supervising the election of the prince. They are, also, to exercise together the guarantee, accorded by existing treaties to Russia, of the privileges enjoyed by the Christian population of Turkey. Another of the four points, (the remaining one relating to the free navigation of the Danube,) proposes a revision of the treaty of 1841, which recognizes, as the ancient rule of the Ottoman Empire, the closing to ships of war, in time of peace, of the Straits of the Dardanelles and the Bosphorus—a matter which, from their territorial possessions around the Blank Sea, would, under ordinary circumstances, be within the exclusive control of Turkey and Russia; but which, as we have seen, has been recognized by both these States, as within the congnizance of the general policy of the great European powers. Turkey had, indeed, by the treaty of Unkiar Skelessi, (when the Czar volunteered to put down, in Mehemmet Ali, the Pasha of Egpt, the establishment of a new Mohammedan dynasty, whose success might delay the consummation of his long deferred designs,) agreed to close these Straits against foreign ships at the request of the Emperor of Russia, by way of reciprocity for his covenanting to assist the Porte with a naval and military force, whenever required so to do.

How far the political institutions of the Ottoman Empire and its international relations, permitting the continued intervention of foreign States in its internal affairs, are from being assimilated to those of the rest of Europe, is furthermore apparent from the fact that the existing war was preceded by the revival of conflicting pretensions of Russia and France, in behalf of the Greek and Latin Churches, respectively, to the holy places, connected with the nativity and important passages, in the life of the common Saviour of Christians, situated in the territory forming an integral part of the Turkish dominions; while Austria, as well as Russia, was intervening in the relations between the Porte and Montenegro, whose new prince had just repudiated the ecclesiastical character which, in his predecessors, had been blended with the civil magistracy. England was then, also, as she had long been, engaged in obtaining for the Armenians and other subjects of the Porte a separate recognition. Indeed, her Parliamentary papers, for several years back, are replete with reports from her diplomatic and consular agents in Turkey, showing for several years back, are replete with reports from her diplomatic and consular agents in Turkey, showing an active surveillance by them over the internal administration of affairs, and that they were constantly menacing the local authorities of Syria with the intimation of insurrectionary movements on the part of the Christian population, and to which, they were given to understand, that their co-religionists might not remain strangers. Nor can it be forgotten in this connection that it was a violation of stipulations of the treaty of Bucharast in favor of the Servians, which led, in 1813, when the protecting power was occupied with the war with France, to that insurrection, the cruelties of which, equally with the atrocities exercised in the Morea, aroused the sympathy of all Christendom against Turkey.

It has been our duty to point out, in the annotations, the important changes that have occurred, since Mr. Wheaton's time, in the maritime law of nations. At least, for the present war, the most liberal course has been adopted by all the belligerents. In reference to the rule, "free ships free goods," which has been usually connected, for no better reason, it would seem, than that it formed a verbal antithesis, with the proposition, "enemy ships enemy goods," the conflicting views of England and France have been conciliated in a way resulting greatly to the benefit of neutrals; while Russia has, by a treaty with the United States, and to which all other nations have been invited to become parties, consecrated anew those principles of which the Emperor Nicholas had a claim to be the hereditary champion.

By the treaty of July 22, 1854, immunity is given to neutral property on board of enemy's vessels, as well as to enemy's property on board of neutral vessels, with the exception of contraband of war, which may be confiscated, whether on board of neutral or enemy vessels. Though it is to be presumed that the penalty, in the case of contraband found on board of a neutral carrier, is by the treaty limited to the confiscation of the interdicted article, and is not to be extended, as by the Russian decrees at the commencement of the war, to the condemnation in all cases of the vessel carrying it, and in which respect the ordinances of that power differ from those of the allies; yet it is to be regretted that, by continuing to subject to capture under the term of contraband of war, the definition of which has varied in the maritime codes of different nations, and of the same nation at different times, articles on board of a neutral vessel destined to an enemy's port though not blockaded, the evils to neutrals, inseparable from a right of search, are perpetuated, without any correspondent benefit to the belligerent. The law of blockade, it is conceived, effects the exclusion of contraband of war in the only cases in which, in the present state of commerce and the arts, the prohibition can be of any importance as regards belligerent operations.

A treaty, in the same terms with the one between the United States and Russia, was signed with Mexico, on the 8th of January, 1855; and another, with the King of the Two Sicilies, on the 13th of that month.

Other points of maritime law have also been recently discussed in the cabinets of Europe. Much greater liberality prevailed, at the commencement of the present hostilities, than on any previous occasion, in reference to the property of one belligerent found in the country of the other; and which would, according to the former practice of England, have been confiscated as droits of Admiralty. Though privateering has not been formally abolished, and such a proposition cannot be acceded to by a power, situated like the United States, with a great mercantile marine, without a correspondent navy, while the capture of private property by government ships is tolerated; yet England and France, the superiority of whose fleets over those of Russia give to them the command of the ocean, have continued to adhere to the course adopted by them at the commencement of war, and have abstained from issuing commissions to private armed vessels.

Great changes have, likewise, been introduced, in reference to trade with an enemy. This, in the last war between England and France, was forbidden by the recognized law of nations, to the merchants of the contending belligerents, under the penalty of confiscation; while it was effectually interdicted to neutrals, under the plea of the rule of the war of '56, interpolated by Great Britain into maritime law, and by Orders in Council and retaliatory decrees. Now, instead, every facility, consistent with a state of hostilities, is accorded by the maritime powers, as well to their own subjects as to neutrals, for the continuance of the ordinary commercial intercourse with all places not blockaded, and in all articles not contraband of war. And, it may not be irrelevant here to state that, in the most recent discussions in the British Parliament, the proposition for a recurrence to the system of former wars was most emphatically repudiated, and those views, which had been so ably elucidated at the previous session by Sir William Moles-worth, were defended by the Minister of the Crown, to whose department the subject appropriately belongs.

Nor have the negotiations of our government with foreign powers been confined to matters relating to a state of war. The immense additions made to the Union, with the revolution produced in the nature of the precious metal by the substitution of an Anglo-American population in territory long, for little purpose, under the dominion of Spain and Mexico—the acceptance by that power, with which our most extensive trade is carried on, (and which had previously given its adhesion to liberal principles by the abolition of prohibitory enactments in relation to the importation of articles that contribute directly to the sustenance of human life,) of the proffer made by us to all the world, more than a quarter of a century ago, of the reciprocal abolition of discriminating duties on navigation, without reference to the origin of the cargo, and which has been followed by England's going beyond us in the march of free trade, and laying open her coasting trade—the expansion given to our commerce by the treaty with Japan and the measures adopted to confirm our diplomatic relations with China and the other countries of the remote east—the treaties for opening the great rivers of South America to the enterprise of our citizens, and the application, between us and England, to the St. Lawrence of the principles of public law recognized at the Congress of Vienna as to the rivers of Germany, with the removal of restrictions from a free reciprocal interchange of commodities with our neighbors on this continent, with whom we are connected by the ties of a common origin, language, and religion, and which, by the increased intercourse, must lead to a commercial union, if not ultimately to a more intimate association—these are all among the events comprised in the brief period, that has intervened, since the last publication in America of the "Elements of International Law."

In the preparation of the present edition, that of Leipzig, of 1848, which had received the latest corrections of the Author, has been adopted as the standard, though matter contained in previous editions and there omitted, as being specially applicable to the United States, is now retained. No liberty has been taken with the original text, except to translate and insert such additions as were made to the French publication, and of which no English manuscript could be found.

The new notes, which are marked in brackets, have been confined almost exclusively to a reference to events which have occurred since the last edition, or to works which were not published, when the Author's emendations were made. IN this connection, the Editor would state that, not only have the papers of Mr. Wheaton been placed at his disposal, but that, through the courtesy of the Secretary of State, he was enabled to examine the portion of his correspondence with the government, of which copies are not in possession of the family.

W. B. Lawrence.

Ochre Point, Newport, Rhode Island,

March17, 1855.

附录五

Editor's Preface[①]

As the text of this work may be supposed to have now becoame, by the death of Mr. Wheaton, unalterable, it has been thought judicious to adopt a new mode of division, forthe greater convenience of reference. The text is accordingly divided into short sections, the numbering of which is continued through the book; so that hereafter, the sections being permanent and the text unaltered, the book may be cited by the sections, without regard to editions or to pages.

It was Mr. Wheaton's practice, in new editions, to revise his text, and not to put new matter into notes. It will be found, therefore, that his notes are short, and contain rarely any thing more than references to the authors discussed in the text.

This edition contains nothing but the text of Mr. Wheaton, according to his last revision, and the original matter contributed by the editor. Mr. Wheaton's notes are indicated by letters. The original contributions of the editor are all in the form of notes, which are indicated by numbers, enclosed in brackets and signed with the letter D. For convenience in referring to the

---

① [美] Henry Wheaton, *Elements of International Law*, Oxford: At The Clarendon Press. London: Humphrey Milford, 1936.

editor's notes, the numbering is continuous through the book.

It will not be expected, that this preface should furnish an extended biography of Mr. Wheaton; still less, that the editor should enter upon an analysis of his mind, or a eulogy of his merits and services. These have their appropriate places, in which all that his warmest admirers can wish has been said by those best qualified to speak of him.

Nothing more will be undertaken than it may be an assistance to the reader to have at hand, ---a history of the work itself, and such a sketch of the author's life as will show his public relations, and in what circumstances and under what influences the book was written.

HENRY WHEATON was born in Providence, Rhode Island, Nov. 27, 1785. His family was one of the most respectable and influential in that State. His father was a merchant of high standing and competent fortune, and was able to give his son the advantages not only of a liberal education, but, what was not so common then as now, of early travel and study in Europe. Mr. Wheaton was educated at Providence College (now Brown University), where he took his degree in 1802. During the next three years, he studied law, and, in 1805, went abroad to complete his studies, and especially to make himself familiar with the languages, history, and literature of Europe. While in France, he gave attention to the subject of the codes, then greatly discussed, and to the international questions that attracted the attention of both worlds; and letters of introduction were such as to place him on intimate terms with the leading public men of his country then in Europe, ---a position which he maintained by his own merits.

On his return to the United States, he entered on the practice of the law in the city of New York. Continuing his interest in international questions, he published, in 1815, his small work on the Law of Maritime Captures, which gained him an early and lasting reputation. From 1816 to 1827, he was the reporter of the decisions of the Supreme Court of the United States, during what no one can be offended by hearing called the great period of the Federal

Bench and Bar. The reporter was the friend and associate of the judges and the most eminent counsel; and, in respect to learning on foreign and international questions, and general culture, he held an enviable reputation throughout the country. In 1820, he delivered the annual address before the Historical Society of New York, taking for his subject the science of Public and International Law. This address, with his treatise on Captures, was the germ of his great work. For some time, he was engaged on a commission to revise the statute law of New York, during which he was a diligent student of the subject of codification, and of legislation generally. In 1827, he was appointed, by President Adams, Charge d'Affaires at the court of Denmark, and resided at Copenhagen until 1835, when he was transferred to Berlin, first as Minister Resident, but the office was afterwards raised to the rank of Plenipotentiary. This post he held until 1846, when his diplomatic career was closed by one of the most unfortunate sacrifices our government ever made to mere party routine.

Notwithstanding his long residence abroad, and at the courts of Europe, his patriotism suffered no diminution: but distance and absence seemed to present his country more as a unit, and with stronger hold on his imagination and affections; and he preserved not only with fidelity, but enthusiasm, the republican principles with which he began life.

Remaining a year in France, Mr. Wheaton returned to America in 1847. He was at once appointed Lecturer on International Law at Harvard University, and was to have had the professorship, then about to be founded and permanently endowed for him, of Civil and International Law: but rapidly declining health obliged him to break off from all his labors; and he died at Dorchester, in Massachusetts, on the 11th, 1848.

During the twenty years that Mr. Wheaton resided abroad in the diplomatic service, he was engaged in negotiations of great importance to his own country and Europe. He conducted the well-known controversy respecting the captures at Kiel, which ended in Treaty of Indemnity of 1830, and led the way to other treaties of indemnity to the United States, based on a similar principle. While at Copenhagen, he was practically the American representative for all Germany, as we had no minister in Prussia or Austria, or any other of the German States; and he gave constant attention to the internal concerns as well as the foreign policy of those powers. For many years he observed carefully the affairs of the Zollverein, and succeed at last in effecting the treaty of 1844, which was thought by diplomatists and publicists to do him great honor, and the rejection of which by the United States Senate caused him no little great, —the more, perhaps, from the fact that its defeat was understood to have been an accident of party politics, against the judgment of the ablest men of the country.

The reader of this book will see, at almost every stage in the questions of the last thirty years, traces of the labors of Mr. Wheaton, especially in the subjects of the abolition and capitalizing of the Sound Dues and the Scheldt Dues and the tolls on the Elbe, the extradition of criminals, and the lines of distinction established as to the exemption of naturalized citizens of the United States from certain claims of their former sovereigns. But there was scarcely a topic affecting the interests of his country, or the science of international and public law, or the political and social condition of his kind, in which he did not interest himself; contributing pamphlets to the press, articles to the leading journals of Europe and America, and maintaining a correspondence with the philosophical and literary societies on both sides of the Atlantic, of which he was an honored member. In 1831, he published his valuable History of the Northmen, which was afterwards published in French at Paris. In 1838 appeared the History of Scandinavia—the joint work of himself and Dr. Crichton.

In 1841, Mr. Wheaton wrote an essay for a prize offered by the French Institute, on the subject, 'L' Histoire Du Droit des Gens en Europe, depuis la Paix de Westphalie jusqu' au Congres de Vienne. ' He afterwards enlarged it into a treatise on the History of the Law of Nations in Europe and

America, from the earliest times to the treaty of Washington in 1842. This was published in English, in New York, in 1845, —the preface being dated at Paris in 1843; and in French, in 1846, at Leipsic and Paris.

To his great work, the Elements of International Law, Mr. Wheaton, in some from or other, gave the greater part of his life after his twenty – fifth year. For the duties of a commentator on that branch of science, he combined advantages which, in no one of his countrymen, were ever before united. He was familiar with the four languages in which the stores of international law are gathered. He had the early preparatory discipline successively of a practising lawyer, and a reporter of judicial decisions, followed by twenty years of diplomatic experience at one of the political centres of Europe. He maintained an intimate personal acquaintance and familiar correspondence with the most eminent statesman, publicists, and scholars of Europe and America; and kept himself thoroughly informed of the current history of whatever bore upon the relations of States. In short, he combined the advantages of the discipline of a barrister, the culture of a scholar, the experience of a diplomatist, and the habits of a man of society. And it is no small thing to add, that, to a subject essentially moral, he brought a purity of nature, candor, and fidelity to truth and duty, as remarkable as his learning, industry, and philosophy.

This work, under the title of The Elements of International Law, was first sent to the press in 1836, in two editions, —one at Philadephia, and the other at London; the preface being written at Berlin, and dated Jan. I, 1836.

The third edition was published in Philadephia in 1846; the preface being dated at Berlin, November, 1845.

IN 1846 and 1847, Mr. Wheaton prepared an edition in French; the preface being dated at Paris, April 15, 1847, just before his final return to America. It was published at Leipsic and Paris, in 1848, —the year of the author's death.

A second edition of the work, in French, was published at the same places in 1853.

The next foreign edition conferred a singular distinction upon the author: ie was a translation into Chinese, executed and published in 1864, under the auspices of the Imperial Government. See note 8.

In 1855, an edition, which has always been called the sixth edition (counting the French editions as the fourth and fifth), was prepared in Boston, with notes by Mr. W. B. Lawrence.

In 1863, the seventh edition was published in Boston, also with notes by Mr. Lawrence.

The present is therefore the eighth edition. The notes of Mr. Lawrence do not form any part of this edition. It is confined, as has been said, to the text and notes of the author, and the notes of the present editor, who undertakes his work at request of the widow of Mr. Wheaton, recently deceased, and of his only surviving children, his daughters.

Adhering to the course proposed, no attempt is made to discuss the character of this work, or to enter upon an examination of the more strictly literary labors of the distinguished jurist; still less, to report the tributes which have been paid to him by bodies politic, literary and scientific societies, or eminent individuals. Yet, among the honors his memory has received, one may be selected for mention, as peculiarly gratifying. His native State has resolved to place his statue in the Capitol of the Union, as one of the two assigned to it in the gallery of the public men of America.

The son of Mr. Wheaton, who gave so fair promise of continuing the honor of his name in another generation, survived him but afew years. Yet it is hoped that too much is not claimed in expressing a belief, that his name will still remain so long as the science which regulates the relations of States shall be studied among men.

RICHARD H. DANA, JR.

BOSTON, *July* 2, 1866.

附录六

PREFACE[1]

The republication of the classic works connected with the history and development International Law was undertaken by the Carnegie Institution of Washington in 1906 at the suggestion of the undersigned, then Solicitor for the Department of State, under whose supervision as General Editor the series has since been published. On January 1, 1917, the project was transferred to the Carnegie Endowment for International Peace, and the publication of the series is being continued by the Endowment's Division of International Law.

One reason for republishing the classics of International Law is the difficulty in procuring the texts in convenient form for scientific study; the libraries in the United States have been searched with the result that few of the earlier works were to be found. The same difficulty exists in Latin America, Japan, and in a less degree in many European countries. Another reason is that some of the foreign works selected for republication have never been translated into English.

Eminent publicists, European and American, who have been consulted as to the usefulness of the plan to republish the classics, have endorsed the

---

[1] [美] Henry Wheaton, *Elements of International Law*, Oxford: At The Clarendon Press. London: Humphrey Milford, 1936.

project and have pledged their personal co-operation. The works to be included in the series have not only been approved but even suggested by them, so that the undertaking is international in scope, in selection, and in execution.

The underlying principle of selection has been to reissue those works which can be said to have contributed either to the origin or to the growth of International Law, and the term classic has been used in a broad rather than in the narrow sense. In general, the text of each author is reproduced photographically, so as to lay the source before the reader without the mistakes which creep into a newly printed text. In the case of some early authors the photographed text will be accompanied by a revised text whenever that course shall seem desirable. An Introduction, prefixed to each work, gives the necessary biographical details and states the importance of the text and its place in International Law; errata in the original are indicated, and notes deemed necessary to clear up doubts and ambiguities or to correct mistakes in the text are supplied.

Each non-English work is accompanied by an English version made expressly for the series by a competent translator.

It is hoped that the series will enable specialists as well as general readers to trace International Law from its faint and unconscious begining to its present ample proportions, and to forecast with some degree of certainty its future development into that law which Mirabeau tells us will one day rule the word.

Henry Wheaton's *Elements of International Law* was first published in the year 1836, and its inclusion in this series one hundred years later is appropriate not only as marking the centenary of its original publication but also as a recognition of the fact that it has stood the test of time and may therefore properly be considered a classic in the literature of International Law.

The present edition has been prepared by George Grafton Wilson, an eminent American publicist and authority on International Law and for many years professor of that subject at Harvard University. The text chosen for reproduction, as indicated in Professor Wilson's Introduction, is that of Dana's edition of 1866. It should, perhaps, be added that the choice in question represents a departure from the practice heretofore followed in the series of reproducing, whenever possible, the last edition issued during the lifetime of the author because it might fairly be presumed to contain the text which had his final approval. In the case of Wheaton's Elements of International Law, however, it was felt that the famous edition of 1866, containing Dana's voluminous and frequently cited notes, should be chosen for reproduction because it has for many decades been more widely known and used than any pther edition.

In issuing the present volume the purpose has been, not to add to the number of revised editions of Wheaton, but to reproduce what has come to be considered the standard and, indeed, classical text of his treaties. Therefore, in preparing the edition, Professor Wilson has taken great care to keep the reproduction intact with respect to both Wheaton's text and Dana's notes. With this in view all editorial corrections have been made in footnotes. The reader will in consequence have before him a literal reproduction of Dana's edition, with its errors corrected in such a way as not to alter the original text.

In addition to his editorial notes and Introduction, Professor Wilson has supplied a sketch of the life of Dana and a chronological list of the editions of Wheaton's Elements of International Law in various languages. The Endowment is indebted to him also for the likeness of Wheaton which appears as a frontispiece to the volume.

Washington.
January I, 1936.

James Brown Scott,
General Editor.

附录七

HENRY WHEATON AND INTERNATIONAL LAW[①]

Elements of International Law with a Sketch of the History of the Science, by Henry Wheaton was published concurrently in London and in Philadelphia in 1836. Many editions of the Elements of International Law have appeared since that time. In the edition between 1836 and 1846 changes and addition were made by Wheaton. The edition of 1848 published in French at Leipzig and at Paris was revised by Wheaton himself before his death and may, therefore, with the English edition of 1846, be considered his latest utterance upon international law.

In the Advertisement of the first edition, which is dated Berlin, January I, 1836, just one hundred years ago, Wheaton said: 'The object of the Author in the following attempt to collect the rules and principles which govern, or are supposed to govern, the conduct of States in their intercourse in peace and in war, and which have therefore received the name of International Law, has been to compile an elementary work for the use of persons engaged in diplomatic and other forms of public life, rather than for mere tech-

---

① [美] Henry Wheaton, *Elements of International Law*, Oxford: At The Clarendon Press. London: Humphrey Milford, 1936.

nical lawyers, although he ventures to hope that it may not be found wholly useless even to the latter. ' The weight of Wheston's opinion in diplomatic affairs and in judicial decisions has since proven that the author's anticipations were far too modest.

In the editions of 1836 there appeared a*Sketch of the History of International Law*. This was based upon an anniversary discourse which the author had delivered before the New York Historical Society at its meeting of December 28, 1820.

This sketch does not appear in later editions as Wheaton had published in the meantime, in 1845, his*History of the Law of Nations* covering in a comprehensive manner the material touched upon in the *Sketch of the History of International Law*. While omitting the *Sketch* in subsequent editions, Wheaton does, however, transfer to the text some historical material.

The two editions of 1836, one appearing in London and one in Philadelphia, are alike so far as contents are concerned, though ordinarily the London edition is in two volumes and the Philadelphia edition in one volume.

Of the third edition, issued in 1846, Wheaton says, in the preface: ' In preparing for the press the present edition of the Elements of International Law, the work has been subjected to a careful revision, and has been considerably augmented. The author has endeavoured to avail himself of the more recent question which have occurred in the intercourse of States, the discussion and decision of which have contributed to throw new light upon that system of rules by which all civilized nations profess to be bound in their mutual intercourse. ' In the third edition some of the material formerly in the footnotes appears in the text and in general the changes are comprehensive.

In this and the later French edition of 1848, prepared by Wheaton, there is a tendency to pay more attention to principles as set forth in adjudicated cases and to give less weight to natural law doctrines. Healso in the third edition drops the term ' law of nations ' as the alternative to ' international law ' in his definition and follows Bentham's lead in adopting ' international law', while supporting Savighy. s recognition of its positive character though admitting that it is 'imperfect.' The influence of the work of Heffter and other writers of the period is also evident.

Official opinions of governmental advisers are recognized as among the sources of international law. Wheaton's distinction between state and nation and his idea of sovereignty is made clearer in this third 'Right of Self Preservation' and on 'Right of Independence' are combined and a new chapter on 'Rights of Civil and Criminal Legislation' is inserted. This chapter contains some of the material from the combined chapters, give much more attention to the law of *res judicate*, and in particular shoes the influence of the then recently published work of Foelix. Chapters are also enlarged by material relating to fisheries and other maritime matters with some of which Wheaton's negotiations had given him special familiarity. Wheaton's retirement from the diplomatic service made it possible for him to write more freely upon diplomatic matters in the third edition and to illustrate from his own experience.

In treating 'Rights of War', Wheaton write much more fully of the war of 1812 and other nineteenth – century differences than in the earlier editions, specially discussing the questions of capture and enlarging on the discussion of 'free ships, free goods'.

The other chapters are not greatly changed from the text of the earlier editions though throuhout there is evidence that the opinions of reviewers of these editions received from Wheaton careful and discriminating attention.

There are added, in appendices, the Mariime Convention of 1801 between Great Britain and Russia, covering many of the disputed questions to which the Armed Neutralities had given rise, and the Final Act of the Congress of Vienna, 1815, which fixed the state of Europe for the time being. An index also increases the value of the third edition.

The texts of the French edtions of 1848 and 1852, commonly reckoned the fourth and fifth editions, are practically identical as are the subsequent French editions, though there is some change in paging. The French edition published in 1848, in which the preface bears the date April 15, 1847, is the last edition to which Wheaton gave revision, as he died within the year.

The first American edition after the death of Wheaton, edited by William Beach Lawrence, appeared in 1855 and was republished in 1857. In his 'Introductory Remarks', pp. Xiii – clxxxiv, Lawrence offers a 'brief sketch' of Wheaton's 'public career and preliminary pursuits'. Lawrence says: 'In the preparation of the present edition, that of Leipzig, of 1848, which had received the latest corrections of the Author, has been adopted as the standard, though matter contained in previous editions and there omitted, as being specially applicable to the United States, is now retained. No liberty has been taken with the original text, except to translate and insert such additions as were made to the French publication, and of which no English manuscript could be found'. The text of the third edition of 1846 is used as the basis for this edition.

Lawrence, in this edition, inserts notes additional to those of Wheaton referring to matters which had occurred or had become public since Wheaton's death and also refers to more recent publications. The discussion in these notes is sometimes more extended than that in the original text of Wheaton and touches many points on which Lawrence had decided opinions. Indeed the total number of pages of Lawrence's notes is about one hundred in small type as compared with about five hundred pages of Wheaton's large – type text. These notes, with the 'Introductory Remarks' of Lawrence, make his contribution to this edition about two hundred and eighty – five pages, exclusive of the appendix.

This edition of 1855 of Lawrence has a table of cases from English and American Reports and an index.

Lawrence issued what he called a 'Second Annotated Edition' in 1863, which was reprinted in London in 1864. Of this edition and referring to his edition of 1855, Lawrence says: 'Much of what appeared as "Introductory Remarks" in the last edition, is now incorporated in notes or in the "notes of the Author". Some extended notes will be found in the Appendix. ' In general the notes in this edition are more extended and at times somewhat controversial. It is not infrequently the case that a few lines of text have below them a long note, and Lawrence's appendixes cover more than one hundred and thirty pages and a supplement of nearly fifty pages is also added.

During the period between the first and second editions of Lawrence's Wheaton, there was issued a French edition of Wheaton in 1858, which was another reprint of the edition of 1848.

In 1860 an Italian edition translated by Arlia from the French edition of 1848 was issued at Naples.

In 1864 there appeared another reprint of the French edition, in two volumes, *'suivie d'un commentaire par William Beach Lawrence en quater volumes'*

There was also in 1864 a striking evidence of the influence of Wheaton's work in the translation into Chinese, under the general advice of Dr. W. A. P. Martin, assisted by a commission of scholars appointed by Prince Kung, of Wheaton's Elements of International Law in four volumes. The work when published was sent to a large number of Chinese officials for their general guidance. When it was published the American Minister, Anson Burlingame, making of the event a special note, wrote to the State Department, 'The Chinese did not address me in writing, but called in person to mark their sense of the importance of the completion of the work, and when the Prince and suit kindly sat for their photographs, Fung Sun, who had superintended the translation, desired to be taken with a copy of Wheaton in his hand.'

The edition published in China was quickly exhausted. The work had been received with much favour in Japan. An edition of this Chinese text reprinted and adapted for Japanese use was published in Kyoto, Japan, in 1865, and other editions were issued in the East.

Other translations into foreign languages were also made, not all of which have been published.

Dana's edition of Wheaton was issued in 1866.

Lawrence's *Commentaries on the Elements of International Law and History of the Progress of the Law of Nations* appeared in French in four volumes between 1868 and 1880 in which, with much new material, there was published material from Lawrence's earlier editions of Wheaton. Many matters treated in these volumes, while having incidental bearing on international law, are primarily of importance to other branches.

Another French edition of Wheaton was published in 1874.

A large number of English editions have been issued. Those of 1878, 1880, and 1889 were by A. C. Boyd, in each of which there were notes and appendice bringing the work down to the respective dates. In 1904 J. B. Atlay continued the work of Boyd. These editions contained much valuable material. An edition called the fifth English edition by Coleman Phillipson was issued in 1916. This is unlike the earlier English editions in removing 'all distinction between the original author's writing and that of his editions'. An edition called the sixth English edition following a plan somewhat similar was issued by A. Berriedale Keith in two volumes in 1929.

The numerical sequence of editions of Wheaton's Elements of International Law is not always chronological even if in the same Language, and unauthorized editions add further confusion. The family of Mr. Wheaton requested Mr. Dana to call his edition the eighth.

Wheaton's Elements of International Law, commonly called the eighth edition, edited, with notes, by Richard Henry Dana, Jr., Boston: Little, Brown, and Company, 1866, is the edition chosen for a place among the Classics of International Law. Of all the edition of Wheaton's text but also Dana's notes have been cited in many legal decisions. The text of this edition is the same as that of the earlier edition of Lawrence, and the issue of Dana's edition was the ground of long litigation between Lawrence and Dana involving the Wheaton family and the publishers.

The text of Dana's edition being identical with that of Lawrence is based on the third edition, 1846, with the later changes and additions introduced in the French edition of 1848.

Dana says in the 'Editor's Preface' that the text 'may be supposed to have now become, by the death of Mr. Wheaton, unalterable'. Dana does, however, number the sections consecutively, 'foe greater convenience of reference'. He further says, 'This edtion contains nothing but the text of Mr. Wheaton, according to his last revision, his notes and the original matter contributed by the editor'.

In the 'Editor's Preface' there is a brief sketch of Wheaton's life to which the present editor has added certain notes marked G. G. W. to distinguish these from other notes.

The text followed in Dana's eidtion as compared with the first edition shows the influence of German writers upon Wheaton. Slavery and other contemporary questions received more attention. Wheaton's changes from the text of the previous editons are more common in the earlier than in the later chapters. There are changes in order of material indicating a tendency to emphasize less the natural law ideas of the prior period and to place more weight upon positive law. The discussion of sovereignty became more clear and some matter which had been added to the third edition is omitted in the sixth. There is a growing recognition of the field of conflict of law and some recent cases on the rights of property are considered, particularly property at sea. Many long discussions of the first edition are reduced to a paragraph or to a brief note.

Dana's notes are indicated by the letter D. These refer particularly to publications and events since the death of Wheaton and discuss certain topics at length.

The period of the middle of the nineteenth century afforded new material for Dana's notes, The Monroe Doctrine had been somewhat intervention in Mexico under the convention of 1861 to which France, Great Britain, and Spain were parties. The question of slavery, recognition of belligerency, contraband, blocked, continuous voyage, convoy, the *Trent* affair, and other questions arising during the American Civil War, 1861 – 5, offered Dana much new material for notes, and many of these topics received elaborate treatment. The same is true of matters arising during the period 1840 to 1860 and involving naturalization, extradition, and recent practices in civil and criminal legislation. As Dana's edition went to press the feeling between the United States and Great Britain over the *Alabama* affair was acute and his long note of more than forty pages on the Foreign Enlistment Act gives a comprehensive idea of this controversy at a time before the method of settlement had been arranged. Later, in 1877, in his argument before the Halifax Fishery Commission, Dana had opportunity to use some of the material which he had gathered upon the long – atanding North Atlantic Fisheries dispute.

Dana's notes constitute about one – fifth of the volume called the eighth edition. Some of these notes have been reprinted elsewhere, as in the case of his note on the Monroe Doctrine, which appeared in pamphlet from and later with additions by his son as Chapter XIV in *Speeches in Stirring Times.*

In many respects Dana's preparation for work in the field of international law was similar to that of Wheaton. His education, training in the law, contact with men at home and abroad qualified him, like Wheaton, to take a broad view of of the subject, while appreciating the importance of its technical aspects. Dana's period – he was born in the year of the Congress of Vienna and died in 1882 – covered years full of international events which tested treaties and principles. His participation in American Civil War cases and other cases involving the application of international law gave to his notes vitality and an authority like that which Wheaton's text gained from his experience in international affairs.

Dana's studies in international law continued after the publication of the eighth edition of Wheaton and during his later sojouns in Europe he was actively ebgaged in the preparation of a work upon international law. He had already begun writing this work. His manuscript notes showed ample evidence of the careful method with which he was laying the foundation for this work and promised a further valuable contribution to the science of international law of which his death deprived the world.

Like Grotius, Wheaton made contribution to other fields of knowledge. His *History of the Law of Nations*, 1845, became the standard. His other writings in history, literature, and biography received immediate recognition. His high ideas of public and private conduct compelled respect from all parties and in negotiations brought forth justice. Wheaton may be named with Grotius as one of the great expounders of the science of international law.

GEORGE GRAFTON WILSON

CAMBRIDGE, MASSACHUSETTS,

January 1, 1936.

附录八

SKETCH OF THE LIFE OF RICHARD HENRY DANA, JR. [1]

RICHARD HENRY DANA, Jr., who edited the eighth edition of Wheaton's *Elements of International Law*, was born in Cambridge, Massachusetts, August I, 1815, and died in Rome, Italy, January 6, 1882. His family had been associated with public affairs in America since the days of settlement of Massachusetts. Mr. Dana entered Harvard College in 1831. His course was broken by a voyage to California which subsequently became the basis for the book which has a high place in American narrative writing, *Two Years Before the Mast*. Mr. Dana, returning, graduated from Harvard College with the Class of 1837, attaining the highest standing. Immediately after graduating he enrolled in Dana Law School (now Harvard Law School), where he had the advantage of close contract with such men as Story and Greenleaf.

In 1840 Mr. Dana entered actively upon the practice of law. In this year also appeared his book, *Two Years Before the Mast*, and in the following year a book, *The Seaman's Friend*. His personal experience in maritime affairs as well as these books brought him business relating to shipping. Mr. Dana's prac-

---

[1] ［美］Henry Wheaton, *Elements of International Law*, Oxford: At The Clarendon Press. London: Humphrey Milford, 1936.

tice steadly increased, though, owing to his conscientious defence of positions often unpopular or opposed to the dominant commercial and business interests, his practice was not always highly lucrative. As Dana said of a fellow member of the bar, so it could be said of him, 'He seems to be a gentleman practising law and not a mere lawyer.'

Mr. Dana was married in 1841 to Miss Sarah Watson, of Hartford, Connecticut.

Mr. Dana's active work in many lines seriously impaired his health, and in 1859 he stated upon a trip around the world. On his return, Much benefited, he again entered actively into work. From 1861, during the trying period of the American Civil War, he held the responsible office of United States District Attorney for Massachusetts. During this period Mr. Dana was in close touch with international affairs. He was keenly conscious of the significance of cases before the courts as he said in 1863 of the Prize Cases, 'So the judiciary is actually, after a war of twenty – three months' duration, to decide whether the government has the legal capacity to exert these war powers. This is the result of a written Constitution, as a supreme law, under which there is no sovereign power, but only coordinate departments.' Mr. Dana's argument in the case of the *Amy Warwick* was clear and convincing, and his conduct of the case on behalf of the government called forth the highest commendation even from President Lincoln.

The position of Judge of the United States District Court was open to Mr. Dana, but he did not feel it expedient to take this place. He, however, retained the office of United States District Attorney till September 1866.

Before resigning this office, he had undertaken, at the urgent request of Mrs. Wheaton, the editing of a new edition of her husband's work on international law. Up to this time the copyright of the work was in Mrs. Wheaton's name. He made extended notes. These the considered with his father, whose criticisms on style and method the particularly valued, and with his brother Edmund, who was familiar with European systems of law. He consulted the books relating to the sublect in the libraries, but he says,' I did my work at my study in Cambridge, which for two years was a workshop and depot of international law, my table, chairs, and floors being mainly covered with borrowed books or my own in immediate use, while I wrote at a standing desk'; and he further said,' However long Imay live, Ican never expect to try harder and give more original power to any subject than I did to those notes.' THe result of these labours was the eighth edition of Wheaton's *Elements of International Law*, edited with notes by Richard Henry Dana, Jr., LL. D., Boston: Little, Brown, and Company, 1866.

In 1866 Mr. Dana, partly in recognition of his work upon Wheaton's *International Law*, received the degree of Doctor of Laws from Harvard College.

Of this eighth edition of Wheaton, which he edited, he said: 'The presen, is therefore, the eighth edition, The notes of Mr. Lawrence do not form any part of this edition. It is confined, as has been said, to the text and notes of the author, and the notes of the present editor, who undertakes his work at the request of the widow of Mr, Wheaton, recently deceased, and of his only surviving children, his daughters.'

This statement in the preface to Dana's edition was probably made in view of the fact that it had, at first, been proposed to use all the material of Mr. Lawrence's edition of which the text was used and merely to bring that edition to date.

Mr. William Beach Lawrence, to whose editions of Wheaton's *International Law* reference is made, immediately took exception to the statement of Mr. Dana. Along controversy, involving legal proceedings between Mr. Lawrence and Mrs. Wheaton, the publishers, and Mr. Dana, followed. Mr. Lawrence also endeavored to obtain an injuunction against the issue of Dana's edition of Wheaton. The matter relating to this case would fill several volumes. The deposition of Mr. Dana in 1868 covered 222pages, and Mr. Lawrence's reply, 255 pages.

A decision was handed down by the court, September 20, 1869. This decision declared Mr. Lawrence had an equitable right by what amounted to an assignment to him from Mrs. Wheaton of copyright in his notes; that Mr. Dana, though not actually notified, might be held to have a 'constructive' knowledge of this assignment; that Mr. Lawrence had no claim to copyright in the text of the edition; and that the sale of Dana's edition should not be stopped pending a report from a Master as to the question of the extent to which Mr. Dana may have infringed upon Mr. Lawrence's right to the notes in his preceding editions. To the Master's report, made in 1877, legal exceptions were taken. The final report was not filed till January, 1881, and adds more than 200 pages to this controversial material. This report was filed January 14, covering 211 quarto pages, but not printed. The case was not appealed to the Supreme Court. The Master said in his report on the notes to Dana's edition of Wheaton (Lawrence *us.* Dana *et al.* 15 Fed. Cas. 63):' It must be remembered that D. [ana] was to cover by his notes a period of eighteen years, since Wheaton published his last edition in 1848, fifteen years of which had been covered by the learned and exhaustive notes of the complainant. It is apparent, therefore, that if the second annotator discharged his duty with diligence and fidelity, there must inevitably be strong resemblance between the two sets of notes, and a large proportion of the citations must be common to both. Direct and positive proof as to where the second annotator found his citations, or as to how far he traced them back, is not attainable.' Of the great number of notes included in Dana's edition, the Master, venturing an opinion with 'much hesitation' after long investigation under the strict and technical rules laid down by the court, reports that of more than two hundred and fifity references and citations thirteen may be considered as infringing the complainant's equitable rights. Even as these points the question involved is not of using Mr. Lawrence's own writing, but of using references and paragraphs in citations where in some instances neither editor had exactly followed the original text.

Mr. Lawrence's demand for an injunction on the sale of Dana's edition was denied by the court. The edition was sold before the final report of the Master, which was fifiteen years after the issue of the book. Interests in the case had for the most part disappeared. The editions were left to win their place upon yheir merits. Dana's edition of Wheaton's *International Law* came to be recognized as one of the leading authorities cited in the courts of the world during the nineteenth century.

In 1873 Mr. Dana, writing of himself, said, 'I should like to be relieved from the time – wasting of ordinary lawsuits—for they are no better to man at my age, —and to be able, the next eight or ten years, to use my powers and knowledge in a larger sphere. Or, if I am not to be so employed, to give my mind and study to a work on international law. ' The politics of this period were not particularly attractive or suited to a man of Mr. Dana's habits or character, and his political campaigns at this time were not satisfactory or happy. In 1876 President Grant, not conversant with the plans of certain influential senators and without previous consultation, nominated Mr. Dana as Minister of the United States to Great Britain, but this nomination was not confirmed by the Senate. In the following year Mr. Dana served as one of Article XXII of the Treaty of Washington of 1871.

The longing to devote himself to the preparation of a work on international law was often expressed, and in 1878 Mr. Dana gave up the the practice of law and with members of family went to Europe, there to further elaborate his plans. The death of his father in 1879 caused Mr. Dana to revisit Cambridge for a short time, after which he returned to Europe to continue gathering and arranging material for his proposed treatise on international law.

The manuscript notes which Mr. Dana made during these years show careful attention to historical preparation in the events and institutions with which international law deals. (The writer, through the courtesy of Mr. Dana's son, Richard Henry Dana, 3d, has these notes before him.) Mr. Dana's notes on Grotius' *de jure belli ac pacis* refer to what Mr. Dana regards as the main points from page to page and raise queries as to positions which he does not regard as clear, sound, or with a review of Grotius with detailed notes was indicative of the nature of the work for which he was planning.

Funck – Brentano and Albert Sorel had recently, in 1877, issued *Precis du droit des gens*. To this Mr. Dana gave attention as presenting late points of view, particularly as emphasizing war as the main sanction of international law. To many of the positions in this book, Mr. Dana raised decided objections in his notes.

Mr. Dana then seems to have read critically Sir Edward Creasy's *First Platform of International Law* which had been issued in 1876. To this book he does, not give much attention. He also made a careful study of Wheaton's *History of the Law of Nations*. After this Mr. Dana turned to a familiar field and reviewed Wheaton's *Elements of International Law* as edited by Boyd. He then endeavored to obtain the German point of view as shown in a late edition of Heffter's Volkerrecht in the translation by Bergson as republished in 1873. He finds much in Heffter which would be serviceable in his plans for a tratise om international law, though there are positions to which Mr. Dana is entirely opposed, especially in the matter relating to prize courts. His interest in maritime law led him to make many notes on Ortolan's *Diplomatie de La Mer*. Mr. Dana naturally gave very careful attention also to Kent, using Abdy's edition and finding much suggestive material. The notes on Twiss's *Law of Nations* are extended and detailed, with many observations to the merit of the text. The recent translation of Bluntschli's work on international law by Lardy was the more interesting to Mr. Dana because of its references to Wheaton's *International Law* and because Bluntschili had been led to make the attempt to codify international law through Dr. Lieber's successful drafting of Instructions for the Government of the Armies of the United States in 1863. In this systematic work he finds many suggestive points. William Edward Hall's *International Law* appeared in 1880, and Mr. Dana saw much of value in this new and somewhat pro – British treatise.

Mr. Dana did not confine himself himself to treatises, but supplemented these by reading monographs, recent cases, and journals containing articles on special topics. Which he particularly studied in Paris, he visited other parts of Europe, greatly enjoying Italy. He had his material well in mind and had begun to put it on paper, but his contribution was never given to the world, for he was stricken with pneumonia in Roma and didi not recover.

The simple tablet in the old Protestant cemetery where Shelley and Keats lie buried bears the following inscription:

RICHARD HENRY DANA

of Boston

UNITED STATES OF AMERICA

BORN AUGUST 1, 1815,

Died in Rome

JANUARY 6, 1882.

January 1, 1936.   GEORGE GRAFTON WILSON.

附录九

NOTE[①]

The capitalization and punctuation of the eighth edition of Wheaton's *Elements* of *International Law* varies somewhat from that of earlier editions, and in those editions there are also many differences in printing. Such minor typographical variations have not been indicated in this revision, but in other respects some corrections, though seemingly insignificant, may be helpful and have been made. Occasionally a reference to a book commonly available at the time of publication is indicated rather than an earlier edition which the author may have used, but where different editions of tha same book are referred to in succeeding pages without indication, in making corrections the edition most frequently cited is followed. In some instances the citation mentioned is expanded in order that it may be identified more easily. For corrections in Wheaton's text, editions of books referred to are prior to 1845, and for Dana's notes editions prior to 1866.

IN this edition notes are indicated as follows:

Wheaton's notes, as in the edition of 1866, by (*a*), (*b*), (*c*).

Dana's notes, as in the edition of 1866, by superior numerals and foot-

---

① [美] Henry Wheaton, *Elements of International Law*, Oxford: At The Clarendon Press. London: Humphrey Milford, 1936.

note – brackets followed by—D. , as [I] —D

Wilson's notes by superior numerals in angle – brackets and footnote – brackets followed by—G. G. W. , as [i] —G. G. W.

An efforts has been made in order that errors and possibly misleading statements which have reappeared in successive editions of Wheaton may not be further perpetuated.

参考文献

一　史料类

爱汉者：《东西洋考每月统记传》，中华书局1997年版。

陈学恂：《中国近代教育史教学参考资料》，人民教育出版社1987年版。

《海上墨林 广方言馆全案 粉墨丛谈》，上海古籍出版社1985年版。

花之安：《自西徂东》，上海书店出版社2002年版。

《康熙与罗马使节关系文书影印本》，北京故宫博物院1932年版。

李书源整理：《筹办夷务始末》，中华书局1979年版。

魏源：《海国图志》，海南国际新闻出版中心1996年版。

徐继畬：《瀛环志略》，上海书店2001年版。

于宝轩：《皇朝蓄艾文编》，上海官书局1903年版。

［法］毕利干：《法国律例》，日本司法省1894年版。

［美］丁韪良：《公法便览》，光绪四年同文馆聚珍版。

［美］丁韪良：《公法会通》，光绪六年同文馆聚珍版。

［美］丁韪良：《陆地战例新选》，上海书局石印1897年版。

［美］丁韪良：《天道溯源》，伦敦圣教书类会社1880年版。

［美］丁韪良：《西学考略》，光绪九年同文馆聚珍版。

［美］丁韪良：《星轺指掌》，光绪二年同文馆聚珍版。

［美］丁韪良著，沈弘等译：《花甲记忆》，广西师范大学出版社2002年版。

［美］惠顿：《万国公法》，［美］丁韪良译，何勤华点校，中国政法大学出版社2003年版。

［意］艾儒略著，谢方校释：《职方外纪》中华书局 1996 年版。

Henry Wheaton, Elements of International Law, Boston: Little, Brown and Company, 1855.

Henry Wheaton, Elements of International Law, London: B. Fellowes, Ludgate Street, 1836.

Henry Wheaton, Elements of International Law, Oxford: At The Clarendon Press. London: Humphrey Milford, 1936.

W. A. P. Martin, D. D., Lld. Hanlin Papers—Essays on the History, Philosophy, and Religion of the Chinese. ShangHai: Kelly Walsh The Tientsin press, 1894 年版。

二 著作类

陈顾远：《中国国际法溯源》，商务印书馆 1933 年版。

陈向阳：《晚清京师同文馆组织研究》，广东高等教育出版社 2004 年版。

程道德主编：《近代中国外交与国际法》，现代出版社 1993 年版。

林学忠：《从万国公法到公法外交：晚清国际法的传入、诠释与应用》上海古籍出版社，2019 年

田涛：《国际法输入与晚清中国》，济南出版社 2001 年版。

王铁崖主编：《国际法》，法律出版社 1995 年版。

杨焯：《丁译〈万国公法研究〉》，法律出版社 2015 年版。

邹振环：《影响中国近代社会的一百种译作》，中国对外翻译出版公司 1996 年版。

三 论文类

曹刚华、张美华：《清末传教士丁韪良早期对中国传统文化的理解》，《历史教学问题》2005 年第 6 期。

段琦：《丁韪良与西学东渐》，《世界宗教研究》2006 年第 1 期。

方维规：《东西洋考自主之理》，《中外法学》2000 年第 3 期。

郭世佑：《近代法制与中国社会转型的互动》，《史学月刊》2004 年第

8 期。

韩礼刚：《丁韪良生平简介以及对他的重新评价》，《内蒙古师范大学学报》2005 年第 3 期。

何芳川：《华夷秩序论》，《北京大学学报》1998 年第 6 期。

何勤华：《法律翻译在中国近代的第一次完整实践——以 1864 年〈万国公法〉的翻译为中心》，《比较法研究》2014 年第 2 期。

何勤华：《万国公法与清末国际法》，《法学研究》2001 年第 5 期。

李长莉：《晚清同文馆对人才的培养，《河北师范大学学报》1987 年第 1 期。

李贵连：《法国民法典的三个中文译本》，《比较法研究》1993 年第 1 期。

李祝环：《清末翻译外国法学著作述评》，《中外法学》2000 年第 3 期。

田涛：《晚清国际法输入述论》，《天津社会科学》1999 年第 6 期。

王开玺：《1864 年清廷翻译万国公法所据版本问题考异》，《北京师范大学学报》2005 年第 6 期。

王美秀：《丁韪良的中国宗教观》，《北京大学学报》1995 年第 2 期。

王维俭：《普丹大沽口船舶事件和西方国际法传入中国，《学术研究》1985 年第 5 期。

文正邦：《论权利及权力》，《外国法学研究》1996 年第 1 期。

余来明：《历史文化语义学：理论与实践》，《光明日报》2007 年 3 月 30 日。

张燕清：《丁韪良与万国公法》，《新闻出版交流》2003 年第 2 期。

后　　记

　　本书是 2011 年教育部人文社会科学研究一般项目结题成果。2004 年 9 月，年近不惑的我考入武汉大学历史学院攻读博士学位，师从人文社会科学资深教授冯天瑜先生，围绕京师同文馆输入的法学术语展开研究（国家社科基金结题书稿"京师同文馆输入的国际法术语研究"已于 2021 年中国社会科学出版社出版）。为了搜集史料，我整天泡在武汉大学樱顶老图书馆内，当发现印刷精美的"同文馆聚珍版"《万国公法》、《星轺指掌》、《公法便览》、《公法会通》时，喜悦、激动之情溢于言表，即便时隔近二十年后的今天，仍能体会。特别应予以感谢的是那位图书管理员，她允许我进入地下书库，馆外骄阳似火，室内温馨清凉。我在里面慢慢浏览、摘抄。冯先生远在扶桑讲学，也将《万国公法》英、日对译本相关章节邮寄给我，让我备受鼓舞。此外，台湾地区同胞刘正中博士委托在哈佛大学的好友，给我复印了部分英文版 *Elements of International Law*，聂长顺兄在日本国立国会图书馆帮我找到了许多史料。先后同居一室的林志鹏教授（中国台湾）、王书强（马来西亚）、唐详勇诸君以及同时求学于武汉大学的罗惠缙教授、戚学英教授、关培凤教授、鲁家亮教授、祁怀高教授、蔡双泉教授、张才圣教授、江田祥教授，也给予我诸多帮助。该书的出版还得到了惠州学院政法学院蒋炜院长、董立山教授、李实书记、罗传宝副书记的大力支持，在此一并感谢！一起切磋多年的周海英教授、黄静秋女士、周丽红女士、宋少兵先生，让研究工作之余的生活丰富多彩，轻松愉快，这也是该书得以顺利出版不可或缺的因素，自然应该铭记于心。

万齐洲

2022年8月19日下午3点19分